Marriage and Family in Transition

Edited by

JOHN N. EDWARDS
DAVID H. DEMO

Virginia Polytechnic Institute and State University

ALLYN AND BACON
Boston London Toronto Sydney Tokyo Singapore

For Pat
    —J. N. E.

For Mom, Leslie, Michael, and Brian
    —D. H. D.

Series Editor: Karen Hanson
Series Editorial Assistant: Laurie Frankenthaler
Production Administrator: Annette Joseph
Production Coordinator: Holly Crawford
Editorial-Production Service: Laura Cleveland, WordCrafters Editorial Services, Inc.
Cover Administrator: Linda K. Dickinson
Cover Designer: Suzanne Harbison
Manufacturing Buyer: Megan Cochran

Copyright © 1991 by Allyn and Bacon
A Division of Simon & Schuster, Inc.
160 Gould Street
Needham Heights, MA 02194

All rights reserved. No part of the material protected by this copyright notice may be reproduced or utilized in any form or by any means, electronic or mechanical, including photocopying, recording, or by any information storage and retrieval system, without the written permission of the copyright owner.

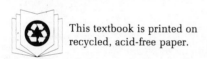

This textbook is printed on recycled, acid-free paper.

Library of Congress Cataloging-in-Publication Data

Marriage and family in transition / [editors] John N. Edwards, David
  H. Demo.
    p. cm.
  Includes bibliographical references.
  ISBN 0-205-12641-3
    1. Family—United States. 2. Marriage—United States. 3. Life
cycle, Human. I. Edwards, John N.   II. Demo, David H.
HQ535.M36   1991
306.8'0973—dc20   90-46803
                                                                         CIP

Printed in the United States of America
10 9 8 7 6 5 4 3 2 1 95 94 93 92 91 90

Contents

Foreword, *Alan Booth* **vi**
Preface **vii**

Introduction: Dating, Marriage, and Divorce in the 1990s 1

PART ONE   DATING AND MATING

Initiating and Dissolving Relationships

1. Dating: Attracting and Meeting, *Bernard I. Murstein,* 13
2. Loving and Leaving: Sex Differences in Romantic Attachments, *Zick Rubin, Letitia Anne Peplau, and Charles T. Hill,* 29
3. The Courtship Game: Power in the Sexual Encounter, *Naomi B. McCormick and Clinton J. Jesser,* 43

Date Violence

4. The Incidence of Violence and Acquaintance Rape in Dating Relationships among College Men and Women, *Marta Aizenman and Georgette Kelley,* 67

Premarital Sex

5. The Sexualized Society, *John D'Emilio and Estelle B. Freedman,* 77

Cohabitation

6. Cohabitation: Recent Changes in the United States, *Graham B. Spanier,* 94

PART TWO   MARRIAGE AND FAMILY RELATIONS

Changing Marital Roles

7. Coming Apart: Radical Departures Since 1960, *Steven Mintz and Susan Kellogg,* 107
8. American Couples, *Philip Blumstein and Pepper W. Schwartz,* 117
9. The Division of Labor in Contemporary Marriage: Expectations, Perceptions, and Performance, *Dana V. Hiller and William W. Philliber,* 129
10. Marriage, Family Life, and Women's Employment, *Jane Riblett Wilkie,* 143

Marriage over the Life Cycle

11. The Changing Family Life Cycle, *Betty Carter and Monica McGoldrick,* 165
12. Sexuality in the Early Years of Marriage, *Cathy Stein Greenblat,* 175
13. The Sexual Stages of Marriage, *Ellen Frank and Carol Anderson,* 186
14. Factors in Long-Term Marriages, *Robert H. Lauer and Jeanette C. Lauer,* 191
15. Extramarital Sex, *Anthony P. Thompson,* 198
16. The Marriage License as a Hitting License, *Murray A. Straus, Richard J. Gelles, and Suzanne K. Steinmetz,* 215
17. The Family in an Aging Society, *Matilda White Riley,* 230
18. Widowhood, *Starr Roxanne Hiltz,* 242

Parent-Child Relations over the Life Cycle

19. Folk Beliefs about Parenthood, *E. E. LeMasters and John DeFrain,* 251
20. Making Difficult Choices Easier: Day Care and Children's Development, *Donna King and Carol E. MacKinnon,* 267
21. America's Youth: A Changing Profile, *Luther B. Otto,* 284
22. When Parent Becomes Peer: Loss of Intergenerational Boundaries in Single Parent Families, *David S. Glenwick and Joel D. Mowrey,* 299
23. Fatherhood and Social Change, *Ralph LaRossa,* 306
24. Parent Care as a Normative Family Stress, *Elaine M. Brody,* 322
25. Styles and Strategies of Grandparenting, *Andrew J. Cherlin and Frank F. Furstenberg, Jr.,* 343

PART THREE DISSOLUTION AND ITS AFTERMATH

Divorce: Its Causes and Consequences

26. Major Variations in the Family Life Cycle: Divorce and Remarriage, *Betty Carter and Monica McGoldrick,* 353
27. Uncoupling, *Diane Vaughan,* 358
28. The Divorce Process, *Paul K. Rasmussen and Kathleen J. Ferraro,* 376
29. Divorce and Marital Instability over the Life Course, *Alan Booth, David R. Johnson, Lynn K. White, and John N. Edwards,* 389
30. The Impact of Divorce on Children, *David H. Demo and Alan C. Acock,* 403

The Second Time Around: Remarriage and Stepfamilies

31. The Six Stations of Remarriage: Developmental Tasks of Remarriage after Divorce, *Ann Goetting,* 428
32. From Nuclear to Stepfamily Ideology: A Stressful Change, *Barbara Fishman and Bernice Hamel,* 436
33. Children in Stepfamilies, *Marilyn Ihinger-Tallman and Kay Pasley,* 453

PART FOUR INTIMATE ALTERNATIVES AND ISSUES FOR THE FUTURE

34. Multiple Marriage, Swinging, Adultery, and Open Marriage, *Robert N. Whitehurst,* 473
35. The Intimate Relationships of Lesbians and Gay Men, *Letitia Anne Peplau and Steven L. Gordon,* 479
36. Asexual Reproduction and the Family, *John N. Edwards,* 497
37. Age Wars: The Coming Battle between Young and Old, *Phillip Longman,* 506
38. The Politics of the Family, *Steven Mintz and Susan Kellogg,* 512

Appendix: Correlation Chart   518

Foreword

AS A STUDENT enrolled in a marriage or family course, you will find between the covers of this book a set of articles that is both interesting and unique. You will find the book interesting because the articles commence by focusing on premarital relations and then proceed on to marriage itself as it changes over the life course. Divorce and remarriage have become the norm in Western society, and this fact is reflected in the contents of the book.

I know that great care has gone into the selection of the materials. Not only are the selections from some of the leading social science publications, but they were chosen because they are well written, thorough, and imaginative.

In the editors' comments that introduce each section, comparative and historical research have been summarized and brought to bear on the topic. This increases the scope of the book and fills in important areas you will find of interest.

From your own experience, you know that the family changes in some ways and remains remarkably consistent in others as people progress through the life cycle. These changes and consistencies are amply covered in the readings. It should be easy for you to relate these materials to your own experience.

The final section of this anthology offers a glimpse of the future. The institutions of marriage and family are going through a number of profound changes. As a result, family policy has become the center of much debate. Legislators, lobbyists, and citizens alike have a stake in the decisions and their consequences. The contents of this volume should aid you in understanding the source of the debate and the possible outcomes of legislative action.

Whether you are planning to work in human services where families are a key component, or you want to become informed about marriage and family for personal reasons, you will find the materials in this book helpful in preparing for the future.

Alan Booth

Preface

THIS BOOK GROWS out of our many years of collective experience in teaching undergraduate courses on marriage and the family, subjects of infinite fascination to us. Marriage and the family provide the most important relationships in most people's lives, and understanding how these relationships are affected by the social context—and how they in turn affect that context—is a fundamental issue.

One of the most obvious, but least understood, aspects of family life today is its changing character. For this reason, we have selected articles that emphasize the nature of the many transitions people are experiencing today in their marriages and family relations. These changes are affecting not only the ways in which people go about finding a mate but are altering the nature of the relationships formed in marrying and becoming parents. While there are many historical continuities in marriage and the family, it is change that people find most problematic in their daily lives.

Our understanding of marriage and the family is enriched by viewing these relationships in a life-cycle or life-course perspective. This perspective, which we hope most instructors will find compatible with their own approach to teaching about marriage and the family, makes explicit the transitional character of intimate relationships.

Following from the life-course perspective, we have divided the book into four major parts. Part One deals with the formation of intimate relationships, and the articles in this section discuss various aspects of dating. Part Two contains selections on marriage and parent-child relations over the life cycle. In Part Three, we provide several selections concerning divorce and its aftermath, including remarriage and the formation of stepfamilies. In devoting equal space to marital dissolution and its consequences, we provide students with a broad range of materials on events that increasingly touch their lives and are an ever more prevalent part of the typical family life cycle. The final section of the book, Part Four, deals with alternatives to monogamous marriage and a few of the impending issues bearing on future families. Throughout the book, we have deliberately included selections that discuss the "darker side" of dating, marriage, and divorce to provide some balance to what we view as the rather saccharine treatments that some textbooks give to contemporary family life. In order to facilitate use of the selections, a correlation chart appears at the end of the anthology keying each reading to the relevant chapters of some of the most widely used texts.

Preceding each major section, there is a brief editors' introduction, which attempts to give a broad overview of the topics discussed in the articles to follow. Especially in the first three parts, we have tried to provide an historical and cultural perspective to marriage and family relationships in the United States. Diversity in dating, marriage, and divorce is also emphasized, particularly in terms of how these phenomena vary by race, social class, and gender. Instructors may wish to elaborate on these introductions, for we believe that only by understanding the historical and cultural context in which we live can we begin to grasp the meaning of the marital and family transitions taking place around us.

In compiling these readings, we have incurred several debts. We are grateful to the authors and their publishers who permitted us to include their works. We thank Elaine David, Barbara Peters, Paula DuPrey, Carolyn Vaughan, and Anna Zajicek-Wagemann for their invaluable assistance in collecting and preparing the materials for this book. We are grateful for the constructive comments and suggestions of the reviewers: Barbara Risman at North Carolina State University, Rita Phylliss Sakitt at Suffolk County Community College, and Constance Sheehan at the University of Florida. Annette Joseph ably guided the production of the manuscript, and we wish to express our appreciation to Karen Hanson, sociology editor of Allyn and Bacon, for her enthusiastic support throughout the project.

J. N. E.
D. H. D.

Introduction: Dating, Marriage, and Divorce in the 1990s

VALUES AND ATTITUDES concerning marriage and family life changed dramatically in the three decades from the late 1950s to the late 1980s. In the United States, opposition to abortion and divorce weakened, while singlehood, cohabitation, childlessness, premarital and extramarital sexual relations, and egalitarian gender roles became widely endorsed (Thornton, 1989). The reasons for these changes are many, and the consequences are profound. We briefly discuss some of the major reasons why our ideas about family life have changed so dramatically, and we then highlight some of the consequences for individuals and families moving through the family life cycle in the 1990s and beyond.

An important dimension of the changing social fabric is the increasing emphasis on individual interests and aspirations. Through the 1960s and 1970s, several countercultural movements generated national awareness of hedonistic values and self-fulfillment, facilitating what social psychologists refer to as a "me" orientation. One of the ramifications of individualism is that people can lose sight of social commitments and responsibilities, in a sense detaching themselves from social relationships and institutions, such as marriage and family. While people continue to value and to derive satisfaction from marriage, parenthood, and family life, today there is greater tolerance of individual choice in deciding whether and when to marry, whether and when to have children, and whether to remain married or divorce. In a penetrating analysis of modern American society, Robert Bellah and colleagues (1985) conclude that there are at least two ways of viewing this more tolerant atmosphere:

> To the extent that this new atmosphere creates more sensitive, more open, more intense, more loving relationships, as it seems to have done, it is an achievement of which

Americans can justly be proud. To the extent that the new atmosphere renders those same relationships fragile and vulnerable, it threatens to undermine those very achievements. (p. 110)

Marriage and family life have been influenced by a number of other social changes as well. The women's movement focused attention on women's rights to educational and occupational equality, and dual-earner marriages replaced traditional male-breadwinner families as the norm in American society. Abortion and divorce laws were liberalized, the birth rate fell to 1.8 children for every married woman, and religion became much less important in the lives of many Americans.

What does all this mean? What are the consequences of rapidly changing values, social expectations, and household composition? History tells us that the importance of the family as a source of social integration and social support waxes and wanes over time, and as we enter the 1990s there is every indication that marriage and parenthood will continue to be highly valued. There is also reason to believe that people will continue to have very high expectations for passionate and romantic marriages and for harmonious families that provide a nostalgic and peaceful haven of love and tenderness. At the same time, however, most people are not willing to invest substantial amounts of time and energy in pursuit of meaningful and rewarding intimate relationships, the consequences of which include marital conflict, dissatisfaction, instability, and divorce.

The guiding assumption of this book is that dating, marriage, and divorce are life-cycle phenomena; that is, marriage and family relationships can be understood by examining the trajectories of these relationships and by examining families in their social context. The family life-cycle perspective emphasizes that families change over time as individuals and families progress through a sequence of developmental stages. At each stage there are developmental tasks that must be accomplished before making the transition to the next stage. The transition to parenthood, for example, is smoother for couples who are able to make the adjustments to marriage successfully. As children and adults mature, develop, and age, their relationships change. It is also important to note that developmental processes unfold in a social context complete with socially constructed timetables for appropriate behavior.

Many of the idealistic and overly romanticized notions of marriage and family life are learned in early socialization experiences and are crystallized in the dating process, thereby influencing dating relationships and mate-selection decisions. To better understand how these processes are set in motion, let's consider the social context of dating in the 1990s.

DATING

During adolescence and young adulthood, ideas of marriage and family life are molded by parents, peers, television sitcoms, soap operas, and love stories, as well as rock and roll lyrics. Although definitions of gender-appropriate behavior have broadened in the past three decades, one of the most pervasive messages delivered through the popular culture is that there are separate roles for males and females. Males are expected to be in control, strong, dominant, assertive, and sexually active, while females are expected to be passive, submissive, physically and interpersonally attractive, nurturant, thoughtful, and understanding. For females, especially, the importance of romantic attachments is communicated in Hollywood movies, romance novels, and rock lyrics, such as "I can't live without you," and "I can't get over you." For males, the corresponding message in the popular culture is that love is desirable but not essential, that a real man doesn't need a woman, at least he doesn't need a *relationship* with a woman.

Norms regarding premarital sexual behavior became much more permissive in the 1960s and 1970s, with high rates of premarital sexual intercourse continuing in the 1980s. By age eighteen, two out of three boys and two out of five girls have experienced sexual intercourse (Dornbusch, 1989). Black adolescents become sexually active earlier than their white counterparts, and sporadic use of contraceptives among both groups leads to alarming rates of teenage pregnancy and childbearing.

The contradiction for most adolescents and young adults involved in heterosexual relationships is that males and females bring different expectations to their relationships: Males are encouraged to seek sex but not necessarily a relationship and females are encouraged to seek relationships, preferably without sex. Although many males and females do not conform exactly or entirely to these stereotypes, there are numerous situations in which dating partners act out these expectations, with a definite power imbalance to the males' advantage. Different expectations and priorities strain communication in dating relationships, and when expectations are not fulfilled, violence often results. Contrary to the stereotype of romantic and pleasure-oriented dating relationships, approximately one out of four college women report that they have experienced some form of physical violence or sexual assault, often date or acquaintance rape.

Males and females also take different approaches in evaluating relationships and deciding whether to continue dating or to dissolve the relationship. Again our stereotypes are misleading: Females are depicted as emotional and capable of being "swept away" by their suitors; males are portrayed as strong, rational, and realistic. However, research demonstrates that females are more cautious and practical in making commitments, and males are more romantic in the sense of wanting to keep the relationship together. As we illustrate in Part One of this book, the unrealistic and idealistic expectations that dating partners and cohabiting couples bring to relationships have profound consequences for decisions regarding mate selection. Moreover, these expectations also have long-term implications for the dynamics of marital relationships themselves.

MARRIAGE

Marriage has changed dramatically over the last few decades. The cohort of young men and women who married in the 1980s waited longer to marry and waited longer to have children than their predecessors. They are having fewer children, more of the wives are working outside the home, and both men and women can expect to live longer than previous generations. The rapid pace of social, demographic, and technological change has profoundly altered the family life cycle, creating discontinuities between the values, life styles, and social expectations of the succeeding generations.

Compared to couples who married for the first time during the 1950s and 1960s, couples who began their marriages in the 1970s and 1980s devote much less time to raising children, and they spend significantly greater amounts of time looking after their elderly parents. Despite changing gender roles, women are still expected to do most of the caregiving, for both their children and their parents. Research evidence clearly demonstrates that wives still do most of the caregiving, even though there are increased demands on their time because of employment outside the home. Changing gender roles have influenced our expectations regarding what men should do as fathers. But even as fathers engage in a wider range of parenting behaviors than previously, in most contemporary families it is the mothers who are more directly involved in childrearing responsibilities.

Changing gender roles have led to greater flexibility, but these changes have not uniformly permeated the society. The movement from traditional to more egalitarian gender roles is largely a white, middle-class phenomenon. Among working-class whites, and among blacks and Hispanics, traditional gender roles prevail. Even in the segment of society where the most change has occurred—white, middle-class, dual-earner families—there are strong reminders of a patriarchal society in which males are dominant and females are subordinate. Husbands are expected to fulfill instrumental roles: They exert the most power in the family, make the important decisions, and serve as financial providers. Wives, even those who work outside the home, are generally expected to be the social-emotional leaders of the family, to be nurturant and passive. As these arrangements are challenged, there are profound consequences for marriage and family relations, as well as for the wider society.

There are also important consequences associated with the new norm of dual-earner marriages. Both husbands and wives invest substantial amounts of time and energy in work-related activities, draining resources that could otherwise be devoted to the marital relationship. The time that marriage partners do spend together is disrupted by negotiations over household tasks and childrearing responsibilities. Marital communication is strained, leisure time and "quality time" are rare, sexual frequency declines after the initial years of marriage, and marital conflict is common. Dissatisfaction with marriage and with sexual relations also may lead spouses to look beyond the marriage for stimulation in the form of extramarital sex. Another consequence of strained marital and family relations is the alarming incidence of family violence, most notably wife abuse and child abuse.

In studying the family life cycle, we find that relationships among family members are strongly influenced by age-graded social expectations and developmental processes. In the early years of marriage, when romantic feelings are normally intense, spouses are required to make a series of adjustments associated with living together on a daily basis. Routines and procedures are established for a wide range of behaviors, including family decision-making, work schedules, a domestic division of labor, recreational activities, and sexual relations. Nine out of ten couples decide to have children, creating additional stresses on the couple's intimate relationship. Although children provide meaningful sources of happiness and social support, the emotional and financial resources required to raise children in modern society means that there are fewer resources available to invest in the marital relationship. Many young, dual-earner (mostly middle-class) couples opt to send their children to daycare, further reducing the amount of time children spend with their parents and sparking national concern about the effects daycare has on children's development during the "formative years."

First marriages that endure beyond a decade encounter a fresh set of challenges and transitions. Often, varying degrees of stability, momentum, and inertia characterize marriage during this stage. Children become involved in a variety of extrafamilial contexts—especially during adolescence—spending most of their time in school, with peers, and enjoying extracurricular activities. But for adults during the midlife years, the freedom they gain from the growing independence of their teenage children is accompanied by the increasing dependence of their aging parents. Middle-aged women, especially, often feel obligated to reverse parent-child roles and do whatever they can to provide personal care and emotional support for their aging parents. Once dependent-aged children leave home and parents enjoy an "empty nest," the marital relationship typically regains some of its privacy and spontaneity, and couples at this stage report increasing levels of marital satisfaction through the retirement years.

Grandparenthood has emerged as a major family role in the late twentieth century. Usually spanning the middle-adult and late-adult years, grandparenting can be a very gratifying social role. Although many grandparents are unable to spend as much time with their children and grandchildren as they would like—largely as a result of social and geographical mobility—other grandparents are actively involved. Many grandparents find that the time they spend with the younger generations is pleasurable. They can play with young children or watch their grandchildren in recreational activities and leave the disciplining to the children's parents! However, contrary to myth, older adults also derive satisfaction from many other activities, notably leisure time spent with each other and sexual relations.

A high percentage of marriages are terminated by death (as opposed to separation or divorce), with most postmarital families headed by widows aged sixty-five and over. Widowhood is a difficult transition that often presents severe emotional and financial difficulties. Widows and widowers commonly experience loneliness, social isolation and depression. At the same time, they must make numerous adjustments to restructure their social networks and their lives. For a small minority, widowhood, as a major social status, ends with remarriage, marking the beginning of another family life cycle.

DIVORCE

The divorce rate in the United States accelerated rapidly in the 1960s and 1970s, then stabilized in the 1980s. At the current rate, however, one of every two marriages initiated in the 1990s will end in divorce. Because many people view divorce as a serious threat to the American family, it is important to address several questions: What kinds of marriages are most prone to divorce, how are men and women affected as they dissolve their marriages, how does divorce affect children, how are remarriages different from first marriages, and what kinds of relationships exist in stepfamilies?

In terms of proneness to divorce, couples who marry very young (especially teenagers, but also couples who marry in their early twenties) are more vulnerable than couples who marry in their mid- to late twenties. Marrying at a later age allows individuals to mature, learn about themselves, make more realistic judgments of their partners, complete their education, and prepare themselves occupationally. Further, couples who have been married a long time are less vulnerable to divorce than couples who only have been married a few years. Research on marital instability and divorce indicates that accumulation of assets (e.g., home, cars, savings) is an important factor in keeping marriages together.

When divorce occurs, the experience is usually an unpleasant and stressful one for spouses and children alike. Interpersonal problems and tensions in the nuclear family broaden, even intensify, as friends and relatives are drawn into a typically conflictual situation and are themselves divided along various lines. Emotional wounds are compounded by legal complexities and financial considerations involving custody, visitation, and the division of assets. Emotional adjustments are typically easier for the spouse who initiates the divorce than for his or her partner, and older children typically have an easier time adjusting than younger children. Unhappily, the financial consequences suffered by women and children in single-parent families can be both severe and longlasting.

Because divorce terminates the marital relationship, in many ways it signifies the end of the family life cycle. But, in other ways, divorce can be viewed as reorganizing old relationships and setting the stage for new relationships. Currently, five out of six divorced men and three out of four divorced women remarry, with most remarriages involving young children. Blended or reconstituted families are formed, creating new family life cycles. Research indicates that marital quality is quite comparable in remarriages as compared to first marriages, but stepfamily life presents a fresh set of challenges. The norms are unclear for stepparents and stepchildren, stepsiblings and half-siblings, straining interaction and contributing to higher divorce rates for remarriages than for first marriages.

In sum, dating, marriage, and divorce are social processes embedded in the family life cycle. As individuals engage in these processes, they simultaneously progress through periods of social and historical change, individual and family development. Lifelong socialization processes accompany the acquisition of new roles, while long-held roles are transformed or lost, generating continuities and discontinuities, transitions and disruptions through the life course. Parts One through Three of this book are organized to illustrate the dynamics of dating, marriage, and divorce. They highlight the intricate ways in which these three processes are interrelated. In Part Four, we address some of the commonly practiced alternatives to traditional marriage and family arrangements and explore the possible consequences and implications of emerging patterns of family life as we approach the twenty-first century.

REFERENCES

Bellah, Robert N., Richard Madsen, William M. Sullivan, Ann Swidler, and Steven M. Tipton. 1985. *Habits of the Heart: Individualism and Commitment in American Life*. New York: Harper & Row.
Dornbusch, Sanford. 1989. "The Sociology of Adolescence." *Annual Review of Sociology* 15: 233–259.
Thornton, Arland. 1989. "Changing Attitudes Toward Family Issues in the United States." *Journal of Marriage and the Family* 51: 873–893.

PART ONE
Dating and Mating

EVERY SOCIETY, of necessity, has established ways for people of the opposite sex to meet, pair off, and eventually marry. How they do this, however, differs from one society to the next. One basic difference between societies is whether mate selection is arranged or participant-run. Arranged marriage, at its extreme, means that the prospective spouses have little, if any, say in the decision. It is the duty of family elders, usually the fathers, to find suitable mates for their offspring. In such systems, love and marriage are unrelated. Marriage unites families or kin groups, not merely two individuals. Therefore, the elders go to considerable lengths to ensure that a suitable match is made. In fact, since love is a universal potential, societies with arranged marriages seek to control it. Some do so by bethrothing their children, sometimes even when they are infants. Some have very strict rules about who is eligible to marry whom, thus narrowing the field of possible acceptable partners. Still other societies physically segregate the sexes to prevent the "wrong" people from getting together and possibly forming an emotional attachment to each other. This practice often is accompanied by a system of chaperonage, further ensuring that only those acceptable to the parents will meet and eventually marry.

Participant-run systems of mate selection represent the opposite extreme. The responsibility of finding a mate is squarely placed on each individual, although subject to indirect parental control. Romantic love is actively encouraged. Love is a prerequisite for marriage. Marriage is the end result of being in love. And even if love does not conquer all, it justifies the establishment of a relationship between two people. In mate-selection systems of this type, what is important, in the final analysis, is what the other person is like as an individual. Physical attractiveness and the individual's personality are crucial considerations. Family concerns, if they are considered at all, are secondary.

Until recently, arranged systems of mate selection have been prominent in societies around the world. However, as more societies industrialize and become urbanized, extended family systems tend to break down. As this happens, families have less and less stake in whom their offspring marry, and the frequency of arranged marriages has begun to decline.

In the strictest sense, American society never had a system of arranged marriage. But we have undergone considerable change in the degree to which our system is participant-run. During the seventeenth century and most of the eighteenth, parents exerted considerable influence over their children's choice of a mate. Parental approval of a would-be spouse was an absolute necessity, giving parents at least veto power over whom their offspring would marry. Inheritance and the transfer of property were at the heart of the matter. A young man could not marry until he was capable of supporting a family. Usually this meant waiting until he inherited land or developed a skill that would enable him to make a living. The "wrong" choice of a mate could mean being disinherited. For the young woman's part, parental disapproval could result in refusal to provide a dowry. In either case, it meant that individuals who defied their parents' wishes started off at a disadvantage. If the withdrawal of property was not enough to deter young people from choosing someone that their parents did not approve of, the colonial courts were empowered to levy fines and, in some cases, to decree physical punishment for the offenders.

The frontier conditions of the nineteenth century, along with increasing industrialization, effectively eroded such direct parental control over the selection of a mate. Greater geographical mobility and the lack of family control over earning a livelihood substantially reduced any parental threat to withhold property. This signaled the beginning of a truly participant-run system, ushering in a new, twentieth-century phenomenon. It was called dating.

Dating may start as early as grade school, governed mainly by the norms of peers rather than parents. As a process, and for most people, it begins with casual relationships with many partners, gradually narrowing to a few individuals and more exclusive relationships. Finally, the field is narrowed to a single person. As the articles in Part One suggest, however, it is often a process many people find to be anxiety-producing, emotionally difficult, and sometimes highly exploitive.

To a degree, dating is a process that varies with social class. In general, the higher the class, the greater the stake parents have in whom their offspring will marry, and the greater the control parents exert in the dating activities of their children. The upper class, in particular, lives in a relatively isolated social world that provides boundaries around whom their offspring will meet and date. Exclusive neighborhoods, vacation resorts, private schools, and clubs ensure that date activities will take place among social equals.

Middle-class youth have greater latitude in dating choices. But they, too, are subject to more parental control than their lower class counterparts. In comparison with the latter, middle-class dating activities are more likely to be associated with school-, church-, and civic-sponsored events. Lower class dating also tends to be more informal and more likely to consist of "hanging out." Dating activities themselves are less structured than among middle-class youth.

There are few, if any, differences in dating patterns along racial and ethnic lines. White, black, and Hispanic dating patterns vary by social class. However, since blacks and Hispanics are overrepresented among the poor, dating patterns for most blacks and Hispanics resemble those of lower class youth.

More prominent differences in dating are evident between males and females. Although gender roles are changing, traditional norms and behavior patterns structure the dating of many. Traditionally, men have been the aggressors. In terms of dating, this means that men ask for dates, they control the activities engaged in, monopolize conversations, and initiate sex. Men pay and men dominate. Women, in contrast, traditionally have been passive. They are to be pursued. Women accept or decline dates; they do not initiate them. Above all, they are to be submissive.

Plainly, these traditional gender-role expectations and patterns of behavior are breaking down. Today, women often initiate dates rather than waiting passively to be asked. Men are more likely to accept women as their intellectual equals. Dating relationships are more egalitarian, rather than being characterized by the dominance-submission pattern of the past. Yet, differences remain.

As the articles in Part One attest, dating and finding a mate is not an easy process for many. Meeting a person to one's liking may be problematic. Because traditional patterns are breaking down, many questions arise as to how one is to behave. Who is to initiate a relationship? Is the relationship egalitarian? Who has the power? In our increasingly sexualized society, sex becomes a major issue for many couples. What role is it to play in the relationship? Who initiates it? When? Not having ready answers, many dating relationships turn violent. As relationships become more serious and involve more commitment, increasingly the issue arises as to whether a couple should live together and to what purpose. While the unmarried have greater freedom today than ever before, it is an uneasy freedom. The old norms guiding dating may be considered passé, but the new norms are not firmly established.

ARTICLE 1
Dating: Attracting and Meeting

BERNARD I. MURSTEIN

This article details some of the ways in which finding a mate has changed from our colonial past to today. Despite a move toward more egalitarian relations between men and women, important gender differences remain. Attraction, however, is crucial to both sexes, and Murstein describes how this comes about.

HOW DO PEOPLE interested in marriage get to meet someone who might make a suitable marriage candidate? In colonial America, marriage was still more a question of necessity than of interpersonal needs being fulfilled. Men needed help on the farm and received it in the labor provided by wives and offspring. Women needed status and economic support because few jobs were open to them. Thus, marriage was more businesslike than today. Because of the need to earn a livelihood, poor travel conditions, and close chaperoning of adolescents, there was not much time available for courtship. To be sure, there were "hoedowns," barnraising, fairs, and Sunday Church, but compared to the present day, the frequency and extent of interaction among the young was limited.

Among the poor, less formal business arrangements were needed and in the middle of the eighteenth century, the custom of "bundling" flourished along the eastern seaboard.

Bernard I. Murstein, "Dating, Attracting, and Meeting." In *Paths to Marriage* (Newbury Park, Calif.: Sage, 1986): pp. 64–77. Copyright 1986 by Sage Publications, Inc. Reprinted by permission of Sage Publications, Inc.

Bundling

Suppose a young man was interested in a young woman. Daylight was too precious to spend on courting. It must be reserved for work. Farms were far apart, it was dangerous to travel at night, and in any event, most families retired shortly after dark. A parlor and sofa were unknown in a farm house, not to mention guest rooms. With the permission of a woman's parents, however, a young man could spend the evening with a young lady in whom he was interested, including bedding down with her.

Various ways were devised to forestall physical contact: a wooden board might be placed in the middle of the bed; the young girl might be encased in a type of long laundry bag up to her armpits; or, her garments might be sewn together at strategic points.

Although premarital sex was quite prevalent, particularly among the betrothed in colonial America, it is doubtful that sex in the beginning of a relationship was an automatic product of such arrangements. Certainly the girl was in little danger, for a well-placed scream would have brought instant aid. The idea of the couple in bed, however, brought prurient visions to the minds of many, who imagined the worst. In time, bundling jokes made the rounds; in one of them, a mother asked her daughter if she had kept her limbs in the bundling bag, and the innocent Miss replied, "Ma, dear, I only took one out" (Aurand, 1938).

We noted earlier that technology and mass education gave young men and women the occasion to interact and to have privacy (i.e., bicycle, telephone, car). But the disappearance of the chaperone system did not mean that the young were ready to disregard the customs and wishes of their parents. The 1920s were a transition period in which the custom of marrying the culturally "right" person at the right time (after the man had a job) was still largely adhered to among the upper middle class. A theory of dating was suggested by Willard Waller, a sociologist (1937, 1938). He saw dating as a time of dalliance. College students were sexually mature, but by custom were delayed in sexual expression until they finished their schooling and married. Meanwhile, they passed the time by dating for prestige, fun, status, and above all, thrills.

Dating was more than lighthearted recreation. It was competitive. Each participant tried to get the better of the other by bargaining, deception, or whatever it took. The man, in search of a thrill, might try to "go all the way" with a girl, but he rarely expected to succeed. An evening with a date could be successful, however, if he got at least a kiss and perhaps a "feel."

To achieve the highest possible status, it was necessary for him to date only Class A girls—those from sororities with the highest prestige. It was helpful for a man not only to be handsome, wealthy, neat, and to possess a car, but to also have a good "line." The line was intended to show the girl how sophisticated, suave, desirable and admirable he was, and to get her to fall in love with him while he remained calm and detached. According to what Waller called the "principle of least interest," the individual least interested in the continuation of the relationship exercised the most power over the other person.

The Class A sorority woman was not without her own weapons. She could parry the "line" of the boy with her own. Also, she tried to make herself as beautiful as possible, wear chic clothes, dance well, and achieve or give the semblance of being highly popular. For example, a girl receiving a telephone call allows herself to be paged several times so that every girl in the sorority house knows just how popular she is. A Class A girl never accepts a date on short notice no matter how interesting the boy. Being available on short notice marks one as of low status.

On a date, the girl must be seen with the right escort at the right place, get her date to spend freely on her, showing how highly she is valued, and grant nothing, or next to nothing, in sexual favors. In sum, Waller saw dating more as a fencing match than a wholesome encounter. Each combatant warily stalks the other and tries to exploit assets, mask liabilities, and get the upper hand. If a Class A man dates a lower status girl, he often tries to trade his superior assets for sexual yielding on her part. On the other hand, a Class A woman may "gold dig" a man of mediocre status as the price for the privilege of a date.

Although dating is not intended to lead to marriage, it often, mysteriously, does lead to it. Waller cannot explain this result. Perhaps in the middle of the "line," individuals discover they really mean what they say.

Many distinguished writers on the dating scene supported Waller's theory, but most researchers have been highly critical. The crux of the criticisms was that dating is more than dalliance. It can be a search for a marital partner or at least an educational experience in interpersonal relationships. Individuals dating tend to pair on the same variables that people who marry do, hardly a sign of dalliance (Hansen & Hicks, 1980). Moreover, the characteristics considered by Waller so important for dating (line, car, grooming, good dancer) are not rated as essential by daters (Blood, 1955; Krain, Cannon, & Bagford, 1977). Friendship, intimacy, being able to listen, and having one's self-esteem raised are more important (Vreeland, 1972).

Yet Waller was not entirely wrong. He was speaking of his observations of Pennsylvania State University around 1929. The male-female ratio was 6 to 1, and fraternities flourished and competed with each other for the small pool of women. College was reserved more for the upper middle class than today, and ambitious college students often postponed marriage. Thus, it is possible that rating and dating was a minority phenomenon on some campuses for a brief period (Gordon, 1981).

Last, Waller's understanding of the dynamics of attraction and power and the tactics of men and women with each other has a core of truth if we focus on initial contacts. When individuals don't know each other, they are often wary, apt to "play games" and assess the market value of the other before committing themselves to a relationship.

HOW DO THEY MEET TODAY?

College

A study of university students indicated how college students met at a southeastern college (Knox & Wilson, 1981). As shown in Table 1, most men and women used

TABLE 1 How 334 University Students Met Their Dating Partners

Ways of Meeting	% Female (n = 227)	% Male (n = 107)
Through a friend	33	32
Party	22	13
At work	12	5
Class	6	9
Other	27	41

Source: D. Knox and K. Wilson, "Dating Behaviors of University Students." *Family Relations, 30* (1981) p. 256. Copyrighted 1981 by the National Council on Family Relations, 3989 Central Ave. N.E., Suite #550, Minneapolis, MN 55421. Reprinted by permission.

a large number of ways to meet, with the most popular being through a friend. Another study several years earlier had reported fairly similar findings except that "blind date" had been the most frequently used method, with 35% of the women and 28% of the men using this method (Bell, 1975). However, many people have had bad luck with blind dates. Half of the dating failures men reported in one study were blind dates whereas for women the figure was 25% (Albrecht, 1972). The reasons for this trauma may be that the best adjusted good looking persons easily establish social contacts, leaving the shy, withdrawn, and unattractive as a residual pool from which blind dates are drawn.

Currently, on many college campuses, students tend to do things in heterosexual groups from which individuals eventually pair off. This more relaxed approach results in fewer persons dated but more successful dates, in that background and compatibility are more carefully scrutinized before pairing.

Noncollege Dating

Individuals who have graduated from college, unlike college students, do not have a built-in clientele from which to choose, and must work harder. Friends and relatives are a source of dates, as is the job, but much more initiative may be required. The basic goal stressed in the book *How to Get Married* is to be visible in as many contexts as possible (Weiss & Davis, 1983). The authors advise women (apparently they don't expect men to read their book) to start conversations whenever possible, frequent health gyms, interest clubs, museums, acquire a dog (cats don't have to be walked), go to dance clubs, shop a lot, and go on tour vacations.

Commercial Dating

If all else fails, there is always the commercial route. This includes bars, computer matchups, video interviews, lonely hearts clubs, personals, social clubs, and singles' complexes.

Singles' Bars
The singles' bar is a haven for white postcollegiate middle-class individuals. There is little room in the popular bars, the noise is deafening, and one nods the head earnestly and guesses what is being said.

"Looks" and "line" are everything. "Let me tell you a secret" says a man. Puzzled, the woman leans over and receives a kiss on the ear much to her surprise (Gordon, 1976). Exchange is the order of the day. If a woman lets a man buy her a few drinks, she "owes" him something—time spent talking to him, perhaps going out to dinner, or even to bed. There is always a chance of meeting someone "permanent" at a bar, although this writer in numerous interviews with people has heard that this is very infrequent.

Computer Matchups
Clients are furnished with questionnaires in which they check off interests, qualities desired in a date and/or spouse, and some background information. The information goes into "memory storage," and when a comparable person of the opposite sex is encountered (the criteria are rarely revealed), the computer records this fact. At some point, the applicant gets three or more "compatible" names to contact.

Video Interviews
Recently, computers have been supplanted in some locales by five-minute videotapings in which a client looks at another client responding to questions asked by the company's interviewer. Clients, after looking at a number of tapes, choose any they would be interested in, and if there is mutual interest, the telephone numbers are exchanged.

Matrimonial Bureaus
These are geared to marriages more than "meaningless" dates. Although compatibility is desired and necessary, it is assumed that clients are interested in marriage as a status and are not going to get hung up over whether their psyches are meshing properly or whether one partner doesn't like classical music.

Lonely Hearts Clubs
These are mail-order houses dispensing human merchandise (Godwin, 1973). The stock is lists and photographs. Misrepresentation is likely, photographs may be old, and the lists of clients offered also may be slightly tarnished with age.

Advertisements
Many individuals today prefer to do their own shopping. They may put an ad in a singles' magazine or in a periodical in which they extol their virtues, omit their deficiencies, and wait for a reply.

Social Clubs
These are quasi-permanent groupings in which socials (dances) are the mainstay. They are held periodically for members, who fend for themselves at the affair.

Singles' Complexes

A number of housing developments have sprung up that cater to singles. They feature game rooms, tennis, swimming, and other sports. Rents tend to be high, but there are more men than women in these complexes. In a sense, encounters are more natural in such an environment, but many individuals are wary of getting involved with a neighbor whom it may be embarrassing to encounter at the pool after the affair is over.

Evaluation of Commercial Matchups

The data reveal a male-dominated situation. Men seek younger, trim partners, offer less attractiveness, and more status and financial security. Women more often state what they want in a partner in personality rather than focus on themselves as much as men do (Harrison & Saeed, 1977; Bolig, Stein, & McKenry, 1984; Green, Buchanan, & Heuer, 1984; Lynn & Shurgot, 1984). They also are less demanding of physical characteristics aside from preferring tall men.

Computer matchups suffer from the fact that favorable distortions are in the interest of clients who desire choice partners. One individual told me, "If I revealed that I wasn't good looking they might match me with Frankenstein's bride." Also, the matchups are made on the basis of habits, race, religion, and the characteristics we reviewed earlier, but they can't deal with interpersonal attraction. Thus, one gentleman wrote, "Your computer was right. Mitzi and I like all the same things . . . : same food, . . . opera, bike-riding, . . . dogs . . . there was only one thing we didn't like—each other" (Godwin, 1973, p. 87).

The commercial enterprises are all happy to boast of their successes in matching, but in truth the vast majority of clients cannot expect much success.

The reason is age. Men listing themselves in ads on the average want a woman seven years younger than themselves, whereas women want a man three years older (Cameron, Oskamp, & Sparks, 1977). But the average age of women advertisers was more than nine years older than male advertisers (Jedlicka, 1978). Few members of either sex advertise in magazines in their 20s. Starting at age 30, the men advertise more than would be expected. They are competing with younger men for the same pool of women in their 20s. But when men are in their 50s, they find it easier to find women. As women get older, their marriage marketability drops more rapidly than men's marketability. Middle-aged men want younger women, not age mates. Moreover, as men are biologically more fragile than women, they decline in numbers leaving a glut of women 45 and over fighting for a dwindling supply of older men, many of whom are looking for women below 45.

SEX DIFFERENCES

Anxiety

Men and women show many differences in their expectations of dating and their feelings about it. A study of several thousand Arizona college students indicated that 37% of the men but only 25% of the women suffered from anxiety about dating (Machlowitz, 1981). Why men should be more anxious is not hard to fathom. Traditionally, men have had more responsibility for initiating courtship. With this "privilege," however, runs the greater risk of rejection. The self-assured may pass rejection off as the woman's loss, but most teenagers are not self-assured and take rejection as a sign of their own inadequacy.

Initiation of Date

A researcher gave college men and women the names of the opposite sex to call for a date, specifying only that one of them should call the other within a week (Machlowitz, 1981). In over 90% of the time, the man called the woman. But times are changing. Another study reported that 87% of the college men had been asked for a date by a college woman, and 86% of these men accepted (Kelley, Pilchowicz, & Bryne, 1981).

Feminists are more likely than nonfeminists to initiate dates and pay for themselves (Korman, 1983). A majority of both feminists and nonfeminists believed that men expected women to engage in more sexual activity when the man paid for his date.

Most women think that a man prefers to ask a woman out, but of 106 men polled, 53 preferred the woman to ask, 52 preferred her to hint, and only 1 preferred her to wait passively until asked (Muehlenhard & McFall, 1981). The chief determinant of accepting these female-initiated dates was how the man felt about the woman. The more he liked her, the more likely he was to accept. Thus, it appears that initiative by a woman in asking or making clear her feelings for a man is not harmful to her dating life and may even be helpful.

The Subject of Sex

There is almost total agreement in the studies undertaken that, at least initially, men are far more interested in sex than women are, and this causes a problem (Klaus, Hersen, & Bellack, 1977; Knox & Wilson, 1983; McCabe & Collins, 1984). Men not only often equate dating with sex (Whitehurst & Frisch, 1974), they believe that women expect them to make passes at them and would not consider them masculine if they didn't try (Balswick & Anderson, 1969). Thus, men exhibit positive pressure, whereas women determine the rate of progress toward this goal (Peplau, Rubin, & Hill, 1977).

At the first date, both sexes manifest little expectation that sex will occur. Thereafter, when the age sampled is 17–19, men exceed women in expecting sex after several dates or when going steady. By the time the age level of 20–24 is reached, however, the women have accepted the men's attitudes towards sex. In short, men's attitudes do not vary much as a function of age except on the first date. Women's expectations of sex become more convergent toward the men's attitudes with increasing age (Collins, Kennedy, & Francis, 1976).

Expressing Intimate Feelings

The majority of studies indicate that, in a heterosexual relationship, women tend to express more intimate feelings before men do (Klaus, Hersen, & Bellack, 1977). This tendency develops quite early in heterosexual relationships (around puberty), although in their 20s men do show a tendency to catch up (McCabe & Collins, 1979, 1983). There is not complete agreement because McCabe and Collins (1983) found no difference between the sexes in affectional behavior from age 17 to 24. Whether the difference in their findings and those of others (cited in Sharabany et al., 1981) is due to the different countries sampled or different scales used is unknown.

In sum, sex differences in dating persist. Men still initiate more dates, although absolute hegemony in this regard is weakening. Men still lag in expressing intimate feelings. However, once a couple is established, the differences seem to dwindle. Men's greater interest initially in instituting a sexual relationship is not due to a lack of interest in the affectional aspects of the relationship, but is in addition to it. In time, the established dating couple becomes more balanced in the affectional-sexual components of the relationship.

ATTRACTION

Attraction and dating are tied together in a circular fashion. If attraction is present, dating will often result. Sometimes, however, a date may be arranged without much prior attraction, as on a blind date. Here dating may lead to attraction. One way or the other, attraction is considered a necessary antecedent to marriage, at least in the United States where it is expected to lead to love and thence to marriage. In this section, we investigate the personal characteristics of the individuals leading to attraction including their physical characteristics, their emotional states, and the tactics used to attract others. We close by considering physical signs of attraction that precede verbal expression of it.

Culturally Determined Qualities Leading to Attraction

The culturally accepted qualities desirable in a spouse have been determined mainly by researcher-generated lists. The most useful list is that of Hoyt and Hudson (1981), who, using earlier researchers' work as well as their own, have traced the ranking of personal characteristics from 1939 to 1977, as shown in Table 2. This table reveals that "dependable character" and "emotional stability" have been vital since 1939. "Mutual attraction" has become increasingly important over time as have "sociability" and "education-intelligence," and partner's "good looks" for men. "Chastity" has dropped for both sexes as has "good cook-housekeeper" for men.

Other studies indicate that college women are increasingly attracted to men favoring egalitarian sharing of house chores and a career for women (Holahan,

TABLE 2 Rank of 18 Personal Characteristics in Mate Selection Based on Mean Value by Year and Sex

	Male				Female			
	1939	1956	1967	1977	1939	1956	1967	1977
(1) Dependable character	1	1	1	3	2	1	2	3
(2) Emotional stability	2	2	3	1	1	2	1	2
(3) Pleasing disposition	3	4	4	4	4	5	4	4
(4) Mutual attraction	4	3	2	2	5	6	3	1
(5) Good health	5	6	9	5	6	9	10	8
(6) Desire for home-children	6	5	5	11	7	3	5	10
(7) Refinement	7	8	7	10	8	7	8	12
(8) Good cook-housekeeper	8	7	6	13	16	16	16	16
(9) Ambition-industriousness	9	9	8	8	3	4	6	6
(10) Chastity	10	13	15	17	10	15	15	18
(11) Education-intelligence	11	11	10	7	9	14	7	5
(12) Sociability	12	12	12	6	11	11	13	7
(13) Similar religious background	13	10	14	14	14	10	11	13
(14) Good looks	14	15	11	9	17	18	17	15
(15) Similar educational background	15	14	13	12	12	8	9	9
(16) Favorable social status	16	16	16	15	15	13	14	14
(17) Good financial prospect	17	17	18	16	13	12	12	11
(18) Similar political background	18	18	17	18	18	17	18	17

Source: L.L. Hoyt and J.W. Hudson, "Personal Characteristics Important in Mate Preference among College Students." *Social Behavior and Personality,* 9 (1981), p. 95. Reprinted by permission of the Society for Personality Research.

1984; Martin & Martin, 1984). Thus, current surveys indicate that egalitarianism, steadiness, and mutual involvement are the characteristics most desired, with little difference between the sexes.

Physically Attracting Qualities

Physical Attractiveness

There are countless studies that show the very first thing most people respond to in a dating situation is the physical attractiveness of the other. Men respond more to this quality than women. The beautiful people of the world also get a bonus, as if they needed it. Attractive individuals compared to less attractive ones are seen as sexy, warm, sensitive, kind, modest, and competent (Dion, Berscheid, & Walster, 1972).

Body Language

Messages such as "I have it, I'm available, and I want you" can be telegraphed through body language:

> For the male, it may be . . . an arrogant grace, a thrust of his hips, touch, gestures, extra long eye contact, carefully looking at the woman's figure, open gestures and movements . . . or showing excitement and desire in fleeting facial expressions. For the woman, it may be . . . sitting with her legs symbolically open, crossing her legs to expose a thigh, engaging in flirtatious glances, stroking her thighs, protruding breasts, using appealing perfume, showing the "pouting mouth" in her facial expressions, opening her palm to the male, using a tone of voice which has "an invitation behind the words." (Knapp, 1972, p. 17)

Eyes

The eye is important in courtship in two ways. We look intently at those to whom we are attracted. Men's pupils dilate when looking at pictures of attractive women but not when regarding photos of men or babies. Women's pupils expand in response to pictures of both men and babies but not to those of women (Hess, 1965).

Women in medieval times thought that eyes with pupils dilated were more attractive and, consequently, took the drug *belladonna* ("beautiful woman" in Italian) to enlarge their pupils (Cook & McHenry, 1978). They were right. One study had men rate two photos of a woman identical except that one had been retouched so as to make the pupils larger. The men preferred the retouched photo although unable to say why they preferred it (Hess, 1965).

Eye contact is also an indication of interest in the early stages of a relationship (Brust, 1975). The more one is involved with another, the longer one gazes at their eyes (Rubin, 1970; Walsh, Meister, & Kleinke, 1977). However, shy and uncomfortable individuals may not make eye contact because attraction is confounded with anxiety.

Physical Closeness

Sir Francis Galton in 1884, observing people at dinner parties, concluded that the more one individual liked another, the more the individual inclined toward the other (Wilson & Nias, 1976). This observation has been supported for new "dates" in which attraction ratings were correlated with the distance the individuals stood from one another (Byrne, Erwin, & Lamberth, 1970).

Exposure

Seeing someone many times over a period of time increases familiarity, and familiarity tends to breed attraction (Zajonc, 1968). Thus, mere exposure is enough to make someone liked. This finding has been documented numerous times (Harrison, 1969; Harrison & Zajonc, 1970, among many others).

Memory

If individuals are asked to recall acquaintances having the same first name (e.g., John), the order of recall is almost invariably the same as the order of liking (Cromwell, 1956). An experiment done with dating couples had every individual turn up a series of cards each containing a word and read the word out loud. When tested for recall, individuals did best on words they had read out loud, and next best on words read by their partners. The best recall was made by couples observed touching each other who had also reported the strongest liking for each other (Brenner, 1971). Thus, how well our behavior is remembered may be an index of how well we are liked by our partners.

Clothes

We clearly send out messages by the clothes we wear and being well dressed gives one more power than being poorly dressed. A smartly dressed person is more likely to induce others to cross against the light (Lefkowitz et al., 1955) or to jaywalk (Bull, 1974), and is more highly regarded than a poorly dressed person (Hamid, 1969). Even individuals known fairly well by their classmates are seen as having changed in personality when they change their style of dress (Bull, 1974). Women fashionably dressed are seen as having different dating patterns and sexual morals (Gibbins, 1969).

In sum, we convey a great deal consciously or unconsciously without uttering a word. In the next section we shall consider tactics consciously employed by individuals seeking to attract a partner.

TACTICS FOR ATTRACTION

Initiating Contact

Suppose a young man sees an attractive young woman in the park. How does he initiate the relationship? He must if possible discover if she is *cleared* for the encounter. If she is wearing a wedding band, she may not be cleared. Assuming she is cleared, he must find an opener that engages the attention of the prospect—a compliment, or a remark about the weather. But it is necessary to go further—to find an *integrating topic* that interests the woman. He must also project a *come-on self* that will make him appear to be someone she would like to know better. If time is limited, a second encounter must be scheduled (Davis, 1973).

I have outlined a possible approach. But what about specific tactics such as flattery or playing hard to get?

How Far Does Flattery Get One?

The answer is, it depends on how aware and sure the flattered persons are of their shortcomings or strengths. Positive evaluations from strangers generally make us like them, even if we know they are somewhat too kind ("they are good souls to say it even if we don't deserve it"). However, flattery is most effective when we aspire to be somebody we're not sure we are. For example, it's fruitless to tell Miss America she's beautiful. She knows it. However, if she's studying to be a violinist and we tell her convincingly that she sounds like a concert artist, we have probably made a friend (Berscheid & Walster, 1978).

Playing Hard To Get

Contrary to what most people think, women who play hard to get are not all the more attractive for it, to the average man. Too much difficulty is intimidating. However, if the woman is hard to get for other men, but indicates or hints that she would be amenable to wooing by the man in question, she becomes quite attractive to him (Walster, Walster, Piliavin, & Schmidt, 1973).

EMOTIONAL STATES CONDUCIVE TO ATTRACTION

Are there any emotional states that are conducive to attraction? Yes there are, and one is a rather common occurrence.

Attraction After Rejection

A number of experiments have involved raising or lowering subjects' self-esteem by contrived reports on how they did in alleged personality or intelligence tests. The effect is generally that lowered self-esteem women are more receptive to men's affection (Walster, 1965). Lowered self-esteem men are more likely to attempt to establish contact with an unattractive woman as opposed to an attractive one (Kiesler & Baral, 1970), and lowered self-esteem men are more hostile to a rejecting woman than are raised self-esteem men (Jacobs, Berscheid, & Walster, 1971). In sum, rejected individuals in a broken love match are probably apt to lower their standards and thresholds for latching onto someone new in an effort to restore their self-esteem.

SUMMARY AND CONCLUSION

Although relationships between men and women take place more naturally and on a more equal basis than ever before, dating still seems to be an anxiety-provoking experience to many. The paradox is resolved by noting that networks of intimacy formerly provided by family and community are often missing for many individuals in a highly mobile society. Women are more equal and, therefore, more choosy than ever before, and an affluent society can look beyond mere subsistence. Most individuals make emotional intimacy and family their top priority. With so much at stake, individuals are wary of contributing to the high divorce statistics without careful evaluation of potential partners.

Dating services have mushroomed but have not solved the needs of the majority. These services have demonstrated little validity, are expensive, and in an achievement-oriented society, there is a stigma to needing help to find a date.

Dating behavior has lagged behind changes in the social and economic status of the sexes. Men still largely initiate dates, but women are slowly starting to initiate more or to hint more actively. Women may not realize that most men would welcome a more active initiating role by women.

Men still press early for sex, whereas women are more slow to accept sexuality, although as relationships develop, the majority engage in sex. Men's earlier interest in sex does not mean that they are disinterested in the affectional aspects of the relationship. Women express intimate feelings earlier than men but men improve somewhat in this regard with time.

There are many nonverbal cues to attraction: body movements and posture, eyes, distance between members of a couple, exposure, memory, and clothes.

Initiating contacts requires some thought and planning as well as knowledge of the emotional state of oneself and the other.

REFERENCES

Albrecht, R. (1972). A study of dates that failed. In R. E. Albrecht & E. W. Brock (Eds.), *Encounter: Love, marriage, and family* (pp. 57–63). Boston: Holbrook Press.

Aurand, A. M., Jr. (1938). *Little known facts about bundling in the new world*. Lancaster, PA: Aurand Press.

Balswick, J. O., & Anderson, J. A. (1969). Role definition in the unarranged date. *Journal of Marriage and the Family, 31*, 776–778.

Bell, R. R. (1975). *Marriage and family interaction* (4th ed.). Homewood, IL: Dorsey.

Berscheid, E., & Walster, E. H. (1978). *Interpersonal attraction* (2nd ed.). Reading, MA: Addison-Wesley.

Blood, R. O., Jr. (1955). A retest of Waller's rating complex. *Marriage and Family Living, 17*, 41–47.

Bolig, R., Stein, P. J., & McKenry, P. C. (1984). The self-advertisement approach to dating: Male-female differences. *Family Relations, 33*, 587–592.

Brenner, M. (1971). Caring, love, and selective memory. *Proceedings of the 79th Annual Conference of the American Psychological Association, 6*, 275–276.

Brust, R. G. (1975). Liking, love, and similarity of humor preference. Unpublished master's thesis, Connecticut College.

Bull, R. (1974). The importance of being beautiful. *New Society, 30*, 412–414.

Byrne, D., Erwin, C. R., & Lamberth, J. (1970). Continuity between the experimental study of attraction and real life computer dating. *Journal of Personality and Social Psychology, 16,* 157–165.

Cameron, C., Oskamp, S., & Sparks, W. (1977). Courtship American style: newspaper ads. *Family Coordinator, 26,* 27–30.

Collins, J. K., Kennedy, J. R., & Francis, R. D. (1976). Insights into a dating partner's expectations of how behavior should ensue during the courtship process. *Journal of Marriage and the Family, 38,* 373–378.

Cook, M., & McHenry, R. (1978). *Sexual attraction.* Oxford: Pergamon Press.

Cromwell, R. J. (1956). Factors in the serial recall of names and acquaintances. *Journal of Abnormal and Social Psychology, 53,* 63–67.

Davis, M. (1973). *Intimate relationships.* New York: Free Press.

Dion, K., Berscheid, E., & Walster, E. (1972). What is beautiful is good. *Journal of Personality and Social Psychology, 24,* 285–290.

Gibbins, K. (1969). Communication aspects of women's clothes and their relation to fashionability. *British Journal of Social and Clinical Psychology, 8,* 301–312.

Godwin, J. (1973). *The mating trade.* New York: Doubleday.

Gordon, M. (1981). Was Waller ever right? The rating and dating complex reconsidered. *Journal of Marriage and the Family, 43,* 67–76.

Gordon, S. (1976). *Lonely in America.* New York: Simon & Schuster.

Green, S. K., Buchanan, D. R., & Heuer, S. K. (1984). Winners, losers and choosers: A field investigation of dating initiation. *Personality and Social Psychology Bulletin, 10,* 502–511.

Hamid, P. N. (1969). Changes in person perception as a function of dress. *Perceptual and Motor Skills, 29,* 191–194.

Hansen, S. L., & Hicks, M. W. (1980). Sex role attitudes and perceived dating-mating choices of youth. *Adolescence, 15,* 57–83.

Harrison, A. A. (1969). Exposure and popularity. *Journal of Personality, 37,* 359–376.

Harrison, A. A., & Saeed, L. (1977). Let's make a deal: An analysis of revelations and stipulations in lonely hearts advertisements. *Journal of Personality and Social Psychology, 35,* 257–264.

Harrison, A. A., & Zajonc, R. B. (1970). The effects of frequency and duration of exposure on response competition and affective ratings. *The Journal of Psychology, 75,* 163–169.

Hess, E. H. (1965). Attitudes and pupil size. *Scientific American, 212,* 46–54.

Holahan, C. K. (1984). Marital attitudes over 40 years: A longitudinal and cohort analysis. *Journal of Gerontology, 39,* 49–57.

Hoyt, L. L., & Hudson, J. W. (1981). Personal characteristics important in mate preference among college students. *Social Behavior and Personality, 9,* 93–96.

Jacobs, L., Berscheid, E., & Walster, E. (1971). Self-esteem and attraction. *Journal of Personality and Social Psychology, 17,* 84–91.

Jedlicka, D. (1978). Sex inequality, aging, and innovation in preferential mate selection. *The Family Coordinator, 27,* 137–140.

Kelley, K., Pilchowicz, E., & Bryne, D. (1981). Response of males to female-initiated dates. *Bulletin of the Psychonomic Society, 17,* 195–196.

Kiesler, S. B., & Baral, R. L. (1970). The search for a romantic partner: The effects of self-esteem and physical attractiveness on romantic behavior. In K. Gergen & D. Marlowe (Eds.), *Personality and social behavior* (pp. 155–165). Reading, MA: Addison-Wesley.

Klaus, D., Hersen, M., & Bellack, A. S. (1977). Survey of dating habits of male and female college students: A necessary precursor to measurement and modification. *Journal of Clinical Psychology, 33*, 369–375.

Knapp, M. (1972). *Nonverbal communication in human interaction*. New York: Holt, Rinehart & Winston.

Knox, D., & Wilson, K. (1981). Dating behaviors of university students. *Family Relations, 30*, 255–258.

Knox, D., & Wilson, K. (1983). Dating problems of university students. *College Student Journal, 17*, 225–228.

Korman, S. K. (1983). Nontraditional dating behavior: Date-initiation and date expense-sharing among feminists and nonfeminists. *Family Relations, 32*, 575–581.

Krain, M., Cannon, D., & Bagford, J. (1977). Rating-dating or simply prestige homogamy? Data on dating in the Greek system on a midwestern campus. *Journal of Marriage and the Family, 39*, 663–674.

Lefkowitz, M., Blake, R. R., & Mouton, J. S. (1955). Status factors in pedestrian violation of traffic signals. *Journal of Abnormal and Social Psychology, 51*, 704–706.

Lynn, M., & Shurgot, B. A. (1984). Response to lonely hearts advertisements: Effects of reported physical attractiveness, physique, and coloration. *Personality and Social Psychology Bulletin, 10*, 349–357.

Machlowitz, M. (1981, May 4). Researchers explore dating woes. *The Day*, New London, CT: p. 40.

Martin, D., & Martin, M. (1984). Selected attitudes toward marriage and family life among college students. *Family Relations, 33*, 293–300.

McCabe, M. P., & Collins, J. K. (1979). Sex role and dating orientation. *Journal of Youth and Adolescence, 8*, 407–425.

McCabe, M. P., & Collins, J. K. (1983). The sexual and affectional attitudes and experiences of Australian adolescents during dating: The effects of age, church attendance, type of school, and socio-economic class. *Archives of Sexual Behavior, 12*, 525–539.

McCabe, M. P., & Collins, J. K. (1984). Measurement of depth of desired and experienced sexual involvement at different stages of dating. *The Journal of Sex Research, 20*, 377–390.

Muehlenhard, C. L., & McFall, R. M. (1981). Dating initiation from a woman's perspective. *Behavior Therapy, 12*, 682–691.

Peplau, L. A., Rubin, Z., & Hill, C. T. (1977). Sexual intimacy in dating relationships. *Journal of Social Issues, 33*, 86–109.

Rubin, Z. (1970). Measurement of romantic love. *Journal of Personality and Social Psychology, 16*, 265–273.

Sharabany, R., Gershoni, R., & Hoffman, J. E. (1981). Girlfriend, boyfriend: Age and sex differences in intimate friendship. *Developmental Psychology, 17*, 800–808.

Vreeland, R. S. (1972). Is it true what they say about Harvard boys? *Psychology Today, 5*(8), 65–68.

Waller, W. (1937). The rating and dating complex. *American Sociological Review, 2*, 727–734.

Waller, W. (1938). *The family: A dynamic interpretation*. New York: Cordon.

Walsh, N. A., Meister, L. A., & Kleinke, C. L. (1977). Interpersonal attraction and visual behavior as a function of perceived arousal and evaluation by an opposite sex person. *Journal of Social Psychology, 103*, 65–74.

Walster, E. (1965). The effects of self esteem on romantic liking. *Journal of Experimental Social Psychology, 1*, 184–197.

Walster, E., Walster, G. W., Piliavin, J., & Schmidt, L. (1973). "Playing hard to get":

Understanding an elusive phenomenon. *Journal of Personality and Social Psychology, 26,* 113–121.

Weiss, H., & Davis, J. (1983). *How to get married.* New York: Ballantine.

Whitehurst, R. N., & Frisch, G. R. (1974). Sex differences in dating orientation: Some comparisons and recent observations. *International Journal of Sociology of the Family, 4,* 213–219.

Wilson, G., & Nias, D. (1976). *The mystery of love.* New York: Quadrangle.

Zajonc, R. B. (1968). Attitudinal effects of mere exposure. *Journal of Personality and Social Psychology, 9,* 2–27.

ARTICLE 2
Loving and Leaving: Sex Differences in Romantic Attachments

ZICK RUBIN, LETITIA ANNE PEPLAU, AND CHARLES T. HILL

According to prevailing stereotypes of males and females, women are the lovers and men are the leavers. The authors, following a sample of college students as their dating relationships progressed or deteriorated, find evidence that the opposite may be more true. Men fall in love more quickly, and women are more likely to end a troubled relationship. Women, in loving relationships, tend to be more cautious, practical, and realistic. Contrary to the stereotype, men are the "romantics."

THIS REPORT COMPARES men's and women's orientations toward beginning and ending close male-female relationships. Specifically, it considers whether there is any general difference between the sexes in the propensity or ability to fall in love in the first place, and in the propensity or ability of one who is in love to fall out of it.

This is an area of inquiry which has perhaps been explored most thoroughly by songwriters, comicbook creators, and other producers of popular culture both today and in times gone by. It is an area in which stereotypes reign supreme. If our reading of the popular wisdom is correct, the most common set of perceptions holds

Zick Rubin, Letitia Anne Peplau, and Charles T. Hill, "Loving and Leaving: Sex Differences in Romantic Attachments." *Sex Roles*, 7 (1981): 821–835. Reprinted by permission of Plenum Publishing Corporation.

that of the two sexes, women are the more starry-eyed and sentimental, while men are the most hardhearted and rational. A woman, according to this stereotype, is more likely to fall in love at first sight and to experience such symptoms as a heightened pulse, a trembling hand, and an itching in her heart. Meanwhile, the male object of the woman's affection is presumed to remain impassive and even unaware of the strange transformation that she is undergoing. Men have also been known to experience some of these physiological symptoms of love, but they are generally thought to be less likely to experience them than women are. A related pair of stereotypes portray the man as a ruthless exploiter who falls out of love, if he ever was in it, quickly and casually, moving on to new conquests while the woman who loves him tearfully watches him ride off into the distance. Women, according to the stereotype, are the lovers, men the leavers.

Do these stereotypes contain a kernel of truth? Our research leads us to propose not only that these stereotypes of female lover and male leaver are unjustified but also that there is a notable difference between men and women that goes in precisely the opposite direction. Our hypothesis can best be stated as a two-part empirical generalization: (a) Men tend to fall in love more readily than women. (b) Women tend to fall out of love more readily than men. Before we proceed to the evidence for these hypothesized differences, several specifications are in order.

First, the terms "fall in love" and "fall out of love" are not being used in a very special or mysterious way. They simply refer to people's ability or propensity to enter into and to give up romantic attachments. Several different indicators of falling in and out of love will be introduced as we examine the relevant evidence.

Second, these generalizations were suggested primarily by the results of a longitudinal study of 231 college student dating couples in the Boston area. The hypothesized differences are seen as being most relevant to such dating or premarital relationships in middle-class America today. They would not necessarily be found in different times, different cultures, different age groups, different social class groups, or different sorts of relationships (such as marriage). As we will suggest later, comparisons with other segments of the population might be of great interest in formulating different explanations of sex differences in love.

Third, even among the sample of dating couples that we will be considering, the sex differences to be reported are not massive ones. On all the measures to be discussed, there is a great deal of overlap between the distributions of the two sexes, and the overall differences are modest ones. Nevertheless, the various strands of evidence combine to suggest that the postulated differences are real ones, if they are viewed as actuarial propositions about a preponderance of cases. These actuarial propositions may be of considerable interest not as social facts in their own right, but for what they imply about the socialization of the two sexes for close relationships in contemporary America.

With these specifications in mind, let us turn to the evidence for our two-part hypothesis. First, we will describe the research program that provides our main source of data. Then we will discuss the evidence bearing on each of the two parts of our empirical generalization. Finally, we will consider several possible lines of explanation for the observed differences.

THE BOSTON COUPLES STUDY

Through a series of letters and advertisements in the spring of 1972, we recruited a sample of 231 couples who were "dating" or "going together" at four colleges in the Boston area. The four colleges were chosen with a view toward diversity. They included a small private college, a large private university, a Catholic university, and a state college enrolling commuter students. The large majority of participants came from middle-class backgrounds. About half of the participants' fathers had graduated from college and about one-fourth of the fathers held graduate degrees. The modal couple consisted of a male junior and a female sophomore who had been dating for about eight months. Almost all the couples were dating one another exclusively, but few had any concrete plans about marriage. Further details of the sampling procedure and characteristics of the sample have been reported elsewhere (Hill, Rubin, & Peplau, 1976).

We proceeded to follow up these couples through extensive questionnaires in fall 1972, spring 1973, and (by mail) in spring 1974. The response rates on the follow-up questionnaires remained high, even though by 1974 many of the participants had left the Boston area. In 1974 the mailed questionnaires were returned by 83% of the women and 75% of the men in the initial sample. In all cases, each partner was asked to complete the questionnaire individually. Subjects were assured that their responses would be kept in strict confidence, and that their replies would never be revealed to their partners.[1]

The questionnaires covered a wide range of events, experiences, attitudes, and feelings. On the follow-up questionnaires we also asked participants to reflect on changes in the relationship over time. These questions are of particular interest in cases in which the couple had broken up in the interim. We also interviewed a subset of the participants more intensively. Of special relevance to this report is a series of interviews conducted in fall 1972 with 18 people whose relationships had ended since the previous spring.

Proposition 1: Men Tend to Fall in Love More Readily than Women

In spite of prevailing stereotypes about "romantic" women, or women "out to catch a man," there is converging evidence that men tend to fall in love more readily than women do. Men have consistently been found to have higher scores than women on measures of "romanticism" (Hobart, 1958; Knox & Sporakowski, 1968; Z. Rubin, 1969). In the Boston Couples Study men were again found to score significantly higher than their girlfriends on such a romanticism scale (paired $t = 4.10$, $df = 230$, $p < .001$). This scale assesses the degree to which a person adheres to such tenets of romantic ideology as the belief that love strikes at first sight and overcomes bars of race, religion, and economics. Men's greater belief in this romantic ideology suggests that they may be more ready than women to fall in love quickly and with a wider range of partners, while women may tend to be more deliberate and discriminating about entering into a romantic relationship.

This difference in ideology may be paralleled by a difference in dating goals. We asked participants in the Boston Couples Study to indicate how important each of a variety of goals was as a reason for entering their relationship. Surprisingly, in light of the prevailing stereotype of romantic women, men rated the "desire to fall in love" as a significantly more important reason for entering the relationship than did women (paired $t = 2.21$, $df = 227$, $p < .05$).

The suggestion that men tend to fall in love more readily than women is also supported by more direct reports of attraction in the early stages of relationships. In an extensive study of engagement and marriage conducted by Burgess and Wallin (1953) in the 1930s and 1940s, many more men than women reported that they had been strongly attracted to their eventual fiancées at their first meeting or shortly thereafter. In a "computer-dance" study conducted at Iowa State University in the 1960s (Coombs & Kenkel, 1966), men were more satisfied with their randomly assigned partners on all criteria; indicated that they felt more "romantic attraction" toward them; and, when asked to speculate about the possibility that they could have a happy marriage, were more optimistic. In a study conducted at the University of Michigan in 1968-1969, Z. Rubin administered a self-report "love scale" to a large sample of dating couples. This scale is a 9-item self-report attitude scale calling on the respondent to assess the degree to which he or she feels attached to, cares about, and feels intimate with a particular other person (Z. Rubin, 1970). In the total sample the average love scores of men and of women proved to be approximately equal. But among the 40 couples who had been dating for only a short time (up to three months), boyfriends' love scores were significantly higher than those of their girlfriends (Z. Rubin, 1969). All these findings seem consistent with the proposition that men tend to fall in love more readily than women. In the earliest stages of a relationship, men tend to report greater attraction and love for their girlfriends than they receive in return. This is true both in relationships that later become more intimate (as in the Burgess and Wallin study) and in relationships that typically never get beyond an initial date (as in the Iowa State study).

Proposition 2: Women Tend to Fall Out of Love More Readily than Men

Proposition 2 refers specifically to the ending of close relationships. We were able to keep in touch with at least one member of all but 10 of the 231 couples in the Boston Couples Study over a two-year period, from spring 1972 to spring 1974. By spring 1974, 20% of the couples about whom we had information had married, 33% were still dating or going together, and the remaining 47% (103 couples) had broken up. In considering the evidence for the second proposition, we will focus on the couples who had ended their relationship. We will consider evidence from several different domains—participants' self-report love scores before and after the breakup, their perceptions of problems in the relationship, reports concerning which of the

FIGURE 1 Women's and men's mean love scores in 1972 and 1973 for those who stayed together and those who broke up during this interval. The means are based on individuals who filled out the love scale in both years (121 women and 118 men in couples who stayed together, 31 women and 39 men in couple who broke up). The maximum possible score is 117.

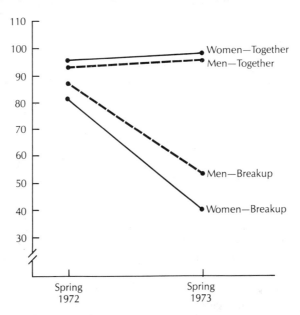

partners most wanted to break up, reports of emotional reactions to the breakup, and reports of whether or not the former partners "stayed friends" after the breakup.

Love Scale Scores

Z. Rubin's love scale was administered to men and women in the sample at two points in time, separated by one year (spring 1972 and spring 1973; the love scale was not readministered in 1974). Within this interval, approximately one-third of the total sample of 231 couples had broken up. Figure 1 presents average love scores of men and women in couples who stayed together over the course of the year (Togethers) and in couples who broke up (Breakups). The members of Together couples were reporting their feelings of attachment, caring, and intimacy toward a current dating partner at each of two points in time. The members of Breakup couples were responding to a current dating partner in 1972 and a former dating partner in 1973. Not surprisingly, the love scores of men and women in Breakup couples plummeted over the one-year period, while those of men and women in Together couples stayed at high levels (Time × Together-Breakup interaction $F = 107$, $df = 1, 129$, $p < .001$). Of greater relevance are the differences between the average scores of men and women. Among couples who stayed together over the one-year period, women's scores were initially slightly higher than their boyfriends' scores. Among couples who were to break up over the one-year period, in contrast, the women's love scores were somewhat lower than their boyfriends' scores. Thus, it would have been possible to do a better job of predicting whether a couple would stay together on the basis of women's than of men's scores. In addition, among couples who broke up over the one-year period, the women's scores remained lower than the men's—and dropped even more sharply. (The overall Sex $\times$ Together-Breakup interaction is significant; $F = 7.83$, $df = 1, 129$, $p < .01$). The total pattern of scores points to two related conclusions: First, a woman's love was a better predictor or barometer of the continuation of a relationship than a man's love; and, second, as a prelude to and/or as a consequence of the ending of a close relationship, women's love tended to diminish more than men's. Both these conclusions seem consistent with the proposition that women tend to fall out of love more readily than men do.

Perception of Problems in the Relationship
One likely reason for—or concomitant of—falling out of love is the perception that one's relationship is beset with problems. We gave the members of couples who had broken up a list of 13 common problem areas and asked them to indicate which of these problems had contributed to the breakup. We found that women indicated more problems had contributed to the breakup than men did (paired $t = 3.15$, $df = 77$, $p < .003$). In particular, more women than men cited "differences in interests," "differences in intelligence," "conflicting ideas about marriage," "my desire for independence," and "my interest in someone else" as contributing factors. The only problem that men cited more frequently than women was "living too far apart." These reports are retrospective and clearly susceptible to distortion. Nevertheless, they suggest that women tended to be more sensitive than men to problem areas in their relationship, and that women were more likely than men to compare the relationship to alternatives, whether hypothetical or actual. These tendencies seem consistent with the postulated tendency of women to fall out of love more readily than men.

Who Precipitated the Breakup?
If women tend to fall out of love more readily than men, we would expect them to precipitate the breakups (i.e., to play the role of "breaker-upper") more frequently than men. Combining men's and women's independent reports of "who wanted to break up more," we were able to estimate that the woman was more interested in breaking up in 51% of the couples, the man in 42%, and the breakup was reported as being mutual in 7%. This preponderance is a small one and could be written off as a statistical accident. It is given greater credence, however, by the fact that our participants' reports of the breakups of their closest opposite-sex relationship prior to our study (with over 200 cases for each sex) suggested a similar preponderance of female-initiated breakups (Hill, 1974). And in his study at the University of Michigan, Z. Rubin (1969) found that 17 of 25 nonmutual breakups had been precipitated by women.

TABLE 1 Who Wanted to End the Relationship, as a Function of the Couple's Relative Involvement Before the Breakup[a]

	Man was more involved	Woman was more involved	Total
Man wanted to end	7	26	33
Mutual ending	4	1	5
Woman wanted to end	23	16	39
Total	34	43	

[a]Measures were derived by averaging men's and women's independent reports; 18 cases in which the two partners were "equally involved" are omitted.

This preponderance of female-precipitated breakups might be easily understood if women tended to have been less involved in their relationships than men. This was not the case. Once the relationships of the couples in our study had proceeded beyond their early stages, the women were by all indications at least as involved as the men. Combining the two partners' reports before the time of the breakup, women were categorized as the more involved partner in 45% of all couples and men as more involved in 36%; in the remaining 19% the two partners were classified as being equally involved. As Peter Blau has suggested, a relationship in which there is unequal involvement will not always be ended by the less involved partner: "Whereas rewards experienced in the relationship may lead to its continuation for a while, the weak interest of the less committed, *or the frustrations of the more committed* probably will sooner or later prompt one or the other to terminate it" (Blau, 1964, p. 84, italics added). Our data, presented in Table 1, suggest that both of Blau's postulated patterns describe a substantial number of breakups precipitated by women. Many women ended their relationship when they were the less involved partner and wanted to move on to better alternatives. But in a substantial minority of cases, relationships were ended by women who had been the more involved partner, when they finally realized that their commitment was not reciprocated. When breakups were precipitated by men, in contrast, only the first pattern was common. Relationships were frequently ended by men when they were the less involved partner, but only rarely when they were the more involved. In asymmetrical situations in which one's own love was not reciprocated, women seemed to be more able than men to relinquish their love and to take the initiative in ending the relationship.

Seeing It Coming
Apparently related to women's ability to give up love more readily than men do is the fact that women tended to see the breakup coming sooner than men did. There was an overall tendency for women to report that the breakup was more "gradual" (as opposed to "abrupt") than their boyfriends reported (paired $t = 2.10$, $df = 76$, $p = .039$). As the means in Table 2 indicate, this difference was most clear when the woman was the breaker-upper and when the breakup was mutual. When the man was the breaker-upper, the breakup was perceived by both sexes as being about

TABLE 2 Mean Ratings of Perceived Gradualness of the Breakup, as a Function of Who Wanted to Break Up[a]

	Man wanted to break up (N = 31)	Both wanted to break up (N = 5)	Woman wanted to break up (N = 37)
Women's perceived gradualness	4.23	6.00	5.05
Men's perceived gradualness	4.29	3.80	3.89

Scale: 1 = ending was "extremely abrupt"; 9 = ending was "extremely gradual."
[a] Only couples in which we have reports from both partners are included.

equally abrupt (interaction $F = 3.02$, $df = 2, 70$, $p = .056$). On the whole, then, women seem to have had more a warning that a breakup was coming than men did, and perhaps more time to prepare themselves to fall out of love.

Emotional Reactions to Breaking Up
Our proposition about sex differences in falling out of love would suggest that breaking up tends to be a more traumatic experience for men than for women. Unfortunately, the quantitative data available to test this proposition are limited to the 15 couples from whom we obtained reports of emotional reactions to the breakup from both partners on the one-year follow-up. These data suggest that men were hit harder by the breakup than were women. In the wake of the breakup, men tended to report that they felt more depressed, more lonely, less happy, and less free than did their former girlfriends (paired ts median $p = .15$). Even women who had been more involved in the relationship than their boyfriends tended to feel greater equanimity after the breakup than did men in comparable situations. For example, one woman ended her relationship with her boyfriend when she could no longer tolerate his continuing neglect of her. Ruth later told us that she had no regrets about her relationship with David or its ending. "It's probably the most worthwhile thing that ever happened to me in my 21 years," she said, "so I don't regret having the experience at all. But after being in the supportive role, *I* want a little support now." Ruth added that "I don't think I ever felt romantic [about David]—I felt practical. I had the feeling that I'd better make the most of it because it won't last that long." In contrast, men in such situations were more likely to regret that they had not been able to give the relationship another chance, and more likely to act with incredulity to indications that their love was not reciprocated. Women who were rejected were also likely to react with considerable grief and despair, but they seemed less likely to retain the hope that their rejectors really loved them after all.

In this connection, it is of interest to consider the clinical impressions of George W. Goethals (1973), based on his experience counseling young people: "The notion that the young adult male is by definition a heartless sexual predator does not

TABLE 3 "Staying Friends," as a Function of Who Wanted to Break Up[a]

Did the couple "stay friends"?	Who wanted to end the relationship?			
	Man	Mutual	Woman	Total
Yes	28 (70%)	5 (71%)	23 (46%)	56
No	12 (30%)	2 (29%)	27 (54%)	41

[a]"Staying friends" was assessed by pooling the two partners' reports. If either partner said "No," the couple was categorized as nonfriends.

bear examination. In point of fact some of the most acute cases of depression I have ever had to deal with occurred in attempting to help young men with their betrayal by a young woman in whom they had invested a great deal and who had, as the relationship developed, exploited them rather ruthlessly" (p. 94).

Our proposition about a sex difference in the readiness to give up love may provide part of the explanation for Goethals' observation. It is unlikely that women are by nature any more "exploitative" or "ruthless" than men are. But if men are in fact less ready or able to give up love, men may be particularly likely to be mystified, hurt, and ultimately crushed by rejection.

Staying Friends

If men find it more difficult than women to renounce their love, we might also expect relations between former partners to be more strained after the woman has rejected the man than vice versa. Whereas a rejected woman may be able to redefine her relationship with her boyfriend from "love" to "friendship"—which, as Davis (1973) notes, is often a euphemism for acquaintanceship—a rejected man may find such a redefinition more difficult to accomplish. In such cases, "staying friends" is likely to be impossible. The data are clearly consistent with this expectation. As shown in Table 3, a couple was much more likely to report that they stayed friends if the man had been the one who precipitated the breakup or if the breakup had been mutual than if the woman had precipitated the breakup ($\chi^2 = 5.83$, $p < .06$).

POSSIBLE EXPLANATIONS

Having summarized the evidence for both parts of our generalization—men tend to fall in love more readily than women, and women tend to fall out of love more readily than men—let us turn to possible explanations for it. We will consider three lines of explanation for the observed differences, from the standpoints of psychoanalytic theory, the social and economic context of mate selection, and the socialization of men and women in the management of their own emotions.[2]

When we reported these findings to our psychoanalytically oriented colleagues, they welcomed them, because they provide support for a psychoanalytic notion about sex differences in the capacity for love. This is the notion that because of the strength of their initial love for their mothers, men have a greater capacity for complete heterosexual commitment than women do. Women, in contrast, are believed to handle the Oedipal conflict in a more gradual way, first shifting their sexual interest from mother to father, and later from father to substitute objects of love. Working from this set of assumptions, Nancy Chodorow (1976) argues that "Women have a richer, ongoing inner world to fall back on, and the man in their life does not represent the intensity and exclusivity which the woman represents to the man" (p. 463). Because of their richer reserve of internalized emotional objects and their lesser emotional dependence on men, women may tend to enter romantic relationships more cautiously, to leave them more readily, and to rebound more easily after a rejection. We remain skeptical of this psychoanalytic position, because there is very little firm evidence for the set of early childhood events that it presumes to occur. Nevertheless, the psychoanalytic position may have a grain of truth, and it suggests that the sex difference that we have been discussing may be general, extending far beyond the specific domain of campus courtship. There just may be some deeply rooted aspects of men's and women's personality that make it likely for men to make more complete heterosexual commitments than women—or, at least, to do so more quickly—and that makes it harder for men to get over the loss of such a love relationship.

A different explanation of our propositions derives from an examination of the social and economic context of mate selection. Rather than presupposing any deep personal or emotional differences between men and women, this explanation focuses on the peculiarities of the institution of courtship in Western society. According to this approach, women must be more cautious, practical, and realistic than men in the process of mate selection for simple social and economic reasons. In most marriages, the wife's status, income, and life chances are far more dependent on her husband's than vice versa. As a result, in a "free choice" system of mate selection (like that in contemporary America) the woman must be especially discriminating. She cannot allow herself to fall in love too quickly; nor can she afford to stay in love too long with the "wrong person." The woman must carefully evaluate her partner's strengths and weaknesses and must compare him to potential alternative partners, in order to be sure that she is getting the best possible "bargain" in the marriage market. Men, on the other hand, being in a position of greater power both in the larger society and in the marriage market, do not need to worry so much about such rational calculations. Instead, the man can better afford the luxury of being "romantic." This sociological explanation is by no means a new one. It was stated most bluntly by Willard Waller (1938) in the 1930s: "There is this difference between men and women in the pattern of bourgeois family life. A man, when he marries, chooses a companion and perhaps a helpmate, but a woman chooses a companion and at the same time a standard of living. It is necessary for a woman to be mercenary" (p. 243).

We suspect that there is a great deal of truth in this analysis. In spite of the recent movement toward more egalitarian sex-role attitudes, the marriage marketplace in the 1980s is still characterized to a large extent by the same basic inequities that characterized it in the 1930s. This socioeconomic explanation remains incomplete, however, because it does not deal with the links between the social and economic requirements of mate selection and the differences in emotional capacities that we have been discussing. To fill out the explanation, therefore, we also need to focus on what men and women learn about the experience and management of emotions.[3] Evidence from a variety of studies suggests that women come to be more socially sensitive than men. Women tend to be more empathic than men (Hoffman, 1977) and more sensitive to nonverbal communication (Hall, 1978). In addition, women have been found to make sharper distinctions between interpersonal sentiments, such as those of "liking" and "loving" than men do (Z. Rubin, 1970). These sex differences are in accord with the traditional assignment of women to the role of social-emotional specialists, while men are the traditional task specialists (Parsons & Bales, 1955). The emphasis on social-emotional matters in women's socialization may lead them to be more sensitive than men to the quality of their interpersonal relationships, both in the present and projecting into the future. Thus, women may evaluate their relationships more carefully than men do, and their criteria for falling in love—and for staying in love—may be higher than men's.

In addition, Hochschild (1975) has argued convincingly that women come to be more adept than men at cognitively managing their own feelings. In self-report accounts of emotional experience that Hochschild collected, women were more likely than men to write about actively managing their own feelings, using such terms as "I made myself feel . . .," "I snapped myself out of it," and "I tucked my feelings in." Men seemed to be less closely in touch with their own feelings and to take a less active stance with regard to them. Hochschild's analysis suggests that women are also more likely to exert cognitive control over such events as falling in and out of love. Such greater cognitive control would help to explain our findings that women tended to be (1) less likely to be swept off their feet into a deep love relationship; (2) more likely to perceive the problems of a relationship and, if necessary, to end it; (3) better able to get over their feelings of loss when a relationship ends; and (4) when rejected, better able to accomplish the transition from love to friendship. Women presumably develop this greater cognitive control as a result of socialization experiences which emphasize that they have a considerable degree of power in the emotional domain, whereas such emotional socialization is neglected for men. It can also be argued that a greater degree of control for women in the domain of their own emotions is a necessary adaptation to their lesser degree of power and control in other domains.

SUMMARY AND CONCLUSION

We proposed a two-part generalization about sex differences in love: (1) Men tend to fall in love more readily than women; and (2) women tend to fall out of love more readily than men. We then presented data from a longitudinal study of 231 student dating couples in support of these propositions. The data suggest that women were less "romantic" than men, more cautious about entering into romantic relationships, more sensitive to the problems of their relationships, more likely to compare their relationships to alternatives, more likely to end a relationship that seemed ill fated, and better able to cope with rejection. Psychoanalytic theorists might account for these differences in terms of underlying differences between men and women in the capacity for complete heterosexual commitment. A socioeconomic explanation, in contrast, focuses on the need for women to be more practical and discriminating than men in the marriage marketplace. A final explanation refers to socialization experiences through which women learn to control and manage their own emotions more effectively than men do.

To evaluate these (and any other) explanations of sex differences in love, it would be valuable to investigate the generalizability of the present findings to other segments of the population. Our sample was restricted to college students of predominantly middle-class background. Almost all these students deferred marriage until or beyond the end of their college years. Would similar sex differences be found among working-class couples who do not attend college and who typically marry earlier? To the extent that the sex differences we observed reflect deeply rooted aspects of men's and women's personality, we might expect them to generalize beyond the boundaries of social class. It might be, however, that women in working-class couples tend to feel a greater pressure to marry early and are less likely, as a result, to exhibit the degree of caution and cognitive control in their love relationships that the women in our sample displayed (cf. L. B. Rubin, 1976). It would also be interesting to determine whether the sex differences we observed would also be found among older unmarried couples or among previously married men and women who are considering remarriage.[4] It is hoped that future research will extend the present investigation to couples of different social class backgrounds, ages, and marital histories, as well as of different cultures and historical periods. Such comparative research would help us to choose more knowledgeably among the various explanations of sex differences in love that have been or might be offered. Such research would also help to create a fuller appreciation of the ways in which psychological, social structural, and cultural forces join to shape intimate relationships between men and women.

NOTES

1. In many cases, the partners decided to discuss their responses with one another after they had turned in their questionnaires. This was one way in which participation in the research had an effect on couples' relationships, in some respects similar to the effects of couples counseling. For a discussion of "couples research as couples counseling," see Z. Rubin and Mitchell (1976).

2. Another possible line of explanation derives from sociobiological speculations about sexual selection. Our finding that women tended to be more "selective" than men, being more

cautious about entering a romantic relationship and quicker to extricate themselves from a relationship that seemed ill fated, might be seen as an instance of the general tendency for females in the large majority of animal species to be more selective than males in their choice of mate. See, for example, Barash (1977). It would involve a rather large jump from the data at hand, however, to argue that the human sex difference under discussion is a product of natural selection.

3. It is, of course, possible that some aspects of sex differences in the experience and management of emotions build on differences in genetic predispositions. For example, Hoffman (1977) has summarized evidence that newborn female infants are more likely than newborn males to cry in response to another infant's cry, suggesting the possibility of a constitutional precursor of sex differences in empathy. That sex differences in the experience and management of emotions build on such constitutional differences remains highly speculative, however. In contrast, it is hard to doubt that social learning in early and late life plays a major role in the development of emotional differences.

4. Zeiss and Zeiss (1978) have recently reported data on sex differences in initiating and adjusting to divorce that closely parallel our findings of sex differences in falling out of love.

REFERENCES

Barash, D. P. *Sociobiology and behavior*. New York: Elsevier, 1977.
Blau, P. M. *Exchange and power in social life*. New York: Wiley, 1964.
Burgess, E. W., and Wallin, P. *Engagement and marriage*. Philadelphia: Lippincott, 1953.
Chodorow, N. Oedipal asymmetries and heterosexual knots. *Social Problems*, 1976, *23*, 454–468.
Coombs, R. H., and Kenkel, W. F. Sex differences in dating aspirations and satisfaction with computer-selected partners. *Journal of Marriage and the Family*, 1966, *28*, 62–66.
Davis, M. S. *Intimate relations*. New York: Free Press, 1973.
Goethals, G. W. Symbiosis and the life cycle. *British Journal of Medical Psychology*, 1973, *46*, 91–96.
Hall, J. A. Gender effects in decoding nonverbal clues. *Psychological Bulletin*, 1978, *85*, 845–857.
Hill, C. T. *The ending of successive opposite-sex relationships*. Doctoral dissertation, Harvard University, 1974.
Hill, C. T., Rubin, Z., & Peplau, L. A. Breakups before marriage: The end of 103 affairs. *Journal of Social Issues*, 1976, *32*(1), 147–168.
Hobart, C. W. The incidence of romanticism during courtship. *Social Forces*, 1958, *36*, 362–367.
Hochschild, A. R. *Attending to, codifying and managing feelings: Sex differences in love*. Paper presented at the meeting of the American Sociological Association, San Francisco, August 1975.
Hoffman, M. L. Sex differences in empathy and related behaviors. *Psychological Bulletin*, 1977, *84*, 712–722.
Knox, D. H., Jr., & Sporakowski, M. J. Attitudes of college students toward love. *Journal of Marriage and the Family*, 1968, *30*, 638–642.
Parsons, T., & Bales, R. F. *Family, socialization, and interaction processes*. Glencoe, Ill.: Free Press, 1955.

Rubin, L. B. *Worlds of pain: Life in the working-class family.* New York: Basic Books, 1976.

Rubin, Z. *The social psychology of romantic love.* Doctoral dissertation, University of Michigan, 1969.

Rubin, Z. Measurement of romantic love. *Journal of Personality and Social Psychology,* 1970, *16*, 265–273.

Rubin, Z., & Mitchell, C. Couples research as couples counseling. Some unintended effects of studying close relationships. *American Psychologist,* 1976, *31*, 17–25.

Waller, W. *The family: A dynamic interpretation.* New York: Dryden, 1938.

Zeiss, A. M., & Zeiss, R. A. *Sex differences in initiation of and adjustment to divorce.* Paper presented at the meeting of the Western Psychological Association, San Francisco, April 1978.

ARTICLE 3
The Courtship Game: Power in the Sexual Encounter

NAOMI B. McCORMICK AND CLINTON J. JESSER

Dating is a crucial aspect of courtship in the United States. While recently dating has changed in significant ways, McCormick and Jesser discuss how power is an important dynamic in the courtship process. They note fundamental differences in how males and females act as they move from flirtation to seduction, frequently falling back on traditional gender-role stereotypes to guide their behavior.

THE BOUNDARIES OF HETEROSEXUAL COURTSHIP—the institutional way that men and women become acquainted before marriage—have changed dramatically since a physician (Robinson, 1929, p. 262) offered the following advice:

> Fortunate are you, my young girl friend, if you come from a well-sheltered home. . . . But if you have lost your mother at an early age, or if your mother is not the right sort . . . if you have to shift for yourself, if you have to work in a shop, in an office, and particularly if you live alone and not with your parents, then temptations in the shape of men, young and old, will encounter you at every step; they will swarm about you like flies about a lump of sugar; they will stick to you like bees to a bunch of honeysuckle.

In the 1800s and the beginning of this century, courtship among middle-class North Americans was a sober process that strongly emphasized the end goal of

"The Courtship Game: Power in the Sexual Encounter." From *Changing Boundaries: Gender Roles and Sexual Behavior*, edited by Elizabeth Rice Allgeier and Naomi B. McCormick by permission of Mayfield Publishing Company. Copyright © 1983 by Mayfield Publishing Company.

marriage. Almost everyone, including feminists, valued sexual self-control (Hersh, 1980). Unmarried people were severely restricted as to *whom* they might court and *what* went on during courtship (Gordon, 1980). Because the respectable unmarried woman was constantly supervised by older adults, sexual experience with her courtship partner was unlikely (Kinsey et al., 1953).

Power—the ability to influence another person's attitudes or behavior—is an essential component of courtship. As societies become increasingly industrialized and urbanized, family and kin exercise less power over the young. "The world, as a whole, seems to be moving toward the idea of free choice in marriage" (Murstein, 1980, p. 778). The absence of parental power does not imply that courtship has become a free-for-all. Now, unmarried people have most of the power in determining the course of their own courtship.

To some extent, the sexual revolution is the result of this shift in power. As premarital sex has gained peer acceptance, increasing numbers of youthful North Americans, especially women, have sexual intercourse before marriage (Zelnik & Kantner, 1977, 1979, 1980). Sex and intimacy, not always leading to marriage, may be the new end goals of courtship.

We look at the ways people use power in courtship. Given the limited research in the area, some of our discussion is more relevant to never-married, heterosexual, middle-class youth than to other groups.

We examine gender differences in using and responding to power, and explore all levels of courtship, from meeting someone to having sex. We focus predominantly on new dating relationships (such as how people flirt and ask dates out). We ask who holds most of the power in a dating relationship, the man or the woman. After this inquiry, we subject the sexual encounter itself to rigorous power analysis. We view sexual expression in political terms. And we inquire how and why people use particular strategies for having and avoiding sex and prefer some coital positions over others.

POWER AND COURTSHIP

Power is one person's ability to impose wishes on another more than that other can impose his or her wishes (Weber, 1964, p. 152). The exercise of power is effective when one person succeeds in changing another person's thoughts, attitudes, or behavior (Raven, 1965, 1971). People acquire power and dominance in many ways. Sometimes they acquire and use power in a heavy-handed way. They use physical strength, social position in organizations and politics, and control over land and money, and often take unfair advantage of an influencee, or target (Collins & Raven, 1968; French & Raven, 1959).

Rape occurs when an influencing agent uses physical strength or the threat of violence to influence a victim (influencee) to have sex. Using superior wealth or the authority one has acquired as the boss or leader to convince a less-than-willing influencee to have sex is also heavy-handed. In the very least, such a use of power is sexual harassment. At its most extreme, it is rape.

Students sometimes balk when we suggest that nice people, not just sadists, use power during courtship. "If both the man and the woman like each other or want sex," they argue, "then power is irrelevant." According to these romantic students, lovers just happen to meet, just happen to get carried away and have sex. Characteristic of this attitude, some California college students are unable to relate to the question "Assuming you are very desirous of sexual intercourse . . . describe how you would try to influence your date to have sex" (McCormick, author's files):

- I don't think I would try to influence my date to have sex. If it's time and everything is right, sex will follow its own pattern.
- I would not try. In time we would make it.
- It must come about naturally. No persuasion should be necessary. Otherwise, lovemaking is not a sign of affection but rather a disgusting sexual act.

Not everyone sees dating and mating in the same romantic light as these three students. Many, ourselves included, speculate that people are able to plan strategies carefully for attracting and seducing sexual partners. Power, the potential to influence another person's attitudes or behavior, may be an essential component of any romantic attraction or sexual relationship.

As we said before, there is more than one way to acquire and use power. The development of skills and knowledge, being perceived as attractive and likeable, and even acting helpless or "needy" can all be used to influence someone else (Collins & Raven, 1968; French & Raven, 1959). Often, these less obvious kinds of power are more effective because they avoid hitting the influencee over the head.

People often assume that their behavior is self-motivated when they receive relatively little feedback indicating that they are being influenced by someone else (Bem, D. J., 1972). For this reason, the effective strategies for influencing courtship tend to be subtle enough to convince a partner that he or she wanted what happened as much as the influencing agent wanted it. Flirtation in bars is an excellent example:

> We begin with a woman entering a bar. She is nicely dressed, and perhaps she expects to meet someone. As she enters, she characteristically stops, and nearly always adjusts some item of clothing, an accessory, or her hair. Then she looks around the bar, a deliberate scan, not a casual glance. . . . Then, she goes to the bar itself, walking directly to it and ends up standing next to some man. . . . If he fails to look at her, or if he turns away, the interaction is likely to cease immediately. But we assume that he moves slightly, perhaps looking at her briefly, perhaps just shifting his weight. His seeming trivial action is essential, since it has communicated to her that she has been noticed. . . . If things go further, he may well believe that *he* picked up *her*. [Perper & Fox, 1980a, p. 12]

MEN AS PURSUERS, WOMEN AS PURSUED

Sex and the broader conditions of life cannot be separated. This fact is especially important today with the changing circumstances and opportunities in men's and women's lives. Because societies vary greatly, it is difficult to generalize about the relationship between sex and power.

Where or under what conditions do women have the most control over their sexual lives? Generally speaking, in five specific situations women have greater say over who they have sex with and how they have sex (see Hacker, 1975, pp. 212–214). First, women enjoy more sexual freedom where there is little or no emphasis on warfare and militarism. Second, women control their own sexuality more where men participate in child rearing or where child-care services are available. Third, women have greater power in their sexual relationships when they have political representation. Fourth, women enjoy greater sexual freedom where they have helped mold the mythology, religious beliefs, and world view of their groups. Finally, women are more sexually emancipated where they have economically productive roles such as control over tools, land, produce, and products.

In most societies, women's sexuality is more restricted than that of men (Safilios-Rothschild, 1977). A *double standard*—the expectation that premarital and extramarital sex is more permissible for men—has been employed. The cultural conditions just cited modify the extent to which the double standard is enforced. On the other hand, cultures that emphasize male dominance in society as a whole severely penalize premarital sex by women (Safilios-Rothschild, 1977). For example, in some Arab societies, women who break sexual conventions may be executed, sometimes by their brothers or fathers (Critchfield, 1980, p. 67).

Fortunately, not all societies oppress the sexual choices of women. The more power women have in society as a whole, the weaker the double standard is. The double standard is weak or absent in matrilineal societies, where descent and inheritance occur through the mother and land is owned or controlled by women (see Jesser, 1972, pp. 248–249). The double standard is also on the wane in societies that reward women for bearing children by encouraging them to be sexually permissive, as in Polynesia. Finally, the double standard dies in societies that have an overabundance of men. For example, in the Marquesa Islands, where men greatly outnumbered women at one time, men did all the work, including housework and child care. In contrast, Marquesan women spent their time attracting and pleasing sexual partners. In glaring contrast to North American culture, Marquesan men catered to women's whims, women were viewed as hypersexual, and sex started only after the woman gave the signal (Leibowitz, 1978).

Intriguing as they were, the Marquesans were unusual. Most societies are politically controlled by men. Consequently, sexual access to women is part of the property system (see Stephens, 1963, pp. 240–259). In societies in which women are regarded as property, men try to "enrich" themselves by having sex as frequently and with as many women as possible. Correspondingly, women try to keep themselves "precious" by staying beautiful or desirable while they refuse to give themselves to any but the "right" men—their present or future husbands (Safilios-Rothschild, 1977).

Male-dominated societies seem to permit men to use power to have sex with women while women are allowed to exercise power only to avoid sex with unsuitable partners. In such a society, a woman who uses power to seduce a man openly is regarded as "bad" and possibly dangerous. A man who uses power to avoid sex with a "turned-on" woman is regarded as "religious" at best, and inept, stupid, and unmanly at worst. This selection explores the extent to which this value system about power in sexual encounters survives in North American society.

POLITICS OF COURTSHIP IN NORTH AMERICA

It would be difficult to describe adequately the conditions of North American society that have affected the status of women and, consequently, their sexual relations with men. Essentially, what happened is that the industrial system has become so successful during the last 70 years that men's and women's spheres of work have separated. Except for lower-class women and during times of war, many women were eliminated from the expanding workforce. Place of work and place of residence separated under industrialization, and for the "secure and successful" workforce, a man's paycheck became adequate for the support of the family (see Deckard, 1975, pp. 199–375). A "cult of domesticity" emerged (Degler, 1980), supposedly reigned over by women. This involved the attempt on the part of the middle class to upgrade (professionalize) full-time housework.

Such developments were not without strains, which have become especially noticeable within the last 25 years. Middle-class women became dissatisfied with the "gilded cage"—the house—in the midst of their declining and unrewarding domestic functions. More educated than ever before and trying their best to manage while the family's income was eaten away by inflation, housewives did not find their lot easy. As a more companionate marriage of equality became the ideal, middle-class homemakers became even more sharply aware of their unhappiness.

Divorce, when it did break the trap, sometimes resulted in more difficulties than it solved. Outside employment or going back to college also posed dilemmas for women. Domestic duties could be reduced but not completely eliminated (Davidson & Kramer-Gordon, 1979); instead of having one job, working and student mothers now had two. Eager to pacify insecure husbands, employed women retained major responsibility for child care and housework (Berkove, 1979; Hooper, 1979; Pleck, 1979).

Just as the balance of power between the genders influences sexual relations in other cultures, North American women's subordinate economic and political status severely limits their sexual freedom. It should come as no surprise that the "battle of the sexes" in the living room spills over into the bedroom.

Although it is less severe in North America than in the Third World, a double standard—unfavorable to women's premarital and extramarital sexual expression, while favorable to such expression by men—has prevailed. Admittedly, this standard is looser than in the past (Hopkins, 1977; Komarovsky, 1976; Peplau, Rubin, & Hill, 1977). Also, it is important to remember that the double standard is stronger among white, lower-middle-class people. It is rare among certain ethnic or racial groups, including working-class U.S. blacks, who do not stigmatize children who are born out of wedlock (Broderick, 1979); Scanzoni & Scanzoni, 1976). Here, too, women's relative power outside of sexual relationships is important. Although economically oppressed in their own right, lower-class black women are less dependent on men for their livelihood than are white women. Consequently, they may enjoy sex for its own sake rather than expecting it to be an economic bargaining tool (Coleman, 1966).

Unlike their lower-class black counterparts, middle-class white women use sex as a bargaining tool with some hazard to themselves because of the lingering double standard: Specifically, they are tacitly expected to exchange sexual and emotional companionship for economic support from men (Scanzoni, 1970, pp. 4–25). The sexual revolution hasn't changed matters much. Instead of waiting until she marries the "right man" before having sex, today's middle-class woman waits until she *finds* the "right man" to have *premarital* sex (Hunt, 1974).

For some, the goal of courtship continues to be finding the right man to marry. Such arrangements give women veto power over sex and thus a bargaining lever for other things for which sex might be exchanged. The extent to which this veto power operates successfully, or even the desirability of that kind of power in the first place (as compared to true independence and initiative power), can be questioned (Gillespie, 1971, p. 448). Nevertheless, current researchers continue to find that women are less interested in having sex than men (Mancini & Orthner, 1978; Mercer & Kohn, 1979) and have greater power than men when a couple makes the decision to abstain from sexual intercourse (Peplau et al., 1977). If men are really more enthusiastic about sex, it is likely that the traditional pattern of bargaining continues.

CHANGING BOUNDARIES OF COURTSHIP

Not all North American women view sex as a bargaining tool for finding men who will take care of them. Courtship patterns are changing and these changes could alter the balance of power between the genders. The decrease in the number of people marrying early and staying married weakens the once close connection between successful courtship and marriage. Courtship now occurs for a variety of other purposes, such as for having "a good time," for sexual release only, and for proving one's competence and status. Nevertheless, these changes in themselves may not lead to substantial social change.

The sexual politics of courtship may be especially resistant to change because couples beginning to court often engage in posing—the tendency to fall back on those gender roles that are stereotypically appropriate or safe (Heiss, 1968, p. 82). For example, even if such stereotyped behavior is uncharacteristic, a woman might be careful to appear as sweet and unassertive as possible on the first date so as to make a good impression.

In the next two major sections, we question the extent to which "posing" continues in sexual encounters (in bars, bedrooms, or the back seats of cars). The following types of questions arise:

1. Do men and women desire (seek) different types of benefits, satisfactions and goals in the courtship process, and if so, what are they, and who actually achieves them?
2. Who may touch whom, and how or where?
3. When sex and sexual signaling occur, to what extent do the values of the society and the gender roles disadvantage one or the other party in the form, content, timing of the acts or in the benefits to be derived?

DYNAMICS OF DATING

Despite some speculation that the traditional date is disappearing (Murstein, 1980, p. 780), dating remains a crucial part of courtship for many young people (Bell, 1979, p. 49), although now, with more mixed gender places available and more casualness as the norm; people don't date as much, or they just call it "going out." Dating enables courting partners to get away from their parents and have the opportunity to know each other better. However, there is more to dating than just being alone together. Dating is also a bargaining process in which the man provides certain goods and services in exchange for others provided by the woman. In other words, dating is similar to marriage because it requires negotiations to take place. Perhaps this point would be much clearer if we analyze how the genders use power on the typical date. The best and most enjoyable way to do this is to imagine a traditional date.

When we imagine the classic North American date, the following narration comes to mind. On Tuesday, Herbert Dumple makes the first move. He calls Mildred Smedly, doing his best to sound sophisticated and desirable over the telephone. Herbert asks Mildred out for the following Saturday. Mildred accepts, especially impressed that he phoned a few days in advance. She assesses that this means that Herbert *values* her. She might have refused, even if she had nothing to do but wash her hair, if he phoned only one day before.

On Saturday, Herbert arrives at Mildred's home promptly at 7 P.M. He is neatly attired in a sports jacket and dress slacks. His neat appearance brings home the fact that he values Mildred (jogging shoes and old jeans would be a "putdown") and that he himself is valuable. Herbert's middle-class status or aspirations are clear from his respectable appearance. In other words, he looks like "a good catch."

Mildred isn't ready yet, accidentally on purpose. Consequently, Herbert has about ten minutes to chat with her family. He sits on the loveseat, somewhat anxious about making a good impression, and tries to sound intelligent and responsible. Meanwhile, Mildred's Mom and Dad look him over. The assessment process is so critical that the family has turned off the television set and are even checking out Herbert's manners, asking, "Would you like a snack while you wait?"

Mildred finally comes down to the living room at 7:10 P.M. However, perhaps we are jumping the gun. Before we describe her entrance, it might be useful to speculate about her reasons for being late. Actually, Mildred has two reasons for taking her time, both of which are relevant to our previous discussion of courtship as a bargaining process. First, by being late, she has more time to make herself attractive (put on make up, fix her hair, make sure she has chosen the right outfit). Second, by being late, she is telling Herbert that she is a valuable person, a woman *worth* waiting for.

At last, Mildred comes down the stairs from her room. She looks "beautiful," at least according to Herbert and her father. Some parent-child negotiations take place concerning where the couple is going and when Mildred can be expected home. "Oh, Mom!" she says, "Can't you trust me?" Finally, the awkward process is over, and Herbert escorts Mildred to his car. He opens the door for her, an excellent example of the posing we described earlier.

Mildred is relieved that Herbert has a car. This increases his marketability. Apparently, he might have some money. She dislikes dating men who expect her to travel on the bus. After all, dates are potential husbands, and it is important to find a good provider.

Mildred and Herbert go to dinner. Again, Herbert provides evidence of his potential as a good provider by taking her somewhere expensive and paying for their meals. Furthermore, he shows that he is appropriately masculine (posing again) by ordering their meals and taking responsibility for assessing the quality of the wine.

During dinner, Mildred tries her best to be a good conversationalist. This means that she asks Herbert about school or his job, focusing on *his* interests and trying her best to sound enthusiastic. Mildred's selfless concern for Herbert's interests is not accidental. After all, she wants to present herself as a valuable person, a potential spouse. She has already established that she is attractive ("beautiful"); her market value could only increase if she also seems empathic and emotionally supportive.

After dinner, the couple goes to Herbert's apartment. He has carefully made sure that his roommates are out so that the two of them can be alone. Mildred and Herbert smoke a couple of joints and share a small bottle of imported wine. Then Herbert begins to make some sexual moves. Now Mildred must make a choice. It is up to Mildred (the woman) to decide "how far to go" (Peplau, Rubin, & Hill, 1977).

Back in the 1950s, Mildred would probably have gone along with Herbert until they engaged in heavy petting. She would have been unlikely to have had sexual intercourse. In those days, many women remained "technical virgins" until marriage because coital experience would have "cheapened them" or decreased their market value for marriage.

The values of the 1950s are over. . . . More and more women, including young adolescents, are having sex before marriage. Today, a woman's market value might be increased by being a good lover (providing, of course, that she has sex with only one man at a time in a relationship). There are still strong prejudices against women who have many partners.

If Mildred really likes Herbert (she may convince herself she loves him), she will probably have sex. However, she will let Herbert make most of the moves. Although it is acceptable for today's woman to have sex, it is still risqué for her to ask for it.

Mildred and Herbert do have sex. Before they straighten out their hair and clothing, trying to look innocent for the benefit of parents, it is appropriate to analyze the power implications behind Mildred's decision to have sex. Mildred's potential power during her sexual encounter depends heavily on her age. If she is a young adolescent, she is probably trading off sex for Herbert's esteem. Indeed, if this is the case, Mildred may have traditional gender-role attitudes and be looking toward Herbert to fulfill multiple dependency and status needs (Scanzoni & Fox, 1980). Young adolescent women who wait until they are older before having sex often have higher self-esteem and more profeminist attitudes than their more coitally experienced peers (Cvetkovich et al., 1978; Larkin, 1979; Scanzoni & Fox, 1980).

Putting on your Sherlock Holmes hats, you may be confused at this point. How could Mildred be a young teenager? Wasn't she able to order wine at the restaurant? Well, if Mildred wasn't "passing" as an older woman, you have a good point. More importantly, the power implications of having sex are completely different for older, college-age women. If Mildred is a college student, having sex suggests that she feels good about herself. In contrast with younger women, sexually active college women are more independent, autonomous, assertive, and profeminist than their less sexually active peers (Scanzoni & Fox, 1980).

DATING, POWER, AND EQUITY

Our description of Herbert and Mildred's date provides some insight into how men's and women's different interests are reflected in their experience of power during courtship. Equity theory, which predicts that people prefer relationships in which each party receives equal relative gains (Hatfield & Traupmann, 1980), is useful at this point. Will Mildred and Herbert become a couple? Will they feel secure enough about each other to have sex again? Will Herbert and Mildred eventually have one of those long-term relationships?

According to equity theory, people in inequitable (or "unfair") relationships (both those receiving too little and those receiving too much) become distressed enough to either balance or end the relationship. According to equity theory, then, Herbert and Mildred will be likely to seek a balanced or fair relationships, especially if they have already made a heavy investment in one another (Walster, Walster, & Berscheid, 1978, p. 6).

As their dating relationship develops, if either Herbert or Mildred feels that he or she is getting a "raw" deal, the injured party will use power ploys to achieve a better position. For example, if Herbert "cheats" on Mildred by sleeping with another woman, she will let him have it during an argument. Mildred will continue to feel distressed until Herbert makes it up to her for cheating, perhaps by being especially considerate or even by purchasing an engagement ring. Such actions would help balance the relationship and would lead to greater happiness for both members of the couple (Hatfield & Traupmann, 1980).

Suppose, however, that Mildred's power ploys have failed. Despite her entreaties, Herbert goes out with even more women. Her friends tell her that he is sleeping around with everyone. Moreover, Herbert is into drugs quite heavily and appears to have become an insensitive lout. Unless she can convince herself that she deserves such treatment (alas, some women do this and stay around), Mildred may end or withdraw from what has become an unsatisfactory relationship. Inequitable relationships are unstable. Both the overbenefited, cheating Herbert and the underbenefited, jealous Mildred are not satisfied with the way things are going (Hatfield & Traupmann, 1980). Motivated by anger and guilt, such people would be more likely than equitable couples to use power ploys or attempt to end their relationships (see Walster, Walster, & Traupmann, 1978).

Another important issue for Herbert and Mildred is their evaluation of each other's value or marketability with different dating partners. As described earlier, Herbert and Mildred are constantly assessing each other and themselves. Early on, even Mildred's parents get into the act. This evaluation process continues throughout their relationship. Herbert and Mildred are more likely to stay together if they are well-matched in age, intelligence, educational plans, and good looks (Hill, Rubin, & Peplau, 1976).

Finally, equity theory is relevant to the quality of Herbert and Mildred's sex life together. They are more likely to continue having sex if neither partner feels "ripped off" or overbenefited. Actually, having sex in the first place suggests that this couple feels they are a good match. Couples in inequitable relationships are more likely to stop before "going all the way" (Walster, Walster, & Traupmann, 1978, p. 89). Even more relevant to power during sexual encounters, Mildred and Herbert will have very different feelings about *why* they had sex, depending on whether their relationship is equitable or unfair. If Herbert and Mildred truly make up after their argument about Herbert's affair, they will say that they had sex because *both* wanted to, citing reasons such as "mutual physical desire" and "enjoyment" (Walster, Walster, & Traupmann, 1978, p. 89). On the other hand, if their sexual relationship continues, despite the fact that Mildred still feels she is getting the short end of the stick, sex too would be seen as unfair. Herbert, for example, might feel that Mildred obliged him to make love to her to apologize for his indiscretion. In contrast, if Herbert wanted sex more than Mildred, she might blame him for taking advantage of her here, too.

STRATEGIES FOR INITIATING NEW RELATIONSHIPS

The discussion of equity theory helps explain the balance of power in long-term relationships. However, it provides very little information about how people actually use power, especially in beginning new relationships. Focusing first on flirtation and then on the process during which one person asks another for a date, we will discuss *how* men and women actually use power with new dating partners.

Flirtation

A flirtation "is a sequence of behavior, mostly nonverbal, which brings two people into increasing sociosexual intimacy" (Perper & Fox, 1980a, p. 23). To date, the best research on what actually happens during flirtation (as opposed to what people think happens) is by Timothy Perper and Susan Fox.

Clocking over 300 hours of observations of working-class and middle-class single people of varying ages in New Jersey and New York City bars, Perper and Fox have overturned two of our most beloved cultural myths. The first overturned cultural myth is that the man is always the sexual aggressor, eagerly pressing himself on the coy but reluctant woman. At least in the beginning of the flirtation process, men do not "swarm around a woman like bees about a lump of sugar." Instead, the woman often makes the first move. Because her move is subtle—usually nothing more than standing close to her target—it is understandable that the man might erroneously come to believe that *he* started the interaction.

According to the second overturned myth, men know more about flirtations and sex than women. In glaring contrast with this expectation, women are the experts:

> Typically, women are exquisitely familiar with what occurs during flirtations while men are generally quite ignorant. Women can describe in great detail how they and other women flirt and pick up men, and what men do (and just as frequently, what men do *not* do). In contrast, . . . [most] men were unfamiliar with all or most of the events of flirtations. Even quite successful men had no idea how they attracted women and what happened during a flirtation. Often men create vast and complex theories . . . but they seem to possess little or no information. [Perper & Fox, 1980b, p. 4]

Now that we have established that women know more about flirting, at least in bars, it is still appropriate to ask, "Which gender has the most power?" Egalitarians should be delighted to know that flirtations are not under the control of one person. Instead, both genders have equal power.

A successful flirtation is one that will probably result in a new dating or sexual relationship. Such a flirtation depends on the influencee or target signaling that the flirt's influence attempts are welcome at *each* stage of the flirtation. To clarify this, we have described the stages of a flirtation in Figure 1.

As you can see, neither gender dominates a successful flirtation. Indeed, it is hard to separate the influencing agent from the influencee. Each person takes a turn at influencing the partner and at signaling that the other's influence attempts are welcome. As the couple's relationship becomes more secure, flirtation strategies become more obvious:

> [A woman] commonly touches the man before he touches her. Her touch is made, typically with the palm of the hand flat, and not with the fingertips, in a light, fleeting and pressing gesture. . . . She might brush against him with her hip or back, she may lean on him briefly, or she might brush against him while she turns to look at something. An alternative is for the woman to remove an otherwise nonexistent piece of lint from

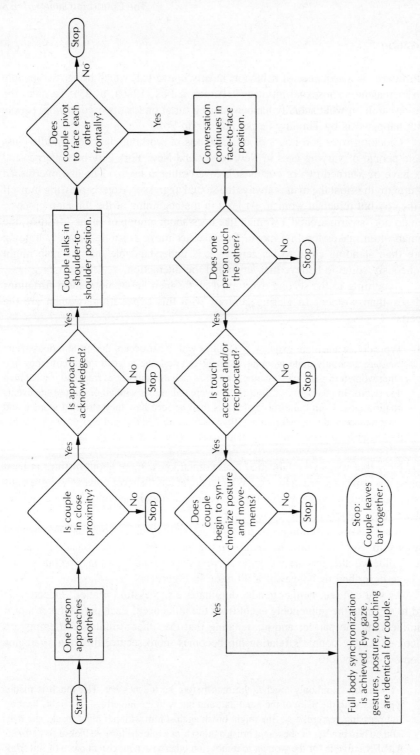

FIGURE 1 Flirtation in Bars (Note that either gender may initiate a flirtation. Power is shared; neither partner dominates the outcome.)

Based on work published in Timothy Perper, *Sex Signals: The Biology of Love* (Philadelphia: ISI Press, 1985). Used by permission of the author.

the man's jacket (men's jackets in bars collect such lint very readily). [Perper & Fox, 1980a, p. 18]

An important aspect of touching is that it is safe, in that it can be interpreted as accidental. This saves face for the influencing agent should the flirtation prove unsuccessful. Touching during flirtation is similar to body language, a popular strategy for both men and women when they approach a date to have sexual intercourse (McCormick, 1979). This strategy relates to a point made earlier; less obvious kinds of sexual power may be preferred because they are subtle enough to convince a partner that he or she wanted what happened just as much as the influencing agent did.

Asking for a Date

As you recall, Herbert Dumple asked Mildred Smedly out. North American gender-role norms are rather strict about who initiates a date. The traditional woman can, at most, make herself attractive. She is not allowed to call the man or start a new relationship. In contrast, the traditional man (shy or not) is responsible for initiating any and all relationships with women. Does the man still have all the power when it comes to initiating a new dating relationship? Perhaps not. Current research sheds light on this issue.

Research fails to clarify whether or not women take more assertive roles in dating than in the past. Nevertheless, there are strong indications that traditional gender-role norms prevail. Men are more likely to say that they would initiate new heterosexual relationships than women are (Green & Sandos, 1980). Moreover, both gender-typed and androgynous college students report that men typically initiate dates and pay for expenses incurred on dates (Allgeier, 1981).

Men still have most of the power when it comes to initiating new dating relationships. However, not everyone is happy with this situation. Already, some college students are pushing for change (see Allgeier, 1981). Liberals are experimenting with innovative dating patterns. Androgynous people, especially men, tend to have more experiences with female-initiated dates than do gender-typed individuals. Also, some men express dissatisfaction with the traditional date. Men are more positive about women initiating and paying for dates than women are.

In any event, the times may be ripe for change. A recent study at a southern university suggests that college men welcome female sexual initiation. In this study, women students approached strangers with this line: "I have been noticing you around campus. I find you very attractive." After saying this, most of the women are extremely successful in gaining men's verbal compliance with requests to go out on dates, to go to the women's apartments, and especially to go to bed with the women (Clark & Hatfield, 1981). Apparently, more than a few college men enjoy being propositioned. However, as we shall see, wishes aren't always realities.

Women are well advised to be cautious when contemplating whether or not to ask men out. The gender-role norms for male initiative in courtship are far from dead. When college students are asked how they feel about someone who either starts a friendly conversation or invites a co-worker to dinner at a restaurant, responses are stereotyped (Green & Sandos, 1980). Both men and women feel that it is more appropriate for the man than for the woman to take the initiative in either situation. Perhaps this helps explain why women are so conservative. Not surprisingly, women are more positive about men initiating dates than men are (Allgeier, 1981).

There is more to power in courtship than asking someone out. People also have the power to refuse. Women are more pragmatic than men about courtship. They want to size men up before committing themselves to relationships. Moreover, the double standard may still be operating. Women may be especially reluctant to go along with a man's sexual advances when he comes on "too strong." Clark & Hatfield's (1981) study supports this idea. When men ask strangers on a college campus for dates, they are successful. However, when they ask the new acquaintances to go to their apartments or go to bed with them, they are not greeted with the warm enthusiasm that men give women for these same requests. Instead, most are flatly refused, with such responses as "You've got to be kidding" or "What is wrong with you? Leave me alone" (p. 17).

Changing Boundaries of Dating

We may conclude at this point that North American courtship is not as rigidly bound to the double standard as many of us suspected. Traditional gender-role norms are being challenged in three ways. First, with the exception of young adolescents, sexually active women are not exploited by men. Instead, the coitally experienced woman is likely to be independent and profeminist. Also, she is unlikely to have sex outside of an equitable or balanced relationship. Second, men are not the experts when it comes to picking up dates. If knowledge is power, then women are more powerful than men when it comes to signaling men with whom they would like to become better acquainted. Finally, although it is not known if women are asking men out more than in the past, the times are ripe for change. Some men are highly receptive to women's invitations for dates and sex (Hite, 1981). Probably, the main thing that holds women back is the continued stereotype that such behavior is unfeminine or inappropriate.

Courtship has changed, at least in its preliminary stages. However, what happens once a couple does have sex? In the remainder of this chapter, we focus more specifically on the relationship between men and women during sexual intercourse. We also further identify and document the sexual value system—society's evolving rules for playing the courtship game.

ROLES AND POWER DURING SEXUAL INTIMACY

In general, dominant and extroverted people report engaging in more varied sexual behavior and with more frequency than submissive, introverted people (De Martino,

1963; Eysenck, 1971, 1972; Maslow, 1963). Extroverts of both genders are more likely than passive individuals to be sexual nonconformists, willing to deviate from expected gender roles in their sexual encounters. For example, unlike her passive counterpart, the dominant and extroverted woman may be more likely to take the active sexual role. She is also more willing to experiment with nontraditional coital positions, such as being on top of her partner during sex.

Traditionally, women have been expected to play a relatively passive role in sexual encounters in our own and in some other societies (Ford & Beach, 1951; Rainwater, 1971; Rubin, 1976, pp. 134–154). It is no accident that the stereotype of the sexually passive woman is consistent with both the sexual double standard we have alluded to previously and our culture's idealization of the "passive-receptive" woman (Broverman et al., 1972; McKee & Sherriffs, 1957; Rosenkrantz et al., 1968).

Consistent with the double standard and idealization of the passive-receptive woman, most dating and married couples report that a woman seldom actively initiates a couple's first intercourse (Peplau, Rubin, & Hill, 1977). Generally, the woman is less likely to initiate sex than the man (Bell, 1976; Carlson, 1976; Crain & Roth, 1977). These findings still leave many questions unanswered, however. For example, the need to look feminine might lead a woman to overlook or forget some subtle strategies she uses to give her partner the idea that *he* wants sex. What are the politics of deciding whether and how to have sexual intercourse?

Seduction and Rejection

Historically, the whole scenario of the sexual encounter, from initiation and timing to positioning of the bodies, was expected to be initiated by men (Long-Laws, 1979). In contrast, the woman has been expected either to passively go along with men's sexual advances or to refuse to have sex (Ehrman, 1959; Gagnon & Simon, 1973; Komarovsky, 1976; Peplau, Rubin & Hill, 1976, 1977).

Young people's sexual vocabularies characterize men as sexual actors and women as sexual objects. According to Sanders and Robinson (1979, p. 28), women describe the penis with "cute little euphemisms" such as "Oscar," "penie," "ding-a-ling," and "babymaker." In contrast, young men are more likely to use power slang such as "womp," "rod," "pistol," and "stick." Similarly, men use slang for sexual intercourse, such as "poking," "stroking a hole," and "hosing," suggesting that men perceive sex as demonstrations of power. Their language contrasts strongly with women's vague, passive, and romantic images of sex: "doing it," "being inside," "going all the way," and "loving."

Women's typical words for describing sexuality (that is, "penis," "vagina," and "make love") reveal attitudinal constraints that contrast strongly with men's verbal flexibility. Unlike women, men are able to communicate about sex with a variety of audiences (Sanders & Robinson, 1979). Less free to talk about sex, women may also feel less free to be sexual actors than are men.

On the other hand, women may feel more comfortable about being sexual actors than they did in the past. A large proportion of both men and women in ongoing relationships report persuading their partners to have sex using such straightforward approaches as touching, snuggling, kissing, allowing their hands to wander, and asking directly (Jesser, 1978). When asked how men respond to their sexual advances, women who ask directly to have sex are *not* more likely to report being rebuffed than those who fail to report asking directly. Predictably, women who are opposed to female sexual modesty and the need for women to pursue their interests inconspicuously are especially likely to consider directly asking their dates to have sex. Equally predictable, men whose partners had directly asked them to have sexual relations are also those who disagreed with the view that women must regard their bodies more modestly than men. These same men are especially likely to disagree with the position that men's dominant interest in women is sexual (Jesser, 1978).

Could sexual role playing be on the wane among today's courting couples? Another study finds strong similarities between men's and women's use of influence in sexual encounters. When asked how they would influence a date to have sex in a hypothetical sexual encounter, both male and female college students prefer indirect strategies. For instance, one student said, "I would test my limits by holding hands, sitting closer to this person, etc." (McCormick, 1979, p. 199). As you recall, using touch as an approach is also popular in flirtations.

Indirect strategies are preferred for good reasons. In their very subtlety, these strategies provide the influencing agent with a haven from possible rejection. For example, imagine that Mildred Smedly uses another indirect approach—environmental manipulation—to influence Herbert Dumple to have sex. After doing her best to set the stage for sex by dimming the lights, providing some liquor, and playing sensual music on the stereo, she is shocked when Herbert makes fun of her. Fortunately, her strategy permits her to avoid the hot seat when Herbert ridicules her.

> *Herbert (in challenging voice):* Mildred, are you coming on to me?
>
> *Mildred (firmly):* No, Herbert. I just like that record a lot. Also, candlelight is good for my eyes after a long day of typing my term paper.

Clearly, indirect strategies are useful for having sex. However, seduction, a highly direct and arousal-oriented strategy, is also popular with both men and women for influencing a hypothetical partner to have sex. Here are two quotes from students' essays describing how they would seduce their dates (McCormick, author's file):

> [*Female college student*:] I would start caressing his body and start kissing his chest, maybe stomach. I would try to be very sexy, doing this especially with lots of eye contact. Probably a few sighs here and there to let him know I feel sexually stimulated. This would probably be all I would do aside from wearing something slinky and bare. I could not get myself to perhaps start unbuckling his pants.
>
> [*Male college student*:] I would proceed to use my charm and bodily contact to get what I want. (1) If she shys away in a huff, I would stop and try to talk it out. If we got nowhere from there, I would take my ass home. (2) If she gives me the come on, then I would proceed very vigorously. (3) If she pushed away gently, I would tell her

what a good time we had, that we are not children, and since we relate so well, we should "Get it on."

Consistent with the stereotype that men are sexual actors and women are sex objects, men say they would use seduction significantly more than women say they would. However, both genders prefer seduction over all other strategies for influencing a potential partner to have sex. Women are clearly capable of experiencing men as sex objects.

Gender differences also disappear when college students are asked how they would avoid sexual intercourse with a turned-on partner. Both men and women prefer direct, obvious strategies. Moralizing—using religious convictions or moral opposition to argue against having sex—is one such strategy. As one volunteer put it, "I would state directly that that type of relationship is reserved for marriage" (McCormick, 1979, p. 199).

Clearly, some of today's young singles are breaking out of sexual role playing. At any rate, the previously discussed findings suggest that male and female college students have the *potential* to enjoy courtship interactions that are free of gender-role stereotypes. Nevertheless, egalitarian readers should be advised to hold their applause. It is important to note that regardless of their gender-role attitudes, the overwhelming majority of college students stereotype men as using all possible strategies to have sex and women as using every strategy in the book to avoid having sex (LaPlante, McCormick, & Brannigan, 1980; McCormick, 1976, 1979). If such stereotyping persists, it is likely that students believe that others want them to engage in sexual role playing and that such behavior will be common with future dating partners.

In contrast with their lack of sexual role playing when asked what they would do within hypothetical sexual encounters with imaginary or future partners, students report strict adherence to gender-role stereotypes during their actual courtship experiences. When describing their personal use of power via various strategies, men use strategies significantly more than women do to influence dates to have sex, and women use strategies significantly more than men do when the goal is avoiding sexual intercourse. Complementing this finding, when asked to describe their experiences as influencees within sexual encounters, men are more likely than women to report being influenced by all strategies for avoiding sex. Also, women report being more likely than men to be influenced by the majority of strategies for having sex (LaPlante, McCormick, & Brannigan, 1980; McCormick, 1977).

The continued importance of gender roles in sexual encounters is supported by the fact that a higher proportion of women than men say that they use extraordinarily subtle or indirect signals to indicate their sexual interest. For instance, they report using eye contact, changes of appearance or clothing, and changes in tone of voice. Could it be that these women are fearful of "turning off" their partners if they are more sexually assertive? Consistent with such an opinion, many women are hesitant about being assertive with dates with whom they want to have sex, perceiving this as unacceptable to men. Ironically, women may be holding themselves back sexually more than men would desire. Relatively unoffended by sexually assertive women (Jesser, 1978), college men are more positive about women initiating sex than are women (Allgeier, 1981). Just as they would welcome greater female initiative in dating, men also desire more assertive sexual partners. For instance, many older men agree that "it's exciting when a woman takes the sexual initiative" (Tavris, 1978, p. 113).

Overall, the research on strategies for having and avoiding sex has disappointing implications for those who prefer sexual behavior liberated from gender roles. It may be that courtship is a bastion for the strict performance of stereotyped gender-role behavior. However, before we accept this conclusion, let us look at the research on coital positions.

Coital Positions: Who's on Top

The "missionary position," in which the woman lies on her back while the man is on top of her, seems to be the most common coital position in North American society (Allgeier, 1981; Ford & Beach, 1951, p. 23). A few decades ago, many people never attempted to use any but the man-on-top position for sexual intercourse (Kinsey, Pomeroy, & Martin, 1948). Although contemporary couples are more likely to experiment with other positions (Hunt, 1974), the man-on-top coital position may have some symbolic value. This position closely fits the stereotype in our society that the male should be active while the female remains passive during sexual intercourse.

Little is known about the relationship between gender-role identity and coital position. Recent research sheds some light on this issue. Unmarried college students were asked to give their opinions of couples who are having sexual intercourse in various positions including the ever-popular man-above and the nontraditional woman-above coital positions. Interestingly enough, women are more conservative than men in their evaluation of the woman who is on top of her partner during sexual intercourse. Women, but not men, have a real distaste for the couple in the woman-above position. They rate the woman as "dirtier, less respectable, less moral, less good, less desirable as a wife, and less desirable as a mother when she is on top than when she is beneath the man during intercourse" (Allgeier & Fogel, 1978a, p. 589). Given these feelings, it is not surprising that women report having sex with the man on top more frequently than do men. Possibly, gender-role stereotypes color their reasons for preferring this position. Women claim that the man-above position offers greater "emotional satisfaction" than the woman-above position (Allgeier, 1981, p. 326).

Advocates of social change may be even more disappointed with some additional findings. Allgeier (1981) found no relationship between gender-role identification and feelings about various coital positions. Moreover, both androgynous and gender-typed college students are likely to have greater experience with the man-above coital position than with the woman-above position. As Allgeier and Fogel suggest,

> Aside from giving birth, there is probably no other arena in which gender differences have more importance to us than in our sexual interaction. "Vive la difference"

expresses our pleasure with the ways in which males and females *do* differ; and perhaps this attitude is so strong that it overwhelms the potential influence of [androgyny]. [Allgeier & Fogel, 1978b, p. 13]

Allgeier and Fogel's findings parallel McCormick's (1979) failure to find a relationship between being profeminist and rejecting the stereotype that men always initiate sex and women do everything they can to avoid sex. In addition, their findings bear some strong similarities to Jesser's research. Both Jesser and Allgeier find that women are more attached to the gender-role norms that prescribe female sexual submissiveness. Women's attitudes may present greater barriers to egalitarian sexual behavior than do men's attitudes.

ARE THE RULES FOR COURTSHIP CHANGING?

The courtship game has changed in three ways. First, thanks to the weakening of the double standard and encouragement from feminists, women are freer to make the first move in a flirtation and to have premarital sex than in the past. Second, men seem to be encouraging women to be more assertive in initiating sexual relationships. Third, given the opportunity, men would reject sex and women would try to have sex with the same strategies that are characteristically used by the other gender.

Despite these changes, the courtship game continues to follow gender-role stereotypes. Men ask women out more than vice versa. Men are more likely to influence a date to have sex; women are more likely to refuse sex. The persistence of gender-role playing is associated with a number of factors, such as women's more conservative attitudes toward sexuality. Another factor that contributes to the courtship game is that North American society views people who behave "out of role" (that is, passive men and assertive women) as less well adjusted and popular (Costrich et al., 1975).

As the women's liberation movement gains increasing acceptance, the courtship game will probably become less rigid. For instance, although women prefer masculine over feminine men, male college students are not more attracted to feminine women than they are to masculine women (Seyfried & Hendrick, 1973). Even more indicative of social change, recent research contradicts earlier reports (Goldberg, Gottesdiener, & Abramson, 1975; Johnson et al., 1978) that men are turned off by profeminist women. Johnson, Holborn, and Turcotte (1979) found that men were more attracted to women who support the feminist movement than they were to those who are described as nonsupporters. As attitudes toward feminist women become more liberal, people may try out more egalitarian ways of dealing with courtship. However, such experimentation is likely to be minimal at first because out-of-role behavior is especially risky within sexual encounters where people already feel emotionally vulnerable.

Some insight into future directions for male-female courtship is provided by a vocal and liberal group of physicians and sex therapists. In the past decade, a number of therapists have contributed their ideas in opinion articles with titles such as "Do men like women to be sexually assertive?," "Who should initiate sexual relations, husband or wife?," and "Who should take the sexual lead—the man or the woman?" In many of these articles, medical personnel and sex therapists indicate that they favor sexual equality in the bedroom for all but those few patients who would experience emotional turmoil as a result of such equality. The following statement is characteristic:

> The assumption that the male must be the aggressor in sexual intercourse and the female passive is simply not valid. Each partner must be both passive and aggressive and must participate mutually and cooperatively in the interaction. The unfortunate persistence of labels attributable to one sex as opposed to another has led to untold misery, creating feelings of guilt, inferiority, inadequacy, or even suspicions of homosexuality when one's inclinations are somewhat different from prevailing notions concerning sex roles. [Salzman, 1976, p. 23]

If the public continues to be exposed to these liberal ideas, values of future generations will slowly but surely change. It may not be overly optimistic to predict that college students in the year 2000 will be less likely to stereotype strategies for having sex as something only men would do and strategies for avoiding sex as something only women use. Furthermore, women in the year 2000 may be less likely to put down those who experiment with nontraditional coital positions. Before we get carried away with optimism, however, it is important to note that not all opinion leaders reject the sexist courtship game. Indeed, a powerful backlash by psychiatrists and other sex therapists has indicated that they are highly alarmed by the supposedly explosive impact of the women's liberation movement on power in the sexual encounter. According to this backlash, women who are assertive about sex endanger the security of otherwise solid relationships and make men neurotic, anxious, or insecure. Ruminating about the new impotence allegedly caused by sexually aggressive women, these conservative sex experts advise women to remain sexually passive in the bedroom or, at the very least, to be cautious when taking the sexual initiative with men (Ginsberg, Frosch, & Shapiro, 1972; also see F. Lemere's and G. Ginsberg's commentary in Kroop, 1978). Clearly, if the stereotyped courtship game does die, it will have an agonizing and elongated death rattle.

Hopefully, this . . . has shed a little light on the complexities of power in courtship. If you are still perplexed, consider this popular dirty joke: " 'I nearly fainted last night when my date asked me to kiss him,' exclaimed the sweet young thing to her escort. 'Really?' laughed the boy. 'Then you're gonna die when you hear what I have in mind' " (Fry, 1977, p. 64). Are you laughing? If you are, what tickled you? Would this joke be just as amusing if the sweet young thing was an adolescent boy and the escort was an adolescent girl?

REFERENCES

Allgeier, E. R., The influence of androgynous identification on heterosexual relations. *Sex Roles*, 1981, 7, 321–330.

Allgeier, E. R., & Fogel, A. F. Coital position and sex roles: Responses to cross-sex behavior in bed. Expanded version of an article that appeared in *Journal of Consulting and Clinical Psychology*, 1978. Unpublished manuscript, 1978. (Available from Dr. Elizabeth R. Allgeier, Department of Psychology, Bowling Green State University, Bowling Green, Ohio 43403). (b)

Allgeier, E. R., & Fogel, A. F. Coital position and sex roles: Responses to cross-sex behavior in bed. *Journal of Consulting and Clinical Psychology*, 1978, *46*, 588–589. (a)

Bell, R. R. Changing aspects of marital sexuality. In S. Gordon & R. W. Libby (Eds.), *Sexuality today and tomorrow*. Belmont, Calif.: Wadsworth, 1976.

Bell, R. R. *Marriage and family interaction*. Homewood, Ill.: Dorsey Press, 1979.

Bem, D. J. Self-perception theory. In L. Berkowitz (Ed.), *Advances in experimental social psychology* (Vol. 6). New York: Academic Press, 1972.

Berkove, G. F. Perceptions of husband support by returning women students. *The Family Coordinator*, 1979, *28*, 451–458.

Broderick, C. B. *Marriage and the family*. Englewood Cliffs, N.J.: Prentice-Hall, 1979.

Broverman, I., Vogel, S., Broverman, D., Clarkson, F., & Rosenkrantz, P. Sex role stereotypes: A current appraisal. *Journal of Social Issues*, 1972, *28*, 59–78.

Carlson, J. The sexual role. In F. I. Nye (Ed.), *Role structure and analysis of the family*. Beverly Hills, Calif.: Sage, 1976.

Clark, R. D., III, & Hatfield, E. *Gender differences in receptivity to sexual offers*. Unpublished manuscript, 1981. (Available from Dr. Elaine Hatfield, Psychology Department, 2430 Campus Road, Honolulu, HI 96822).

Coleman, J. S. Female status and premarital sexual codes. *American Journal of Sociology*, 1966, *72*, 217.

Collins, B. E., & Raven, B. H. Group structure: Attraction, coalition, communication, and power. In G. Lindzey & E. Aronson (Eds.), *The Handbook of social psychology* (2nd ed., Vol. 4). Reading, Mass.: Addison-Wesley, 1968.

Costrich, N., Feinstein, J., Kidder, L., Maracek, J., & Pascale, L. When stereotypes hurt: Three studies of penalties for sex-role reversals. *Journal of Experimental Social Psychology*, 1975, *11*, 520–530.

Crain, S., & Roth, S. *Interactional and interpretive processes in sexual initiation in married couples*. Paper presented at the meeting of the American Psychological Association, San Francisco, August 1977.

Critchfield, R. Sex in the third world. In C. Gordon & G. Johnson (Eds.), *Readings in human sexuality: Contemporary perspectives* (2nd ed). New York: Harper & Row, 1980.

Cvetkovich, G., Grote, B., Lieberman, E. J., & Miller, W. Sex role development and teenage fertility-related behavior. *Adolescence*, 1978, *13*, 231–236.

Davidson, L., & Kramer-Gordon, L. *The sociology of gender*. Chicago: Rand McNally, 1979.

Deckard, B. S. *The women's movement*. New York: Harper & Row, 1975.

Degler, C. *At odds: Women and family in America from the revolution to the present*. New York: Oxford University Press, 1980.

DeMartino, M. F. Dominance-feeling, security-insecurity, and sexuality in women. In M. F. DeMartino (Ed.), *Sexual behavior and personality characteristics*. New York: Grove Press, 1963.

Ehrmann, W. *Premarital dating behavior*. New York: Holt, Rinehart & Winston, 1959.

Eysenck, H. Introverts, extroverts, and sex. *Psychology Today*, 1971, *4*, 48–51; 82.

Eysenck, H. L. Personality and sexual behavior. *Journal of Psychosomatic Research*, 1972, *16*, 141–152.

Ford, C. S., & Beach, F. A. *Patterns of sexual behavior*. New York: Harper & Row, 1951.

French, J. R., Jr., & Raven, B. H. The bases of social power. In D. Cartwright (Ed.), *Studies in Social Power*. Ann Arbor: University of Michigan Press, 1959.

Fry, W. F. Psychodynamics of sexual humor: Seduction. *Medical Aspects of Human Sexuality*, 1977, *11*, 64; 69–71.

Gagnon, J. H., & Simon, W. *Sexual conduct: The social sources of human sexuality*. Chicago: Aldine, 1973.

Gillespie, D. L. Who has the power? The marital struggle. *Journal of Marriage and the Family*, 1971, *33*, 445–458.

Ginsberg, G. L., Frosch, W. A., & Shapiro, T. The new impotence. *Archives of General Psychiatry*, 1972, *26*, 218–220.

Goldberg, P. A., Gottesdiener, M., & Abramson, P. R. Another put-down of women? Perceived attractiveness as a function of support for the feminist movement. *Journal of Personality and Social Psychology*, 1975, *32*, 113–115.

Gordon, M. The ideal husband as depicted in the nineteenth-century marriage manual. In E. H. Pleck & J. H. Pleck (Eds.), *The American man*. Englewood Cliffs, N.J.: Prentice-Hall, 1980.

Green, S. K., & Sandos, P. *Perceptions of male and female initiators of relationships*. Paper presented at the meeting of the American Psychological Association, Montreal, September 1980.

Hacker, H. M. Gender roles from a cross-cultural perspective. In L. Duberman (Ed.), *Gender and sex in society*. New York: Praeger, 1975.

Hatfield, E., & Traupmann, J. Intimate relationships: A perspective from equity theory. In S. Duck & R. Gilmour (Eds.), *Personal relationships*. London: Academic Press, 1980.

Heiss, J. (Ed.), *Family roles and interaction*. Chicago: Rand McNally, 1968.

Hersh, B. G. A partnership of equals: Feminist marriages in 19th-century America. In E. H. Pleck & J. H. Pleck (Eds.), *The American man*, Englewood Cliffs, N.J.: Prentice-Hall, 1980.

Hill, C. T., Rubin, Z., & Peplau, L. A. Breakups before marriage: The end of 103 affairs. *Journal of Social Issues*, 1976, *32*, 147–168.

Hite, S. *The Hite report on male sexuality*. New York: Knopf, 1981.

Hooper, J. O. My wife, the student. *Family Coordinator*, 1979, *28*, 459–464.

Hopkins, J. R. Sexual behavior in adolescence. *Journal of Social Issues*, 1977, *33*, 67–85.

Hunt, M. *Sexual behavior in the 1970s*. Chicago: Playboy Press, 1974.

Jesser, C. J. Women in society: Some academic perspectives and the issues therein. *International Journal of Sociology of the Family*, 1972, *2*, 246–259.

Jesser, C. J. Male responses to direct verbal sexual initiatives of females. *Journal of Sex Research*, 1978, *14*, 118–128.

Johnson, R. W., Doiron, D., Brooks, G. P., & Dickinson, J. Perceived attractiveness as a function of support for the feminist movement: Not necessarily a put-down of women. *Canadian Journal of Behavioral Science*, 1978, *10*, 214–221.

Johnson, R. W., Holborn, S. W., & Turcotte, S. Perceived attractiveness as a function of active vs. passive support for the feminist movement. *Personality and Social Psychology Bulletin*, 1979, *5*, 227–230.

Kinsey, A. C., Pomeroy, W. B., & Martin, C. E. *Sexual behavior in the human male*. Philadelphia: Saunders, 1948.

Kinsey, A. C., Pomeroy, W. B., Martin, C. E., & Gebhard, P. H. *Sexual behavior in the human female*. Philadelphia: Saunders, 1953.

Komarovsky, M. *Dilemmas of masculinity: A study of college youth*. New York: Norton, 1976.

Kroop, M. When women initiate sexual relations. *Medical Aspects of a Human Sexuality*, 1978, *12*, 16, 23; 28–29.

LaPlante, M., McCormick, N., & Brannigan, G. Living the sexual script: College students' views of influence in sexual encounters. *Journal of Sex Research*, 1980, *16*, 338–355.

Larkin, R. *Suburban youth in cultural conflict*. New York: Oxford University Press, 1979.

Leibowitz, L. *Females, males, families: A biosocial approach*. Belmont, Calif.: Wadsworth, 1978.

Long-Laws, J. *The second X: Sex role and social role*. New York: Elsevier, North Holland, 1979.

Mancini, J. A., & Orthner, D. K. Recreational sexuality preferences among middle-class husbands and wives. *Journal of Sex Research*, 1978, *14*, 96–106.

Maslow, A. H. Self-esteem (dominance feeling) and sexuality in women. In M. F. DeMartino (Ed.), *Sexual behavior and personality characteristics*. New York: Grove Press, 1963.

McCormick, N. *Impact of sex and sex role on subjects' perceptions of social power in hypothetical sexual interactions*. Paper presented at the meeting of the Western Psychological Association, Los Angeles, April 1976.

McCormick, N. B. Gender role and expected social power behavior in sexual decision-making (Doctoral dissertation, University of California at Los Angeles, 1976). *Dissertation Abstracts International*, 1977, *37*, 422-B. (University Microfilms No. 77-1646, 151)

McCormick, N. B. Come-ons and put-offs: Unmarried students' strategies for having and avoiding sexual intercourse. *Psychology of Women Quarterly*, 1979, *4*, 194–211.

McCormick, N. Author's files. Unpublished data, 1976. (Information available from N. McCormick, Ph.D., Department of Psychology, State University of New York College at Plattsburgh, Plattsburgh, NY 12901).

McKee, J., & Sherriffs, A. The differential evaluation of males and females. *Journal of Personality*, 1957, *25*, 356–371.

Mercer, G. W., & Kohn, P. M. Gender difference in the interpretation of conservatism, sex urges, and sexual behavior among college students. *Journal of Sex Research*, 1979, *15*, 129–142.

Murstein, B. I. Mate selection in the 1970s. *Journal of Marriage and the Family*, 1980, *42*, 777–792.

Peplau, L., Rubin, Z., & Hill, C. The sexual balance of power. *Psychology Today*, 1976, *10*, 142–147; 151.

Peplau, L. A., Rubin, Z., & Hill, C. T. Sexual intimacy in dating couples. *Journal of Social Issues*, 1977, *33*, 86–109.

Perper, T., & Fox, V. S. *Special focus: Flirtation behavior in public settings*. Paper presented at the meeting of the Eastern Region of the Society for the Scientific Study of Sex, Philadelphia, April 1980. (a)

Perper, T., & Fox, V. S. Flirtation and pickup patterns in bars. Paper presented at the meeting of the Eastern Conference on Reproductive Behavior, New York, June 1980. (b)

Pleck, J. H. Men's family work: Three perspectives and some new data. *Family Coordinator*, 1979, *28*, 481–488.

Rainwater, L. Marital sexuality in four cultures of poverty. In D. S. Marshall & R. C. Suggs (Eds.), *Human sexual behavior: Variations in the ethnographic spectrum*. New York: Basic Books, 1971.

Raven, B. H. Social influence and power. In D. Steiner & M. Fishbein (Eds.), *Current studies in social psychology*. New York: Holt, Rinehart, & Winston, 1965.

Raven, B. H. The comparative analysis of power and power preference. Paper presented at the meeting of the Albany Symposium on Power and Influence, Albany, New York, October 11–13, 1971.

Robinson, W. J. *Woman: Her sex and love life* (17th ed.). New York: Eugenics Publishing, 1929.

Rosenkrantz, P., Vogel, S., Bee, H., Broverman, I., & Broverman, D. Sex role stereotypes and self-concepts in college students. *Journal of Consulting and Clinical Psychology*, 1968, *32*, 287–295.

Rubin, L. B. *Worlds of pain: Life in the working class family*. New York: Basic Books, 1976.

Safilios-Rothschild, C. *Love, sex, and sex roles*. Englewood Cliffs, N.J.: Prentice-Hall, Spectrum Books, 1977.

Salzman, L. Sexual aggressivity vs. passivity. *Medical Aspects of Human Sexuality*, 1976, *10*, 16–17; 23; 28–29.

Sanders, J. S., & Robinson, W. L. Talking and not talking about sex: Male and female vocabularies. *Journal of Communication*, 1979, *29*, 22–30.

Scanzoni, J. H. *Opportunity and the family*. New York: Free Press, 1970.

Scanzoni, J. H., & Fox, G. L. Sex roles, family, and society: The 70s and beyond. *Journal of Marriage and the Family*, 1980, *42*, 743–756.

Scanzoni, L., & Scanzoni, J. H. *Men, women, and change*. New York: McGraw-Hill, 1976.

Seyfried, B. A., & Hendrick, C. When do opposites attract? When they are opposite in sex and sex-role attitudes. *Journal of Personality and Social Psychology*, 1973, *25*, 15–20.

Stephens, W. N. *The family in cross-cultural perspective*. New York: Holt, Rinehart & Winston, 1963.

Tavris, C. 40,000 men tell about their sexual behavior, their fantasies, the ideal woman, and their wives. *Redbook Magazine*, February 1978, pp. 111–113.

Walster, E., Walster, G. W., & Berscheid, E. *Equity: Theory and research*. Boston: Allyn & Bacon, 1978.

Walster, E., Walster, G. W. & Traupmann, J. Equity and premarital sex. *Journal of Personality and Social Psychology*, 1978, *36*, 82–92.

Weber, M. [*The theory of social and economic organization*] (A. M. Henderson and T. Parsons, Eds. and trans.). New York: Free Press, 1964.

Zelnik, M., & Kantner, J. F. Sexual and contraceptive experience of young unmarried women in the United States, 1976 and 1971. *Family Planning Perspectives*, 1977, *9*, 55–71.

Zelnik, M., & Kantner, J. F. Reasons for nonuse of contraceptives by sexually active women aged 15–19. *Family Planning Perspectives*, 1979, *11*, 289–296.

Zelnik, M. & Kantner, J. F. Sexual activity, contraceptive use and pregnancy among metropolitan-area teenagers: 1971–1979. *Family Planning Perspectives*, 1980, *12*, 230–237.

ARTICLE 4
The Incidence of Violence and Acquaintance Rape in Dating Relationships among College Men and Women

MARTA AIZENMAN AND GEORGETTE KELLEY

Intimate relationships presumably are harmonious. Yet, more and more studies, such as those described in this article, are reporting high levels of violence in dating relationships. About one-quarter of all college women indicate they have been physically abused by a date. Of these, nearly half have been raped or forced to have sexual intercourse against their will.

VIOLENCE BETWEEN MEN AND WOMEN who are intimately related has been increasingly noted by mental health clinicians, as well as in studies about couples interaction. During the last decade, research conducted on relationships shows a high incidence of violence among couples in dating, as well as in marital life. Gelles (1972), for example, found that the incidence of abuse among married couples was as high as 60%. Other studies using a national sample estimated that about 2 million husbands per year abuse their wives (Straus, Gelles, & Steinmetz, 1980).

Marta Aizenman and Georgette Kelley, "The Incidence of Violence and Acquaintance Rape in Dating Relationships among College Men and Women." *Journal of College Student Development,* 29 (1988): 305–311. Copyright © 1988 by the American Association for Counseling and Development. Reprinted by permission of the American Association for Counseling and Development.

The violent behavior encountered among the general population seems to be present in college dating relationships. In a study of violence in dating relationships, Makepeace (1981) reported that 21% of the students who participated in the study were personally involved in a violent episode in a dating relationship, and 61% knew someone who was involved in such a relationship. Matthews (1984), replicating the Makepeace study, found that 22% of the students surveyed had been directly involved in at least one incidence of dating violence. Bernard and Bernard (1983), who also surveyed college students concerning violence in their relationships, concluded that violence is as much a part of life among college students as it is a part of life in the American marriage.

Violence in college relationships seems to be manifested not only in dating behavior but also in the amount of acquaintance rape cases that occur on campuses. Recent studies on acquaintance rape show that a high percentage of the female college population has suffered sexual victimization, usually by a person they previously knew. For example, Rappaport and Burkhart (1984) found that more than 22% of all the freshman and sophomore women in their study had been forced to have sex against their will. Koss (1985), in a national survey on relationships between men and women, reported that one-fourth of the women studied were victims of rape, and almost 90% of them knew their assailant.

Although researchers who have studied sex differences tend to agree that men are, in general, more aggressive than women, there is a discrepancy among various studies on the targets of this aggression. Maccoby and Jacklin (1974), after analyzing different studies, concluded that male aggression is primarily directed toward males. They offered as an explanation the existence of a tacit assumption throughout the socialization process that women should not be aggressed against. Other studies, which have focused more specifically on relationships between the sexes, either in fantasy or in real life (Berk, Berk, Loeske, & Rauma, 1983; Gilligan, 1982; May, 1980), indicate that men do take women as the target of their aggression. Most studies reviewed by Maccoby and Jacklin were based on observations of children, and none concerned aggressive behavior in ongoing romantic relationships. This suggests the possibility of a change in attitude when the young boy becomes a man, raising the question of whether or not this transition occurs at a time such as late adolescence, when relationships between the sexes become more intimate. It seems important, therefore, to study the incidence, the attitudes, and the objects of violence that exist at this developmental stage.

A contributing factor to aggressive behavior in adulthood seems to be the degree of earlier exposure to physical aggression. For example, several authors indicated that there is a relationship between the level of physical punishment experienced in childhood and the violence individuals exercise at later stages (Becker 1964; Herbert, 1986; Walker, 1983). Moreover, a significant relationship between having been beaten or having witnessed family violence and becoming an abuser with adult partners (Kalmuss, 1984; Laner & Thompson, 1982) has also been found. This research suggests the possibility that harsh punishment received as a child may also increase the likelihood of becoming the recipient of violence in a dating relationship.

The studies previously discussed raise potential issues about the occurrence of violence in dating relationships among college students. In this study, the following questions were investigated:

1. What is the incidence of violence and acquaintance rape among college students?
2. What type of violent behavior is occurring and under what circumstances?
3. What are students' attitudes and beliefs in regard to the presence of violence in a romantic relationship?
4. Are there sex-related differences in being the victim or the perpetrator of violence?
5. Is there any relationship between punishment and sexual violence that the students suffered as children, and perpetrating or receiving abuse in a dating relationship?
6. Is violence in dating relationships associated with personality-related variables such as feelings of well-being, sense of control, and comfort with one's sexuality?

METHOD

A total of 800 undergraduate students at Rutgers University was randomly selected to participate in the study—400 male students at a co-educational college and 400 female students at an all-female college. The 800 students were mailed a packet that included a letter, which described the study and requested the students' anonymous cooperation, and a questionnaire.

In the questionnaire, students were asked to indicate whether they had been abused or had abused their partner in a romantic relationship, the type of abuse received, and whether the relationship was a casual or a steady one. Other questions addressed the students' attitudes toward the use of violence in relationships. In addition, students were asked whether they had (a) been involved in a situation they could call acquaintance rape, (b) successfully avoided such a situation, (c) been forced to have intercourse against their will, and (d) ever been pressed to have unwanted sexual contact when they did not want to. Issues such as childhood experiences of inappropriate sexual contact and types of punishment were also explored. Finally, the students were asked to rate their feelings of well-being, depression, self-confidence, sense of control over their behavior, loneliness, comfort with their sexuality, and their ability to express feelings directly, using 5-point Likert type scales (with low points indicating a positive attitude). These items were taken from the intake questionnaire given at the counseling centers of both colleges.

The validity of the scales was tested by comparing the responses of a random sample of students with those given by students seeking counseling. (Students in this last group had expressed concerns in the areas covered by the scales.) The scores obtained by the counselees were significantly higher ($p<.05$) than those of the random sample. Test-retest reliability was .92 for a random sample of college students during a 6-week period. For each item of the questionnaire, the responses of the female and male students were compared. Chi-square tests were used to analyze the data.

RESULTS

Of the 400 men and 400 women who were randomly selected to participate in the study, 43% (51% women, 35% men) returned the questionnaire. All were undergraduates. The mean age of the sample was 20.32 for women and 20.88 for men, with standard deviations of 1.73 and 2.14, respectively. Of the entire sample, 98% were single, 1% married, and 1% divorced. Most of the men and women in the sample were Catholic (62% women, 63% men); some were Protestants (12% women, 16% men) and Jews (11% women, 11% men). Also, most were White (90% women, 89% men), followed by Blacks (6% women, 5% men), Hispanics (3% women, 4% men), and Orientals (1% women, 2% men).

The percentage of students in the sample who had been abused in a relationship was higher for women than for men [women = 25%, men = 7%, $\chi^2(1) = 16.66$, $p<.05$]. More than 75% of abused women and more than 50% of abused men indicated that the abuse was physical rather than verbal [for women, $t(49) = 1.73$, $p<.05$; for men, $p<.05$, using binomial distribution because of the small sample size of abused men]. Of those who were physically abused, 43% reported being pushed, 28% slapped, 19% punched, 8% struck with an object, and 2% struck with a weapon.

There was no significant difference between the sexes in the number of students who had been perpetrators of abuse (women = 5%, men = 6%). The nature of this abuse was not ascertained.

Most of the cases of violent behavior in a romantic relationship were reported in steady, ongoing relationships. Of the students who reported abuse, 44% described the relationship as a steady one, 30% as a dating one, and 26% as a casual one. Violent behavior tended to occur most frequently for both men and women during their senior year in high school (11%) or during their freshman year in college (27%). When a violent relationship was cited, 61% of the students mentioned that it had occurred on numerous occasions; almost 50% of the total sample reported that the relationship continued after the abuse occurred.

For both sexes, being abused in a romantic relationship relates to (a) lacking a sense of control over their own behavior [Women: $\chi^2(3) = 7.83$; Men: $\chi^2(4) = 18.01$, $p<.05$], and (b) becoming the perpetrators of abuse [Women: $\chi^2(1) = 17.57$, $p<.05$; Men: $\chi^2(1) = 4.21$, $p<.05$]. Alcohol was involved in the episodes of violence for more than 35% of the men and 32% of the women.

The large majority (95% of the students) objected to the use of violence. Although a significant difference existed between the number of male students who indicated that violence can be helpful in a relationship (7%) and the number of

TABLE 1 Percentage of Students Who Reported Being Sexually Abused According to Sex and Type of Abuse

Type of Abuse	Women	Men[a]
Fondled as a child	19	1
Acquaintance rape	22	6
Successfully avoided acquaintance rape	51	18
Forced to have intercourse against their will	29	14
Pressed to have sexual contact when they did not want to	43	17

[a]$\chi^2(1) p<.05$.

female students who consider it so (1%), $\chi^2(1) = 9.48$, $p<.05$, both percentages were small. There were no significant relationships between the men that professed a belief that violence could be helpful in a relationship (7%) and those who indicated that they had been abusers (6%).

Students seem to be aware of the existence of violence in campus romantic relationships. At least 52% of the male sample and 51% of the female sample indicated that they knew a fellow student who was involved in a violent relationship. Also, 80% indicated that if they were witnessing violence in an acquaintance's dating relationship, they would take action against it. Another 30% reported that they have, in fact, intervened after witnessing someone acting violently.

More women than men were touched sexually or fondled as children and were involved later in life in forced sexual contact on dates, including acquaintance rape. Among the female sample, 19% were sexually fondled as children, in contrast to only 1% of the men, $\chi^2(1) = 19.04$, $p<.05$. Also, 22% of the female students and 6% of the male students [$\chi^2(1) = 16.02, p<.05$] responded positively to the question, "Have you been involved in a situation that you would call acquaintance rape?" Of the women, 51% indicated that they had successfully avoided an acquaintance rape, 29% mentioned that they had been forced to have intercourse against their will, and 43% reported having been pressed to have sexual contact when they did not want to (see Table 1). In addition, significant relationships were found for women between the following variables: (a) lacking a sense of well-being with having been inappropriately fondled as a child [$\chi^2(14) = 12.30$, $p<.05$] and (b) being inappropriately fondled as a child with being involved in an acquaintance rape [$\chi^2(1) = 11.44$, $p<.05$].

Although the number of female students who reported having been forced to have sexual interactions, not necessarily intercourse, was greater than the number of male students, the men also apparently experienced some degree of abuse, force, and violence from women in relationships. Of the male students, 14% mentioned having been forced to have intercourse against their will, and 17% indicated that they had been pressed to have sexual contact when they did not want to.

Women reported being punished as children to a greater extent than did men [Women = 84%, Men = 71%, $\chi^2(1) = 8.4$, $p<.05$]. The punishment received was mostly a mixture of physical and verbal for both sexes (Men = 83%, Women =

64%); however, more women (30%) than men (13%) were punished only by verbal threats [$\chi^2(2) = 11.36, p<.05$].

Men and women in the sample seemed to react differently to the punishment they received in childhood. There was a significant relationship for the female sample between being punished as children and lacking a feeling of well-being [$\chi^2(4) = 10.69, p<.05$] and between perceiving punishment received in childhood as abusive and being abused in romantic relationships [$\chi^2(2) = 7.61, p<.05$]. The relationships between these variables were not significant for the male sample. Instead, a relationship existed for men between considering the punishment received in childhood as abusive and not feeling very comfortable with their sexuality [$\chi^2(4) = 12.51, p<.05$].

DISCUSSION

The incidence of violence in relationships revealed in this study (25% for women, 7% for men), similar to that reported in comparable studies (Makepeace, 1981; Matthews, 1984), indicates its occurrence among college students. Although most of the students (85%) seemed to oppose the use of violence in romantic relationships, at least one-fourth of the women had encountered it some time in a relationship, and half of the sample reported knowing a student who was involved in one. Furthermore, the high incidence of acquaintance rape on campus today is another indication of the presence of violence in dating relationships. The percentage of women who have been involved in acquaintance rape (22%), and the percentage of women who have successfully avoided it (51%), is also consistent with the results found by other researchers (Koss & Oros, 1982; Rappaport & Burkhart, 1984). Given that the return rate in the study was modest, however, particularly for men, generalization of the findings should be made cautiously.

There are several important points raised by the results of this study. For example, the fact that more women than men report being in an abusive relationship brings up the question of what this difference can be attributed to. One possibility is that the same type of incident may be viewed differently by each sex. In other words, a man's definition of abuse behavior may involve more violence than that of a woman. Another reason may be the reluctance of men to acknowledge the existence of an abusive relationship. Since men tend to be abusers in such a situation, it is possible that they fear admitting to their behavior.

The high percentage of students who, after being subjected to abuse, chose to continue the relationship suggests that violence is accepted by those who have experienced it. The fact that violent behavior appears more frequently in long-term relationships (44% of the cases) may indicate, as Cate, Henton, Koval, Christopher, and Lloyd (1982) suggested, that the likelihood of aggression increases with the seriousness of the relationship. It may, however, also point to additional interpretations. For example, it is possible that for some young people, violence is not seen as a factor of enough importance to interrupt the relationship or that they do not perceive alternative means of dealing with problems. The frequency of violent incidents in dating relationships during the last year of high school and the freshman year in college would suggest that immaturity can be considered as a factor contributing to poor communication and coping skills in relationships.

The vast majority of men and women indicated that they are comfortable with their sexuality; however, the number involved in forced sexual contact and the percentage of students who have been in an acquaintance rape situation might suggest that considerable numbers of young people are suffering from a lack of good communication in the area of sexuality and a lack of confidence in asserting their sexual rights and needs.

Women are more vulnerable targets than men. The fact that they are subjected to more disciplinary punishment in childhood and suffer child molestation to a higher degree than men may contribute to their readiness to accept more abuse later in life. The physical differences in size between the sexes, as well as in sexual aggressiveness, are also relevant factors. When attempting to explain the high incidence of men as perpetrators of violence in relationships, it is important to note that men and women are often victims of sex-role stereotyping. For example, although women often are taught to be passive and nonassertive, men are encouraged to be aggressive. As a result, men may perceive violence in more positive terms. Thus, their use of force in relationships may be a way in which the developing adolescent reassures himself and others of his own masculinity.

The discipline received in childhood, when perceived as abusive, may reinforce in both men and women attitudes that are carried into adult romantic relationships. The effect on women seems to be a learned helplessness syndrome. Women who have been in abusive dating relationships frequently report having been abusively punished as children. The lack of comfort with sexuality among men who have been abusively punished as children may be an indication that abusive discipline may have a negative impact on the development of a masculine identity in men. These relations, and the fact that women who have been punished as children tend to lack a general sense of well-being, raise questions for further research about the possible long-range effects of punishment practices that take place during childhood. The relationship found for both sexes between having been abused and becoming a perpetrator of abuse suggests that for some victims of violence in dating relationships, the abuse reinforces a nonassertive attitude; in others, it only generates more anger, sometimes transforming the abused into an abuser, creating a vicious cycle.

IMPLICATIONS

Violence is playing a role in college dating relationships. Because these experiences occur in a developmental period when values and identities are consolidated, the issue has many implications for college educators, particularly those who deal with student programming. Because many of these violent behaviors may be taking place on campus, trained residence hall staff and health center personnel need to recognize symptoms of dating violence. It is also important that students be made aware of the campus resources available to them in situations where dating violence occurs. Finally, some attempts should be made to provide procedural guidelines for residence hall staff intervention in cases of violence.

Because a large majority of students has either witnessed violence in relationships or has been involved in such behavior, more emphasis should be placed on presenting programs dealing with the topic of relationships. These programs and workshops should also include topics related to sexual abuse and violence, emphasizing the likelihood of becoming the victim of abuse or being abusive in current romantic relationships when abuse has previously occurred. Second, issues dealing with better communication and mutual interaction between partners should be addressed. The ideal of mutual interaction in a relationship and equality in sexual encounters may not be in conformity with the sex-role stereotypes and social conditioning that students bring from their families, home environment, and the media. Programs developed for dealing more openly with these topics in co-educational groups can model more direct and honest communication between men and women.

Because most violent acts seem to occur during the beginning years of college, it would be advisable to present these topics early, perhaps in the freshman orientation program. Clearly there is a need to alert freshman and sophomore women to the high incidence of acquaintance rape during those 2 years. In addition, given that the consumption of alcohol tends to be present when violent acts take place, it is also of primary importance to draw students' attention to this issue when presenting programs on violence and prevention of alcohol abuse.

An important factor contributing to the occurrence of violence in relationships is sex-role stereotyping. In dealing with the higher incidence of men as perpetrators of violence in relationships, it is helpful to realize that men are often victims of stereotyping. That is, our culture encourages men to be aggressive, to be a "real" man, and this may be the way that a developing adolescent reassures himself and others of his own masculinity. The female sex-role stereotype establishes the expectation that women should be more passive and nonassertive. This encourages women to fall into the role of the victim, being unable to be assertive, say no, or directly state what they want in a relationship. Creative programming must confront sex-role stereotypes and common communication problems for couples with the awareness that they may be suggesting changes in relationships that are not common in western society. For instance, they may have to struggle against the assumption many people hold that someone, generally the man, has to be the dominant one in a relationship. (Because there is a stress for men to be in control of their lives, to be in charge, and to be strong, they usually assume this role). Programs must stress that men are also being abused in dating relationships. Relating the incidence of violence toward men might lower their defensiveness, emphasizing that it is a more common problem than students may realize. Working on co-educational programs for sororities and fraternities could also add an important contribution in this direction.

The recent publicity given to acquaintance rape might provide an opener for these issues. There has been considerable work on video presentations that can be used in these discussions. Other topics of violence in dating relationships should be included as well; however, because the issue of acquaintance rape is only one manifestation of much deeper problems. Finally, in dealing with the victims of violence and sexual abuse in ongoing relationships, college counseling centers might provide groups in which the degree of isolation and guilt these victims suffer could be addressed through group treatment and educational sessions.

One of the most interesting findings of this study is the similar percentage of male and female students who reported having abused someone in a romantic relationship. One of the shortcomings of the questionnaire was the students' not being specific about the type of abuse they were inflicting—physical or emotional. This statistic, coupled with the reported abuse to male students, betrays any notion that violence is entirely an issue for women in the area of intimacy and relationships.

The results of the study raise questions for future research. One potential area for subsequent exploration will be to consider whether or not violence is occurring more frequently in dating relationships when there is sexual involvement. Another important area to examine would be the relationship between violence in the home among the parents and dating violence. Moreover, other issues for further investigation might be the relationship between alcoholism in the family and future behavior on the part of the children. Finally, it would be interesting to determine the impact the suggested programs would have on the development of the students' communication patterns in their dating relationships.

REFERENCES

Becker, W.C. (1964). Consequences of different kinds of parental discipline. In M.C. Hoffman & L.W. Hoffman (Eds.), *Review of child development research* (Vol. I). New York: Russell Sage Foundation.

Berk, R.A., Berk, S.F., Loseke, D.R., & Rauma, D. (1983). Mutual combat and other family violence myths. In D. Finkelhor, R. Gelles, G. Hotaling, & M. Strauss (Eds.), *The dark side of families*. Beverly Hills, CA: Sage Publications.

Bernard, M.L., & Bernard, J.L. (1983). Violent intimacy: The family as a model for love relationships. *Family Relations, 32,* 283–286.

Cate, R.M., Henton, J.M., Koval, J., Christopher, F.S., & Lloyd, S. (1982). Premarital abuse: A social psychological perspective. *Journal of Family Issues, 3*(1), 79–90.

Gelles, R.J. (1972). *The violent home: A study of physical aggression between husbands and wives*. Beverly Hills, CA: Sage Publications.

Gilligan, C. (1982). In a different voice. Cambridge, MA: Harvard University Press.

Herbert, M. (1986). The pathology of human behavior. In W. Sluckin (Eds.), *Parental behavior*. Oxford, England: Basil Blackwell.

Kalmuss, D. (1984). The intergenerational transmission of marital aggression. *Journal of Marriage and the Family. 46,* 11–19.

Koss, M.P. (1985). The hidden rape victim: Personality, attitudinal, and situational characteristics. *Psychology of Women Quarterly, 9,* 193–212.

Koss, M.P., & Oros, C.J. (1982). The sexual experiences survey: A research instrument investigating sexual aggression and sexual victimization. *Journal of Consulting and Clinical Psychology, 50*(3), 445–457.

Laner, M.R., & Thompson, J. (1982). Abuse and aggression in courting couples. *Deviant Behavior: An Interdisciplinary Journal, 3,* 229–244.

Maccoby, E.E., & Jacklin, C.N. (1974). *The psychology of sex differences.* Stanford, CA: Stanford University Press.

Makepeace, J.M. (1981). Courtship violence among college students. *Family Relations, 30,* 97–102.

Matthews, W.J. (1984). Violence in college couples. *College Student Journal, 18*(2), 150–159.

May, R. (1980). *Sex and fantasy.* New York: Norton.

Rappaport, K., & Burkhart, B. (1984). Personality and attitudinal characteristics of sexually coercive college males. *Journal of Abnormal Psychology, 93*(2), 216–221.

Straus, M.A., Gelles, R.J., & Steinmetz, S.K. (1980). *Behind closed doors: Violence in the American family.* Garden City, NY: Anchor.

Walker, L.E. (1983). The battered woman syndrome. In D. Finkelhor, R.G. Gelles, G.T. Hotaling, & M.A. Straus (Eds.). *The dark side of families: Current family violence research.* Beverly Hills, CA: Sage Publications.

ARTICLE 5
The Sexualized Society

JOHN D'EMILIO AND ESTELLE B. FREEDMAN

Changes in the 1960s and 1970s reshaped our sexuality, altering both our attitudes and behavior. This selection chronicles those changes and discusses some of the cultural contradictions of the sexual revolution.

TOWARD THE END of the 1960s John Williamson, a successful engineer in southern California, purchased a fifteen-acre retreat in the Santa Monica mountains. Graced with a view of the ocean, the secluded site sported a two-story mansion, several smaller houses, and a building that contained an Olympic-sized pool. Williamson intended to make the property the setting in which to implement an experiment in sexual freedom. For years, a group of people "had met regularly at his house to discuss and explore ways of achieving greater fulfillment in marriage." They were all "middle-class people," many of them prosperous professionals like himself, "who held responsible jobs in the community [and] were integrated in the social system."[1] Over time, the discussions led to action, including the swapping of marital partners for sexual excitement and group sex. Williamson's newly acquired property, Sandstone, would give the venture institutional expression.

In the succeeding years, Sandstone became something of an underground tourist attraction, bringing through its doors upper-middle-class adventurers in search of new kinds of personal fulfillment and erotic delights. Those who made the trek could take off their clothes or leave them on. They could sip wine, smoke marijuana, and converse by the fireplace upstairs, or wander downstairs where they would find, in the words of one visitor, "a parlor for pleasure-seekers, providing sights and

"The Sexualized Society" from INTIMATE MATTERS: A HISTORY OF SEXUALITY IN AMERICA by John D'Emilio and Estelle B. Freedman. Copyright © 1988 by John D'Emilio and Estelle B. Freedman. Reprinted by permission of Harper and Row, Publishers, Inc.

sounds that . . . [they] had never imagined they would ever encounter under one roof during a single evening." They would see

> shadows and faces and interlocking limbs, rounded breasts and reaching fingers, moving buttocks, glistening backs, shoulders, nipples, navels, long blond hair spread across pillows, thick dark arms holding soft white hips, a woman's head hovering over an erect penis. Sighs, cries of ecstasy could be heard, the slap and suction of copulating flesh, laughter, murmuring, music from the stereo, crackling black burning wood.

Perhaps the only thing more surprising than Sandstone itself was the fact that a prominent journalist would write about it. Gay Talese's *Thy Neighbor's Wife,* from which this description is taken, became a widely reviewed, much discussed bestseller.[2]

Although Sandstone was unusual, the attraction of successful professionals to it and the marketing of it by Talese suggest that the liberal consensus about sex had dissolved. Feminists and gay liberationists were not the only ones challenging its assumptions. By the late 1960s the belief in sex as the source of personal meaning had permeated American society. The expectation that marriage would fulfill the quest could no longer be sustained. Aided by the values of a consumer culture and encouraged by the growing visibility of sex in the public realm, many Americans came to accept sexual pleasure as a legitimate, necessary component of their lives, unbound by older ideals of marital fidelity and permanence. Society was indeed becoming sexualized. From the mid-1960s to the 1980s, as the liberal consensus disintegrated, the nation experienced perhaps the greatest transformation in sexuality it had ever witnessed. The marketing of sex, important shifts in attitudes, and major changes in the life cycle of Americans all encouraged alterations in patterns of sexual behavior.

THE BUSINESS OF SEX

One unmistakable sign of the reorganization of sexuality came through the large-scale invasion by entrepreneurs into the field of sex. The tension in sexual liberalism, between the celebration of the erotic as the peak experience in marriage and the effort to contain its expression elsewhere, made sex ripe for commercial exploitation. Since the mid-nineteenth century, the erotic had attracted entrepreneurs. But, as we have seen, it mostly remained a marginal, illicit industry. As the Supreme Court in the 1950s and 1960s shook the legal edifice that kept sexual imagery within certain limits, the capitalist impulse seized upon sexual desire as an unmet need that the marketplace could fill. Wherever Americans looked, it seemed, the erotic beckoned in the guise of a commodity.

Pornography provides one convenient measure of the dynamic that was underway. Long confined to a shadowy underground, and formerly taking the shape of a home industry, it became in the 1970s highly visible. Thousands of movie houses featuring triple-"X"-rated films dotted the country, ranging from drive-ins on the outskirts of towns, and theaters in the central city, to fancy establishments in modern shopping malls. North Carolina and South Carolina boasted the largest concentration of adult theaters, belying the notion that pornography was the product of big-city decadence. Some of the films, such as *Deep Throat* and *The Devil in Miss Jones,* achieved respectability of sorts, becoming cult favorites that attracted large audiences. In most cities, adult bookstores sold hard-core sex magazines and paperbacks without the literary pretensions or journalistic substance to which *Playboy* and its competitors aspired. A substantial portion of newsstand sales came from publications that the police would have seized a decade earlier. Technological advances offered new opportunities and new audiences for the distribution of pornography. The introduction of video-cassette recorders in the late 1970s opened the door to a booming business in sex films for home consumption. As one maker of pornographic videos remarked, "there are some people who would like to frequent sex theaters, but for various reasons they don't. They're either ashamed to be seen going in, they don't want to take their wives with them, or whatever. This way, they're able to see the X material in the privacy of their own home, and it doesn't seem so distasteful to them." Men brought their wives or girlfriends to help them select the evening's viewing fare. Soon, the rental of pornographic movies was providing the essential margin of profit for many video stores. The spread of cable television, meanwhile, allowed producers to avoid the constraints of the federally regulated networks. A subsidiary of Time, Inc., for instance, used cable television to distribute a weekly program, *Midnight Blue,* that featured couples having sex.[3]

By the 1980s, economic analysts were referring to the "sex industry." A multi-billion-dollar endeavor, it featured high-salaried executives, a large work force, brisk competition, board meetings, and sales conventions. Al Goldstein, the publisher of *Screw* who "diversified" in the 1970s, remarked on the contrast between the sleazy image of the industry and its more prosaic—and profitable—reality. "People come into my office,' he said, "and they think there are supposed to be 12 women under my desk. If there is anybody under there, it's 12 tax accountants. Or 12 attorneys. I'm a capitalist. I'm good at what I do." Industry boosters promoted the field as they would any other. Dennis Sobin, who edited *The Adult Business Report,* the chief trade magazine of the industry, commented that "the sex business has the same potential for sales and profits as the food industry. It is a growth industry that cannot go backwards."[4]

One reason, perhaps, for the confidence of this new breed of entrepreneur was that they could arguably see themselves as simply the least hypocritical of an entire spectrum of marketers of sexuality. Not only had pornography moved into the light of day, but sexual imagery had become incorporated into the mainstream of American life. Advertisers broke new ground in their use of the erotic to excite consumers. In newspaper ads, clothing manufacturers and department stores featured pre-pubescent girls in flirtatious poses. Record companies enticed buyers with sexually suggestive album covers. Calvin Klein commissioned billboards with models naked from the waist up, their buttocks snugly fitted into his designer jeans. "The tighter they are, the better they sell," he commented.[5] By the 1980s, male bodies, too, were being used to promote sales. On television, commercials for any number of products projected the message that consumption promised the fulfillment of erotic fantasies and appetites.

The visual entertainment media also made sex a staple of their shows. An evening of television might begin with game shows in which attractive female models draped themselves over prizes representing a consumer's dreams, progress to situation comedies where the plot revolved around the titillating possibilities of sexual encounters, and end with steamy adult dramas. Instead of *I Love Lucy,* viewers laughed at the innuendo of *Three's Company,* in which a man and two women cohabited, or they might wonder when Sam and Diane, the main characters in *Cheers,* would make it into bed. Rather than the simple cops-and-robbers plots of *The Untouchables,* the award-winning *Hill Street Blues* closed many episodes in the bedroom of its chief protagonists. Popular nighttime soap operas combined the themes of money, power, and sex into high Nielsen ratings. Potboiler novels became mini-series, with titles such as *Sin,* or *Hollywood Wives,* in which the characters trotted around the globe in search of sexual adventure. Multi-million-dollar budgets and the absence of frontal nudity were about the only differences between these network specials and their prodigal pornographic cousins.

The permeation of sex throughout the culture made itself felt in other ways. In the morning newspapers, "Dear Abby" and Ann Landers found themselves addressing more and more explicit sexual scenarios. A series of articles in one midwestern daily advised single men and women that "there is nothing wrong with sharing physical pleasure with somebody else. Sure, old moralistic rules flash by, but for a growing number of us they can satisfactorily be put aside. For once, it's exhilarating to be the 'bad' kid. . . . By having a variety of partners we learn there are interesting variations on the theme."[6] In the early 1980s, Dr. Ruth Westheimer, a radio personality with a grandmotherly wholesomeness, became something of a national hero, as well as a highly paid lecturer, through her enthusiastic prescriptions for sexual happiness. Magazines made space for pages of personal ads where a "DWM" (divorced white male) might seek "SF" (single female) for walks, talks, and an afternoon affair. Cars sported bumper stickers ("firemen have long hoses," "elevator operators like to go down," "teachers do it with class") that jocularly associated occupational identity with sexual prowess.

So much openness about sexuality had an impact on the prescriptive literature to which Americans were so partial. By the 1970s, marital advice books were fast losing their audience to popular sex manuals. Many of them—*Everything You Always Wanted to Know about Sex, The Sensuous Man, The Sensuous Woman*— became runaway best-sellers. Dispensing with the genteel language and scientific descriptions characteristic of midcentury books for the married, they endorsed sexual experimentation in language that twenty years earlier had been the province of pornography. "Put your girl in a soft, upholstered chair," the author of *The Sensuous Man* advised,

> and kneel in front of her so your head comes about to the level of her breasts . . . Now slide her off the chair and right onto that beautiful erect shaft. The feeling is dizzying. She is wet and very, very hot; you are face to face and in about as deep as you can be.

... [It's] an exciting way to come. When you do explode, you'll find yourself in each other's arms—exhausted, wet, beautiful—a total state of A.F.O.—all fucked out.[7]

Alex Comfort's *The Joy of Sex* played on the theme of a popular cookbook by offering menus of its own for the sexual gourmet. Liberally illustrated with erotic drawings, it depicted naked men and women in an endless variety of sexual positions. Comfort's success propelled publishers to commission companion volumes for gay men and lesbians. Even books aimed at supposedly traditional Americans dispensed with reticence. Marabel Morgan's *The Total Woman* may have held that woman's place was in the home, but it also instructed housewives to greet their husbands at the end of the day dressed in a transparent nightgown.[8]

CHANGING LIFE CYCLES AND NEW SEXUAL PATTERNS

As entrepreneurs were weaving sexuality into the fabric of public life, Americans were simultaneously experiencing dramatic demographic changes. Between the 1960s and the 1980s, the life cycle of many Americans became considerably more complex and unpredictable. The timing of marriage and childbearing, control over fertility, the instability of the traditional nuclear family, and innovations in living arrangements all encouraged a reorganization of sexual standards.

The unusual demographic patterns of the baby-boom era reversed themselves with startling rapidity in the 1970s. Between 1960 and 1980, the marriage rate declined by a quarter. By 1985, the median age of marriage for men had risen to 25.5 years, while for women it jumped to 23.2. Along with later marriage came an overall decline in fertility. Beginning in the mid-1970s, the fertility of American women hovered at the replacement level, far below the peaks reached in the late 1950s. The accessibility of legal abortions, the accelerating trend toward sterilization, and the availability of reliable contraceptives put absolute control of fertility within reach for the married. Especially within the middle class, childlessness emerged as a serious option to consider. As one couple noted, "we are the only people we know who have a child, or at least the only people we know well. . . . Some [of our friends] are married, a few might as well be, others aren't totally opposed to the idea—and they have all either ruled out families entirely or postponed them until the very distant future." By the end of the 1970s more than a quarter of married women in their late twenties remained childless.[9]

Not only were Americans marrying later and having fewer children, but families were much less likely to remain intact. Aided by the liberalization of state laws, the divorce rate began a steep climb in the mid-1960s. Between 1960 and 1980, the number of divorced men and women rose by almost two hundred percent; the divorce rate itself jumped ninety percent. For blacks, the impact of divorce was even more widely felt. In 1980, over a quarter of black men and women between the ages of twenty-five and fifty-four were divorced, in comparison to less than ten percent of whites. Many of the divorced remarried eventually, yet second marriages had even less chance of surviving. Although the rush to divorce had slowed somewhat by 1980, marriages of the late seventies had only a one-in-two chance of surviving.

All of these shifts affected the size and structure of American households, which tended to grow smaller and become more diversified in composition. During the 1970s, over half of the new households created were nonfamily ones. The traditional two-parent family with children accounted for only three-fifths of all living arrangements by 1980. Even that figure tended to overstate its predominance, since many of those families would experience dissolution, and most Americans could expect to spend a portion of their childhood and adult years in "nontraditional" situations.

One widely touted demographic innovation of the 1970s was the rise of cohabitation among men and women. Hardly noted by 1960 census-takers, it became a highly visible phenomenon in the 1970s, tripling in frequency. Although cohabiting couples constituted only three percent of American households, the chances of an individual participating in such an arrangement were much higher. One study found that almost one in five American men had lived for at least six months with a woman other than their spouse. The phenomenon was more common among blacks than whites, and a majority of the men had been previously married. Surveying the changing nature of American lifestyles, the sociologists Philip Blumstein and Pepper Schwartz confidently predicted that cohabitation "will probably become more visible and more common."[10]

In the midst of this reorganization of household and family structure, one element of change elicited special comment—the rise of the working mother. White married women had been steadily entering the labor force since World War II, and for black wives work outside the home had always been a common experience. But the rapid movement of mothers into paid employment surprised most observers. By the early 1980s a majority of mothers, including those with children of preschool age, were working for wages. Some of this change owed its origin to feminism, which validated the choices of mothers who sought employment. Some of it was due to financial necessity. As inflation escalated in the 1970s, and the changing structure of economic and social life raised the consumption needs of many families, the pressure for mothers to work mounted. Among married couples in 1980, wives with family incomes between twenty-five thousand and fifty thousand dollars were most likely to be employed. The absence of female employment consigned many families to subsistence living. Moreover, as the divorce rate mounted and more women found themselves heading households, many mothers had no choice but to work.

Whatever the motives, the high proportion of women in the work force promised upheavals in the realm of personal life and heterosexual relations. Working women were both cause and effect of many demographic changes—the rising age of marriage, later childbearing, the decline in fertility, the spread of single-person households, and cohabitation. Unhappy marriages, in which spouses felt compelled out of duty or desperation to remain together, might more readily dissolve. As Paul Glick, a Census Bureau demographer who had studied marriage and divorce for a generation, commented, "women who enter the marketplace gain greater confidence, expand their social circles independent of their husbands' friends, taste independence and are less easy to satisfy, and more likely to divorce." Or, as one Indiana wife put it, "women don't have to put up with [men's] crap—they can support themselves."[11] Working women brought greater confidence and more power to their relationships with men. Although conflict might ensue as couples readjusted their expectations, surveys indicated nevertheless that younger males in particular preferred the more egalitarian results that came with the modification of traditional sex roles.

These demographic shifts hit the black community with special force. Although black-white differentials in family structure actually narrowed in the 1970s, nontraditional living arrangements still appeared with much greater frequency among blacks. Overall incidence rates of divorce, female-headed households, and out-of-wedlock births remained higher. By 1980 almost half of black households were female-headed, a majority of black infants were born to unmarried women, and only a minority of black children were being raised in two-parent households. Approximately half of black adults were not married and living with their spouse. In assessing these statistics, one sociologist was moved to comment that "all is not well between black men and women." In contrast to the mid-1960s, when the Moynihan report provoked so much controversy within the civil rights movement, black leaders in the eighties felt freer to air their own concerns. By the early 1980s, many were rating the issue of family life equally with jobs and education as a critical concern of the community. Eleanor Holmes Norton, who served in the Carter administration, called it "the most serious long-term crisis in the black community."[12]

When combined with the invasion of sexuality into so much of the public realm, these new demographic patterns among Americans presaged a major shift in sexual behavior and attitudes. The later age of marriage increased the likelihood that women as well as men would enter the institution sexually experienced. The rise in divorce meant that more and more Americans would be searching for new sexual partners as mature adults. Children and adolescents would know that their parents were having sex outside of marriage; the openness with which heterosexual cohabitation, lesbianism, and male homosexuality were discussed provided visible alternatives to marriage. Postponed childbearing and low fertility made obvious the distinction between sex for procreation and for pleasure. Women who worked and had more sexual experience were better placed to negotiate the terms of a sexual relationship with a partner. The new explicitness of so much popular literature about the erotic almost guaranteed that many Americans would have their sexual repertoires greatly enhanced. Perhaps most significantly, the growing complexity of the American life cycle substantially weakened the hegemony of marriage as the privileged site for sexual expression. As one longitudinal study of families in Detroit concluded, "the decision to marry or remain single is now considered a real and legitimate choice between acceptable alternatives, marking a distinct shift in attitude from that held by Americans in the past."[13]

Survey data from a variety of sources confirm a striking shift in sexual values toward approval of nonmarital sexuality. As late as the 1950s, for instance, polls suggested that fewer than a quarter of Americans endorsed premarital sex for men and women. By the 1970s, these figures had been reversed. Especially among the young, substantial majorities registered their approval. Although males, blacks, the college-educated and higher-income families were more likely to accept premarital sexuality, the differences between groups were disappearing. Only older Americans and religiously devout whites tended to maintain a stance of moral disapproval. The generation gap was especially pronounced over some of the more radical departures from past orthodoxy. One study found that three-quarters of Americans over sixty-five opposed the practice of cohabitation, while the figures were reversed for the under-thirty population. Similarly, when confronted with the contemporary openness of the gay community, younger Americans proved more than three times as likely as their seniors to display tolerance for homosexuality. In their study of American couples, Blumstein and Schwartz found that among married couples, cohabiting heterosexuals, gay men, and lesbians, majorities of everyone except wives expressed approval for sexual relationships devoid of love.[14]

One important ideological source for the revamping of sexual beliefs was feminism. Particularly among younger heterosexuals, traditional notions of male and female differences weakened in the 1970s. Most looked forward to marriages in which roles blurred. Many younger males abandoned the allegiance to a double standard of behavior for their female peers. For both men and women, expectations about sexuality and intimacy changed. As Sophie Freud Loewenstein, a Boston social worker, explained it,

> Women who have taken it for granted that their sexual satisfaction was unimportant are now reading about women having multiple orgasms. Many men realize that they've been ripped off by being programmed to deny their expressive aspects. It becomes a possibility to throw out some of the old sex roles and change drastically. That change can be very frightening, but the atmosphere makes it more permissible.[15]

As its critique of sex-role conditioning spread throughout the culture, feminism altered the attitudes of Americans about the proper behavior of men and women.

Demographic change, shifts in attitudes, and the eroticism that so much of the public realm displayed contributed to a major alteration in the sexual life of many Americans. Unmarried youth as well as conjugal pairs, urban male homosexuals as well as heterosexual couples, experienced important modifications in their patterns of sexual behavior. Among other things, sexual experience was beginning at a younger age, acts once considered deviant were more widely incorporated into heterosexual relations, and the gap between the sex lives of men and women was narrowing.

The behavior of the young and the unmarried dramatically illustrates the extent of change. From the mid-1960s onward the incidence of premarital intercourse among white females zoomed upward, narrowing substantially the disparity in experience between them and their male peers. Survey after survey of white college students in every part of the country confirmed this shift. By 1980 large majorities of female students were engaging in coitus, often in relationships that held no expectation of marriage. Among black women, too, there was evidence of change, though primarily in the age at which coitus began. Between 1971 and 1976, fifteen- and sixteen-year-olds were half again as likely to have engaged in intercourse. In the early 1970s, a much broader survey that included men and women of varying educational levels also documented the rise in premarital coitus among women. By then young women were as likely to have sex as were the men in Kinsey's study a generation earlier. Morton Hunt, the author, also confirmed a greater variety in practices. Where Kinsey had found few heterosexuals who had tried fellatio or cunnilingus, by the 1970s it was a commonplace experience among those in their twenties. The frequency of intercourse for young men and women was also substantially higher, while masturbation, especially among women, was starting earlier and had become more widespread.[16]

Evidence of other sorts substantiates these survey findings. On college campuses, health services routinely distributed contraceptive information and devices to students. For those who began having intercourse earlier, or who did not attend college, Planned Parenthood clinics offered an alternative source of assistance. In Muncie, Indiana, for example, a third of teenage girls used the services of Planned Parenthood in 1979. The rise in births to unmarried teenagers, as well as the large number who sought abortions, also suggest that a growing proportion of the young were sexually active.[17]

These changes in patterns of behavior took place in a social context different from that which had shaped the behavior of youth between the 1920s and the 1960s. For one, formal dating evinced a sharp decline. Teenage youth socialized casually in groups without pairing off; friendships between males and females were more common. As one high school boy described it, in drawing a contrast between himself and his father:

> Once he told me that he wasn't brought up to think about women the way guys like me do, and it was vice versa back then. 'We were scared of each other; we didn't really have *friends* of the opposite sex' is the way he said it to me. Now that's changed! I can talk with girls I'm not dating—I mean, be real friendly with them. There's one girl at school who's the person I feel easiest with there. We're pals, but I've never wanted to make out with her!

This ease of interaction had implications for the progress of sexual experience. When the young did pair off, it tended to signal an already serious relationship. They were less likely to move gradually through the stages of kissing, necking, and petting before deciding to have intercourse. In fact, one observer of the young concluded that petting, so important in the sexual initiation of midcentury adolescents, "seems destined to take its place as a historical curiosity."[18]

The demographic patterns of the late 1960s and 1970s, as well as the less measurable effects of feminist ideology, also contributed to the shape of change. As women became sexually active earlier in life, as the age of marriage rose, and their participation in the labor force promised greater autonomy, more of them could approach sexual experience with different expectations. One twenty-eight-year-old blue-collar female, cohabiting with a male partner, firmly expressed her right to an erotic life. "I may have had an unusual upbringing, but it never occurred to me that a man wouldn't let me be sexy," she said. "I have the same needs and moods as a man, and I am not going to let some chauvinist pig stifle them." Another single woman, also in her twenties, justified nonmonogamy on the basis of her strong sexual desires. "I have a roving eye and sometimes I give in to it. . . . I consider myself a very sexual person and I need an adventure from time to time. And I think [my cohabiting partner] does too. But that's all it is—fun and a little bit of an ego thrill."[19] Their comments suggest that at least some women had moved a long distance from the 1950s, when sexual intercourse had to be justified as a sign of an abiding romantic attachment.

Not surprisingly, the erotic dimension of marriage also changed profoundly during these years. Although some elements of the past persisted, especially concerning gender differences in initiating sex, the conjugal relationship was moving rapidly in the direction of greater variety, higher levels of satisfaction, and more frequent intercourse. For instance, a study comparing the sexual practices of married couples in the early 1970s with those in the Kinsey reports found twice as many couples departing from the missionary position. Except among black couples, oral sex—both cunnilingus and fellatio—had been incorporated into the sexual repertoire of husbands and wives to such an extent that the author of the study, Morton Hunt, called the change an "increase . . . of major and historic proportions." Among whites, the move toward variety in technique and position extended across the social spectrum, narrowing considerably the class differences that Kinsey had noted. The frequency of intercourse had also risen, in a reverse of the trend displayed by Kinsey's respondents. As Hunt explained,

> Although in [Kinsey's] time the frequency of marital coitus was declining due to the wife's rising status and her growing right to have a voice in sexual matters, the regularity of her orgasm in marital intercourse was rising. . . . This increase in orgiastic reliability and overall sexual satisfaction eventually offset the forces that caused the initial drop in coital activity.

Only ten percent of the wives in Hunt's survey described their sexual relations of the preceding year as unpleasant or of no interest to them. Of the ninety percent claiming satisfaction, three quarters were content with the frequency while one-quarter wished for more.[20]

The visibility of sex in the culture certainly contributed to these trends. Not only did it encourage an interest in the erotic, but it also made information much more readily available to adults. Particularly among working-class wives, who as late as the 1940s and 1950s were often dependent on their husbands to lead the way, the barriers to active sexual agency were dropping. A waitress in her mid-thirties described the initiative she took:

> What changed our sex life was that a bunch of us girls on the same block started reading books and passing them around—everything from how-to-do-it sex books to real porno paperbacks. Some of the men said that the stuff was garbage, but I can tell you that

my husband was always ready to try out anything. . . . Some of it was great, some was awful . . . and some was just funny, like the honey business.

Another woman, married to a blue-collar worker, had him buy sex manuals to spice up their love life. "We found all different ways of caressing and different positions, and it was very nice because we realized that these things weren't dirty," she explained. "Like I could say to my husband 'Around the world in eighty days!' and he'd laugh and we'd really go at it." Moreover, much of the literature written in the 1970s, such as *The Hite Report* and Nancy Friday's *My Secret Garden,* presented sex from women's vantage point. The emphasis in these works shifted from simultaneous orgasm through intercourse to forms of pleasuring suitable for women, or what one commentator called "separate but equal orgasms." Thus, even the supposedly immutable "sex act" underwent redefinition in ways that weakened a male monopoly over the nature of sex.[21]

As couples experimented with different techniques of lovemaking, the erotic became a vehicle for exploring new realms of intimacy and power. Some men enjoyed the sensation that came from knowing they were satisfying their partners. "The whole process [of oral sex] makes me feel good about myself," said one husband. "I take serious pride in being a good lover and satisfying my partner, giving her pleasure." A businesswoman remarked that "I like oral sex very much because it is extremely intimate and I'm moved by it as an act of intimacy." For some women, oral sex evoked feelings of power. "I do feel powerful when he does it. I feel quite powerful,' said one. "Sort of the Amazon mentality—all-powerful woman." Another experienced similar emotions when performing fellatio. "I'm exerting power. I'm rewarding him," she commented. "The giving of pleasure is a powerful position, and the giving of oral sex is a real, real gift of pleasure."[22]

The cultural validation of erotic pleasure also contributed to a historic shift in expectations. Among earlier generations, men and women had found themselves at odds about the frequency of sex in marriage. At the turn of the century, at least among the white middle class, many women submitted to their husbands' desires; by midcentury, many men felt themselves sexually deprived. But a survey of couples conducted in the late 1970s found virtual agreement among men and women about sexual satisfaction and frequency. Eighty-nine percent of married men and women who had sex three or more times a week expressed contentment with their sex life; among those who had sex once a week or less, the figure dropped to fifty-three percent for each gender. The responses of unmarried cohabiting couples provided roughly similar findings. Not only were most men and women indicating similar preferences, but they expected relatively high frequencies of sex. According to Blumstein and Schwartz, among all the couples they studied—heterosexual, gay male, and lesbian—"a good sex life is central to a good overall relationship," and infrequent sex provoked discontent with all aspects of the relationship. Even the readers of a mainstream women's magazine such as *Redbook* had incorporated high expectations about sex into their lives. After polling 100,000 women, the editors found that "women are becoming increasingly active sexually and are less likely to accept an unsatisfactory sex life as part of the price to be paid for marriage."[23]

One reason, undoubtedly, for the shifts in heterosexual relationships was the availability of birth control. The dramatic move in the 1960s toward effective contraception continued into the 1970s. By mid-decade three out of four married couples relied on the pill, the IUD, or sterilization.[24] Then, too, the legalization of first-trimester abortions provided a measure of last resort for wives whose contraceptive efforts failed. Though it is difficult to know how great an increase in the incidence of abortion took place in the seventies, the fact that it was medically safe and legal at least removed the dangers that formerly attached to it. The near universality of birth control practices had virtually eliminated the constraints that fears about pregnancy had imposed on the sex life of married women. It also highlighted the degree to which the erotic had been divorced from procreation.

The separation of sex from reproduction also emerged from another quarter. Not only could couples safely have sex without the expectation of conception, but technological innovations were making it possible to have babies without sex. Science was upsetting age-old certainties about the natural connection between sex and procreation. "Remember when there was only one way to make a baby?" an advertisement for a 1979 CBS special report asked. "That was yesterday. Today, nature's role is being challenged by science. Conception without sex. Egg fertilization outside the womb. 'Surrogate' mothers who can bear other couples' children. Frozen embryos stored in 'supermarkets' for future implantation."[25] Among other things, scientific change was allowing lesbian couples to have children, without choosing marriage, through the cooperation of male sperm donors. Public policy added another dimension to technological change, as welfare agencies allowed single women and single men to adopt children, thus emphasizing the distinction between biological and social parenting. Though the new technology would raise some vexing problems of its own, as the controversy over Baby M revealed, people were nonetheless making choices that seemed to confirm that making love and making babies were not the same.

The new visibility that gay life achieved in the 1970s also emphasized the weakened link between procreation and the erotic. Although it is difficult to measure change in this area with any degree of precision, certainly the social life of gay men and lesbians had altered considerably. The many organizations that existed throughout the country allowed greater ease in making friends and acquaintances, and in embarking upon relationships. Less police harassment made it safer for bars to open and stay in operation. Regional music festivals brought thousands of lesbians together for several days of companionship; annual rituals such as the gay pride marches each June became celebrations of community cohesiveness even as they made a political statement. Church attendance, political club membership, and professional caucuses all contributed to a broadening of an identity in which the erotic played a prominent role. But the historic invisibility of gay male and lesbian life makes it impossible to compare the erotic dimension of gay experience from one generation to another. Even in the 1970s there were few studies that moved beyond the impressionism of journalistic observations.

A study that did, the work of Philip Blumstein and Pepper Schwartz, is interesting in part because of the comparison it allows between men and women, and between heterosexuals and homosexuals. The researchers found that a good sexual adjustment was as important to a successful relationship among gay male and lesbian respondents as among heterosexuals, and that the higher the frequency of sex the greater the sense of satisfaction. But lesbians seemed content to have sex less often, and after two years in a relationship, the lesbian couples tended to see a significant decline in the frequency of sex. Young lesbians were more likely to engage in oral sex than were older women, and among all the couples, gay men placed the greatest stock in variety in sexual technique. Lesbians proved very similar to heterosexual men and women in the extent of nonmonogamy—twenty-eight percent of lesbians, twenty-five percent of husbands, and twenty-one percent of wives—whereas for gay men, nonmonogamy was a way of life. Furthermore, among couples that did not practice monogamy male homosexuals tended to have sex with a far larger number of partners. One percent of the lesbians, seven percent of the husbands, but more than two-fifths of the gay men, had sex with more than twenty partners while living with a mate.[26]

Even in an era that witnessed an expansion of erotic opportunities, the experience of some urban gay men appeared to stand outside the norm. When Kinsey undertook his study in the 1940s he found that although male homosexuals on average had sex less frequently than heterosexual men, some of them had far more partners in the course of a lifetime. In the 1970s, as the urban gay subculture became larger and more accessible, the chances for sexual encounters multiplied. Heterosexuals may have had their singles bars where they could meet a partner for an evening of sex, but in large cities, gay bathhouses, bars with back rooms, and stores showing pornographic films allowed gay male patrons to have sex with a series of men in rapid succession. For many, sexual promiscuity became part of the fabric of gay life, an essential element holding the community together. Yet the fact that such sex businesses could operate in the 1970s relatively free of police harassment and that the media could spotlight them in discussions of gay life says as much about heterosexual norms as about those of gay men. In the larger metropolitan areas, male homosexuals were no longer serving as symbols of sexual deviance; their eroticism no longer divided the good from the bad. Heterosexuals sustained a vigorous singles nightlife, and advertised in magazines for partners; suburban couples engaged in mate-swapping; sex clubs were featuring male strippers, with women in the role of voyeur. By the end of the decade, some "straight" men and women were even patronizing a heterosexual equivalent of the gay bathhouse, as the success of places like Plato's Retreat in New York demonstrated. The experience of the urban gay subculture stood as one point along a widened spectrum of sexual possibilities that modern America now offered.

Although it would be foolhardy to deny the depth and breadth of the changes that had occurred by the end of the 1970s, one must also acknowledge the continuities with the past. Blumstein and Schwartz, for instance, found that "there *are* new men and new women, among both heterosexual and homosexual couples, who are dealing with sexual responsibilities in new ways and trying to modify the traditions that their maleness and femaleness bring to their relationships." But they were fewer in number than the pair of sociologists expected to find, and the persistence of tradition was particularly hard for some heterosexual women whose partners proved "less 'liberated' than she—or he—thought he was."[27] Marriages were happier and more intimate than a generation earlier, but partly because so many unhappy ones ended in divorce. In a culture that was coming to identify frequent, pleasurable, varied, and ecstatically satisfying sex as a preeminent sign of personal happiness, the high rate of marital dissolution could easily mean that large numbers of Americans were failing to reach these standards. The differences in the patterns of behavior of gay men and lesbians also pointed to the continuing salience of gender in shaping sexual meanings. Moreover, while lesbians and male homosexuals had carved out some space for themselves in society, the frequency of physical assaults upon visibly gay men and women suggested that their form of nonprocreative sex still provoked outrage. Feminism, too, may have opened new realms of sexual expressiveness for women, but the extent of rape and other forms of male sexual violence still made sex an arena of danger for them. The much-vaunted "sexual revolution," though real in many ways, was hardly complete.

Two issues, in particular, were emerging by the end of the 1970s to suggest the contradictory emotions that still enshrouded sex. Since the advent of penicillin in the 1940s, the threat of venereal disease had, to a significant degree, faded as an inhibitor of nonmonogamous sexual expression. But, in the midst of Americans' recently acquired sexual "freedom," the media spotlighted a new venereal scourge. Herpes, which *Time* magazine labeled "today's scarlet letter" and the "new leprosy," was reaching epidemic proportions among young urban heterosexuals. Though the condition posed far less physical danger than syphilis, it provoked guilt and panic as well as a pulling back from erotic encounters for some. A medical professional reported that "we hear it over and over: I won't have sex again." Among victims, the disease elicited feelings of self-pollution—"you never think you're clean enough," said one. The *Soho Weekly News,* a New York paper popular among young professionals in the city, was moved to proclaim "current sexual practice" as "the real epidemic." For many, the spread of herpes came to symbolize the inherent flaws in an ethic of sexual permissiveness. Pleasure brought retribution; disease became a marker of weak moral character.[28]

Another "epidemic," that of teenage pregnancy, also highlighted ambivalence about the erotic. Although most Americans tended to look benignly upon sex between unmarried adults, the spread of sexual experience among teenagers troubled them. To a large extent, adolescents were pursuing the erotic without the approval or the guidance of their elders. Despite the visibility of sex in the culture, the acquisition of knowledge by the young remained sporadic and haphazard, largely "a private, individually motivated and covert affair," in the opinion of one sex researcher. Some parents felt it was simply wrong, despite their own experience. As one middle-class mother in Muncie had phrased it, "just because it was right for me doesn't make it okay for my kids." A survey of high school youth in the early 1980s found that almost half had learned nothing about sex from their parents. Nor were schools rushing to fill the gap. By the late 1970s only half a dozen states mandated sex education; in most places, curriculum remained up to the local school districts, which generally displayed the same caution or disregard that occurred in the home. In one New York City suburb, a high school principal refused to let the editor of the school paper print an article about birth control methods. A California school district provided sex instruction in conjunction with drivers education, indicating how marginal it was to the academic curriculum. "In order to avoid controversy," according to the authors of *Sex and the American Teenager*, "schools embrace boredom."[29]

The result of this abdication of responsibility by schools and parents was that the young were often left to drift into sexual activity without guidance and with little knowledge. Teenagers whose parents were unwilling to talk with them about sex, or who did not receive sex education in school, were more prone to engage in intercourse. Yet they were also likely to be ignorant of how conception occurred or how to prevent it. Even when schools did provide instruction, they often acted too late. One North Carolina fifteen-year-old learned about condoms in a junior high school class, after he had been having intercourse for two years. "And then I realized, man, I've been taking a lot of chances. Thirteen, fourteen, fifteen . . . Lord's been good to me," he said. Others were not so lucky, as the incidence of teenage pregnancy revealed. In 1976, among the premaritally sexually active, twenty-seven percent of white girls and forty-five percent of blacks had become pregnant by the age of eighteen. Ironically, in view of the laissez-faire stance that adults seemed to take, the young were looking for advice. As Robert Coles and Geoffrey Stokes concluded on the basis of their work with high school students,

> it seems clear from our interviews that some kids who are planning to enter sexual relationships *want* to be told to wait. But those who can't talk to their parents hear either nothing or a ritualized naysaying that has no bearing on their *immediate* situation—and those who can may find their parents unwilling to take the responsibility for saying anything more than "Be careful."[30]

Meanwhile, for those who had made their choice to have sex, accurate information about reproduction, conception, and birth control might at least save them from the tragedy of unwanted pregnancies.

That so many teenage girls were becoming pregnant in an age when reliable contraception was available says much about the contradictions within the sexually permissive culture of the 1960s and 1970s. From everywhere sex beckoned, inciting desire, yet rarely did one find reasoned presentations of the most elementary consequences and responsibilities that sexual activity entailed. Youth had more autonomy from adult supervision than ever before, allowing them to explore the erotic at a time of profound physiological changes, but adults seemed to respond by implicitly drawing a boundary at sexual activity during adolescence. Perhaps one could not stop the young from experimenting, but neither would society endorse their behavior. The result was a social problem of tragic dimensions, one that placed in bold relief the ambivalence of American society toward sex. And, the fact that young girls were left to pay a higher price for sexual activity served as a poignant commentary on the persistence of gender in the structuring of sexuality in the post-liberal era.

The reshaping of sexuality in the 1960s and 1970s was of major proportions. The marketing of sex, new demographic patterns, and the movements of women and homosexuals for equality all fostered a substantial revision in attitudes and behavior. In some ways, the process of sexualization represented pushing the logic of sexual liberalism to its extreme: once sex had been identified as a critical aspect of happiness, how could one justify containing it in marriage? Even before the 1960s, the behavior of youth and the commercial manipulation of the erotic had suggested the vulnerability of the liberal consensus. By the end of the 1970s, it was obvious that the consensus had dissolved. As Americans married later, postponed childbearing, and divorced more often, and as feminists and gay liberationists questioned heterosexual orthodoxy, nonmarital sexuality became commonplace and open. And, all of this took place in a social environment in which erotic imagery was ubiquitous.

The collapse of sexual liberalism did not, however, lead to a new, stable consensus. By the end of the 1970s, conservative proponents of an older sexual order had appeared. Their efforts to stem the tide of change and, indeed, to restore sexuality to a reproductive marital context would demonstrate the continuing power of sex to generate controversy.

NOTES

1. Gay Talese, *Thy Neighbor's Wife* (Garden City, N.Y., 1980; paperback, 1981), p. 188.
2. *Ibid*, p. 398.
3. New York *Times,* April 5, 1979, p. B15.
4. New York *Times,* February 10, 1981, p. B6, and February 9, 1981, p. B6.
5. New York *Times,* February 9, 1981, p. B6.
6. Theodore Caplow et al., *Middletown Families* (Minneapolis, 1982), pp. 173–74.
7. Quoted in Morton Hunt, *Sexual Behavior in the 1970s* (New York, 1974), p. 9.
8. Alex Comfort, ed., *The Joy of Sex: A Gourmet Guide to Love Making* (New York, 1972); Marabel Morgan, *The Total Woman* (Old Tappan, N.J., 1975).
9. *New York Times Sunday Magazine,* May 25, 1975, p. 10. Unless otherwise noted, the demographic information in this and the following paragraphs is from Andrew Hacker, ed., *U/S: A Statistical Portrait of the American People* (New York, 1983).
10. Richard R. Clayton and Harwin L. Voss, "Shacking Up: Cohabitation in the 1970s," *Journal of Marriage and the Family* 39 (1977), pp. 273–83; Philip Blumstein and Pepper Schwartz, *American Couples: Money, Work, Sex* (New York, 1983; paperback, 1985), p. 36.
11. New York *Times,* November 27, 1977, p. 74; Caplow et al., *Middletown Families,* p. 131.
12. Robert Staples, *Black Masculinity* (San Francisco, 1982), p. 115; New York *Times,* August 13, 1984, p. B4.
13. New York *Times,* December 23, 1982, p. C5.
14. See Hunt, *Sexual Behavior in the 1970s,* p. 21; B. K. Singh, "Trends in Attitudes toward Premarital Sexual Relations," *Journal of Marriage and the Family* 42 (1980), pp.

387–93; New York *Times,* November 27, 1977, p. 75; Norval D. Glenn and Charles N. Weaver, "Attitudes Toward Premarital, Extramarital, and Homosexual Relations in the U.S. in the 1970s," *Journal of Sex Research* 15 (1978), pp. 108–18; Blumstein and Schwartz, *American Couples,* pp. 255, 272.

15. New York *Times,* November 28, 1977, p. 36.

16. Ira E. Robinson and Davor Jedlicka, "Change in Sexual Attitudes and Behavior of College Students from 1965 to 1980: A Research Note," *Journal of Marriage and the Family* 44 (1982), pp. 237–40; Robert R. Bell and Kathleen Coughey, "Premarital Sexual Experience Among College Females, 1958, 1968, and 1978," *Family Relations* 29 (1980), pp. 353–57; Melvin Zelnick, Young J. Kim, and John F. Kanter, "Probabilities of Intercourse and Conception Among Teenage Women, 1971 and 1976," *Family Planning Perspectives* 11 (1979), pp. 177–83; Hunt, *Sexual Behavior in the 1970s,* pp. 150, 166, 77, 87.

17. Caplow et al., *Middletown Families,* pp. 169–70, 185.

18. Robert Coles and Geoffrey Stokes, *Sex and the American Teenager* (New York, 1985), p. 7; Hunt, *Sexual Behavior in the 1970s,* p. 142.

19. Blumstein and Schwartz, *American Couples,* pp. 208, 282.

20. Hunt, *Sexual Behavior in the 1970s,* pp. 202, 198, 187, 192.

21. *Ibid,* pp. 183–84; Barbara Ehrenreich, Elizabeth Hess, and Gloria Jacobs, *Re-Making Love: The Feminization of Sex* (Garden City, N.Y., 1986), p. 100.

22. Blumstein and Schwartz, *American Couples,* pp. 232, 236.

23. *Ibid.,* pp. 201–3; Ehrenreich et al., *Re-Making Love,* p. 164.

24. New York *Times,* July 22, 1977, p. 1.

25. New York *Times,* October 31, 1979, p. C19.

26. Blumstein and Schwartz, *American Couples,* pp. 202–3, 236, 273. For another study see Karla Jay and Allen Young, *The Gay Report: Lesbians and Gay Men Speak Out About Sexual Experiences and Life Styles* (New York, 1979).

27. Blumstein and Schwartz, *American Couples,* p. 305.

28. Allan M. Brandt, *No Magic Bullet: A Social History of Venereal Disease in the United States Since 1880* (New York, 1985), pp. 170–74, 179–82.

29. Hunt, *Sexual Behavior in the 1970s,* p. 130; Caplow et al., *Middletown Families,* p. 171; Coles and Stokes, *Sex and the American Teenager,* p. 38.

30. Coles and Stokes, *Sex and the American Teenager,* pp. 37, 99.

ARTICLE 6
Cohabitation: Recent Changes in the United States

GRAHAM B. SPANIER

One consequence of the sexual revolution and the increasing sexualization of American society was the significant increase in unmarried cohabitation, resulting in a profound change in our courtship system. This article describes the trends in cohabitation and offers some explanations of why unmarried individuals are more prone to live together.

SOCIAL SCIENTISTS CAN POINT to few trends in contemporary American society that have manifested such a dramatic pace of change and that have exhibited such consistent upward growth as the trend in unmarried cohabitation. . . .

About four million American adults are living with a partner of the opposite sex whom they have not married (U.S. Bureau of the Census 1983a, 1984). Some observers may regard the number as small in a population of 238 million. Yet cohabitation usually involves persons who are eligible for an important life transition—marriage—or who have recently experienced another critical transition—divorce. Thus the study of the features of marriage entails at least some study of cohabitation.

By definition, an unmarried cohabiting individual is an adult sharing living quarters with one unrelated adult of the opposite sex. No other adult may be present in the household although children may or may not be present. The data are drawn

Taken from "Cohabitation in the 1980s: Recent Changes in the United States," by Graham B. Spanier in CONTEMPORARY MARRIAGE: COMPARATIVE PERSPECTIVES ON A CHANGING INSTITUTION, Kingsley Davis and Amyra Grossbard-Shechtman, editors. © 1986, The Russell Sage Foundation. Used with permission of the Russell Sage Foundation.

primarily from the March 1980 *Current Population Survey* conducted by the U.S. Bureau of the Census and secondarily from more recent *Current Population Surveys*. It is reasonable to assume that most heterosexual unmarried couples with no other adults in the household live together because they are romantically involved. This assumption is important to note because the data featured here are demographic and do not provide the respondents' reports of their attitudes, motivations, and plans. The demographic data, however, do allow us to address many of the questions raised in this chapter. For example, although our definition of unmarried cohabitation encompasses such arrangements as an elderly woman who rents a room to a male college student or an elderly man who employs a live-in nurse or housekeeper, fewer than 1 percent of unmarried cohabiting couples fit this profile. Most unmarried couples differ in age by no more than a few years.

TRENDS IN UNMARRIED COHABITATION

A profound increase in unmarried cohabitation occurred during the 1960s and 1970s and has continued into the 1980s; only recently are there signs that the rate of increase may be leveling off.

Table 1 compares figures for 1970, 1980, and 1984. In 1980 three times as many unmarried couples lived together as in 1970, the number nearly doubling between 1975 and 1980. In 1980 the trend continued to grow, showing a 14 percent increase by 1981. In 1984, there were two million unmarried-couple households (U.S. Bureau of the Census 1984), a 25 percent increase since 1980. About 4 percent of all couples living together in the United States are unmarried.

Table 1 also reveals that about 27 percent of all unmarried-couple households have at least one child in the household. When children as well as adults are included, more than 4.6 million persons live in the households of unmarried couples.

Table 2 verifies a finding noted in earlier data, namely that primarily young adults find unmarried cohabitation attractive as a living arrangement. One-fourth of

TABLE 1 Households with Two Unrelated Adults of Opposite Sex Sharing Living Quarters, by Presence of Children: 1970, 1980, 1984

	1984		1980		1970	
	Number (in thousands)	Percent	Number (in thousands)	Percent	Number (in thousands)	Percent
Total	1,988	100.0	1,589	100.0	523	100.0
No children present	1,373	69.1	1,159	72.9	327	62.5
Children present[a]	614	30.9	431	27.1	196	37.5

Source: U.S. Bureau of the Census, *Current Population Reports,* Series P-20, No. 391, 1984.

[a] For the year 1970, children in unmarried-couple households are under 14. For the years 1980 and 1984, children are under 15.

TABLE 2 Partners in Unmarried Couple Households, By Sex, Age, and Marital History: 1981 (Numbers in Thousands)

	Men		Women	
	Number	*Percent*	*Number*	*Percent*
Total	1,808	100.0	1,808	100.0
Age				
Under 25	435	24.1	687	38.0
25–34	780	43.1	686	37.9
35–44	252	13.9	151	8.4
45–64	232	12.8	181	10.0
65 years or more	111	6.1	99	5.5
Marital history				
Never married	958	53.0	991	54.8
Ever married	850	47.0	817	45.2

Source: U.S. Bureau of the Census, *Current Population Reports,* Series P-20, No. 372, 1982.

the men and nearly two-fifths of the women are under 25 years old; two-thirds of the men and three-fourths of the women are under 35. Although unmarried couples consist of persons of all ages, the phenomenon continues to involve younger persons disproportionately.

Between 1970 and 1981 one particularly noteworthy trend was a significant decline in the proportion of unmarried couples involving persons 65 and over. The absolute number of elderly persons remained relatively constant. For example, in 1970 approximately 115,000 persons 65 or older were unmarried and cohabiting, constituting 22 percent of all households with no children present. In 1981 there were approximately 120,000 such couples, only 7 percent of those with no children present. Given a possibly greater reluctance to report such a living arrangement in 1970 than in 1981, the negligible change in the number of unmarried cohabiting older persons during a period when the elderly population increased significantly is noteworthy. Changes in Social Security regulations, which make remarriage more practical for the elderly, may account for some of the inertia in cohabitation.

Another interesting subgroup are persons legally married to someone other than the person they live with. In 1981 there were an estimated 282,000 such individuals—about 8 percent of the total number of persons cohabiting. The partners of individuals in this category most frequently either have never married or have been divorced. To a lesser extent, the partners share the same status, namely, still married to someone else.

Contrary to previous speculation suggesting that unmarried couples typically involve never-married persons, Glick and Spanier (1980) found that about half of the individuals living together had been married previously. More recent data confirm this finding. Although never-married cohabiting individuals tend to be young (81 percent of the men and 88 percent of the women are under 35), those who have been married are more evenly distributed across the adult years—40 percent of the men and 31 percent of the women are 35–54 years old, and 24 percent and 22 percent, respectively, are 65 or older. One of the more notable changes between 1975 and 1980 is the increase in the proportion of cohabitants under 35 who have been married. In other words, among the ever-married, a larger share of the increase can be attributed to those under 35. This change undoubtedly stems somewhat from the continuing high divorce rate, which rose from 4.9 to 5.2 per 1,000 population during the period (National Center for Health Statistics 1981, 1982). The change may also reflect a possibly longer period between divorce and remarriage, although such a trend has not yet been established. Since divorce disproportionately affects younger adults, a growing pool of previously married individuals now has the option of remarrying or of living with someone as an unmarried couple.

Glick and Spanier (1980) reported that between 1960 and 1975 the number of unmarried couples in households with children present had not varied much. The increase in nonmarital cohabitation was accounted for primarily by young couples without children. This pattern changed between 1975 and 1980 when both the number and the proportion of households with children increased. Thus, the recent growth in nonmarital cohabitation comes both from couples with children and from couples without children.

As with married couples, most young unmarried cohabiting adults live with someone of the same race. In 1980 nearly 98 percent of married couples and 95 percent of unmarried couples were of the same race. In 1980 about 2.2 percent of all marriages with the woman under 35 involved persons of different races, compared to 1.2 percent in 1975. The largest share of this increase occurred among couples with a white man or woman married to a person who designated a race other than black or white. Black men are far more likely to be living with white women than are black women to be living with white men. Individuals neither black nor white are as likely to have a partner of a different race as of the same race.

Unmarried partners generally are in the same or an adjacent age group. The ages of the partners tend to be widest apart when the man was previously married and least widely apart when he was never married. Whereas 45 percent of the previously married cohabiting men are in an older five-year age cohort than their wives, 71 percent of the previously married cohabiting men are in an older category than their unmarried partners. These findings reflect a tendency for men either to live with and then marry younger women or simply to live with a younger woman following a disrupted marriage.

It is interesting to point out that whereas only 4 percent of married women are in an older five-year cohort than their husbands, about 12 percent of the couples with a never-married man, and about 6 percent with one previously married, have such a profile. In general, therefore, young unmarried women, regardless of their marital history, are more likely than married women to be older than their partners.

The increase in cohabitation in recent years has encompassed persons of all educational backgrounds, but particularly has involved those with less than a college degree. In 1975, for example, 25 percent of the men and 21 percent of the women of cohabiting couples involving a never-married man were college graduates; in 1980 the percentages had dropped to 18 and 16.

Unemployment in 1980 was about twice as high for unmarried cohabiting women as it was for married men. An unmarried working man or woman exhibits a much higher tendency to live with an unemployed partner than does his or her married counterpart. However, unemployment does not seem to afflict both members of a cohabiting relationship simultaneously. Only 2 percent of unmarried-couple households possessed both an unemployed man and an unemployed woman.

The statistics are similar for both partners' participation in the labor force. In 1980, in only 3 percent of unmarried-couple households both the man and the woman were not in the labor force. However, unmarried women are much more likely than married women to be supporting a man who is not in the labor force. On the other side of the coin, married men are more likely than their cohabiting counterparts to support a woman not in the labor force.

Of all unmarried couples in which the woman is under 35 years old, nearly half are ones in which neither partner has ever been married. This represents an increase (48 percent compared to 43 percent) between 1975 and 1980. In another 15 percent of the cases, both the man and the woman have been divorced and in another 23 percent one partner has never been married while the other has been divorced.

Among these relatively young couples, widowhood is rare, as are relationships involving individuals still married to another partner. Cohabiting men and women who are still married to another person are much more frequent among couples in which the woman is over 35.

In 1980 in unmarried households, the proportion of separated persons was only half of what it had been in 1975, while the proportion of divorced persons was larger. This shift suggests that individuals are now more likely than before to terminate a failing marriage by divorce rather than to allow it to continue legally. Divorce may be sought sooner by persons who wish to live with someone else; moreover, divorce laws now more readily permit a speedy dissolution of a marriage.

EXPLAINING THE TREND

Increased unmarried cohabitation suggests that attitudes have changed. Cohabitation is viewed as a more acceptable form of living, and individuals are now more willing to live together. If so, if both attitude and behavior have changed, what are the causes of the change?

One factor has been the increase in the average age at first marriage, which has accompanied the rising incidence of cohabitation. After the 1950s, when the median age at first marriage reached a low for both men and women in the United States, the marital age rose steadily. In the most recent twenty-five-year period the median age climbed by more than two full years for both men and women (U.S. Bureau of the Census 1983a). It can be argued that among never-married persons cohabitation provides a contemporary extension of the courtship process, perhaps contributing to the postponement of marriage. Of course, if individuals first decide to postpone marriage, then cohabitation has more time to flower. Thus additional explanations are in order as to why these trends have covaried.

Several trends pertaining to sexual behavior and fertility have been well-documented during the last twenty-five years. In particular, the incidence of premarital coitus has increased, effective contraception is more readily available, fertility rates among young women have declined, and young married women are waiting longer after the wedding to commence childbearing (U.S. Bureau of the Census 1983b; Zelnik and Kantner 1980).

The prospect of sexual intimacy probably offered young adults of a generation ago a powerful incentive to consider marriage and to schedule it with some dispatch. Since the significant upward trend in cohabitation appears to have begun in the early 1960s, let us consider the 1950s as a period of comparison with today. In the 1950s, as Andrew Cherlin points out (Cherlin 1981), home and family life were highly regarded. It was a period of prosperity, high birth rates, and geographical dispersion to family-centered suburbs. In these and other ways, society provided a climate conducive to early marriage, early childbearing, and relatively high birth rates. Cohabitation had no prominent place given the norms of the time. Since the public consciousness largely disapproved of sexual intercourse outside of marriage—although it was fairly common—marriage provided young people with the only pragmatic route to sexual intimacy on a continuing basis. Since the 1950s, however, premarital sexual activity has become more prevalent, has involved less risk, and has tended to begin earlier. Society accepts such behavior more readily. Contraception more readily available to young people reduces or even eliminates the fear of pregnancy. The availability of abortion and the increased awareness of abortion as a method of controlling fertility undoubtedly also play some role.

Society's changing views of sex and marriage have made it possible to deemphasize or even to eliminate access to a sexual partner as a primary motivation for marriage. With this motivation removed, it is logical on the average that marriage would tend to occur later. Simultaneously, the period during which cohabitation can occur has extended and there now exists a diminished need for a cohabitational relationship to be formalized. Since a woman can almost completely eliminate the risk of pregnancy, the couple also can avoid what in the 1950s would have been a very compelling reason for early marriage—a birth out of wedlock or premarital pregnancy.

Society has changed in another way that may contribute to increased unmarried cohabitation. In the 1950s people assumed that women would marry relatively early, in part to begin childbearing, and that most mothers would remain at home to raise the children. The impressive movement of women into the labor force during the intervening years has changed this picture. Women now possess a much greater propensity to have attended college in order to pursue a career or to have an interest in working during their early adult years. Consequently, they have a diminished desire to marry during their early twenties or to have children at a time when their careers are being launched. With the internal and external pressures to marry and have children lessened, it is likely that young women would want to consider other options, such as cohabitation without marriage, during the years when their counterparts a generation ago were already married and beginning families.

Higher education, in its own right, may also influence cohabitation in two ways. First, since more young women leave home for college today than did so in the 1950s, they are more likely to become socially independent of their parents. The contemporary woman has increased opportunities to interact with eligible men, usually in an environment that tends to be less restrictive than that at home. Second, women attending college today expect to integrate both family and career, whereas women a generation ago viewed college as a transition to marriage. The college climate today directs women toward careers, not toward mate selection and marriage.

Urbanization, similarly, may be conducive to nonmarital cohabitation. The urban environment and its characteristic anonymity allow for cohabitation with fewer sanctions than a small town or rural environment might provide. Men and women may live together out of wedlock with little concern about what others will think. With urbanization, the level of surveillance of personal behavior has declined, thus making cohabitation easier to consider.

Finally, we may cite the increased prospect of divorce as a contributor to the upward trend in cohabitation. Although few brides and grooms expect to get divorced, there is now a very real awareness of the increased propensity to divorce. Many young men and women have experienced a divorce in their own families of orientation. The delay in marriage and the increased likelihood of cohabitation as a temporary alternative to marriage reflect to some degree a reluctance to rush into a relationship that runs some risk of divorce. In other words, young couples today may be weighing the prospects for marriage more carefully, deciding to marry only after reaching a degree of commitment higher than that required two or three decades earlier.

Although the discussion above focuses on young adults never yet married, parallel arguments can be presented for the phenomenon of divorced persons cohabiting after their marriages have been dissolved. One common trend in all of these explanations is that couples do not necessarily equate living together with a permanent and lasting alternative to marriage, but rather associate it with a postponement of marriage or regard it as a temporary matter of convenience without an explicit understanding of what lies ahead. Indeed for many couples, the link between cohabitation and marriage is unclear from the outset because of other overriding concerns such as educational or job mobility. Couples may wish to delay marriage because one individual is preparing to go to graduate school and views marriage as a distant possibility. They may delay marriage because of job offers in differing locations. Economic concerns also suggest why a couple may prefer temporary cohabitation. They may be reluctant to marry before they are financially secure or when one or both partners are unemployed. Cohabitation can thus be viewed as an extension of the traditional courtship process, having many of the same conceptual features as engagement.

This discussion suggests that nonmarital cohabitation increased over the course of a generation when other fundamental changes also took place in society. Cohabitation, I believe, is best viewed not as a cause or effect of such changes, but rather as a phenomenon that occurred simultaneously and logically with other changes. We may generalize that cohabitation allows for intimacy without the commitment of marriage, providing for some couples the opportunity to satisfy the needs traditionally met in a family context. Cohabitation also affords the opportunity to terminate a relationship without the messy legal tangles (although they are not always avoided) and without the stigma that can accompany divorce. Cohabitation may serve an important economic function, since two individuals living together can usually live more cheaply than two individuals living apart. It may also be more economical than living together as a married couple due to the structure of our income tax system. Unmarried cohabitation may be like engagement in that it signifies to others that a formal, committed relationship short of marriage exists. It can be a period where the advisability of marriage is determined. Unlike engagement, however, which implies an imminent wedding, cohabitation may function in a contrary manner, allowing the indefinite postponement of a wedding date.

Some aspects of the demography of cohabitation must be viewed in a broader historical context. For example, the racial differences in social and economic characteristics of unmarried cohabitants are so substantial that they cannot be explained solely in terms of contemporary history. It is likely that nonmarital unions have different meanings for blacks and whites. The history of black family life in Africa and during the period of slavery in the United States suggests that black women and men possessed a greater degree of independence than did men and women in traditional European society. Of course, other fundamental differences exist between blacks and whites that may be responsible for the cohabitational variation. Differing employment patterns for black men and women, a higher rate of economic instability for blacks than for whites, the higher rate of illegitimate births among blacks, and the sex ratio resulting in fewer black men available for marriage to black women as compared to whites may all play some role in explaining the differences presented. . . .

CONCLUSION

What lies in the future? An overall increase in cohabitation is likely to occur, although more slowly than in recent years, since the conditions that have been conducive to nonmarital cohabitation or that perhaps have contributed to its increase will continue to be present. Since the age at first marriage probably will continue its increase, cohabitation will remain prominent in our society. If the divorce rate continues at its current level, or even declines slightly, a large population of previously married individuals will be free to cohabit, many in a transition to remarriage. The beginnings of a trend toward postponement of remarriage, undoubtedly corresponding with the trend in postponement of first marriage, is likely to continue, thus increasing unmarried cohabitation arrangements.

Although the pace of the increase shows signs of deceleration, the large numbers of individuals who now cohabit and who have caused significant changes in our society have bequeathed to us a demographic history that will not go unnoticed by the next generation. Future cohorts will find the freedoms and flexibility of cohabitation attractive, and, almost certainly, behavior across social class lines will converge. To the extent that social and economic conditions improve, cohabitation for lower-status individuals should level off or decline. Yet a continuing increase in cohabitation due to other factors mentioned certainly will compensate for this leveling effect. The collective outcome is likely to be one of convergence among social classes within the larger framework of a continuing increase nationally in cohabitation. A comparison of 1975, 1980, and later data indicates that this prediction may have some merit.

REFERENCES

Cherlin, A. J. *Marriage, Divorce, Remarriage*. Cambridge, Mass.: Harvard University Press, 1981.

Glick, P. C., and Spanier, G. B. "Married and Unmarried Cohabitation in the United States." *Journal of Marriage and the Family* 42(1980):19–30.

National Center for Health Statistics. "Annual Summary of Births, Deaths, Marriages, and Divorces: United States, 1980." *Monthly Vital Statistics Report*, Vol. 29, No. 13, September 17. Washington, D.C.: Department of Health and Human Services, 1981.

National Center for Health Statistics. "Births, Marriages, Divorces, and Deaths for 1981." *Monthly Vital Statistics Report*, Vol. 30, No. 12, March 18. Washington, D.C.: Department of Health and Human Services, 1982.

U.S. Bureau of the Census. "Marital Status and Living Arrangements: March 1980." *Current Population Reports*, Series P-20, No. 365. Washington, D.C.: U.S. Government Printing Office, 1981a.

U.S. Bureau of the Census. "Household and Family Characteristics: March 1980." *Current Population Reports*, Series P-20, No. 366. Washington, D.C.: U.S. Government Printing Office, 1981b.

U.S. Bureau of the Census. "Marital Status and Living Arrangements: March 1981." *Current Population Reports*, Series P-20, No. 372. Washington, D.C.: U.S. Government Printing Office, 1982.

U.S. Bureau of the Census. "Marital Status and Living Arrangements: March 1982." *Current Population Reports*, Series P-20, No. 380. Washington, D.C.: U.S. Government Printing Office, 1983a.

U.S. Bureau of the Census. "Fertility of American Women: June 1981." *Current Population Reports*, Series P-20, No. 378. Washington, D.C.: U.S. Government Printing Office, 1983b.

U.S. Bureau of the Census. "Households, Families, Marital Status, and Living Arrangements: March 1984 (Advance Report)." *Current Population Reports*, Series P-20, No. 391. Washington, D.C.: U.S. Government Printing Office, 1984.

Zelnik, M., and Kantner, J. F. "Sexual Activity, Contraceptive Use and Pregnancy Among Metropolitan-Area Teenagers: 1971–1979." *Family Planning Perspectives* 12 (1980):230–237.

PART TWO
Marriage and Family Relations

BECOMING MARRIED marks one of the most profound transformations an individual can undergo. Marriage represents not only the establishment of a new relationship but the creation of a new identity—a coupled identity. With it comes a whole new set of social relationships with the spouses' parents, relatives, and friends. In joining two people, a new piece of social fabric is woven.

Humans have been marvelously inventive in putting the two sexes together. Although there always must be two people, a husband and a wife, to constitute a marriage, it does not follow that marriage consists of only two individuals. In various places and times, all of the logical possibilities have been tried and practiced. Aside from monogamy (one husband and one wife), marriage has taken three different forms. Polygyny is the wedding of one husband and two or more wives, polyandry involves one wife with two or more husbands, and group marriage consists of two or more husbands with two or more wives.

While we may think of monogamy as being "normal," polygyny is in fact the most commonly preferred type of marriage. This probably is due to the economic advantages polygyny has over the other forms. Whatever else a marriage may be to its participants, it is always an economic arrangement. If the labor of women makes a major contribution to a family's economic well-being, then there are obvious advantages to having multiple wives: the more, the better. Polygyny also has reproductive benefits, inasmuch as one man can impregnate several women. If children are economic assets, polygyny has clear advantages over the other forms of marriage. Under the pressures of industrialization, however, these conditions are being rapidly eroded, so that in terms of statistical frequency most marriages are monogamous in character.

Cross-culturally, there is one other noteworthy variation in marriage. This concerns the extent to which marriage is socially defined as being instrumental or expressive in character. Marriage tends to be instrumental when the relationship, no matter how many spouses are involved, is viewed as a means to other ends. Those ends may have to do with forming alliances between family groups, with enhancing economic well-being, or may simply concern the desire to reproduce. When marriage has a more expressive character, it is viewed as being intrinsically rewarding, not as a means to other ends. It is an emotionally intimate relationship, based on common interests and intended to be mutually rewarding. In reality, of course, marriages tend to be a mixture of these extremes. But at the societal level, we can clearly differentiate between the two types of marriage systems.

Historically, in the United States, we have moved from expecting marriage to be more instrumental to anticipating that it will fill expressive needs. If we use the colonial era as a comparative baseline, the expectation then was that marriage was foremost an economic partnership. With the more direct influence of parents in the mate-selection process, making a "good match" meant taking into account a person's social rank, which was largely based on property or the eventual prospects for it. Upon marriage, women lost many of the legal rights they previously had, and husbands had virtual control over any property wives brought to the marriage. Since economic production was mostly a family enterprise, wives and children alike constituted economic assets. This is not to say that romance was unknown in the colonies, but in most instances, it clearly took a back seat to economic considerations.

The more instrumental character of colonial marriage also can be seen in the role of sex in marriage. Today, of course, sex is seen as a crucial element in marriage, considered by many as the ultimate expression of intimacy and expressiveness. It is less clear that it had such a central role in colonial times. While the Puritans and other colonists were far from being prudes, the limited privacy in colonial homes probably minimized the pleasurable aspects of sex. The need for reproduction and large families was certainly more imperative, suggesting that sex in marriage may have had a different meaning than it does today.

Beginning in the last quarter of the nineteenth century, the instrumental character of American marriage began to give way. Some of the first indications of change were in the altered perceptions of sex. There was a growing acknowledgment of female sexuality and a new evaluation of marital sexuality as an expression of love and affection. From this followed a new conception of marriage emphasizing the importance of love, affection, and compatibility. Spurred by the feminist movement, companionship and individual fulfillment through marriage became paramount goals.

The trend toward a companionate and more expressive type of marriage continues. We are moving toward a symmetrical form of marriage. The roles of husbands and wives have become more alike. In ever increasing proportions, wives have moved into the paid labor force. Husbands have begun to assume more of the housework traditionally associated with the wife's role. Fathers have become more visible as they become more involved in child care and rearing. Significant alterations in the life cycle have occurred (compression of the childbearing period and the prolongation of the retirement years), permitting couples to spend more of their leisure time together.

These changes, however, have not affected—at least in equal proportions—all segments of American society. Social-class differences remain, as do racial and ethnic differences. Lower class and upper class marriages do not exhibit the same amount of symmetry as found among middle-class couples. For one thing, there is a greater rigidity in the division of labor. Especially in the upper class, marriage conforms more to the traditional model, with the husband acting as the breadwinner and the wife being responsible for domestic affairs. In comparison to the middle class, working and lower class couples are more segregated by gender in socializing outside the home and in their pursuit of leisure-time activities. Thus, at both ends of the social-class spectrum, the roles of husbands and wives tend to complement each other rather than having a symmetrical character.

Throughout the American class structure, even in the middle class, one prominent asymmetry remains. This concerns who has the power. Our past is patriarchal; men have dominated in all arenas of social life. Although there have been significant inroads in changing this patriarchal past, especially in the economic realm, wives and women in general are still disadvantaged. It is proper to speak of "his" and "her" marriages, for they are divided realities. This, along with the issue of how labor is to be allocated in the home, is likely to be a central contention among couples well into the twenty-first century.

We begin Part Two with articles that describe some of the recent developments affecting marriage in the United States. These selections also note some important continuities, particularly with respect to an inequitable distribution of domestic labor. We next present articles dealing with marital changes over the life cycle, proceeding from the early years of marriage to its later phases, including widowhood. We then turn to parent-child relations. The articles in this part range from a discussion of the myths surrounding parenthood and the problems of child care, to the experience of being the "sandwich generation" and the styles of grandparenting.

ARTICLE 7
Coming Apart: Radical Departures Since 1960

STEVEN MINTZ AND SUSAN KELLOGG

In the short span of three decades, the traditional family has all but disappeared. The breadwinner father and housewife mother, with one or more children, constitute less than one-sixth of current households. Mintz and Kellogg attribute this dramatic transformation to a massive upheaval in our cultural values. The "new morality," they contend, set in motion a revolution in family values and behavior.

A GENERATION AGO Ozzie, Harriet, David, and Ricky Nelson epitomized the American family. Over 70 percent of all American households in 1960 were like the Nelsons: made up of dad the breadwinner, mom the homemaker, and their children. Today, less than three decades later, "traditional" families consisting of a breadwinner father, a housewife mother, and one or more dependent children account for less than 15 percent of the nation's households. As American families have changed, the image of the family portrayed on television has changed accordingly. Today's television families vary enormously, running the gamut from traditional families like "The Waltons" to two-career families like the Huxtables on "The Cosby Show" or the Keatons on "Family Ties"; "blended" families like the Bradys on "The Brady Bunch," with children from previous marriages; two single mothers and their children on "Kate and Allie"; a homosexual who serves as a surrogate father on "Love, Sidney"; an unmarried couple who cohabit in the same house on "Who's the Boss?";

"Coming Apart: Radical Departures since 1960." Reprinted with permission of The Free Press, a division of Macmillan, Inc. from DOMESTIC REVOLUTIONS: A Social History of American Family Life by Steven Mintz and Susan Kellogg. Copyright © 1988 by The Free Press.

and a circle of friends, who think of themselves as a family, congregating at a Boston bar on "Cheers."[1]

Since 1960 U.S. families have undergone a historical transformation as dramatic and far reaching as the one that took place at the beginning of the nineteenth century. Even a casual familiarity with census statistics suggests the profundity of the changes that have taken place in family life. Birthrates plummeted. The average number of children per family fell from 3.8 at the peak of the baby boom to less than 2 today. At the same time, the divorce rate soared. Today the number of divorces each year is twice as high as it was in 1966 and three times higher than in 1950. The rapid upsurge in the divorce rate contributed to a dramatic increase in the number of single-parent households, or what used to be known as "broken homes." The number of households consisting of a single woman and her children has doubled since 1960. A sharp increase in female-headed homes was accompanied by a steep increase in the number of couples cohabiting outside marriage; their numbers have quadrupled since 1960.[2]

Almost every aspect of family life seems to have changed before our eyes. Sexual codes were revised radically. Today only about one American woman in five waits until marriage to become sexually active, compared to nearly half in 1960 who postponed intercourse. Meanwhile, the proportion of births occurring among unmarried women quadrupled. At the same time, millions of wives entered the labor force. The old stereotype of the breadwinner-father and housewife-mother broke down as the number of working wives climbed. In 1950, 25 percent of married women living with their husbands worked outside the home; in the late 1980s the figure is nearly 60 percent. The influx of married women entering the labor force was particularly rapid among mothers of young children. Now more than half of all mothers of school-age children hold jobs. As a result, fewer younger children can claim their mother's exclusive attention. What Americans have witnessed since 1960 are fundamental challenges to the forms, ideals, and role expectations that have defined the family for the last century and a half.[3]

Profound and far-reaching changes have occurred in the American family in behavior and in values. Contemporary Americans are much more likely than their predecessors to postpone or forgo marriage, to live alone outside familial units, to engage in intercourse prior to marriage, to permit marriages to end in divorce, to permit mothers of young children to work outside the home, and to allow children to live in families with only one parent and no adult male present. Earlier family norms—of a working father, a housewife, and children—have undergone major alterations. The term "family" has gradually been redefined to include any group of people living together, including such variations as single mothers and children, unmarried couples, and gay couples.[4]

All these changes have generated a profound sense of uncertainty and ambivalence. Many Americans fear that the rapid decline in the birthrates, the dramatic upsurge in divorce rates, and the proliferation of loose, noncontractual sexual relationships are symptoms of increasing selfishness and self-centeredness incompatible with strong family attachments. They also fear that an increased proportion of working mothers has caused more children to be neglected, resulting in climbing rates of teenage pregnancy, delinquency, suicide, drug and alcohol abuse, and failure in school.[5]

Today fear for the family's future is widespread. In 1978 author Clare Boothe Luce succinctly summarized fears about the fragility of the family that continue to haunt Americans today:

> Today 50% of all marriages end in divorce, separation, or desertion. . . . The marriage rate and birth rate are falling. The numbers of one-parent and one-child families are rising. More and more young people are living together without benefit of marriage. . . . Premarital and extramarital sex no longer raises parental or conjugal eyebrows. . . . The rate of reported incest, child molestation, rape, and child and wife abuse, is steadily mounting. . . . Runaway children, teenage prostitution, youthful drug addiction and alcoholism have become great, ugly, new phenomena.[6]

What are the forces that lie behind these changes in family life? And what are the implications of these transformations?

NEW MORALITY

The key to understanding the recent upheavals in family life lies in a profound shift in cultural values. Three decades ago most Americans shared certain strong attitudes about the family. Public opinion polls showed that they endorsed marriage as a prerequisite of well-being, social adjustment, and maturity and agreed on the proper roles of husband and wife. Men and women who failed to marry or who resented their family roles were denigrated as maladjusted or neurotic. The message conveyed by the broader culture was that happiness was a by-product of living by the accepted values of hard work and family obligation.[7]

Values and norms have shifted. The watchwords of contemporary society are "growth," "self-realization," and "fulfillment." Expectations of personal happiness have risen and collided with a more traditional concern (and sacrifice) for the family. At the same time, in addition to its traditional functions of caring for children, providing economic security, and meeting its members' emotional needs, the family has become the focus for new expectations of sexual fulfillment, intimacy, and companionship.[8]

Today a broad spectrum of family norms that prevailed during the 1950s and early 1960s is no longer widely accepted. Divorce is not stigmatized as it used to be; a large majority of the public now rejects the idea that an unhappily married couple should stay together for their children's sake. Similarly, the older view that anyone who rejected marriage is "sick," "neurotic," or "immoral" has declined sharply, as has the view that people who do not have children are "selfish." Opinion surveys show that most Americans no longer believe that a woman should not work if she has a husband who can support her, that a bride should always be a virgin when she marries, or that premarital sex is always wrong.[9]

Economic affluence played a major role in the emergence of a new outlook. Couples who married in the 1940s and 1950s had spent their early childhood years in the depression and formed relatively modest material aspirations. Born in the late 1920s or 1930s, when birthrates were depressed, they faced little competition for jobs at maturity and were financially secure enough to marry and have children at a relatively young age. Their children, however, who came of age during the 1960s and 1970s, spent their childhoods during an era of unprecedented affluence. Between 1950 and 1970, median family income tripled. Increased affluence increased opportunities for education, travel, and leisure, all of which helped to heighten expectations of self-fulfillment. Unlike their parents, they had considerable expectations for their own material and emotional well-being.[10]

In keeping with the mood of an era of rising affluence, philosophies stressing individual self-realization flourished. Beginning in the 1950s, "humanistic" psychologies, stressing growth and self-actualization, triumphed over earlier theories that had emphasized adjustment as the solution to individual problems. The underlying assumptions of the new "third force" psychologies—a name chosen to distinguish them from the more pessimistic psychoanalytic and behaviorist psychologies—of Abraham Maslow, Carl Rogers, and Erich Fromm, is that a person's spontaneous impulses are intrinsically good and that maturity is not a process of "settling down" and suppressing instinctual needs but of achieving one's potential.[11]

Even in the early 1960s, marriage and family ties were regarded by the "human potential movement" as potential threats to individual fulfillment as a man or a woman. The highest forms of human needs, contended proponents of the new psychologies, were autonomy, independence, growth, and creativity, all of which could be thwarted by "existing relationships and interactions." Unlike the earlier psychology of adjustment, associated with Alfred Adler and Dale Carnegie, which had counseled compromise, suppression of instinctual impulses, avoidance of confrontations, and the desirability of acceding to the wishes of others, the new humanistic psychologies advised individuals to "get in touch" with their feelings and freely voice their opinions, even if this generated feelings of guilt.[12]

The impulse toward self-fulfillment and liberation was further advanced by the prophets of the 1960s counterculture and New Left, Normal O. Brown and Herbert Marcuse. Both Brown and Marcuse transformed Sigmund Freud's psychoanalytic insights into a critique of the constraints of liberal society. They were primarily concerned not with political or economic repression but rather with what they perceived as the psychological repression of the individual's instinctual needs. Brown located the source of repression in the ego mechanisms that controlled each person's instincts. Marcuse, in a broader social critique, believed that repression was at least partially imposed by society.[13]

For both Brown and Marcuse, the goal of social change was the liberation of eros, the agglomeration of an individual's pleasure-seeking life instincts, or, as Marcuse put it, the "free gratification of man's instinctual needs." Brown went so far as to challenge openly the basic tenets of "civilized sexual morality," with its stress on genital, heterosexual, monogamous sex, and extolled a new ideal of bisexualism and "polymorphous perversity" (total sexual gratification). For a younger affluent, middle-class generation in revolt against liberal values, the ideas of Brown and Marcuse provided a rationale for youthful rebellion.[14]

An even more thoroughgoing challenge to traditional family values was mounted by the women's liberation movement, which attacked the family's exploitation of women. Feminists denounced the societal expectation that women defer to the needs of spouses and children as part of their social roles as wives and mothers. Militant feminist activists like Ti-Grace Atkinson called marriage "slavery," "legalized rape," and "unpaid labor" and denounced heterosexual love as "tied up with a sense of dependency." The larger mainstream of the women's movement articulated a powerful critique of the idea that child care and housework was the apex of a woman's accomplishments or her sole means of fulfillment. Feminists uncovered unsettling evidence of harsher conditions behind conventional familial togetherness, such as child abuse and wife beating, wasted lives and exploited labor. Instead of giving the highest priority to their families, women were urged to raise their consciousness of their own needs and abilities. From this vantage point, marriage increasingly came to be described as a trap, circumscribing a woman's social and intellectual horizons and lowering her sense of self-esteem. Homemaking, which as recently as the early 1960s had been celebrated on such television shows as "Queen for a Day," came under attack as an unrecognized and unpaid form of work in contrast to more "serious" occupations outside the home. And, as for marital bliss forevermore, feminists warned that divorce—so common and so economically difficult for women—was an occurrence for which every married woman had to be prepared. In general the feminists awakened American women to what they viewed as the worst form of social and political oppression—sexism. The introduction of this new awareness would go far beyond the feminists themselves.[15]

The challenge to older family values was not confined to radical members of the counterculture, the New Left, or the women's liberation movement. Broad segments of society were influenced by, and participated in, this fundamental shift in values.

Although only a small minority of American women ever openly declared themselves to be feminists, there can be no doubt that the arguments of the women's movement dramatically altered women's attitudes toward family roles, child care, marital relationships, femininity, and housework. This is true even among many women who claim to reject feminism. Polls have shown a sharp decline in the proportion of women favoring large families and a far greater unwillingness to subordinate personal needs and interests to the demands of husbands and children. A growing majority of women now believe that both husband and wife should have jobs, both do housework, and both take care of children. This represents a stunning shift of opinion in a decade and a half. A new perception of woman in the family has taken hold. In extreme imagery she is a superwoman, doing a full-time job while managing her home and family well. The more realistic image is of the wife and mother who works and struggles to manage job and family with the help of spouse, day care, and employer. Thus, as women increasingly seek employment outside the home, the family itself shifts to adjust to the changing conditions of its members while striving to provide the stability and continuity it had traditionally afforded.[16]

During the 1960s a sexual revolution that predated the counterculture swept the nation's literature, movies, theater, advertising, and fashion. In 1962, Grossinger's resort in New York State's Catskill mountains introduced its first singles-only weekend, thereby publicly acknowledging couples outside marriage. That same year Illinois became the first state to decriminalize all forms of private sexual conduct between consenting adults. Two years later, in 1964, the first singles bar opened on New York's Upper East Side; the musical *Hair* introduced nudity to the Broadway stage; California designer Rudi Gernreich created the topless bathing suit; and bars featuring topless waitresses and dancers sprouted. By the end of the decade, a growing number of the nation's colleges had abolished regulations specifying how late students could stay outside their dormitories and when and under what circumstances male and female students could visit with each other.[17]

One of the most important aspects of this latter-day revolution in morals was the growth of a "singles culture"—evident in a proliferation of singles bars, apartment houses, and clubs. The sources of the singles culture were varied and complex, owing as much to demographic shifts as to the ready availability of birth control, cures for venereal diseases, and liberalized abortion laws. The trend toward postponement of marriage, combined with increased rates of college attendance and divorce, meant that growing numbers of adults spent protracted periods of their sexually mature lives outside marriage. The result was that it became far easier than in the past to maintain an active social and sex life outside marriage. It also became more acceptable, as its patterns became grist for the popular media and imagination.[18]

Sexually oriented magazines started to display pubic hair and filmmakers began to show simulated sexual acts. *I Am Curious (Yellow)* depicted coitus on the screen. *Deep Throat* released in the 1970s, showed cunnilingus and fellatio. Other manifestations of a relaxation of traditional mores included a growing public tolerance of homosexuality, a blurring of male and female sex roles, increasing public acceptance of abortion, the growing visibility of pornography, a marked trend away from female virginity until marriage, and a sharp increase in the proportion of women engaging in extramarital sex. Within one decade the cherished privacy of sexuality had been overturned and an era of public sexuality had been ushered in.[19]

Increasingly, values championed by the women's movement and the counterculture were adopted in a milder form by large segments of the American population. A significant majority of Americans adopted permissive attitudes on such matters as premarital sex, cohabitation outside of marriage, and abortion. Fewer women aspired to motherhood and homemaking as a full-time career and instead joined the labor force as much for independence and self-fulfillment as from economic motives. The preferred number of children declined sharply, and to limit births, the number of abortions and sterilizations increased sharply. A revolution had occurred in values and behavior.[20]

NOTES

1. The statistics on changes in family composition can be found in Daniel Yankelovich, *New Rules: Search for Self-Fulfillment in a World Turned Upside Down* (New York, 1981), xiv–xv.

2. Stephen L. Klineberg made a similar argument in a public lecture "American Families in Transition: Challenges and Opportunities in a Revolutionary Time" delivered at Rice University, February 15, 1983. Also see Andrew Hacker, *The End of the American Era* (New York, 1971), 174; James J. Lynch, *The Broken Heart: The Medical Consequences of Loneliness* (New York, 1977), 8–10; *Time* (December 2, 1985), 41; *NYT,* June 27, 1979, I, 1; *NYT,* May 26, 1981, I, 1.

It must be emphasized that despite the dramatic changes that have taken place, the institution of the family is not an endangered species. Today, commitment to marriage remains strong and 90 percent of young Americans marry. Despite rising divorce rates, the majority of marriages do not end in divorce, most divorced individuals remarry, and only a small percentage marry more than twice. Even when divorces occur, they do not necessarily produce grave social problems. Forty percent of all divorces occur within four years of marriage and usually involve no children. At the same time, the desire to have children remains as high as ever. Today only 1 percent of American women say that the ideal number of children in a family is none. And despite concern about the fragility of family ties, the increase in the divorce rate has been largely offset by a decline in death rates. As a result, marriages today are only slightly more likely to be disrupted by divorce, desertion, or death than they were earlier in the century. Indeed, even with the rising divorce rate, fewer children today are raised in institutions or by relatives or by mothers barely able to support them than formerly. In spite of the rising divorce rate, the prevalence of single-parent households has not increased markedly among the middle class because women today are much more likely to remarry after a divorce.

Even in the controversial areas of child care and sexuality, behavior has changed less than newspaper headlines suggest. Today most preschoolers are cared for by full-time mothers or mothers who work part-time. Most mothers of young children accommodate their work schedules to the needs of their children. Continuity is also apparent in sexual behavior. Despite the increasing incidence of premarital sex and widespread public discussion of swinging, wife swapping, and illegitimacy, the overwhelming majority of women who have premarital sex have just one or two partners, usually a fiance or a steady date. Nor has the proportion of unmarried white women having babies increased dramatically. In 1950, 99.5 percent of white teenage women did not have illegitimate births; thirty years later, 98.1 percent of this group did not. See Mary Jo Bane, *Here to Stay: American Families in the Twentieth Century* (New York, 1976), 12–13, 30; Sar A. Levitan and Richard S. Belous, *What's Happening to the American Family?* (Baltimore, 1981), 21, 63; Mary Jo Bane et al., "Child Care Settings in the United States" in *Child Care and Mediating Structures,* eds. Brigitte Berger and Sidney Callahan (Washington, D.C., 1979), 19: Carol Tavris and Carole Offir, *The Longest War: Sex Differences in Perspective* (New York, 1977), 64–69.

3. Tavris and Offir, *The Longest War,* 64–69; Peter Uhlenberg and David Eggebeen, "Declining Well-Being of American Adolescents," *The Public Interest* (Winter 1986), 32–33; Lynch, *Broken Heart,* 8–10; *Time* (December 2, 1985), 41; *NYT,* June 27, 1979, I, 1; *NYT,* May 26, 1981, I, 1; *NYT,* March 16, 1986, I, 18.

4. The impact of these changes is most readily apparent in the lives of a key "pacesetting" segment of the population: educated career women. These women are four times less likely to marry than women of lower economic and educational status and 50 percent more likely to divorce. See Andrew Hacker, "Goodbye to Marriage," *New York Review of Books* (May 3, 1979), 23–27. Peter Clecak, *America's Quest for the Ideal Self: Dissent and Fulfillment in the 60s and 70s* (New York, 1983), 93–94.

5. Yankelovich, *New Rules,* 104, 184.

It is easy to exaggerate the significance of rising rates of divorce, working mothers, and single parent households and to conclude that these changes are bad for the family. But it is also possible to view these developments in a more favorable light. Declining birthrates mean that Americans are less likely to bear children by accident or because it is socially expected than earlier Americans, while rising divorce rates mean that people today are less willing to tolerate unhappy and empty marriages. See Klineberg, "American Families in Transition."

6. Ben J. Wattenberg, *The Good News is the Bad News is Wrong* (New York, 1985), 290–91.

7. Joseph Veroff, Elizabeth Douan, and Richard A. Kulka, *The Inner American: A Self Portrait from 1957 to 1976* (New York, 1981), 191, 192, 194, 196; Yankelovich, *New Rules*, 5, 68, 97, 99.

8. Yankelovich, *New Rules*, 5. The rapid rise in the divorce rate is clearly a legacy of changing social values. When individuals are asked why they have decided to get a divorce, a new set of reasons predominates. A survey conducted by the Family Service Association found that the major source of conflict in marriages involved "communications." Conflict over sex was another reason commonly cited in explanations of divorce. More traditional areas of conflict, such as disputes over children or family finances, lagged far behind. See *NYT,* January 3, 1974, I, 16.

It should be noted, however, that the best predictors of a marital breakup remain what they have always been: a teenage marriage, a wife pregnant before marriage, and a low level of family income. Psychological stress continues to be a leading cause of divorce, since many marriages fail following an acutely stressful experience, such as an unexpected death in the family, revelation of an infidelity, or loss of a job. See Arthur J. Norton and Paul C. Glick, "Marital Instability in America: Past, Present, and Future," in *Divorce and Separation: Context, Causes, and Consequences,* eds. George Lebinger and Oliver C. Moles, (New York, 1979), 6–19; Bane, *Here to Stay,* 22, 32–33, 36.

Traditional causes of marital stress were aggravated by social and legal changes during the 1970s. Economic instability produced conditions conducive to high divorce rates. Instability in a husband's employment or earnings is a major source of strain in the marriages of poorer couples, producing friction because of the husband's inability to fulfill his family's expectations. Divorce is more likely as well when a wife's earnings are higher than her husband's, in part because independent earnings add to a woman's sense of self-esteem and in part because this contributes to the husband's sense of insecurity. As more wives entered the labor force after 1970, this factor became a growing source of marital strain. Increased rates of social mobility across ethnic, religious, and geographical lines also contributed to the rising rates of marital instability. Census statistics disclose that more and more people are marrying partners who come from outside their ethnic or religious group or their area of birth. After marriage an increasing number of couples pull up stakes and move to new parts of the country, particularly to the Sunbelt, disrupting ties with family and friends. Divorce statistics show that the twelve metropolitan areas with the highest divorce rates are all located in Southern and Western states. Victor R. Fuchs, *How We Live* (Cambridge, Mass., 1983), 147–50; *NYT,* November 13, 1981, I, 12.

Changes in law also contributed to the rising number of divorces. Legal changes that made it easier to obtain a divorce included enactment of no-fault divorce laws in every state except South Dakota, "do-it-yourself" divorce kits that allow couples to dissolve a marriage without the help of a lawyer, a tendency toward lower alimony awards, and a trend toward making property settlements less contingent on who was at fault in breaking up the marriage. *NYT,* January 5, 1974, I, 16; *NYT,* March 19, 1975, I, 33; *NYT,* February 7, 1983, I, 1; Joan Anderson letter, *NYT,* December 5, 1981, I, 24; Lenore J. Weitzman and Ruth B. Dixon,

"The Transformation of Legal Marriage Through No-Fault Divorce: The Case of the United States," in *Marriage and Cohabitation in Contemporary Societies: Areas of Legal, Social, and Ethical Change,* eds. John M. Eekelaar and Sanford N. Katz (Toronto, 1979), 143–53; Lynne Carol Halem, *Divorce Reform: Changing Legal and Social Perspectives* (New York, 1980), 233–83.

Finally, the current upsurge in divorces may be a product of the early marriages contracted during World War II and the early postwar period, when an unprecedented number of very young couples were joined together in wedlock. The high number of divorces during and after the World War II may have contributed to the high divorce rate during the 1970s, because the children of divorce face a substantially higher risk than others of having their own marriages fail. Norton and Glick, "Marital Instability in America," 6–19; *NYT,* November 27, 1977, I, 1; *NYT,* April 13, 1982, C1.

9. Veroff, Douan, and Kulka, *The Inner American.,* 191, 192, 194, 196; Yankelovich, *New Rules,* 5.

10. Richard A. Easterlin, "The American Baby Boom in Historical Perspective" Occasional Paper no. 79 (Washington, D.C., National Bureau of Economic Research, 1962); "Relative Economic Status and the American Fertility Swing," in *Social Structure, Family Life Styles, and Economic Behavior,* ed. Eleanor B. Sheldon (Philadelphia, 1972); Easterlin, "The Conflict Between Aspirations and Resources," *Population and Development Review,* 2 (September/December 1972), 417–26; Arthur A. Campbell, "Baby Boom to Birth Dearth and Beyond," *Annals,* 435 (January 1978), 52–53.

11. Russell Jacoby, *Social Amnesia: A Critique of Conformist Psychology from Adler to Laing* (Boston, 1975); Ehrenreich, *Hearts of Men,* 89–98, 122, 147, 164–65; Yankelovich, *New Rules,* 235.

12. Refer to note 11. For an example of the new viewpoint on marriage and divorce, see a popular textbook *Essentials of Life and Health* (New York, 1972): "Far from being a wasting illness, divorce is a healthful adaptation, enabling monogamy to survive in a time when patriarchal powers, privileges and marital systems have become unworkable; far from being a radical change in the institution of marriage, divorce is a relatively minor modification of it. . . ."; quoted in Lynch, *The Broken Heart,* 10.

13. Allen J. Matusow, *The Unraveling of America: A History of Liberalism in the 1960s* (New York, 1984), 277–80, 321–23.

14. Refer to note 13. If a single term gave expression to the growing influence of young people during the 1960s, it was the phrase the "generation gap." It referred to the appearance among the young of a separate culture, a distinct language, and a distinctive outlook, apart from the world of adults. A shift in generational experience may have contributed to the perceived gulf between old and young. Young people of the 1960s, unlike their parents, had escaped the years of hardship, austerity, and sacrifice of the depression and World War II. Also contributing to a generation gap was the rising level of education attained by younger Americans. Many studies conducted during the 1960s concluded that those who had attended college were generally more liberal in their social, religious, and moral attitudes than those who had not.

It would be a mistake, however—a mistake made by many social commentators—to exaggerate the dimensions of the generation gap during the 1960s. Little persuasive evidence was uncovered during the sixties showing extensive alienation between adolescents and their parents. Survey research found a deep cleavage within the younger generation itself, dividing young college students from those who had entered blue collar jobs directly from high school, who were reportedly appalled "by the collapse of patriotism and respect for the law." Altogether, little evidence was found to indicate that younger Americans had abandoned traditional moral frameworks. Even in the most controversial and highly publicized areas of change—sex and drug-taking—truly dramatic shifts would have to wait for the 1970s. Studies of sexual behavior in the late 1960s detected only a modest liberalization in sexual practices compared to findings of twenty years before, while surveys of drug use found that only about 10 percent of young Americans had experimented with marijuana.

A number of influential studies of college students also argued that younger people's rejection of the strict norms that prevailed in the 1950s did not constitute a generation gap. According to these studies, students were simply giving expression to suppressed elements in their parents' lives. See Yankelovich, *New Rules,* 174; Kenneth Keniston, *Young Radicals* (New York, 1968; *NYT,* February 4, 1971, I, 1; *NYT,* January 17, 1972, I, 33; *NYT,* August 18, 1977, C13; *NYT,* December 1, 1968, VI, 129; *NYT,* November 2, 1969, VI, 32ff.; *NYT,* January 18, 1970, VI, 10.

15. Manchester, *Glory and the Dream,* 1221, 1355, 1463–68. The literature on the women's movement is vast. A useful introduction is William H. Chafe, *Women and Equality: Changing Patterns in American Culture* (New York, 1977). On the ideology of feminism, see Barbara Sinclair Deckard, *The Women's Movement: Political, Socioeconomic, and Psychological Issues* (New York, 1975); Sara Evans, *Personal Politics: The Roots of Women's Liberation in the Civil Rights Movement and the New Left* (New York, 1979); Jo Freeman, *The Politics of Women's Liberation: A Case of an Emerging Social Movement and Its Relation to the Public Policy Process* (New York, 1975); Judith Hole and Ellen Levine, *Rebirth of Feminism* (New York, 1971); *Radical Feminism,* eds. Anne Koedt, Ellen Levine, and Anita Rapone (New York, 1973); Gayle Graham Yates, *What Women Want: The Ideas of the Movement* (Cambridge, Mass., 1971).

16. On the impact of feminism, see Judith M. Bardwick, *In Transition: How Feminism, Sexual Liberation, and the Search for Self-Fulfillment Have Altered America* (New York, 1979); Chafe, *Women and Equality,* ch. 5; Cynthia Fuchs Epstein, "Ten Years Later: Perspectives on the Women's Movement," *Dissent,* 22 (Spring 1975); 169–76; Janet Giele, *Women and the Future: Changing Sex Roles in Modern America* (New York, 1978); Elinor Lenz and Barbara Myerhoff, *The Feminization of America: How Women's Values Are Changing Our Public and Private Lives* (Los Angeles, 1985); Jane de Hart Mathews, "The New Feminism and the Dynamics of Social Change," in *Women's America: Refocusing the Past,* eds. Linda Kerber and Jane de Hart Mathews (New York, 1981), 397–421.

17. Manchester, *Glory and the Dream,* 1035–36. On the sexual revolution, see "Sex and the Contemporary American Scene," *Annals of the America Academy of Political and Social Science,* 376 (March 1968).

18. *NYT,* February 10, 1971, I, 48. On the growth of a "single culture," see *NYT,* January 3, 1974, I, 16; *NYT,* April 21, 1977, C1. Homosexual rights ordinances were adopted in Ann Arbor, Michigan; Berkeley, California; Columbus, Ohio; Detroit, Michigan; Minneapolis, Minnesota; San Francisco, California; Seattle, Washington; and Washington, D.C., between 1972 and 1974. In 1973, the American Psychiatric Association removed homosexuality from its list of mental disorders.

19. Manchester, *Glory and the Dream,* 1035–36; "Sex and the Contemporary American Scene," *Annals of the American Academy of Political and Social Science,* 376 (March, 1968); *NYT,* February 10, 1971, I, 48; *NYT,* January 3, 1974, I, 16; *NYT,* April 21, 1977, C1.

20. Yankelovich, *New Rules,* xiv, 88, 97, 99, 100, 103, 104.

ARTICLE 8
American Couples

PHILIP BLUMSTEIN AND PEPPER W. SCHWARTZ

Marriage in the United States has undergone numerous changes in recent decades, fostering diversity in male-female and same-sex relationships. Blumstein and Schwartz describe the variation that exists in heterosexual and homosexual relationships today and discuss the influence of gender on the relationships people form. They point to a number of problems modern couples face and to the barriers that stand in the way of their contentment.

WE DID THIS STUDY because we, like many others in this country, were becoming increasingly aware that relationships in general and marriage in particular were in flux, that they seemed to be getting more fragile, and that we were witnessing social change that needed to be understood. We wanted to know if the institution of our past—marriage—would be the institution of the future. We wanted to know whether any intimate relationship could meet modern challenges, be satisfying, and last for a lifetime.

What do we mean by *institution*? An institution is a way of life that is very resistant to change. People know about it; they can describe it; and they have spent a lifetime learning how to react to it. The *idea* of marriage is larger than any individual marriage. The *role* of husband or wife is greater than any individual who takes on that role.

Institutions set up standards and practices that let people fall neatly into niches, giving them roles and rules of conduct that help interaction proceed smoothly. Each relationship does not have to deal with the same problem as if it has never occurred

"American Couples." Pp. 318–330 from AMERICAN COUPLES by Philip Blumstein and Pepper W. Schwartz. Copyright © 1983 by Philip Blumstein and Pepper W. Schwartz. Reprinted by permission of William Morrow & Co.

before. Trust can be assumed because of the nature of the rules. This is illustrated by one of the major differences between marriage and cohabitation: Marriage has no need for the kind of financial bookkeeping so common among cohabitors because the rules help keep people together and help make for an orderly exit if the relationship ends. Bookkeeping is alienating. It implies the possibility of a breakup or suggests that partners will not do their share unless watched, or that the relationship has to be fifty-fifty and that anything else is a bad bargain.

At the present time, marriage is an institution that seems to be in danger of collapse. We understand it in its pure form. Indeed, every schoolchild understands what marriage is supposed to be like. Ask a young child to explain marriage and he or she can tell its essential parts: that there are a husband and wife, and eventually a mommy and a daddy, that it entails a ceremony, and that the two people live together for the rest of their lives. The child knows just as well as the adult that there are marriages that do not look like this. He may have seen his own parents divorce. But he will not describe real life when he describes marriage—he will describe the "ideal type." The question is, Is that ideal type disappearing because of the exceptions to it? Is marriage becoming less an institution because of the prevalence of divorce, because of new roles for husbands and wives, and because society is debating what relationships are and should be? Are there now different types of marriage, and if so, does that strengthen the institution or weaken it? Moreover, if institutionalization is intrinsically good—if it gives shape to a relationship so that partners know what to expect of one another and can predict what their future together will be like—is this something that our other three kinds of couples should aim for? Indeed, do any of these three already have institutional aspects to their relationships?

TYPES OF RELATIONSHIP

In looking at marriage in the last part of the twentieth century, we see that there are different marital forms. At one end of the continuum there is traditional marriage, with the man working outside the home and having unquestioned authority, the woman a homemaker, and no possibility of divorce. At the other end of the continuum are the most experimental forms of marriage.

It may be that this continuum will start to break off into little clusters, each a different kind of marriage. We may see, for example, that "voluntary marriage' will take on a recognizable profile. These are the marriages that last only while the couple is in love. Based as they are on "happiness" and "compatibility," they may be expected to be less stable than relationships grounded in a presumption of permanence. Such marriages might be seen as requiring special contracts, renewable every year or every five years. Partners would anticipate the fact that their high expectations made permanence improbable. If voluntary marriage became an institution people would say, "I'm entering into a voluntary marriage," to their friends and their friends would immediately know this was different from any other form of marriage. For example, economic arrangements might be quite specific and separate.

The question is, however, Does voluntary marriage simply create a new form of marriage, or does it have deeper implications? Does the mere concept of voluntary marriage undermine the institution so thoroughly that even the most traditional of vows lose their effect, thereby bringing the permanence of the marital institution, its most critical aspect, into question?

Another modern variation may be cohabitation as a "trial marriage." Trial marriages, as we have seen, are quite conservative and it might be said that they are exactly like marriage except that the couple has not yet made the final decision. But trial marriage is really quite different from the *institution* of marriage. It is not the mere anticipation of marriage but the actual experience of it that shapes people's lives. A woman who intends to quit her job will not do so until the marriage has occurred. No children will be born until their future can be assured by the safeguards of marriage. While trial marriage may be the nonmarital form closest to marriage (because it presumes an eventual lifetime commitment), it is still not marriage.

Traditionalists see voluntary marriage and trial marriage as truly threatening alternatives because they *seem* to be supportive of the institution while in fact they are not. Allowing such variation erodes the historic nature of marriage. And society does not sit by complaisantly and allow its institutions to change radically. Those who champion voluntary marriage and argue that what modern society needs is many different forms of intimate life-style are ignoring the fact that such a development would be a revolutionary one.

There have already been revisions in the concept of marriage that may prove shattering. Society now questions whether husbands should have absolute authority. Soon it may be taken for granted that the working wife will be a financial partner, sharing even the man's provider role. This gives a woman more power because many of the justifications for the couple's division of labor were predicated on one person, the male, directing the relationship because his work made survival possible. If he is no longer the provider, he may lose his legitimacy as ultimate decision-maker. Other decisions, such as who chooses where they will live become problematic. (We are already, for example, seeing one outcome of such a situation, wherein couples commute rather than live together because each partner values his or her job and neither will compromise success by moving to the other person's location.) Changes such as these do not simply modify the institution; they alter the very meaning of marriage so drastically that it may cease to be an institution in the way we have always known it. We are not arguing that these changes should not occur. We are merely saying that if and when they do, the institution may fail and need to be reconstructed according to a different model.

What about other kinds of couples? It could be argued that cohabitators who plan never to marry are attempting to create a new institution. The whole idea behind lifetime cohabitation is that people who love each other can create a bond that does not need the state's participation and can be durable and satisfying. But relationships are both public and private. It is difficult to create an institution without support from society and this society still recognizes only marriage as an institution.

Furthermore, to be an institution, cohabitation would have to have a predictable shape, and at present cohabitation takes too many forms. The fact that two partners often have very different concepts of what cohabitation means is evidence that it is not yet institutionalized. It is not recognized as a stable *form* by law or society; it is seen as a *situation* which may change at any moment. Its lack of predictability and the absence of clear understandings about what the relationship means to the participants themselves make establishing the institution of cohabitation very difficult.

Before cohabitation can become an institution, its properties must be clear to any schoolchild. It must be seen as legitimate. Both partners must have the same level of commitment (or lack thereof) to the future. At the present time, we think that because there are so many possible permutations of cohabitation, partners may have trouble being sure they both want the same things out of the relationship. There is often no basis for trust, no mutual cooperation, and no ability to plan.

Currently, cohabitation as a way of life is unstable. Cohabitors may be dismayed by this because they feel their love is enough and that all it takes to create a way of life is two people who see eye to eye. But they do not take into account the importance of society's reactions and how poorly society is equipped to accommodate them. For example, parents may not want to acknowledge a cohabitor's partner as a family member. Even if they want to be welcoming, they may be unsure of what to expect of such a person; they may not know how to act toward him or her. One symptom of this confused state of affairs is that cohabitation has been widely discussed and openly practiced for the past fifteen years, and yet we still do not have a term the two people can use for one another. Couples who want to create an institution should be aware of what an awesome task they have taken on. It is very hard to anticipate the results when one tries to create a new tradition and it is very hard to maintain one's resolve in the face of an unsupportive society. After all, it has taken a long time for Western marriage to evolve the features that it has. Institutions are not made or redesigned overnight.

Moreover, we think it will be hard for cohabitation to become an institution while the traditional model of marriage still exists. As long as marriage retains its image as the highest form of commitment, it acts as a lure to cohabiting couples who want to prove their love for each other. So they are likely either to get married or to break up once their commitment falters. If cohabitation is to be a unique institution, it must be perceived as different from marriage, and marriage cannot be allowed to be seen as a better or next step in the relationship. But, the establishment of cohabitation as a lifetime alternative to marriage is an implied criticism of the latter, and hence is likely to be resisted by government and society in an attempt to defend the concept of matrimony. Society accepts cohabitation now only because it is thought of as a phase in a person's life. It is not understood as challenging the legitimacy of marriage.

Do same-sex couples exist as an institution? Certainly not in the general community. Neither schoolchildren nor heterosexual adults can explain accurately how such couples function. Furthermore, because of the general antipathy toward homosexuality in American society, gay men and lesbians are not encouraged to be open about their sexual preference or about their relationships. Hence they are seldom extended such commonplace courtesies as having a partner invited to an office party or to a retirement banquet. Even heterosexuals who might like to welcome a gay friend's partner may not know how to go about doing so.

Are same-sex couples an institution with the gay and lesbian community? At present, we think not. There is a general fear in both gay and lesbian circles that relationships are unlikely to last. Long-lasting relationships are seen as quite special. They are unexpected, and therefore newly formed couples are not treated as though they will remain together for fifty years. People are less likely to ask, "How's Jerry?" and more likely to say, "Are you still with your lover?" This is particularly true for gay men. But it happens with both men and women, and when a couple is not treated as inviolate, the less likely it is that the partners will see themselves that way.

We might expect that the existence of a gay culture would help the development of "couple" status. A community could offer the support of public opinion, the reinforcement of a relationship by friends, and censure of a person who treats his or her partner badly or dissolves a well-thought-of partnership. Conventions could be established and a couple who violated them would have an awareness that they might be headed for trouble. Role models would be present to show that relationships can last, and more important, to show how.

The problem with gay male culture is that much of it is organized around singlehood or maintaining one's sexual marketability. Meeting places like bars and baths promote casual sex rather than couple activities. The problem with the lesbian world is quite different. Women are often in tight-knit friendship groups where friends and acquaintances spend so much intimate time together that, it seems to us, opportunities arise for respect and companionship to turn into love and a meaningful affair. Thus, gay men imperil their relationships because of the availability of a singles market that draws men out of their relationships; lesbians are in jeopardy because of opportunities to fall in love. We have found that when gay women are involved in the gay world, they break up more, not less. If couplehood were an institution, participation in the gay world would not be detrimental; it would be supportive.

What would give institutional status to gay relationships? They would not need to look like marriage or to have the same rules as marriage. But they would have to have some predictable elements so that couples could agree on their obligations. Ideally there might be a public witness to the couple's vows to one another, perhaps even a ceremony. The couple might want to be legally joined by the state and have reciprocal legal responsibilities that would make it emotionally and financially harder to break up. Sometimes gay men and lesbians have put each other in their wills; sometimes one has adopted the other. These are attempts to give the relationship stronger ties than the couple's private promises to one another.

The chance to marry legally, however, is denied to gay people. We think the courts, as agents of the broader society, have resisted same-sex petitions to wed, partly because of anti-homosexual precedents and prejudices and partly because it would be the most fundamental change ever made to the institution of marriage. The judiciary understands that if gay people were allowed to marry, it would help institutionalize their relationships; the courts do not want to do this. Nor do they want to create parallel institutions to marriage. Just as the courts once enforced laws that forbade blacks and whites to marry because white America feared an interracial society, so they also prohibit gay marriage, fearing that it would in some way encourage homosexuality. Courts are by nature conservative; they enforce the status quo and resist change. They do not want to redefine marriage.

This is very upsetting to many gay people, but they should also remember that there are some minuses to balance the pluses institutions provide. For one thing, when relationships become institutions, this reduces pluralism. There becomes only one model of how to live as a couple. In addition, the more the couple is extolled, the more the single person is excluded. At present, the fluidity of couple status in the gay community makes it easier to be a single gay man or lesbian than it is to be a single heterosexual person. Institutional standing for same-sex couples may reduce some of the freedom the gay community offers.

A more important drawback is that the institution of marriage, at least until now, has been organized around inequality, and attempts to change this framework have not yet been very successful. The traditional married couples in our study often laid their solid foundation on roles that stabilized the relationship but gave the woman some of the less pleasant responsibilities, such as housework, and assigned her duties, such as the buyer role. If tasks were allotted on the basis of efficiency or affinity, we would expect that married couples could reassign household chores and have the institution remain as durable as ever. We have found, however, that when roles are reversed, with men doing housework and women taking over as provider, couples become dreadfully unhappy. Even couples who willingly try to change traditional male and female behavior have difficulty doing so. They must not only go against everything they have learned and develop new skills, but they have to resist the negative reaction of society. Thus we have learned that while the institution is bigger than the individuals within it, it may not be bigger than the assignment of roles by gender.

GENDER

Gender has been a second theme running through this study. We have described many differences among the four types of couples, but we have also observed that heterosexual men have traits in common with homosexual men, and this is also true of heterosexual and homosexual women. It has been clear that a person's gender affects what he or she desires in a relationship and how he or she behaves in one. It is equally clear that the way people expect their partners to behave depends on whether the partner is male or female; thus gender requirements set the stage for how individuals will interact as a couple.

An extremely important effect of having one male and one female in heterosexual couples is that each gender is automatically assigned certain duties and privileges. A couple does not have to think about how the house is going to be cleaned or money is going to be earned, if they depend on tradition to guide the male's efforts in one direction and the female's in another. All this is taken for granted except when people are trying to reject tradition or when they have no gender differences to guide them. Then the true complexity of running a household and running a relationship become evident. Each element of the couple's life—from cooking a meal to initiating sex to writing Christmas cards—becomes a potential point of debate. Both may want to take on a responsibility or neither may be so inclined. Both may have been trained to do certain things, or neither may know anything about them. For heterosexual couples, gender provides a shortcut and avoids the decision-making process.

With this enormous advantage comes two enormous disadvantages. First, while the heterosexual model offers more stability and certainty, it inhibits change, innovation, and *choice* regarding roles and tasks. Second, the heterosexual model, which provides so much efficiency, is predicated on the man's being the dominant partner. Giving one person the final say guarantees less argument about the organization of the relationship—as long as neither partner sees this as unfair. Historically the man's authority was questioned by neither the man nor the woman. But today, the right of men to have authority over women is widely debated and it is not as clear what the internal organization of the relationship will be. Same-sex couples cannot, obviously, rely on gender to guide their decisions about who will do what in the relationship. But they do not have the inequality that gender builds into heterosexual relationships. Some individual gay male or lesbian couples may not have equality, but that is either the happenstance of that individual relationship or perhaps the result of modeling their relationship on marriage. It is not thrust upon them as part of the nature of their relationship. Same-sex couples who wish to build a relationship based on equality are a step ahead of heterosexual couples, but the price they pay is the lack of traditions or guidelines.

When asked how they came to organize their relationship the way they do, same-sex couples usually refer to trial and error, both partners minimizing the number of tasks they hate doing, or say they had to discover which partner was more talented in one area or another. If heterosexual couples today wish to avoid the hierarchy that gender places on them and to escape from adherence to notions of "men's work" and "women's work," they often arrange their lives so that each performs the jobs he or she prefers or to which he or she is better suited. They do not fully realize, however, that growing up male or female shapes one's preferences and one's skills, so choosing tasks on the basis of personal preference still brings them within the traditional framework.

What is there about men's and women's roles that enhances relationships, and what is there that undermines them? What are the properties of gender that men and women prize in their relationships, and which do they wish to discard? Among the heterosexuals we find that men are still invested in their work and treat it as a major focus of their lives. The provider role, however, is in jeopardy. Husbands are still in the work force supporting their families, but many are now joined by their wives who help carry financial responsibility. Many husbands told us in the interviews that they no longer wish to be totally responsible for a partner's economic well-being.

Looking at the cohabitors, we can see that when relationships between men and women are less scripted, men can, and indeed do, cast off that responsibility. Their ambition to achieve, however, is not diminished even though they are no longer the sole support of their partners. The world of work has not lost its allure for men, even though a major reason for conquering it is disappearing. It is too important a source of respect for them. What may be lessening, however, is their ability to use their responsibilities to family or relationship as a rationale for devoting themselves to work. In the future a man's excessive attachment to his work may be viewed as selfish rather than selfless.

There is another reason why work is an important part of a man's self-image. For most married couples, it is still the man's work that remains sacrosanct. His superior earning power means it is in the couple's best interest to make choices that will support his presence in the work world. It is interesting that even when the couple shares the provider responsibility, the husband's career will probably continue to be put first. This is extremely important for gender hierarchy. This assures that he will remain a dominant force in the relationship.

His work gives him a great deal of influence. Historically, a husband's influence came from the fact of his being male and therefore the head of the household. While there is a residue of this kind of authority left, it seems to us that it is fast disappearing and that it is being shored up by a man's achievements. Thus men may be even more attached to their work because they now derive their influence from how well they do as well as from who they are.

When the husband was making the only money the couple had, it was traditional for the wife to make his life at home as comfortable as possible. Since his labor was synonymous with the couple's welfare, doing things for him was doing something for the whole family. Men learned to be indulged without feeling particularly selfish. They learned to make decisions without consulting the rest of the family because of their authority and the importance of their comforts. They felt it was their due to be taken care of in return for the burdens they carried. They became accustomed to doing no housework unless they wished to be magnanimous, and it was unquestionably their right to have their sexual needs and desires shape the couple's sex life. Although times are changing, it is still difficult for men to give up these privileges. The assumption that they should be indulged shapes the lives of heterosexual men, both married and cohabitors. Men are starting to give up the costs of being male, but they are moving much more slowly in giving up benefits that were their due in an earlier age.

Women in relationships with men increasingly see employment as part of their self-image, although this does not yet include taking on the provider role. We believe that this role is still foreign to most of them. They wish to work, but not as the primary support of the family. Further, while some women in our study are "work-centered," it remains a minority. We think that most employed women continue to value their role as companion and caretaker. Women in the study seem to want respect for both roles and are seeking a way to perform them both successfully. They also want to preserve part of men's traditional commitment to the world of work: They still want their partners to achieve. When they enter the world of work, they do not want him to leave. Women want to look up to, or at least directly across at, their male partner if they are to respect him.

Women, like men, want to be admired for their success at their jobs. Men, however, are more likely to see their own work as more important and the woman's work as auxiliary. This is partly because she generally earns less money, but it may also reflect the belief that her work is more voluntary or done more for her self-fulfillment than for the couple's welfare. In established married couples, if the woman wanted to quit working, if it were financially feasible, her husband would probably acquiesce. If the man wanted to quit working, it would be considered a central change in the relationship. There is still some residue of the provider role, and in a man any reluctance to work would be seen as abandoning his responsibilities.

Cohabiting men and women feel that neither should be responsible for the other's economic welfare and so they are more likely to see the woman's work as a duty rather than as a choice. Cohabiting men and women do not give the woman or the man a provider role. They are likely to invoke the rule of doing one's fair share. Cohabiting women seem pleased to be as self-sufficient as possible and to contribute to the financial needs of the relationship, but their desire for equality is often stymied by the fact that women still do not earn as much as men. The woman with a high income may easily do her fair share and more, but in general, cohabiting women are struggling to keep up with their partners. Until women earn as much as men, even cohabiting women would like to base their financial participation on what they can afford. These women have rejected most aspects of traditional female subordination and they do not like to be in a less than equal position in the relationship. But while some cohabiting men subscribe to an equitable arrangement of splitting expenses, many prefer absolutely equal contribution. This is frustrating to a woman because it puts her at a disadvantage and gives her less influence. The fact that the woman brings in less income keeps the couple from operating along egalitarian lines, and it is a reminder to her that she is in a second-class position. There are of course more traditional cohabitors, those intending to marry, who are not as taken up with the idea of equality, but most cohabiting women want respect for their ability to pay their own way. It seems to us that this may be evidence that dependency, financial or otherwise, will eventually cease to be such a large part of the female role.

Furthermore, it seems likely that women will press for some changes in men's roles. Women, in exchange for sharing financial responsibilities, want more help with burdensome chores, and in most of the areas we have studied, would like to move closer to equality. They do not want to dominate their men any more than men want to be dominated. But they want enough power so that they can have their desires considered and so the relationship does not always operate on their partner's terms. This may be accomplished as work plays a more important role in their lives and, by making them less dependent, moves the relationship more toward equal decision-making.

The gay men, like the heterosexual men, derive much of their self-esteem from the world of work and the ability to make a good income. As men, they expect to work. Because they have a male partner, they expect him to work as well. The provider role lapses because it is really suitable only in a heterosexual context. Men do not expect to provide for other men. They ask of their partners the same things they ask of themselves: ambition, earning power, and initiative. This can create a problem for the internal dynamics of couples where one man clearly does better in the world of work than the other or where one man is clearly more powerful than the other. Men do not do well in such relationships. The more dominant man finds it difficult to respect his partner and not punish him for being less successful or for not being forceful and aggressive. The man who is less powerful may have trouble staying in a relationship where he is unable to see himself as an equal. A man might like to cook or keep house, or be less invested in his work, but if these things bring him less respect or power from his partner—as they may well do—this is likely to be disturbing to all but a small proportion of gay men. Relaxing some of the demands of the male role seems to be less of a problem than assuming roles that have traditionally been held by women.

It seemed to us that, at least in some ways, lesbians also find the female role demeaning and wish to change it. Like the other women, they still value being companions and they still want their relationships to be at the center of their lives. These are parts of the traditional female role that they continue to prize. But while we spoke to lesbians who had relationships where one woman supported the other or where one was content to be clearly subordinate, our overwhelming impression is that most lesbians, young or old, affluent or poor, wish to avoid being dependent or having a dependent partner. There is a strong emphasis on being able to take care of oneself. If, for example, one woman seemed to need a lot of help making decisions or was clearly glad to be supported, the more dominant partner was usually unhappy about it. Lesbians are vigilant for signs of weakness or lack of initiative in themselves or in their partners. They want their partners to be ambitious and to enter the world of work, and they are careful to divide evenly the tasks like housework that remind them of women's subordinate status in heterosexual relationships. They do not want a partner to dominate them, and just like heterosexual women, they have no desire to dominate. As we saw when we looked at the data on who broke up, the woman who was in a more dominant role was the woman more likely to leave the relationship. Lesbians are in a double bind: On the one hand, they want a great deal of attention and communication from a partner. On the other hand, they do not want a partner who is so relationship-centered that she has no ambition or attachment to work. Lesbians want an intense home life, but they also want a strong, ambitious, and independent partner. They want to give a great deal, but only if their partner gives as much. They demand a lot, but not more than they can return in kind. They do not want to be provider, but neither do they wish to be provided for.

This gives us a clue to why lesbians have such a high breakup rate. They are the vanguard in changing women's roles in the 1980's. They have many conflicting desires in their relationships, none of which can be solved by reverting to the traditional female role. Both partners are rejecting the comfortable supported position that women have been trained for in favor of being a full and equal partner in a relationship. This endangers their desire to place their relationship at the center of their lives and their need for emotional intensity because it means that both women need to be equally ambitious outside the relationship. Moreover, they are at the same time moving away from male traits that they feel provide inequality. They do not wish to dominate in their relationship or take too much initiative. They know that if they do, their partner may actually relax into what they see as a traditional female dependency, and this they refuse to allow. Thus lesbians are rejecting almost all available gender directives at once.

The lesbians are trying to carve out a new female role. This is an exceptionally difficult challenge and it is a testimony to their persistence that so many of their relationships do thrive. We think that one reason some are successful is because lesbians still retain women's desire for closeness and nurturance. Most are still relationship-centered and are willing to put time and effort into working out their problems and being attentive to their partner's emotional needs.

We have tried to describe some of the major issues that will be confronting couples in this decade and perhaps for far longer. Institutions evolve slowly and change slowly. Gender roles are entrenched, and they are difficult to change even when they are no longer satisfying. We hope that after seeing where the conflicts and successes lie, couples will be more aware of where the directives imposed by gender serve them well and where they serve them badly.

We have focused a great deal of attention on the problems couples face, their sources of conflict, and the factors that stand in the way of their contentment. These are the issues that challenged us as sociologists and these are the issues we felt that couples would most want to understand. What we have not shown is why so many couples can face up to extremely difficult problems and yet endure and be happy. We have been impressed with the energy that human beings are willing to put out to conquer problems against great odds, to make compromises, and to achieve enough satisfaction to stay and work things out. We have tried to stress the reasons why some kinds of couples face greater hurdles than others. We hope that while drawing attention to the conflicts that can erode a couple's relationship, we have also offered insights into what can make them stronger. Many of the problems we have discussed have no easy solution, and this is particularly true because a couple does not live in a vacuum. The modern world in which they are trying to create a life together is full of complexities. There are demands made of men and women by virtue of their gender that they may resist because they see them as an affront to their individual values—only to find it difficult to invoke new, better and fairer guidelines. People may avoid marriage because of the inequalities built into its traditional design only to find that there are pitfalls in not having rules and regulations and social recognition.

Looking at marriage and its alternatives, we see advantages both in the institution and in nonmarital forms. As we look at the impact of being male or female, we see no evidence that historic gender-role traditions and restrictions help solve *all* issues for couples. We believe that the time for orthodoxy is past. Neither, however, do we reject the idea that gender differences may be valuable for a couple in certain areas of their life together. Gay couples face problems that arise from "sameness" of gender; these give us an indication of where it might be wise for partners to be different. Heterosexuals face problems that arise from their "differentness"; these give us guidance about where it might be better for two partners to be more alike.

There is, of course, no perfect composite picture that will fit every couple's needs. But we hope that the findings of this study will help a couple identify roles and develop understandings that will help make their relationship satisfactory and long-lasting. As the institution of marriage loses its predictability for heterosexuals, and while homosexual couples have no institution to enter, each couple will have to establish guidelines for making gender work for, not against, the possibility of a lifetime relationship.

ARTICLE 9
The Division of Labor in Contemporary Marriage: Expectations, Perceptions, and Performance

DANA V. HILLER AND WILLIAM W. PHILLIBER

With a majority of wives employed today, an important issue for couples is the fairness or equity in the way their labor is divided. What do husbands and wives expect of each other? This study finds that while there is widespread agreement that responsibilities should be shared, many spouses maintain a traditional division of labor, and husbands continue to play the dominant role. The authors contend that until women's earnings are more comparable to men's, equity in the division of labor is unlikely.

MARRIED WOMEN HAVE MOVED into the labor market at a dramatic pace during the second half of the twentieth century. In 1950, 12 percent of wives with pre-schoolers were employed while in 1980, 50 percent of this group were employed (Biachi and Spain, 1983). However, the institutions of North American society are still geared to meet the needs of two-parent families with only one employed partner.

Partners in a two-job marriage may be overloaded with demands on their time

Dana V. Hiller and William W. Philliber, "The Division of Labor in Contemporary Marriage: Expectations, Perceptions, and Performance." Copyright © 1986 by the Society for the Study of Social Problems. Reprinted from *Social Problems*, Vol. 33, No. 3, Feb. 1986, pp. 191–201, by permission.

and energy, and that pressure in turn may generate rigid role performances as well as emotional exhaustion. Such conditions create an environment ripe for marital dissent. Two outside jobs demand that couples take time to negotiate a household division of labor that once was a given, while at the same time employment absorbs more time and requires greater efficiency in the performance of household tasks.

The underlying issue for individual spouses is equity and fairness in the distribution of costs and rewards within the relationship. With a majority of wives employed in the United States, a new definition of an equitable marital role bargain is emerging which suggests men should take a more active role in housekeeping and childcare. Yet, sharing the responsibilities for housework, parenting, and nurturing others is difficult when tradition has delegated those tasks solely to women. Not surprisingly, Huber and Spitze (1983) have found that "thought of divorce" is strongly related to division of labor in the family. We believe that the extent to which the role expectations of a husband and wife differ will be critical to their ability to negotiate a mutually acceptable role bargain and, ultimately, to their marital stability.

We interviewed 489 midwestern married couples (two-thirds of them were dual-earner couples) to discern what each partner's expectations were and how they actually behaved, and to determine what factors were likely to influence those expectations and behaviors. Assuming that a couple's situational definitions are also important, we studied the perceptions spouses have of their partners' expectations. The specific purpose of this study was to answer the following questions: (1) Do husbands and wives hold different role expectations?; (2) How accurately does each partner perceive the other's expectations?; (3) How do expectations and behavior differ?; and (4) How is the division of labor between a couple affected by the expectations of husbands or wives? In general, we find that tradition endures even in modern, dual-earner families, and that the husband's view of marital roles strongly influences actual behavior.

PREVIOUS RESEARCH

The literature on gender role attitudes and marital role expectations suggests more attention should be paid to the perceptions partners have of their spouses' attitudes. Research indicates that men and women hold differing marital role expectations, with men tending to have somewhat more traditional expectations (Komarovsky, 1973; Mason and Bumpass, 1975; Osmond and Martin, 1975). Both men and women—but especially women—have come to prefer less rigid gender roles in the labor market and in family relationships (Mason et al., 1976; Parelius, 1975a).

It is unclear whether men really lag behind women in their preference for more egalitarian roles or whether women simply perceive that they do. Very early, McKee and Sheriffs (1959) found that women perceive men as wanting them to show more feminine qualities than men actually do. Parelius (1975b) concluded that women's expectations for themselves have changed, but that women perceive the expectations of men to have changed little. Osmond and Martin (1975) found more men saying their own self-esteem would not be hurt if their wives earned more money, while most women thought that their husband's self-esteem would be hurt.

Others have found that expectations and perceptions of expectations influence married women's decisions to work. Scanzoni (1979) found that a wife's attitude toward her gender role affects the probability that she will participate in the labor force. Spitze and Waite (1981) demonstrated that whether the wife perceived her husband's attitude to be positive or negative was important for her employment.

Husbands and wives also have different perceptions about behavior. Condran and Bode (1982) point out what they call the Rashomon effect—a significant disjuncture between wives' and husbands' perceptions about how much the husbands participate in household duties. Husbands see themselves as participating more than wives believe they do. Regardless of the perceptions, actual behavior with respect to housework and childcare has been slow to change (Meissner et al., 1975; Vanek, 1974). Typically only one partner is interviewed in these studies. Thus, there has been no way to determine whether partners actually differ in their expectations, or whether they just believe that they have different expectations than their partners. By using couples in our sample, we hope to clarify this issue.

SAMPLE

In 1983, personal interviews were conducted with a stratified sample of 489 married couples in Hamilton County (Cincinnati), Ohio. Participants were selected by randomly dialing households in the target area and securing appointments for interviews to be conducted separately but simultaneously with husbands and wives in their home. Men interviewed husbands, and women interviewed wives. The overall acceptance rate was 47 percent.[1] Because we were particularly interested in professional and managerial women, the sample was stratified to over-sample dual-earner couples, and especially dual-earner couples in which wives held professional and managerial positions. This stratified sample was drawn as callers dialed random numbers and screened subjects. In the final sample, husbands only were employed in 153 couples, wives only were employed in 39 couples, both spouses were employed with the wife in a non-professional or non-managerial occupation in 240 couples, and both spouses were employed and the wife held a professional or managerial position in 57 couples.

Comparing this sample with the 1980 census and with a sample of the non-respondents suggests that the socio-economic status of these subjects is somewhat higher than in the general population and among those who refused to participate. The average family income for the comparable population in Hamilton County is $28,711; in the sample it is $38,260. The census indicates this population to be 12.5 percent black; the sample is 7 percent black. Equal percentages in the census data and the sample were in their first marriages. Demographic variables appear sensitive to response rates, but we believe marital variables to be less so (see Hiller and Philliber, 1985). In all analyses the sample has been weighted to match the actual proportions of Hamilton County households which are dual earner households, husband-only-earner households, and wife-only-earner households.

MEASURES

Role Expectations

The four family roles for which expectations were analyzed were childcare, housework, money management, and income earning. The first two are traditionally considered to be in the wife's domain, and the second two in the husband's. Participants were asked to indicate on a five-point scale whether they thought each of these four family roles should be carried out entirely or mostly by themselves, by both partners equally, or mostly or entirely by their spouses.

Perceptions of Spouse's Role Expectations

Using the same five-point scale, we asked participants who they thought their spouses thought should take responsibility for these family roles. In addition, husbands were asked how they felt about their wives being employed, and wives were asked how they thought their husbands felt about their being employed.

Accuracy of Perception

We computed a three-fold difference score for the relationship between an individual's expectation and his or her spouse's perception of that expectation. Individuals were classified either as having a *more traditional* expectation than perceived by their partners, having an expectation *congruent* with their partner's perception, or having a *less traditional* expectation than perceived by their partners.

Attachment to Roles

Marriage partners were asked how important it was to them to be better than their spouses at each of the four family roles: raising children; keeping house; managing finances; and earning income. Responses were scored on a four-point scale from very important to not important at all.

Perception of Division of Household Labor

Both husbands and wives were presented with a list of 20 household and childcare tasks, and were asked whether these tasks were done mostly by themselves, mostly by their spouses, equally by both, mostly by children, or mostly by someone hired. In these analyses, the children and hired help responses are eliminated.

FINDINGS

Differences in Expectations

Within each couple, we compared the spouses' views of who should do what.[2] Table 1 indicates that, irrespective of the family role in question, over two-thirds of the couples had similar expectations. However, for roles traditionally thought to be the wife's, 84 percent agree that childcare should be shared, but only 38 percent agree housework should be. Almost as many couples, 30 percent, agree that housework should be the wife's responsibility. For the roles traditionally assigned to husbands, 69 percent agree that the management of money should be shared, but only 24 percent agree that earning it should be. Almost twice as many—43 percent—agree that earning money is the husband's responsibility.

When couples disagree, the spouses who traditionally perform a given role believe they should continue to do so, while their partners believe those tasks should

TABLE 1 Comparison of Spouses' Expectations About Who Should Perform Marital Roles

Expectations for Wife's Traditional Roles:	Childcare	Housework
Agree job should be shared	84%	38%
Agree it is wife's job	2	30
Husband: wife's job/Wife: should share	7	13
Husband: should share/Wife: wife's job	8	20
Total	101%	101%
(N)	(483)	(488)
Expectations for Husband's Traditional Roles:	Money Management	Income Earning
Agree job should be shared	69%	24%
Agree it is husband's job	9	43
Wife: husband's job/Husband: should share	5	9
Wife: should share/Husband: husband's job	17	25
Total	100%	101%
(N)	(487)	(484)

be shared. A greater number of husbands wish to maintain traditional roles in money matters, and more women than men thought they, the women, should be responsible for domestic matters. This suggests that few husbands or wives want to give up the prerogatives belonging to their traditional marital roles, yet some are interested in expanding their activities into non-traditional roles.

Differences Between Expectations and Partner's Perceptions

Table 2 compares one partner's expectations about the division of family roles with his or her spouse's perceptions of those expectations. First, spouses misperceive their partners' expectations fairly often. In five of the nine comparisons, over 40 percent inaccurately perceive their partner's expectations. In two of those comparisons—wife's perceptions of husband's attitude about her working and about who should manage money—the majority were incorrect. Second, husbands perceive their spouses' expectations more accurately than their wives perceive theirs. On each of the four items which were available for both husbands and wives, husbands were accurate more often than wives.

Third, inaccurate perceptions about housekeeping and childcare roles occur most often because husbands are less traditional and wives more traditional than their partners expect. On the one hand, sizable percentages of wives believe their husbands expect them to do housework and childcare when, in fact, their husbands believe these should be shared roles. On the other hand, husbands are especially likely to believe their wives expect them to share housework when, in fact, wives do not expect this.

Finally, inaccuracies in perceptions of expectations for roles traditionally assigned to men occur most often because husbands are more traditional and wives less traditional than their partners expect. Wives tend to perceive husband's expecta-

TABLE 2 Accuracy of Spouse's Perception of Partner's Expectations for Marital Roles

	Accuracy of Wife's Perception				Accuracy of Husband's Perception			
	Husband More Traditional	Perception Accurate	Husband Less Traditional	Total (N)	Wife More Traditional	Perception Accurate	Wife Less Traditional	Total (N)
Having a working wife	26%	38	36	100% (482)	a	a	a	a
Doing childcare	6%	73	21	100% (483)	11%	82	7	100% (485)
Doing housework	9%	55	36	100% (487)	27%	65	8	100% (487)
Managing money	37%	44	19	100% (488)	18%	51	31	100% (485)
Earning income	22%	55	23	100% (484)	13%	61	26	100% (484)

Note: a. Variable not measured.

tions about managing money to be less traditional than they actually are. Husbands more often perceive wive's expectations about both managing and earning money to be more traditional than they actually are.

Differences Between Expectations and Behavior

How do the expectations spouses have of themselves and each other match the actual behavior in their marriages? The discrepancies between expectations and actual behavior become apparent when Table 1 is compared to data on task performance in Table 3. Fifty-eight percent of husbands say housework should be shared; yet, except for two tasks listed in Table 3, not more than a third of the husbands either share or do regular household tasks, even by their own estimate. Thirty-three percent

TABLE 3 Husband's and Wife's Perceptions of Division of Labor

	Wife's Perception				Husband's Perception				Percent Agreement Between Spouses
	Wife Does %	Both Do %	Husband Does %	(N)	Wife Does %	Both Do %	Husband Does %	(N)	
Regular Household Tasks									
Food shopping	70	20	10	(489)	67	23	10	(489)	86
Meal preparation	85	10	5	(481)	82	13	5	(487)	81
House cleaning	80	17	3	(453)	73	23	4	(456)	78
Washing dishes	66	29	5	(451)	57	36	7	(453)	87
Washing clothes	84	10	6	(475)	81	14	5	(473)	76
Ironing	90	7	3	(489)	90	7	3	(450)	90
Managing money	42	31	27	(489)	30	38	32	(488)	65
Less Regular Household Tasks									
Household repairs	7	13	80	(440)	2	7	91	(458)	82
Yard work	11	29	60	(382)	6	24	70	(405)	71
Supervision of help	72	24	4	(174)	51	34	15	(226)	56
Entertaining preparation	52	48	2	(487)	44	53	3	(489)	61
Major purchases	14	82	4	(489)	9	85	6	(488)	79
Planning recreation	16	80	4	(476)	11	83	7	(476)	72
Planning vacations	8	85	7	(472)	8	82	10	(482)	79
Childcare Tasks									
Arranging activities	61	36	3	(280)	58	40	2	(325)	63
Take kids to doctor	74	23	3	(309)	62	34	4	(333)	73
Stays home when kids are sick	62	36	2	(332)	48	48	4	(340)	52
Get kids ready for bed	60	34	6	(253)	48	47	5	(300)	71
Get kids ready for school	82	11	7	(218)	80	16	4	(267)	81
Help kids with homework	45	41	14	(235)	35	54	11	(266)	65

of the husbands report they shop for food, and 43 percent wash dishes. Note that the percentages of wives who see their husbands doing or sharing these tasks is lower than the percentages of husbands who see themselves doing them (although the percentages tend to vary in the same direction across all tasks). Both husbands and wives report that money management is the only regular household task either done or shared by a majority of husbands.

Although wives perform the more regular household tasks, a number of husbands do household tasks which are less regular or are needed on an occasional basis. Almost all husbands take primary responsibility for household repairs and yard work, and most share in making major purchases, planning recreation, and planning vacations. Many also share in the supervision of help and in preparations for entertainment.

Analyses of perceptions of childcare task performance were limited to those couples who still have children at home (which accounts for the reduced sample size for these items in Table 3). While 84 percent of all these couples agree that childcare should be shared, a majority of fathers say they participate equally or more in only three of the six childcare tasks—staying with ill children, getting children ready for bed, and helping kids with homework. Moreover, according to wives' reports, only about a third of their husbands participate equally or more in any childcare tasks, except for helping with homework.

As shown in the far right-hand column of Table 3, couples generally agree about who does what around the house. With the exception of money management, at least three-quarters agree about whether regular household tasks are done primarily by the wife, the husband, or are shared. There is somewhat lower agreement about who does non-regular household tasks and even less about who does childcare; but for every task the majority of couples agree. Across the board, both husbands and wives see themselves participating more than their spouses see them participating. Husbands are especially more likely to see tasks as shared, while wives see themselves with major responsibility.

Personal Attachment to Roles

Table 4 shows that 58 percent of husbands consider it important to be better than their wives at earning income—suggesting that the men are still very attached to their traditional breadwinning role. Neither husbands nor wives are overwhelmingly attached to the role of managing finances. However, 43 percent of wives still consider it important to be better than their husbands at childcare, and 38 percent feel that way about housekeeping. The majority of wives do not consider it important to exceed their husbands in performance of the traditional female roles.

Table 5 indicates husbands' feelings about their wives' employment. While the majority of men in this sample consider it important to earn more income than their wives, three-fourths of those with employed wives like the fact that their spouses are working, and over a third with unemployed wives would like their wives

TABLE 4 Importance of Superior Role Performance for Husband and Wife

Importance of Role	Childcare		Housework		Money Management		Income Earning	
	Husband	Wife	Husband	Wife	Husband	Wife	Husband	Wife
Very Important	4%	15%	2%	14%	9%	7%	26%	2%
Somewhat Important	22	28	7	26	30	25	32	10
Not Very Important	43	30	43	33	36	41	24	44
Not At All Important	31	27	48	27	25	27	18	44
Total	100%	100%	100%	100%	100%	100%	100%	100%
(N)	(481)	(481)	(488)	(486)	(487)	(486)	(488)	(485)

to be working. Less than a fourth of the total sample of husbands prefer that their wife be unemployed.

Effects of Expectations and Perceptions on Performance

To discern how expectations and perceptions of expectations affect performance, measures of the division of labor in four major areas were subjected to multiple regression analysis. We constructed a summary measure of who does childcare by adding responses to the six childcare items. Similarly, we obtained a measure of who does housework by adding the six regular household tasks, excluding money management. Money management was kept as a separate item. We calculated income earning as the percent of family income earned by the wife. On all four measures, a high score indicates the wife takes greater responsibility for the role.[3]

The four regression equations included as predictors each spouse's expectations for the specific marital role, perceptions of partner's expectations, and husband's and wife's attachments to the role.[4] In addition, we included family income, wife's employment, presence of children in the home, and length of marriage to examine and control their possible effects on performance of each role.

Table 6 indicates that the only variable with a significant effect on childcare

TABLE 5 Husband's Attitude Toward Wife's Employment

	Husbands with Employed Wife	Husbands with Non-Employed Wife	All Husbands
Likes Wife Working	74%	37%	63%
Does Not Care	11	26	15
Dislikes Wife Working	15	37	22
Total	100%	100%	100%
(N)	(341)	(141)	(482)

TABLE 6 Standardized Effects of Independent Variables on Household Division of Labor as Reported by Husband

	Marital Role			
Predictor	Childcare (N = 209)	Housework (N = 336)	Money Management (N = 395)	Income Earning (N = 185)
Family Income	−.01	−.13**	.01	−.19**
Wife's Employment	−.25***	−.14**	.09**	b
Children in the Home	a	.06	−.05	−.11
Length of Marriage	−.10	.07	−.05	−.13
Husband's Role Expectations	.12	.17**	.31***	.02
Wife's Role Expectations	.01	−.09	−.08	−.04
Husband's Perception of Wife's Expectation	−.05	−.23***	−.22***	.21*
Wife's Perception of Husband's Expectation	.11	.27***	.28***	−.18*
Importance of Role to Husband	.09	−.11*	−.09**	−.01
Importance of Role to Wife	.08	.07	.08*	.01
R^2 =	.16	.42	.56	.15

Notes:
a. Analysis limited to couples with children in the home.
b. Analysis limited to couples with an employed wife.
  *p < .05
 **p < .01
***p < .001

is the wife's employment. Specifically, the husband is more likely to share in childcare if the wife is employed than if the wife stays at home.

Several variables significantly affect performance of housework. The wife does more of the housework if she is not employed, has a husband who believes she should do the housework, perceives that to be his expectation, and has a husband who perceives it to be her expectation. She does less housework if her husband feels it is important for him to be able to do it as well, or if the family has a relatively high income. The strongest effect is that of wife's perception of husband's expectation. In general, the husband's attitudes about housework appear to be more important than the wife's.

Money management is affected by expectations, perceptions, and role attachment in much the same way as housework, except that the wife's attitudes are somewhat more important. The wife is more likely to manage the money if she is employed, if both she and her husband feel she should do it and perceive the other to feel that way, and if performance of that role is important to her and unimportant to him. Again, the most influential variables are husband's expectation and wife's perception of that expectation.

Three predictors are significantly related to income earning. First, the lower the total income of a family, the higher the percentage earned by the wife. Also, the percentage of income earned by the wife is greater if (a) the husband perceives that his wife expects to earn money, and (b) the wife perceives that her husband expects her to share in income earning.

DISCUSSION AND CONCLUSIONS

What do partners in contemporary marriages expect of one another? How do they see their spouse's expectations? And, how do these definitions of the marital relationship relate to the traditional division of labor in the household? We have attempted to move beyond previous efforts to answer these questions by basing our inquiry on the perspectives of both husbands and wives. The picture of their marriages portrayed in our results is complex, but it is still heavily colored by traditional expectations about spouses' respective role responsibilities.

We did find widespread agreement among couples that childcare and money management should be shared responsibilities. Most couples expected to share childrearing equally, and two-thirds expected to take equal responsibility for managing money. However, differences between and within couples were more apparent for two other areas of responsibility—housework and income earning. Although many spouses agreed that these tasks should be shared equally, nearly a third of the couples agreed that housework is the wife's job, and 43 percent agreed that income earning is the husband's job. In another third of these couples, partners held different expectations about housework and income earning. In these cases, the wife tended to be more traditional with respect to responsibility for housework, and the husband was more likely to hold traditional expectations toward income earning. These results suggest that many spouses were willing to share in the traditional roles of the opposite sex but did not expect to relinquish primary responsibility for their own traditional roles in marriage.

Focusing specifically on the key issue of income earning in these households, we found that nearly two-thirds of the husbands liked (or would have liked) their wives being employed. Yet, a majority of the men in our sample (58 percent) felt that it is important to earn more than their wives earn, and nearly three-fourths of them held to the traditional view that income earning is the husband's job. Apparently, most husbands were comfortable with having their wives work—as long as the man is still the main breadwinner. While over half of the wives similarly expected the husband to be the primary earner of household income, our results seemingly contradict Osmond and Martin's (1975) finding that women were more likely than men to believe that a husband would be hurt if his wife earned more money.

Turning to the question of how partners perceive their spouses' expectations about household responsibilities, we found that husband's perceptions were consistently more accurate than were wives' perceptions. Perhaps wives are more likely to express their feelings about who should perform household tasks, giving their husbands a better reading of these expectations. When partners misperceived their spouses' expectations, this often occurred because the spouse actually expected to take more responsibility for the traditional roles of the opposite sex than the partner perceived. For instance, many wives underestimated their husbands' willingness to share childcare and housework. Likewise, substantial proportions of the husbands seemed unaware that their wives expected to share in managing and earning household income. On the other hand, spouses tended to be more traditional about their own sex-specific responsibilities—i.e., husbands expecting to manage the money and wives expecting to do the housework—than their partners thought they would be.

Spouses' respective perceptions of the actual division of labor in their household were generally consistent with one another. In those instances where spouses disagreed about who performed a given task, both husbands and wives tended to see themselves as doing more than their spouses said they did. These discrepancies reflect the Rashomon effect noted previously by Condran and Bode (1982). However, the dominant pattern in spouses' ratings of task performance, especially for routine tasks, was one of agreement. Consequently, we focused on husband's reports in our subsequent analyses of the household division of labor.

Even when measured by husbands' reports of behavior, the performance of key household tasks departed markedly from spouses' expectations about shared responsibilities. For instance, over four-fifths of these couples expected to share childcare, but less than half actually did so. Over half of these spouses expected to share housekeeping chores, but only a third of the husbands reported sharing even two tasks equally (dishwashing and shopping). For most couples, then, these activities continued to follow traditional patterns in spite of spouses' expectations for greater equality in their relationship.

This brings us to our final question: What factors do affect the household division of labor? Perhaps the most important and far-reaching finding of our multivariate analysis is that perceptions of partners' expectations strongly influence spouses' behavior. Spouses' views of what their partners expected significantly affected performance of housework, money management, and income earning. Clearly, these definitions of the marital situation have real consequences for the behavior of married men and women, even when they define their partner's expectations incorrectly. This important link between perceptions and behavior in the marital relationship deserves attention in future research.

Our analysis also indicated that the husband's prerogatives continue to have a more pronounced impact on marital role bargains than do the wife's employment or other family characteristics. We found that money management was more strongly affected by the husband's expectations—and by the wife's perception of those expectations—than by whether the wife worked. Similarly the husband's expectations and wife's perceptions of his preferences were the most important factors in the allocation of housework. The only area where the wife's employment had a leading influence was in childcare.

Therefore, despite the fact that 69 percent of the wives in our sample were working outside the home, the traditional division of labor and dominant role of the male "head-of-household" were still very much in evidence in these marriages. Although some signs of change were apparent in spouses' expectations about sharing certain household tasks, we did not find indications of dramatic change in the husband's position as the "primary" wage earner or in the wife's day-to-day responsibilities for housework and childcare. As Pleck (1977) has argued, the traditional priorities of work and marital roles reflected in our results form an interdependent system that will be difficult to alter. Until women's earnings are more comparable to men's, it seems unlikely that role bargaining in the intimate marital relationship will change drastically. Conversely, the ability of women to compete equally with men in the public worlds of work and politics will suffer until they are equally free of—or equally burdened by—the constraints of housework and childcare.

NOTES

1. Callers contacted 1,037 households in which a married couple lived and at least one spouse was employed. Of these, 489 couples agreed to be interviewed, producing an acceptance rate of 47 percent. Both men and women callers screened households between 6 and 9 P.M. weeknights and on Saturdays, and interviews were scheduled at the convenience of the subjects. Addresses were sought from eligible couples who hesitated to make interview appointments, and information about the study was mailed. This letter was followed by a call back, and, if necessary, a second letter and call back. Those who refused to give addresses or who initially refused to answer the screening question were also called a second time. Subjects were not paid but gave their time voluntarily. More details about the sampling and data collection processes for this study appear in Hiller and Philliber (1985) and are presented in a working paper available from the authors upon request.

2. For roles traditionally fulfilled by wives, responses were dichotomized by grouping perceptions that the role should be carried out entirely or mostly by wife as "wife's job," while perceptions that the role should be shared or done entirely or mostly by husband were classified as "shared job." The same procedure was followed for roles traditionally carried out by husbands with the categories reversed accordingly.

3. Because of the reasonably high agreement between husbands and wives, only husband's perception of who does childcare, housework, and money management were analyzed.

4. Zero-order correlations, means, and standard deviations for the variables in the four regression equations are available from the first author. As might be expected, several of the independent variables in these analyses are significantly correlated, but none so highly that multicollinearity would be of great concern. The total N varies across the four analyses because of different levels of missing data (deleted listwise) and sub-sample selection on the dependent variable (i.e., analysis only of couples with children or a working wife).

REFERENCES

Bianchi, Susanne M. and Daphne Spain. 1983. American Women: Three Decades of Change (DCS–80–8). Washington, DC: U.S. Bureau of the Census.

Condran, John G. and Jerry G. Bode. 1982. "Rashomon, working wives, and family division of labor: Middletown, 1980." *Journal of Marriage and the Family* 44:421–26.

Hiller, Dana V. and William W. Philliber. 1985. "Maximizing confidence in married couple sample." *Journal of Marriage and the Family* 47:729–32.

Huber, Joan and Glenna Spitze. 1983. *Sex Stratification: Children, Housework, and Jobs.* New York: Academic Press.

Komarovsky, Mirra. 1973. "Cultural contradictions and sex roles: the masculine case." *American Journal of Sociology* 78:873–84.

Mason, Karen Oppenheimer and Larry L. Bumpass. 1975. "U.S. women's sex-role ideology, 1970." *American Journal of Sociology* 80:1212–19.

Mason, Karen Oppenheimer, John L. Czajka and Sara Arber. 1976. "Change in U.S. women's sex-role attitudes, 1964–1974." *American Sociological Review* 41:573–96.

McKee, John P. and Alex C. Sheriffs. 1959. "Men's and women's beliefs, ideals, and self-concepts." *American Journal of Sociology* 64:356–63.

Meissner, Martin, Elizabeth Humphreys, Scott Meis and William Scheu. 1975. "No exit for wives: sexual division of labor and the cumulation of household demands." *Canadian Review of Sociology and Anthropology* 12:424–39.

Osmond, Marie Withers and Patricia Yancey Martin. 1975. "Sex and sexism: a comparison of male and female sex-role attitudes." *Journal of Marriage and the Family* 37:744–53.

Parelius, Ann P. 1975a. "Change and stability in college women's orientations toward education, family, and work." *Social Problems* 22:420–32.

Parelius, Ann P. 1975b. "Emerging sex-role attitudes, expectations, and strains among college women." *Journal of Marriage and the Family* 37:146–53.

Pleck, Joseph H. 1977. "The work-family role system." *Social Problems* 24:417–27.

Scanzoni, John. 1979. "Sex-role influences on married women's status attainments." *Journal of Marriage and the Family* 41:793–800.

Spitze, Glenna D. and Linda J. Waite. 1981. "Wife's employment: the role of husband's perceived attitudes." *Journal of Marriage and the Family* 42:117–24.

Vanek, Joann. 1974. "Time spent in housework." *Scientific American* 231:116–20.

ARTICLE 10
Marriage, Family Life, and Women's Employment

JANE RIBLETT WILKIE

The majority of women now combine work with marriage and having a family. This article details the wide-ranging effects of female employment on marriage patterns, husband-wife relationships, marital satisfaction, divorce, and the relations between parents and children. The author notes how work differentially affects the lives of white, black, and Hispanic women, concluding with suggestions for needed policy changes that would support today's families.

IN 1980, FOR THE FIRST TIME in the twentieth century, married women's place was, typically, no longer only in the home. In that year, the number of married women working for pay outside the home exceeded the number following the traditional pattern of full-time unpaid service to the family within the home. We have entered an era in which women are likely to work for pay whether or not they marry, rather than choosing *either* a job *or* marriage.

This selection explores some of the profound changes in our family and personal lives that have resulted from women's increasing participation in the paid labor force. (Because my focus here is the impact of women's employment on their family lives, I do not cover, except peripherally, how women's family lives affect their employment, or the relationship between wives' and husbands' employment. . . . I consider first the impact of women's employment on the incidence and timing

"Marriage, Family Life, and Women's Employment." From *Women Working: Theories and Facts in Perspective* (2nd ed.), edited by Ann Helton Stromberg and Shirley Harkess by permission of Mayfield Publishing Company. Copyright © 1988, 1978 by Mayfield Publishing Company.

of marriage. Then I focus on the married to examine whether paid employment of married women alters power relations within the family and the distribution of household work. I ask what the effect of women's employment is on marital satisfaction and whether women who work outside the home are more likely to divorce than full-time housewives.

Next I turn to the relations between women's employment and parenthood. These two roles are often difficult to reconcile in industrial societies where home and paid work are typically in separate locations, so I first examine whether employed women are less likely to have children and whether they have smaller families than full-time homemakers. Then I examine the effect of women's increased labor force participation on the care of children and on their emotional, cognitive, and social development, as well as sex role attitudes. I also consider the effect of women's employment on the economic welfare of families. I conclude by discussing the public policy implications of these findings.

Throughout, where data are available, I describe and contrast the experiences of white, black, and Hispanic women, and, with respect to parenthood, the growing number of women who are raising families alone. In addition, again where data permit, I look at how women's employment affects the family life of lesbian couples.

THE EFFECTS OF WOMEN'S EMPLOYMENT ON MARRIAGE

Economic and Social Bases of Marriage

Expectations regarding marital roles have changed significantly over the past 35 years. In 1950, the predominant family pattern involved substantial role division by gender. The economic provider role was assigned primarily to men, and only 18 percent of married women with children worked outside the home, usually out of economic necessity. Managing the household and caring for the children were assigned to women, and men typically did only a few household tasks such as lawn mowing and automobile repair. This role specialization in the family reflected social beliefs that men and women have substantially different characteristics, interests, and abilities. Men were assigned their tasks because they were assumed to be independent, achievement-oriented, and technologically inclined, while women's roles reflected their assumed social and emotional skills. Few families followed this pattern completely, but it was a model many tried to emulate.

The typical husband-wife family in the 1980s has two wage earners. In only one-third of these families is the husband the sole wage earner (Hayghe, 1981); and in families where the wife is under 45, only 16 percent of husbands have been the sole wage earner since marriage. Employment is strongly expected of unmarried women and young childless wives (Waite, 1980), and, although it may not be "required" of them, over half (59 percent) of married women with children are employed. Black married women with children are even more likely to work for pay

(70 percent) than either white (58 percent) or Hispanic (49 percent) mothers (Hayghe, 1984).

For those whose marital arrangements have changed from role division to role sharing, the reasons for marrying and the bases of mate selection have probably also changed. When women gain economic security and social placement from marriage, and men get emotional support, sexual gratification, and someone to raise the children and manage the home, mate selection emphasizes the economic prospects of men and the social, emotional, and physical attributes of women. People who have rejected these goals tend to seek a marital relationship that provides mutual love, companionship, and emotional support based on cooperation and shared responsibility.

Women's increased employment, by altering the basis of the marital exchange, has had widespread effects on many aspects of married life. We begin our consideration of these effects by looking at trends in marriage rates.

Effects of Women's Employment on Marriage Patterns

Almost all American women marry. In the mid-1980s, only 5 percent of women between the ages of 40 and 44 had never married, a proportion not significantly different from that for their mothers' and older sisters' generations (U.S. Bureau of the Census, 1985c). What has changed with the increasing employment of women is *when* women marry and their likelihood of remaining married.

Since the mid-1950s, the median age at first marriage for women has increased from 20 to 23 years, and there is reason to believe that women's increased employment may be a significant cause of this trend. One view holds that employment offers women an alternative to marriage, and as the economic benefits of women's employment begin to offer them greater economic security and personal satisfaction than traditional marriage, they delay marriage in order to give greater priority to occupational goals. An alternative view holds that women's increased employment outside the home and the increase in the age of marriage both result from another trend—the greater difficulty for recent generations of achieving the life-style they have come to expect. According to this view, the post-World War II baby-boom cohorts experience greater difficulty establishing themselves in well-paying jobs and in achieving living standards comparable to their parents' because they exceed in size the cohorts of their parents, and thus the number needing jobs exceeds the number of positions left vacant by smaller prior generations (Easterlin, 1973). This has led many young people to defer marriage until they have completed an adequate education and worked to save a nest egg. Furthermore, consumption aspirations are rising as two-income households increasingly provide the standard by which all householders judge how well they are doing (Oppenheimer, 1982).

The increased education and employment experience of young women have also changed the aspirations of women and made them less exclusively oriented toward family roles. Early labor force experience makes women more likely to plan to work for pay throughout marriage (Waite, 1980), and it changes what they want from, and what they are prepared to give to, a marital relationship. We turn next to a discussion of the specific ways in which relationships between husbands and wives have been altered by wives' employment.

Employment and Husband-Wife Relationships

In the past, traditional gender roles involved substantial subordination of women's interests to the interests of their husbands. Gender stratification was pervasive, and more or less spontaneous consensus existed that since the family depended upon the husband's income, the common good of the family required that the husband's breadwinning sphere have primacy. The demands of the husband's occupation affected where the family lived, whether they moved, how they spent disposable income, whether the wife worked, and so forth.

In fact, the husband's primacy went well beyond this. Men enjoyed greater power in other, non-job-related spheres of the marital relationship. A woman's only spheres of authority and influence were household management and child rearing, and often these tasks were delegated to her by her husband or adopted by her without question because they were prescribed by the strong normative expectations surrounding her. Social norms defined the exchange between husbands and wives, and they legitimized males' greater power, thus granting husbands greater authority. This role pattern still characterizes most marriages, even those with an employed wife (Huber and Spitze, 1980).

Contemporary Power Relations
The employment of women outside the home has begun to undermine the economic basis of the traditional, normative sources of male power. Areas that in the past were consensually agreed upon have become areas of conflict and negotiation for many younger couples. For example, a substantial increase has occurred in the proportion of wives who (often not very realistically, as we shall see) expect their husbands to share household tasks (Mason, Czajka, and Arber, 1976). Further, married women's employment creates new situations for which no norms exist, such as how to divide family finances when there are two paychecks and whether to set up two homes to accommodate two careers some distance apart. Thus, many more areas require joint decision making.

Employment also increases women's ability and opportunity to act independently. Employed wives are much more likely than housewives to have made their own decisions about whether to take a job or to stay at home (Rank, 1982). An income permits women to establish their own credit, make independent financial decisions, and provides them with the basis for a greater say in family purchasing decisions (Bahr, 1975). Employment also increases women's social resources: women establish social contacts through work that provide alternative bases of support. These resources make women less likely to feel they should, or must, give in to their husbands, and more willing to risk their husbands' displeasure (Ferree, 1976).

Employed women are also more likely to win arguments with their husbands because several features of paid work increase women's skill and assertiveness in pursuing their own interests. First, paid work sharpens women's instrumental skills, making employed women more effective bargainers than housewives (Scanzoni, 1978). Further, employment increases a woman's self-esteem and feeling of self-worth (Kessler and McRae, 1982), contributing to the employed woman's increased sense of legitimacy of her own interests (Ferree, 1976) and to her greater assertiveness in bargaining (Scanzoni, 1978).

While employment outside the home increases women's autonomy, power resources, and negotiating skills, it may not be sufficient to achieve an egalitarian marriage. Gender stratification limits wives' resources even when they are employed. Their employment provides them with, on the average, only 44 percent of the earnings of their husbands (U.S. Bureau of the Census, 1986). Further, as women work in less prestigious jobs than men, they accrue less social power and sense of self-worth. Moreover, even employed women are often expected to defer to men, and this disadvantages them psychologically in the struggle for marital power (Gillespie, 1971). There has been improvement, but the deck remains stacked against women.

The power structure in black families differs somewhat from the model just described, but there is little support for the stereotype of a "black matriarchy" of dominant women. Black couples are more accurately characterized as egalitarian than matriarchal: housekeeping, child-care, and wage-earning roles are most typically shared (Staples, 1981), as is decision making (Willie and Greenblatt, 1978). Black couples *are* less husband-dominated than white couples (Cromwell and Cromwell, 1978). This is not surprising: black men have benefited less from the norms of male superiority because American society has traditionally accorded blacks less status than whites, and racial discrimination has diminished their economic resources. The meager wages of many black men increase the likelihood that two incomes will be needed to support the family, and black women's greater labor force participation has increased their social and economic independence.

In contrast to the stereotype of black families as matriarchal, the Hispanic family has been characterized as patriarchal. Traditional Hispanic values have been assumed to legitimize the authority of the husband over the wife and prescribe strict sex role segregation within the family. A growing body of empirical evidence, however, challenges the notion that male dominance is typical in marital relationships among Mexican Americans (Mirandé, 1977). (Research on Hispanics in the United States has focused on Mexican Americans, who represent 60 percent of the U.S. Hispanic population.) Egalitarian decision making is far more prevalent than male dominance (Ybarra, 1982). Cromwell and Cromwell (1978) found that about 70 percent of Mexican American wives reported egalitarian decision making, the same proportion as white wives, although Mexican American husbands were more likely than white husbands to report they made most family decisions (20 percent compared to 13 percent). Baca Zinn (1982) has argued that structural factors such as age, education, and women's employment are more important than cultural values in accounting for differences in gender roles among Mexican Americans, just as they are among whites. For instance, egalitarian role structure and decision making is more frequently found among Mexican American families where the wife is employed outside the home (Ybarra, 1982).

For lesbian couples, normative sources of power appear to be of greater importance than economic resources. Blumstein and Schwartz (1983), in a study of heterosexual and homosexual couples, found that only lesbian couples avoided allocating more power to the main provider. Most lesbians rejected the notion that their worth is determined by the amount of money they earn. They made a conscious effort to free their relationships from domination by either partner, and they were particularly opposed to domination based on money. In contrast, in all other types of couples, money tended to bring power. Among married couples and cohabiting heterosexual couples, the greater the economic contribution of the woman, the greater, in general, her clout.

Division of Labor

Most research finds that while a wife's employment does increase her power in family decision making, it does not produce role equity in the household (Miller and Garrison, 1982). Major studies conducted from the mid-1960s to the early 1970s consistently found that employed wives still did most of the housework and that husbands did not increase their participation in housework and child care when their wives were employed. As a result, employed wives experienced considerable role overload compared to their husbands. Vanek (1980) calculated that employed wives worked, on the average, 71 hours per week at household tasks and paid work, 8.5 hours per week longer than their husbands. In families with young children the gap increased to 15 hours, with employed mothers averaging an 80-hour week.

Recent research suggests, however, that the amount of household labor contributed by wives and husbands is becoming somewhat more similar (Pleck, 1982). Robinson (1980) found that wives, both full-time housewives and those employed, spent 2.5 fewer hours per week in family work in the mid-1970s than in the mid-1960s. He found, however, no increase in men's contribution to housework over this period. Barnett and Baruch (1984), in contrast, found that husbands with employed wives participated on the average 1.3 hours more per week in household work than did husbands with nonemployed wives. Both studies point to changing role expectations as the major source of these changes; wives today are more likely to want husbands to participate in household tasks.

While these studies indicate that employed women's role overload in terms of hours is decreasing, the practical impact of these changes may be limited. Husbands' and wives' contributions to household work still differ in traditional ways. Men are more likely to contribute to the less regular, less demanding, and more pleasurable household and child-care tasks, and women still tend to be the ones primarily responsible for the household (LaRossa and LaRossa, 1981).

Other aspects of family organization are also unfavorable to women. First, women's disproportionate contributions to domestic production are not limited to housework and child care. Wives provide unpaid support services, such as entertainment of colleagues and clients, that contribute to husbands' career success (Papanek, 1973), and they maintain and enhance family status by such activities as the training of children, gift giving, and ritual observance (Papanek, 1979). Second, women are more likely than men to choose jobs that accommodate their families. They more frequently work part-time or intermittently when they have children (Hayghe, 1984), they select jobs close to home or with hours that permit them to integrate domestic and occupational responsibilities (Ericksen, 1977), and they move when their husbands' career advancement demands it, although that disrupts their own employment and career advancement.

Several alternative explanations, . . . have been offered for these inequities in the division of labor. Resource-based power theories suggest that the greater resources of men are viewed as justification for inequity. For example, Lein and Blehar (1979) found that both husbands and wives often viewed women's longer hours of housework as a compensation for their lower wages in the marketplace and consequent lesser contribution to family finances. However, even when women have high resources, as is the case for those professionally employed, an equitable division of labor in the home does not result. Dual-career families may purchase outside labor to replace that of the wife rather than increase the husband's share of household tasks, thus maintaining men's advantage. Family priorities also still favor men. Women in high-status occupations, just as other women, experience the negative income and occupational effects of family migration (Lichter, 1983). The inability of women to translate their wages into an equal work week and their educational and occupational resources into equal family investment in their careers suggests that traditional, normative power advantages of men persist (Hartmann, 1981).

Exchange and bargaining theories, on the other hand, suggest that the mutual expectation of husband and wife as to who ideally should fill the provider role is pivotal in the reallocation of household work. One study of 128 Swedish couples found that breadwinning responsibility was a more important determinant of domestic role sharing than was the wife's employment status (Haas, 1982). At present, most American couples do not expect the husband and wife to be coproviders. Two-job couples are willing to relieve the husband of some of his provider role responsibility and to acknowledge that the wife's contribution is important and perhaps even necessary, but only a minority will agree that the duty to provide should be shared equally (Hood, 1986).

Effects of Women's Employment on Marital Satisfaction and Divorce

Empirical studies on the effect of wives' employment on marital satisfaction show no consistent effects, most likely due to the limitations of the various measures used. Evidence exists, however, that employment is associated with lower marital satisfaction for wives when it violates role expectations or creates role conflict (Houseknecht and Macke, 1981). This explains why women of the lower class, who are more likely to be employed out of necessity, score lower on marital adjustment ratings when they have jobs (Rallings and Nye, 1979), while women of the middle class, who are more likely to be employed out of choice, do not (Bahr and Day,

1976). Further, employed women are more satisfied in their marriages when their husbands are more supportive and share child care and when they have fewer children or their children are older (Kessler and McRae, 1982).

Whether men's marital satisfaction increases or decreases with the employment of their wives also depends on whether it violates their role expectations. Kessler and McRae (1982) found that employment of wives is most likely to distress married men who hold traditional sex role attitudes. These findings suggest that it is not the wife's employment per se that determines marital satisfaction but rather whether the husband and wife achieve their preferences.

Not surprisingly, in general, men's marital satisfaction does not decrease when their wives are employed. Counterbalancing the loss of sole-breadwinner status and the personal services of their wives, are the advantages of decreased economic responsibility, few additional household chores, increased leisure time (men whose wives are employed spend fewer hours at paid work and no more hours at household work, and thus have more leisure hours than men whose wives are full-time homemakers [Robinson, 1977]), and a higher family income. Since, in general, marital satisfaction is positively related to such factors, these effects of wives' working often counterbalance any ego loss. And as more and more married women enter the labor force, the potential ego loss diminishes and the economic gains become more salient.

Despite the fact that wives' employment is not associated with higher marital dissatisfaction, given a certain level of satisfaction or dissatisfaction, marriages with an employed wife are more unstable than those in which the wife is a full-time housewife. Both men and women are more likely to have had thoughts of divorce when the wife has had work experience (Huber and Spitze, 1980), and the effect of employment is significant: 26 percent of employed wives were found in one study to have had thoughts of divorce, compared to 18 percent of full-time housewives (Booth et al., 1984). Thus, wives' employment increases marital instability, and this association is heightened by women's high earnings or potential earnings (Cherlin, 1979), and advanced education (Glick and Norton, 1977).

Several studies have found that it is not women's employment per se but rather the financial independence women gain from employment that contributes to higher rates of marital instability and divorce. Booth et al. (1984) found that the negative influence of wives' employment on marital stability is almost completely accounted for by its indirect effects. It increases wives' income and spousal disagreement, which in turn increase marital instability. These findings suggest that divorce is higher among employed married women than full-time housewives due to several factors associated with wives' employment. First, the family changes that occur when the wife enters the labor force increase marital disagreement, especially at the present time when there are few guidelines and institutional supports for two-earner families. Second, the increased independence women gain from an income lowers the threshold of satisfaction at which divorce is considered and provides women with the financial ability and psychological strength to end a relationship they are not satisfied with.

To summarize this section, I have found that the employment of wives has important effects on marriage. The change from marital role division toward role sharing alters the basis of marriage for some couples. Women marry later, but they appear to be just as likely to marry as earlier generations when fewer women were in the labor force. Employment has, however, changed the relationship between husbands and wives. Employed women have more power in marital relationships, although they have not yet achieved equal power and they still retain primary responsibility for the domestic sphere. Marital satisfaction is not consistently affected by wives' employment; it depends on whether a wife's job violates role expectations of the husband or the wife. However, marriages with an employed wife are more likely to end in divorce, probably because employed women are more likely than housewives to have the financial and other resources to end a relationship they are not satisfied with.

THE EFFECT OF WOMEN'S EMPLOYMENT ON PARENTHOOD

I will now consider the effects of women's employment on parenthood. This issue has generated great controversy and concern, in part because early research findings (for example, Bowlby, 1952) on atypical samples linked maternal employment to emotional deprivation and delinquent behavior in children, associations later found to be spurious. I begin by examining how employment has affected women's childbearing patterns.

Women's Employment and Childbearing

A strong negative relationship exists between female employment and childbearing. Indeed, Blake (1965:1197) has described this relationship as "one of the strongest, most persistent over time and space, and most theoretically reasonable" in the study of differential fertility. Employed women, and women who plan to enter the labor force, expect to have and do have fewer children (Waite and Stolzenberg, 1976), begin their families later (Wilkie, 1981), and are more likely to remain permanently childless than women who do not work outside the home. Women in the labor force completing their childbearing in the mid-1980s had, on the average, 20 percent fewer children than women not in the labor force, and double their rate of childlessness (16 percent compared to 8 percent). Among younger women, those 18 to 34, over half of those in the labor force had delayed having a first child compared to only a quarter of those at home, and twice as many (13 percent compared to 6 percent) expected to remain childless (U.S. Bureau of the Census, 1985b).

The lower fertility of employed women holds for women of all racial and ethnic groups. Black and Hispanic women have more children than white women, but within each race and ethnic group, employed women have smaller completed families than housewives. For example, in 1984, employed black women aged 35 to 44 averaged 2.5 children, compared to 3.5 children for black housewives. The comparable figures for Hispanic women were 2.7 and 3.1, and white women averaged 2.1 children if they were employed and 2.6 children if they were not (U.S. Bureau of the Census, 1985b).

Four different explanations have been offered for the lower fertility of employed women. The first argues that the causal direction is from fertility to employment. This model suggests that mother and employee roles are incompatible in modern industrial societies as few alternatives to mother-care of infants exist and the occupational structure does not provide the flexibility women need to combine both roles. Since normative expectations require that women give precedence to the child-rearing role, having children decreases the likelihood that they will be employed (Sweet, 1973). This model also implies that women who do not want or cannot have children are likely to be employed.

A second model similarly argues that mother and employee roles are incompatible, but it postulates that employment decisions determine fertility decisions (Blake, 1965). This view is supported by findings that employment reduces actual and expected fertility (Cramer, 1980), and women who plan to enter the labor force intend to have smaller families than women who do not plan to (Waite and Stolzenberg, 1976).

A third view attempts to reconcile the preceding models by postulating a reciprocal causal relationship between fertility and employment (Cramer, 1980). For example, Hout (1978) found that in the short run, the discomforts of pregnancy and the demands of newborns account for the lower labor force participation of mothers with young children. In the long run, however, he found that career commitments lead to curtailed fertility. Thus, women who are employed are more likely to revise downward their preferred family size after two children (Jones, 1981). This suggests that fertility and labor force decisions are not static, but are made sequentially, with parents reevaluating employment and family plans after the birth of each child.

A fourth view suggests that other, antecedent factors explain both employment and the number of children a woman bears. For example, highly educated women start childbearing later and have smaller families (Rindfuss, Bumpass, and St. John, 1980), and education also affects labor force participation. Women with a college degree, for example, are twice as likely to be employed as women with only a high school degree. Thus, higher education leads to both higher labor force participation and lower fertility.

The relationship between women's employment and childbearing is likely much more complicated than any one of these models suggests. Individual decisions are based upon complex considerations, and many of the factors specified in the models are changing. For example, traditionally, married women with children of preschool age have had substantially lower employment rates than women with children of school age, and they in turn have had lower employment rates than women with no children under 18. But this difference has been decreasing, and a sizeable increase in employment of mothers with young children has occurred (see Figure 1). Thus, children are less a deterrent to maternal employment today than they were just 10 years ago. Further, having older children may actually increase

Marriage, Family Life, and Women's Employment   **153**

FIGURE 1   Labor Force Participation Rates of White, Black, and Hispanic Wives under Age 35, 1950 to 1983, by Presence and Age of Children

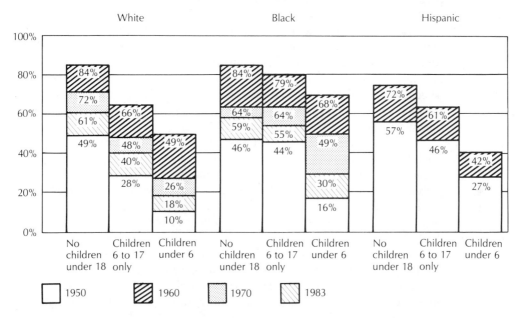

Sources: U.S. Bureau of the Census, 1950 Census of Population, *General Characteristics of Families,* Tables 12 and 13 (1955), 1950 Census of Population, *Fertility,* Tables 25 and 27 (1955), 1960 Census of Population, *Families,* Table 11 (1963), 1970 Census of Population, *Characteristics of the Population,* Table 216 (1973); U.S. Department of Labor, Bureau of Labor Statistics, *Families at Work: The Jobs and the Pay,* Table B-5 (1984).

Note: Excludes married women with spouse absent and, in women married more than once. In 1950 and 1960, data on Hispanic women are not available and data on blacks include other nonwhite groups.

women's labor force participation due to the high costs of raising adolescents (Oppenheimer, 1982). Thus, the assumptions of the first model are less accurate than they once were.

Because of these trends, more and more families face the problem of finding child care, and increasingly, the child care they need is for younger and younger children. In the next section we consider how families are solving this problem.

Child Care Arrangements of Employed Mothers

In 1983, for the first time, half of all mothers with children under age six were in the labor force. This means that 7.6 million families now face the problem of arranging alternative care for 8.9 million preschool-age children, and this is a growing problem. It is a particularly severe problem for the more than 2 million mothers of preschoolers who are maintaining a family alone, and whose income may be crucial to support their children. One of every nine white preschoolers, nearly one out of every two black preschoolers, and one out of every five Hispanic preschoolers live in families without a father present (U.S. Department of Labor, 1984).

How do these families manage? According to the U.S. Census Bureau (1983), most preschool children under five years of age with employed mothers in 1982 were cared for by family members: the parents themselves cared for 23 percent of the children and 29 percent were cared for by other relatives. An additional 28 percent were cared for by an unrelated person, either in the child's home or in that person's home, and 15 percent were cared for in group facilities, either nursery schools or day care centers.

This represents a shift away from family care and an increase in group care since 1965. At that time, over 60 percent of children under six years of age with mothers in the labor force were cared for by parents or other relatives and only 6 percent were in group care (U.S. Bureau of the Census, 1982). Moreover, the increase in the use of group care is underestimated because of the difference in the age groups reported at the two dates. The 1965 data include five-year-olds, while the 1982 data do not, and older children are more likely to be placed in group care.

Part of the shift away from care in the home to group care arrangements is due to the reduced availability of traditional home care providers, relatives and neighbors. Grandmothers and neighbor women whose children are grown are now more likely to be employed themselves. Further, the increase in one-parent families, now 16 percent of all families, has reduced the likelihood that a father will be available to care for the child. Employed women who are raising children alone are much more likely to rely on group care facilities than those in two-parent families (20 percent compared to 13 percent). As these women have substantially lower financial resources than other mothers, they can probably least afford this type of care. Other groups of employed women who are more likely to use group care are well-educated women, those who work full-time, and those with high family incomes. These women can afford high-quality group care and they may also feel more favorable toward a group facility because they see it as an extension of the child's schooling to the preschool years, rather than as a substitute mother.

Black employed mothers of preschool children are particularly likely to use other relatives (45 percent) and group care (20 percent) and least likely to have parents (11 percent) and nonrelatives (16 percent) care for their children (U.S. Bureau of the Census, 1983). These child care arrangements in part reflect the greater ties to extended kin in black family life and the high proportion of black families (43 percent) that are headed by a woman, making parental care less available. Hispanic employed mothers are also likely to use other kin (46 percent) as well as parents (18 percent) and are least likely to use group care (9 percent). This may reflect the high proportion of two-parent families among most Hispanic groups except Puerto Ricans.

The trend toward maternal employment and the increasing use of group care rather than parental or other home care of children has made it vitally important to study the effects of these changes on children. The next section examines how maternal employment and alternative care affect children. Paternal employment, unlike maternal employment, has not been viewed as problematic for children, and so unfortunately, little research has examined its effect.

Effect of Maternal Employment on Children

How does mothers' employment affect children? Little evidence exists that mothers' employment has a general adverse effect on children. Research has typically found few significant differences, or inconsistent differences, between children whose mothers are employed and those whose mothers are not. The effects of mothers' employment may, however, differ by the characteristics of the child, the conditions of the mother's employment, and the type and quality of the substitute care, among other things.

The age, sex, and social class of children may mediate or change the effect of maternal employment. Infants' needs are different from those of adolescents, males may respond differently from females, and lower-class children react differently from the way middle-class children do (Gold and Andres, 1978a, 1978b; Cochran and Gunnarsson, 1985). In addition, children respond differently depending on whether their mothers prefer or prefer not to be employed (Farel, 1980). Further, the effect of maternal employment depends on the type and quality of substitute care. Group care of children is improved when the ratio of children to caretakers is lower and there is greater responsiveness to individual children; when caretakers have greater experience and training, more positive attitudes toward children, and lower turnover; and when the caretaking environments are more stimulating (Clarke-Stewart, 1982).

However, the effect of all the factors mentioned depends on the outcome one examines. In the following paragraphs we consider the effect of maternal employment on three principal dimensions of child development: emotional and cognitive development, social adjustment, and sex role attitudes; we contrast the effects for different age, sex, and social class groups when data permit.

Early research found that maternal separation had negative effects on the emotional and cognitive development of children, especially infants. However, these findings were based on poorly designed studies of children who were institutionalized in extremely understaffed facilities, and thus they are not applicable to most alternative child care situations. More recent research has found that infants of employed mothers establish normal attachments (Schwartz, 1975), and mothers' employment does not adversely affect the stability of the parent-child relationship (Easterbrooks, Chase-Lansdale, and Goldberg, 1984). Furthermore, there is no evidence that it is better if the caretaker is the mother or that multiple attachments interfere with a primary attachment to the mother (Lamb, 1977). Infants and preschool children with employed mothers are not significantly different from those with nonemployed mothers with respect to most developmental measures: for example, language development (Schachter, 1981), motor development (Hock, 1980), and intelligence, as measured by standard tests (Belsky and Steinberg, 1978). Day care may, in fact, intellectually benefit disadvantaged children, at least in the short run (Golden et al., 1978).

These findings may be due to the fact that, contrary to common assumptions, employed mothers spend almost as much time with their children as other mothers do (Clarke-Stewart, 1977), and no significant difference exists in the quality of care provided by employed mothers and full-time homemakers (Stith and Davis, 1984). The amount and kind of stimulation given a child may vary more by the educational level of the parent and the type of substitute care than by the mother's employment status (Moore and Hofferth, 1979).

With respect to social adjustment, a number of studies have found that school-age and adolescent children benefit from the behaviors and attitudes encouraged by employed mothers. Employed mothers are more likely to encourage independence in their children, have structured rules for them, and require that they help around the house (Hoffman, 1974). These parenting styles likely serve to smooth household functioning when the employed mother is absent and may also reflect the lesser investment of employed mothers in their household roles. Full-time homemakers with school-age children may overinvest in the mother role because it is the only one from which they derive a sense of self-worth (Hoffman, 1979). These mothers may unwittingly encourage dependency in their children to enhance and justify their role (Gold and Andres, 1978a).

The role model effect of employed mothers on adolescent daughters appears to be particularly positive. Daughters of employed mothers are more outgoing, independent, active, highly motivated, score higher on a variety of indexes of academic achievement, have higher educational aspirations, and appear better adjusted on social and personality measures than daughters of full-time homemakers (Hoffman, 1979).

The picture for sons is more complicated, as the findings differ by social class and age. The positive effect of mother's employment on sons is stronger for the lower class than for the middle class, and adolescents fare better than younger boys. The effect of having an employed mother on an adolescent boy is particularly positive. Gold and Andres (1978a) found that adolescent sons of employed mothers had better social and personality adjustment, a greater sense of personal worth and belonging, better family relations, and better interpersonal relations in school than sons of full-time housewives.

Finally, with respect to sex role attitudes, children with mothers in the labor force clearly view women and women's employment more positively than do children of full-time homemakers (Powell and Steelman, 1982). Further, both sons and daughters of employed women tend to have less traditional views of marriage and sex roles than do children of full-time homemakers (Stephan and Corder, 1985).

In summary, no evidence exists that mothers' employment has systematic, negative effects on children. In fact, for school-age, particularly adolescent, children, the effects of mothers' employment are generally positive. Much more research is needed, however, on the effects of various types of alternative care for infants and other preschool children. This is a growing population requiring alternative care, and few definitive studies exist to guide parents in the choices they must make.

Women's Employment and the Economic Welfare of Families

Employed wives and mothers make substantial contributions to their families' economic welfare. Families in which the wife or mother is employed have higher incomes and are less likely to be in poverty than families where the wife or mother is not employed. The earnings of women are particularly crucial for families maintained by women. During the 1970s, the rising incidence of marital breakup and of births to unmarried women increased the proportion of families maintained by women. Women now head 16 percent of all families and 43 percent of all black families. These families have, on the average, one-third the income of those headed by a husband and wife ($8,712 compared to $27,538), and more than a third live in poverty. Families maintained by employed mothers, however, have more than twice the income of those where the mother is not employed (see Figure 2), and their chances of living in poverty decrease from 47 percent to 20 percent (U.S. Bureau of the Census, 1985a).

For several reasons, however, income differences between families in which the wife or mother is employed and those in which she is a full-time housewife overstate differences in standards of living. First, two-earner families are penalized by the income tax system; two-earner couples generally pay more taxes than they would if they were permitted to file as two single individuals, while one-earner couples with the same total family income pay less than they would if filing separately (Gordon, 1979a). Second, there are costs related to employment, such as transportation to work, clothing expenditures, and retirement payments. Two-earner couples pay substantially more in social security taxes for roughly the same benefits as one-earner couples (Gordon, 1979b). Finally, families of employed women must purchase some of the services provided by women who work at home. For families with preschool-age children, child care can be a sizeable expense, especially for women who maintain families alone. Altogether, work-related expenditures, increased income taxes, and purchased household services decrease the average woman's paycheck by an estimated one-third (Vickery, 1979).

To summarize this section, we found that mothers' employment has few adverse effects on children. Employed women have fewer children and these children are increasingly likely to be cared for by nonrelatives and in group facilities. But virtually no evidence exists that maternal employment has systematic negative effects on younger children, and for older children the effects are generally positive. In addition, mothers' employment raises the living standard of families. It increases the family income and it significantly decreases the likelihood that the family will live in poverty.

CONCLUSIONS AND POLICY IMPLICATIONS

Women's increasing labor force participation shows no signs of abating. In fact, women who were least likely to be employed in the past—married women, especially

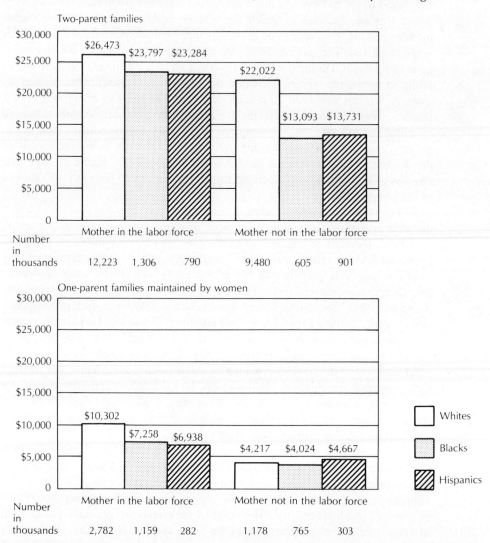

FIGURE 2 Median Family Income, 1982, for Families with Children under 18, by Type of Family, Mother's Labor Force Participation, Race and Hispanic origin

Source: U.S. Department of Labor, Bureau of Labor Statistics, *Families at Work: The Jobs and the Pay* (1984).

those whose husbands have high income, and mothers, especially those with preschool-age children—comprise the fastest-growing segments of the female labor force. Increasingly, the paid work lives of women parallel those of men, while at the same time women continue to assume the major share of household and family responsibilities.

Our literature review has found that women have managed both home and work responsibilities with considerable success. By shouldering a greater burden in family work than their husbands, employed women cushion men's loss of relative power and personal services. By managing to spend "quality time" with their children despite a long work week, employed women continue to provide the love, involvement, and stimulation necessary for the successful development of their children. In addition, employed mothers provide their families with many positive benefits. Their child-rearing methods and the role models they provide produce independence, high aspirations, and an enhanced sense of self-worth in their children. And their earnings increase the economic security and well-being of their families.

Women's success in combining paid work and family roles has been, however, at the expense of their leisure time and their careers. Employed women work longer hours than men or full-time housewives, they are more likely to interrupt their employment for family responsibilities, and they choose jobs they believe make fewer demands so they can better combine their work and family lives. The costs to women are significant. Women experience greater psychological distress than men when they combine employment, marriage, and parenthood (Thoits, 1986) and women's domestic labor time often results in reduced wages and limited labor force achievement (Coverman, 1983). A more equitable division of family labor is necessary before wage labor inequalities between the sexes can be improved.

Women in the past have disproportionately assumed the costs to the family of the loss of a full-time homemaker, but younger married women are less likely to be willing to take dead-end and low-paying jobs so that they can manage family responsibilities. Women are increasing their educational attainment at a faster rate than men and some are beginning to move into nontraditional jobs. Moreover, an increasing number of families are maintained by women, and a disproportionate share of these are poor. These women, particularly, need support to enable them to assume better-paying jobs and keep their families out of poverty. The question then becomes, What social policies are needed to produce a more equitable sharing of family responsibilities and to ensure that women have equal opportunity in the work world?

Child care is the issue that causes families with employed mothers the most difficulty. One-third of employed mothers surveyed in a national study reported that child care was a problem (National Commission on Working Women, 1979), and child care services for employed parents are not keeping up with the increasing number of children in need of services. The Children's Defense Fund (1982) has estimated that 13 million children 13 years of age and under are in households where the parent or parents are employed full-time. Currently, child care centers can serve fewer than 1 million children, and care for children in private homes serves close to 7 million children. This leaves more than 5 million children to care for themselves. As women's labor force participation increases, the need for alternative child care will increase at the same time that the number of traditional providers will decrease.

Until now, the response of government and industry to this growing problem has been minimal. The United States is the only industrialized country in the world with no policy guaranteeing women the right to maternity leave and job protection and no explicit policy on child care. Fewer than 40 percent of working mothers are entitled to some paid leave at the time of childbirth, usually six to eight weeks (Kamerman, 1984), and currently only two thousand out of the six million employers in the United States provide any form of child care assistance ("Child Care Finds," 1985). Clearly, the scope of the problem demands greater involvement of government and industry in the provision of direct or indirect financial support of child care.

Government and industry could help employed parents cope with child care responsibilities by several family-friendly policies. First, a national policy on maternity and paternity leaves is needed to guarantee parents the right to return to their jobs. Second, child care options could be expanded by government incentives to employers, grants to assist public and nonprofit agencies to develop child care programs, and the use of public schools to provide supervised activities for children before and after school. Currently, inadequate maternity benefits and the absence of provisions for combining employment and child care at the end of maternity leaves, coupled with few affordable child care facilities, force many women to choose between caring for their young children and maintaining their job and seniority.

Employers could also provide support for families. First, industry could expand options or flexible work hours and part-time work to enable employees to better combine job and family responsibilities, especially during their children's preschool years. Second, employers could permit a parent to stay home with a child when the child is too sick to attend day care or school. Such policies have been shown to benefit families: workers spend more time with their children and spouses and participate more in family work (Bohen and Viveros-Long, 1981). Furthermore, these supports for employed parents need to be made available without perpetuating the segregation of women into low-paying, dead-end jobs.

Such policies are needed to respond to the reality that most women now work outside the home, and to give substance to society's commitment to support families, ensure the well-being of children, and guarantee equity for women in the labor market. Without such policies, women's other victories will prove to be hollow.

REFERENCES

Baca Zinn, M. 1982. "Chicano Men and Masculinity." *Journal of Ethnic Studies* 10:29–43.
Bahr, S. J. 1975. "Effects on Power and Division of Labor in the Family." In *Working Mothers*, ed. L. W. Hoffman and I. F. Nye. San Francisco: Jossey-Bass.
Bahr, S. J., and R. D. Day. 1976. "Sex Role Attitudes, Female Employment, and Marital Satisfaction." *Journal of Comparative Family Studies* IX:53–68.
Barnett, R. C., and G. K. Baruch. 1984. "Determinants of Fathers' Participation in Family Work." Working Paper No. 136, Wellesley College Center for Research on Women.
Belsky, J., and L. Steinberg. 1978. "The Effects of Day Care: A Critical Review." *Child Development* 49:929–49.

Blake, J. 1965. "Demographic Science and the Redirection of Public Policy." *Journal of Chronic Diseases* 18:1181–1200.

Blumstein, P., and P. Schwartz. 1983. *American Couples*. New York: Morrow.

Bohen, H., and A. Viveros-Long. 1981. *Balancing Jobs and Family Life: Do Flexible Work Schedules Help?* Philadelphia: Temple University Press.

Booth, A., D. Johnson, L. White, and J. Edwards. 1984. "Women, Outside Employment, and Marital Instability." *American Journal of Sociology* 90:567–83.

Bowlby, J. 1952. *Maternal Care and Mental Health*. World Health Organization Monograph Series, No. 2. New York: World Health Organization.

Cherlin, A. 1979. "Work Life and Marital Dissolution." In *Divorce and Separation*, ed. G. Levinger and O. Moles. New York: Basic Books.

"Child Care Finds a Champion in the Corporation." 1985, August 4. *New York Times*, section 3, p. 1.

Children's Defense Fund. 1982. *Employed Parents and Their Children: A Data Book*. Washington, DC: Author.

Clarke-Stewart, A. 1977. *Child Care in the Family: A Review of Research and Some Propositions for Policy*. New York: Academic Press.

_____. 1982. *Daycare*. Cambridge, MA: Harvard University Press.

Cochran, M., and L. Gunnarsson. 1985. "A Follow-up Study of Group Day Care and Family-based Childrearing Patterns." *Journal of Marriage and the Family* 47:297–309.

Coverman, S. 1983. "Gender, Domestic Labor Time, and Wage Inequality." *American Sociological Review* 48:623–37.

Cramer, J. C. 1980. "Fertility and Female Employment." *American Sociological Review* 345:167–90.

Cromwell, V. L., and R. Cromwell. 1978. "Perceived Dominance in Decision-Making and Conflict Resolution Among Anglo, Black and Chicano Couples." *Journal of Marriage and the Family* 40:749–59.

Easterbrooks, N., L. Chase-Lansdale, and W. Goldberg. 1984. "The Relationship Between Maternal Employment Status and the Stability of Attachments to Mother and Father." *Child Development* 55:1894–1901.

Easterlin, R. 1973. "Relative Economic Status and the American Fertility Swing." In *Fertility and Family Planning: A World View*, ed. E. Sheldon. Ann Arbor, MI: University of Michigan Press.

Ericksen, J. 1977. "An Analysis of the Journey to Work for Women." *Social Problems* 24:428–35.

Farel, A. M. 1980. "Effects of Preferred Maternal Roles, Maternal Employment, and Sociodemographic Status on School Adjustment and Competence." *Child Development* 51:1179–86.

Ferree, M. M. 1976. "Working Class Jobs: Housework and Paid Work as Sources of Satisfaction." *Social Problems* 23:431–41.

Gillespie, D. 1971. "Who Has the Power? The Marital Struggle." *Journal of Marriage and the Family* 33:445–58.

Glick, P., and A. J. Norton. 1977. "Marrying, Divorcing, and Living Together in the U.S. Today." *Population Bulletin* 32:3–39.

Gold, D., and D. Andres. 1978a. "Comparisons of Adolescent Children with Employed and Nonemployed Mothers." *Merrill-Palmer Quarterly* 24:243–54.

_____. 1978b. "Relations Between Maternal Employment and Development of Nursery-School Children." *Canadian Journal of Behavioral Science* 11:116–29.

Golden, M., L. Rosenbluth, M. Grossi, H. Policare, H. Freeman, and E. Brownlee. 1978.

The New York City Infant Day Care Study. New York: Medical and Health Research Association of New York City.

Gordon, N. M. 1979a. "Institutional Responses: The Federal Income Tax System." In *The Subtle Revolution*, ed. R. E. Smith. Washington, DC: The Urban Institute.

———. 1979b. "Institutional Responses: The Social Security System." In *The Subtle Revolution*, ed. R. E. Smith. Washington, DC: The Urban Institute.

Haas, L. 1982. "Wives' Commitment to Breadwinning in Sweden." Paper presented at the 10th World Congress of Sociology, Mexico City.

Hartmann, H. 1981. "The Family as the Locus of Gender, Class and Political Struggle: The Example of Housework." *Signs* 6:366–94.

Hayghe, H. 1981, February. "Husbands and Wives as Earners: An Analysis of Family Data." *Monthly Labor Review* 104:46–59.

———. 1984, December. "Working Mothers Reach Record Number in 1984." *Monthly Labor Review* 107:31–34.

Hock, E. 1980. "Working and Nonworking Mothers and Their Infants: A Comparative Study of Maternal Caregiving Characteristics and Infant Social Behavior." *Merrill-Palmer Quarterly* 26:79–101.

Hoffman, L. W. 1974. "Effects of Maternal Employment on the Child—A Review of the Research." *Developmental Psychology* 10:204–28.

———. 1979. "Maternal Employment: 1979." *American Psychologist* 10:859–65.

Hood, J. 1986. "The Provider Role: Its Meaning and Measurement." *Journal of Marriage and the Family* 48:349–59.

Houseknecht, S., and A. Macke. 1981. "Combining Marriage and Career: The Marital Adjustment of Professional Women." *Journal of Marriage and the Family* 43:651–61.

Hout, M. 1978. "The Determinants of Marital Fertility in the United States, 1968–1970: Inferences from a Dynamic Model." *Demography* 15:139–60.

Huber, J., and G. Spitze. 1980. "Considering Divorce: An Expansion of Becker's Theory of Marital Instability." *American Journal of Sociology* 86:75–89.

Jones, E.F. 1981. "The Impact of Women's Employment on Marital Fertility in the U.S., 1970–75." *Population Studies* 35:161–73.

Kamerman, S. B. 1984. "Child Care Services: A National Picture." In *Families at Work: The Jobs and the Pay*, U.S. Department of Labor, Bureau of Labor Statistics, Bulletin 2209. Washington, DC: U.S. Government Printing Office.

Kessler, R. C., and J. A. McRae. 1982. "The Effect of Wives' Employment on the Mental Health of Married Men and Women." *American Sociological Review* 47:216–27.

Lamb, M. E. 1977. "The Development of Mother-Infant and Father-Infant Attachments in the Second Year of Life." *Developmental Psychology* 13:637–48.

LaRossa, R., and M. LaRossa. 1981. *Transition to Parenthood*. Beverly Hills, CA: Sage.

Lein, L., and M. Blehar. 1979. "Working Couples as Parents." In *Families Today: A Research Sampler on Families and Children*, vol. 1, ed. E. Corfman. Washington, DC: U.S. Department of Health and Human Services.

Lichter, D. 1983. "Socioeconomic Returns to Migration Among Married Women." *Social Forces* 62:487–503.

Mason, K., L. Czajka, and S. Arber. 1976. "Change in U.S. Women's Sex Role Attitudes, 1964–1974." *American Sociological Review* 41:573–96.

Miller, J., and H. H. Garrison. 1982. "Sex Roles: The Division of Labor at Home and in the Workplace." *Annual Review of Sociology* 8:237–62.

Mirandé, A. 1977. "The Chicano Family: A Reanalysis of Conflicting Views." *Journal of Marriage and the Family* 39:747–56.

Moore, K. A., and S. L. Hofferth. 1979. "Women and Their Children." In *The Subtle Revolution*, ed. R. E. Smith. Washington, DC: The Urban Institute.

National Commission on Working Women. 1979. *National Survey on Working Women*. Washington, DC: National Manpower Institute.

Oppenheimer, V. K. 1982. *Work and the Family: A Study in Social Demography*. New York: Academic Press.

Papanek, H. 1973. "Men, Women and Work: Reflections on the Two-Person Career." *American Journal of Sociology* 78:852–72.

———. 1979. "Family Status Production: The "Work" and "Non-work" of Women." *Signs* 4:775–81.

Pleck, J. 1982. "Husbands' and Wives' Family Work, Paid Work, and Adjustment." Working Paper No. 95, Wellesley College Center for Research on Women.

Powell, B., and L. C. Steelman. 1982. "Testing an Undertested Comparison: Maternal Effects on Sons' and Daughters' Attitudes Toward Women in the Labor Force." *Journal of Marriage and the Family* 44:349–55.

Rallings, E. M., and F. I. Nye. 1979. "Wife-Mother Employment, Family and Society." In *Contemporary Theories About the Family: Research-Based Theories*, vol. 1, ed. W.R. Burr et al. New York: Free Press.

Rank, M. 1982. "Determinants of Conjugal Influence in Wives' Employment Decision Making." *Journal of Marriage and the Family* 44:591–604.

Rindfuss, R. R., L. Bumpass, and C. St. John. 1980. "Education and Fertility . . . Roles Women Occupy." *American Sociological Review* 45:431–47.

Robinson, J. P. 1977. *How Americans Use Time: A Social-Psychological Analysis*. New York: Praeger.

———. 1980. "Housework Technology and Household Work." In *Women and Household Labor*, ed. Sarah Fenstermaker Berk. Beverly Hills, CA: Sage.

Scanzoni, J. 1978. *Sex Roles, Women's Work, and Marital Conflict*. Lexington, MA: Lexington Books.

Schachter, F. F. 1981. "Toddlers with Employed Mothers." *Child Development* 52:958–64.

Schwartz, J. C. 1975, October. "Social and Emotional Effects of Day Care: A Review of Recent Research." Paper presented to the Society for Research in Child Development, University of Michigan, Ann Arbor.

Staples, R. 1981. "Race and Marital Status: An Overview." In *Black Families*, ed. H. P. McAdoo. Beverly Hills, CA: Sage.

Stephan, C. W., and J. Corder. 1985. "The Effects of Dual-Career Families on Adolescents: Sex-Role Attitudes, Work and Family Plans, and Choices of Important Others." *Journal of Marriage and the Family* 47:921–29.

Stith, S. M., and A. J. Davis. 1984. "Employed Mothers and Family Day Care Substitute Caregivers: A Comparative Analysis of Infant Care." *Child Development* 55:1340–48.

Sweet, J. A. 1973. *Women in the Labor Force*. New York: Seminar Press.

Thoits, P. 1986. "Multiple Identities: Examining Gender and Marital Status Differences in Distress." *American Sociological Review* 51:259–72.

U.S. Bureau of the Census. 1982. *Trends in Child Care Arrangements of Working Mothers* (Current Population Reports, Series P–23, No. 117). Washington, DC: U.S. Government Printing Office.

———. 1983. *Child Care Arrangements of Working Mothers: June 1982* (Current Population Reports, Series P–23, No. 129). Washington, DC: U.S. Government Printing Office.

———. 1985a. *Characteristics of the Population Below the Poverty Level* (Current Population Reports, Series P–60, No. 147). Washington, DC: U.S. Government Printing Office.

———. 1985b. *Fertility of American Women: June 1984* (Current Population Reports, Series P–20, No. 401). Washington, DC: U.S. Government Printing Office.

———. 1985c. *Marital Status and Living Arrangements: March 1984* (Current Population Reports, Series P–20, No. 399). Washington, DC: U.S. Government Printing Office.

———. 1986. *Earnings in 1983 of Married-Couple Families, by Characteristics of Husbands and Wives* (Current Population Reports, Series P–60, No. 153). Washington, DC: U.S. Government Printing Office.

U.S. Department of Labor. Bureau of Labor Statistics. 1984. *Families at Work: The Jobs and the Pay* (Bulletin 2209). Washington, DC: U.S. Government Printing Office.

Vanek, J. 1980. "Household Work, Wage Work, and Sexual Equality." In *Women and Household Labor*, ed. Sarah Fenstermaker Berk. Beverly Hills, CA: Sage.

Vickery, C. 1979. "Women's Economic Contribution to the Family." In *The Subtle Revolution*, ed. R. E. Smith. Washington, DC: The Urban Institute.

Waite, L. 1980. "Working Wives and the Family Life Cycle." *American Journal of Sociology* 86:272–94.

Waite, L. J., and R. M. Stolzenberg. 1976. "Intended Childbearing and Labor Force Participation of Young Women: Insights from Nonrecursive Models." *American Sociological Review* 41:235–52.

Wilkie, J. R. 1981. "The Trend Toward Delayed Parenthood." *Journal of Marriage and the Family* 43:583–91.

Willie, C., and S. Greenblatt. 1978. "Four Classic Studies of Power Relationships in Black Families: A Review and Look to the Future." *Journal of Marriage and the Family* 40:691–94.

Ybarra, L. 1982. "When Wives Work: The Impact on the Chicano Family." *Journal of Marriage and the Family* 44:169–78.

ARTICLE 11
The Changing Family Life Cycle

BETTY CARTER AND MONICA McGOLDRICK

The traditional American family, with the male as breadwinner and the female acting solely in a domestic capacity, is fast disappearing. In fact, families today are highly diverse. Most, however, still go through predictable developmental stages. Each phase represents a significant transition, requiring individual change and alterations in relationships. Carter and McGoldrick point out some of the typical marital and family problems associated with the various life-cycle stages.

WITHIN THE PAST GENERATION, the changes in family life cycle patterns have escalated dramatically, due especially to the lower birth rate, the longer life expectancy, the changing role of women, and the increasing divorce and remarriage rate. While it used to be that child rearing occupied adults for their entire active life span, it now occupies less than half the time span of adult life prior to old age. The meaning of the family is changing drastically, since it is no longer organized primarily around this activity.

The changing role of women in families is central in these shifting family life cycle patterns. Women have always been central to the functioning of the family. Their identities were determined primarily by their family functions as mother and wife. Their life cycle phases were linked almost exclusively to their stages in child-rearing activities. For men, on the other hand, chronological age has been seen as

"The Changing Family Life Cycle." From *The Changing Family Life Cycle: A Framework for Family Therapy*, Betty Carter and Monica McGoldrick (eds.), 2nd ed., Allyn and Bacon, Inc., Boston, 1989, pp. 10–20. Copyright © 1989 by Allyn and Bacon, Inc. Excerpted and reprinted by permission of the publisher.

a key variable in life cycle determinations. But this description no longer fits. Today women are moving through the parenting cycle more rapidly than their grandmothers; they may put off developing personal goals beyond the realm of the family, but they can no longer ignore such goals. Even women who choose a primary role of mother and home-maker must now face an "empty nest" phase that equals in length the years devoted primarily to child care. Perhaps the modern feminist movement was inevitable, as women have come to need a personal identity. Having always had primary responsibility for home, family, and child care, women necessarily began to struggle under their burdens as they came to have more options for their own lives. Given their pivotal role in the family and their difficulty in establishing concurrent functions outside the family, it is perhaps not surprising that women have been the most prone to symptom development at life cycle transitions. For men the goals of career and family are parallel. For women these goals conflict and present a severe dilemma. While women are more positive than men about the prospect of marriage, they are less content than men generally with the reality of it (Bernard, 1972). Women, not men, are likely to become depressed at the time of childbirth: this appears to have a great deal to do with the dilemma that this shift creates in their lives. Women, more than men, seek help during the child-rearing years, and as their children reach adolescence and leave home and as their spouses retire or die. And women, not men, have had primary responsibility for older relatives. Surely women's seeking help for problems has much to do with the different ways in which they are socialized, but it also reflects the special life cycle stresses on women, whose role has been to bear emotional responsibility for all family relationships.

Actually, at an ever-accelerating pace over the decades of this century, women have radically changed—and are still changing—the face of the traditional family life cycle that had existed for centuries. In fact the present generation of young women is the first in history to insist on their right to the first phase of the family life cycle—the phase in which the young adult leaves the parents' home, establishes personal life goals, and starts a career. Historically women were denied this most crucial step in adult development and were handed, instead, from their fathers to their husbands. In the next phase, that of the newly married couple, women are establishing two-career marriages, having children later, having fewer children, or choosing not to have children at all. In the "pressure cooker" phase of the family life cycle—that of families with young children—the majority of divorces take place, many of them initiated by women; in the next phase, that of families with adolescents, couples have the fastest growth in divorce rates at present. It is during this phase that the "midlife crisis" has sent unprecedented numbers of women back to school and work. Finally, when the children are gone, a married couple—if they are still married—can expect an average of 20 years alone together, the newest and longest phase of the family life cycle. In former times one spouse, usually the husband, died within two years of the marriage of the youngest child. Old age, the final phase of the family life cycle, has almost become a phase for women only, both because they outlive men and because they live longer than they used to. At ages 75–79, only 24% of women have husbands whereas 61% of men have wives.

At ages 80–84, 14% of women have husbands and 49% of men have wives. At age 85, 6% of women have husbands and 34% of men have wives (Bianchi & Spain, 1986; Glick, 1984b; U.S. Senate Special Committee Report, 1985).

The recent changes in these patterns make our task of defining the "normal" family life cycle even more difficult. An ever increasing percent of the population are living together without marrying (3% of couples at any one point in time), and a rapidly increasing number are having children without marrying. At present 6% or more of the population is homosexual. Present estimates are that 12% of young women will never marry, three times the percent for their parents' generation; 25% will never have children; 50% will end their marriages in divorce and 20% will have two divorces. Thus families often are not going through the "normal" phases at the "normal" times. If one adds to this the number of families that experience the death of a member before old age and those that have a chronically ill or handicapped or alcoholic family member, which alters their life cycle pattern, the number of "normal" families is even smaller. Another major factor affecting all families at one time or another is migration (Sluzki, 1979; McGoldrick, 1982). The break in cultural and family continuity created by migration affects family life cycle patterns for several generations. Given the enormous number of Americans who have immigrated within the past two generations, the percentage of "normal" families is diminished still further.

Thus our paradigm for middle-class American families is currently more or less mythological, though statistically accurate, relating in part to existing patterns and in part to the ideal standards of the past against which most families compare themselves. . . .

It is time . . . to give up attachments to the old ideals and to put a more positive conceptual frame around what *is*: two paycheck marriages; permanent "single-parent" households; unmarried couples and remarried couples; single-parent adoptions; and women of all ages alone. It is past time to stop thinking of transitional crises as permanent traumas, and to drop from our vocabulary words and phrases that link us to the norms and prejudices of the past: children of divorce, out-of-wedlock child, fatherless home, working mother, and the like.

THE STAGES OF THE INTACT MIDDLE-CLASS AMERICAN FAMILY LIFE CYCLE

Our classification of family life cycle stages of American middle-class families in the last quarter of the 20th century highlights our view that the central underlying process to be negotiated is the expansion, contraction, and realignment of the relationship system to support the entry, exit, and development of family members in a functional way. We offer suggestions about the process of change required of families at each transition, as well as hypotheses about the clinical fallout at each phase.

The Launching of the Single Young Adult

In outlining the stages of the family life cycle, we have departed from the traditional sociological depiction of the family life cycle as commencing at courtship or marriage and ending with the death of one spouse. Rather, considering the family to be the operative emotional unit from the cradle to the grave, we see a new family life cycle beginning at the stage of "young adults," whose completion of the primary task of coming to terms with their family of origin most profoundly influences who, when, how, and whether they will marry and how they will carry out all succeeding stages of the family life cycle. Adequate completion of this requires that the young adult separate from the family of origin without cutting off or fleeing reactively to a substitute emotional refuge. Seen in this way, the "young adult" phase is a cornerstone. It is a time to formulate personal life goals and to become a "self" before joining with another to form a new family subsystem. The more adequately young adults can differentiate themselves from the emotional program of the family of origin at this phase, the fewer . . . stressors will follow them through their new family's life cycle. This is the chance for them to sort out emotionally what they will take along from the family of origin, what they will leave behind, and what they will create for themselves. As mentioned above, of greatest significance is the fact that until the present generation this crucial phase was never considered necessary for women, who had no individual status in families. Obviously the tradition of caretaking has had profound impact on the functioning of women in families, as the current attempt to change the tradition is now also having.

We have found it useful to conceptualize life cycle transitions as requiring second-order change, or change of the system itself. Problems within each phase can often be resolved by first-order change, or a rearranging of the system, involving an incremental change. We have summarized the shifts in status required for successful accomplishment of life cycle transitions in column 2 of Table 1, which outlines the stages and tasks of the life cycle. . . . In the young adult phase, problems usually center on either young adults' or their parents' not recognizing the need for a shift to a less hierarchical form of relating, based on their now all being adults. Problems in shifting status may take the form of parents' encouraging the dependence of their young adult children, or of young adults' either remaining dependent or rebelling and breaking away in a pseudo-independent cutoff of their parents and families.

For women, problems at this stage more often focus on short-circuiting their definition of themselves in favor of finding a mate. Men more often have difficulty committing themselves in relationships, forming instead a pseudo-independent identity focused around work.

It is our view, following Bowen (1978), that cutoffs never resolve emotional relationships and that young adults who cut off their parents do so reactively and are in fact still emotionally bound to rather than independent of the family "program." The shift toward adult-to-adult status requires a mutually respectful and personal form of relating, in which young adults can appreciate parents as they are, needing neither to make them into what they are not nor to blame them for what they could not be. Neither do young adults need to comply with parental expectations and

TABLE 1 The Stages of the Family Life Cycle

Family Life Cycle Stage	Emotional Process of Transition: Key Principles	Second-Order Changes in Family Status Required to Proceed Developmentally
1. Leaving home: Single young adults	Accepting emotional and financial responsibility for self	a. Differentiation of self in relation to family of origin b. Development of intimate peer relationships c. Establishment of self re work and financial independence
2. The joining of families through marriage: The new couple	Commitment to new system	a. Formation of marital system b. Realignment of relationships with extended families and friends to include spouse
3. Families with young children	Accepting new members into the system	a. Adjusting marital system to make space for child(ren) b. Joining in childrearing, financial, and household tasks c. Realignment of relationships with extended family to include parenting and grandparenting roles
4. Families with adolescents	Increasing flexibility of family boundaries to include children's independence and grandparents' frailties	a. Shifting of parent child relationships to permit adolescent to move in and out of system b. Refocus on midlife marital and career issues c. Beginning shift toward joint caring for older generation
5. Launching children and moving on	Accepting a multitude of exits from and entries into the family system	a. Renegotiation of marital system as a dyad b. Development of adult to adult relationships between grown children and their parents c. Realignment of relationships to include in-laws and grandchildren d. Dealing with disabilities and death of parents (grandparents)
6. Families in later life	Accepting the shifting of generational roles	a. Maintaining own and/or couple functioning and interests in face of physiological decline; exploration of new familial and social role options b. Support for a more central role of middle generation c. Making room in the system for the wisdom and experience of the elderly, supporting the older generation without overfunctioning for them d. Dealing with loss of spouse, siblings, and other peers and preparation for own death. Life review and integration

wishes at their own expense. . . . Only when the generations can shift their status relations and reconnect in a new way can the family move on developmentally.

The Joining of Families Through Marriage: The Couple

The changing role of women, the frequent marriage of partners from widely different cultural backgrounds, and the increasing physical distances between family members are placing a much greater burden on couples to define their relationship for themselves than was true in traditional and precedent-bound family structures. While any two family systems are always different and have conflicting patterns and expectations, in our present culture couples are less bound by family traditions and freer than ever before to develop male-female relationships unlike those they experienced in their families of origin. Marriage tends to be misunderstood as a joining of two individuals. What it really represents is the changing of two entire systems and an overlapping to develop a third subsystem. As Jessie Bernard pointed out long ago, marriage represents such a different phenomenon for men and for women that one must really speak of "his" and "her" marriage. Women tend to anticipate marriage with enthusiasm, although statistically it has not been a healthy state for them. Men, on the other hand, approach marriage typically with much ambivalence and fear of being "ensnared," but, in fact, do better psychologically and physically in the married state than women. Marriage has traditionally meant the wife taking care of the husband and children, providing for them a haven from the outside world. The traditional role of "wife" provides low status, no personal income and a great deal of work for women and typically has not met women's needs for emotional comfort. This is part of the reason for the recent lowering rate of marriage and later age of marriage, as well as the trend for women to delay child bearing, or even to choose not to have children at all. A rise in women's status is positively correlated with marital instability (Pearson & Hendrix, 1979) and with the marital dissatisfaction of their husbands (Burke & Weir, 1976). When women used to fall automatically into the adaptive role in marriage, the likelihood of divorce was much lower. In fact it appears very difficult for two spouses to be equally successful and achieving. There is evidence that either spouse's accomplishments may correlate negatively with the same degree of achievement in the other (Ferber & Huber, 1979). Thus achieving a successful transition to couplehood in our time, when we are trying to move toward the equality of the sexes (educationally and occupationally), may be extraordinarily difficult.

Although we hypothesize that failure to renegotiate family status is the main reason for marital failure, it appears that couples are very unlikely to present with extended family problems as the stated issue. Problems reflecting the inability to shift family status are usually indicated by defective boundaries around the new subsystem. In-laws may be too intrusive and the new couple afraid to set limits, or the couple may have difficulty forming adequate connections with the extended systems, cutting themselves off in a tight twosome. At times the inability to formalize a living-together couple relationship in marriage indicates that the partners are still too enmeshed in their own families to define a new system and accept the implications of this realignment.

It is useful in such situations to help the system move to a new definition of itself . . . rather than to get lost in the details of incremental shifts they may be struggling over (sex, money, time, etc.).

Becoming Parents: Families with Young Children

The shift to this stage of the family life cycle requires that adults now move up a generation and become caretakers to the younger generation. Typical problems that occur when parents cannot make this shift are struggles with each other about taking responsibility, or refusal or inability to behave as parents to their children. Often parents find themselves unable to set limits and exert the required authority, or they lack the patience to allow their children to express themselves as they develop. Often, parents with children who present clinically at this phase are somehow not accepting the generation boundary between themselves and their children. They may complain that their four-year-old is "impossible to control." Or, on the other hand, they may expect their children to behave more like adults, reflecting too strong a generational boundary or barrier. In any case, child centered problems are typically addressed by helping parents gain a view of themselves as part of a new generational level with specific responsibilities and tasks in relation to the next level of the family.

The central struggle of this phase, however, in the modern two-paycheck (and sometimes two-career) marriage is the disposition of child-care responsibilities and household chores when both parents work full-time. The pressure of trying to find adequate child care when there is no satisfactory social provision for this family need produces serious consequences: the two full-time jobs may fall on the woman; the family may live in conflict and chaos; children may be neglected or sexually abused in inadequate child-care facilities; recreation and vacations may be sharply curtailed to pay for child care; or the woman may give up her career to stay home or work part-time. This problem is at the center of most marital conflict presented at this stage, and often leads to complaints of sexual dysfunction and depression. It is not possible to work successfully with couples at this phase without dealing with the issues of gender and the impact of sex-role functioning that is still regarded as the norm for most men and women. It is not really surprising that this is the family life cycle phase that has the highest rate of divorce. . . .

The shift at this transition for grandparents is to move to a back seat from which they can allow their children to be the central parental authorities and yet form a new type of caring relationship with their grandchildren. For many adults this is a particularly gratifying transition, which allows them to have intimacy without the responsibility that parenting requires.

The Transformation of the Family System in Adolescence

While many have broken down the stages of families with young children into different phases, in our view the shifts are incremental until adolescence, which ushers in a new era because it marks a new definition of the children within the family and of the parents' roles in relation to their children. Families with adolescents must establish qualitatively different boundaries than families with younger children, a job made more difficult in our times by the lack of built-in rituals to facilitate this transition (Quinn et al., 1985). The boundaries must now be permeable. Parents can no longer maintain complete authority. Adolescents can and do open the family to a whole array of new values as they bring friends and new ideals into the family arena. Families that become derailed at this stage may be rather closed to new values and threatened by them and they are frequently stuck in an earlier view of their children. They may try to control every aspect of their lives at a time when, developmentally, this is impossible to do successfully. Either the adolescent withdraws from the appropriate involvements for this developmental stage, or the parents become increasingly frustrated with what they perceive as their own impotence. For this phase the old Alcoholics Anonymous adage is particularly apt for parents: "May I have the ability to accept the things I cannot change, the strength to change the things I can, and the wisdom to know the difference." Flexible boundaries that allow adolescents to move in and be dependent at times when they cannot handle things alone, and to move out and experiment with increasing degrees of independence when they are ready, put special strains on all family members in their new status with one another. This is also a time when adolescents begin to establish their own independent relationships with the extended family, and it requires special adjustments between parents and grandparents to allow and foster these new patterns. . . . The central event in the marital relationship at this phase is usually the "midlife crisis" of one or both spouses, with an exploration of personal, career, and marital satisfactions and dissatisfactions. There is usually an intense renegotiation of the marriage, and sometimes a decision to divorce. A focus on parent-adolescent complaints by either the family or the therapist may mask an affair or a secretly pondered divorce, or may prevent the marital problems from coming to the surface. This is not to say that common adolescent symptoms, such as drug and alcohol abuse, teenage pregnancy, or delinquency or psychotic behavior, should not be carefully assessed and dealt with.

Families at Midlife: Launching Children and Moving On

This phase of the family life cycle is the newest and the longest, and for these reasons, it is in many ways the most problematic of all phases. Until about a generation ago, most families were occupied with raising their children for their entire active adult lives until old age. Now, because of the low birth rate and the long life span of most adults, parents launch their children almost 20 years before retirement and must then find other life activities. The difficulties of this transition can lead families to hold on to their children or can lead to parental feelings of emptiness and depression, particularly for women who have focused their main energies on their children and who now feel unprepared to face a new career in the work world. The most significant aspect of this phase is that it is marked by the greatest number of exits and entries of family members. It begins with the launching of grown children and proceeds with the entry of their spouses and children. It is a time when older parents are often becoming ill or dying. This, in conjunction with the difficulties of finding meaningful new life activities during this phase itself, may make it a particularly difficult period. Parents not only must deal with the change in their own status as they make room for the next generation and prepare to move up to grandparental positions, but also with a different type of relationship with their own parents, who may become dependent, giving them (particularly women) considerable caretaking responsibilities. This can also be a liberating time, in that finances may be easier than during the primary years of family responsibilities and there is the potential for moving into new and unexplored areas—travel, hobbies, new careers. For some families this stage is seen as a time of fruition and completion and as a second opportunity to consolidate or expand by exploring new avenues and new roles. For others it leads to disruption, a sense of emptiness and overwhelming loss, depression, and general disintegration. The phase necessitates a restructing of the marital relationship now that parenting responsibilities are no longer required. As Solomon (1973) has noted, if the solidification of the marriage has not taken place and reinvestment is not possible, the family often mobilizes itself to hold onto the last child. Where this does not happen, the couple may move toward divorce.

The Family in Later Life

. . . Few of the visions of old age we are offered in our culture provide us with positive perspectives for healthy later-life adjustment within a family or social context. Pessimistic views of later life prevail. The current myths are that most elderly people have no families; that those who do have families have little relationship with them and are usually set aside in institutions; or that all family interactions with older family members are minimal. On the contrary, the vast majority of adults over 65 do not live alone but with other family members. Over 80% live within an hour of at least one child.

Another myth about the elderly is that they are sick, senile, and feeble and can be best handled in nursing homes or hospitals. Only 4% of the elderly live in institutions (Streib, 1972), and the average age at admission is 80. There are indications that if others did not foster their dependence or ignore them as functional family members, even this degree of dependence would be less.

Among the tasks of families in later life are adjustments to retirement, which not only may create the obvious vacuum for the retiring person, but may put a special strain on a marriage that until then has been balanced in different spheres. Financial insecurity and dependence are also special difficulties, especially for family members who value managing for themselves. And, while loss of friends and relatives is a particular difficulty at this phase, the loss of a spouse is the most difficult adjustment, with its problems of reorganizing one's entire life alone after many years as a couple and of having fewer relationships to help replace the loss.

Grandparenthood can, however, offer a new lease on life, and opportunities for special close relationships without the responsibilities of parenthood.

Difficulty in making the status changes required for this phase of life are reflected in older family members' refusal to relinquish some of their power, as when a grandfather refuses to turn over the company or make plans for his succession. The inability to shift status is reflected also when older adults give up and become totally dependent on the next generation, or when the next generation does not accept their lessening powers or treats them as totally incompetent or irrelevant. The evidence suggests that men and women respond very differently to their roles in aging and this too must be carefully assessed (Hesse-Biber & Williamson, 1984).

Even when members of the older generation are quite enfeebled, there is not really a reversal of roles between one generation and the next, because parents always have a great many years of extra experience and remain models to the next generations for the phases of life ahead. Nevertheless, because older age is totally devalued in our culture, family members of the middle generation often do not know how to make the appropriate shift in relational status with their parents. . . .Helping family members recognize the status changes and the need for resolving their relationships in a new balance can help families move on developmentally.

REFERENCES

Bernard, J. (1972). *The future of marriage.* New York: Bantam.

Bianchi, S.M. & Spain, D. (1986). *American women in transition.* New York: Russel Sage.

Bowen, M., (1978). *Family therapy in clinical practice.* New York: Aronson.

Burke, R.J., & Weir, T. (1976). The relationships of wives' employment status to husband, wife and pair satisfaction. *Journal of Marriage and the Family* 38:279–287.

Ferber, M., & Huber, J. (1979). Husbands, wives and careers. *Journal of Marriage and the Family*, 41:315–325.

Glick, P. (1984b). Marriage, divorce, and living arrangements. *Journal of Family Issues* 5(1):7–26.

Hesse-Biber, S., & Williamson, J. (1984). Resource theory and power in families: Life Cycle Considerations. *Family Process* 23(2):261–278.

McGoldrick, M. (1982). Overview. In M. McGoldrick, J.K. Pearce, & J. Giordano, (Eds.), *Ethnicity and family therapy.* New York: Guilford Press.

Pearson, W., & Hendrix, L. (1979). Divorce and the status of women. *Journal of Marriage and the Family*, 41:375–386.

Quinn, W.H., Newfield, N.A., & Protinsky, H.O. (1985). Rites of passage in families with adolescents. *Family Process*, 24(1):101–112.

Sluzki, C. (1979). Migration and family conflict. *Family Process* 18(4):379–390.

Solomon, M. (1973). A developmental conceptual premise for family therapy. *Family Process* 12:179–188.

Streib, G. (1972). Older families and their troubles: Familial and social responses. *The Family Coordinator*, 21:5–19.

U.S. Senate Special Committee on Aging and American Association of Retired Persons. (1985). *Aging America.* Washington, D.C.: U.S. Government Printing Office.

ARTICLE 12
Sexuality in the Early Years of Marriage

CATHY STEIN GREENBLAT

How important is sex in marriage? How frequently do young marrieds have intercourse? What happens over time? This article suggests that most people in the early years of marriage think sex is important, but this is not reflected in the frequency of intercourse, a frequency that declines with time for most couples. Several factors, the author notes, conspire to reduce sexual intimacy: children, jobs, commuting, housework, and financial worries.

STUDIES UNIFORMLY REPORT a linear decline in frequency of marital intercourse by age. Whatever scientists such as Masters and Johnson may have told us of the "mythology" of declining biological potential, the evidence clearly suggests that the older people are, the lower their rates of marital intercourse.

These findings are to some degree puzzling. We know that the *range* of reported experiences is very great . . . yet we know very little about how rates are set in the early years of marriage or what the meaning and importance of sex is in those early years. In addition, it is unclear why the decline in frequency with age takes place. In particular, we do not know if it is really an *age-related* phenomenon or an example of a confounding of age effects and duration-of-marriage effects. That is, it may be that what is really evidenced is an outcome not of increased age but rather of longer times with the same partner. If people marry or remarry at "later

---

Cathy Stein Greenblat, "Sexuality in the Early Years of Marriage." *Journal of Marriage and the Family,* 45:289–299. Copyrighted © 1983 by the National Council on Family Relations, 3989 Central Ave. N.E., Suite #550, Minneapolis, MN 55421. Excerpted and reprinted by permission.

ages," for example, are their rates similar to those of their age peers or duration-of-marriage peers? . . . Answers to some of these questions must wait for a longitudinal study with a sample that is large and diverse in social characteristics and in which respondents have been married varying periods of time. Some suggestive insights, however, may be gained from less ambitious (and less expensive) studies which focus on one or more of these dimensions. The material presented here represents one such smaller attempt to explicate the processes of rate-setting in the early years of marriage and to suggest how and why the decline is set in motion.

METHODS

Troubled by some of the anomalies discussed above, I included some questions about sex in a larger study of emotional relationships in the early years of marriage. . . . A subcontract was let to Opinion Research Corporation of Princeton, New Jersey for the random-digit dialing (cf. Dillman, 1978) of telephone numbers in the telephone area of New Brunswick, New Jersey—an eight-community area. With this procedure, names, addresses, and telephone numbers for 97 persons (41 males and 56 females) who were married five years or less were obtained. . . . Respondents were diverse in terms of ethnicity, religion, education, income, occupation, parental status, and virtually all other major social characteristics. . . . In-depth, structured interviews with open-ended questions were conducted with 30 males and 50 females (not married to one another). They ranged from two hours to five hours in length, averaging about two hours and 45 minutes, and were tape-recorded. Most interviews were conducted in the respondents' homes when the spouses were not present; a few were done at our offices at the university.

Almost all of the respondents appeared comfortable when answering questions about frequency of intercourse in the first year and at present, although they appeared less at ease when asked about changes they would like in their sexual relationships and about difficulties or sexual problems they had experienced with their spouses. By the time the questions about sex were posed, most had spoken in great detail about a wide range of nonsexual difficulties, disappointments, and marital crises, as well as about positive experiences and sentiments. . . .

FREQUENCY AND CHANGE IN FREQUENCY

The First Year of Marriage

The most striking finding concerning the frequency of intercourse during the first year of marriage is the wide *range* of responses. The men reported monthly frequencies from 1 to 43, while the women's reports ranged from 2 to 45. This is not an instance of a few aberrant cases creating a picture belied by the bulk of the cases;

rather, the responses are widely scattered through the range. . . .No differences in first-year marital coitus rates were reported by those married different amounts of time at the moment the interview was conducted. That is, there appear to be no serious errors of inflation or deflation in the retrospective reports when these are compared to reports of those still in the first year and thus giving current rates. . . .

Rates After the First Year

In examining the intercourse rates after the first year, the striking finding is the degree of decline in frequency of intercourse. . . .Both first-year and current rates were available for 62 persons who had been married for more than one year. The current frequency was divided by the first-year frequency for each of them, yielding a percentage. This revealed that: (a) 6% reported current rates *higher* than their first-year rates; (b) 24% reported current rates *the same* as their first-year rates; (c) 32% reported rates from *60%–99%* of their first-year rates; and (d) 37% reported rates of *less than 60%* of their first-year rates (including 6% for whom the rates were less than 30% of the first-year rates). Men's and women's distributions were similar. . . .

Interpretation and Discussion

What, then, has been found, and what does it signify? It has been shown that the frequency of intercourse in the first year of marriage is highly variable, ranging from once a month for some couples to 45 times a month for others. Furthermore, there appears to be little relationship between the frequency of early marital coitus and other social characteristics of the respondent or couple. Knowing such things about a newlywed as age, education, whether he or she has been married before, religious preference, and degree of prior sexual experience does not help much to predict the frequency of marital intercourse in the first year.

In some ways this is not surprising. Indeed, while the premarital sexual world is replete with proscriptions and prescriptions, there is little to guide the newlywed couple in how to develop a sexual pattern. Few people are aware of the findings of that handful of research studies that describe what is the "typical" frequency. Bridal magazines and guides, premarital counseling, and sex manuals may endorse the idea that marital sex is important and may offer suggestions about good sexual technique and/or etiquette, but none of them say anything about how *often* to do it! Finally, few people talk with others to obtain the personal advice that on other topics is so abundant (or overabundant) as the nuptials approach (Greenblat and Cottle, 1981). In short, the marital sex domain has few cultural norms.

Furthermore, most people experience considerable difficulty *discussing* their sexual desires, preferences, and behaviors, even with those persons with whom they are most intimate, emotionally and physically (Gagnon, 1977). What these data suggest, then, is that the initial rates are set fairly idiosyncratically by each couple, through a relatively mute or, at least, indirect communication/negotiation process.

While there was not a steady, clear pattern of decline from year to year, far fewer persons, male or female, reported that they were having intercourse with their spouses more than twice a week at the present time. While approximately 75% had reported such rates for the first year, only 40% reported such current frequencies. Once more, there is considerable variation in the reports, which ranged from once a month to 20–25 times a month; again, little of the variance is explained by respondents' social characteristics. Rather, the best predictor of frequency in years 2–6 proved to be frequency in the first year.

It appears, then, that a pattern (or habit) is set in the first year. From then on almost everything—children, jobs, commuting, housework, financial worries—that happens to a couple conspires to *reduce* the degree of sexual interaction, while almost nothing leads to increasing it. Thus, some couples with children have high rates while others have low rates; but most couples who have children will experience a *decline* in the frequency of intercourse. They are not likely to know whether their initial rates or their current rates are high or low in comparison to others, nor are they likely to realize that others *without* children are also experiencing a decline in the frequency of intercourse. Instead, for them as for most persons, their own prior experience represents the only known and relevant comparison. Even if they might fall into the "high" category compared to others, they are unlikely to know this; they do know that sex between them is less frequent than it used to be. A self-explanation is required; and in this case, an explanation to an outsider also was requested, as seen in the next section. . . .

What do the respondents themselves report about the changes (or lack of changes) in coital frequency? As indicated, there were only four cases in which respondents indicated that the frequency of intercourse had *increased* from the first year. In one case the couple had decided that they now wanted to have children, and the procreative character of the act changed its meaning to the wife. Another respondent who reported an increase was very unhappy in his marriage from its start, having married someone his family approved of rather than a woman he loved. He reported intercourse once a month in the first year. Now, feeling even more trapped in the marriage, he drinks a great deal, comes home drunk a few times a week, and reports intercourse about twice a week. The other two respondents indicated they now had *fewer* external obligations and more relaxed time together; this permitted more frequent sexual relations.

Fifteen respondents reported that the current frequency was the same as that of the first year. In response to the question of why there had been no decline, four types of reasons were offered: habit; deliberate effort to maintain the frequency; the absence of negative factors in their lives which would decrease it; and finally, the positive values they see in their sexual relationship. . . . Those responses considered to represent "habit" were offered largely by those who had lived together prior to marriage. Their statements included: "It declined before we were married" (F); "it declined while we were living together" (F); "we settled into a routine" (M); and "we established a pattern before we were married, and marriage didn't change much of our lives" (M).

One respondent spoke of the couple's deliberate efforts to maintain the early rates, inspired by the sickness of a friend:

We went through a couple of months where it was lower, about once a week; and then one of Dave's friends went into shock after having her third child. Her pituitary gland collapsed and she had no desire for sex at all. It was a one in a million type thing that happened and I don't know if it's temporary or not—she's still having tests. But it's been hard on her husband because it's a once a month thing now. And that made Dave and me definitely more aware of each other and about showing our love physically.

Several people saw their constant rates as being the result of the absence of those elements that they believe lead to declines: "There's been no friction between us" (M); "we eased into marriage and things have been smooth since then" (M); "in the beginning we had so many pressures from life, and if anything they've eased up in the last few years."

The most frequent type of response dealt with positive elements of their sex lives: "It's a way of expressing your love" (F); "we have a relaxed feeling about it" (F); "he's a good man with a lot of sexual needs; he's a good lover, and I enjoy it" (F); "we enjoy each other and enjoy sex" (F); . . . and "we still have a need for each other—it's a way of expressing our love—it's fun and we enjoy it" (M).

One additional response must be noted here. Although it was the lone one of its sort from someone whose rates had stayed the same, it is strongly echoed in the interpretations of those whose rates have declined. This woman noted that their rates had stayed the same because "we didn't start as sex maniacs!" In other words, by not having "overdone it" at first, they were able to avoid the typical decline!

Far more common, of course, were responses to the question about decline. . . . Again, the responses fell into four major categories: birth-control and pregnancy-related reasons; children; work; and familiarity (including settling into a routine). A few responses did not fit into one of these categories, including three persons who reported medical problems or medication which affected sexual desire or behavior, one person whose husband's views of sex and religion became more powerful in the intervening years; and one person who reported that phone interruptions were now more common and prevented spontaneity!

The birth-control and pregnancy-related responses were given almost exclusively by the women. Two men referred to their wives' current pregnancies as reasons current rates were low, and two women reported the same thing. In general, however, the women's responses in this category were more varied: "The pill ruined my desire"; "I wasn't interested for a while after the pregnancy, and he got used to it less often"; "I had an undesired pregnancy and froze after that; first we abstained for six months, and then we did it a little—and I got pregnant *again*!"; "I was afraid of getting pregnant and couldn't discuss it"; "I had an abortion, and that lowered my trust in him in general."

Children were reported as directly responsible for declines in coital frequency be several men and women. Some just said "the kids!" assuming that was self-explanatory. Others who said "fatigue" connected that statement to child-care tasks (while others connected it to labor-force work); and some pointed to particular elements of the parental role: "Our kid hasn't slept through the night for 16 months . . . " (F); "our child doesn't take naps anymore" (M). One woman explained why the presence of children affected their sex lives as follows:

> *Our sex life is still good because for me it's the same as for him—we enjoy sex together and we can express ourselves without any inhibitions, and we're comfortable. There's no problem there. Also, it's not just that we're going to bed, you know—it's that we're making love, and that's a big thing. But we don't like to just jump into it, and we don't just do it and that's it, go to sleep—we'll watch TV and take our time saying good night after. But it's hard because with kids you have to get up a lot and you can't just relax and enjoy it . . . .*

Work responsibilities, long hours, and the resulting fatigue were also common responses. People reported that one or both had new jobs with heavy work schedules; some couples had opposite work hours (i.e., he works a night shift, and she works days); some men were working two jobs to pay for child-related or housing expenses; some people had long commutes or traveled extensively, reducing the amount of time they had together. In general, these respondents reported that their schedules were far busier now than when they were first married, with both being active at home, at work, or in a range of activities. Thus, many others, having earlier described these enterprises just said "fatigue" or "not enough energy when everything I have to do is done" or "exhaustion," clearly tying this state to work-related demands. Some were more specific, making it clear that it was work that caused the reduction, as in the case of the woman who said, "Tiredness. When he comes home he's exhausted. He just goes from 8:00 in the morning till 10:00 at night, and it's not fair for me to say 'All right, let's go!' He needs his sleep."

A few people saw this drain of energy and time as temporary. Others thought it might be longer term but were able to talk about it:

> *Exhaustion is a very big problem. I never thought it could happen. When I'm working and running my business, it is totally absorbing and it takes me a long time to decompress at night, by which time Jerry is usually sound asleep! And I guess Jerry, unlike when we first got married, he has a lot of responsibility in his position—so it's work that's taking its toll in our sex life! But we both get very tired, and that is really a very large problem for us. We mostly joke about our sex life, and when things get serious we sit down and have serious talks about it. The fatigue is a problem. The lack of frequency doesn't really trouble either of us most of the time, and when it does we just talk about it. We make a date!*

Yet others were resigned to this as a more permanent condition and were unhappy about it:

Oh, it's getting worse all the time. Maybe it's three or four times a month now instead of three or four times a week. But I guess it's natural—it's like "I'm tired, you're tired, let's forget it."

Finally, others felt the reduction wasn't really a problem. The male who reported the highest first-year rates (40–45 times a month) said his current frequency was 20–25—about half—but then explained:

It's because of my job. As far as an overall picture, as far as whether it's still satisfying or still exciting, it pretty much is. I know what you're talking about—I have friends, and these guys tell me, "Forget it—after the first year the honeymoon's over." But it's really not like that for us. It's pretty good. I'm only going by what I know, but I have friends who tell me they go home and they're tough out of luck, whereas with me, even if my wife is tired and she doesn't want to, she still will to keep me happy. It's that kind of a deal. So it's job related, or we wouldn't be too far off the first year. And she likes it better now, too, because she's gotten over her hesitation; and before I was getting the best part of the deal, but now it's improved for her. . . .

In many instances, of course, both the presence of children and heavy work schedules were simultaneous; the wife left her job, children were born, and husbands often took on additional jobs or spent longer hours. For example, one respondent who reported a drop in frequency from almost daily to about twice a week reported:

The first year it was between five and seven times a week, but Danny's working two jobs right now. Since the baby's been born and with Danny's schedule, we do it when we can. . . . So maybe once or twice a week. But it's not out of choice, but out of circumstances being what they are. She's not a very good sleeper at all—she wakes up quite frequently. I would say the baby is the main reason, and lately since Danny's been working an early morning job he's very, very tired at night. . . .

The most common responses, however, were those that referred in one way or another to familiarity and availability. Sometimes these were said with a negative cast, sometimes neutral, and sometimes positive. The negative tones were found almost exclusively in the men's responses. For example: "We're not together as much, so our moods aren't as similar, as synchronized"; "we've gotten into a routine with each other and it's not as exciting anymore"; "it's like a routine"; "that's as much as she wants and will give now"; "familiarity—the spark isn't as big." A woman gave a similar reason: "He spends a lot of nights at the lab and I have more activities, too, like dancing lessons twice a week and what not. We're just busy I guess. When you're first married it's something unique—now it's not."

One man and several women suggested more neutral reasons: "It's easier to admit if you're tired or don't feel like it" (M); "we have options now—he's home every night, so we're together a lot and, thus, we don't have that now-or-never sense" (F); "we're available to each other now—so we can say, if not tonight, tomorrow—and sometimes we do the same thing tomorrow!"(F).

Another set of persons stressed that the decline represented something *positive*. Comments included: "It's better because it's more relaxed" (F); "it's more the quality now than the quantity" (F); "not having it regularly or daily makes it more interesting" (M); "I get a good feeling just being with her in bed, so it's not as important now" (M); "there are other things that satisfy us besides sex: reading to each other, listening to music together . . . " (M). One woman explained it as follows:

Maybe it's not a necessity anymore. We have other ways of expressing our feelings, and intercourse is one of the ways. When we first got married we thought it was the only way, and now we realize it's not. And the quality of our sex life has improved. Now it gives us so much satisfaction, it's not really necessary that we have it every single night. . . .

Finally, one set of these responses must be singled out. A number of people suggested that the reason for the decline was that the first-year rates were artificial—they didn't represent what these people would "normally" do; for at that time sex had a "novelty" element, or they felt pressure to have frequent sex. They responded with such statements as "Familiarity—it's not new, it's normal now" (F); "it's not new anymore" (F); "at first it was almost like we had a quota! Now we do it because we enjoy each other " (F); "the newness the first year . . . " (F). Three respondents elaborated on this theme:

Sex has become less important now—in the beginning there was a feeling that newlyweds screw a lot; therefore, we ought to. It was great and I loved it, but now I think that other things have become more important as we found other things that are satisfying to do besides sex. [M]

The quantity is probably related to familiarity. It's really nothing new now. I think when you find new things, different things, it tends to be more interesting, and sometimes we do that. But it really depends on the time of the month. Sometimes I feel like I'm horny all the time and twice a day just wouldn't be enough. Other times I think, "Do we really have to do it now? Couldn't we do something else? I'm sure there's something more interesting around!"—that type of feeling. I think, all in all, it's okay the way it is. Sometimes I think, "Oh wouldn't it be nice to be terrifically passionate all the time like when we were first together!" but then I think "Oh my God! I don't think I'd have the energy!" I feel like I'm getting older—well, of course I am, but it's not really age, but sometimes when I think of the amount of effort and energy needed. . . !

Looking back at it now, it seems like it was kind of silly. It was, ah, I don't know, not silly, but it was just like a new toy in a way. The present figure is the more real one.

Accounts and Salience

Some of the accounts given were quite predictable: the presence of children and the demands of work are "acceptable" reasons. Both are understood to be draining of energy and time, and both reduce spontaneity. Furthermore, work and child-care are usually anti-erotic enterprises. Since couples who are similar in having heavy occupational and parental responsibilities vary so widely in the frequency of intercourse, however, neither form of "extra work" can be said to be responsible for low rates. Rather, it seems fairer to say that people establish an initial sexual pattern and few of them maintain these initial sexual commitments (or act on them) in the face of work and parental pressures. Furthermore, with serious occupational and parental responsibilities, it is extremely difficult to *increase* these sexual commitments.

As shown earlier, neither low coital rates nor high declines in frequency are limited to persons who have heavy work schedules or young children. Overall, the rates after the first year are fairly low, and declines are typical. The evidence suggests that even without additional work and parental responsibilities the frequency of intercourse will decline. While these two factors provide acceptable accounts, they are not an adequate explanation even where they are "appropriate." Rather, the findings of this study suggest that after the first year sex is not very salient to many people. To the extent that people do not *make time* for sex, do not maintain their early commitments to sex, we might well conclude that, in general, sex has decreasing importance after the first year of marriage.

There is an alternative explanation for the decline—one offered by several of the respondents: the *first-year* frequencies are not good indicators of the importance of sex. They represent a temporary aberration; they are inflated figures stemming from novelty. Thus, the current lower rates are not a source of dismay; they do not represent a decline in the importance of sex but a return to reality. In retrospect, the early rates are a source of amusement.

CONCLUSION: THE RELATIVE IMPORTANCE OF MARITAL SEX

Examining data on frequency of marital intercourse, we have seen that marital sex does not appear to be very important to many people. Despite the highly sex-oriented media and social environment, the frequency of intercourse in these couples, all in the early years of marriage, is not very high. Furthermore, first-year rates are not maintained by most persons, particularly in the face of increased work and parenthood pressures. Others discount the first-year rates as inflations, temporary phenomena.

One might ask, however, do these respondents consider sex to be important? Surely there are other measures of importance than the frequency of intercourse. Near the end of the interviews, respondents were queried about what they thought marriage *should* be like. One question in this section asked how important they thought the sexual aspect of a marital relationship is. A few respondents (15%) indicated that "it depended." The rest of the responses were almost equally split between those that could be classified as "important" and those that could be classified as "very important." Once again, these responses were not related to the frequencies.

People who describe sex as important stressed that there are *other* ways to show love or stressed that closeness, tenderness, love, companionship or affection are more important. Some said they had found that just cuddling or lying together was rewarding and they didn't require the specifically sexual interaction much of the time. These sort of sentiments are shown in the following quotations:

> *I think it's very important, but I don't think its number one or even number three on the list. On my list it would come fourth. Marriage, as far as I'm concerned, is friendship and companionship: that ranks first. Then there's consideration for one another, and then trust and then fourth I'd say your physical relationship. And those three that come before hopefully enhance what you experience in your physical relationship. [F]*

> *It's important but I think love, affection, tenderness, and all that other stuff is better to have than sex, because who's to say who's good and who's not. If you never had it with anybody else, you know? [F]*

Those who said it was "very important" stressed the special character of sex as a form of intimacy or bonding for a husband and wife, as in the following cases:

> *I think it's really important. You don't have to do it constantly all the time and hanging from the mirror. You don't have to have that kind of sex life, but you need that physical contact—it brings you closer together. Like when the baby is first born, having his mother holding him is very important; in that way I think that a husband and wife need that contact. They get out their frustrations, and it does bring them closer. [F]*

> *I think it's very important. It's a form of assurance; it's a form of communication, aside from language. You can communicate with your bodies better than verbally, I believe. It's very important. It's communicating an inner feeling of oneness, I guess, of something shared, of giving, and a willingness to be totally open with each other. [M]*

One person noted that she felt it was important because of the consequences of *poor* sexual relations:

> *I think it's very important because if you have sexual frustrations it comes out in other ways. I think it does anyway. [F]*

Several of those who said "it depends" referred to the *stage* of the relationship, suggesting it was much more important in the early stages (time undefined) of a marriage, or in the first year. Others said it depends on the particular individuals and what they want from life and from their sex life in particular.

Finally, three people pointed to a critical element—it depends on the *quality* of the sexual relationship. Even here, however, there was disagreement. One respondent suggested marital sex is important only if it is particularly *good*:

Quite. If it is not intensely pleasurable, then it's not terribly important. But if it is intensely pleasurable, the relationship and love is pleasant. Then sex is among the pleasures that has led to this and, therefore, it has some high degree of importance.

On the other hand, one man and one woman suggested sex was important in marriage only if the sex was *poor*, as in the following:

If you've got it, it's not important. If you don't, it's extremely important. It's one of those things that if you're happy with what you have, it just sort of blends in with the rest of your life; it's of no importance to you. If you don't have what you want, then it's like a toothache. It just gnaws at you.

REFERENCES

Dillman, D.A. 1978. *Mail and Telephone Surveys: Total Design Method*. New York: Wiley.
Gagnon, J.H. 1977. *Human Sexualities*. Glenview, IL: Scott Foresman.
Greenblat, C. and Cottle, T.J. 1981. *Getting Married*. New York: McGraw Hill.

ARTICLE 13
The Sexual Stages of Marriage

ELLEN FRANK AND CAROL ANDERSON

The sexual attitudes and behavior of husbands and wives, Frank and Anderson observe, vary and change in different ways over the life cycle. This article details what happens early in marriage, during the middle years, and during the later years. It points out how performance and sexual satisfaction vary by gender through these various stages.

LAST MONTH two of our good friends got married. It was an ideal type of wedding in many ways—a small knot of close friends huddled expectantly in an imposing Gothic chapel; the bride, serene and lovely in a short chiffon dress; the groom glowing; the minister—a woman—offering sage advice about love, marriage, sexuality, commitment and how all of those fit together.

At the warm, informal reception, when the last glass of champagne had been downed, conversation turned to what sort of life our two friends would have together.

Since we've recently been involved in research on marriage sexuality, we wondered what to predict about the sexual relationship of these newlyweds. What would happen to their attraction, interest and performance over the years?

If most of us predicted what would happen to a man's and a woman's sexual adjustment over the course of their marriage, we would probably say that sex would be frequent, fun, but somewhat awkward and unsatisfying in the beginning. Then

Ellen Frank and Carol Anderson, "The Sexual Stages of Marriage," in *Marriage and Family in a Changing Society* (3rd ed.) (New York: The Free Press, 1989), pp. 190–195. Reprinted by permission of the authors.

it would gradually increase in satisfaction over the years as each partner became more aware of the other's needs and more skilled at communicating their own desires. Also, interactional difficulties, such as finding the best kind of foreplay or choosing the right time for sex, would decrease as the couple got to know one another more intimately and learned to read each other's signals. We would also think that, since sex takes two, spouses' periods of dissatisfaction would probably correspond. But it turns out that things are *not* quite so "logical."

When we asked 100 relatively well-educated, middle-class couples whose marriages were "working" to describe their relationships in a number of areas, we were surprised by many of their responses about sexual adjustment.[1] Here are three findings:

- First, it is clear that men and women are indeed different. Husbands and wives appear to have different sexual attitudes and behaviors that change in different ways during the course of their marriage.
- Second, there is neither a *coordinated* increase nor decrease in the overall satisfaction of a couple over the years of their marriage.
- Third, while sex may be symbolically important throughout a marriage, performance factors are not as important as we once believed.

Now, let's look more closely at the different stages of marriage and the sexual attitudes unique to them, and see as well how the crises of adult life have their impact in the master bedroom.

EARLY MARRIAGE—YEARS OF SATISFACTION

Almost all newlyweds like sex in the beginning. Ninety-one percent of the women and 95% of the men married less than five years describe their sex lives as either satisfying or very satisfying, using words like "excitement," "pleasurable anticipation," and "confidence" when talking about their sexual relationships. No male in this early-marriage group reports difficulty with erections, and only 24% report premature ejaculation, compared with over 40% of those men married five years or longer. Despite the fact that in most of these new marriages both partners work (78% of the women have a full-time job), they have a relatively high frequency of intercourse. Approximately 18% report a frequency of four to five times a week, over a third report a frequency of two to three times a week, and another third report a frequency of once a week. The major sexual complaint of these couples revolves around the arousal and orgasmic difficulties of the women. But although women in this early period of marriage have as many difficulties becoming excited or reaching orgasm as women married longer (50% of the women in each marriage stage seem to have this problem), the newlyweds are more optimistic, believing that these problems will dissipate with time.

Another interesting finding is that among those newly married, 97% of the women and 90% of the men feel they *know* what pleases their spouses sexually. Fewer individuals in the middle and late periods of marriage express the same confidence. Either a spouse's sexuality becomes a greater enigma over time, or communication becomes more difficult as novelty lessens and other priorities compete for attention. Interestingly, recently married women are likely to report that they feel their [spouses do] not know what pleases *them* sexually. Recently married men (93%), in contrast, feel that their [spouses do] know what pleases *them*. Later on, these trends reverse: More women feel understood while more men do not.

THE MIDDLE YEARS—THE ERA OF DISTRACTIONS

Things seem to fall apart a bit in the middle years, when more husbands and wives report that they are distracted from their sexual relationship with one another. But men and women express this distraction in different ways. Men maintain an interest in sex, but are troubled by attractions to women other than their wives. Women seem to lose interest in sex itself and report that it is more difficult to relax prior to intercourse. Many studies have indicated that women may reach their "sexual peak" in their 30's in terms of their capacity to respond sexually. Yet it does not appear that their life circumstances necessarily foster their enjoyment of that capacity.

At first this seems surprising, since these women apparently have more time to devote to husband and family. Only 39% of them have a full-time job. But these middle years of marriage are also years of child-rearing. The never-ending responsibilities and interruptions of child-caring may be a much greater distraction from sexual pleasure than holding a full-time job.

Also, a woman's working outside the home may contribute to sexual stimulation. Certainly, this stimulation could be related to the increased self-esteem many women derive from a rewarding job. People who feel good about themselves invariably experience greater sexual pleasure.

These middle years are certainly a time in which nonsexual priorities are likely to be higher. The honeymoon is over: Women are devoting their time to child-rearing and men are interested in career advancement. This concentration on children and career also helps explain why, during the middle years of marriage, foreplay becomes more important for both women and men. Yet more than one-third of the men and 40% of the women in this phase of marriage report that there is too little foreplay in their sexual relationship.

Still, like their younger counterparts, individuals in this middle period of marriage are more satisfied than dissatisfied sexually. They, too, use "excitement," "pleasurable anticipation," and "confidence" in describing their sexual relationships. However, while only 9% of women in the early phase of marriage and only 4% in the late period report anxiety about their sexual lives, approximately 20% of those in the middle period report such feelings. Women in this group are also more likely than their more recently married counterparts to report fears about their own sexual inadequacy. This worry prevails among the men as well. These fears, however, apparently grow stronger still in the later period of marriage, when age may well contribute to self-doubts for those who view sexual adequacy in terms of performance.

THE LATER YEARS—A TIME FOR TENDERNESS

The couples in our study who have been married 20 years or more tend to include husbands settled professionally and wives working outside the home (79% or more). Most of their children are about to leave home or have already left. Although these couples give their marriages high marks in terms of satisfaction and compatibility, the picture they paint of their sex lives is less glowing. For instance, although the men report less trouble with premature ejaculation, they have more difficulty in both getting and maintaining erections. Intercourse becomes less frequent: Only 20% of those married 20 years or longer report a frequency of intercourse greater than once a week (as compared to 59% of those married less than 10 years).

But despite this decrease in potency *and* frequency, older males do not report decreased satisfaction with their sex lives. Apparently these men find alternate sources of pleasure in marriage or simply accept the inevitability of change with age.

Women, on the other hand, tell another story: They agree with their husbands about the decreasing frequency of intercourse but report more dissatisfaction. They more often describe themselves as less excited, less confident and more resigned. In fact, over half the women in their 40's use the word "resignation" to describe their feelings about their sexual relationship. This may be because about 50% of women in this age group still report difficulty in getting excited and in having orgasms. This, combined with their husbands' becoming less potent, may cause the couple to discontinue a sexual encounter in which erection is elusive, leaving the woman unsatisfied.

Some decline in frequency of intercourse is normal, and while those who are unhappily married may be very upset by it, happily married couples are less so. For more content couples, the issue seems to become tenderness in this later phase of marriage. It is sought by both the men and women in our study who have been married 20 years or more.

HAS THERE BEEN A SEXUAL REVOLUTION?

If the much-discussed sexual revolution really has occurred, we would expect the sexual experience of our younger couples to differ dramatically from those who are older. This does *not* seem to be the case. In fact, the young marrieds have almost as many anxieties and not that much more pleasure than those who have been together for years.

What does seem to be affected by the increased sexual freedom in our culture is *pre*marital experience. Seventy-five percent of women in their 20's had an ongoing sexual relationship with their partner before marriage. This compares with 50% of those in their 30's, only 25% of those in their 40's and 19% of those in their 50's and 60's. Eighty-two percent of the men in their 20's, 56% of those in their 30's, 35% of those in their 40's and 25% of those in their 50's and beyond reported an ongoing sexual relationship with their partner prior to marriage.

Does premarital sex contribute to sexual adjustment when one marries? Apparently not. Those groups with a higher percentage of premarital activity do not appear to have fewer sexual complaints or more sexual fulfillment in their marriages. Practice, in this case, does not make perfect.

WHAT DOES ALL THIS MEAN?

What do we conclude from our study of the sexual stages of our couples?

In an earlier study we found that it is not so much the quality of *sexual performance* that counts within a relationship, but rather the quality of *feeling* that goes with it. This appears to hold across all periods of marriage.

Also, there appears to be a kind of curvilinear sexual relationship in marriage, implying that if couples can weather the middle years, then sexual intimacy, if not performance, can improve even after years of marriage.

What advice might the couples we studied pass on to our young friends whose marriage we toasted? They can tell them that there will be some phases in which sex will be extremely important, other phases when it will not matter so much. And that all of these sexual stages are "normal" and do not mean that the total relationship they have together is not special indeed. . . .

NOTE

1. The researchers interviewed a hundred couples who consider themselves to be happily married. The couples were predominately white (95 percent), Christian (32 percent Catholic and 47 percent Protestant), and well educated (78 percent of the women and 97 percent of the men had attended college).—Ed.

ARTICLE 14
Factors in Long-Term Marriages

ROBERT H. LAUER AND JEANETTE C. LAUER

While there are numerous studies of divorce, few investigations have explored long-term intact marriages. We know far more about why marriages come apart than about what keeps them together. Lauer and Lauer find that commitment to marriage and to one's spouse is central to longlasting relationships among both happily and unhappily married couples. But for happily married people, there are additional ingredients, including the consideration of the mate as a best friend and having positive regard for that individual.

OVER A DECADE AGO, Wallis (1970, p. 53) wrote that "we have still not quite come to grips with what it is that makes marriages last, and enables them to survive." His observation is still valid. There are numerous studies that deal with marital satisfaction (see Rice, 1983, p. 172, for a summary of the factors). And there are numerous prescriptions for building a happy marriage that come out of a clinical context. That is, many of the available books that advise people how to create a lasting and happy marriage are based on inferences from work with troubled marriages.

But there have been few studies that directly examine long-term marriages to identify the factors that may account for the enduring relationship. Among those in recent years, Sporakowski and Hughston (1978) reported a study of 40 couples who had been married for 50 years. They found that the long-term couples were similar to couples who are satisfied at earlier stages of marriage—they scored high on the

Robert H. Lauer and Jeanette C. Lauer, "Factors in Long-Term Marriages." *Journal of Family Issues*, 7 (1986): 382–390. Copyright © 1986 by Sage Publications, Inc. Reprinted by permission of Sage Publications, Inc.

Locke-Wallace scale and tended to agree in their perceptions of their relationship. Roberts (1979) surveyed 55 couples who had been married an average of 55.5 years. The couples indicated that the factors that contributed to their enduring relationship included their commitment to each other, companionship, and qualities of caring. Finally, Mudd and Taubin (1982) report a longitudinal study of 59 families over a 20-year period. Such things as commitment, altruism, egalitarianism, and affection characterized the couples that were still together.

It would appear, then, that the kinds of factors that contribute to marital satisfaction at any stage of the relationship are important to stability. Indeed, Lewis and Spanier (1979) offer a theory of marital stability in which marital quality is the most important factor. "The central proposition of the theory . . . can be stated in propositional form as follows: 'The greater the marital quality, the greater the marital stability' " (Lewis and Spanier, 1979, p. 288).

Nevertheless, we know that many marriages that rank high in marital quality at some point will eventually end in divorce. Moreover, we know that a certain number of marriages that are low in marital quality will endure. The question that arises, and that is the purpose of the present study, is What factors are involved in marriages that persist, and what factors differentiate persisting and satisfying marriages from persisting, unhappy unions?

METHOD

Sample

We used a nonrandom sample of 351 couples who had been married for 15 years or more. We chose 15 years as the minimum for two reasons. First, 15 is slightly more than double the median number of years that American couples who break up are married prior to the dissolution of the marriage. It seemed reasonable therefore to consider 15 years as sufficiently long to be considered long term. Second, the 15-year minimum is sufficiently low that it allowed us to use couples who were married in the 1960s, when the divorce rate rose dramatically and attitudes toward divorce altered considerably. The range of years married for the final sample was 15 to 61, with a median of 25.

The couples were identified through personal contacts. Approximately 80% of the couples reside in Southern California, and the remainder live in the Midwest and East. They are predominantly white (93.5%), middle- and upper-middle class (34.6% have family incomes of $50,000 or more). Religiously, they are similar to the national population: 58% are Protestant, 25.6% are Roman Catholic, 8.9% are Jewish, and 7.4% claim no religious affiliation. Of the couples, 300 claimed to be happily married. In 32 of the marriages, one of the spouses rated the union as less than happy. And in 19 cases, both spouses said they were unhappy to some extent.

Instruments

As Kitson, Babri, and Roach (1985, p. 278) point out in their review of the divorce literature, varied methods yield somewhat different perspectives on the issue. But there have been a number of recent efforts to investigate the reasons for marital breakdown from the point of view of the divorced themselves. From a symbolic interactionist viewpoint (Lauer and Handel, 1983), reported reasons are an important perspective on any issue because people's definitions of situations have consequences for their behavior.

We used three different methods to get at the reported reasons for an enduring marriage. Of the couples, 305 filled out a questionnaire that included both forced-choice and open-ended questions; 24 of the couples were interviewed in depth, and the rest wrote up an account of their marriage and the reasons for its stability. For those who filled out the questionnaires, we asked each spouse to respond individually and separately. More than half of the questionnaires were filled out with the researchers or their assistants present. The others were mailed in. The questionnaire contained the Dyadic Adjustment Scale (Spanier, 1976) as the first 32 items. This scale contains one item on self-reported happiness with the marriage that was used to categorize the couples into happy, mixed, and unhappy. We added seven additional Likert-type questions on attitudes toward the spouse (appreciating spouse's achievements; viewing spouse as best friend; liking spouse as a person; and believing that spouse has grown more interesting over time) and toward marriage (viewing marriage as a long-term commitment, a sacred obligation, and an important factor in societal stability). Respondents were asked to identify which of the 39 items were most important in accounting for their long-term marriage and to explain why those items were important.

The open-ended questions asked respondents to identify any other factors that they considered important in their marriages; to draw a graph of their satisfaction with their marriage over time and explain high and low points; to discuss how they and their spouses changed over time; and to indicate how they dealt with problems and with conflict.

RESULTS

Table 1 shows the reasons given by at least 10% of each group. For happily married couples, the most frequently mentioned reason for staying together was the perceived nature of the relationship: In essence, the individuals said, "I am involved in an intimate relationship with someone I like as a person and enjoy being with." The second most frequently named reason was a belief that marriage is a long-term commitment. Among the mixed and unhappy marriages, the most frequently named reason was the belief that marriage involves a long-term commitment. Nineteen percent of those in mixed marriages and 47% of those in unhappy unions added that

TABLE 1 Ranking of Reasons for Staying Together, by Marital Satisfaction

Happy (508)	*Unhappy* (38)
Mate best friend (188)	Marriage is a long-term commitment (20)
Like mate (167)	Children (18)
Marriage is a long-term commitment (157)	Marriage sacred (8)
Marriage sacred (87)	Enduring marriages are important to a stable society (5)
Agree on aims and goals in life (77)	Mate best friend (4)
Mate more interesting now (67)	
Want to succeed (66)	
Laugh together (59)	

Mixed (64)

Happy (32)	*Unhappy* (32)
Marriage is a long-term commitment (11)	Marriage is a long-term commitment (10)
Mate best friend (8)	Children (8)
Children (6)	Like mate (5)
Like mate (5)	Marriage sacred (4)
Marriage sacred (3)	
Want relationship to succeed (3)	
Enduring marriages are important to a stable society (3)	
Shared outside interests (3)	

Note: Numbers in parentheses are the number of respondents who gave that reason.

they stayed together because of their children. The differences between the happy and the unhappy spouses in a mixed marriage were not as different as we expected.

DISCUSSION

The results of the research add to the considerable body of evidence indicating that marital quality is not the only factor in marital stability. Cuber and Harroff (1965) noted long ago that many long-term marriages become "devitalized" or are characterized by habitual conflict. The couples remain together although one or both are dissatisfied with the relationship. The unhappy respondents in our survey indicated that they stayed in the marriage primarily because of family and social values and children. The importance of children is consistent with other research that shows differential rates of divorce depending on the number of children (Thornton, 1977; Waite, Haggstrom, and Kanouse, 1985). Some of our respondents, incidentally, admitted that when the children have all left home they may separate from or divorce their spouse.

The commitment to marriage of the unhappily married arose from both religious and family values. For example, a housewife with five children said "We are Catholic, and do not believe in divorce. If all people remained married and raised their children properly there would be less crime." Both she and her husband reported themselves somewhat unhappy with the marriage. A wife in a mixed marriage (her husband said he was happy with the relationship) said that she stayed with her husband "because of children and religion as well as family pressures from my parents and brothers and sisters. No one in my family has ever been divorced, and the social stigma would be worse than staying in an unhappy relationship."

It is interesting to note that some of the unhappy individuals still consider their spouses their best friend and that they like them as persons (some also said candidly that they did not like their spouses). In a number of these cases, the unhappy spouse suggested that it was simply a matter of a relationship that was not working. "We're both likeable people," said a man married 35 years. "And I would expect to be her friend if we got divorced. But we're not a good couple. It just doesn't work." Just as two troubled individuals can have a good marriage, two healthy individuals can fail to construct a satisfying relationship. In other cases, there was a resignation based on a definition of the individual's overall situation. A woman cried as she spoke of the problems in her marriage, but said she had no friends and no family to whom she could turn: "He's all I've got." Another woman noted "We are about as happy as most other couples we know."

Those who have long-term, happy marriages report that the qualities of the spouse, the "best-friend" nature of the relationship, and their commitment to the relationship are the most important factors in their marriages. In the report of their nationwide survey, Pietropinto and Simenauer (1979, p. 150) pointed out that nearly all couples will say that they love each other, "but occasionally you find a pair who clearly indicate that there is no one on earth they could possibly be more compatible with or consider a better friend." Our happy couples stressed that point again and again. They *like* the kind of people to whom they are married. As one wife put it, "The liking was probably more important than the loving in the long run." Another wife described the qualities of her husband that were the basis of liking him: "Don is a kind and generous person. He gives me a lot of freedom to grow. He is a person I would like to know even if we weren't married. He has all the attributes I value in another person."

The open-ended questions shed some additional light on the reasons mentioned by our respondents. First, with respect to perceptions of the spouse, our respondents tended to emphasize the same valued qualities, namely, they tend to see their mates as individuals who are caring, giving, honest, and who have a sense of humor. As one husband said, "I have found in my mate a growing and exciting friendship. . . . She is a kind and compassionate person. She is genuinely concerned about people and their needs. She has an honest, forthright outlook on life."

Second, the meaning of commitment includes a willingness to endure difficult times. In charting their marital satisfaction over time, virtually all of the respondents indicated high and low points. They also pointed out that one of the requisites for an enduring and satisfying relationship is the willingness to work through the low points. "I'll tell you why my marriage has lasted," said one woman. "I'm just too damned stubborn to give up." "You can't run home to mama," said another wife, "the first time you have problems. You have to work them out." In other words, our respondents recognized the fact that being happily married does not mean a problem-free, untroubled relationship. Their dreams were not shattered by difficulties because they did not expect to escape them in the first place, and when the difficulties came they did not expect to deal with them by breaking up the relationship.

Third, the eighth item in the list of reasons given by those happily married was laughing together. As noted above, one of the valued qualities of a spouse most frequently mentioned was a sense of humor. Nearly three-fourths of the happily married respondents said that they laugh together once a day or more. None of the unhappy respondents listed humor and only one person in a mixed marriage put it down as a reason for the endurance of the marriage. The role of humor and playfulness in a marriage has recently been stressed by Betcher (1981), a clinical psychologist, who noted that playfulness helps stabilize a marriage by avoiding the extremes of alienation and suffocating intimacy.

Finally, while they did not list it as an important element in the stability of their marriage, our happily married respondents' description of their methods for handling conflict suggests that this too is an important factor. In essence, whether by nature or by learning through trial and error, they tended to take a problem-solving approach to conflict. They stressed such points as attacking the issue and not the mate, maintaining calmness and flexibility, and keeping issues in perspective.

CONCLUSIONS

Commitment to one's spouse and to marriage as an institution is one of the most important reported reasons for marital stability among both our happily and unhappily married respondents. Children also keep a marriage together even if one or both spouses are unhappy. For a long-term, happy marriage, a number of additional factors appear to be important. The two most important factors are viewing one's mate as a best friend and liking one's mate as a person. In addition, happily married couples indicate that they agree on life goals and strive to maintain humor and playfulness in their marriages. And because every long-term relationship involves times of conflict, good conflict-management skills are undoubtedly of considerable importance; the happily married couples employed such skills although they did not explicitly identify them as one of the significant factors in their marriages.

Finally, the research underscores the point that we cannot simply infer the factors in marital stability and satisfaction from studies of instability and dissatisfaction. The most common reasons given for divorce include extramarital sex, personality and financial problems, and various interpersonal problems such as lack of communication and role conflict (Kitson, Babri, and Roach, 1985, p. 269). Combining these reasons with those given by people in enduring marriages, however, gives us a more comprehensive portrait of the factors defined by people as important in maintaining or threatening a long-term, satisfying relationship.

REFERENCES

Betcher, R. William. 1981. "Intimate Play and Marital Adaptation." *Psychiatry* 44 (February): 13–33.
Cuber, John F. and Peggy B. Harroff. 1965. *The Significant Americans: A Study of Sexual Behavior Among the Affluent.* New York: Appleton-Century.
Kitson, Gay C., Karen Benson Babri, and Mary Joan Roach. 1985. "Who Divorces and Why: A Review." *Journal of Family Issues* 6 (September): 255–293.
Lauer, Robert H. and Warren H. Handel. 1983. *Social Psychology: The Theory and Application of Symbolic Interactionism.* Englewood Cliffs, NJ: Prentice-Hall.
Lewis, Robert A. and Graham B. Spanier, 1979. "Theorizing About the Quality and Stability of Marriage." Pp. 268–294 in *Contemporary Theories About the Family*, Vol. 1, edited by Wesley R. Burr et al. New York: Free Press.
Pietropinto, Anthony and Jaqueline Simenauer. 1979. *Husbands and Wives: A Nationwide Survey of Marriage.* New York: Times Books.
Rice, F. Philip. 1983. *Contemporary Marriage.* Boston: Allyn & Bacon.
Roberts, William L. 1979. "Significant Elements in the Relationship of Long-Married Couples." *International Journal of Aging and Human Development* 10(3): 265–271.
Spanier, Graham B. 1976. "Measuring Dyadic Adjustment: New Scales for Assessing the Quality of Marriage and Other Dyads." *Journal of Marriage and the Family* 38(February): 15–25.
Sporakowski, Michael J. and George A. Hughston. 1978. "Prescriptions for Happy Marriage: Adjustments and Satisfactions of Couples Married for 50 or More Years." *Family Coordinator* 27(October): 321–327.
Thornton, Arland. 1977. "Children and Marital Stability." *Journal of Marriage and the Family* 39(August): 531–540.
Waite, Linda J., Gus W. Haggstrom, and David E. Kanouse. 1985. "The Consequences of Parenthood for the Marital Stability of Young Adults." *American Sociological Review* 50(December): 850–857.
Wallis, J. H. 1970. *Marriage Observed.* London: Routledge & Kegan Paul.

ARTICLE 15
Extramarital Sex

ANTHONY P. THOMPSON

This article provides a broad overview of what we know and don't know about extramarital sex. It focuses in particular on the factors associated with extramarital involvement, including social background characteristics, marital characteristics, personal readiness, the differences between males and females, and the attitudes people have about sex outside of marriage.

THE FOLLOWING IS A REVIEW of the literature in an area that many refer to broadly as "extramarital sex" (Macklin, 1980). To the extent that it is possible to separate the topic of extramarital sex from that of other alternatives to traditional marriage, this paper focuses primarily on the former.

DEFINITIONAL ISSUES

Extramarital relationship and extramarital involvement, as terms, refer to a wide range of behaviors outside of the traditional marriage bond (Edwards, 1973; Neubeck, 1969). Edwards, for example, states that extramarital involvement has, as its referent, behaviors ranging from flirtation through to coitus. Such broad terms do not specify the exact emotional/sexual nature of the behavior, although commonly the assumption of sexual involvement is made (Sprey, 1972). To emphasize the sexual nature of contacts with persons other than a spouse, the term extramarital sex has been widely applied (e.g., Maykovich, 1976; Whitehurst, 1969). Extramarital

Anthony P. Thompson, "Extramarital Sex." *The Journal of Sex Research 19* (1983):1–22. Published by permission of *The Journal of Sex Research,* a publication of The Society for the Scientific Study of Sex.

coitus (e.g., Bell, Turner, & Rosen, 1975; Johnson, 1970b) defines the sexual contact even more precisely.

The emphasis of most of this terminology is on extramarital heterosexual intercourse. The term extramarital intercourse has been defined to include a variety of activities and to depend upon conditions such as frequency of the behavior and the number of partners (Bernard, 1974; Cuber, 1969; Sprey, 1972). The nonsexual components of extramarital relations have received minor attention (Weis & Slosnerick, 1981). There has also been little consideration of extramarital relationships which are intensely emotional (to the point of love) but sexually continent, even though such relationships have been described (Bernard, 1968; Bernard, 1974; Kessler & Clark, 1976).

Extramarital sex, by definition, focuses upon the married dyad. Thus, the terms "adultery" and "infidelity" have found usage (Green, Lee, & Lustig, 1974; Peck, 1975; Salzman, 1972; Wasserstrom, 1975). Adultery, defined as sexual relations with anyone other than one's spouse, arises from legal usage. Infidelity is distinguishable from adultery in that it represents the violation of a promise or vow. Bernard (1974) points out that, in its strictest interpretation, infidelity occurs not only with extramarital sexual relations but also whenever one or both spouses cease to love, honor, cherish, or comfort one another. Boylan's (1971) definition of infidelity also encompasses the fulfillment of extramarital emotional and psychological needs. All of this terminology refers to couples who formalize their commitment to each other through marriage. Parallel behaviors occur among those who choose to live together as cohabiting couples. The population of cohabiting couples is ever increasing (Glick & Spanier, 1980), yet the extra-behavior of this group has received little attention. Buunk (1980) has included cohabitors in his research, and Thompson (1982a) uses the term extradyadic relations to include the behavior of married and cohabiting couples.

Extramarital sex most frequently occurs without the awareness or sanction of both spouses (Hite, 1981; Hunt, 1974; Pietropinto & Simenauer, 1977; Yablonsky, 1979). Secrecy, however, is not always involved. Co-marital sex refers to any type of extramarital sex in which knowledge and consent is shared with the spouse (Knapp, 1975; Ziskin & Ziskin, 1975). Co-marital (consensual) sex is frequently a basis for alternatives to monogamous marriage, such as sexually open marriage, swinging, multilateral relations, and group marriage (e.g., Constantine & Constantine, 1971; Smith & Smith, 1973). In this context, Ramey (1975, 1976, 1977) has introduced "intimate friendships" as a term which refers to otherwise traditional friendships in which sexual intimacy is considered appropriate behavior and is, therefore, consensual. Ramey's term is quite broad, applying to married and nonmarrieds, singles, dyads, and groups.

It is evident from the above citations that there is a confusing array of terminology in the field of extramarital relations. Continued use of the popular term "affair" (Lake & Hills, 1979; Strean, 1976; Vaughan & Vaughan, 1980; Whitehurst, 1969) adds further to the definitional ambiguity. Primarily, the lack of definitional clarity limits the degree to which research findings can be compared. For example, survey investigations which have examined extramarital intercourse (Hunt, 1974), extramarital sex/affairs (Yablonsky, 1979), and cheating (Pietropinto & Simenauer, 1977) are not directly comparable. Buunk (1980) has attempted to introduce some order by proposing a continuum of extramarital erotic and sexual behavior. Buunk's behavioral continuum includes flirting, light petting, falling in love, sexual intercourse, and prolonged sexual relationship. Even some of these behaviors are nonspecific, which increases the likelihood of perceived differences in their placement along a continuum of "more serious involvement." Buunk found that respondents placed "falling in love" at different points on his behavioral and behavioral intention continua.

Conclusions: Definitional Issues

The existing definitional ambiguity and related interpretive complications demonstrate the need to apply more systematic and precise terminology to the field of extramarital relations. It is important for all terminology in this field to specify at least three conditions: first, the consensual or secretive nature of the behaviors; second, the nature of the relationship outside of which the behavior occurs; third, a description of the outside behavior. Thus, extramarital relations could be defined by applying a three-part system of descriptors. The first term would be a sanction descriptor (e.g., consensual versus non-consensual); the second term would be a relationship descriptor (e.g., extramarital, extracohabiting, extramultilateral); and the third term would describe the behavior (e.g., intercourse, petting, homosexual genital contact). It would also be important to provide a precise elaboration of the behavioral descriptor identifying important characteristics such as frequency, number of partners, and self-reported degree of emotional involvement. Under this system of terminology, "extrarelationships" (a broad term used by Nass, Libby, & Fisher, 1981) are specified according to key characteristics thereby overcoming existing definitional difficulties.

INCIDENCE SURVEYS OF EXTRAMARITAL BEHAVIORS

Interest in the phenomenon of extramarital behaviors has quite naturally lead to investigation by survey techniques. Apart from epidemiological considerations, such research has been guided by a widespread desire to know what other people are doing. This knowledge, in itself, can prove therapeutic since, "ignorance of what the other fellow does often breeds guilt, inhibitions and in some cases despair" (Athanasiou, Shaver, & Tavris, 1970, p. 52). In many ways, the studies of Kinsey, Pomeroy, Martin (1948) and Kinsey, Pomeroy, Martin, and Gebhard (1953) marked a new era in the systematic study of human sexual behavior. Since Kinsey, many recent surveys have investigated extramarital behaviors (Athanasiou et al., 1970; Bell, Turner, & Rosen, 1975; Buunk, 1980; Hite, 1981; Hunt, 1974; Johnson, 1970a, 1970b; Levin, 1975; Maykovich, 1976; Pietropinto & Simenauer, 1977;

Tavris & Sadd, 1975; Wolfe, 1980; Yablonsky, 1979). As indicated in the previous section of this review, survey respondents have not always been approached with specific questions about extramarital behavior. Consequently, across surveys the extramarital behavior referent has included cheating, affairs, extramarital sex, and extramarital sexual intercourse. Although the authors of these surveys appear to have been predominantly referring to non-consensual, extramarital sexual intercourse, it cannot be assumed that respondents always took this meaning. Table 1 summarizes the results of 12 surveys of extramarital behavior indicating sample characteristics, the behavioral referent, and incidence rates.

Incidence rates in Table 1 reveal that the extramarital behaviors studied are common in all samples. However, survey figures represent conservative estimates for several reasons. First, socially desirable responses refuting extramarital behavior are often evoked by the intimate nature of questions in this area and respondent concern regarding confidentiality and public sanction (Johnson, 1970a). Green, Lee, and Lustig (1974) report that in a study of 750 case histories only 30% initially reported unfaithfulness, but during intensive therapy an additional 30% revealed secret affairs. Secondly, most of the incidence figures of Table 1 do not reflect lifetime accumulative incidence. In other words, as young non-extramaritally involved subjects grow older there is the continuing possibility that they will become extramaritally involved. Thus, survey results underestimate accumulative incidence rates which would require laborious longitudinal methods to determine accurately. Hunt (1974) does make a lifetime accumulative extramarital intercourse estimate of 50% for males, and he projects that within the next 20 years the female figure will be more or less at the same level. Ramey's (1977) guestimates are very similar to those of Hunt, whereas Nass, Libby and Fisher (1981) make an educated guess that 50 to 65 percent of married men and 45 to 55 percent of married women engage in extramarital sex by age 40.

Another limitation of available survey data is that questionnaires have typically left no room for cohabiting, defacto partners to respond to questions regarding involvements outside of a permanent relationship. With cohabitation being viewed as an alternative to legalized marriage by large numbers of people (Clayton & Voss, 1977), it is clear that a good deal of data and information are being missed by strict adherence to the term extramarital. In a similar vein, the decidedly heterosexual bias of investigators has excluded consideration of extramarital homosexual involvements along with the responses of homosexuals living in permanent relationships.

Finally, another way of reporting incidence rates for extramarital behaviors would be to consider the married (or cohabiting) couple as the observational unit rather than the individual male or female. For example, extramarital intercourse occurs if either the male or the female, or both, are involved in extramarital intercourse. Incidence rates for this type of statistic have not been gathered, but probability estimates can be made from some of the data in Table 1. Using the figures of Anthanasiou et al. (1970), if 40% of the married males and 36% of married females are involved in extramarital intercourse, then the probability of at least one partner in a marriage having such an involvement is $[P(A \cup B) = P(A) + P(B) - P(A \cap B)]$ somewhere between 40% and 76% [$P(A \cap B)$ is not calculable from published survey

TABLE 1 Incidence of Extramarital Behaviors in Selected Studies

Study, Behavioral Referent, Sample	Married Men	Married Women
Kinsey (1948, 1953), extramarital intercourse. Approximately 3088 married men of all ages. Approximately 2000 married women up to the age of 40.	50%	26%
Anthanasiou, Shaver, and Tavris (1970), extramarital intercourse. Approximately 8000 married men and women of all ages, but three-quarters of the sample younger than 35 years.	40%	36%
Johnson (1970a, 1970b), extramarital intercourse. 100 middle-aged couples, well educated, fairly affluent, and, as a group, experienced considerable stability in their marriages.	20%	10%
Hunt (1974), extramarital intercourse. 982 males and 1044 females, 18 years of age and over, representative of the adult American population.	41%	18%
Bell, Turner, and Rosen (1975), extramarital intercourse. 2262 married women, average age of 34.5 years, average length of marriage 13.2 years, reasonably distributed by education and religious affiliation.	—	26%
Levin (1975); Tavris and Sadd (1975), extramarital sex. Married female *Redbook* readers in the United States, 40 years of age and older.	—	39%
Maykovich (1976), extramarital sexual relations. 100 white, middle-class, married American women, aged 35 to 40.	—	32%
100 middle-class married, Japanese women, aged 35 to 40.	—	27%
Pietropinto and Simenauer (1976), cheating on wife or steady girlfriend. 4066 men in a nationwide United States sample.	47%	—
Yablonsky (1979), extramarital sex/affairs. 771 married men from various United States geographic regions; average age 36 years, average marriage approximately 11 years.	47%	—
Buunk (1980)[a] 125 males and 125 females in non-random Dutch sample.	26-43%	18-32%
Wolfe (1980), extramarital sex. Married female *Cosmopolitan* readers; age 35 and older.	—	69%
Hite (1980), extramarital sex. Married men in an overall sample of 7239 men representative of the male population of the United States.	66%	—

Note. The designation "married" frequently includes presently married as well as previously married.

[a]Buunk included married and cohabiting individuals. The percents are ranges for sexual intercourse and/or prolonged sexual relationship. These categories are not mutually exclusive in Buunk's study.

results]. The value of such couple statistics is that they relate the behavior back to the dyad from which they are defined. The conceptual importance of specifying the unit out of which the extra-behavior occurs has already been made. Also, unit (e.g., married couple) statistics have added meaning for clinicians and counsellors who frequently deal with consequences of extramarital behavior at the couple level (Hunt, 1974; Thompson, 1982a).

Conclusions: Surveys of Extramarital Behaviors

It is unlikely that there is much more to be gained than currently exists from large surveys which have as their major objective the investigation of incidence rates and wholesale correlates. Such efforts are best saved until there are considerable empirical and theoretical advances in the understanding of extramarital behaviors. Even then, it is possible that validity and generalizability research will rely on smaller samples carefully chosen to maximize specific key variables. With this in mind, empirical and theoretical developments in the area of extramarital sex are examined next.

EMPIRICAL STUDIES OF EXTRAMARITAL SEX

Efforts to understand EMS have naturally focused upon many of the variables identified as potentially relevant in survey studies. The major dependent variable has been the occurrence of EMS, and statistical comparisons are typically made between EMS and non-EMS subjects. Edwards and Booth (1976) underscore the rationale of this approach, "an empirical assessment of these variables should afford us some insight into the major conceptual components of a theory concerning marital and extramarital sex, and yield a more parsimonious model of these relationships which may prove useful in future attempts at theory-building in this area" (p. 73). A variable by variable account of the EMS research presents a diffuse array of results which are difficult to integrate. Consequently, this view draws together variables with an underlying commonality into four categories: social background characteristics, characteristics of the marriage, personal readiness characteristics, and sex and gender differences. In addition to conceptual convenience, this approach brings together, on an *a priori* basis, variables which might be expected to show higher correlations within their own category than across categories. Table 2 provides a category by research study summary of recent empirical work which focuses upon EMS behavior. The table shows which studies are relevant to assessing the conceptual importance of each group of variables in a model of EMS. The rationale for each variable category and the research findings follow.

TABLE 2 Categories of EMS Variables Under Investigation in Selected Studies

	Variable Category			
Study	Social Background	Marital	Personal Readiness	Sex and Gender
Neubeck & Schletzer (1962)		*	*	
Whitehurst (1969)		*	*	
Johnson (1970 a, b)		*	*	*
Bell, Turner, & Rosen (1975)	*	*		
Edwards & Booth (1976)	*	*	*	*
Maykovich (1976)	*	*	*	
Glass & Wright (1977)		*		*
Atwater (1979)[a]	*	*	*	
Gerstel (1979)[a]		*	*	
Buunk (1980)	*	*	*	*

Note: An * indicates the variable category was considered.
[a]These studies are based on qualitative analysis.

Social Background Characteristics

A large group of variables has been investigated which encompasses social background factors. Included in this category are measures of occupational status, educational achievement, rural-urban residence, ethnicity, wife's employment, age, religion, political orientation, general liberality, and premarital sexual experience. These measures seem to be predominantly indices of socialization, and many were categorized as such by Edwards and Booth (1976). Buunk (1980) refers to some of the variables as demographic. Atwater (1979) claims that these variables frequently represent early socialization factors rather than adult socialization factors. Friends who engage in EMS, for example, serve as adult socialization agents whose influence is more immediate and specific than the role models that have influenced educational achievement and general liberality. The descriptor used here, "social background characteristics," incorporates both the early and demographic nature of variables in this category. Although some of the variables, such as occupational status, are "present-day" measures, they usually represent the culmination of earlier socialization experiences.

The research studies cited in Table 2 indicate that social background characteristics are minimally useful in accounting for EMS. Some significant correlations are found. In the Bell et al. (1975) study, political orientation and geographic location were significantly related to women's extramarital intercourse. Conservative women living in mountain and prairie regions of the United States were less likely to engage in extramarital intercourse. Edwards and Booth found age negatively related to extramarital intercourse for husbands, but not for wives. Buunk's subjects with higher education and lower levels of church attendance were more likely involved in extramarital sexual and erotic behavior. However, there has been no confluence of significant results. Of the large number of social background variables investigated, few have been found significant and, in the great majority of cases, significant correlations account for less than 10% of overall EMS variance. Considering these findings, the conclusions of Edwards and Booth seem warranted—indicators of early socialization and presumed differences in values and attitudes associated with demographics do not carry over in any marked way to influence EMS.

Characteristics of the Marriage

A second, large group of variables reflects contextual and qualitative characteristics of the marriage. For example, the dominance structure of the dyad, marriage type (Cuber & Harroff, 1965), length of marriage, divorce history, number and age of children, perceived decline in love for spouse, spousal threats to leave home, self-reported marital satisfaction/need fulfillment, romanticism, frequency of marital intercourse, quality of marital intercourse, sexual values/liberality/preferences in marriage, and space and time apart from the spouse. These variables operationalize various characteristics of marriage and have consistently been referred to as marital context or marital relationship variables. Most of the variables in this category have emerged from what might be described as a deficit model of EMS. More precisely, low rated characteristics of the marriage (deficits) have been explicitly, or implicitly, hypothesized to have a role in promoting and sustaining EMS.

Findings consistently show that characteristics of the marriage bear a significant relationship to EMS. The lower the evaluation of aspects of the marital relationship related to marital satisfaction and the lower the frequency and quality of marital intercourse the more likely the occurrence of EMS. Such characteristics of the marriage reliably account for approximately 25% of the variance of the dependent measure (EMS versus no EMS). Of those quantitative studies investigating marital variables (Table 2), only Neubeck and Schletzer (1962) found no significant relationship between marital satisfaction and the incidence of EMS. However, Neubeck and Schletzer did find a significant relationship between marital satisfaction and EMS fantasy involvement. Subjects less satisfied with their marriage fantasized more about extramarital involvements. Other marital variables such as dominance structure of the dyad, threats to leave home, and perceived decrement in love reveal significant, although weaker, correlations (Edwards & Booth, 1976). It is possible that marital satisfaction and coital satisfaction are the two major variables and that the influence of many secondary marital characteristics are incorporated in these broader evaluations.

Although, on the basis of current research, marital variables bear a strong relationship to EMS, this relationship is not always direct. Maykovich (1976) and Whitehurst (1969) both find support for considering personal alienation (or a sense of isolation and powerlessness) in conjunction with evaluations of the marital and coital relationship. In other words, the data of these authors suggest that marital and coital dissatisfaction lead to EMS only when combined with a sense of personal alienation. Edwards and Booth (1976), Glass and Wright (1977) and Johnson (1970b) find that the relationship between marital/coital dissatisfaction and EMS is neither as strong, nor as consistent, for females as it is for males. Atwater (1979) and Bell et al. (1975) point out that, among their subjects, EMS was not necessarily related to a poor marital relationship. However, the latter observations are based upon individual differences rather than overall significant correlations.

Personal Readiness Characteristics

Another group of variables seems to represent personal readiness characteristics. Whitehurst (1969) was one of the first to postulate a sequence of changes in the personal values system of the individual which could lead to EMS as an extension of normal behavior. Included in this category are personality variables (Macklin, 1980) and related opportunity factors (Gerstel, 1979) which facilitate a personal readiness for EMS. Variables which have been investigated include perceived desire of others for involvement, strength of conscience/justification for involvement, alienation/sense of isolation, perceived opportunity for involvement, knowing someone who has engaged in EMS, and perceiving sexual activity as separable from love. Some of the personal readiness variables emerge from a view of EMS that stresses positive motives. For example, personal growth and humanistic, expressive motives for EMS have been defined by measures of need for intimacy, need for relational variety, sex role egalitarianism, and emotional independence.

One personal readiness variable, alienation, has already been found to interact significantly with marital characteristic variables (see Maykovich, 1976; Whitehurst, 1969, as discussed in the previous section). Other personal readiness characteristics are equally important. Buunk's (1980) measures of need for intimacy, emotional independence, and sex role egalitarianism were stronger correlates of extramarital sexual and erotic involvement than marital need deprivation. Buunk's correlation coefficients for these personal readiness variables ranged between .39 and .70 and were generally higher for intentional involvement than actual involvement. Atwater (1979) found that the personal readiness characteristics of knowing someone who had engaged in EMS, talking to someone about EMS, and thinking about EMS for an extended period of time were important EMS precursors for women. Atwater's qualitative analysis of the motives of 40 women involved in EMS needs further empirical validation with both male and non-EMS control samples.

Perceived opportunity for EMS involvement has found support in more than one study as another significant variable to be considered (Johnson, 1970b; Maykovich, 1976; Whitehurst, 1969). However, perceived opportunity needs more rigorous scrutiny. Johnson (1970b) asked his subjects, "Have you ever been in a position where you could easily have had sexual relations with someone other than your spouse?" (p. 451). It is clear that if respondents were answering honestly, then all those having had EMS would have answered affirmatively to this question; whereas non-EMS subjects were not bound by this condition. Hence, the procedure begs the research question since the variable is predisposed to produce a positive relationship with EMS. Gerstel (1979) also makes this point. A true test of the relationship between perceived opportunity for involvement and EMS would start with a non-EMS sample at one point in time and follow them longitudinally to see if at a later time those with greater perceived opportunity were more likely to have experienced EMS. An alternative strategy for investigating personal readiness variables, such as perceived opportunity, is suggested by Buunk, who recommends the use of "intentional EMS involvement" as the most appropriate dependent variable in correlational research. Perceived opportunity, for example, is more consistent with the time frame of intentional involvement than it is with actual EMS involvement which is always a past behavior. Also, intention to perform a behavior is the immediate determinant of the behavior (Ajzen & Fishbein, 1980; Fishbein & Ajzen, 1975). A focus upon EMS intent may provide better understanding of the EMS phenomenon than attempts to predict the actual behavior.

Sex and Gender

The final variable category examines EMS differences between males and females. Survey data has revealed numerous male and female differences in EMS attitudes and behaviors. Moreover, sex specific gender role expectations continue to influence many people. However, on the basis of current research findings, it is difficult to draw uniform conclusions about such differences. Often the "males vs. females" variable has been found to qualify direct relationships between other variables. For example, Edwards and Booth (1976) found employment status to significantly influence the frequency of reported EMS among wives but not among husbands. Glass and Wright (1977) found that, for males, EMS is associated with lower marital satisfaction in young and middle length marriages, but, for females, EMS is associated with lower marital satisfaction in middle length and older marriages. Buunk (1980) found income level significantly related to extramarital experience for men but not for women. These examples typify the nature of sex differences in EMS research. There is no convergence of results, but the sex variable is consistently found to qualify and moderate other empirical relationships. As in the above citations, male/female interaction effects are observed more often when EMS is correlated with social background characteristics than with marital context and personal readiness measures. It may be that differences are more noticeable with variables that account for small proportions of EMS variance. However, this is a tentative hypothesis in need of further verification.

EMS research also should attempt to reduce differences between males and females to more specific gender related constructs. For example, Atwater (1979) suggests that role definitions of "passivity vs. aggressiveness" influenced women's ability to initiate EMS. Similar gender linked differences affected the degree to which Atwater's subjects felt guilty about their EMS, as opposed to viewing EMS as a humanistic-expressive form of self-fulfillment. Male/female differences in EMS may be largely related to such gender role expectations, and the delineation of differences in terms of component constructs seems fruitful.

Conclusion: EMS Research

On the basis of current EMS research, characteristics of the marriage and personal readiness variables bear the strongest relation to EMS. Social background characteristics do not influence EMS in any major way. Sex and gender differences are important but their relationship to EMS varies from study to study. Thus, characteristics of the marriage and personal readiness emerge as variable categories that are integral to an understanding of EMS. The correlational nature of most EMS research limits the development of explanatory models incorporating these variables. Furthermore, the interplay between characteristics of the marriage and personal readiness characteristics is not clear. For example, does marital dissatisfaction lead to expressive needs for intimacy, or does personal growth in expressive needs contribute to marital dissatisfaction? Part of the difficulty in answering these questions is that EMS has not always been defined precisely. Intercourse is the most common EMS behavioral referent. However, intercourse is only one of many behaviors that constitute the process of extramarital sexual involvement. The sequence of events that lead to personal readiness for EMS, and the related sequence of behaviors that lead to and follow intercourse should be identified and studied more closely. Research strategies need to concentrate upon how people become involved rather than why people become involved if EMS is to be understood beyond the isolation of significant correlates.

EXTRAMARITAL SEXUAL PERMISSIVENESS

Numerous studies have focused upon attitudes toward extramarital relations rather than investigating actual extramarital behavior. There has been particular interest in examining degree of approval for extramarital sex. This dimension is usually referred to as extramarital sexual permissiveness (Singh, Walton, & Williams, 1976). As such, extramarital sexual permissiveness (EMSP[1]) can be thought of as an attitude continuum ranging from repressiveness to permissiveness. In general, many people disapprove of extramarital sexual behavior (Glenn & Weaver, 1979; Klemmack & Roff, 1980). However, research interest in EMSP is based upon the proposition that the higher the degree of EMSP the more likely is extramarital sexual involvement (Athanasiou & Sarkin, 1974; Edwards, 1973). In other words, an approving attitude toward extramarital sex is viewed as an important precursor of extramarital sexual behavior. This approach has been encouraged by a social and cultural support theory of deviance (Reiss, 1967, 1970) which has found application in the study of premarital sexual permissiveness and premarital sexual behavior.

Singh, Walton, and Williams (1976) reviewed 10 selected studies that dealt with EMSP. In their own research, Singh et al. elaborated on the contexts and conditions under which extramarital sexual relations are either approved or disapproved. Their major significant findings were that the more liberal a person the greater the chances of their approval of EMSP and that the greater the approval of premarital sexual permissiveness the greater the approval of EMSP. Singh et al.

found negligible association (less than 10% of the variance) between EMSP and age, sex, race, marital status, social class, and religiosity. In a nine-culture sampling of student opinion toward marital infidelity, Christensen (1973) found that males gave more approval to extramarital coitus than females and that students with premarital sexual experience were more permissive towards infidelity than students without such experience. Bukstel, Roeder, Kilmann, Laughlin, and Sotile (1978) similarly found that premarital sexual behaviors and attitudes were the variables most strongly related to EMSP (as measured by projected extramarital involvement). Reiss, Anderson, and Sponaugle (1980) found premarital sexual permissiveness significantly correlated with EMSP. These authors also found happiness in marriage, religiosity, gender equality, political liberality, education, gender, and age as significant antecedents of EMSP. Their suggestions for future EMSP research and theory development include the investigation of new antecedent variables such as marital power and intimacy conception. Indeed, Weis and Slosnerick (1981) investigated a measure of intimacy conception they call "sex-love-marriage association," and found it to be the best predictor ($r = .40$) in a multivariate analysis of attitudes toward sexual and non-sexual extramarital involvement. Individuals who dissociated sex, love, and marriage were more likely to approve of a variety of extramarital behaviors. Weiss and Slosnerick also found premarital sexual permissiveness significantly correlated with EMSP ($r = .37$).

The EMSP research rather convincingly shows premarital sexual permissiveness as the most significant correlate of EMSP. Although this variable is a major predictor of EMSP in a statistical sense, its overall significance in relation to actual extramarital behavior may be quite minimal. Singh et al. found premarital sexual permissiveness accounted for 18% of the EMSP variance. The eight antecedent variables examined by Reiss et al. explained only 17% of the EMSP variance. Relationships of this magnitude are typical. Even if more substantial correlates/antecedents of EMSP can be established, their saliency will depend upon the directness of the EMSP—behavior link.

The EMS research examined in this review did not support a strong attitude-behavior relationship based upon social background indices of attitude. Also, Maykovich (1976) found considerable attitude-behavior discrepancy for extramarital sex in Japanese and American samples. American women were more inclined toward approval without practice, whereas Japanese women were more inclined toward practice without approval. Such attitude-behavior discrepancies are common, particularly when intense emotional/sexual matters are involved (Rodman, 1969; Safilios-Rothschild, 1969). Fishbein and Ajzen (1975) and Ajzen and Fishbein (1980) address the problems of attitude research, and their analysis is relevant to the EMSP research.

Fishbein and Ajzen propose a model of "reasoned action." Central to their model is the distinction between personal attitudes (an individual's evaluation of personally performing a behavior) and normative attitudes (an individual's perception of the social norm pertaining to the behavior). Some of the EMSP research focuses upon personal attitudes (e.g., Bukstel et al., 1978; Weis & Slosnerick, 1981); other studies assess normative attitudes (e.g., Singh et al., 1976; Reiss et al., 1980). Ajzen and Fishbein propose that behavioral intention depends upon the relative importance of personal and normative attitudes. In this way, attitude-behavior discrepancies can be explained. For example, Hartnett, Mahoney and Berstein (1977) have shown that the motivation for an extramarital affair may be crucial in the evaluation of it. Subjects in the Harnett et al. study perceived participation in an extramarital affair more favorably if love was involved than if the affair was loveless. Christensen (1973) found commitment to influence attitude. Subjects were more approving of extramarital relations for sexual release during long periods of separation than for an extramarital love-sex involvement with an unmarried person; still fewer subjects approved of an extramarital love-sex involvement with another married person. These studies help elucidate conditions under which personal attitudes toward extramarital behavior might outweigh the normative proscription.

Conclusions: Extramarital Sexual Permissiveness

EMSP research has focused upon identification of attitudinal correlates, and premarital sexual permissiveness has emerged as the major predictor in a statistical sense. There is little evidence to suggest that EMSP predicts behavior. One of the problems in this area is that personal attitude toward extramarital behavior has not been distinguished from normative attitude toward extramarital behavior. Fishbein and Ajzen's model of reasoned action emphasizes the role of both attitudinal factors in determining behavior. The model also makes sense of some of the EMSP research identifying conditions which qualify general disapproval of extramarital behavior. Thus, EMSP research needs to clearly distinguish between personal and normative attitudes, to identify the factors which underlie both attitudes, and to understand the interplay between personal and normative attitudes as they influence behavior.

SUMMARY

As is apparent from the current review, the phenomenon of extramarital sex (EMS) has received considerable research attention. The progression of investigations in this area has taken various forms, although most efforts are either (a) surveys which have examined incidence rates and wholesale correlates of extramarital sexual behaviors, (b) empirical studies which have attempted to account for EMS in terms of a variety of predictor variables and have tested such hypotheses by comparing EMS and non-EMS samples, and (c) studies which have viewed extramarital sexual permissiveness (EMSP) as a significant attitudinal precursor of EMS and have focused upon this attitudinal component. The purpose of the foregoing review has not been to resolve definitively research issues in the complex area of EMS. Rather, the primary motive for this discussion has been the organization and critical analysis of an ever growing body of research literature. In the process of presenting this review, some attempts at synthesis and suggestions for resolving research problems have been made. The following comments summarize the major points of the review.

(a) Extramarital sex (EMS) incorporates a variety of extramarital behaviors which have frequently remained undefined. Some of those investigating EMS have specified extramarital sexual intercourse. Rarely has the consensual or non-consensual nature of extramarital intercourse been a consideration. Parallel behaviors among unmarried dyads have likewise been overlooked. Definitional and topographical issues will be settled only if EMS research studies identify the specific sexual or non-sexual behaviors under investigation, the dyad or groups outside of which the behavior occurs, and the consensual or non-consensual nature of the behavior. Precision at the definitional level is crucial for an understanding of the phenomenon under investigation.

(b) Since 1970, the published results of 11 surveys of extramarital sexual behaviors attest to the current extent of these phenomena. Only half of the surveys specify intercourse in questioning their respondents about extramarital sex. Population parameters for extramarital coitus seem to be at least 50% for married men, and the figure for married women is rapidly approaching the same level. Surveys investigating extramarital behaviors always have a place as barometers of social and cultural standards. At early research stages, global survey data also help generate theoretical and empirical hypotheses. However, survey investigations will not yield further useful data until precise questions about extramarital behavior can be formulated on the basis of theoretical and empirical advances.

(c) An important objective has been to identify and to operationalize the key correlates of extramarital sex (EMS). The rationale for much of this research has been that variables which discriminate between EMS and non-EMS subjects are conceptually important for any model of EMS. Existing research of this kind strongly indicates that characteristics of the marriage and personal readiness characteristics are of prime importance in understanding EMS. These variables deserve a high priority in ongoing empirical work. Similarly, sex and gender differences are likely to qualify major empirical relationships as they have regularly in the EMS research literature. Future EMS research strategies need to concentrate upon defining and examining the sequence of events that constitute extramarital sexual involvement. In this way, key EMS variables can be fitted into a working model of EMS.

(d) Extramarital sexual permissiveness (EMSP) is an attitude continuum ranging from repressiveness to permissiveness. Attitudinal research strongly supports premarital sexual permissiveness as the most significant correlate of EMSP. Evidence in support of other predictors of EMSP is tenuous; although indices of intimacy conception, such as the ability to dissociate sex, love, and marriage, have recently proved noteworthy. A major concern in EMSP research is the nature of the attitude-behavior (EMSP-EMS) link which existing research indicates is neither direct nor simple. Ajzen and Fishbein's distinction between personal and normative attitudes provides some direction for unraveling these complexities.

NOTE

1. EMSP is a more appropriate abbreviation than ESP (Singh, Walton, & Williams, 1974) as the latter may be confused with extrasensory perception.

REFERENCES

Ajzen, I., & Fishbein, M. *Understanding attitudes and predicting social behavior*. Englewood Cliffs, New Jersey: Prentice-Hall, 1980.

Athanasiou, R., & Sarkin, R. Premarital sexual behavior and postmarital adjustment. *Archives of Sexual Behavior*, 1974, *3*, 207–225.

Athanasiou, R., Shaver, P., & Tavris, C. Sex. *Psychology Today*, July, 1970, 37–52.

Atwater, L. Getting involved: Women's transition to first extramarital sex. *Alternative Lifestyles*, 1979, *2*, 33–68.

Bell, R. R., Turner, S., & Rosen, L. A multivariate analysis of female extramarital coitus. *Journal of Marriage and the Family*, 1975, *37*, 375–384.

Bernard, J. *The sex game*. New York: Prentice-Hall, 1968.

Bernard, J. Infidelity: Some moral and social issues. In J. R. Smith & L. G. Smith (Eds.), *Beyond Monogamy*. Baltimore: Johns Hopkins University Press, 1974.

Boylan, B. R. *Infidelity*. Englewood Cliffs, N.J.: Prentice-Hall, 1971.

Bukstel, L. H., Roeder, G. D., Kilmann, P. R., Laughlin, J., & Sotile, W. M. Projected extramarital sexual involvement in unmarried college students. *Journal of Marriage and the Family*, 1978, *40*, 337–340.

Buunk, B. Extramarital sex in the Netherlands: Motivation in social and marital context. *Alternative Lifestyles*, 1980, *3*, 11–39.

Christensen, H. T. Attitude toward marital infidelity: A nine-culture sampling of university student opinion. *Journal of Comparative Family Studies*, 1973, *4*, 197–214.

Clayton, R., & Voss, H. Shacking up: Cohabitation in the 1970's. *Journal of Marriage and the Family*, 1977, *39*, 273–283.

Constantine, L., & Constantine, J. M. Sexual aspects of multilateral relations. *The Journal of Sex Research*, 1971, *7*, 204–225.

Cuber, J. F. Adultery: Reality versus stereotype. In G. Neubeck (Ed.), *Extramarital relations*. Englewood Cliffs, N.J.: Prentice-Hall, 1969.

Cuber, J. F., & Harroff, P. B. *The significant Americans: A study of sexual behavior among the affluent*. New York: Appleton-Century-Crofts, 1965.

Edwards, J. N. Extramarital involvement: Fact and theory. *The Journal of Sex Research*, 1973, *9*, 210–224.

Edwards, J. N., & Booth, A. Sexual behavior in and out of marriage: An assessment of correlates. *Journal of Marriage and the Family*, 1976, *38*, 73–81.

Fishbein, M., & Ajzen, I. *Belief, attitude, intention and behavior: An introduction to theory and research*. Reading, Massachusetts: Addison-Wesley, 1975.

Gerstel, N. R. Marital alternatives and the regulation of sex: Commuter couples as a test case. *Alternative Lifestyles*, 1979, *2*, 145–176.

Glass, S. P., & Wright, T. L. The relationship of extramarital sex, length of marriage and sex differences on marital satisfaction and romanticism: Athanasiou's data reanalyzed. *Journal of Marriage and the Family*, 1977, *39*, 691–703.

Glenn, N. D., & Weaver, N. Attitudes toward premarital, extramarital and homosexual relations in the U.S. in the 1970's. *The Journal of Sex Research*, 1979, *15*, 108–119.

Glick, P. C., & Spanier, G. B. Married and unmarried cohabitation in the United States. *Journal of Marriage and the Family*, 1980, *42*, 19–30.

Green, B. L., Lee, R. R., & Lustig, N. Conscious and unconscious factors in marital infidelity. *Medical Aspects of Human Sexuality*, September, 1974, pp. 87–91; 97–98; 104–105.

Hartnett, J., Mahoney, J., & Bernstein, A. The errant spouse: A study in person perception. *Perceptual and Motor Skills,* 1977, *45,* 747–750.

Hite, S. *The Hite report on male sexuality.* New York: Alfred A. Knopf, Inc., 1981.

Hunt, M. *Sexual behavior in the 70's,* Chicago: Playboy Press, 1974.

Johnson, R. E. Extramarital sexual intercourse: A methodological note. *Journal of Marriage and the Family,* 1970, *32,* 279–282 (a).

Johnson, R. E. Some correlates of extramarital coitus. *Journal of Marriage and the Family,* 1970, *32,* 449–456 (b).

Kessler, S., & Clark, J. Createmates. *Personnel and Guidance Journal,* 1976, *55,* 37–39.

Kinsey, A. C., Pomeroy, W. B., & Martin, C. E. *Sexual behavior in the human male.* Philadelphia: W. B. Saunders, 1948.

Kinsey, A. C., Pomeroy, W. B., Martin, C. E., & Gebbhard, P. H. *Sexual behavior in the human female.* Philadelphia: W. B. Saunders, 1953.

Klemmack, D. L., & Roff, L. L. Heterosexual alternatives to marriage: Appropriateness for older persons. *Alternative Lifestyles,* 1980, *3,* 137–148.

Knapp, J. Some non-monogamous marriage styles and related attitudes and practices of marriage counselors. *The Family Coordinator,* 1975, *24,* 505–514.

Lake, T., & Hills, A. *Affairs: The anatomy of extramarital relationships.* London: Open Books, 1979.

Levin, R. J. The *Redbook* report on premarital and extramarital sex. *Redbook,* October, 1975, pp. 38, 40, 42, 190, 192.

Macklin, E. D. Nontraditional family forms: A decade of research. *Journal of Marriage and the Family,* 1980, *42,* 905–920.

Maykovich, M. K. Attitudes versus behavior in extramarital sexual relations. *Journal of Marriage and the Family,* 1976, *38,* 693–699.

Nass, G. D., Libby, R. W., & Fisher, M. P. *Sexual choices.* Belmont, California: Wadsworth, 1981.

Neubeck, G. The dimensions of the "extra" in extramarital relations. In G. Neubeck (Ed.), *Extramarital relations.* Englewood Cliffs, N.J.: Prentice-Hall, 1969.

Neubeck, G., & Schletzer, V. M. A study of extramarital relationships. *Journal of Marriage and the Family,* 1962, *24,* 279–281.

Peck, B. B. Therapeutic handling of marital infidelity. *Journal of Family Counselling,* 1975, *3,* 52–58.

Pietropinto, A., & Simenauer, J. *Beyond the male myth.* New York: Times Books, 1977.

Ramey, J. W. Intimate groups and networks: Frequent consequences of sexually open marriage. *The Family Coordinator,* 1975, *24,* 515–530.

Ramey, J. W. *Intimate friendships.* Englewood Cliffs, N.J.: Prentice-Hall, 1976.

Ramey, J. W. Alternative lifestyles. *Society,* 1977, *14,* 43–47.

Reiss, I. L. *The social context of premarital sexual permissiveness.* New York: Holt, Rinehart and Winston, 1967.

Reiss, I. L. Premarital sex as deviant behavior: An application of current approaches to deviance. *American Sociological Review,* 1970, *35,* 78–87.

Reiss, I. L. Some observations on ideology and sexuality in America. *Journal of Marriage and the Family,* 1981, *43,* 271–283.

Reiss, I. L., Anderson, R. E., & Sponaugle, G. C. A multivariate model of the determinants of extramarital sexual permissiveness. *Journal of Marriage and the Family,* 1980, *42,* 395–411.

Rodman, H. Fidelity and forms of marriage: The consensual union in the Caribbean. In G. Neubeck (Ed.), *Extramarital relations.* Englewood Cliffs, N.J.: Prentice-Hall, 1969.

Safilios-Rothschild, C. Attitudes of Greek spouses toward marital infidelity. In G. Neubeck (Ed.), *Extramarital relations*. Englewood Cliffs, N.J.: Prentice-Hall, 1969.

Salzman, L. Female infidelity. *Medical Aspects of Human Sexuality,* February, 1972, pp. 118–120; 125; 128; 133; 136.

Singh, B. K., Walton, B. L., & Williams, J. S. Extramarital sexual permissiveness: Conditions and contingencies. *Journal of Marriage and the Family,* 1976, *38,* 701–712.

Smith, L. G., & Smith, J. R. Co-marital sex: The incorporation of extramarital sex into the marriage relationship. In J. Money & J. Zubin (Eds.), *Critical issues in contemporary sexual behavior*. Baltimore: Johns Hopkins Press, 1973.

Sprey, J. Extramarital relations. *Sexual Behavior,* 1972, *2,* 34–40.

Strean, H. S. The extramarital affair: A psychoanalytic view. *Psychoanalytic Review,* 1976, *63,* 101–113.

Tavris, C., & Sadd, S. *The Redbook report on family sexuality.* New York: Dell, 1975.

Thompson, A. P. Extramarital relations: Counselling considerations and a developmental perspective. *Australian Journal of Family Therapy,* 1982, *3,* 141–147.

Vaughan, J., & Vaughan, P. *Beyond affairs.* New York: Bantam Books, Inc., 1980.

Wasserstrom, R. *Today's moral problems.* New York: Macmillan Publishing Company, 1975.

Weis, D. L., & Slosnerick, M. Attitudes toward sexual and nonsexual extramarital involvements among a sample of college students. *Journal of Marriage and the Family,* 1981, *43,* 349–358.

Whitehurst, R. N. Extramarital sex: Alienation or extension of normal behavior. In G. Neubeck (Ed.), *Extramarital relations*. Englewood Cliffs, N.J.: Prentice-Hall, 1969.

Wolfe, L. The sexual profile of that Cosmopolitan girl. *Cosmopolitan,* September, 1980, 254–265.

Yablonsky, L. *The extra-sex factor. Why over half of America's married men play around.* New York: Times Books, 1979.

Ziskin, J., & Ziskin, M. Co-marital sex agreements: An emerging issue in sexual counseling. *The Counseling Psychologist,* 1975, *5,* 81–84.

ARTICLE 16
The Marriage License as a Hitting License

MURRAY A. STRAUS, RICHARD J. GELLES, AND SUZANNE K. STEINMETZ

What goes on behind closed doors? This study by Straus, Gelles, and Steinmetz suggests that it is not always harmonious and loving. Every year, in approximately one out of every six couples, one partner commits at least one violent act against the other, and the true incidence of violence may be double that. A large part of these acts involves pushing and slapping, but a startling number cause serious injury.

WIFE-BEATING IS FOUND in every class, at every income level. The wife of the president of a midwestern state university recently asked one of us what she could do about the beatings without putting her husband's career in danger. Japan's former Prime Minister Sato, a winner of the Nobel Peace Prize, was accused publicly by his wife of many beatings in their early married life. Ingeborg Dedichen, a former mistress of Aristotle Onassis, describes his beating her till he was forced to quit from exhaustion. "It is what every Greek husband does, it's good for the wife," he told her.

What is at the root of such violent attacks? Proverbs such as "A man's home is his castle," go a long way in giving insights into human nature and society. The home belongs to the man. It is the woman who finds herself homeless if she refuses further abuse.

The image of the "castle" implies freedom from interference from outsiders.

Murray A. Straus, Richard J. Gelles, Suzanne K. Steinmetz, "The Marriage License as a Hitting License." In *Behind Closed Doors* (Newbury Park, Calif.: Sage, 1980): pp. 31–50. Reprinted by permission of Murray A. Straus.

What goes on within the walls of the castle is shielded from prying eyes. And a modern home, like a medieval castle, can contain its own brand of torture chamber. Take the case of Carol, a Boston woman who called the police to complain that her husband had beaten her and then pushed her down the stairs. The policeman on duty answered, "Listen, lady, he pays the bills, doesn't he? What he does inside of his house is his business."

The evidence we documented . . . suggested that, aside from war and riots, physical violence occurs between family members more often than it occurs between any other individuals. At the same time we also pointed out the limitations of the data. In particular, no research up to now gives information on how often each of the different forms of family violence occurs in a representative sample of American families.

THE OVER-ALL LEVEL OF HUSBAND-WIFE VIOLENCE

Violence Rates

A first approach to getting a picture of the amount of violence between 2,143 husbands and wives in this study is to find out how many had engaged in any of the eight violent acts we asked about. For the year we studied this works out to be 16 per cent. In other words, every year about one out of every six couples in the United States commits at least one violent act against his or her partner.

If the period considered is the entire length of the marriage (rather than just the previous year), the result is 28 per cent, or between one out of four and one out of three American couples. In short, if you are married, the chances are almost one out of three that your husband or wife will hit you.

When we began our study of violence in the family, we would have considered such a rate of husbands and wives hitting each other very high. In terms of our values—and probably the values of most other Americans—it is still very high. But in terms of what we have come to expect on the basis of the pilot studies, this is a low figure. *It is very likely a substantial underestimate.*

Later in this chapter we will give the reasons for thinking it is an underestimate. But for now, let us examine the violent acts one by one. This is important if we are to get a realistic picture of the meaning of the overall rates of 28 per cent. One needs to know how much of the violence was slaps and how much was kicking and beating up. This information is given in Figure 1.

Slaps, Beatings, and Guns

Figure 1 shows that in almost seven of every hundred couples either the husband or the wife had thrown something at the other in the previous year, and about one out of six (16 per cent) had done this at some point in their marriage.

FIGURE 1 Rate at Which Violent Acts Occurred in the Previous Year and Ever in the Marriage

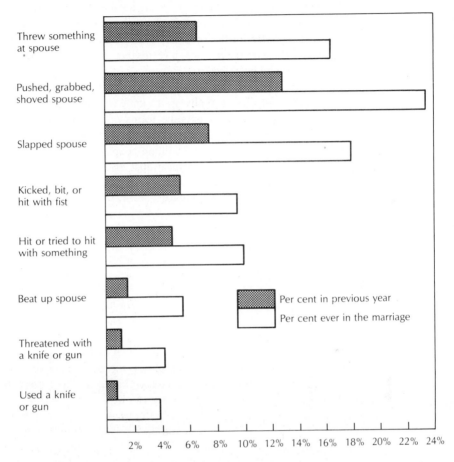

The statistics for *slapping* a spouse are about the same: 7 per cent in the previous year and 18 per cent at some time.

The figures for pushing, shoving, or grabbing during an argument are the highest of any of the eight things we asked about: 13 per cent had done this during the year, and almost one out of four at some time in the marriage.

At the other extreme, "only" one or two out of every hundred couples (1.5 per cent) experienced a *beating-up* incident in the previous year. But a "beating-up" had occurred at some time in the marriages of one out of every twenty of the couples we interviewed.

The rates for actually *using a knife or gun* on one's spouse are one out of every two hundred couples in the previous year, and almost one out of twenty-seven couples at some point in the marriage.

We were surprised that there was not a bigger difference between the rate of occurrence for "mild" violent acts (such as pushing and slapping) and the severe acts of violence (such as beating up and using a knife or gun). This is partly because the rates for the more violent acts turned out to be greater than we expected, and partly because the rates for the "ordinary" acts of husband-wife violence were less than expected. Whatever the reasons, it seems that couples are using more than slaps and shoves when violence occurs.

Indeed, the statistics on the number of husbands and wives who had ever "beaten up" their spouses or actually used a knife or gun are astoundingly high. The human meaning of these most extreme forms of violence in the family can be understood better if we translate the percentages into the total number of marriages affected. Since there were about 47 million couples living together in the United States in 1975, the rates just given mean that *over 1.7 million Americans had at some time faced a husband or wife wielding a knife or gun, and well over 2 million had been beaten up* by his or her spouse.

How Accurate Are the Statistics?

It is difficult to know how much confidence to put in these statistics because several different kinds of error are possible. First, these are estimates based on a sample. But the sample is reasonably large and was chosen by methods which should make it quite representative of the U.S. population. Comparisons with characteristics reported in the U.S. census show that this in fact is the case.

Still, there is the possibility of sampling error. So we computed what is known as the "standard error" for each of the rates in Figure 1. The largest standard error is for the over-all violence index. Even that is low: there is a 95 per cent chance that the true percentage of couples *admitting to* ever having physically assaulted one another is somewhere between 26.8 and 28.8 per cent of all couples.

"Admitting to" was italicized to highlight a much more serious and more likely source of error, that of an underestimate. The 26.8 to 28.8 per cent figure assumes that everyone "told all." But that is very unlikely. Three of the reasons are:

(1) There is one group of people who are likely to "underreport" the amount of violence. For this group a slap, push, or shove (and sometimes even more severe violence) is so much a normal part of the family that it is simply not a noteworthy or dramatic enough event always to be remembered. Such omissions are especially likely when we asked about things which had happened during the entire length of the marriage.

(2) At the opposite end of the violence continuum, there is another group who fail to admit or report such acts because of the shame involved if one is the victim, or the guilt if one is the attacker. Such violent attacks as being hit with objects, bitten, beaten up, or attacked with a knife or gun go beyond the "normal violence" of family life and are often unreported.

(3) A final reason for thinking these figures are drastic underestimates lies in the nature of the sample. We included only couples currently living together. Divorced people were asked only about their present marriage. Since "excessive" violence is often a cause of divorce, the sample probably omits many of the high violence cases.

The sample was selected in this way because a major purpose of the study was to investigate the extent to which violence is related to other aspects of husband-wife interaction. Questions were limited to current marriages because of interview time limits and limits on what people could be expected to remember.

The figures therefore could easily be twice as large as those revealed by the survey. In fact, based on the pilot studies and informal evidence (where some of the factors leading to underreporting were not present), it seems likely that *the true rate is close to 50 or 60 per cent of all couples than it is to the 28 per cent who were willing to describe violent acts to our interviewers.*

MEN AND WOMEN

Traditionally, men have been considered more aggressive and violent than women. Like other stereotypes, there is no doubt a kernel of truth to this. But it is far from the clear-cut difference which exists in the thinking of most people. This is also the case with our survey. About one out of eight husbands had carried out at least one violent act during the course of a conflict in the year covered by the survey, *and* about the same number of wives had attacked their husbands (12.1 per cent of the husbands versus 11.6 per cent of the wives).

Mutual Violence

One way of looking at this issue is to ask what percentage of the sample are couples in which the husband was the only one to use violence? What per cent were couples in which the only violence was by the wife? And in what percentage did both use violence?

The most common situation was that in which both had used violence.

One man, who found himself in the middle of a family battle, reported it this way:

> *It started sort of slowly . . . so I couldn't tell for sure if they were even serious. . . . In the beginning they'd push at each other, or shove, like kids—little kids who want to fight but they don't know how. Then, this one time, while I'm standing there not sure whether to stay or go, and them treating me like I didn't exist, she begins yelling at him like she did.*
>
> *"You're a bust, you're a failure, I want you out of here, I can always get men who'll work, good men, not scum like you." And they're pushing*

and poking with their hands, like they were dancing. She pushes him, he pushes her, only she's doing all the talking. He isn't saying a word.

Then all of a sudden, she must have triggered off the right nerve because he lets fly with a right cross that I mean stuns. I mean she goes down like a rock! And he's swearing at her, calling her every name in the book. Jesus, I didn't know what the hell to do.

What I wanted to do was call the police. But I figured, how can I call the police and add to this guy's misery, because she was pushing him. . . . She was really pushing him. I'd have done something to her myself.

Of those couples reporting any violence, 49 per cent were of situations of this type, where both were violent. For the year previous to our study, a comparison of the number of couples in which only the husband was violent with those in which only the wife was violent shows the figures to be very close: 27 per cent violent husbands and 24 per cent violent wives. So, as in the case of the violence rates, there is little difference between the husbands and wives in this study.

Specific Violent Acts

Figure 2 compares the men and women in our study on each of the eight violent acts. Again, there is an over-all similarity. But there are also some interesting differences, somewhat along the lines of the stereotype of the pot- and pan-throwing wife.

I got him good last time! He punched me in the face and I fell back on the stove.

He was walking out of the kitchen and I grabbed the frying pan and landed it square on his head. Man, he didn't know what hit him.

The number of wives who threw things at their husbands is almost twice as large as the number of husbands who threw things at their wives. The rate for kicking and hitting with an object is also higher for wives than for husbands. The husbands on the other hand had higher rates for pushing, shoving, slapping, beating up, and actually using a knife or gun.

WIFE-BEATING—AND HUSBAND-BEATING

Wife-beating has become a focus of increased public concern in the last few years. In part this reflects the national anguish over all aspects of violence, ranging from the Vietnam war to the upward surge of assault and murder. Another major element accounting for the recent public concern with wife-beating is the feminist movement.

FIGURE 2 Comparison of Husband and Wife Violence in Previous Year

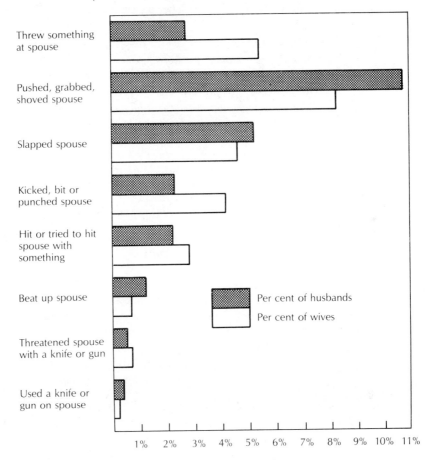

Behind that are the factors which have given rise to the rebirth of the feminist movement in the late 1960s and early 1970s.

What Is Wife-Beating?

To find out how much wife-beating there is, one must be able to define it in a way which can be objectively measured. When this is tried, it becomes clear that "wife-beating" is a political rather than a scientific term. For some people wife-beating refers only to those instances in which severe damage is inflicted. Less severe violence is not considered violence or it is laughed off. A joke one of us heard while driving across northern England in 1974 is no doubt familiar to many readers of this book. It goes like this in the BBC version: One woman asks another why she feels her husband doesn't love her any more. The answer: "He hasn't bashed me in a fortnight." Or take the following letter to Ann Landers:

> *Dear Ann Landers:*
> *Come out of the clouds, for Lord's sake, and get down here with us humans. I am sick to death of your holier-than-thou attitude toward women whose husbands give them a well deserved belt in the mouth.*
> *Don't you know that a man can be pushed to the brink and something's got to give? A crack in the teeth can be a wonderful tension-breaker. It's also a lot healthier than keeping all that anger bottled up.*
> *My husband hauls off and slugs me every few months and I don't mind. He feels better and so do I because he never hits me unless I deserve it. So why don't you come off it?*—REAL HAPPY.
>
> *Dear Real Happy:*
> *If you don't mind a crack in the teeth every few months, it's all right with me. I hope you have a good dentist.*

So a certain amount of violence in the family is "normal violence." In fact, most of the violent acts which occur in the family are so much a part of the way family members relate to each other that they are not even thought of as violence.

At what point does one exceed the bounds of "normal" family violence? When does it become "wife-beating"? To answer this question, we gathered data on a series of violent acts, ranging from a slap to using a knife or gun. This allows anyone reading this book to draw the line at whatever place seems most appropriate for his or her purpose.

Measuring Wife-Beating

This "solution," however, can also be a means of avoiding the issue. So in addition to data on each violent act, we also combined the most severe of these into what can be called a Severe Violence Index. If these are things done by the husband, then it is a "Wife-beating Index." The Wife-beating Index consists of the extent to which the husband went beyond throwing things, pushing or grabbing, and slapping and attacking his wife by kicking, biting, or punching; hitting with some object; beating her up; threatening her with a gun or knife; or using a knife or gun (the last five behaviors in Figure 1).

Why limit the Wife-beating Index to "only" the situations where the husband went beyond throwing things, pushing, grabbing, and slapping? Certainly, we don't want to imply that this reflects our conception of what is permissible violence. None of these are acceptable for relationships between husband and wife—just as they are unacceptable between student and teacher, minister and parishioner, or colleagues in a department. In short, we follow the maxim coined by John Valusek: "People are not for hitting."

What then is the basis for choosing kicking, biting, or punching; hitting with an object; beating up; threatening with a knife or gun; and using a knife or gun for the Wife-beating Index? It is simply the fact that these are all acts which carry with them a high risk of serious physical injury.

What Percentage Are Beaten?

How many husbands and wives experience the kind of attack which is serious enough to be included in the Wife-beating and Husband-beating Indexes? A remarkably large number. In fact, since our survey produced a rate of 3.8 per cent, this means that about one out of twenty-six American wives get beaten by their husbands every year, or a total of almost 1.8 million per year.

Staggering as are these figures, the real surprise lies in the statistics on husband-beating. These rates are slightly higher than those for wife-beating! Although such cases rarely come to the attention of the police or the press, they exist at all social levels. Here is an example of one we came across:

> A wealthy, elderly New York banker was finally granted a separation from his second wife, 31 years his junior, after 14 years of marriage and physical abuse. According to the presiding judge, the wife had bullied him with hysteria, screaming tantrums and vicious physical violence.
> The husband wore constant scars and bruises. His ear had once been shredded by his wife with her teeth. She had blackened his eyes, and on one occasion injured one of his eyes so badly that doctors feared it might be lost.

From 4.6 per cent of the wives in the sample admitted to or were reported by their husbands as having engaged in an act which is included in the Husband-beating Index. That works to be about one out of twenty-two wives who attacked their husbands severely enough to be included in this Husband-beating Index. That is over 2 million very violent wives. Since three other studies of this issue also found high rates of husband-beating, some revision of the traditional view about female violence seems to be needed.

How Often Do Beatings Happen?

Let us look at just the couples for which a violent incident occurred during the year previous to our study. Was it an isolated incident? If not, how often did attacks of this kind occur?

It was an isolated incident (in the sense that there was only one such attack during the year) for only about a third of the violent couples. This applies to both wife-beating and husband-beating. Almost one out of five of the violent husbands and one out of eight wives attacked their partner this severely twice during the year. Forty-seven per cent of the husbands who beat their wives did so three or more times during the year, and 53 per cent of the husband-beaters did so three or more times.

So, for about half the couples the pattern is that if there is one beating, there are likely to be others—at least three per year! In short, violence between husbands and wives, when it occurs, tends to be a recurrent feature of the marriage.

Was There Ever a Beating?

A final question about how many beatings took place can be answered by looking at what happened over the entire length of the marriage. Did something that can be called a beating *ever* happen in the marriage?

There are several reasons why even a single beating is important. First, even one such event debases human life. Second, there is the physical danger involved. Third is the fact that many, if not most, such beatings are part of a struggle for power in the family. It often takes only one such event to fix the balance of power for many years—or perhaps for a lifetime.

Physical force is the ultimate resource which most of us learn as children to rely on if all else fails and the issue is crucial. As a husband in one of the families interviewed by LaRossa said when asked why he hit his wife during an argument:

> . . . *She more or less tried to run me and I said no, and she got hysterical and said, "I could kill you!" And I got rather angry and slapped her in the face three or four times and I said, "Don't you ever say that to me again!" And we haven't had any problem since.*

Later in the interview, the husband evaluated his use of physical force as follows:

> *You don't use it until you are forced to it. At that point I felt I had to do something physical to stop the bad progression of events. I took my chances with that and it worked. In those circumstances my judgment was correct and it worked.*

Since greater size and strength give the advantage to men in such situations, the single beating may be an extremely important factor in maintaining male dominance in the family system.

We found that one out of eight couples (12.6 per cent) experienced at least one beating incident in the course of marriage. That is approximately a total of 6 million beatings. However, as high as that figure is, the actual statistics are probably higher. This is because things are forgotten over the years, and also because (as we pointed out earlier) the violent acts in question are only about the current marriage. They leave out the many marriages which ended in divorce, a large part of which were marked by beatings.

Wives and Husbands as Victims

This study shows a high rate of violence by *wives* as well as husbands. But it would be a great mistake if that fact distracted us from giving first attention to wives *as victims* as the focus of social policy. There are a number of reasons for this:

(1) The data in Figure 2 shows that husbands have higher rates of the most dangerous and injurious forms of violence (beating up and using a knife or gun).
(2) Steinmetz found that abuse by husbands does more damage. She suggests that the greater physical strength of men makes it more likely that a woman will be seriously injured when beaten up by her husband.
(3) When violent acts are committed by a husband, they are repeated more often than is the case for wives.
(4) The data do not tell us what proportion of the violent acts by wives were in self-defense or a response to blows initiated by husbands. Wolfgang's study of husband-wife homicides suggests that this is an important factor.
(5) A large number of attacks by husbands seem to occur when the wife is pregnant, thus posing a danger to the as yet unborn child. This isn't something that happens only on Tobacco Road:

> The first time Hortense Barber's husband beat her was the day she told him she was pregnant with their first child. "He knocked out my two front teeth and split open my upper lip," the 32 year old honors graduate told a New York Senate Task Force on Women. Later Mrs. Barber's husband regularly blackened her eyes during her pregnancy and threw a knife at her "in jest," cutting her knee.

(6) Women are locked into marriage to a much greater extent than men. Women are bound by many economic and social constraints, and they often have no alternative to putting up with beatings by their husbands. The situation is similar to being married to an alcoholic. Nine out of ten men leave an alcoholic wife, but only one out of ten women leave an alcoholic husband.

Most people feel that social policy should be aimed at helping those who are in the weakest position. Even though wives are also violent, they are in the weaker, more vulnerable position in respect to violence in the family. This applies to both the physical, psychological, and economic aspects of things. That is the reason we give first priority to aiding wives who are the victims of beatings by their husbands.

At the same time, the violence *by* wives uncovered in this study suggests that a fundamental solution to the problem of wife-beating has to go beyond a concern with how to control assaulting husbands. It seems that violence is built into the very structure of the society and the family system itself. . . . Wife-beating . . . is only one aspect of the general pattern of family violence, which includes parent-child violence, child-to-child violence, and wife-to-husband violence. To eliminate the particularly brutal form of violence known as wife-beating will require changes in the cultural norms and in the organization of the family and society which underlie the system of violence on which so much of American society is based.

NORMS AND MEANINGS

Just as we need to know the extent to which violent *acts* occur between husbands and wives, parents and children, and brothers and sisters, it is also important to know how family members feel about intrafamily violence. Just how strongly do they approve or disapprove of a parent slapping a child or a husband slapping a wife? To what extent do people see violence in the family as one of those undesirable but necessary parts of life?

It is hard to find out about these aspects of the way people think about family violence. One difficulty is there are contradictory rules or "norms." At one level there are norms strongly opposed to husbands and wives hitting each other. But at the same time, there also seem to be implicit but powerful norms which permit and even encourage such acts. Sometimes people are thinking of one of these principles and sometimes the other.

Another thing is that violence is often such a "taken for granted" part of life that most people don't even realize there are socially defined rules or norms about the use of violence in the family.

The existence of these implicit norms are illustrated by the case of a husband who hit his wife on several occasions. Each time he felt that it was wrong. He apologized—very genuinely. But still he did it again. The husband explained that he and his wife got so worked up in their arguments that he "lost control." In his mind, it was almost involuntary, and certainly not something he did according to a rule or norm which gives one the right to hit his wife.

But the marriage counselor in the case brought out the rules which permitted him to hit his wife. He asked the husband why, if he had "lost control," he didn't stab his wife! This possibility (and the fact that the husband did not stab his wife despite "losing control") shows that hitting the wife was not just a bubbling over of a primitive level of behavior. Although this husband did not realize it, he was following a behavioral rule or norm. It seems that the unrecognized but operating norm for this husband—and for millions of other husbands—is that it is okay to hit one's wife, but not to stab her.

There is other evidence which tends to support the idea that the marriage license is also a hitting license. For example, "Alice, you're going to the moon," was one of the standard punch lines on the old Jackie Gleason "Honeymooners" skits which delighted TV audiences during the 1950s, and which are currently enjoying a revival. Jokes, plays, such as those of George Bernard Shaw, and experiments which show that people take less severe actions if they think the man attacking a woman is her husband are other signs.

It has been suggested that one of the reasons neighbors who saw the attack didn't come to the aid of Kitty Genovese in the 1964 Queens murder case was because they thought it was a man beating his wife!

Or take the following incident:

> Roy Butler came over to help his bride-to-be in preparations for their wedding, which is why the wedding is off.
>
> Roy, 24, made the mistake of going to a stag party first.
>
> On the way to fiancée Anthea Higson's home, he dropped the wedding cake in the front garden.
>
> In the shouting match that followed, he dropped Anthea's mother with a right cross to the jaw.
>
> Anthea, 21, promptly dropped Roy. She said the wedding was off and she never wanted to see him again.
>
> *"If he had hit me instead of my mother, I probably would have married him all the same,"* [italics added] she said yesterday after a court fined Butler $135 for assaulting Mrs. Brenda Higson.
>
> "But I'm not having any man hitting my mum," Anthea said.

Interesting as are these examples, none of them provide the kind of systematic and broadly representative evidence which is needed. That is what we attempted to get in this study.

Measuring the Meaning of Violence

To find out how our sample felt about violence in the family, we used the "semantic differential" method. For husband-wife violence, we asked subjects to rate the phrase "Couples slapping each other." They were asked to make three ratings: unnecessary . . . necessary; not normal . . . normal; and good . . . bad.

How many of the husbands and wives rated "Couples slapping each other" as "necessary," "normal," or "good"? Over all just under one out of four wives and one out of three husbands (31.3 and 24.6 per cent) saw this type of physical force between spouses as at least somewhat necessary, normal, or good.

These statistics are remarkably close to those from a national sample studied by the U.S. Violence Commission. The Violence Commission found that about one quarter of the persons interviewed said they could think of circumstances in which it would be all right for a husband to hit his wife or a wife to hit her husband. This is slightly lower than the percentages for our sample. But if the Violence Commission survey data had been analyzed in the way we examined our data, the results could well have been almost identical.

The separate ratings for violence being necessary, normal, or good are interesting in the contrast they provide with each other and in the way men and women think about violence. On the other hand, there are big differences in the percentage of husbands as compared to wives who could see some situations in which it is necessary for a husband or wife to slap each other (see Figure 3). There is also a larger percentage of husbands who could see some situations in which this would

FIGURE 3 Per Cent of Husbands and Wives Who Rated "A Couple Slapping Each Other" as at Least Somewhat Necessary, Good, or Normal

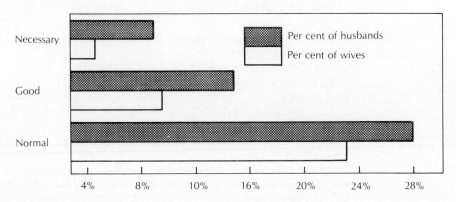

not be a bad thing to do. In fact, for both these ratings, twice as many husbands as wives felt this way.

On the other hand, the percentages for the not normal . . . normal rating are particularly interesting because they are larger and because there is little difference between men and women. The figures in the chart show that a large proportion of American husbands and wives see violence as a normal part of married life. It may not be good, and it may not be necessary, but it is something which is going to happen under normal circumstances. The marriage license is a hitting license for a large part of the population, and probably for a much greater part than could bring themselves to rate it as "normal" in the context of this survey.

SUMMING UP

We are reasonably confident that the couples in the study are representative of American couples in general. But we suspect that not everyone told us about all the violence in his or her family. In fact, the pilot studies and informal evidence suggest that the true figures may be double those based on what people were willing to admit in a mass survey such as this. If this is the case, then about a third of all American couples experience a violent incident every year, and about two thirds have experienced such an incident at least once in the marriage.

Of course, a large part of these "violent incidents" are pushes and slaps, but far from all of them. A large portion are also actions which could cause serious injury or even death. We know from the fact that so many murderers and their victims are husband and wife that this is not just speculation. For the couples in this sample, in fact, almost one out of every twenty-five had faced an angry partner with a knife or gun in hand.

If the "dangerous violence" is not limited solely to use of a knife or gun, and includes everything *more serious* than pushing, grabbing, shoving, slapping, and throwing things, the rate is three times as high. In short, almost one out of every eight couples admitted that at some point in the marriage there had been an act of violence which could cause serious injury.

Another way of grasping this is to compare the rates of wife-beating and husband-beating in our survey with assaults which are reported in official statistics. The Uniform Crime Reports on "aggravated assault" are given in rate per 100,000. But the rates in this chapter are percentages, i.e., rates per 100, not per 100,000.

We can translate the rates for this survey into rates per 100,000 per year. They are 3,800 per 100,000 for assaults on wives, 4,600 for assaults on husbands, and a combined rate of 6,100 per 100,000 couples. Compare this with the roughly 190 per 100,000 aggravated assaults of all kinds known to the police each year.

Of course, many crimes are not reported to the police. So there have been surveys asking people if they were the victims of a crime. The rate of aggravated assault coming out of the National Crime Panel survey is very high: 2,597 per 100,000. But our rate for wife-beating and husband-beating of 6,100 per 100,000 is almost two and a half times higher. Also, since the Uniform Crime Reports, and especially the National Crime Panel data, include many within-family assaults, the amount by which husband-wife assault exceeds any other type of assault is much greater than these rates suggest.

Leaving aside the fact that our figures on husband-wife violence are probably underestimates, and even leaving aside the psychological damage that such violence can produce, just the danger to physical health implied by these rates is staggering. If any other crime of risk to physical well-being involved almost 2 million wives and 2 million husbands per year, plus a much larger amount at some point in the marriage, a national emergency would probably be declared.

ARTICLE 17
The Family in an Aging Society

MATILDA WHITE RILEY

Due to unprecedented increases in longevity, kin linkages are potentially extended across the generations. Kin ties, however, no longer carry with them strict obligations. The ties have become more voluntary, creating what Riley refers to as a "matrix of latent relationships." How the linkages are actually created and recreated have important consequences for the shape and dynamics of contemporary families.

OVER TWO-THIRDS of the total improvement in longevity from prehistoric times until the present has taken place in the brief period since 1900 (Preston, 1976). In the United States, life expectancy at birth has risen from less than 50 in 1900 to well over 70 today. Whereas at the start of the century most deaths occurred in infancy and young adulthood, today the vast majority of deaths are postponed to old age. Indeed we are approaching the "squared" mortality curve, in which relatively few die before the end of the full life span. For the first time in all history, we are living in a society in which most people live to be old.[1]

Though many facts of life extension are familiar, their meanings for the personal lives of family members are elusive. Just how is increasing longevity transforming the kinship structure? Most problematic of all, how is the impact of longevity affecting those sorely needed close relationships that provide emotional support and socialization for family members (see Parsons and Bales, 1955)? To answer such questions, I must agree with other scholars in the conclusion that we

Matilda White Riley, "The Family in an Aging Society." *Journal of Family Issues*, 4:439–454. Copyright 1983 by Sage Publications, Inc. Reprinted by permission of Sage Publications, Inc.

need a whole new way of looking at the family, researching it, living in it, and dealing with it in professional practice and public policy.

Indeed, an exciting new family literature is beginning to map and interpret these unparalleled changes; it is beginning to probe beneath the surface for the subjective implications of the protracted and intricate interplay of family relationships. As the kinship structure is transformed, many studies are beginning to ask new questions about how particular relationships and particular social conditions can foster or inhibit emotional support and socialization—that is, the willingness to learn from one another. They are asking how today's family can fill people's pressing need for close human relationships.

From this developing literature, four topics emerge as particularly thought-provoking: (1) the dramatic extension of the kinship structure; (2) the new opportunities this extension brings for close family relationships; (3) the special approaches needed for understanding these complex relationships; and (4) the still unknown family relationships of older people in the future. I shall touch briefly on each of these topics. From time to time I shall also suggest a few general propositions—principles from the sociology of age (see M. W. Riley, 1976; forthcoming) that seem clearly applicable to changing family relationships. Perhaps they will aid our understanding of increasing longevity and the concomitant changes about us. The propositions may guide us in applying our new understanding in research, policy, and practice.

THE CHANGING CONFIGURATIONS OF THE KINSHIP STRUCTURE

I shall begin with the kinship structure as influenced by longevity. The extent and configurations of this structure have been so altered that we must rethink our traditional view of kinship. As four (even five) generations of many families are now alive at the same time, we can no longer concentrate primary attention on nuclear families of young parents and their children who occasionally visit or provide material assistance to grandparents or other relatives. I have come to think of today's large and complex kinship structure as a matrix of latent relationships—father with son, child with great-grandparent, sister with sister-in-law, ex-husband with ex-wife, and so on—relationships that are latent because they might or might not become close and significant during a lifetime. Thus I am proposing a definition of the kinship structure as a latent web of continually shifting linkages that provide the *potential* for activating and intensifying close family relationships.

The family literature describes two kinds of transformations in this structure that result from increasing longevity: (1) The linkages among family members have been prolonged, and (2) the surviving generations in a family have increased in number and complexity.

Prolongation of Family Relationships

Consider how longevity has prolonged family relationships. For example, in married couples a century ago, one or both partners were likely to have died before the children were reared. Today, though it may seem surprising, couples marrying at the customary ages can anticipate surviving together (apart from divorce) as long as 40 or 50 years on the average (Uhlenberg, 1969, 1980). As Glick and Norton (1977: 14) have shown, one out of every five married couples can expect to celebrate their fiftieth wedding anniversary. Because the current intricacy of kinship structures surpasses even the language available to describe it (our step-in-laws might not like to be called "outlaws"), it sometimes helps to do "thought experiments" from one's own life. As marital partners, my husband and I have so far survived together for over 50 years. What can be said about the form (as distinct from the content) of such a prolonged relationship?

For one thing, we share over half a century of experience. Because we are similar in age, we have shared the experience of aging—biologically, psychologically, and socially—from young adulthood to old age. Because we were born at approximately the same time (and thus belong to the same cohort), we have shared much the same historical experiences—the same fluctuations between economic prosperity and depression, between periods of pacifism and of war, between political liberalism and reactionism, and between low and high rates of fertility. We have also shared our own personal family experiences. We shared the bearing and raising of young children during our first quarter century together; during our second quarter century we adjusted our couplehood to our added roles as parents-in-law and grandparents. The third quarter-century of our married life, by the laws of probability, should convert us additionally into grandparents-in-law and great-grandparents as well. In sum, prolonged marriages like ours afford extensive common experiences with aging, with historical change, and with changing family relationships.

Such marriages also provide a home—an abiding meeting place for two individuals whose separate lives are engrossed in varied extrafamilial roles. Just as longevity has prolonged the average duration of marriage, it has extended many other roles (such as continuing education, women's years of work outside the home, or retirement). For example, Barbara Torrey (1982) has estimated that people spend at least a quarter of their adult lives in retirement. Married couples, as they move through the role complexes of their individual lives, have many evening or weekend opportunities either to share their respective extrafamilial experiences, to escape from them, to (though certainly not in my own case) to vent their boredom or frustration on one another (see Kelley, 1981).

Thus two features of protracted marriages become apparent. First, these marriages provide increasing opportunity to accumulate shared experiences and meanings and perhaps to build from these a "crescive" relationship, as suggested by Ralph Turner (1970) and Gunhild Hagestad (1981). But second, they also present shifting exigencies and role conflicts that require continual mutual accommodation and reaccommodation. As Richard Lazarus (DeLongis, et al., 1982) has shown, "daily hassles" can be more destructive of well-being than traumatic family events. And

Erving Goffman (1959: 132) warns that the home can become a "backstage area" in which "it is safe to lapse into an asociable mood of sullen, silent irritability."

Many marriages, not ended by death, are ended by divorce. The very extension of marriage may increase the likelihood of divorce, as Samuel Preston (1976: 176–177) has shown. Returning to my personal experience, I was the only one of four sisters who did not divorce and remarry. But as long as their ex-husbands were alive none of my sisters could ever entirely discount the remaining potential linkages between them. These were not only ceremonial or instrumental linkages, but also affective linkages that could be hostile and vindictive, or (as time passes and need arises) could renew concern for one another's well-being. Whatever the nature of the relationship, latent linkages to ex-spouses persist. Thus, a prolonged marriage (even an ex-marriage) provides a continuing potential for a close relationship that can be activated in manifold ways.

The traditional match-making question—"Will this marriage succeed or fail?"—must be replaced and oft-repeated as the couple grows older by a different question: "Regardless of our past, can we—do we want to—make the fresh effort to succeed, or shall we fail in this marriage?"

Here I will state as my first proposition: *Family relationships are never fixed*; they change as the self and the significant other family members grow older, and as the changing society influences their respective lives. Clearly, the longer the relationship endures (because of longevity) the greater the opportunity for relational changes.

If, as lives are prolonged, marital relationships extend far beyond the original nuclear household, parent-offspring relationships also take on entirely new forms. For example, my daughter and I have survived together so far for 45 years of which only 18 were in the traditional relationship of parent and child. Unlike our shorter-lived forebearers, my daughter and I have been able to share many common experiences although at different stages of our respective lives. She shares a major portion of the historical changes that I have experienced. She also shares my earlier experience of sending a daughter off to college, and will perhaps share my experience of having a daughter marry and raise children. Of course, she and I differ in age. (In Alice Rossi's study of biological age differences, 1980, the consequences for parent-offspring relationships of the reciprocal tensions between a pubescent daughter and her older mother who is looking ahead to the menopausal changes of midlife were explored.)[2] Although the relational age between me and my daughter—the 26 years that separate us—remains the same throughout our lives, the implications of this difference change drastically from her infancy to my old age.

Number and Stability of Generations

I have dwelt at length on the prolongation of particular relationships to suggest the consequent dramatic changes in the family structure. Longevity has, in addition, increased the stability and the number of generations in a family. A poignant example of this instability (Imhof, 1982) can be found in an eighteenth-century parish where a father could spawn twenty-four offspring of whom only three survived to adulthood—a time in which "it took two babies to make one adult." With increased longevity each generation becomes more stable because more of its members survive. For the young nuclear family in the United States, for example, though the number of children born in each family has been declining over this century, increased longevity has produced a new stability in the family structure. In an important quantitative analysis, Peter Uhlenberg (1980) has shown how the probability of losing a parent or a sibling through death before a child reaches age 15 has decreased from .51 in 1900 to .09 in 1976. Compared with children born a century ago, children born today are almost entirely protected against death of close family members (except for elderly relatives). To be sure, while mortality has been declining, divorce rates have been increasing but less rapidly. Thus, perhaps surprisingly, Uhlenberg demonstrates that disruptions of marriage up through the completion of child rearing have been declining since 1900. In other words, many marriages have been broken by divorce, but overall more have remained intact because of fewer deaths! Thus the young family as well as each of the older generations becomes more stable through survival.

At the same time, the number of older generations has been increasing. Looking up the generational ladder, increasing numbers of a child's four grandparents survive. Among middle-aged couples, whereas back in 1900 more than half had no surviving elderly parents, today half have two or more parents still alive (Uhlenberg, 1980: 318). Conversely, looking down the generational ladder, each set of elderly parents has adult children with spouses and children of their own. Meanwhile, the increase in divorce and remarriage (four out of five divorced people remarry) compounds the complexity of this elaborate structure, as Andrew Cherlin (1981) has shown. In my own family, for example, each of our two middle-aged children have their own children, and they also have us as two elderly parents; my daughter's husband also has two parents; and my son (who has married twice) has his ex-wife's parents and his current wife's mother, father, and step-mother in addition to us. A complex array!

Of course, as these surviving generations proliferate and overlap, each generation is continually growing older and moving up the generational ladder to replace its predecessor until ultimately the members of the oldest generation die. Because of longevity, every generation—the oldest as well as the youngest—is increasingly stable and more likely to include its full complement of surviving members.

CHANGING DYNAMICS OF CLOSE FAMILY RELATIONSHIPS

What, then, are the implications of this greatly expanded kinship structure for the dynamics of close family relationships? How does the matrix of latent kinship linkages provide for close ties between particular individual lives, as these lives weave in and out of the intricate and continually shifting kinship network? Under what conditions do some family members provide (or fail to provide) recognition, advice, esteem, love, and tension release for other family members?

The answer, it seems to me, lies in the enlarged kinship structure: It provides many new opportunities for people at different points in their lives to select and activate the relationships they deem most significant. That is, the options for close family bonds have multiplied. Over the century, increased longevity has given flexibility to the kinship structure, relaxing both the temporal and the spatial boundaries of optional relationships.

Temporally, new options have arisen over the course of people's lives because, as we have seen, particular relationships have become more enduring. Particular relationships (even following divorce) are bounded only by the birth and death of the members. Now that the experience of losing family members by death is no longer a pervasive aspect of the full life course (and is in fact rare except in old age), people have greater opportunity to plan their family lives. They have time to make mutual adjustments to personal crises or to external threats such as unemployment or the fear of nuclear war. Here we are reminded of my first proposition: Family relationships are never fixed, but are continually in process and subject to change. As family members grow older, they move across time—across history and through their own lives—and they also move upward through the generations in their own families and the age strata of society.[3] As individual family members who each pursue a separate life course, thoughts and feelings for one another are developed; their lives weave together or apart so as to activate, intensify, disregard, or disrupt particular close relationships. Thus the relationship between a mother and daughter can, for example, become close in the daughter's early childhood, her first years of marriage, and again after her children have left home although there may be interim lapses. Or, as current norms permit, couples can try each other out through cohabitation, before deciding whether or not to embark upon marriage.

Just as such new options for close ties have emerged from the prolongation of family relationships, other options have arisen because the number and variety of latent linkages has multiplied across the entire kinship structure. Spatially, close relationships are not bounded by the nuclear households that family members share during their younger lives. Given the intricacy of current kin networks, a wide range of linkages can be activated—between grandchild and grandparent, between distantly related cousins, between the ex-husbands of sisters, or between a child and his or her new step-parent. (Only in Grimm's fairy tales, which reflected the earlier frequency of maternal deaths and successive remarriages, were step-mothers always "wicked.") Aided by modern communication and transportation, affection and interaction can persist even during long periods of separation. On occasion, long-separated relatives or those not closely related may arrange to live together or to join in congregate housing or communes.

Given these options, let me now state a second general proposition: As active agents in directing the course of their own lives, *individuals have a degree of control over their close family relationships*. This control, I submit, has been enhanced because longevity has widened the opportunities for selecting and activating relationships that can provide emotional support and advice when needed.

This part of my discussion suggests a new view of the family. Perhaps we need now to think of a family less as the members of one household with incidental linkages to kin in other households and more as a continuing interplay among intertwined lives within the entire changing kinship structure. The closeness of these intertwined lives and the mutual support they provide depend on many factors (including the predispositions of each individual and the continuing motivation to negotiate and renegotiate their joint lives) but the enlarged kinship structure provides the potential.

NEW APPROACHES TO FAMILY RESEARCH AND PRACTICE

Before considering how the oldest family members—those in the added generation—fit into these intertwined lives, let me pause to ask how we can approach these complex and changing family relationships. If the tidy concept of the nuclear family is no longer sufficient, how can we deal in research and in professional practice with the newly emerging concepts? Clearly, special approaches are required for mapping and understanding the centrifugal and centripetal processes of family relationships within the increasing complexity of the kinship matrix. Such approaches must not only take into account my first two propositions (that relationships continually change, and that family members themselves have some control over this change) but must also consider a third proposition: *The lives of family members are interdependent* such that each person's family life continually interacts with the lives of significant relatives. Though long-recognized by students of the family, this proposition takes on fresh significance in the matrix of prolonged relationships.

As case examples, I shall describe two or three studies that illustrate how we can deal with the family as a system of interdependent lives. These studies are also important as they add to our understanding of emotional support and socialization under current family conditions.

In one study of socialization outcomes, Mavis Hetherington et al. (1977) have shown how parental disruption through divorce has a complex impact on the still-intertwined lives of the spouses and on the socialization of their children. Over a two-year period, detailed investigations were made of nursery school boys and girls and their parents, half of whom were divorced and the other half married. Differences were detected: Divorced parents showed comparatively less affection for their children, had less control over them, and elicited more dependent, disobedient, and aggressive child behavior—particularly in mother-son interactions. But relations between the parents also made a difference in these parent-child relationships: If divorced couples kept conflict low and agreed about child rearing, their ineffectiveness in dealing with children could be somewhat offset. This two-year tracing of the three-way interrelationships among spouses and children in disrupted families yields many insights into the interdependence of life course processes.

As family relationships are prolonged, socialization is more frequently recognized as a reciprocal process that potentially extends throughout the lives of parents and children as well as of marital partners. How can socialization operate across generations that belong to differing periods of historical change? How can parents teach their growing children the norms of the future? One key mechanism, as Marilyn Johnson (1976) has demonstrated, is normative expectations. Parents can influence offspring by expecting behavior that is appropriate to social change, and can in turn be guided by offspring in formulating these expectations. Such subtleties of intergenerational influence are illustrated in a small study which Johnson and I made of high school students in the early 1960s (see Riley, 1982). Just as women's careers were burgeoning, we found that most girls looked forward to combining a career with marriage, whereas most boys did not anticipate marrying wives who worked. How had these young people been socialized to such sharply conflicting norms? We questioned their mothers and fathers to find out. Indeed we learned that, on the whole, parents wanted self-fulfillment for their daughters both in marriage and in work outside the home, while for their sons they wanted wives who would devote themselves fully to home and children. These slight yet provocative findings did presage the future impact of the women's movement on family lives, but I note them here as another instance of research that fits together the differing perspectives of the several interdependent family members.

Analyzing such studies of close relationships impresses one with the problems of studying families from what is often called the "life course" or "lifespan perspective" (see Dannefer, forthcoming). We are indeed concerned with people moving through life. Yet we are concerned not with a single life or a statistical aggregate of lives, but with the dynamic family systems of interdependent lives. An example I often use in teaching comes from the early work of Cottrell and Burgess in predicting success or failure in marriage. Starting with a case study, Cottrell (1933) saw each partner in a marriage as reenacting his or her childhood roles. He showed how the outcome of the marriage depended upon the mesh between these two different sets of early-life experiences—that is, how nearly they would fit together so that each partner met the role expectations of the other. Unfortunately, however, these researchers subsequently departed from this admirable model by questioning large samples of men and women as individuals and then analyzing the data for separate aggregates of men and of women rather than for male-female pairs. Each individual was given a score of likely success in marriage, but without considering the success of a marriage between a particular man and a particular woman! Because the interdependent lives were not examined jointly, the central objective of the project was lost.

This difficulty, which I now call "life-course reductionism," still persists. Although many studies purport to study families as systems, they in fact either aggregate individual lives (as Cottrell and Burgess did) or reason erroneously from the lives of single members about the lives of other family members significant to the relationship. The danger of not considering a key family member is highlighted, for example, in Frank Furstenberg's (1981) review of the literature on kinship relations after divorce. Some studies had suggested that divorce disrupts the relations with parents-in-law (that is, with the parents of the ex-spouse) but these studies failed to include the children of the broken marriage. Only after examining the children's generation was it learned that they, by retaining contact with both sets of their grandparents, could help to link divorced spouses to their former in-laws. Supporting this clue from a small study of his own, Furstenberg found that the ties between grandparents and grandchildren did continue to exist in most cases, even though for the divorced parents (the middle generation) the former in-law relationships were largely attenuated or broken. In reconstituted families, then, grandparents can perhaps serve as "kinkeepers."

Among the studies that pursue close relationships across three generations is a national survey of divorce and remarriage now being conducted by Frank Furstenberg, Andrew Cherlin, Nicholas Zill, and James Peterson. In this era of widespread divorce and remarriage, this study is examining the important hypothesis that new intergenerational ties created by remarriage will balance—or more than balance—the losses incurred as a result of divorce. Step-relationships may replace disrupted natural relationships. The intricacy of interdependent lives within our proliferating kinship structure is dramatized by the design of this study. Starting with a sample of children aged 11 to 16 and their parents (who were originally interviewed five years earlier) the research team will now also question these children's grandparents; note that there can be two sets of grandparents where the parents are in intact first marriages or have been divorced, three sets if one parent has remarried after divorce, and four sets (no less than eight grandparents) if both have remarried. Thus, as surviving generations proliferate, their part in the family system will be explored in this study by questioning the many members of the grandparent generation. Surviving generations cannot be fully understood (as many studies of three generations have attempted) by examining a simple chain of single individuals from each of the generations.

These studies, as models for research, reflect the complex family relationships within which people of all ages today can seek or can give affection, encouragement, companionship, or advice.

OLDER GENERATIONS OF THE FUTURE

About the fourth generation (great-grandparents) that is being contributed by longevity, I want to make three final points.

First, it is too early to tell how an enlarged great-grandparent generation will fit into the kinship structure, or what close family relationships it may form. It is too early because the marked increases in longevity among the old began only in recent decades and are still continuing at a rate far-exceeding earlier predictions (Preston, 1976; Manton, 1982; Brody and Brock, n.d.). Will this added generation be regarded as the more familiar generation of grandparents has been regarded—either as a threat to the young adult generation's independence, or as a "social problem" for family and community, requiring care from the mid-generation that is "squeezed" between caring for both young children and aging parents? Or will an added fourth generation mean new coalitions and new forms of personal relationships? And what of five-generation families in which a grandmother can be also a granddaughter (see Hagestad, 1981)? It is still too early to tell what new family norms will develop (see Riley, 1978).

Second, while we do not know how a fourth or even a fifth generation may fit in, we do know that most older family members are not dependent or disabled (some 5% of those 65 and over are in nursing homes). For those requiring care or instrumental support, families generally make extraordinary efforts to provide it (see Shanas, 1979). Yet most of the elderly, and especially those who are better educated and more active, are stronger, wiser, more competent, and more independent than is generally supposed. Public stereotypes of old people are far more negative than old people's assessments of themselves (National Council on the Aging, 1981). Healthy members of this generation, like their descendants, must earn their own places in the family and create their own personal ties. They cannot expect obligatory warmth or emotional support.

Third, at the close of their lives, however, old people will need advice and emotional support from kin. This need is not new in the annals of family history. What is new is the fact that terminal illness and death are no longer scattered across all generations but are concentrated in the oldest one. Today two-thirds of all deaths occur after age 65, and 30% after age 80 (Brody and Brock, n.d.). And, although most deaths occur outside the home, programs such as the hospice movement are being developed for care of the dying in the home where the family can take part (see J. W. Riley, forthcoming).

In conclusion, I have attempted to trace the impact of the unprecedented increases in longevity on the family and its relationships. In our own time the kinship structure has become more extensive and more complex, the temporal and spatial boundaries of the family have been altered, and the opportunities for close family relationships have proliferated. These relationships are no longer prescribed as strict obligations. They must rather be earned—created and recreated by family members throughout their long lives. Each of us is in continuing need of advice and emotional support from one another, as we contend with personal challenges and troubles, and with the compelling effects of societal changes in the economy, in technology, in culture, and in values. We all must agree with Mary Jo Bane (1976) that the family is here to stay, but in forms that we are beginning to comprehend only now. As members of families and students of the family—whether we are theorists, researchers, counsellors, or policy makers—we must begin to realign our thinking and our practice to incorporate the new realities that are being engendered by increasing longevity.

NOTES

1. Note that increasing longevity in a society is not necessarily the same as increasing proportions of old people in the population, a proportion influenced in the long-term more by

fertility than by mortality. Longevity affects individual lives and family structures, while population composition affects the total society.

2. Gunhild Hagestad (1982) talks even of menopausal grandmothers with pubescent granddaughters.

3. Of course, divisions between generations are only loosely coterminous with age divisions (see the discussion of the difference between "generations" and "cohorts" in the classic piece by Duncan, 1966, and a definitive formulation of this distinction in Kertzer, forthcoming). As Gunhild Hagestad (1981) puts it, "people do not file into generations by cohorts." There are wide ranges in the ages at which particular individuals marry and have children. In addition to the recognized differences by sex, there are important differences by social class. For example, Graham Spanier (Spanier and Glick, 1980) shows how the later marriage age in upper as compared with lower socioeconomic classes postpones many subsequent events in the lives of family members, thus slowing the proliferation in numbers of surviving generations.

REFERENCES

Bane, M. J. 1976. *Here to Stay: American Families in the 20th Century*. New York: Basic Books.

Brody, J. A. and D. B. Brock. n.d. "Epidemiologic and statistical characteristics of the United States elderly population." (unpublished)

Cherlin, A. J. 1981. *Marriage, Divorce, Remarriage*. Cambridge, MA: Harvard University Press.

Cottrell, L. S., Jr. 1933. "Roles and marital adjustment." *American Sociological Society* 27:107–115.

Dannefer, D. Forthcoming. "The sociology of the life course." *Annual Review of Sociology*.

DeLongis, A., J. C. Coyne, G. Dakof, S. Folkman, and R. S. Lazarus. 1982. "Relationship of daily hassles, uplifts, and major life events in health status." *Health Psychology* 1:119–136.

Duncan, O. D. 1966. "Methodological issues in the analysis of social mobility," pp. 51–97 in N. J. Smelser and S. M. Lipsett (eds.) *Social Structure and Mobility in Economic Development*. Chicago, IL: Aldine.

Furstenberg, F. F., Jr. 1981. "Remarriage and intergenerational relations," pp. 115–142 in R. W. Fogel et al. (eds.) *Aging: Stability and Change in the Family*. New York: Academic Press.

Glick, P. C. and A. J. Norton. 1977. "Marrying, divorcing, and living together in the U.S. today." Population Bulletin 32. Washington, D.C. Population Reference Bureau.

Goffman, E. 1959. *The Presentation of Self in Everyday Life*. Garden City, NY: Doubleday.

Hagestad, G. O. 1982. "Older women in intergenerational relations." Presented at the Physical and Mental Health of Aged Women Conference, October 21–22, Case Western University, Cleveland, OH.

———, 1981. "Problems and promises in the social psychology of intergenerational relations," pp. 11–46 in R. W. Fogel et al. (eds.) *Aging: Stability and Change in the Family*. New York: Academic Press.

Hetherington, E. M., M. Cox, and R. Cox. 1977. "The aftermath of divorce," in J. H. Stevens, Jr. and M. Matthews (eds.) *Mother-Child, Father-Child Relations*. Washington, D.C.: National Association for the Education of Young Children.

Imhof, A. E. 1982. "Life course patterns of women and their husbands—16th to 20th century." Presented at the International Conference on Life Course Research on Human Development, September 17, Berlin, Germany.

Johnson, M. 1976. "The role of perceived parental models, expectations and socializing behaviors in the self-expectations of adolescents, from the U.S. and West Germany." Dissertation, Rutgers University.

Kelley, H. H. 1981. "Marriage relationships and aging," pp. 275–300 in R. W. Fogel et al. (eds.) *Aging: Stability and Change in the Family*. New York: Academic Press.

Kertzer, D. I. Forthcoming. "Generations as a sociological problem." *Annual Review of Sociology*.

Manton, K. G. 1982. "Changing concepts of morbidity and mortality in the elderly population." *Milbank Memorial Fund Q.* 60:183–244.

National Council on the Aging. 1981. *Aging in the Eighties: America in Transition*. Washington, D.C.: Author.

Parsons, T. and R. F. Bales. 1955. *Family, Socialization and Interaction Process*. New York: Free Press.

Preston, S. H. 1976. *Mortality Patterns in National Population: With Special References to Recorded Causes of Death*. New York: Academic Press.

Riley, J. W., Jr. Forthcoming. "Dying and the meanings of death: sociological inquiries." *Annual Review of Sociology*.

Riley, M. W. 1976. "Age strata in social systems," pp. 189–217 in R. H. Binstock and E. Shanas (eds.) *Handbook of Aging and the Social Sciences*. New York: Van Nostrand Reinhold.

———. 1978. "Aging, social change, and the power of ideas." *Daedalus* 107, 4:39–52.

———. 1982. "Implications for the middle and later years," pp. 399–405 in P. W. Berman and E. R. Ramey (eds.) *Women: A Developmental Perspective*. NIH Publication No. 82-2298. Washington, D.C.: Dept. of Health and Human Services.

———. Forthcoming. "Age strata in social systems," in R. H. Binstock and E. Shanas (eds.) *The New Handbook of Aging and the Social Sciences*.

Rossi, A. S. 1980. "Aging and parenthood in the middle years," in P. B. Baltes and O. G. Brim, Jr. (eds.) *Life-Span Development and Behavior 3*. New York: Academic Press.

Shanas, E. 1979. "Social myth as hypothesis: the case of the family relations of old people." *The Gerontologist* 19:3–9.

Spanier, G. B. and P. C. Glick. 1980. "The life cycle of American families: an expanded analysis." *J. of Family History:* 97–111.

Torrey, B. B. 1982. "The lengthening of retirement," pp. 181–196 in M. W. Riley et al. (eds.) *Aging from Birth to Death*, vol. II: *Sociotemporal Perspectives,* Boulder, CO: Westview.

Turner, R. H. 1970. *Family Interaction*. New York: John Wiley.

Uhlenberg, P. R. 1969. "A study of cohort life cycles: cohorts of native born Massachusetts women, 1830–1920." *Population Studies* 23, 3:407–420.

———. 1980. "Death and the family." *J. of Family History* (Fall):313–320.

ARTICLE 18
Widowhood

STARR ROXANNE HILTZ

Due to the difference in the longevity of males and females, most women spend part of their lives as widows, a role for which there are no clear expectations. In addition to the emotional trauma of the spouse's death, widows typically face financial problems, the need to find new social roles, and strains in their relations with other family members. These problems are especially acute among women who are lower class, who were unprepared for the death, and who had recently experienced some other life crisis.

THE DEATH OF A SPOUSE is one of the most serious life crises a person faces. The immediate emotional crisis of bereavement, if not fully worked through, may result in symptoms of mental disorder. During the first few days of bereavement, sacred and secular guidelines define the proper mourning role for the widow. Over the longer term, however, there is generally a need for a total restructuring of the widow's life, as she finds herself much poorer, socially isolated, and left without a meaningful life pattern. . . . Widowhood is best conceptualized as a negatively evaluated social category where the individual loses the central source of identity, financial support, and social relationships. It is a "roleless role."

Currently, American women have a life expectancy of 79, about seven years longer than American men. If demographic patterns were used to suggest marital arrangements, it would make sense for older women to marry younger males. However, our cultural norms and opportunities are such that the initial mortality differences are compounded by the tendency for women to marry older men. . . .

Starr Roxanne Hiltz, "Widowhood." *Marriage and Family Review,* 1(6):1, 3–10. Copyright 1978 by The Haworth Press. Reprinted by permission of The Haworth Press, 10 Alice Street, Binghamton, NY 13904.

WIDOWHOOD ROLES

Most preindustrial societies have very clear roles for widows. For example, in traditional Indian society, [in the past] a Brahmin widow was supposed to commit *suttee* by throwing herself on her husband's funeral pyre. If she did not do this, she was condemned to live out her life dressed in a single course garment, with shaven head, eating only one meal a day, and shunned by others as "unlucky." Another extreme solution, practiced in many African societies, was an immediate (automatic) remarriage, in which the wife and children were "inherited" by a younger brother of the deceased or by some other heir, and the widow became one of his wives in a polygamous family. . . . Even if such prescribed actions and roles were not particularly desirable from the widow's point of view, at least it was clear what she was to do with the rest of her life.

The new widow in American and other (Western) industrialized societies has lost not only a husband, but her own main functions, reason for being, and self-identity. In spite of the [large number of women in the work force], most women who are becoming widows have defined themselves primarily as wives and mothers. Lopata sums up the situation in *Widowhood in an American City,* a study of Chicago widows:

> In spite of the rapid industrialization, urbanization, and increasing complexity of the social structure of American society, the basic cluster of social roles available to, and chosen by, its women has been that of wife-mother-housewife. This fact imposes some serious problems upon the last stage of their lives, similar to the problems of retirement in the lives of men who had concentrated upon their occupational roles. The wife-mother-housewife often finds herself with children who are grown, absent from her home, and independent of her as a basic part of their lives; her husband has died, and her household no longer contains a client segment. (Lopata, 1973, pp. 87–88)

Caine, in her poignant account of her own bereavement and eventual readjustment with professional help, has written a most moving description of the effects of the wrenching away of one's social and self-identity that occurs with the death of a husband:

> "Widow" is a harsh and hurtful word. It comes from the Sanskrit and means "empty." . . .
> After my husband died, I felt like one of those spiraled shells washed up on the beach. Poke a straw through the twisting tunnel, around and around, and there is nothing there. No flesh. No life. Whatever lived there is dried up and gone.
> Our society is set up so that most women lose their identities when their husbands die. Marriage is a symbiotic relationship for most of us. We draw our identities from our husbands. We add ourselves to our men, pour ourselves into them and their lives. We exist in their reflection. And then . . . ? If they die . . . ? What is left? It's wrenching enough to lose the man who is your lover, your companion, your best friend, the father of your children, without losing yourself as well. (Caine, 1974, pp. 181, 1)

It should be noted that Caine had a fine job for many years before her husband died, but . . . this did not alleviate the necessity and pain of totally restructuring her social role.

Remarriage is not a likely solution. There are fewer than two million widowers in the United States, one for every five widows, and they are likely to marry younger women. Cleveland and Gianturco (1976), in a retrospective study of North Carolina data, for instance, concluded that less than 5% of women widowed after age 55 ever remarry.

As Lopata points out:

> Life styles for American widows are generally built upon the assumption that they are young and can soon remarry or that they are very old and removed from the realm of actual involvement. The trouble is that most widows are neither, but the society has not taken sufficient cognizance of this fact to modify the facilities and roles available to them. (Lopata, 1973, p. 17)

A woman is likely to spend as much time as a widow as she does raising children. Although she was socialized all through her early life for the wife-and-motherhood role, she typically has had no preparation at all for the widowhood role. The whole subject has been taboo, and few women prepare ahead of time for widowhood. . . .

GRIEF AS A KIND OF ILLNESS: EFFECTS ON ROLE PERFORMANCE

The emotional and psychological traumas of grief and mourning involve "letting go" of the emotional ties and roles centered on the husband. If this working through of grief is successfully accomplished, the widow can face a second set of problems having to do with building a new life, a new set of role relationships, and a new identity.

Much of the psychological literature on grief represents an elaboration of Freud's theories. For Freud, grief or "grief work" is the process by which bereaved persons struggle to disengage the loved object. The emotional bond is fused with energy, bound to memories and ideas related to former interactions with the loved person. The mourner has to spend time and effort to bring to consciousness all of these memories in order to set free the energy, to break the tie (Freud, 1917/1957). . . .

At one time "grief," as in the extended "pining away," . . . was recognized as a cause of death and listed on death certificates. As Glick et al. (1974, p. 10) have concluded from their extensive studies of bereavement, "the death of a spouse typically gives rise to a reaction whose duration must be measured in years rather than in weeks." . . .

A variety of grief reactions may occur when the mourner does not express emotion or refuses to deal with the loss. These include delay of the grief reactions for months or even years; overactivity without a sense of loss; indefinite irritability and hostility toward others; sense of the presence of the deceased; acquisition of the physical symptoms of the deceased's last illness; insomnia, apathy, psychosomatically based illnesses such as ulcerative colitis; and such intense depression and feelings of worthlessness that suicide is attempted (Parkes, 1972, p. 211 . . .).

One tendency is to reconstruct an idealized version of one's deceased husband and of the role relationship with him before the death. Referred to as "husband sanctification," Lopata [1976, pp. 4–5] reports that three-quarters of the Chicago area current and former beneficiaries of Social Security define their late husband as having been "extremely good, honest, kind, friendly, and warm." . . . Sanctification is especially likely among women who rank the role of wife above all others. It is an attempt to continue defining oneself primarily in terms of the now-broken role relationship. Lopata views this as an effort to "remove the late husband into an other-worldly position as an understanding but purified and distant observer" (p. 30), so that the widow is able to go about reconstructing old role relationships and forming new ones.

There are several factors related to severe or prolonged grief. Sixty-eight widows and widowers under the age of 45 were interviewed shortly after the spouse died and again a year later [for] the Harvard Bereavement Study. An "outcome score" was obtained from in-depth interview material and answers to questions on health; increased consumption of alcohol, tranquilizers, and tobacco; self-assessment as "depressed or very unhappy"; and "wondering whether anything is worthwhile anymore." Three classes of strongly correlated and intercorrelated variables predict continued severe bereavement reactions 13 months after the death (Parkes, 1975, pp. 308–309):

1. Low socioeconomic status, i.e., low weekly income of the husband, Spearman's rho correlation of .44; low occupational status, .28.
2. Lack of preparation for loss due to noncancer deaths, short terminal illness, accident or heart attack, or failure to talk to the spouse about the coming death, correlations of .26 to .29.
3. Other life crises preceding spouse's death, such as infidelity and job loss, correlations of .25 to .44.

It is interesting that a poor outcome is likely if the marriage relationship was troubled before the death; folk wisdom would have it that the widow would be "glad to be rid of him." Psychologically debilitating guilt over having wished the death of the husband seems to be very strong in such cases, however. Another problem is the amount of "unfinished business" (Blauner, 1966) left by the removal of the husband through death. Parkes concludes that for his young respondents, including widowers as well as widows, "When advance warning was short and the death was sudden, it seemed to have a much greater impact and to lead to greater and more lasting disorganization" (Parkes, 1975, p. 313). . . .

Emotional problems related to grief or bereavement . . . are not independent of the problems relating to income, friends, and family. Disturbance and dissolution of the widow's main social relationships and removal of the main source of income require finding new friends and activities, a job, often less expensive housing; and similar adjustments. Any major change in role relationships and living patterns is stressful, and causes emotional disturbance. But many changes in one's life circumstances and behavior patterns simultaneously are especially likely to be associated with extreme emotional stress and such symptoms as mental illness, heart attacks, and suicide. . . .

FINANCIAL PROBLEMS

The subsequent life changes and problems faced by the widow indicate that widowhood is a role for which there is no comparable role among males. Glick et al. (1974, p. 262), summarize the difference between their samples of widows and of widowers: "Insofar as the men reacted simply to the *loss of a loved other,* their responses were *similar* to those of widows, but insofar as men reacted to the *traumatic disruption of their lives,* their responses were *different."* . . . This differential impact is found in the financial impact of the death. For the widow, it almost always means the loss of the main source of financial support for the family and a consequent lowering of the standard of living. . . .

By two to three years after the onset of widowhood, the incomes of the widows' families were down an average of 44% from previous levels, and 58% had incomes that fell below the amount that would have been necessary to maintain their family's former standard of living. This occurred even among those who received life insurance benefits. After final expenses, 44% had used up part of this for living expenses, and 14% had consumed all of it.

In addition to financially devastating final expenses which wipe out savings, widows are entitled to no Social Security benefits at all unless they have dependents or are over 60. After 60 years of age, they are entitled only to a portion of what would have been their husband's benefits. The final explanation for the high probability of poverty among widows is that because of age, low level of skill and education, and lack of experience, they are often unable to obtain employment. In other words, neither the private economy nor the public welfare system is currently structured to provide economic support to widows in late middle age.

FINDING NEW SOCIAL ROLES

Before widowhood, a married woman defines herself and relates to others mainly in terms of her status as somebody's wife. At widowhood, most of her role relationships will have to adjust and some will terminate. She will have to establish new role relationships if her life is to be a satisfying one. For example, she is unlikely to maintain close ties with friends and relatives who belonged to social circles maintained with her husband. Changes in finances can require changes in other spheres of life, such as movement into the work force. A change in residence may result in loss of contact with neighbors. Often, in settling her husband's estate, she has to deal with lawyers and insurance agents and has to take on the role of businesswoman (Lopata, 1975, p. 48).

The difficulties an older woman in our society is likely to encounter in establishing such a new set of role relationships is affirmed by Professor Lopata. She found that half of the widows in her sample considered loneliness their greatest problem, and another third listed it second. Social isolation was listed by 58%, who agreed with the statement "One problem of being a widow is feeling like a 'fifth wheel' " (Lopata, 1972, pp. 91, 346).

Lopata's work focuses on the widow's role relationships in regard to motherhood, kin relationships, friendship, and community involvement, including employment. Among her findings are that "women who develop satisfactory friendships, who weather the transition period and solve its problems creatively, tend to have a higher education, a comfortable income, and the physical and psychic energy needed to initiate change" (Lopata, 1972, p. 216). These women are not the "average" widow, who is likely to have a high school education or less, low income, depleted physical energy due to advancing age, and depleted psychic energy due to the trauma of bereavement and its associated problems.

The importance of maintaining or establishing supportive role relationships with an understanding "other," such as an old friend, neighbor, or supportive professional or paraprofessional, has been emphasized in many studies. For instance, Maddison and Raphael (1975, p. 29) emphasize their "conviction that the widow's perception of her social network is an extremely important determinant of the outcome of her bereavement crisis". . . . "Bad outcome" women had no one to whom they could freely express their grief and anger.

DISRUPTION OF FAMILY RELATIONSHIPS

The death of the husband tends to cause strain in relationships with children, in-laws, and even one's own siblings and other relatives. . . . The problems with children were twofold: a perceived coldness or neglect to give the widow as much "love" and support and time as she thought she was entitled to (17%), and what the widow considered serious behavioral problems with the children, such as taking drugs or withdrawing from employment and from communication with the mother (15%) (Hiltz, 1977, pp. 64–65).

What is seen as "neglect" or "coldness" by the widow may be viewed as an unfair and unpleasant burden by the children, especially sons. For example, Adams (1968) found that grown middle-class sons perceived their obligations to their mothers as a "one-way" or unreciprocated pattern of aid and support-giving. This typically results in a son's loss of affection for the mother and his resentment of her dependence upon him.

For younger widows with dependent children, there are difficulties in maintaining the maternal role of effectively responding to the child's needs. . . . Silverman and Englander [1975, p. 11] found that most parents and children avoided talking about the death to one another. Common reactions of the child were fear that they would lose the surviving parent, too; the assumption by the child of new family responsibilities; and poor school work related to rebellion and social withdrawal. . . .

INTERVENTION STRATEGIES AND THEIR EFFECTIVENESS

Findings from recent research projects have sustained the premise that social service or intervention programs to help the widow cope and build a satisfactory network of role relationships do work. One such project involving intervention in the life of the widow is the "Widow-to-Widow" program. Five widows were originally recruited as aides, chosen as having personal skills in dealing with people and as representatives of the dominant racial and religious groups in the community. The aide wrote the new widow a letter saying that she would call on her at a particular time. This usually occurred three weeks after the death, unless the widow telephoned and requested no visit. Of the 91 widows located in the first seven months of the program, 64 accepted contact, half by visit and half by telephone, an overall acceptance rate of 60%. The aides offered friendship as well as advice and assistance with specific problems. In addition, group discussion meetings and social events such as a cookout were organized to which all of the widows were invited (Silverman, 1969, pp. 333–337). As Silverman describes the role of the aide, she "encourages, prods, insists, and sometimes even takes the widow by the hand and goes through the motions with her" (1972, p. 101).

On the basis of this project and one other, Silverman and Cooperband [1975, p. 11] conclude that "the evidence points to another widow as the best caregiver. . . . This other widow . . . can provide a perspective on feelings; she provides a role model; she can reach out as a friend and neighbor." . . .

Some psychiatrists and social workers question the advisability of using untrained recent widows to give aid to other widows, without available referral to professionals. For instance, they point to abnormal grief reactions experienced by widows visited by aides, including two who died, who may have responded to professional intervention. Also, unresolved elements of her own grief might lead the widow-aide to excessive reliance upon her own methods of coping, overlooking or negatively responding to other possibilities (Kahana, 1975). "The danger is that unresolved or unrecognized grief may adversely influence the aide in trying to assist the newly bereaved widow. . . . Some of the people who say 'I know how you feel' may really mean 'I know how I feel' " (Blau, 1975, pp. 36–37). . . .

Group discussion or therapy sessions, with groups of three to ten widows, met weekly with a professional leader [from the Casework Service of the Widows Consultation Center, New York City]. They varied, depending upon the participants, from fairly casual sharing of experiences as widows to explicitly therapeutic groups. (See Hiltz, 1975, for a description of these groups.)

Social activities and recreational events were organized for the Center's clients. These social get-togethers were initiated slowly, with the first year's activities most typically a monthly tea at the Center preceded by a brief lecture on some topic of apparent interest to widows, such as a book on widowhood. By the third year, a part-time social worker was hired to organize and conduct social activities, such as Sunday afternoon sessions at the local "Y," weekend bus trips, and free theater parties.

Special professional consultation about legal or financial problems was arranged through caseworkers, who made appointments for clients who seemed to need expert advice. The financial consultant was a well-known writer on personal finance, who did not recommend specific investments but gave generalized advice on types of investments, budgeting, and allocation of funds.

The main criterion of effectiveness used in this study was the widows' own feelings about whether or not the [Center] had helped them with each problem area identified by each widow at the time she came to the Center. . . .

When asked "Overall, would you say that the Widows Consultation Center was a great deal of help to you, of some help, or no help at all?"; 33% said "of some help"; and 30% said "no help." These results become more favorable as the number of private interviews, group therapy sessions, or social activities attended increases. For example, less than a third of those who had only one or two private interviews felt that the Center had given them a "great deal of help," compared to 79% of those who had five or more private consultation sessions. These findings support the feelings of the caseworkers that they achieved much more success in helping their clients with a supportive casework process that extended over some period of time, rather than a one- or two-visit process. . . .

SUMMARY

Studies of widowhood during the last decade have given us an understanding of the fact that widows in American society must forge a total emotional, financial, and social reorganization of their lives, at a time when their resources for such a task are generally inadequate. There are many areas in which the "broad picture" of the problems faced by widows must be filled in by much more detail. Strategies to prevent deterioration in communication and quality of relationship between the newly widowed mother and her dependent or grown children is one example of an area in which such research would be particularly valuable. At the societal level, we need to explore what mix of private and public efforts can replace the likelihood of poverty created by the current Social Security "blackout period" and lack of job opportunities for older widows with some assurance of financial security. Finally, we need to forge a stronger relationship between social service programs and social research, so that knowledge of successful and unsuccessful strategies in helping widows to build a socially and financially supportive set of role relationships becomes cumulative and shared. . . .

REFERENCES

Adams, B. The middle-class adult and his widowed or still-married mother. *Social Problems*. 1968, *16*, 50–59.

Blau, D. On widowhood: Discussion, *Journal of Geriatric Psychiatry*, 1975, *8*, 29–40.

Blauner, R. Death and social structure, *Psychiatry*, 1966, *29*, 387–394.

Caine, L. *Widow*. New York: Wm. Morrow & Co., 1974.

Cleveland, W. P., & Gianturco, D. T. Remarriage probability after widowhood: A retrospective method. *Journal of Gerontology*, 1976, *31*, 99–103.

Freud, S. Mourning and melancholia. In J. Strachey (Ed. and trans.), *The Standard Edition of the Complete Psychological Works of Sigmund Freud* (Vol. XIV). London: The Hogarth Press and the Institute for Psycho Analysis, 1957. (Originally published 1917.)

Glick, I. O., Weiss, R., & Parkes, C. M. *The first year of bereavement*. New York: John Wiley & Sons, 1974.

Hiltz, S. R. Helping widows: Group discussions as a therapeutic technique. *The Family Coordinator*, 1975, *24*, 331–336.

Hiltz, S. R. *Creating community services for widows: A pilot project*. Port Washington, N.Y.: Kennikat Press, 1977.

Kahana, R. J. On widowhood: Introduction. *Journal of Geriatric Psychiatry*, 1975, *8*, 5–8.

Lopata, H. Z. Role changes in widowhood: A world perspective. In D. Cowgill & L. Holmes (Eds.), *Aging and modernization*. New York: Appleton-Century-Crofts, 1972.

Lopata, H. Z. *Widowhood in An American City*. Cambridge, Mass.: Schenkman Publishing Co., 1973.

Lopata, H. Z. On widowhood: Grief, work, and identity reconstruction. *Journal of Geriatric Psychiatry*, 1975, *8*, 41–55.

Lopata, H. Z. *Widowhood and husband sanctification*. Paper presented at the 71st annual meeting of the American Sociological Association, New York City, August 1976.

Maddison, D., & Raphael, B. Conjugal bereavement and the social network. In B. Schoenberg, I. Gerber, A. Wiener, A. Kutscher, D. Peretz, & C. Carr. (Eds.), *Bereavement: Its psychosocial aspects*. New York: Columbia University Press, 1975.

Parkes, C. M. *Bereavement: Studies of grief in adult life*. New York: International Press, 1972.

Parkes, C. M. Determinants of outcome following bereavement. *Omega: Journal of Death and Dying*, 1975, *6*, 303–323.

Silverman, P. R. The widow-to-widow program: An experiment in preventive intervention. *Mental Hygiene*, 1969, *53*, 333–337.

Silverman, P. R. Widowhood and preventive intervention. *The Family Coordinator*, 1972, *21*, 95–102.

Silverman, P. R., & Cooperband, A. On widowhood: Mutual help and the elderly widow. *Journal of Geriatric Psychiatry*, 1975, *8*, 9–27.

Silverman, P. R., & Englander, S. The widow's view of her dependent children. *Omega: Journal of Death and Dying*, 1975, *6*, 3–20.

ARTICLE 19
Folk Beliefs about Parenthood

E. E. LeMASTERS AND JOHN DeFRAIN

Americans tend to romanticize parenthood. As a result, LeMasters and DeFrain contend, there are many widely held beliefs about parenthood that are not necessarily supported by the facts. In this article, these authors discuss twenty prevalent beliefs. In most cases, these bits of folklore romanticize the truth, but in some instances, reality may not be as dire as the folk beliefs imply.

FOLKLORE CONSISTS OF widely held beliefs that do not necessarily reflect reality. Here are twenty such beliefs about parenthood.

1. REARING CHILDREN IS FUN

No one can teach high school or college courses on the family without being impressed by this common belief that rearing children is fun. It derives from the notion that "children are cute" (to be analyzed later). Young people are often heard to say: "Oh I just cannot wait to have children." The odd thing is that parents do not generally talk that way. This leads one to the conclusion that this belief reflects folklore and has no substantial basis in reality.

The truth is—as every parent knows—that rearing children is probably the

"Folk Beliefs About Parenthood." From PARENTS IN CONTEMPORARY AMERICA: A SYMPATHETIC VIEW, Fifth Edition, by E. E. LeMasters and John DeFrain, © 1989 by Wadsworth, Inc. Reprinted by permission of the publisher. Footnotes were deleted from the original.

hardest, and most thankless, job in the world. No intelligent father or mother would deny that it is *exciting* as well as interesting, but to call it fun is a serious error. The idea of something being fun implies that you can take it or leave it, whereas parents do not have this choice. Fathers and mothers must stay with the child and keep trying, whether it is fun, or whether they are enjoying it or not. Any comparison to bowling, listening to rock 'n' roll records, or sex is strictly coincidental.

In the words of Dorothy Rodgers, the wife of the composer Richard Rodgers: "It's true, I think, as a wise friend told me, that parenthood is a one-way river: parents give and children take. The love of a parent for a child is often the most generous, giving and unselfish love there is."

And, in the wry words of family therapist Frank Farrelly, the child's response is "Gimmie! Lemmie! Iwanna!"

We do not mean to deny that a great many parents enjoy their work and that they derive satisfaction from it. But to describe what parents do as fun is to miss the point. It would be like describing the sweat and tears involved in the artist's creation as fun. The life of Thomas Wolfe or that of almost any serious artist will convey the point.

Brooke Hayward has an interesting way of helping us make our point: "One sleepless night when I was thirteen or fourteen . . . I finally accepted the idea that being a parent might be worse than being a child."

Now that his military service is well in the past, the first author of this book can truthfully say he enjoyed his years in the U.S. Naval Air Corps and he would not have wanted to miss the experience. But it is also true that on almost any day of those three years, he would have accepted his immediate discharge had it been offered. This feeling is very common to the millions of men who served in the armed forces during World War II. We think the sentiment also describes very accurately the feelings of millions of fathers and mothers.

The truth is somewhat as follows: Rearing children is hard work; it is often nerve-racking work; it involves tremendous responsibility; it takes all the ability one has (and more); and once you have begun you cannot quit when you feel like it. It would be helpful to young parents if they could be made to realize all of this before they enlist—or before they are drafted, as the case may be.

In pursuing the analogy between military service and parenthood, the writers have often heard parents refer to married couples who have no children as draft dodgers. The sentiment is similar to that which many veterans of the armed forces have toward able-bodied men who somehow escaped military service in the last war (any last war will do). The veteran often feels military service is a rough experience but it has to be endured for the sake of the country; his feeling toward men who did not have this experience is ambivalent. In a sense, he resents their escaping what he had to go through, but in another sense, he recognizes there may have been valid reasons they were not in the armed forces.

This does not mean, however, most parents regret having had children any more than it means veterans regret having served their country. Of course, we do not hear much from the men who were killed or maimed in the wars, and we also do not hear too much from parents who have suffered much the same fate rearing their children.

Kenneth Keniston says it so well:

> ... The parent today is usually a coordinator without voice or authority, a maestro trying to conduct an orchestra of players who have never met and who play from a multitude of different scores, each in notation the conductor cannot read. If parents are frustrated, it is no wonder: for although they have the responsibility for their children's lives, they hardly ever have the voice, or the power to make others listen to them.

2. CHILDREN ARE SWEET AND CUTE

When young people see small children they are apt to remark: "Your children are so cute!" It is true, of course, that small children *are* cute (at times), but this hardly exhausts the subject—or the adjectives parents use to describe their children when they are *not* being cute. Think back on the other adjectives you have heard used commonly to describe children, some endearing, some impairing.

Several years ago, the first author published the results of a study of young parents titled "Parenthood as Crisis." This report stated that parents in our society have a romantic complex about child rearing and that they tend to suffer from a process of disenchantment after they become parents. When this study was summarized in the *New York Times,* a flood of mail descended on the writer from parents, with the vast bulk of it agreeing with the findings of the study. The response to this paper led the writer to feel that he had struck a responsive chord in the collective bosom of American fathers and mothers.

Robert J. Trotter, in a fine article on infancy, noted:

> Incredible as it may seem . . . infants have not always been seen as bundles of joy. Throughout most of human history, in fact, they were treated as mewling, puking bundles of trouble, easier to be rid of than to rear. Infanticide, the murder of babies, appears to have been a common practice in many ancient societies and was not even outlawed in Rome until A.D. 374.

Even when infants were allowed to live they were not always cared for by their parents. Historical records from the Middle Ages indicate many Western European children were sold as slaves or servants; many others were given away or abandoned to the care of monasteries or nunneries. Well-to-do parents sent their infants to live with wet nurses, rather than be bothered by them. When the youngsters were old enough, they came home from the wet nurses to the care of servants until the age when they were again sent off to school or work.

Are children sweet and cute? It depends on whom you talk with, and in which historical period one is living.

3. CHILDREN WILL TURN OUT WELL IF THEY HAVE "GOOD" PARENTS

Logically, this should be so, and one would certainly like to believe it is so. For that matter, it probably is *usually* a correct statement—but not always. Almost everyone knows of at least one nice family with a "problem child." It seems to be a rare family that has not had some tragic experience with at least one child (assuming the family consists of several children).

It would be comforting to think parents can guarantee happiness and success (the twin gods of our civilization), but the sad truth is they cannot. Children are so complex and so different, and our society is so complicated, that fathers and mothers simply do not have the quality control one finds in industrial production. Parents with skill and ability, of course, probably have a better batting average than those of us with more modest talents—but even the greatest parents do not bat a thousand.

Someone has observed that marriage is perhaps the only game of chance at which both players can lose. It might be that rearing children should be added to this list.

It would be fascinating and interesting (and perhaps frightening) to know what the actual success and failure rate is in rearing children in modern America. The writers have seen no respectable research (including their own) that would answer this question, and in a certain sense it cannot be answered because the terms are so hard to define. When has a parent been successful with any given child? At what age do we judge the product—adolescence, early adulthood, middle age, or the life span? Do we include material success, physical health, mental health, spiritual health, or what?

One strategy for answering these difficult questions bears repeating though. Nick Stinnett, Greg Sanders, John DeFrain, and Karen Strand carefully studied more than 300 families nationwide who perceived their marriage and parent-child relationships to be positive. These strong families volunteered to a request in newspapers across the country, and when asked what qualities made for a strong family commonly responded with the following:

1. Appreciation and affection.
2. Communication.
3. Commitment.
4. Spending time together.
5. Religion and/or shared moral values.
6. Positive coping with stress and crisis.

To see what percentage of parents in the United States believe they have strong parent-child relationships—in essence, that they are successful in parenting—researchers could compare a random sample of American parents with the 300 families in our strong-family study. This would be a laborious task, but useful.

In an extremely unscientific manner, the first writer has surveyed a few families, with very sobering results. Winston Churchill and his wife, for example, appear to have been successful with only two of their children, yet both of these parents were remarkably successful in the other areas of life. Franklin D. and Eleanor Roosevelt, certainly two of the most loved and revered Americans of the modern era, seem to have been only moderately successful in rearing their children—and this appraisal comes from Democrats, not Republicans.

It is true that such families have most unusual family stresses because of the heavy burden carried by the father and mother in discharging their many public responsibilities, but the writers have also studied some families at very modest social levels with somewhat similar results. We know many people who feel they have completely failed as parents. Others report partial failure: Some of their children are okay, others are hopeless. But in all cases, we counsel caution; it is best to reserve judgment. Progress comes slowly in the world, and it may be a while before a child comes around. The second author's seventh-grade science teacher years ago was Henry Goebel, and dear old Mr. Goebel has the best advise of all.

Goebel retired a few years ago after teaching more than forty years. He worked with literally thousands of youngsters and hundreds of their parents.

"Mr. Goebel, Mr. Goebel, we just don't know what to do with Johnny," anxious parents would say to the wise old educator.

"Wait a year," he would reply without flinching. Ninety percent of the problems would disappear in a year's time (or be replaced by new problems), and only ten percent of the parents would dutifully report to Mr. Goebel for further advice.

"Mr. Goebel, Mr. Goebel, we waited a year like you said and we still don't know what do to with Johnny."

"Wait another," Henry Goebel would say with quiet determination.

4. CHILDREN IMPROVE MARRIAGE

It would be nice to think so, but the research available does not support the belief. In his study of divorced women, William J. Goode did not find that children had improved these marriages. In a study of 852 middle- and upper-class parents, Boyd Rollins and Harold Feldman found that only eighteen percent of the husbands and wives reported higher levels of marital satisfaction after parenthood. In an extensive review of the research on this belief, Charles Figley concludes: "A dramatic decrease in marital adjustment and marital communication occurs during the child-rearing period."

Norval Glenn and Sara McLanahan studied the effects of the presence of children on their parents' marital happiness with data from six U.S. national surveys. The researchers, in addition, looked at a number of important subpopulations of parents in these surveys: blacks and whites; males and females; highly educated people versus people with low levels of education; Catholics versus non-Catholics; women employed full time outside the home versus other women; and people who ideally wanted a lot of children versus people who wanted few children. The researchers found no evidence for positive average effects of children on the marriages of any of these subpopulations. "On the average, children adversely affect marital quality," the researchers concluded.

In his study of fatherhood, Leonard Benson decided: "There is no evidence to suggest that having children improves or enhances a couple's ability to handle marriage problems." Jessie Bernard is quoted as having said: "Children rarely make for added happiness between husband and wife."

As S. M. Miller, the behavioral scientist, said: "We had amazing naiveté about the impact of having children—a naiveté, incidentally, that I see today having a similarly devastating effect on many young parents. We just had no idea how much time and emotion children captured, how they simply changed a couple's lives."

One of the most recent studies of the negative correlation between children and marital happiness bears reporting. Lynn K. White, Alan Booth, and J. N. Edwards argued that the presence of children is associated with lower interaction between marital partners; more dissatisfaction with finances and the division of labor; and lower marital satisfaction. Furthermore, having young children keeps unhappily married parents together when they would rather be apart. The birth of a first child and the presence of preschoolers reduces the likelihood that unhappy married people will divorce. So even if the children do not cause the unhappiness, they prolong it because the parents stay together "for the good of the children."

Alice Rossi points out that though marital satisfaction or happiness declines after children are born and continues to decline through the children's adolescence, it increases when the children leave home and the couple settles into the postparental, or "empty-nest," stage of family life.

Rossi says, "The most critical and neglected reason for the increased happiness and improved mental health of a postparental couple is the fact that their children are now older, more settled, employed, and parents themselves, and the parents come to feel they did not do such a bad job of parenting after all."

Douglas Abbott has a number of useful suggestions for couples who are immersed in parenting and want to keep their marriage afloat:

1. *Communicate regularly*. Set aside a specific time to discuss finances and role sharing, and schedule time for joint activities and to iron out relationship problems.
2. *Share child care and household responsibilities*. The major cost of children to parents is an increased workload. By sharing household and child care, the parents can help strengthen their marriage.
3. *Get away together*. Activities don't have to include the children all the time. In fact, it's good for everyone to allow mom and dad time off alone together.
4. *Develop shared interests*. One way to find more time for each other is to look specifically for interests and activities to do with each other—hobbies and tasks that can be done together.
5. *Be sensitive to the affectional and sexual needs of the spouse*. Loss of intimacy and romance is a common problem parents face. Efforts must be

made to gain privacy from the children and to keep the sparkle in the relationship.
6. *Learn together about marriage and parenting.* Many parents recommend that marriage can be strengthened by study: reading and attending educational sessions focusing on marriage and family issues.
7. *Practice resource management skills.* Managing time, energy, and money are major problems for parents. There are classes and workshops available in these areas, also, and couples might benefit from attending some.

5. IF YOU REAR THEM RIGHT, THEY WILL STAY RIGHT

This may have been true in an earlier period of American history, but it seems dubious today. Forrest S. Tennant studied 5,000 American servicemen in Europe in an attempt to determine whether being a Boy Scout, an honor student, or an athlete in earlier years had any relationship to later addiction to alcohol or drugs. He was disillusioned with his findings. "I was hoping to come up with some recipes for parents," he said, "but it didn't turn out that way." A lot of parents would agree with him.

A mother said to the first author: "I am a devout Roman Catholic. I took my four children to church every week for fifteen years and not one of them is a good Catholic today." In another interview a father said: "My wife and I have never used alcohol and have never served it in our home. We thought that if we set a good example, our children wouldn't drink. Now, all four of them go to taverns and bars and our oldest son has been diagnosed as an alcoholic. How do you explain that?"

6. THE NATURE OF THE CHILD BEING REARED IS REALLY NOT VERY IMPORTANT—GOOD PARENTS CAN MANAGE ANY CHILD

Three psychiatrists, after careful research, have concluded that this is a myth. In their book, *Your Child Is a Person,* Stella Chess, Alexander Thomas, and Herbert Birch report that the temperament of the particular child is one of the crucial factors in successful or unsuccessful parental role performance. It is interesting that the subtitle of this book is "A Psychological Approach to Parenthood without Guilt."

Julius Segal and Herbert Yahraes argue that Wordsworth's observation that the child is father to the man should be a caution to modern parents. In their article "Bringing Up Mother," they point out that babies, with their extremely different temperaments, often train parents as much as parents shape them. In fact, we'd love to see, for example, a study of the relationship between colic and child abuse. It is a grisly experience to hear an anguished parent's descriptions of the emotions that wrench one when an infant cries uncontrollably for three, four, even five hours at a time.

Truly, think of all the other special children in the world and how their needs can change the lives of parents. Lynn Wikler, for example, does an excellent job outlining the "Chronic Stress of Families of Mentally Retarded Children." It is almost impossible to imagine what it must feel like to be faced with the probability that one will be involved in very basic-level parenting tasks for the rest of his or her life.

7. TODAY'S PARENTS ARE NOT AS GOOD AS THOSE OF YESTERDAY

It is impossible to prove or disprove this sort of belief, of course, but it does seem to be prevalent. We believe, as shown elsewhere in this study, that standards applied to parents today have been raised, and it is also true that the laboratory in which parents have to operate (the modern world) has become infinitely more complex. All this tends to create the impression that parents as a group have deteriorated since "the good old days" of the eighteenth or nineteenth century. This sort of argument is usually clinched (at least to the satisfaction of the critic) by reference to the family of John Adams or Thomas Jefferson. Actually, nobody knows what most parents were like in "the good old days," but if we can compare them to what doctors and other practitioners of the era were like, it seems possible that they were not supermen or superwomen, but just plain fathers and mothers sweating out every child.

There is always a tendency to romanticize the past, and this seems to have done a very real disservice to modern parents. Thumbing through books on life on the plains and prairies a century ago can be instructive. Invariably there will be a picture or two of a sod house in Kansas, Nebraska, or the Dakotas. The soddie will have a garden, mostly weeds, growing on the dirt roof; a cow may be up there on top munching away, too. The surroundings are unimaginably bleak. No trees or water; just dirt, wind, and sun. The captions under the pictures are usually pretty predictable: "The Jones family on their farm in 1878: Jacob, his wife, Emma, their fourteen children, their cow Bessie, and a hired man." The children back in the days before planned parenthood are too numerous to name. Everyone in the picture is grim faced; each has "tombstones in his eyes." Winter is coming soon, and all seventeen will be cooped up in the one-room dwelling for the better part of four or five months. Could anyone today sincerely believe that child-abuse rates then were less than now?

Though many people may cling to their notion that things were always better in "the good old days," research to prove such an allegation is difficult to obtain. The best research we have on family violence over a period of time indicates quite the contrary. Murray A. Straus and Richard J. Gelles studied the rate of physical abuse of children and spouses in 1975 and repeated their research in 1985. Both studies used national representative samples (2,143 families in 1975 and 3,520 in

1985). Both studies found "an extremely high incidence of violence" in the families, but the 1985 rates were substantially lower than the 1975 rates. Child-abuse rates were down forty-seven percent in the ten-year period, and wife abuse was down twenty-seven percent.

Family violence is relatively common in our society, but Straus and Gelles found a decrease over time. The researchers could not be certain of the reason: Perhaps the different methods used in the two studies artificially produced a difference in the results; perhaps people became increasingly reluctant to report their violent family behaviors between 1975 and 1985; perhaps violence in families actually did lessen over the ten years, due to the increase in prevention and treatment programs across the nation; perhaps violence lessened in families over the ten years because people are getting married at a slightly later age and having fewer children, both of which are associated with a lower likelihood to batter.

The researchers could not be certain. But it is clear the best evidence to date indicates violence in families in recent years has decreased somewhat.

8. CHILDLESS COUPLES ARE FRUSTRATED AND UNHAPPY

This may have been true in the nineteenth century or the early decades of the twentieth century when fertility was more or less a cultural neurosis—but if it was true then, it is certainly not true now. Actually, the very early studies of marital satisfaction by Ernest Burgess and Leonard Cottrell, also by Burgess and Paul Wallin, failed to support this belief: Some of the highest scores on the marital satisfaction scales used in these studies were made by childless couples.

Parenthood today is at last becoming a matter of choice—a man doesn't have to become a father today to prove his virility and a woman doesn't have to become a mother to prove her womanhood. It seems to us that this is a step in the right direction.

9. YOU SHOULDN'T STOP WITH JUST ONE

Folk wisdom dictates that only children are lonely and spoiled. Ellen Peck writes in *The Joy of the Only Child* that, contrary to these beliefs, only children are brighter, get along better with their peers, and are less spoiled.

Judith Blake examined family size and the quality of children. For the purposes of her research, she defined quality as educational attainment among adults and college plans among youngsters. She found that her research supports the so-called dilution model (in the average family, more children means lower quality of each child in terms of education, attainment and college plans). Further, she found that children do not suffer in this realm of quality from the lack of siblings, and that last-borns are not handicapped by a "teaching deficit."

Sharryl Hawke and David Knox take a balanced view of the situation. They studied only children and their parents and found both advantages and disadvantages to such a family style. The advantages include less financial expense and emotional demands on the parents, and more possessions, opportunities, and parental attention for the children. The disadvantages include parents' feelings of giving too much attention and protection to the child, and the child's feelings of loneliness and need for more companionship.

10. THERE ARE NO BAD CHILDREN—ONLY BAD PARENTS

This, in the opinion of the writers, is one of the most destructive bits of folklore relating to parenthood. As Max Lerner points out, parents have become the bad guys in modern America, while children and teachers and other custodians and child-shapers (such as the television station owners) have become the good guys. And, just as on television, the bad guys almost always lose.

Actually, Orville Brim has analyzed a rather lengthy list of factors other than parents that affect the destinies of children. These include genetic factors; siblings; members of the extended family, such as grandparents; schoolteachers; playmates; the youth peer group; and so on. He concludes that parents have been held unduly responsible for shaping the destiny of their offspring.

Lerner takes the position that parental critics tend to be "child worshippers"— the child can do no wrong, all children are potentially perfect (or near perfect), and parents should be able to rear *any* child successfully if they only know enough and try hard enough.

The writers are inclined to the view that some children are doomed almost from the point of birth: Try as they will, their parents seem destined to fail in their efforts to solve the various problems that arise during the child-rearing process. In an earlier America, this was conceptualized as fate, but in contemporary America, there is no such thing as fate; fate is just another word for poor parental role performance. It seems to us that this is folklore or mythology. It is also very unfair to parents who have made valiant efforts to help their children attain a decent and productive life.

We believe it is illogical to view children as good while indicting their parents as bad. In our work with abusive or neglectful parents, we have yet to meet someone currently doing a poor job as a parent who did not as a child have parents who did a poor job rearing them. Rather than blame parents for their failures, we find it much more useful to help them learn new ways to success. One middle-aged black woman comes to mind here: "Two of the kids turned out pretty good," she summarized for us, after telling a long tale of a hard, hard life for her that began in the worked-out farmlands of southern Mississippi in the Depression and was ending up in a lower-class neighborhood in a northern city. She had endured poverty, racism, hunger, and lack of education. "And," she added, "two of the kids just aren't amounting to nothing."

Was it her fault? Did she fail as a parent? we asked intensely, leaning toward her.

"I don't know. Maybe. But I always tried. And always did the best I knew how."

That, to us, is not failure.

11. PARENTS ARE ADULTS

This bit of folklore might depend on the definition of the word *adult,* but the fact is that perhaps forty percent of today's fourteen-year-old girls in the United States will bear a child before their twentieth birthday.

One teenage mother said to us: "My husband and I are just kids. We're growing up with the baby." This experiment may turn out well, but it frightens most child-development specialists.

Then there are the parents who may be adult in terms of chronological age, but in terms of personality are hopelessly immature: impulsive, selfish, lacking in empathy.

12. CHILDREN TODAY REALLY APPRECIATE ALL THE ADVANTAGES THEIR PARENTS ARE ABLE TO GIVE THEM

Oddly enough, the reverse seems to be true: Children today may be less appreciative and not more so. Numerous observers of the American family have come to this conclusion.

Some college students are very frank about this: They regard what they have received as their *right* and not as something to be thankful for.

In a sense, this same sort of psychology is characteristic of all of us living in the modern world; we take for granted inside toilets, painless dentistry, and religious freedom and simply complain when the system fails to deliver what we have come to consider our birthright. Thus, parents derive very little satisfaction from giving children all the modern advantages—they only feel guilty when they *cannot* deliver the goods.

13. THE HARD WORK OF REARING CHILDREN IS JUSTIFIED BY THE FACT THAT THE CHILDREN WILL MAKE A BETTER WORLD

This is a consoling thought, and one most parents need desperately to believe, but there is very little evidence to sustain it. It has more to do with hope than reality.

Whether one looks at crime or alcoholism rates or the prospects of peace in the modern world, the picture is not encouraging.

One can always hope, of course, that the new generation will be braver, wiser, and happier than their parents have been. It is dubious, however, that this will prove to be true.

14. THE SEX EDUCATION MYTH: CHILDREN WILL NOT GET INTO TROUBLE IF THEY HAVE BEEN TOLD THE FACTS OF LIFE

One mother said to us: "I do not see how such a thing (premarital pregnancy) could have happened to our daughter. She has known where babies come from since she was six years old."

This indicates how naïve some parents in our society are about the mystical power of sex education, which, at best, usually covers only the physiology of reproduction. Nothing is said about passion or seduction or the role of unconscious factors in heterosexual interaction. It seems to be assumed by such parents that sex is always a cold, calculating act—as if Freud had never written a word to the contrary.

The truth is that much (if not most) human sexual behavior is nonrational and only partly subject to continuous intellectual control. If this were not the case, illegitimate pregnancies in our society would be much fewer than they are and research data on adultery would be less massive.

A great many human societies, such as the Latin cultures, have always assumed that sex was too powerful for most humans to control, and they therefore arranged that persons for whom sexual relations were taboo were never left alone together. Our society is relatively unique in that we have adopted just the opposite policy—at least for single persons: They are permitted (and even expected) to spend hundreds of hours alone without ever having sexual relations until they marry. Research tells us, of course, that considerable proportions of them do have sexual relations before marriage, but only relatively few ever get pregnant. Or if they get pregnant, they are often married before the birth of the child.

The writers believe in sex education and think it belongs in every school and college curriculum, also in every family. But one should not expect too much of sexual knowledge. Attitudes, values, passion, and a host of factors determine the sexual behavior of any person at any given time with a particular partner. It could well be that the art of seduction has as much to do with premarital sexual relations as sex education does. Certainly the subconscious and unconscious factors analyzed by Freudians have to be taken into account in understanding why people behave the way they do sexually.

15. PARENTHOOD RECEIVES TOP PRIORITY IN OUR SOCIETY

This is a choice bit of folklore. Ask any employee if the company gives priority to his or her role as parent when they need a person in another branch in a different city. Parenthood in American society has always had to defer to military and industrial needs, to say nothing about our community needs. Millions of fathers and mothers have to sandwich their parental role into niches between their other roles in the society.

The wife of a famous authority on the family once said to the first author: "My husband would have made a wonderful father, but he was never home when the children were young. He was always away making speeches on how people should solve their marital problems or rear their children. I took care of the children myself."

A divorced mother with three children put it this way: "My employer couldn't care less about my duties as a mother. The state requires me to be at work at 7:45 which means that I have to leave home an hour before the children go to school. Then I have to work until 4:30, so that the children are out of school over an hour before I get home. And when the schools are closed, I usually have to work because they won't give me time off. Don't tell me parenthood comes first in our society."

16. LOVE IS ENOUGH TO GUARANTEE GOOD PARENTAL PERFORMANCE

Bruno Bettelheim, one of the authorities on child rearing, says love is not enough. His main point is that love has to be guided by knowledge and insight and also tempered with self-control on the part of the parent.

It is quite possible, however, that the reverse proportion is true: No amount of scientific or professional knowledge about child development will do parents (or their children) any good unless it is mixed with love for the child and acceptance of the parental role.

For example, John DeFrain and his wife, Nikki, managed with their first daughter Amie's consent to get the child potty trained by age thirty-one months. Neither John nor Nikki at the time had any particular training in child rearing and picked up tips on a hit-or-miss basis. Seven years later, when a second daughter, Alyssa, was born, the couple was loaded for bear: John was now armed with four years of experience in early childhood education and a Ph.D. in family studies, focusing on parent education and child development; Nikki had completed her training in early childhood education and had a bachelor's degree in human development. The DeFrains concentrated about $30,000 worth of education on the task of potty training Alyssa, and by age twenty-eight months Alyssa succumbed.

In sum, it cost the DeFrains $30,000 to save changing diapers for three months. That's roughly $500 per diaper.

By the time daughter number three, Erica, came around, the DeFrains had completely given up. "Don't push the river," as the book title notes. Erica followed her big sister Alyssa around like a puppy most of the time. By the time Erica was twenty-four months old, four-year-old Alyssa had taught Erica how to use the toilet.

Most parents who fail as parents actually love their children—they fail despite their love.

17. THE ONE-PARENT FAMILY IS PATHOGENIC

No one would deny that it is helpful to have both a father and a mother in the home when children are growing up—this assumes, however, that the two parents are compatible and share the same philosophy of child rearing. In view of the rate of marital failure in our society, this statement is a large assumption.

But has it been proven that children cannot grow up properly in a one-parent family? In a careful review of hundreds of studies of children, Alfred Kadushin reached this conclusion: "The association between single-parent familyhood and psychosocial pathology is neither strong nor invariable." Kadushin's main finding was that our society is not properly organized for the one-parent family—our social institutions were designed for the two-parent family system.

In a study of Head Start children, Joan Aldous did not find significant differences in perception of adult male and female roles between the father-present and the father-absent children when race and social class variables were controlled.

Likewise, John DeFrain, Judy Fricke, and Julie Elmen reviewed the massive research literature on single-parent families and the child's adjustment to divorce. They concluded our society over the years has had a compulsion to "accentuate the negative." The researchers set out to study not only the stresses but also the strengths of single-parent families. In their book, *On Our Own: A Single Parent's Survival Guide,* they concluded after studying testimony from 738 single parents that, "Though the single-parent family in our society has been much maligned, our research and the research of many other professionals indicate that millions of children are successfully raised by parents going it alone."

It does seem well established, however, that the chances of a child being in the so-called poverty group are significantly higher in our society when the father is absent.

18. PARENTHOOD ENDS WHEN CHILDREN LEAVE HOME

It doesn't, of course. The out-of-sight, out-of-mind phenomenon does help though; if you don't *know* that the kids are out late at night at a rock'n'roll concert and that they're probably drinking or stoned, you can probably sleep better. Getting the young adults out of the nest certainly helps in this regard. But they still usually keep coming back: for money, to have their clothes washed, for advice and consolation, and so on. Parents are still giving more, and children are still receiving more, for a long, long time after the nest empties.

To complicate matters, we have what some now are calling the reverse empty-nest syndrome. The children, after a stint in the real world, make a beeline for home. They come home after suffering a divorce; or they come home after college and spend several months hunting up a job while living off mom and dad again; or they get that job and get laid off and they're back again.

This leads to problems. The parents are getting adjusted to the freedom of childlessness. They can sleep through the night soundly, not half-expecting a call like one mother got:

"Mom?"

"Yeah, I guess it's me. But I can't tell for sure this late at night. What's the matter?"

"I got hit by a freight train."

"Oh. . . ."

It seems the young adult went through a railroad crossing a bit thoughtlessly and was broadsided by a 113-car coal train. Somehow he managed to climb free unscathed from his demolished clunker.

A popular writer was in Lincoln recently discussing the possibility of writing a book with the second author on the reverse empty nest. It seems she had just experienced it and was interested in exploring the issues with other parents. She happened to sit down with a very famous politician's wife during a conference and noted she was thinking of doing the book.

"Oh, Lord," the woman moaned. "Our boy just got a divorce and moved back home with us in Washington, and we're going crazy trying to cope!"

There is also much talk today about the so-called caught or sandwiched generation of parents. These are middle-aged parents who still are supporting their adult children for a variety of reasons. And they also are parenting their own aging parents.

For example, a caught couple ages fifty-five and fifty-eight may be financially and emotionally supporting their divorced daughter and two preschool-age grandchildren while the daughter gets back on her feet after the divorce. Meanwhile, this same couple may be trying to figure out how to financially and emotionally support their own aging parents. A very common scenario would have one eighty-seven-year-old great-grandmother in need of tremendous support in her own efforts to remain in her own home and be independent. Besides worrying about the eighty-seven-year-old great-grandmother, the middle-aged parents may also have to worry about a seventy-five-year-old great-grandfather who is showing all the signs and symptoms of Alzheimer's disease. Great-grandpa is "losing his mind," as we say, and the middle-aged parents have to figure out how to ease him into more restrictive care before he hurts himself or someone else.

This story is entirely plausible. One only has to go up to a middle-aged parent and start talking about his or her worries about the older and younger generations in the extended family.

19. THE EMPTY-NEST SYNDROME PLAGUES MANY PARENTS

Psychiatrists coined this delicious term to describe parents, usually mothers, who suffer from the debilitating sadness of losing the little birds to the world. It is certainly true that some parents despair over losing their young and wonder what they will now do besides rearing children to bring meaning into their lives. But researchers in family studies have modified this picture for us.

Bernice and Dail Neugarten argued, "The so-called 'empty nest,' for instance, is not itself stressful for most middle-aged parents. Instead, it is when children do not leave home at the appropriate time that stress occurs in both the parent and the child."

As we mentioned earlier in this chapter, marital satisfaction drops off rapidly with the advent of children. Researchers who follow parents longer into their middle and later years find that the satisfaction curve on the average rises after the children leave home. The pain of losing the young to the world for most parents apparently is more than adequately offset by the newfound freedom from responsibility. And as parents progress into the retirement years and become grandparents, satisfaction increases even more so. When our students study the results of these investigations they often wonder out loud if they should have children at all.

Our reply: Most people don't regret it in the long run. But don't go into this job starry-eyed.

20. PARENTS ALONE SHOULD REAR THE YOUNG

We believe the responsibility is far too great for two people or, increasingly, one person. If we do not have a legal mandate for community responsibility for children, we certainly have an ethical one.

We obviously are not advocating that all the children be shipped off immediately to a huge collective farm and day-care center somewhere out beyond the Salt Flats of Utah next to a hazardous wastes dump. But, in an important sense, we are all "our brothers' and sisters' keepers." It is healthy for our children to have contact with many other people: grandparents, friends, church people, and many more.

Margaret Mead put it so well shortly before she died. She argued that good care for children is unlikely to be given by adults "who find no meaning to life beyond the purchase of equity in a suburban house from which their children will move away, leaving their lives, once narrowly devoted to their own children alone, empty and meaningless."

If we are to change the situation, she argued, society will have to be restructured into communities in which the childless also have a responsibility for children and where parents see beyond the needs of their own biological or adopted children.

ARTICLE 20
Making Difficult Choices Easier: Day Care and Children's Development

DONNA KING AND CAROL E. MacKINNON

One of the most sweeping changes in American society has involved the entrance of women into the paid labor market. Most of them are married with dependent children. Many have had to rely on day care in order to pursue their jobs, and numerous questions have been raised about the consequences such care has for children. This article summarizes much of the recent research on day care.

IN 1978, BELSKY AND STEINBERG published their second major review of research on child care, and for a second time concluded that day care has no apparent deleterious effects on children. About the same time, demographic information on maternal employment and nonmaternal care for young children indicated that day care was, and would increasingly be, a fact of life for children under six (Klein, 1985). Researchers responded by changing their basic research question. People who had been asking, "Should we do day care?" began asking, "How do we do day care?" Methodologically, researchers abandoned the simplistic comparison of children reared exclusively at home by nonworking moms with children reared any other way; they began looking at within-group as well as between-group differences.

Donna King and Carol E. MacKinnon, "Making Difficult Choices Easier: Day Care and Children's Development." *Family Relations,* 37:392–398. Copyrighted © 1988 by the National Council on Family Relations, 3989 Central Ave. N.E., Suite #550, Minneapolis, MN 55421. Reprinted by permission.

They gathered observational data to delineate the actual differences between child care settings. And they began considering variables which might supersede or interact with type of care as an influence on child outcomes.

With Belsky's "reconsideration" of day-care research, the concern that day care harms children has resurfaced in both the scientific and popular literature. While researchers debate the issues in journals, magazines, and on television, parents are faced with immediate and agonizing decisions. Without the comfort of unanimous expert opinion, they must commit themselves and their children to some form of child care. At the same time, politicians looking toward the 1988 elections are formulating proposals for day-care policies that may have far-reaching effects on children and families. Parents and those who influence policy need good information to make appropriate decisions. Both are likely to rely on child and family professionals to provide that information. So, this article reviews day-care research since 1980, focusing on issues critical to personal or policy decisions about child care: the role of family as primary influence on the day-care child's development; the characteristics of high quality day-care environment; and the effects of day care on children's development. Specifically, the review considers how qualities of the home environment interact with qualities of the day-care environment to mediate the effects of day care on children's development.

THE HOME ENVIRONMENT

Despite daily separation of children from families, day care does not mean separate socialization. Rather, child rearing becomes a collaboration between family and day care in which the influence of family variables consistently supersedes the influence of day-care variables (Phillips & Howes, 1987). Family variables include parents' emotional well-being, parenting skills, family SES, and family structure. These variables ultimately affect the child's day-care environment as well, because they influence parental choices about child care. So, they are especially important for the child's development.

Parental Well-Being and Parenting Skills

A mother's emotional well-being and parenting skills influence her own and her child's ability to cope with daily separations, multiple caregivers, and the double load of career and home responsibilities. Working mothers who were rated higher on measures of integration, sensitivity to and acceptance of the child, satisfaction with nonwork time, and positive feelings about their marriages were more likely to have infants who were securely attached, regardless of child care arrangements (Belsky & Rovine, in press; Benn, 1986). Interestingly, a working mother need not have high scores on indices of emotional well-being to help her infant cope successfully with substitute care; 70% of mothers with only moderate levels of integration had sons who were securely attached (Benn, 1986). Perhaps, whether employed or not, mothers need only be "good enough mothers" to rear successful children.

Research on maternal employment and maternal well-being suggests that women who want to work and do work are more satisfied than women who want to work but stay at home. At issue is the consistency between employment attitudes and actual behavior. Similarly, maternal attitudes about substitute care might influence children's response to day care. Findings only partially support this idea. Five months after making their decisions about child care, "inconsistent mothers" (mothers who used child care but were not comfortable with it, or mothers who were comfortable with child care but were not using it) were quicker to anger and less patient than "consistent mothers." Children of inconsistent mothers were more easily frustrated by a task, showed greater distress at separation, and were less compliant. Yet five months later, these differences no longer existed (Everson, Sarnat, & Ambron, 1984).

Family SES and Structures

Typically, day-care research controls for home environment variables like SES and family intactness. Researchers operate from a long-standing assumption that substitute care is beneficial for low SES (including most single-parent families), but a deprivation for high or middle SES children who are leaving maternal care. In a study which confirms that assumption, day care at age three predicted an increase in desire at age five to six for social reinforcement from an unfamiliar adult (suggesting social deprivation) for middle-class children, and a decrease in this desire for lower-class children. Middle-class girls reared at home were more verbal, while middle-class girls in day care were less verbal (Robertson, 1982).

Family variables which influence children directly are also likely to influence day-care choices. Families with little money or information are ill equipped to obtain quality care for their children. In addition, parents probably seek out child care providers whose interactions with children resemble their own. Mothers who are "nurturing and supported" (have more social support, less marital stress, more role satisfaction, and more nurturant child-rearing practices) are likely to choose higher quality and more stable care for boys, while "restrictive and stressed" mothers are more likely to choose low quality, unstable care for girls (Howes & Stewart, 1987).

DAY CARE ENVIRONMENT

Five day-care variables seem important to the day-care child's development: timing of entry into care, extent of care, stability of care, setting of care, and quality of care.

Timing of Entry into Day Care

Because the attachments between parent and child form early, researchers pay special attention to the age at which an infant enters day care. Some research focusing on day care begun prior to age one casts doubt on the advisability of early infant day care. Recent studies using the Strange Situation laboratory test to measure mother/child attachment found that infants who entered day care before age one were at risk for insecure attachments (Belsky, in press; Belsky & Rovine, in press). In a study of Bermudian child care, anxious, hyperactive, and aggressive 5-years-olds were more likely than well-adjusted fives to have entered day care in early infancy (McCartney, Scarr, Phillips, Grajek & Schwartz, 1982). No such findings exist for children entering day care after age one.

Interestingly, other studies that compare entry during the first few months of life with later entry, are not so discouraging. High SES mothers who returned to work earlier ($M = 2.9$ months versus $M = 5.6$ months) were more likely to have securely attached sons, even when controlling for maternal integration (Benn, 1986). Benn speculates that returning to work after 6 months may disrupt predictability and violate the established expectations of the child, especially since the 6-month-old is developing greater cognitive discrimination and stranger anxiety. Day care designed as a positive intervention for low SES, physically nonoptimal infants were more likely to benefit children enrolled by 3 months (Breitmayer & Ramey, 1986). Furthermore, boys entering family day care before 6 months were playing with objects at a higher level as toddlers (Howes, 1987).

Extent of Time in Day Care

Most day-care research focuses on families using full-time child care, 30 or more hours a week. However, two recent studies of attachment (Belsky, in press; Schwartz, 1983) compared infants in part-time day care (less than 20 hours a week) with infants in full-time day care. Children in full-time day care appear to be at risk for insecure attachments, while those in part-time care are no more at risk than children cared for by their mothers. Considering that most employed mothers must work full-time and must place their infants in full-time substitute care, the possibility that infants do better when exposed to limited amounts of day care is perplexing. Mothers may have to weigh the requirements of full-time employment against the attachment needs of their infants.

Stability of Day Care

A stable child care arrangement is more desirable for children and families than one that frequently changes. For toddlers in family day-care homes, frequent changes were associated with less complex peer play; fewer changes were associated with higher levels of object play (Howes, 1987). Presumably, toddlers who were moved frequently had less time to form friendships and thoroughly explore objects in the environment.

Setting of Care

Although most research has been done in day-care centers, only about 10% of day-care children are placed in centers. Most child care is done by sitters in the family home or in family day-care homes, where one caregiver attends to a small group of children. Recently, researchers have been gathering observational data that allows them to compare sitter, family day-care homes, and center care on measures of caregiver characteristics, caregiver/child interactions, and physical environment.

In-home sitters were generally untrained and likely to be related to the child. Two- and three-year-old children at home with a sitter spent more time in one-on-one interaction with an adult, but had limited peer contact. Possibly because homes were organized around adult rather than child interests, sitter children watched more television and did few structured activities (Clarke-Stewart, 1987).

In licensed family day-care homes, caregivers were unlikely to have specialized training, though they were generally better educated than in-home sitters. Caregivers in unlicensed homes were not so well educated. Group size averaged five children, with peers engaging in more parallel than complex cooperative play. Again, homes were organized around adult interests, and children did few structured activities. Still, children in family day care watched less television than children at home with sitters (Clarke-Stewart, 1987; Goelman & Pence, 1987).

In centers, caregivers tended to be professionals with formal training. Groups were larger and play more complex. Children experienced less one-to-one interaction with an adult and more group activities. They were exposed to an average of three caregivers. The physical setting was neat, hazard-free, and organized around children's activities. Activities provided more structure and educational opportunity; children did not watch television (Clarke-Stewart, 1987; Goelman & Pence, 1987).

Center children scored highest on cognitive ability, standardized language tests, social knowledge, and sociability with an adult stranger. They were more independent of their mothers and at the same time demonstrated more social reciprocity and involved interactions with their mothers. Children at home with sitters were least advanced on all measures and most likely to be negative towards peers. Family day-care children's scores were mixed; they were highest in sociability with unfamiliar peers, and least independent of their mothers (Clarke-Stewart, 1987; Goelman & Pence, 1987).

Comparing children in different day-care settings more adequately addresses the research question, "How do we do day care right?" than simply comparing children in any day-care setting with children cared for by their mothers. On the other hand, a global variable like setting has limited usefulness when little is known about the effects of specific features of day-care environments on children. The findings immediately lead to other questions: "What is it about centers that make them more beneficial to children's cognitive development than family day-care homes?" "Why are family day care children more advanced than sitter children?" Studies which consider specific quality variables may help answer questions like these.

Quality of Day Care
Researchers, early childhood practitioners, and parents strive for an incontrovertible definition of high quality child care. Unfortunately, decisions about how to license

and certify quality programs for young children are being made now, although the state of objective knowledge about day-care quality is still uncomfortably meager.

Just how important is day-care quality? The quality of a child's total rearing environment is almost certainly more important than whether or not day care is part of that environment (Rubenstein, 1985). For children in adequate to good day-care situations, quality of the home environment is probably more salient for development than day-care quality (Kontos & Fiene, 1987). However, day-care quality may assume more importance when the quality of day care is extremely good or extremely poor. Unfortunately, much of the day-care research assesses care in relatively high quality, university-based centers, which are probably not typical day-care environments used by most families. LIttle research has been conducted in settings of poor quality because they are generally inaccessible to researchers. Important questions remain: Are relationships between quality and child outcomes linear, or is merely a minimal baseline of quality required (good enough day care)? What specific aspects of quality lead to specific outcomes in the child? Researchers addressing these questions have used global measures of quality as well as measures of regulable quality variables, caregiver/child interactions, and day care's effectiveness as a family support.

Global Measures

In order to study differences between children exposed to day-care situations of varying quality, researchers have had to subjectively operationalize "high quality." Many have used the Harms and Clifford Early Childhood Environment Rating Scale (ECERS), and its equivalent for measuring quality in family day care, the Family Day Care Home Rating Scale (FDCHRS). These instruments are popular with day-care administrators as self-study tools, but their psychometric qualities are unknown. Other researchers have devised their own definitions of high quality, combining scores on variables like teacher/child ratio, group size, physical space, physical facilities, staff training, and caregiver/child interactions to derive a total quality score.

Research across the various global definitions of high quality strongly suggests that good day care can promote children's cognitive and social development. Children in better day-care centers score higher on standardized language and intelligence tests (Goelman & Pence, 1987; McCartney, Scarr, Phillips, & Grajek, 1985; McCartney et al., 1982). They demonstrate more task orientation (McCartney et al., 1985); a higher level of play with objects, adults, and peers (Howes, 1987); more sociability and consideration (McCartney et al., 1982); more compliance and self-regulation (Howes, 1987); higher communicativeness and reciprocity with their mothers (Peterson & Peterson, 1986); and a more positive attitude toward adults (Vandell & Powers, 1983).

All correlations between high quality scores and positive child outcomes were positive, except one, a negative correlation between scores on the ECERS and emotional adjustment. Children who are in centers with higher ECERS scores but less caregiver/child interaction were more likely to be anxious, hyperactive, and aggressive at age five than children in centers scoring lower on the ECERS but higher on interaction (McCartney et al., 1982). Though this finding may be attributable to the inadequacy of the ECERS as a research instrument, it also suggests a need for more research on how quality of day care mediates the effects of day care on emotional development.

Unfortunately, too, the usefulness of the positive findings is limited because of the extreme variability in what different researchers called "high quality" day care. Teacher/child ratios in "high quality" centers ranged from 1:4 to 1:10, and space requirements varied from 40 to 80 square feet per child. Not all of the global definitions included criteria for teacher training, group size, or caregiver interaction. Since little is known about what aspects of high quality affect children, studies which focus on specific regulable qualities may be more useful at present.

Regulable Qualities

Quality of interactions between children and their parents has definite implications for children's development. Similarly, the quality of the interactions between caregivers and children is important for children's development. Unfortunately, interactions per se are difficult to regulate through licensing standards. For that reason, recent research, beginning with the National Day Care Study, 1979, looked at regulable variables which may impact on caregiver/child interactions.

Group Size
Studies since 1980 have confirmed the National Day Care Study's findings that group size is the most important determinant of the quality of children's environments (Ruopp & Travers, 1982). In smaller groups (less than 15), children engage in more classroom activities, in more fantasy play, and more talking with adults; caregivers are more likely to question, praise, and comfort children. In large groups, children play more in small subgroups, and are more often inactive (Smith & Connolly, 1986). These descriptive findings fit logically with correlations found in other studies. Small group sizes were associated with caregivers who were more contingently responsive and positive (Stith & Davis, 1984), and with children who were more sociable with peers and adult strangers (Clarke-Stewart, 1987; Kontos & Fiene, 1987). Children in large groups were less sociable but had more social knowledge (Clarke-Stewart, 1987), knowledge which may come from coping with a large complex of subgroups.

Most early studies which found day-care infants at risk for insecure attachments looked at infants in centers where group sizes ranged from 12 to 20 infants (Rutter, 1982). A group size this large may eliminate the possibility of an infant forming a stable attachment with a single caregiver. In a group of 20 infants with five caregivers, infants were no more likely to interact with their assigned "primary caregiver" than other adults (Wilcox, Staff, & Romain, 1980). If the establishment of a special relationship between a child and one caregiver is important for development, then favorable adult/child ratio cannot adequately compensate for large group size.

Center Size
Findings generally support the notion that day-care centers should be small, more along the proportions of a large family than of a small elementary school. Children in small centers play more elaborately, engage in more fantasy play, show more positive affect, are less avoidant, and less likely to be socially deviant (Kontos & Fiene, 1987; Phillips & Howes, 1987). Children in large centers are less competent socially (Clarke-Stewart, 1987).

Adult/Child Ratio
Research offers qualified support for the use of adult/child ratio as a single standard for high quality. In some studies, poor ratios did seem to handicap caregivers. In centers with many children per adult, caregivers were more prohibitive, less positive, had shorter conversations with children, answered children less, and gave less useful information (Smith & Connolly, 1986). Infants in centers with large groups and poor ratios were more overtly distressed and apathetic, and their caregivers engaged in more management than stimulation (Phillips & Howes, 1987).

Yet other studies contradict these findings. Better ratios were associated with higher anxiety (Phillips, Scarr, & McCartney, 1987) while worse ratios (about 1:15) predicted increased cooperation with peers and adults (Clarke-Stewart, 1987) and increased sociability (Schindler, Moley, & Frank, 1987). Why the mixed findings? A poor caregiver/child ratio probably does exert a negative influence on children's development, and this effect is probably exacerbated by large group size (Belsky, 1984). Often a good ratio means several teachers working in a large group of children. When children have three of four caregivers with whom to form a relationship, they may not form a close, respectful attachment conducive to cooperation and growth. Hence, a small group size might be more predictive of positive outcomes than a good ratio. A group of 10 children with one teacher may provide a higher quality setting than a group of 21 with three.

Caregiver Training
Research since 1980 has not conclusively confirmed the National Day Care Study finding that teachers with specialized training in child development are more responsive and effective. When compared to low quality centers, high quality centers employ teachers with more training and child care experience (Vandell & Powers, 1983). Children with teachers trained in child development scored higher on cognitive ability; however, they were less independent of their mothers and less sociable with adults. Children whose teachers had more general education but less specific training were more competent socially. Possibly, teachers trained in education tend to emphasize cognitive gains, while teachers with a boarder perspective emphasize social skills (Clarke-Stewart, 1987).

Physical Space

Children and caregivers probably function better in ample space which is well organized and well equipped. In larger spaces (75 square feet per child), children were more active and creative; they used objects in unusual ways, and did more running, rough and tumble play, and gross manipulation of objects. In smaller spaces (25 square feet per child), children climb more and make more physical contact with other children and equipment. With only 15 square feet of space per child, children become significantly more aggressive (Smith & Connolly, 1986). When child care environments contain more child than adult items and are organized around children's activities, children score higher on tests of cognitive and social competence (Clarke-Stewart, 1987). Well-organized playgrounds that include a good variety of activities are associated with involved, interactive children and sensitive, friendly teachers (Prescott, 1981).

Group Composition: Age Mix, Peer Interaction, Peer Turnover

Mixed-age grouping has social and cognitive advantages for preschool children in quality day care. Children in mixed-age groups were generally more sociable than children in same-age groups (Schindler et al., 1987). If preschool children had generally positive peer interactions with mature models in their day-care centers, they were likely to be more advanced in cognitive and social competence. Conversely, negative interactions with mature models predicted less competence. The presence of younger children had a negative influence on older children's social competence (Clarke-Stewart, 1987).

Very frequent peer interactions are usually associated with negative outcomes for children, possibly because more interactions with peers means fewer meaningful interactions with significant adults. Higher frequency of play with other children is associated with lower social competence and task orientation and higher dependence, aggression, and anxiety (Clarke-Stewart, 1987; Phillips et al., 1987).

Amount of peer turnover, though rarely studied, may be an important influence on social development in day care. Children's play at home and in day care is more positive and sophisticated with familiar than with unfamiliar peers (Rubenstein & Howes, 1983).

Director's Training and Experience

The relationship of director attributes to child outcome measures seems tenuous. Together with staff experience and group size, director experience explained only 19% of the variance in teacher ratings of sociability for one sample (Kontos & Fiene, 1987). Director variables may be more important for their impact on caregiver job satisfaction and job performance. In that case, perhaps leadership style would be a more predictive director variable than training and experience.

Curriculum

Day-care providers who emphasize divergent aspects of children's development in their curriculums are likely to influence children in different ways. For instance, day-care centers that focus exclusively on cognitive development tend to graduate children with good test scores but inadequate social skills. In one study, curriculum was a stronger predictor of social competence than quality; high quality centers with academic goals proved less likely than moderate quality centers with social goals to produce socially competent children (Schindler et al., 1987). Children who attended a cognitively oriented day-care center from infancy were rated by teachers as intelligent but aggressive when they reached public school (Haskins, 1985).

Curriculum can influence children's behavior in day care. In an unstructured socially oriented curriculum which minimized teacher/child interactions, children formed more peer groups, engaged in more fantasy play, and made more vigorous physical contacts. In a cognitively oriented curriculum emphasizing structured teacher/child interactions, children engaged in more quiet table play, had more contact with adults, did less running, and were more often inactive. Over time, the structured curriculum encouraged a longer attention span and more aggression. Because both curricula seem to offer children some advantages, the high quality day-care curriculum should strike a balance between cognitive and social goals.

Caregiver/Child Interactions

Regulable variables may be important only because they influence caregivers' ability to develop respectful relationships with children, and their willingness to stay on the job. To date, the best predictor of positive outcomes for day-care children is a caregiver who is involved, positive, and stable.

Children develop stronger attachments to caregivers whose interactions with children are typically positive and at close range than to caregivers whose interactions are typically interventions from long distance. In the Strange Situation, children with involved caregivers explored the room while frequently interacting with and contacting their caregivers. Children with low-involved caregivers showed few affiliative or exploratory behaviors in the presence of their caregiver and preferred the stranger (Anderson, Nagel, Roberts, & Smith, 1981). Just as attachment to a caregiver supports children's exploratory behavior in the Strange Situation, it may support their exploration of and adaptation to the day-care environment.

In fact, quality of the caregiver/child relationship does predict a child's ability to benefit from day care. Family day-care children were more socially and cognitively competent when they had more one-to-one conversations with caregivers, and when caregivers read to, touched, and directed them more. When family day-care caregivers were more responsive, children were more positive and reciprocal with their mothers. When these caregivers interacted less with children, the children were less independent of their mothers. (Clarke-Stewart, 1987). For children in centers, the amount of time caregivers spent talking to children individually or in groups strongly predicted higher ratings of task orientation, intelligence, sociability, and consideration, and lower ratings of anxiety, hyperactivity, and aggression (McCartney et al., 1982; Phillips et al., 1987). In these studies, more frequent interaction with adults acted as a positive influence on children.

Other studies find that frequent interactions benefit children only if these interactions are nonrestrictive and positive. In centers where caregivers read, offered choices, encouraged independent manipulation of materials, and abstained from demanding, controlling, punishing, holding, hugging, and helping, children were more advanced congnitively and friendlier with adult strangers (Clarke-Stewart, 1987). Toddlers whose caregivers were more playful and helpful but less intrusive were better adjusted and had better relationships with their mothers two years later. Toddlers with caregivers who provided less praise, less cognitive language stimulation, and more restrictions exhibited more behavior problems, tantrums, and test anxiety at age three and a half (Rubenstein & Howes, 1983).

Typically, caregivers are not stable figures. Staff turnover in day-care centers averages about 40% each year, and in family day-care homes averages 60% (Phillips & Howes, 1987). At the same time, stability may be an important component of high quality care. The positive child/caregiver relationships which benefit children take time to develop. Rubenstein (1985) observed that the longer caregivers are with children, the more like mothers they become. In a study comparing children's responses to stable versus unstable caregivers, Cummings (1980) found that children showed more positive affect with a stable caregiver after separating from their mothers at school.

Day Care As Family Support

Given that family variables and day-care variables both exert important influences on children's development, day care must be most helpful to children when it has positive effects on their families. Day care can have a positive influence on parenting skills. When compared with parents using sitters, parents using child-centered day care were more child centered in their interactions with children at home. Mothers and fathers exposed to male and female child-centered caregivers were higher on play, touching, holding, and proximity to their children (Edwards, Logue, Loehr, & Roth, 1987). Low SES mothers whose children were enrolled in high quality day care from infancy were more likely than mothers in a matched control group to say that children are entitled to opinions, that they learn actively, and that teaching is a parent's job (Ramey, Dorval, & Baker-Ward, 1981).

Day care can also provide social support. High quality child care centers were more effective at alleviating stress in working families than low quality centers (Howes, 1987). Four years after their infants entered a high quality child care center, low SES mothers were less likely than controls to say they were powerless to influence schools or that the future is more important than the present. These mothers also had more education and more semiskilled or skilled jobs (Ramey et al., 1981).

Though little studied, continuity between home and day care may be an important component of high quality; day care should be complementary and supplementary, not contradictory to parents (Ramey et al., 1981). Discontinuity between home and day care in adult behaviors and beliefs, or in physical and social environment, may be disruptive to development unless a child is at risk (Long, Peters, &

Garduque, 1985). Researchers could measure degree of discontinuity by observing children across environments.

Child Outcomes

When reviews of day-care research released in the late 1970s and early 1980s (Belsky & Steinberg, 1978; Rutter, 1982) tentatively concluded that day care was not harmful to children, many researchers diverted their efforts from general studies of day-care effects to studies of day-care quality. Other researchers, committed to existing data bases or bothered by the gaps in previous research, continued to study the effects of day-care attendance on children's emotional, social, and intellectual development. These efforts have drawn criticism from some for dwelling on the practically moot research question, "Should we provide day care?" instead of addressing the more urgent issue, "How do we do day care right?" Even so studies about the effects of day care on children are valuable. If nothing else, their findings on effects of day care in general should help researchers interested in day-care quality pose more penetrating, useful questions.

Emotional Development

Because children in day care experience regular separations from their parents, research on the emotional outcomes of day care has focused on parent/child attachment. Long-established evidence indicates that insecure attachments are not the usual result of day care for children two and older (Rutter, 1982). Findings on infant attachments are less clear, so recent attachment studies have examined the effects of infant day care.

Though at least one recent study found no attachment differences between day care and mother care infants in the Strange Situation (Owen, Easterbrooks, Chase-Lansdale, & Goldberg, 1984), more have found that infants in full-time day care before age one are more likely than mother care infants to be insecure (Barglow, Vaughn, & Moliter, 1987; Belsky & Rovine, in press; Farber & Egeland, 1982; Schwartz, 1983). Belsky (in press) estimates with data combined from four studies that day-care infants are 1.6 times more likely to be insecurely attached.

Evidence from studies using methods other than the Strange Situation yield mixed results. Generally, day-care children look less attached in the lab than at their day-care centers. Day-care children who were separated from and then reunited with their mothers initiated and maintained more distance from mother than home-reared children. In the day-care center, these same children were highly affiliative during reunions, showing significant increases in attachment behavior when mothers arrived in the afternoon. Only a small number of children cried or acted negatively during day-care reunions, and even these children made at least one positive approach to their mothers (Ragozin, 1980). A similar study found that children were much more resistant to being left with a familiar caregiver in a strange lab than they were to being left at the child care center (Cummings, 1980). Another study comparing day-care and mother care children found no differences in attachment behaviors (Hock, 1980).

Findings on attachment have prompted a debate in the day-care community about the methodology and meaning of attachment research. Belsky (in press) argues that the Strange Situation, though artificial, is methodologically superior to various invalidated observation schemes used and considers the Ainsworth test and classification system a valid highly sensitive indicator of a child's emotional status. According to Belsky, the fact that the Strange Situation yields results which naturalistic observations fail to replicate attests to its unique ability to assess a child's vulnerabilities. Researchers like Scarr (1985; informal lecture at Duke University, 1987) point to the ecological irrelevance of the Strange Situation and place more value on behaviors elicited in the actual home and day-care environments of children.

Methodological questions aside, researchers are focusing on the implications of secure or insecure attachment for children. Those concerned with day-care quality, like Scarr (1985; informal lecture at Duke University, 1987) and Clarke-Stewart (1987), see day-care children's avoidant behaviors as adaptive, mature, and independent. Children who routinely separate and reunite with their mothers at day care are comfortable and familiar with separation and so exhibit less overt and intense attachment behaviors. Their avoidance is a habitual reaction to a daily routine, different than the avoidance displayed by an infant cared for exclusively by a mother who is rejecting.

Attachment researchers like Sroufe (1983) point out that attachment theory and research have reliably predicted negative outcomes for infants classified as insecure. Anxious attachments are associated with noncompliance, aggression, social withdrawal, dependency, and negative attention seeking. Positive attachments predict ego reliance, self esteem, positive affect, social competency, popularity with peers, compliance, and empathy.

Scarr and Clarke-Stewart might counter that Sroufe's findings come from studies of children raised exclusively at home. These findings may not apply to avoidant day-care children whose attachment behaviors, though apparently similar, have different nonpathological origins. Belsky (in press) responds to this argument by logically connecting attachment research with research on the social development of day-care children:

> A circumstantial case can be made that extensive infant day-care experience may be associated with increased avoidance of mother, possibly to the point of greater insecurity in the attachment relationship, and that such experience may also be associated with diminished compliance and cooperation with adults, increased aggressiveness, and possibly even greater social maladjustment in preschool and early school years. (p. 37)

Belsky's contention can only be substantiated by longitudinal research. For now, the attachment debate goes on.

Social Development

Children who have attended day care differ from children reared at home on two social dimensions: peer relations and adult-like behaviors. Findings on the peer relationships of day-care children are overwhelmingly positive. From toddlerhood through the early school years, across SES classifications, day-care children exceed home-reared children in frequency of positive social interaction, friendliness, socially mature behaviors, complexity of play, social confidence, interest in peers, and popularity with peers (Ramey et al., 1981; Schindler et al., 1987).

Children with day-care experience are less likely than home-reared children to fully conform to adult standards of behavior and comply with adult requests (Farber & Egeland, 1982; Rubenstein & Howes, 1983) or to respond prosocially to an adult stranger who needed help (Schenk & Grusec, 1987). They tended to be more aggressive (Haskins, 1985), perhaps because in group care they had more opportunities to successfully influence others through aggression (Rubenstein, 1985). In problem-solving situations, day-care children were more often frustrated and less often persistent and enthusiastic (Farber & Egeland, 1982). Day-care infants had more tantrums and were more fearful at age 4, displaying behavior more appropriate for 2-years-olds (Rubenstein & Howes, 1983).

One study indicates that 3- to 5-year-old children with day-care experience may reason differently than home care children about rules and transgressions. Day-care children were less likely to perceive social transgressions as naughty and deserving of punishment. However, they were more likely to recognize moral transgression as wrong and worthy of adult punishment. Furthermore, they were more likely to identify social transgressions as violations of convention and preferred adults to limit their interventions to situations involving moral violations (Siegal & Storey, 1985).

Intellectual Development

Relatively high quality day care has beneficial effects on children's intellectual development, especially for children at risk for declining IQ scores. In two intervention studies, low SES children entering a cognitively oriented day care in infancy scored higher than controls on verbal, perceptual, quantitative, and motor skills (Breitmayer & Ramey, 1986; Ramey et al., 1981). For middle-class toddlers, intellectually valuable experiences in day care, especially language mastery, expressive/artistic, and spatial experiences, explained more than half of the variance in cognitive scores (Carew, 1980). High quality day care has also been associated with higher scores on standardized language tests for middle-class preschoolers (Rubenstein & Howes, 1983).

CONCLUSION

In 1978, when Belsky and Steinberg gave day care a tentative clean bill of health (meanwhile lamenting the limitations of our knowledge about its specific effects), working parents and child care professionals could feel good about the distance developmental psychology had traveled. Knowledgeable people no longer equated day care with institutionalization or maternal employment with abandonment and rejection. Since then, researchers have made some progress towards delineating the relationship of specific day-care features to developmental outcomes. For the most part, they have concentrated on finding out how day care can best serve children and families. Hopefully, researchers will make rapid progress in determining the exact relationships between the many family, day-care, and outcome variables included in this review.

REFERENCES

Anderson, C. W., Nagel, R. J., Roberts, W. A., & Smith, J. W. (1981). Attachment to substitute caregivers as a function of center quality and caregiver involvement. *Child Development*, **52**, 53–61.

Barglow, P., Vaughn, B., & Moliter, N. (1987). Effects of maternal absence due to employment on the quality of infant-mother attachment in a low-risk sample. *Child Development*, **58**, 945–954.

Belsky, J. (1984). Two waves of day care research. Developmental effects and conditions of quality. In R. C. Ainslie (Ed.), *The child and the day care setting* (pp. 1–34). New York: Praeger.

Belsky, J. (in press). The "effects" of infant day care reconsidered. *Early Childhood Research Quarterly*.

Belsky, J., & Rovine, M. (in press). Nonmaternal care in the first year of life and infant-parent attachment security. *Child Development*.

Belsky, J., & Steinberg, L. D. (1978). The effects of day care: A critical review. *Child Development*, **49**, 929–949.

Benn, R. (1986). Factors promoting secure attachment relationships between employed mothers and their sons. *Child Development*, **57**, 1224–1231.

Breitmayer, B. J., & Ramey, C. T. (1986). Biological nonoptimality and quality of postnatal environment as codeterminants of intellectual development. *Child Development*, **57**, 1151–1165.

Carew, J. V. (1980). Experience and the development of intelligence in young children at home and in day care. *Monographs of the Society for Research in Child Development*, **45** (6–7, Serial No. 187).

Clarke-Stewart, A. (1987). Predicting child development from care forms and features: The Chicago study. In D. A. Phillips (Ed.), *Quality in child care; What does research tell us?* (pp. 21–41). Washington, DC: National Association for the Education of Young Children.

Cummings, E. M. (1980). Caregiver stability and day care. *Developmental Psychology*, **16**, 31–37.

Edwards, C., Logue, M., Loehr, S., & Roth, S. (1987). The effects of day care participation on parent-infant interaction at home. *American Journal of Orthopsychiatry*, **57**, 116–119.

Everson, M. D., Sarnat, L., & Ambron, S. R. (1984). Day care and early socialization: The role of maternal attitude. In R. C. Ainslie (Ed.), *Quality variations in day care* (pp. 63–97). New York: Praeger.

Farber, E. A., & Egeland, B. (1982). Developmental consequences of out-of-home care for infants in a low-income population. In E. Zigler & E. Gordon (Eds.), *Day care: Scientific and social policy issues* (pp. 102–125). Boston: Auburn.

Goelman, H., & Pence, A. R. (1987). Effects of child care, family and individual characteristics on children's language development: The Victoria day care research project. In D. A. Phillips (Ed.), *Quality in child care: What does research tell us?* (pp. 89–104). Washington, DC: National Association for the Education of Young Children.

Haskins, R. (1985). Public school aggression among children with varying day care experience. *Child Development*, **56**, 689–703.

Hock, E. (1980). Working and nonworking mothers and their infants: A comparative study of maternal caregiving characteristics and infant social behavior. *Merrill-Palmer Quarterly*, **26**, 79–101.

Howes, C. (1987). Quality indicators in infant and toddler care: The Los Angeles study. In D. A. Phillips (Ed.), *Quality in child care: What does research tell us?* (pp. 81–88). Washington, DC: National Association for the Education of Young Children.

Howes, C. & Stewart, P. (1987). Child's play with adults, toys and peers: An examination of family and child care influences. *Developmental Psychology*, **23**, 423–430.

Klein, R. (1985). Caregiving arrangements by employed women with children under one year of age. *Developmental Psychology*, **21**, 403–406.

Kontos, S., & Fiene, R. (1987). Child care quality, compliance with regulations and children's development: The Pennsylvania study. In D. A. Phillips (Ed.), *Quality in child care: What does research tell us?* (pp. 57–59). Washington, DC: National Association for the Education of Young Children.

Long, F., Peters, D., & Garduque, L. (1985). Continuity between home and day care: A model for defining relevant dimensions of child care. *Advances in Applied Developmental Psychology*, **1**, 131–170.

McCartney, K., Scarr, S., Phillips, D., & Grajek, S. (1985). Day care as intervention: Comparisons of varying quality programs. *Journal of Applied Developmental Psychology*, **6**, 247–260.

McCartney, K., Scarr, S., Phillips, D., Grajek, S., & Schwartz, J. C. (1982). Environmental differences among day care centers and their effects on children's development. In E. Zigler & E. Gordon (Eds.), *Day care: Scientific and social policy issues* (pp. 126–151). Boston: Auburn.

Owen, M. T., Easterbrooks, M. A., Chase-Lansdale, L., & Goldberg, W. A. (1984). The relationship between maternal employment status and the stability of attachment to mother and to father. *Child Development*, **55**, 1894–1901.

Peterson, C., & Peterson, R. (1986). Parent-child interaction and day care: Does quality of day care matter? *Journal of Applied Developmental Psychology*, **7**, 1–15.

Phillips, D., & Howes, C. (1987). Indicators of quality child care: Review of research. In D. A. Phillips (Ed.), *Quality in child care: What does research tell us?* (pp. 1–19). Washington, DC: National Association for the Education of Young Children.

Phillips, D., Scarr, S., & McCartney, K. (1987). Child care quality and children's social development. *Developmental Psychology*, **23**, 537–543.

Prescott, E. (1981). Relationship between physical setting and adult/child behavior in day care. In S. Kilmer (Ed.), *Advances in early education and day care* (pp. 129–157). Greenwich, CT: JAI.

Ragozin, A. (1980). Attachment behavior of day care children: Naturalistic and laboratory observation. *Child Development*, **51**, 409–415.

Ramey, C. T., Dorval, B., & Baker-Ward, L. (1981). Day care and the socially disadvantaged. In S. Kilmer (Ed.), *Advances in early education and day care* (pp. 69–106). Greenwich, CT: JAI.

Robertson, A. (1982). Day care and children's responsiveness to adults. In E. Zigler & E.

Gordon (Eds.), *Day care: Scientific and social policy issues* (pp. 155–173). Boston: Auburn.

Rubenstein, J. (1985). The effects of maternal employment on young children. *Applied Developmental Psychology*, **2**, 99–128.

Rubenstein, J., & Howes, C. (1983). Adaptation to toddler day care. In S. Kilmer (Ed.), *Advances in early education and day care* (pp. 39–62). Greenwich, CT: JAI.

Ruopp, R., & Travers, J. (1982). Janus faces day care: Perspectives on quality and care. In E. Zigler & E. W. Gordon (Eds.), *Day Care: Scientific and social policy issues* (pp. 72–101). Boston, MA: Auburn House.

Rutter, M. (1982). Socioemotional consequences of day care for preschool children. In E. Zigler & E. Gordon (Eds.), *Day care: Scientific and social policy issues* (pp. 155–173). Boston: Auburn.

Scarr, S. (1985). *Mother care, other care*, New York: Warner.

Schenk, V., & Grusec, J. (1987). A comparison of prosocial behavior of children with and without day care experience. *Merrill-Palmer Quarterly*, **33**, 231–240.

Schindler, P., Moley, B., & Frank, A. (1987). Time in day care and social participation of young children. *Developmental Psychology*, **23**, 255–261.

Schwartz, P. (1983). Length of day care attendance and attachment behavior in eighteen-month-old infants. *Child Development*, **54**, 1073–1078.

Siegal, M., & Storey, R. (1985). Day care and children's conceptions of moral and social rules. *Child Development*, **56**, 1001–1008.

Smith, P. K., & Connolly, R. (1986). Experimental studies of the preschool environment: The Sheffield project. In S. Kilmer (Ed.), *Advances in early education and day care* (pp. 22–66). Greenwich, CT: JAI.

Sroufe, L. A. (1983). Infant-caregiver attachment and patterns of adaptation in preschool: The roots of maladaptation and competence. In M. Perlmutter (Ed.), *Minnesota Symposium in Child Psychology* (Vol. 16, pp. 41–81). Hillsdale, NJ: Erlbaum.

Stith, S., & Davis, A. (1984). Employed mothers and family day care substitute caregivers: A comparative analysis of infant care. *Child Development*, **55**, 1340–1348.

Vandell, D. L., & Powers, C. P. (1983). Day care quality and children's free play activities. *American Journal of Orthopsychiatry*, **53**, 493–500.

Wilcox, B., Staff, P., & Romain, M. (1980). A comparison of individual and multiple assignment of caregivers to infants in day care. *Merrill-Palmer Quarterly*, **26**, 53–62.

ARTICLE 21
America's Youth: A Changing Profile

LUTHER B. OTTO

This article sketches how America's youth are changing, characterizing the alterations in a variety of attitudes and behavior. The author points out the implications these changes have for youth services and the larger society.

AMERICA'S YOUTH ARE CHANGING—again. The Baby Boom generation of the late 1940s through the mid-1960s introduced "hippies," then "yippies," the "now" generation, the "pepsi" generation, and the "me" generation. They bought Davy Crockett t-shirts, coonskin caps, and Barbie dolls. They went to Viet Nam, fled to Canada, and poured into Woodstock. Now they've grown up. Gerbers, which once served them baby food, now sells them life insurance. Mattel, which once sold them matchbox toys, now sells them adult electronic toys. Hospitals that once gave them obstetric and pediatric services now offer them coronary care. And McDonalds, for years the malt, burger, and fries feed basket for the nation's young, now serves egg McMuffin breakfasts to the on-the-way-to-work crowd and chicken McNuggets to the cholesterol conscious (Otto, 1984). They were a counter-, indeed a contraculture. Yankelovich (1974) describes them as a generation whose beliefs flaunted "faith in marriage, work, family, patriotism, democracy, competition, and equality of opportunity" (p. 9–10).

Today's young people are as remarkably different as were their predecessors.

Luther B. Otto, "America's Youth: A Changing Profile." *Family Relations*, 37:385–391. Copyrighted © 1988 by the National Council on Family Relations, 3989 Central Ave. N.E., Suite #550, Minneapolis, MN 55421. Reprinted by permission.

This article paints a broad-brushed portrait of today's youth. It sketches them in three dimensions: what characterizes them as a population group or cohort; what distinguishes their attitudes; and what typifies their behaviors. It offers selected comparisons between today's youth and those of decades past. The article addresses youth and family service professionals and suggests implications for youth-service organizations. It shares related observations from recent research on the influence parents have on their son's and daughter's attitudes and behaviors.

YOUTH DEMOGRAPHIC CHANGES

Demographers speak of differential fertility, by which they mean that some groups give birth to more children than do other groups. It takes 2.1 children from every female to maintain the nation's population, but Cubans in our society give birth to 1.3 children per female, whites give birth to 1.7 children per female, blacks give birth to 2.4 children per female, and Mexican-Americans give birth to 2.9 children per female. These fertility differences are heightened by age variation between the same population groups (Hodgkinson, 1985). The average white American is 31 years old. The average black is 25 years old. And the average Hispanic is 22 years old. Thus, white females are moving out of their prime child-rearing years at the same time that Hispanic females are moving into their peak childbearing years. The results are already evident. The state of California, to cite but one example, has a majority of minorities in its elementary schools, as do the 25 largest city-school systems in the country (Plisko & Stern, 1985). Differential fertility is an engine of change. Different birthrates are changing the profile of American's youth, and they will change the face of our nation in the years ahead. Our nation's population stands at 238 million people. We expect 265 million people by the 2020—not a big increase, but 91 million will be minorities, and most of them will be young.

As a nation we have also changed our family living patterns, and young people are caught in the middle of it (Hodgkinson, 1985). In 1955, for example, 60% of all households in the United States consisted of an intact marriage, a working father, a housewife mother, and two or more school-age children. Today, only 7% of all households fit the traditional family image. The normal childhood experience of today's youth is for a child to live with only one parent sometime before reaching age 18. Of every 100 children born today:

- Twelve are born out of wedlock
- Forty-one are born to parents who divorce before the child is age 18
- Five are born to parents who separate
- Two will experience death of a parent before they reach age 18
- Forty-one will reach age 18 without such incidents

What was once America's modal family living pattern has become an exception over the course of a single generation.

A related demographic trend that affects America's youth is the feminization of poverty (Hodgkinson, 1985). Fifty percent of children who live in female-headed households live in poverty compared with 12% who live in male-present households. Two of three poor children are white, but the percentage of minority children who are cared for by one parent and are poor is much higher. Twenty-five percent of the nation's poor are preschool children, and another 21% are school-aged children. By comparison, 14% of the poor are elderly and 12% are nonelderly adults. Almost half of the poor in the United States are children. Indeed, poverty has become more common among children than among any other age group. A child under 6 years old and living in the United States is six times more likely to live in poverty than is a person over 65 years old.

Another major demographic change is the educational achievements of America's youth. Our society has made great strides in raising the educational level of its citizenry. Today, roughly three fourths of young people graduate from high school, and about half attend some form of postsecondary education (Center for Education Statistics, 1987). Two of three of our citizens have high school diplomas, and one of four has a college degree.

But the increases in levels of education exact a cost. Higher levels of education are making the plight of the high school dropout all the more severe. The dropout rate will probably increase in the years ahead because while most states have adopted educational reforms and higher standards, few have passed reform legislation that provides remediation for those who could not meet the lower standards. Since 1980, the national average of all students retained in high school through graduation has been dropping about one half of 1% per year. In 1980 it was 76%. Today it is 73% (Hodgkinson, 1985). School "push-outs" are being added to the list of dropouts.

A direct link is seen between high school retention rates and state levels of economic development. States that retain high percentages of youth in school through graduation enjoy net gains to the state. Young people with diplomas have a high probability of getting a job and repaying the state, even benefiting the state, for the cost of their education through taxable income. But in states with low retention through high school graduation, many young people become a liability to the state. Without a high school diploma, the probabilities of their getting work and of repaying the state through taxes for their education are diminished. Dropouts are also less likely to migrate, which means that they may become a permanent economic burden to the state. And should such young people get into serious trouble, the net loss to the state is even greater. State educational investments in young people are substantial, to be sure. At North Carolina State University, for example, the state of North Carolina pays $15,802.33 per student per year for university education (Poulton, 1987), but the state pays nearly twice as much to care for the imprisoned. And though it may take the average college student 5 years to complete the baccalaureate program, time in prison at double the cost can last a lifetime.

One of the educational contradictions of our age is that at a time when access to some form of postsecondary education is within reach of every high school graduate, higher education is not as appealing as it once was. Hodgkinson (1985) reports that today, one out of eight highly able high school graduates chooses not to attend college. Roughly a third more blacks graduate from high school today than they did a decade ago, but black enrollment in colleges has dropped 11% during the past 10 years. High school graduation rates for Hispanics has increased roughly 40% over the past decade, but Hispanic enrollments in colleges have declined 16% over the same period.

On the positive side, there are as many people formally enrolled in industry-sponsored education and training programs today as there are enrolled in all colleges and universities combined—roughly 12 1/4 million in each; there are three and one-half times as many institutions that award certificates as there are institutions that award degrees (*The College Blue Book*, 1983); and the all-volunteer military provides educational benefits for young people as one of its prime recruitment tools (Bradley, 1983). These compete with formal education, a reminder that changing circumstances do not necessarily mean deteriorating conditions.

Implications

Differential fertility rates have long-term implications for society, but their consequences for youth-serving organizations and professionals are more immediate. The distribution of ethnic groups served by youth organizations will continue to shift. It will increasingly favor minority youth and, within minority cultures, Hispanic youth will become more numerous. Hispanics are likely to replace blacks as the dominant minority presence within the current generation.

As these population dynamics unfold, youth-service professionals and family counselor/therapists will have to learn sensitivities respected in the emerging minority cultures. It is not self-evident what these sensitivities will include, but the national experience with efforts to assimilate blacks over the past quarter of a century offers some hints. Thus, black families challenged our society to a deeper understanding of the implications of father-absent and female-headed households, value differences, even subtleties of vocabulary and body language. So, Hispanics will increasingly challenge youth and family service providers with new beliefs, values, and attitudes. Traditional Hispanic values include commitments to extended families and male machismo. Youth and family services will be on the cutting edge of efforts at resolving how society will integrate ethnic groups with values that fly in the face of prevailing cultural norms. The challenge to serve Hispanic populations is likely to exceed that posed earlier by blacks because Hispanic populations are more heterogeneous. Hispanics include Nicaraguans, Puerto Ricans, Colombians, Mexican Americans, and other groups from Central and South America. Each has its own culture, and the specific needs of these families and youth are not yet well understood.

The literature on socialization and child development is replete with studies of modeling, mentoring, and significant-other influences. Black youth have located their heroes in the athletics and entertainment industries, but it seems unlikely that Hispanics can use the same avenues to establish visible mentors, a national presence, and symbols of ethnic accomplishment and pride. Increasingly youth-service providers and family therapists/counselors will be in the forefront of issues that revolve around the question of whether the American Dream extends to diverse Hispanic populations.

Youth organizations and family practices will face new organizational challenges. These include maintaining resource levels. At the community level, youth and family-service professionals must anticipate the need for increased services to minorities. This means tapping new and additional budget resources, to be sure; but it means more. It also means establishing Hispanic minority presences on governing boards and professional staffs.

Youth-service providers must also anticipate new and revised programming needs. The fact that families with children, especially minorities, are proportionately overrepresented on poverty rolls prescribes an even stronger role for voluntary organizations. Health and fitness, prevention and treatment of drug/alcohol/substance abuse, and pre-employment training are three survival subjects that youth-service organizations have provided, and the changing demographics suggest the need for a redoubling of efforts targeted to Hispanic minorities. Education and training programs in health, drugs, and pre-employment remain peripheral in the nation's schools, but voluntary organizations including churches and youth organizations have responded aggressively, and their programming in these survival areas must be continued, indeed expanded, to new minority populations.

Attention to pre-employment training is especially critical because it effects all of today's young people, young men and young women. Youth unemployment rates are typically two and three times as high as the national average, and minority youth unemployment rates are five and six times the national rate. The problem of youth unemployment is confounded with the problem of educational dropouts. Ours is a credentialing society in which employers sort applicants on the basis of high school diplomas and other forms of certification. Although most employment opportunities in the 1990s will not require a college education, they minimally require a high school diploma and they optimally require additional vocational preparation (Silvestri & Lukasiewicz, 1987). Teaching this world-of-work reality must continue as a high priority agenda item for youth organizations intent upon easing new minority young people through the transitions from school to work and from adolescence to young adulthood.

YOUTH ATTITUDES

Compared with young people during the turbulent years of the late 1960s and early 1970s, today's young people are more laid-back, not as extreme in their dress and behavior, and less vocal in their political behavior.

Today's youth do not face the social, moral, and political issues of a Viet Nam War, or the related personal crisis of the draft. By comparison they have the luxury to dwell on their personal lives and on more immediate issues including their own hopes and plans. Today's young people are back on track in pursuit of the traditional

American Dream complete with stable marriage, children, a secure job, a large and attractive home, and many material advantages.

What is important to today's high school seniors? At the top of the list and in order of importance is being able to find steady work, having strong friendships, being successful in their line of work, having a good marriage and family life, and being able to give their children better opportunities than they have had (Bachman, Johnston, & O'Malley, 1987). "Finding purpose and meaning" is more important to young people today than it was a decade ago (Bachman, Johnston, & O'Malley, 1976), and it is especially important to females.

Today's high school seniors, both males and females, are very traditional in their views of husband/wife roles (Bachman et al., 1987). How would they divide up family responsibilities? Most prefer that husbands and wives take equal responsibility for the day-to-day care of children, but there is also a clear preference that mothers should not work if there are preschool children in the family. Both young men and young women expect that fathers of preschool children will work full-time. Various work arrangements for the wife are acceptable if the marriage is childless, including full-time employment, part-time employment, or no employment. Less than full-time employment by the husbands is unacceptable to the overwhelming majority of young men and young women. Thus, the work role of males continues to be more tightly circumscribed than that of females.

High school seniors feel that their parents agree with many of their ideas including the value of education, what are important values in life, religious beliefs, ideas about what they should do with their lives, views on how they should dress, and their political opinions. Areas of perceived differences between young people and their parents include how young people should use their leisure time, how young people should spend their money, and what is appropriate behavior on a date. Two thirds of the nation's seniors report that they argued or had a fight with their parents at least three times during the last 12 months (Bachman et al., 1987). At the same time, two thirds also indicate that they are satisfied with the way they get along with their parents, and one third say they are completely satisfied (Bachman et al., 1987). Some studies indicate that in recent years young people and their parents enjoy a closer relationship than did parents and children in years now past (Acock & Bengtson, 1980; Elder, 1980; McClelland, 1982).

Young people differ in their attitudes about other people. About a fourth feel that most people can be trusted, another fourth are undecided, but about half feel that "you can't be too careful" (Bachman et al., 1987, p. 38). There is good reason for young people's uncertainty. One of six reports having been threatened by someone with a weapon; one of four says that an unarmed person threatened him or her with injury; and one of six says that someone injured him or her on purpose without using a weapon (Bachman et al., 1987). Threats and injuries are reported most often for males, but 1 of 10 females also reports threats or injuries.

As today's young people look ahead, they see a bleak future for the country and the world, and the pessimism is higher than it was a decade ago (Bachman et al., 1977, 1987). More than half agree that things will get worse in the rest of the world in the next 5 years, and a third believe things will get worse in this country.

Yet, when it comes to their own lives and welfare over the next 5 years, today's young people are incredibly optimistic. None of 10 believe that things will get better for them, and only 1 of 35 thinks that his or her life will get worse. Youthful idealism is alive and well.

Young people expect to do better than their parents (Bachman et al., 1987). Only 1 of 12 expects to own fewer possessions than his or her parents. Half of females and two thirds of males expect to own more. Their materialistic aspirations go further. Half the females and two thirds of the males say that having lots of money is quite important or extremely important to them. Two thirds feel that a house of their own, a big yard, and a well-kept garden and lawn are quite important or extremely important to them. And seniors' expectations for their own children are even higher. Nine of 10 either say that it is either quite important or extremely important for them to be able to give their children better opportunities than they have.

What worries young people today (Bachman et al., 1987)? At the top of the list is crime and violence. In the minds of today's young people, such problems as population growth and pollution are much less a concern than they were a decade ago. Concerns about hunger and poverty are also down. Concerns about energy shortages peaked in 1980 when half of young men and women worried often about energy shortages, but today most young men and young women never or seldom worry about energy shortages. So also, fewer young men and women worry about economic matters today than did a decade ago.

One of the most dramatic changes in young people's worries over the past decade is the large increase in the numbers who worry about the chance of nuclear war (Bachman et al., 1987). Three fourths of young women and two thirds of young men worry sometimes or often about the chance of nuclear war. Very few never worry about it. Almost a third worry that nuclear or biological annihilation will probably be the fate of all mankind within their lifetime. A decade ago, twice as many disagreed as agreed (Bachman et al., 1977).

Most young men and young women want to find purpose and meaning in their lives, and many look for that purpose and meaning in their work. Being successful in their work is important to nearly all of them. Nearly all want to do their best in their jobs even if it means working overtime, and nearly all say they would work even if they had enough money to live comfortably for the rest of their lives (Bachman et al., 1987).

What kinds of jobs do young people want? Almost all say that it is very important that they have a job that is interesting to do, and nearly as many say that it is very important to have a job that makes use of their skills and abilities (Bachman et al., 1987). The high ratings young people give to these job characteristics has been virtually constant over the last decade. But today's young people face a more difficult job market than a decade ago, and they are more concerned about their own individual incomes. The result is that good chances for advancement and a chance to earn a good deal of money are very important to more young people today than they were a decade ago (Bachman et al., 1977).

Young people's work values are very traditional, and their traditional work views extend into sex-typed thinking about the kind of work seniors think they will be doing when they are 30 years old. When it comes to being a clerical or office worker—for example, bank teller, bookkeeper, or secretary— 1 of 5 females sees herself in that role at age 30 compared with only 1 of 75 males. When it comes to being a craftsperson or skilled worker—for example, carpenter, electrician, or mechanic—1 of 6 males sees himself fitting that role by age 30 compared with only 1 in 200 females (Bachman et al., 1987). The notion that some jobs are for women and others are for men continues to be deeply embedded in the way people in our society, including young people, think about work and occupations.

Implications

Many of young people's basic attitudes fly in the face of the demographic and economic realities of the world around them. Logic suggests, for example, that it is unlikely that one's personal circumstances can improve dramatically at the same time that national and world affairs take a turn for the worse. For most people income to support higher standards of living is tied to occupations, and today's youth do aspire to the good jobs to support upscale living; yet employment projections through the close of this century indicate that most employment opportunities will occur in less prestigious occupations that require lower levels of educational achievement and return fewer dollars to the employee (Silverstri & Lukasiewicz, 1987). So also, most females work today; the proportion of females who work is highest among mothers with children; and the labor market is yielding opportunities beyond the traditional female occupations of nursing, teaching, and office work. There are disjunctures between young people's beliefs, values, and attitudes and the world in which they live.

The disjunctures are particularly apparent between the employment outlook and young people's expectations (Otto, 1984). Young people will likely face a problem of adjusting their expectations to the realities around them. In *Birth and Fortune* Easterlin (1980) argues that young people's materialistic expectations are based on the life style they enjoyed when they were young. Easterlin reasons that parents of today's young people developed modest expectations when they were young because they lived in the aftermath of the depression. They also enjoyed America's postwar boom years which enabled them to achieve their modest materialistic expectations with relative ease. By comparison, today's young people were born into the prosperity of the early 1970s and the life styles their parents enjoyed. Thus, young people find themselves in a reversal of circumstances. Instead of learning modest expectations and enjoying great opportunities, today's young people learned great expectations but live in a world of more limited opportunities.

Landon Jones (1980) characterizes such youth as self-protectively conservative. Jones argues that young people aspire to the good jobs and the high incomes because they read the demographic and economic realities correctly. Their materialistic attitudes reflect an awareness and a drive to achieve what, on a cognitive level, they recognize is an increasingly difficult accomplishment.

Astin's (1982) studies of college freshmen indicate that whereas young people went to college in the 1960s to develop a meaningful philosophy, they go to college today to become very well-off financially. It is likely, however, that today's young people will have difficulty achieving their materialistic goals, and that their unrealized aspirations will occur at a time that interest in developing a meaningful philosophy is on the wane. That suggests that youth-service professionals and youth and family counselors/therapists will find themselves increasingly involved in helping young people downsize their materialistic aspirations and in finding avocational avenues that give purpose and meaning to their lives.

This suggests a need for more programming and counseling on life goals and personal values in the years ahead. It may suggest the need to help young people become introspective and to learn to assess themselves on quality considerations other than the accumulation of possessions. Young people may have to rely on inner resources to cope with and to compensate for lower levels of socioeconomic achievement.

One of the by-products of high rates of youth unemployment is that young people, particularly minority youth, are not properly socialized into attitudes appropriate for the work place. By the year 2000 our nation will experience a labor shortage, and industry will be pressed to seek new labor supplies. Minority males, who heretofore have received poor quality educations, who have suffered corresponding high unemployment rates, and who have been poorly socialized for the work place will be in demand, but they will not necessarily be prepared for that opportunity. Youth organizations that provide effective pre-employment training will serve both the short- and long-term needs of the young and the best interests of the larger society.

Youth organizations can offer other human capital development programs. The needs include leadership development of minority youth, rehabilitation programs for offenders, training in communications skills, and literacy programs. Females in general, but minority females in particular, will need guidance in two career decisions: choice of occupational career and choice of a career preparation strategy.

The changing structure of American families, especially the increased numbers of children who grow up in single-parent families headed by working mothers, underscores the need for parent surrogates to teach life's basic lessons, including those that relate to attitudes. Social psychologists distinguish between two kinds of significant others. Role-specific significant others are important because of the roles they play (e.g., teacher, employer, or policeman). Person-specific significant others, by comparison, are important for "personal" reasons, because of whom they are and what they represent in the mind of the other person (e.g., friend and confidant). Most young people affiliate with youth organizations and attach themselves to professional youth workers not because they have to, but because they want to. Youth are attracted, and the youth professionals become person-specific significant others whom some young person has chosen of his/her own volition. Being a person-specific significant other is a powerful role to occupy in the life of a young person, and youth-service professionals often find themselves in that position. They are strategically positioned to influence young people's basic values and attitudes. These influences are likely to be more in demand and increasingly important in youth and family services for Hispanic minorities in the years ahead.

YOUTH BEHAVIORS

Nearly three fourths of today's high school seniors hold a part-time job during the school year (Bachman et al., 1987). The proportion of high school students who work has been rising steadily until recently and, generally speaking, working students have had the support of parents, teachers, and social scientists. "Working is good for them," the conventional wisdom seemed to argue. "It gets them into the real world." "It puts them in touch with all kinds of people, the rich and the poor, the young and the old." "It teaches them the nuts and bolts of holding a job, like getting along, being responsible, being on time." And, of course, "it teaches them the value of a buck."

With the blessing of society, our nation's youth went to work. The number of hours they work rose substantially during the 1970s, before tapering off a bit during the 1980s, but it is still impressively high. Among high school seniors, one of three males works at least 20 hours a week, and one of four females does the same (Bachman et al., 1987). They're working half-time while going to school full-time!

For all the supposed advantages of letting young people work, concerns have also been voiced. Greenberger and Steinberg (1981), for example, conclude that when high school students work more than 15 or 20 hours a week, the negatives begin to outweigh the positives. The negatives include diminished involvement with school, family, and peers, and increased use of cigarettes and marijuana (Steinberg, Greenberger, Garduque, Ruggiero, & Vaux, 1982).

Not only is the number of hours young people work noteworthy, but also how much they earn. Half of young men and a third of young women who work earn more than $50 a week (Bachman et al., 1987). That $200 a month—$2500 a year.

What to they do with the money? The conventional wisdom suggests that young people should also have a lot of freedom about spending their earnings, and they do. Bachman's (1983) research on working youth indicates that young people contribute little to rent, utilities, groceries, real estate taxes, health insurance premiums, dental bills, or orthodontial bills. Most of their earnings become "funny money." Half of high school seniors do not save for future education, and only 1 to 10 saves half of his or her earnings. Among males, automobiles are the biggest expenditure. Females spend substantial monies on automobiles, too, though they save slightly more for education. Over half of high school seniors report that they make no contributions to family expenses of any kind. Overwhelmingly their expenditures are discretionary.

Not surprisingly, one area of life satisfaction that declines among young people during the years after high school is satisfaction with their standard of living (Bachman, 1983). Full-time students after high school feel the pinch of not having enough money, compared to what they had while in high school. Many college graduates also experience a decline in standard of living after they leave the campus with degree in hand.

Drug use continues to be a serious form of problem behavior (Johnston, O'Malley, & Bachman, 1987). Marijuana use reached its highest levels among high school seniors in the late 1970s with daily marijuana use reported by one of seven males and 1 of 14 females. Cigarette use reached its peak a decade ago with one of five young men and women consuming half a pack or more of cigarettes per day. The current rate is about half that high. In recent years, young people have come to believe that there are great physical risks in the regular use of both marijuana and cigarettes. Today, young people believe that the use of marijuana is more harmful than smoking a pack of cigarettes a day. Generally speaking, youth drug use is declining.

That does not mean that the drug problem is resolved, however. The United States continues to have the highest rates of drug use by young people in the world's industrialized nations (Johnston et al., 1987). More than half of high school students try an illicit drug before graduation from high school, more than half try marijuana, and more than a third try an illicit drug other than marijuana. At least 1 in 25 seniors smokes marijuana nearly every day. One in 20 high school seniors consumes alcohol nearly every day, and nearly 4 of 10 say they have been involved in heavy drinking— five or more drinks in a row— in the past few days. Cigarette smoking, which will eventually take the lives of more young people than all other drugs and substances combined, has not dropped in usage among high school seniors since 1984. Nearly a third smoked cigarettes during the past month, a substantial proportion of whom either are, or soon will be, daily smokers. A fifth are daily smokers by the time they leave high school, and more will convert in the years that follow. Compared with past youth patterns in our country and in other countries, these are nontrivial use and abuse levels, and any consideration of the quality of lives young people live must take these realities into account.

The most disturbing change in youth behavior in recent years relates to mortality factors. When young people die, they die violent deaths. Among young people ages 15 to 24 who die, 77% die violently such that death from accidents, suicides, and homicides has passed disease as the leading cause of death for young people (Diegmueller, 1987). Young people are the only age group in the United States that have not enjoyed improved health status over the past 30 years. Death by communicable diseases has decreased appreciably, but the rise in violent deaths has more than offset the reduction in deaths due to disease.

The FBI Uniform Crime Reports for 1986 (Diegmueller, 1987) indicate that half of all homicides and suicides occur in the 15- to 24-year age group. From 1950 to 1980, homicides increased threefold and suicides increased more than fourfold for this age group. Yet, most violent deaths among young people occur on highways. Two thirds of their violent deaths involve car wrecks.

There is a link between substance use and abuse and teen suicides, homicides, and fatal accidents, and that link is alcohol (Diegmueller, 1987). In some areas of the county, the percentage of teen suicides who had been drinking prior to their deaths increased from 13% in the period 1968–1972 to 46% a decade later. The equation becomes even more deadly when firearms are involved. The most common form of teen suicide among those with significant blood alcohol content is use of a firearm. Homicides, suicides, automobile accidents, firearms, and alcohol are pernicious threats to our nation's youth. They represent the most serious forms of problem behavior, especially when the behaviors occur in combination.

Implications

Much has been written in the popular press regarding quality of education in our nation's schools. One of the themes is that test scores, as measured by such standardized instruments as the SAT, have been declining over the past several years. This analysis of youth behaviors adds another dimension to the quality of education issue in pointing out that the proportion of young people who work and the number of hours they work has been increasing over the same time period.

It has been argued that part-time work benefits students. Their earnings provide pocket money to a cohort that lives in poverty, and working may be a better alternative than some other leisure-time activities. Nonetheless, nearly a third of today's young people are exceeding the most liberal estimates of allowances for nondetrimental work time, and nearly half are exceeding the conservative standard. It is not likely that these schedules are in the best interest of our youth. At the heart of the problem is a lack of reliable parental monitoring procedures. The prevalence of single-parent families, problems associated with monitoring other spouse's children in reconstituted families, and young people's erratic schedules exacerbate the situation.

Supplementary mechanisms for monitoring youth behavior can be developed. Parents of young people who abuse drugs have taken the lead and established a model for how parents can act in concert as a support group, as a self-educating/sensitizing group, and as responsible parents who consciously set norms of acceptable behavior for young people. The parental support group model, which has also been adopted by parents with anorexic daughters, can be extended to define other appropriate norms as well, including work norms.

There is a myth, a widely held half-truth, that young people don't listen to their parents. The adolescent society literature of the early 1960s (e.g., Coleman, 1961) contributed to that myth, but more recent reviews of the accumulated research have carefully defined who influences young people about what. In his classic book *Changing Youth in a Changing Society*, Michael Rutter (1980) summarizes as follows: "taken together the findings . . . indicate that adolescents still tend to turn to their parents for guidance on principles and on major values but look more to their peers in terms of interest and fashions in clothes, in leisure activities, and other youth-oriented pursuits" (p. 30). Rutter concludes: "Young people tend both to share their parent's values on the major issues of life and also to turn to them for guidance on most major concerns. The concept of parent-child alienation as a usual feature of adolescence is a myth" (p. 31).

History indicates that myths can be extraordinarily resilient to change, but the notion that parents don't matter must be put to permanent rest. Parents matter, and they matter most on major values. Professional youth workers and family counselors/therapists must guard against the perception that their availability substitutes for the primary influence and responsibility parents have for their children. Practitioners must exercise care that their programming efforts, whether in youth organizations or in family practice clinics, are inclusive rather than exclusive of parents.

The challenge for more adequate monitoring extends beyond work hours to the use of firearms, automobiles, and alcohol. Recent declines in the use of cigarettes, marijuana, and other drugs demonstrate two important points: first, that youth behavior can be changed; and second, that organized parental efforts including information campaigns can make a difference. Moreover, the war on drugs campaign has demonstrated that the entertainment world, the media, even the White House can be enlisted by largely voluntary efforts to clean up the social environment in which we and our children live.

Parents make a difference in the lives of their children, but parents need leadership. Youth and family service agencies can multiply their effectiveness by more actively enlisting and organizing parental support for efforts designed to improve the quality of life for our young people.

CONCLUSIONS

Social historians may some day observe that during the last half of the 20th century, the years in which we live, our society awakened to the need to conserve natural resources. Acid rain, depletion of the ozone layer, oil depletion, contamination of ground water, atmospheric pollution, declining energy reserves, notions of conservation and environmental protection, and commitments to nuclear disarmament have become common topics in newspaper editorials and television features. All have to do with the quality of life we enjoy and destroy.

But news themes have a tendency to obscure the fact that our nation's youth are our most important natural resource. There is no particular reason to manage resources or to improve the quality of life were it not for the fact we want our young people to succeed us. Our youth need the same developmental attention as do our forests and woodlands, our potential energy sources, and our aeronautical and space sciences. To give primary attention to the development of physical resources without being equally attentive to the development of human resources would be a case of misplaced emphasis.

Today's youth offer a different profile than the generations that preceded them. As a cohort they are more diverse. Demographically, minority youth are becoming more numerous, more visible, and more needy. Youth generally and minority youth in particular are more impoverished, they are more often reared in single-parent families, their values derive from new ethnic groups, and the quality of their education is suspect. What is emerging is an increasingly diverse cohort that makes simplistic attention to youth needs ever more problematic. Problems once identified as minority issues are today's societal concerns.

Attitudinally, today's youth are less visible than their earlier counterparts. Today's youth are a more private generation. They aspire to the good life defined in traditional terms of marriage and family, work, and many material advantages; but the opportunity structure will likely deny them their aspirations. Their worries include crime, violence, and nuclear war.

Behaviorially, today's young are a working generation that commands substantial earnings power, nurtures strong appetites for consumables, and satisfies tastes with high levels of discretionary spending. Their patterns of drug and substance abuse have generally declined, but as a group their health status has also declined because of high incidences of accidents, suicides, and homicides compounded by access to firearms and alcohol.

Today's youth present a new and unique challenge to youth and family services. The graying of America, declining proportions of majority-culture youth, and increases in the number of childless families are already colluding to ignore the problems of the emerging youth generation. Social priorities have already shifted to the elderly at some expense to youth and family programs, and the declining proportion of majority culture youth will become increasingly evident in the ballot box and in program budgets. Childless couples, like the elderly, will probably vote their pocketbooks and spend on self-interests. The result is likely to be an increasing indifference towards youth that will make the role of youth and family services both important but also more difficult.

The suggestions offered to meet the changing profile of the nation's youth are primarily programmatic but include a call to more directly incorporate the influence parents have on their children. Conspicuously absent are suggestions for investing in buildings and related capital expenditures. The state of the economy, the numerical decline in youth populations, the changing age structure, and the changing structure of the American family suggest caution in committing to facilities. The primary issues youth and family services must consider are programmatic. Service providers need to think of "facility" not as a noun, but as a verb. The key question must be: How can our facilities facilitate services to the diverse and complex generation of youth at our doorsteps?

REFERENCES

Acock, A. C., & Bengtson, V. L. (1980). Socialization and attribution processes: Actual versus perceived similarity among parents and youth. *Journal of Marriage and the Family*, **42**, 501–15.

Astin, A. (1982). *The American freshman: National norms for fall, 1982*. Los Angeles: Higher Education Research Institute.

Bachman, J. G. (1983). Premature affluences: Do high school students earn too much? (an update through 1985 available from the author), *Economic Outlook*, USA, **10**(3), 64–67.

Bachman, J. G. Johnston, L. D., & O'Malley, P. M. (1977). *Monitoring the future: Questionnaire responses from the nation's high school seniors, 1976.* Ann Arbor, MI: Institute for Social Research.

Bachman, J. G., Johnston, L. D., & O'Malley, P. M. (1987). *Monitoring the future: Questionnaire responses from the nation's high school seniors, 1986.* Ann Arbor, MI: Institute for Social Research.

Bradley, J. (1983). *A young person's guide to military service.* Boston: The Harvard Common Press.

Center for Education Statistics. (1987). *Digest of education statistics 1987.* Washington, DC: U.S. Government Printing Office.

Coleman, J. S. (1961). *The adolescent society: The social life of the teenager and its impact on education.* New York: Free Press.

The college blue book: Occupational education. (1983). Riverside, NJ: Macmillian Publishing Company.

Diegmueller, K. (1987). The violent killing of youths: An adolescent fact of death. *Insight,* 3(32), 18–20.

Easterlin, R. A. (1980). *Birth and fortune.* New York: Basic Books.

Elder, G. (1980). Adolescence in historical perspective. In J. Adelson (Ed.), *Handbook of adolescent psychology* (pp. 3–46). New York: John Wiley.

Greenberger, E., & Steinberg, L. (1981). The workplace as a context for the socialization of youth. *Journal of Youth and Adolescence,* **10**, 185–210.

Hodgkinson, H. L. (1985). *All one system: Demographics of education—Kindergarten through graduate school.* Washington, DC: Institute for Educational Leadership, Inc.

Johnston, L. D., O'Malley, P. M., & Bachman, J. G. (1987). *National trends in drug use and related factors among American high school students and young adults, 1975–1986.* Washington, DC: U.S. Government Printing Office.

Jones, L. Y. (1980). *Great expectations: America and the baby boom generation.* New York: McCann and Geoghegan.

McClelland, K. A. (1982). Adolescent subculture in the schools. In T. Field, A. Huston, H. Quay, L. Troll, & G. Finley (Eds.), *Review of Human Development* (pp. 395–417). New York: John Wiley.

Otto, L. B. (1984). *How to help your child choose a career.* New York: M. Evans and Company.

Plisko, V. W., & Stern. J. D., (Eds.). (1985). *The condition of education: 1985 edition.* Washington, DC: U.S. Government Printing Office.

Poulton, B. R. (1987). *NCSA vital statistics 1982–1988.* Unpublished report to North Carolina State Faculty Meeting, October 29, Raleigh, North Carolina.

Rutter, M. (1980). *Changing youth in a changing society.* Cambridge, MA: Harvard University Press.

Silverstri, G. T., & Lukasiewicz, J. M. (1987). Occupational employment projections: The 1984–95 outlook. *Monthly Labor Review,* Table 2, pp. 45–50, Table 3, p. 51, & Table 4, p. 52.

Steinberg, L., Greenberger, E., Garduque, L., Ruggiero, M., & Vaux, A. (1982). Effects of early work experience on adolescent development. *Developmental Psychology,* **18**, 385–395.

Yankelovich, D. (1974). *The new morality: A profile of American youth in the 70's.* New York: McGraw-Hill Book Company.

ARTICLE 22
When Parent Becomes Peer: Loss of Intergenerational Boundaries in Single Parent Families

DAVID S. GLENWICK AND JOEL D. MOWREY

Following divorce, 90 percent of the children reside with their mother. Frequently under these circumstances, mothers turn to their children for emotional support and solicit their aid in filling the role of the absent parent. In doing so, the usual boundaries between parent and child become blurred, creating a maladaptive situation in which the mother functions as a peer rather than as a parent.

SINCE THE 1960'S, THE NUMBER OF divorces each year in the United States has approximately tripled, from 0.39 million in 1960 to 1.18 million in 1983 (National Center for Health Statistics, 1984), while the number of children who have experienced parental divorce has doubled (Glick, 1979). Currently, one out of five, or approximately 11 million, children live in a single parent home (Ryan, 1981). While the number of annual divorces is leveling off somewhat (i.e., from a peak of 1.22 million in 1981), the high incidence of divorce during the past decade has resulted

David S. Glenwick and Joel D. Mowrey, "When Parent Becomes Peer: Loss of Intergenerational Boundaries in Single Parent Families." *Family Relations*, 35:57–62. Copyrighted © 1986 by the National Council on Family Relations, 3989 Central Ave. N.E., Suite #550, Minneapolis, MN 55421. Excerpted and reprinted by permission. Footnotes were deleted from the original.

in a considerable number of single parent families seeking counseling and therapy. For example, at a community mental health center with which the present authors have been associated, 49% of the child clients in the 1977–81 period had experienced parental divorce (Bush, 1982/1983). The present paper focuses upon one frequently seen subtype of the divorced produced single parent family in which intergenerational boundaries have become blurred, the "Parent Becomes Peer" (PBP) family. . . .

CHARACTERISTICS AND DYNAMICS

In the PBP family, a divorced parent is raising one or more children alone, with the oldest child being 9–13 years of age. Another typical feature is the comparative lack of contact that the child has with the parent who resides outside the home. The emphasis of the present paper is on the mother-run single parent family, as this is the predominant form of divorced family in the United States and the one most commonly encountered in mental health settings. It is this particular child—often bright and verbal—in whom the mother frequently chooses to confide. The child's intelligence and articulateness may, in fact, encourage such maternal behavior, creating the expectation in the parent that the child is more mature than he/she really is. Thus, the parent feels free to transmit and share her feelings on a wide range of personal issues, such as bitterness toward her ex-husband (e.g., for rejecting her or not maintaining support payments); anger at males in general; and frustration with the numerous burdens thrust (or self-imposed) upon her, especially financial concerns and social isolation (Jauch, 1977). The resulting message conveyed by parent to child is that "we're in this together, kid."

The situation is similar to what Minuchin (1974) referred to as an enmeshed mother-child boundary, except that overprotectiveness, normally a feature of such a boundary, is absent in this case. The relationship, then, is much like that of the friendship between "chums," as described by Sullivan (1953), but considerably more one-sided in that only one party's (i.e., the mother's) needs are being addressed (however inappropriately).

Weiss (1979) also referred to this relationship as representing a loss of the "echelon structure," a term coined by Goffman (1966). An echelon structure consists of a hierarchy in which one individual has authority over another. Such a structure usually exists in a two parent family but often is absent in a one parent family due to the parent feeling inadequate and overwhelmed (Hajal & Rosenberg, 1978). The single parent's relationship with her child may become more like that of a peer, friend, or confidant. At its extreme, a reversal of roles occurs in which the child takes care of the parent, providing support and nurturance and assuming parental responsibilities (Weiss, 1979).

Seeking to relate to her child as a peer or partner and abdicating the maternal role, the mother may be having her needs gratified without reciprocally assuming a fair portion of the responsibilities. She may rely on the child for emotional support and for fulfillment of the role and functions of the absent parent (Hetherington,

1979). In addition, to avoid making decisions and commitments and facing her own fears, she may excessively seek out the child's opinion on a variety of matters (e.g., mother's new male friends), in part as an unconscious wish for confirmation of her own predispositions and preferences and perhaps as a means of reducing guilt feelings by including the child in decisions.

With the mother regressing in this fashion to adolescence, the child is simultaneously being pulled up to a pseudoadolescence or pseudoadulthood for which he/she is not prepared. The most apparent sign of this is that, while parental needs are being satisfied (albeit somewhat inappropriately), the child's affective requirements are frequently not met—particularly needs for nurturance and freedom from stresses of adulthood (Weiss, 1979). That is, the mother, though superficially interested and involved, is not genuinely listening and responding to the child's feelings (Wallerstein & Kelly, 1974). Indeed, the mother may not be aware of many of the pressures being placed by her upon the child.

For example, a parent who puts her child into the role of the absent parent may then unconsciously create a parent-child conflict similar to the marital conflict (Anthony, 1974). The child is then caught in a tense, no-win situation as he/she is pressured to assume the absent spouse role but is then treated punitively for behaving like the spouse. Another pressure that may exist in the mother-daughter relationship, especially when the generational hierarchy is abandoned, is that of competition and subsequent jealously in a variety of situations, such as dating and academic achievement (Wallerstein & Kelly, 1974). In addition, certain opinions and attitudes attributed to the child may in actuality be the parent's own perspectives projected onto the child. Thus, a mother's statements to the therapist that her son "would rather not see his father" or that her daughter "doesn't mind when I leave her alone at night with the sitter" are quite possibly a more accurate indication of the mother's feelings and wishes than the child's.

While to the casual observer this parent-child relationship can appear harmonious and even jovial, marked by much wisecracking and good cheer, the banter (especially its more sarcastic tinges) may mask and at times be an indicator of the child's underlying anxiety and discomfort. The literature on children of divorce indicates that while the child will typically initially deny the reality of the divorce and his/her feelings (Anthony, 1974), the denial is followed by feelings of anger, sadness, vulnerability, guilt, shame, embarrassment, betrayal, and resentment. Although anger is the most prominent emotion (Wallerstein & Kelly, 1976), other emotions and concerns are expressed, including a loss of faith, trust, security, and self-worth (Toomin, 1974), loyalty conflicts (Wallerstein & Kelly, 1974), and interpersonal and self-identity concerns (Kurdek, 1981).

In the particular case of the PBP child, these concerns and fears are often not directly expressed and may reveal themselves in a variety of symptomatic behaviors, such as hair pulling, stomach pains and other psychosomatic problems, truancy, sexual and aggressive acting out, withdrawal, running away, sleeping and eating problems, obsessions and/or compulsions, drug use, overcompliance with parental requests, and a decline or unevenness in academic performance. New relationships are often approached with caution due to the fear of being rejected or abandoned

(Sorosky, 1977). The behaviors displayed in a given case will depend upon the age, sex, developmental level, and previous behavioral and emotional history of the child. In some instances, such behaviors may be more apparent in settings other than the home (e.g., school, church group, Scouts). . . .

Two case studies are presented which illustrate the characteristics of the PBP family. The first discusses the modal situation, where an extant PBP family presents itself for therapy. The second demonstrates how experiencing a PBP-type parent may result in ongoing sequelae for the child even after he/she has been physically removed from the PBP family system. The case studies describe each family, as well as the therapeutic interventions utilized by us.

CASE STUDIES

Case 1

Nine-and-a-half-year-old Kim T. was referred for therapy because of hair pulling (resulting in a noticeable bald spot on her head), "bad language," and general "mouthiness" (terms in quotes those of her mother). Her grades had fallen from the B/C to C/F range during the past several months. Mr. and Mrs. T. had recently divorced after 19 years of marriage, with Mrs. T. obtaining custody of Kim and her 8-year-old brother Jason. Interviews and observations indicated that Kim's hair pulling was one of several anxiety provoked habits, others being ear pulling and knuckle cracking. Further exploration with Kim and Mrs. T. revealed considerable ongoing conflict between Mr. and Mrs. T., with Mrs. T. making frequent negative statements to Kim about her father. Additionally, Mrs. T. engaged in crying jags in front of the children, complained of being lonely and tense, and felt burdened by financial pressures. According to Kim, because of her mother's behavior she (Kim) found it difficult to talk with her about the divorce and related issues. Kim also commented that it was hard for her to have to listen to Mrs. T.'s continual critical remarks about Mr. T. Finally, due to Mrs. T.'s job as a cleaning woman and a relationship with a male friend, she was often out of the house, leaving Kim and her brother either alone or with a sitter. Jason's reactions to the situation, though more moderate than Kim's, included increased complaining and displays of anger.

Therapy (lasting 12 sessions) was directed at helping Mrs. T. understand the effects of her actions upon the children, realizing that Kim's feelings regarding the divorce were not identical to her own, and appreciating that Kim was displaying needs that were not currently being met. Mrs. T. was encouraged to channel her anger and resentment toward her ex-husband more appropriately and constructively rather than share it with her children. She began to confide in, and disclose to, friends to a greater extent than previously and joined the local Parents Without Partners chapter, which provided social and emotional support. Instruction in problem solving approaches and stress management enabled Mrs. T. to reduce her tension and gain better control over her real world problems (e.g., finances). With respect to her role as parent, Mrs. T. was given assistance in reassuming maternal responsibilities and structuring the home environment.

Simultaneously with these interventions directed at Mrs. T., counseling with Kim centered on giving her permission to openly discuss her own concerns regarding the divorce and its aftermath. While initially conducted alone with the therapist, such discussions gradually incorporated Mrs. T., with Mrs. T. becoming better able to listen to her daughter without imposing her own desires and preconceptions. Additional components of counseling with Kim included teaching her self-control techniques (e.g., cuing and self-instructions) to decrease her hair pulling and problem solving procedures to apply to some of her divorce-related problems (e.g., getting along with her father's girlfriend's daughter). External reinforcement (e.g., praise, extra treats) delivered by Mrs. T. supplemented the self-control training. At termination, Kim was no longer engaging in hair pulling or the other anxiety derived behaviors noted above. Mrs. T. was evidencing less depressive symptomatology and stating that she felt better able to cope, and a greater degree of stability was present in the household.

Case 2

Ann P. was a bright and verbal 11-year-old referred for therapy because of school truancy, failing grades, smoking, stomach pains, suicide threats, swearing, and failure to comply with adult requests. Ann's parents divorced when she was 10, at which time she lived with her mother while her father moved to a foreign country. Her mother frequently talked with Ann about her current sexual activities and her hatred toward Ann's father and consulted Ann about financial and work related problems. The paternal grandmother reported that Ann was treated "more like a girlfriend than a daughter." Ann was given almost total responsibility for household chores and for the daily care (e.g., feeding, dressing, and babysitting) of her 4-year-old brother. After 1 year with her mother, Ann was sent to live with her paternal grandparents, who brought her for therapy.

The initial problem in therapy with Ann was to overcome her verbalized "hatred" and distrust of her male therapist and her refusal to discuss her parents and the divorce. Thus, early sessions concentrated on permitting Ann to verbally express her feelings, especially anger, while reassuring her that she would still be perceived by the therapist as likable and lovable. A filmstrip on divorce and stories generated by the therapist about the feelings of children from divorced families were used to shift the focus from Ann to a third-person perspective. By doing so, Ann readily volunteered her perceptions, comments, and feelings about the veracity of the stories and filmstrip.

After approximately 2 months of weekly therapy, Ann was able to (a) state a desire to come for sessions and (b) verbalize her feelings, especially the fear of rejection by both the therapist and her parents. Open discussion was then possible regarding Ann's lack of responsibility for the divorce and her parents' problems and imperfections. In particular, she was told that her mother's expectations of her were often unrealistic and unfair. Ann was given permission to express her anger and frustration toward her parents, as well as reassurance that she could have both positive and negative feelings toward them simultaneously.

SUMMARY

Some publications have described the growth producing effects of the divorce process for children, especially an increase in self-esteem and self-reliance (e.g., Weiss, 1979). While it does appear true that a stable one parent home is probably more emotionally fulfilling than a chaotic, acrimonious two parent environment (Anthony, 1974; Parks, 1977; Rosen, 1977), such growth and fulfillment require active concern and involvement by all parties and is not an automatic product of divorce. The present paper has attempted to describe the distinguishing features of one subtype of single parent family that appears with a high degree of frequency in family- and child-oriented community mental health and counseling centers. . . .

REFERENCES

Anthony, E. J. (1974). Children at risk from divorce: A review. In E. J. Anthony & C. Koupernik (Eds.), *The child in his family: Children at psychiatric risk* (Vol. 3), (pp. 461–477). New York: Wiley.

Bush, R. (1983). Evaluating predictors of outcome for children in a community mental health center. (Doctoral dissertation, Kent State University, 1982). *Dissertation Abstracts International*, **43**, 2329B.

Glick, P. C. (1979). Children of divorced parents in demographic perspective. *Journal of Social Issues*, **35**, 170–181.

Goffman, E. (1966). *Asylums*. New York: Doubleday.

Hajal, F., & Rosenberg, E. B. (1978). Working with the one-parent family in family therapy. *Journal of Divorce*, **3**, 259–269.

Hetherington, E. M. (1979). Divorce: A child's perspective. *American Psychologist*, **34**, 851–858.

Jauch, C. (1977). The one-parent family. *Journal of Clinical Child Psychology*, **6**, 30–32.

Kaplan, S. L. (1977). Structural family therapy for children of divorce: Case reports. *Family Process*, **16**, 75–83.

Kurdek, L. A. (1981). An integrative perspective on children's divorce adjustment. *American Psychologist*, **36**, 856–866.

Minuchin, S. (1974). *Families and family therapy*. Cambridge, MA: Harvard University Press.

National Center for Health Statistics. (1984). *Births, marriages, divorces, and deaths, United States 1983* (DHHS Publication No. PHS 84–1120). Hyattsville, MD: U.S. Public Health Service.

Parks, A. (1977). Children and youth of divorce in Parents Without Partners, Inc. *Journal of Clinical Child Psychology*, **6**, 44–48.

Rosen, R. (1977). Children of divorce: What they feel about access and other aspects of the divorce experience. *Journal of Clinical Child Psychology*, **6**, 24–27.

Ryan, P. (1981). *Single parent families* (DHHS Publication No. 79–30247). Washington, DC: U.S. Government Printing Office.

Sorosky, A. D. (1977). The psychological effects of divorce on adolescents. *Adolescence*, **12**, 123–136.

Sullivan, H. S. (1953). *The interpersonal theory of psychiatry*. New York: Norton.

Toomin, M. K. (1974). The child of divorce. In R. E. Hardy & J. C. Cull (Eds.), *Therapeutic needs of the family: Problems, descriptions, and therapeutic approaches* (pp. 56–90). Springfield, IL: Charles C. Thomas.

Wallerstein, J. S., & Kelly, J. B. (1974). The effects of parental divorce: The adolescent experience. In E. J. Anthony & C. Koupernik (Eds.). *The child in his family: Children at psychiatric risk* (Vol. 3), (pp. 479–505). New York: Wiley.

Wallerstein, J. S., & Kelly, J. B. (1976). The effects of parental divorce: Experiences of the child in later latency. *American Journal of Orthopsychiatry*, **46**, 256–269.

Weiss, R. S. (1979). *Going it alone: The family life and social situation of the single parent*. New York: Basic Books.

ARTICLE 23
Fatherhood and Social Change

RALPH LaROSSA

Until recently, fathers have been invisible parents. The so-called "new fathers," however, are said to be not only highly visible but thoroughly involved in the rearing of their children. LaRossa argues that the change is more apparent than real. The ideology surrounding fatherhood has changed, but there is little evidence that the actual behavior of fathers vis-à-vis their children has kept pace.

THE CONSENSUS OF OPINION in American society is that something has happened to American fathers. Long considered minor players in the affairs of their children, today's fathers often are depicted as major parental figures, people who are expected to—people who presumably want to—*be there* when their kids need them. "Unlike their own fathers or grandfathers," many are prone to say.

But, despite all the attention that the so-called "new fathers" have been receiving lately, only a few scholars have systematically conceptualized the changing father hypothesis, and no one to date has marshalled the historical evidence needed to adequately test the hypothesis (Demos, 1982; Hanson & Bozett, 1985; Hanson & Bozett, 1987; Lamb, 1987; Lewis, 1986; Lewis & O'Brien, 1987; McKee & O'Brien, 1982; Plick, 1987; Rotundo, 1985).

Given that there is not much evidence to support the hypothesis, (a) how do we account for the fact that many, if not most, adults in America believe that

Ralph LaRossa, "Fatherhood and Social Change." *Family Relations, 37*:451–457. Copyrighted © 1988 by the National Council on Family Relations, 3989 Central Ave. N.E., Suite #550, Minneapolis, MN 55421. Reprinted by permission.

fatherhood has changed, and (b) what are the consequences—for men, for women, for families—resulting from the apparent disparity between beliefs and actuality? The purpose of this article is to answer these two questions.

THE ASYNCHRONY BETWEEN THE CULTURE AND CONDUCT OF FATHERHOOD

The institution of fatherhood includes two related but still distinct elements. There is the *culture of fatherhood* (specifically the shared norms, values, and beliefs surrounding men's parenting), and there is the *conduct of fatherhood* (what fathers do, their paternal behaviors). The distinction between culture and conduct is worth noting because although it is often assumed that the culture and conduct of a society are in sync, the fact is that many times the two are not synchronized at all. Some people make a habit of deliberately operating outside the rules, and others do wrong because they do not know any better (e.g., my 4-year-old son). And in a rapidly changing society like ours, countervailing forces can result in changes in culture but not in conduct, and vice-versa.

The distinction between culture and conduct is especially relevant when trying to assess whether fatherhood has changed because the available evidence on the history of fatherhood suggests that *the culture of fatherhood has changed more rapidly than the conduct.* For example, E. Anthony Rotundo (1985) argues that since 1970 a new style of American fatherhood has emerged, namely "Androgynous Fatherhood." In the androgynous scheme,

> A good father is an active participant in the details of day-to-day child care. He involves himself in a more expressive and intimate way with his children, and he plays a larger part in the socialization process that his male forebears had long since abandoned to their wives. (p. 17)

Rotundo (1985) is describing not what fathers lately have been doing but what some people would *like* fathers to *begin* doing. Later on he says that the new style is primarily a middle-class phenomenon and that "even within the upper-middle class . . . there are probably far more men who still practice the traditional style of fathering than the new style." He also surmises that "there are more *women* who *advocate* 'Androgynous Fatherhood' than there are *men* who *practice* it" (p. 20). Similarly, Joseph Pleck (1987) writes about the history of fatherhood in the United States and contends that there have been three phases through which modern fatherhood has passed. From the early 19th to mid-20th centuries there was the father as distant breadwinner. Then, from 1940 to 1965 there was the father as sex role model. Finally, since around 1966 there has emerged the father as nurturer. Pleck's "new[est] father," like Rotundo's "androgynous father" is an involved father. He is also, however, more imagined than real. As Pleck acknowledges from the beginning, his analysis is a history of the "dominant *images* [italics added] of fatherhood" (p. 84).

Rotundo and Pleck are clear about the fact that they are focusing on the culture of fatherhood, and they are careful about drawing inferences about the conduct of fatherhood from their data. Others, however, have not been as careful. John Mogey, for example, back in 1957, appears to have mistaken cultural for behavioral changes when, in talking about the emerging role of men in the family, he asserts that the "newer" father's "behavior is best described as participation, the reintegration of fathers into the conspicuous consumption as well as the child rearing styles of family life" (Mogey, as cited in Lewis, 1986, p. 6). Ten years later, Margaret Mead (1967), too, extolled the arrival of the new father:

> We are evolving a new style of fatherhood, in which young fathers share very fully with mothers in the care of babies and little children. In this respect American men differ very much from their own grandfathers and are coming to resemble much more closely men in primitive societies. (p. 36)

And recently there appeared in my Sunday newspaper the comment that "[Modern men] know more about the importance of parenting. They're aware of the role and of how they are doing it. Fifty years ago, fathers didn't think much about what kind of job they were doing" (Harte, 1987), p. 4G).

Neither Mogey nor Mead nor the newspaper presented any evidence to support their views. One can only guess that they were reporting what they assumed—perhaps hoped—was true generally (i.e., true not only for small "pockets" of fathers here and there), for, as was mentioned before, no one to date has carried out the kind of historical study needed to test the changing father hypothesis. If, however, the professional and lay public took seriously the thesis that fathers have changed and if others writing for professional and popular publications have echoed a similar theme, then one can easily understand how the notion that today's fathers are "new" could become implanted in people's minds. Indeed, there is a good chance that this is exactly what has happened. That is to say, Rotundo (1985) and Pleck (1987) probably are correct: there has been a shift in the culture of fatherhood—the way fathers and mothers think and feel about men as parents. But what separates a lot of fathers and mothers from Rotundo and Pleck is that, on some level of consciousness, the fathers and mothers also believe (incorrectly) that there has been a proportionate shift in the conduct of fatherhood.

I say on "some" level of consciousness because, on "another" level of consciousness, today's fathers and mothers *do* know that the conduct of fatherhood has not kept pace with the culture. And I include the word "proportionate" because, while some researchers have argued that there have been changes in paternal behavior since the turn of the century, no scholar has argued that these changes have occurred at the same rate as the ideological shifts that apparently have taken place. These two points are crucial to understanding the consequences of the asynchrony between culture and conduct, and they will soon be discussed in more detail. But first another question: If the behavior of fathers did not alter the ideology of fatherhood, then what did?

The answer is that the culture of fatherhood changed primarily in response to the shifts in the conduct of motherhood. In the wake of declines in the birth rate and increases in the percentage of mothers in the labor force, the culture of motherhood changed, such that it is now more socially acceptable for women to combine motherhood with employment outside the home (Margolis, 1984). The more it became apparent that today's mothers were less involved with their children, on a day-to-day basis, than were their own mothers or grandmothers, the more important it became to ask the question: Who's minding the kids? Not appreciating the extent to which substitute parents (day-care centers, etc.) have picked up the slack for mothers, many people (scholars as well as the lay public) assumed that fathers must be doing a whole lot more than before and changed their beliefs to conform to this assumption. In other words, mother-child interaction was erroneously used as a "template" to measure father-child interaction (Day & Mackey, 1986).

Generally speaking, culture follows conduct rather than vice-versa (Stokes & Hewitt, 1976). Thus, the fact that the culture of fatherhood has changed more rapidly than the conduct of fatherhood would seem to represent an exception to the rule. However, it may not be an exception at all. What may be happening is that culture *is* following conduct, but not in a way we normally think it does. Given the importance that American society places on mothers as parents, it is conceivable that the conduct of motherhood has had a "cross-fertilizing" effect on the culture of fatherhood. There is also the possibility that the conduct of fatherhood is affecting the culture of fatherhood, but as a stabilizer rather than a destabilizer. As noted, research suggests that androgynous fatherhood as an ideal has failed to become widespread. One reason for this may be that the conduct of fatherhood is arresting whatever "modernizing" effect the conduct of motherhood is having. Put differently, the conduct of fatherhood and the conduct of motherhood may, on a societal level, be exerting contradictory influences on the culture of fatherhood.

THE CONDUCT OF FATHERHOOD VERSUS THE CONDUCT OF MOTHERHOOD

Contending that the conduct of fatherhood has changed very little over the course of the 20th century flies in the face of what many of us see every day: dads pushing strollers, changing diapers, playing in the park with their kids. Also, what about the men who publicly proclaim that they have made a conscientious effort to be more involved with their children than their own fathers were with them?

What cannot be forgotten is that appearances and proclamations (both to others and ourselves) can be deceiving; everything hinges on how we conceptualize and measure parental conduct. Michael Lamb (1987) notes that scholars generally have been ambiguous about what they mean by parental "involvement," with the result that it is difficult to compare one study with the next, and he maintains that if we ever hope to determine whether or not fathers have changed, we must arrive at a definition that is both conceptually clear and comprehensive. The definition which he thinks should be used is one that separates parental involvement into three components: engagement, accessibility, and responsibility. *Engagement* is time spent in one-on-one interaction with a child (whether feeding, helping with homework, or playing catch in the backyard). *Accessibility* is a less intense degree of interaction and is the kind of involvement whereby the parent is doing one thing (cooking, watching television) but is ready or available to do another (respond to the child, if the need arises). *Responsibility* has to do with who is accountable for the child's welfare and care. Responsibility includes things like making sure that the child has clothes to wear and keeping track of when the child has to go to the pediatrician.

Reviewing studies that allow comparisons to be made between contemporary fathers' involvement with children and contemporary mothers' involvement with children, Lamb (1987) estimates that in two-parent families in which mothers are unemployed, fathers spend about one fifth to one quarter as much time as mothers do in an engagement status and about a third as much time as mothers do just being accessible to their children. In two-parent families with employed mothers, fathers spend about 33% as much time as mothers do in an engagement status and 65% as much time being accessible. As far as responsibility is concerned, mothers appear to carry over 90% of the load, regardless of whether they are employed or not. Lamb also notes that observational and survey data indicate that the behavioral styles of fathers and mothers differ. Mother-child interaction is dominated by caretaking whereas father-child interaction is dominated by play.

> Mothers actually play with their children more than fathers do but, as a proportion of the total amount of child-parent interaction, play is a much more prominent component of father-child interaction, whereas caretaking is more salient with mothers. (p. 10)

In looking for trends, Lamb relies on one of the few studies which allows historical comparisons to be made—a 1975 national survey that was repeated in 1981 (Juster, 1985). No data apparently were collected on parents' accessibility or responsibility levels, but between 1975 and 1981, among men and women aged 18 to 44, there was a 26% increase in fathers' engagement levels and a 7% increase in mothers'. Despite these shifts, paternal engagement was only about one third that of mothers, increasing from 29% in 1975 to 34% in 1981 (Lamb, 1987).

While there is nothing intrinsically wrong with talking about percentage changes, one should be careful about relying on them and them alone. If, for example, one examines the tables from which Lamb drew his conclusions (Juster, 1985), one finds that the number of hours per week that the fathers spent in child care was 2.29 hours in 1975, compared to 2.88 hours in 1981, which is an increase of about 35 minutes per week or 5 minutes per day. The mothers in the sample, on the other hand, spent 7.96 hours per week in child care in 1975, compared to 8.54 hours per week in child care in 1981, which also is an increase of about 35 minutes per week or 5 minutes per day. Thus, in absolute terms, fathers and mothers increased their child care by the same amount.

Bear in mind also that we are still talking about only *one* component of parental involvement, namely engagement. The two national surveys provide little, if any, information about changes in the accessibility and responsibility levels of fathers and mothers. Perhaps I am being overly cautious, but I cannot help but feel that until we gather historical data which would allow us to compare all three components of fatherhood, we should temper our excitement about surveys which suggest changes in the conduct of fatherhood over time. (For a tightly reasoned alternative viewpoint, see Pleck, 1985.)

Comparisons over time are difficult to make not only because so few scholars have chosen to study the history of fatherhood, but also because the studies carried out over the years to measure family trends provide scant information about fatherhood, per se. For instance, during a recent visit to the Library of Congress, I examined the Robert and Helen Lynd archival collection which I had hoped would include copies of the interview schedules from their two Middletown studies. It had occurred to me that if I could review the raw data from the studies, then I could perhaps plot paternal involvement trends from 1924 to 1935 to 1978, the times of the first, second, and third data collections in the Middletown series (Lynd & Lynd, 1929, 1937; Caplow, Bahr, Chadwick, Hill, & Williamson, 1982). Unfortunately, only four sample interviews from the earlier studies were in the archive. The rest apparently were destroyed. It is a shame that the Middletown data were not saved because the most recent book in the series presents a table which shows an increase in the weekly hours that fathers spent with their children between 1924 and 1987 (Caplow et al., 1982). There is no indication whether this represents an increase in engagement or accessibility or both. Had I been able to look at the interviews themselves, however, I might have been able to discern subtle variations.

What about the dads who are seen interacting with their kids in public (see Mackey & Day, 1979)? A thoughtful answer to this question also must address how we conceptualize and measure paternal involvement. Does the paternal engagement level of fathers in public square with the paternal engagement level of fathers in private, or are we getting an inflated view of fatherhood from public displays? If we took the time to scrutinize the behavior of fathers and mothers in public would we find that, upon closer examination, the division of child care is still fairly traditional. When a family with small children goes out to eat, for example, who in the family—mom or dad—is more accessible to the children; that is to say, whose dinner is more likely to be interrupted by the constant demands to "put ketchup on my hamburger, pour my soda, cut my meat?" And how can one look at a family in public and measure who is responsible for the children? How do we know, for instance, who decides whether the kids need clothes; indeed, how do we know who is familiar with the kids' sizes, color preferences, and tolerance levels for trying on clothes? The same applies to studies of paternal involvement in laboratory settings (see Parke, 1981). What can a study of father-child interaction in, say, a hospital nursery tell us about father-child interaction in general? The fact that fathers are making their presence known in maternity wards certainly is not sufficient to suggest that the overall conduct of fathers has changed in any significant way. Finally, the fact that fathers can be seen in public with their children may not be as important as the question, How much time do fathers spend *alone* with their children? One recent study found that mothers of young children spent an average of 44.45 hours per week in total child-interaction time (which goes beyond engagement), while fathers spent an average of 29.48 hours per week, a 1.5 to 1 difference. If one looked, however, at time spent alone with children, one discovered that 19.56 hours of mothers' child-interaction time, compared with 5.48 hours of fathers' child-interaction, was solo time, a 3.6 to 1 difference. Moreover, while fathers' total interaction time was positively affected by the number of hours their wives worked, fathers' solo time was not affected at all (Barnett & Baruch, 1987).

As for the public proclamations, almost all the books and articles which tout the arrival of "new" fatherhood are written not by a cross-section of the population but by upper-middle class professionals. Kort and Friendland's (1986) edited book, for instance, has 57 men writing about their pregnancy, birth, and child-rearing experiences. But who are these men? For the most part, they are novelists, educators, sculptors, real estate investors, radio commentators, newspaper editors, publishers, physicians, performers, psychologists, social workers, and attorneys. Not exactly a representative sample. As Rotundo (1985) notes, androgynous fatherhood as an ideal has caught the attention of the upper-middle class more than any other group, but that even in this group, words seem to speak louder than actions.

While the perception of fathers in public and the Kort and Friedland (1986) book may not accurately represent what fathers in general are *doing*, they can most certainly have an effect of what people *think* fathers are doing and should be doing. Which brings us back to the question, What are the consequences that have resulted from the apparent disparity between beliefs and actuality?

THE CONSEQUENCES OF ASYNCHRONOUS SOCIAL CHANGE

Thirty years ago, E. E. LeMasters (1957) made the point that parenthood (and not marriage, as many believe) is the real "romantic complex" in our society, and that even middle-class couples, who do more than most to plan for children, are caught unprepared for the responsibilities of parenthood. Later on, he and John DeFrain (1983) traced America's tendency to romanticize parenthood to a number of popular folk beliefs of myths, some of which are: raising children is always fun, children are forever sweet and cute, children will invariably turn out well if they have "good" parents, and having children will never disrupt but in fact will always improve marital communication and adjustment. Needless to say, anyone who is a parent probably remembers only too vividly the point at which these folk beliefs began to crumble in her/his mind.

The idea that fathers have radically changed—that they now are intimately involved in raising their children—qualifies also as a folk belief, and it too is having an impact on our lives and that of our children. On the positive side, people are saying that at least we have made a start. Sure, men are not as involved with their children as some of us would like them to be, but, so the argument goes, the fact that we are talking about change represents a step in the right direction. (Folk beliefs, in other words, are not necessarily negative. The myth that children are always fun, for example, does have the positive effect of making children more valued than they would be if we believed the opposite: that they are always a nuisance.) But what about the negative side of the myth of the changing father? Is there a negative side? My objective is to focus here on this question because up to now scholars and the media have tended to overlook the often unintentional but still very real negative consequences that have accompanied asynchronous change in the social institution of fatherhood.

I am not saying that professionals have been oblivious to the potentially negative consequences of "androgynization" on men's lives, for one could point to several articles and chapters which have addressed this issue (e.g., Benokraitis, 1985; Berger, 1979; Lamb, Pleck, & Levine, 1987; Lutwin & Siperstein, 1985; Pleck, 1979; Scanzoni, 1979). Rather, the point being made is that scholars and the media, for the most part, have overlooked the difficulties associated with a *specific* social change, namely the asynchronous change in the social institution of fatherhood.

The Technically Present but Functionally Absent Father

The distinction between engagement and accessibility outlined by Lamb (1987) is similar to the distinction between *primary time* and *secondary time* in our study of the transition to parenthood (LaRossa & LaRossa, 1981). The social organization of a family with children, especially young children, parallels the social organization of a hospital in that both are *continuous coverage social systems* (Zerubavel, 1979). Both are set up to provide direct care to someone (be it children or patients) on a round-the-clock or continuous basis. And both the family and the hospital, in order to give caregivers a break every now and then, will operate according to some formal or informal schedule such that some person or persons will be "primarily" involved with the children or patients (on duty) while others will be "secondarily" involved (on call or accessible).

Like Lamb, we also found that the fathers' levels of engagement, accessibility, and responsibility were only a fraction of the mothers', and that fathers tended to spend a greater part of their care giving time playing with their children. Moreover, we found that the kinds of play that fathers were likely to be involved in were the kinds of activities that could be carried out at a secondary (semi-involved) level of attention, which is to say that it was not unusual for fathers to be primarily involved in watching television of doing household chores while only secondarily playing with their children.

When asked why they wanted to be with their children, the fathers often would answer along the lines that a father has to "put in some time with his kids" (LaRossa, 1983, p. 585). Like prisoners who "do time" in prison, many fathers see themselves as "doing time" with their children. If, on some level of consciousness, fathers have internalized the idea that they should be more involved with their children, but on another level of consciousness they do not find the idea all that attractive, one would expect the emergence of a hybrid style: the technically present but functionally absent father (cf. Feldman & Feldman, 1975, cited in Pleck, 1983).

The technically present but functionally absent father manifests himself in a variety of ways. One father in our study prided himself on the fact that he and his wife cared for their new baby on an alternating basis, with him "covering" the mornings and his wife "covering" the afternoons. "We could change roles in a night," he said; "it wouldn't affect us." But when this father was asked to describe a typical morning spent alone with his infant son, he gave the distinct impression that he saw fatherhood as a *job* and that while he was "there" in body, he was someplace else in spirit.

> *I have the baby to be in charge of, [which has] really been no problem for me at all. But that's because we worked out a schedule where he sleeps a pretty good amount of that time. . . . I generally sort of have to be with him in the sense of paying attention to his crying or dirty diapers or something like that for anywhere between 30 to 45 minutes, sometimes an hour, depending. But usually I can have two hours of my own to count on each morning to do my own work, so it's no problem. That's just the breaks that go with it.*

Another example: Recently, there appeared an advertisement for one of those minitelevisions, the kind you can carry around in your pocket. Besides promoting the television as an electronic marvel, the man who was doing the selling also lauded how his mini-TV had changed his life: "Now when I go to my son's track meets, I can keep up with other ball games" (Kaplan, 1987, p. 32a). The question is: Is this father going to the track meets to see his son race, or is he going simply to get "credit" from his son for being in the stands? One more example: A newspaper story about a father jogging around Golden State Park in San Francisco who is so immersed in his running that he fails to notice his 3-year-old daughter—whom he apparently had brought with him—crying "Daddy, Daddy" along the side of the running track. When he finally notices her, he stops only long enough to tell his daughter that it is not his job to watch her, but her job to watch for him (Gustatis, 1982).

What will be the impact of the mixed messages that these children—and perhaps countless others—are getting from their fathers? Research capable of measuring and assessing the complexity of these encounters is needed to adequately answer this question (Pleck, 1983).

Marital Conflict in Childbearing and Child-Rearing Families

Because our study was longitudinal, we were able to trace changes over time; and we found that from the third, to the sixth, to the ninth month postpartum, couples became more traditional, with fathers doing proportionately less child care (LaRossa & LaRossa, 1981). It was this *traditionalization* process that provided us with a close-up view of what happens when the bubble bursts; that is, what happens when the romanticized vision of dad's involvement starts to break down.

One father, first interviewed around the third month after his daughter's birth, wanted to communicate that he was not going to be an absentee father like some of his friends were:

> *I've got a good friend of mine, he's the ultimate male chauvinist pig. He will not change a diaper. . . . [But] I share in changing the diapers, and rocking the baby, and in doing those kinds of things. . . . I love babies.*

During the sixth month interview, however, it was revealed that he indeed had become very much the absentee father. In fact, almost every evening since the first interview he had left the house after dinner to play basketball, or participate in an amateur theater group, or sing in the local choir.

Since what he was doing contradicted what he said he would do, he was asked by his wife to "account" for his behavior. *Accounts* are demanded of social actors whose behavior is thought to be out of line. By submitting an account, which in common parlance generally takes the form of an excuse or justification, and having it honored or accepted by the offended party, a person who stands accused can manage to create or salvage a favorable impression (Scott & Lyman, 1968). Because the wife did not honor the accounts that her husband offered, the father was put in the position of either admitting he was wrong (i.e., apologizing) or coming up with more accounts. He chose the latter, and in due course offered no fewer than 20 different explanations for his conduct, to include "I help out more than most husbands do" and "I'm not good at taking care of the baby." At one dramatic point during the second interview, the husband and wife got into a verbal argument over how much of the husband's contribution to child care was "fact" and how much was "fancy." (He, with his head: "I *know* I was [around a lot]." She, with her heart: "[To me] it just doesn't *feel* like he was.")

This couple illustrates what may be happening in many homes as a result of the asynchrony between the culture and conduct of fatherhood. In the past, when (as best we can tell) both the culture and conduct of fatherhood were more or less traditional, fathers may not have been asked to account for their low paternal involvement. If the culture said that fathers should not be involved with their children and if fathers were not involved with their children, then fathers were perceived as doing what they should be doing. No need for an explanation. Today, however, the culture and conduct of fatherhood appear to be out of sync. The culture has moved toward (not to) androgyny much more rapidly than the conduct. On some level of consciousness, fathers and mothers believe that the behavior of fathers will measure up to the myth. Usually, this is early in the parental game, before or just after the birth of the first child. In time, however, reality sets in, and on another level of consciousness it becomes apparent that mom is doing more than planned because dad is doing less than planned. The wife challenges the legitimacy of the (more unequal than she had foreseen) division of child care, demanding an explanation from her husband, which may or may not be offered, and if offered may or may not be honored, and so on.

In short, one would expect more conflict in marriage today centered around the legitimacy of the division of child care than, say, 40 years ago because of the shift in the culture of fatherhood that has occurred during this time. Some may say, "Great, with more conflict there will be needed change." And their point is valid. But what must be kept in mind is that conflict also can escalate and destroy.

Given that at least one recent study has reported that the most likely conflict to lead a couple to blows is conflict over children (Straus, Gelles, & Steinmetz, 1980), family researchers and practitioners would be well advised to pay attention to the possibility that violence during the transition to parenthood may be one negative consequence of asynchronous social change.

Fathers and Guilt

Several years ago, Garry Trudeau (1985), who writes *Doonesbury*, captured to a tee the asynchrony between the culture and conduct of fatherhood when he depicted a journalist-father sitting at his home computer and working on an autobiographical column on "The New Fatherhood" for the Sunday section of the newspaper. "My editor feels there's a lot of interest in the current, more involved generation of fathers," the journalist tells his wife who has just come in the room. "He asked me to keep an account of my experiences." Trudeau's punch line is that when Super Dad is asked by his wife to watch his son because she has to go to a meeting, he says no because if he did, he would not meet his deadline. In the next day's *Doonesbury*, Trudeau fired another volley at the new breed of fathers. Now the son is standing behind his computer-bound father and ostensibly is asking for his father's attention. But again Super Dad is too busy pecking away at his fatherhood diary to even look up: "Not now, son. Daddy's busy" (March 24 & 25).

Trudeau's cartoons, copies of which sit on my wall in both my office and my den, are a reminder to me not to be so caught up in writing about what it means to be a father (thus contributing to the culture of fatherhood) that I fail to *be* a father. The fact, however, that I took the time to cut the cartoons out of the newspaper (and make not one but two copies) and the fact that Trudeau, who is himself a father, penned the cartoons in the first place is indicative of a feeling that many men today experience, namely ambivalence over their performance as fathers.

To feel "ambivalent" about something is to feel alternately good and bad about it. The plethora of autobiographical books and articles written by fathers in the past few years conveys the impression that men do feel and, perhaps most importantly, should feel good about their performance as fathers. A lot of men do seem to be proud of their performance, what with all the references to "new" fatherhood and the like. At the same time, however, men are being almost constantly told—and can see for themselves, if they look close enough—that their behavior does not square with the ideal, which means that they are being reminded on a regular basis that they are *failing* as fathers. Failing not when compared with their own fathers or grandfathers perhaps, but failing when compared with the image of fatherhood which has become part of our culture and which they, on some level of consciousness, believe in.

This is not to suggest that in the past men were totally at ease with their performance as fathers, that they had no doubts about whether they were acting "correctly." For one thing, such an assertion would belie the fact that role playing is, to a large degree, improvisational, that in everyday life (vs. the theater) scripts almost always are ill defined and open to a variety of interpretations (Blumer, 1969). Perhaps more importantly, asserting that men in the past were totally at ease with their performance as fathers would ignore the fact that, contrary to what many think, some of our fathers and grandfathers were ambivalent about the kind of job they were doing. In a study just begun on the history of fatherhood in America, I have come across several cases of men in the early 1900s expressing concern over the quality of their paternal involvement. In 1925, for example, one father wrote to a psychologist to ask whether he was *too involved* with his 2-year-old son. Apparently, he had taught the boy both the alphabet and how to count, and he now wondered whether he had forced his son to learn too much too soon (LaRossa, 1988).

So, what *is* the difference between then and now? I would say it is a difference in degree, not kind. I would hypothesize that, given the asynchrony between the culture and conduct of fatherhood, the number of fathers who feel ambivalent and, to a certain extent, guilty about their performance as fathers has increased over the past three generations. I would also hypothesize that, given it is the middle class which has been primarily responsible for the changes in the culture of fatherhood, it is the middle-class fathers who are likely to feel the most ambivalent and suffer from the most guilt.

There is a certain amount of irony in the proposition that middle-class men are the ones who are the most likely to experience ambivalence and guilt, in that middle-class men are also the ones who seem to be trying the hardest to act according to the emerging ideal. As noted, the testimonials from the so-called androgynous fathers almost invariably are written by middle-class professionals. But it is precisely because these middle-class professionals are trying to conform to the higher standards that one would expect that they would experience the most ambivalence and guilt. Like athletes training for the Olympics, androgynous-striving fathers often are consumed with how they are doing as fathers and how they can do better. For example:

> Should I play golf today, or should I spend more time playing with Scott and Julie? Should I stay late in the office to catch up or should I leave early to go home and have dinner with the children? There is an endless supply of these dilemmas each day. (Belsky, 1986, p. 64)

Some may argue that the parental anxiety that men are beginning to experience is all for the better, that they now may start feeling bad enough about their performance to really change. This argument does have merit. Yes, one positive outcome of asynchronous social change is that ultimately men may become not only more involved with their children but also more sensitive to what it is like to be a mother. After all, for a long time women have worried about *their* performance as parents. It should not be forgotten, however, that the guilt which many women experience as mothers (and which has been the subject of numerous novels, plays, and films) has not always been healthy for mothers—or families. In sum, when it comes to parenthood, today it would appear that both men and women can be victims as well as benefactors of society's ideals.

CONCLUSION

Fatherhood is different today than it was in prior times but, for the most part, the changes that have occurred are centered in the culture rather than in the conduct of fatherhood. Whatever changes have taken place in the behavior of fathers, on the basis of what we know now, seem to be minimal at best. Also, the behavioral changes have largely occurred within a single group—the middle class.

The consequences of the asynchrony between the (comparatively speaking) "modern" culture of fatherhood and the "less modern" or "traditional" conduct of fatherhood are (a) the emergence of the technically present but functionally absent father, (b) an increase in marital conflict in childbearing and child-rearing families, and (c) a greater number of fathers, especially in the middle class, who feel ambivalent and guilty about their performance as fathers.

A number of recommendations seem to be in order. First, more people need to be made aware of the fact that the division of child care in America has not significantly changed, that—despite the beliefs that fathers are a lot more involved with their children—mothers remain, far and away, the primary child caregivers. The reason for publicizing this fact is that if our beliefs represent what we want (i.e., more involved fathers) and we mistakenly assume that what we want is what we have, our complacency will only serve to perpetuate the culture-conduct disjunction. Thus, scholars and representatives of the media must commit themselves to presenting a balanced picture of "new fatherhood."

Second, and in line with the above, men must be held responsible for their actions. In our study of the transition to parenthood, we found that the language that couples use to account for men's lack of involvement in infant care does not simply reflect the division of infant care, it constructs that division of infant care. In other words, the accounts employed by new parents to excuse and justify men's paternal role distance serves as a social lubricant in the traditionalization process (LaRossa & LaRossa, 1981). Thus, when men say things like "I'm not good at taking care of the baby" or "I can't be with Junior now, I have to go to the office, go to the store, go to sleep, mow the lawn, pay the bills, and so forth" the question must be raised, are these reasons genuine (i.e., involving insurmountable role conflicts) or are they nothing more than rationalizations used by men to do one thing (not be with their children) but believe another ("I like to be with my children")? If they are rationalizations, then they should not be honored. Not honoring rationalizations "de-legitimates" actions and, in the process, puts the burden of responsibility for the actions squarely on the person who is carrying out the actions. Only when men are forced to seriously examine their commitment to fatherhood (vs. their commitment to their jobs and avocations) can we hope to bring about the kinds of changes that will be required to alter the division of child care in this country (LaRossa, 1983).

What kinds of changes are we talking about? Technically present but functionally absent fathers are products of the society in which we live. So also, the traditionalization process during the transition to parenthood and the conflict and guilt it apparently engenders cannot be divorced from the socio-historical reality surrounding us and of which we are a part. All of which means that if we hope to alter the way men relate to their children, we cannot be satisfied with individualistic solutions, which see "the problem" as a private, therapeutic matter best solved through consciousness raising groups and the like. Rather, we must approach it as a public issue and be prepared to alter the institutional fabric of American society (cf. Mills, 1959). For example, the man-as-breadwinner model of fatherhood, a model which emerged in the 19th and early 20th centuries and which portrays fathers primarily as breadwinners whose wages make family consumption and security possible, remains dominant today (Pleck, 1987). This model creates structural barriers to men's involvement with their children, in that it legitimates inflexible and highly demanding job schedules which, in turn, increase the conflict between market work and family work (Pleck, 1985). More flex-time jobs would help to relieve this conflict. So would greater tolerance, on the part of employers, of extended paternity leaves (Levine, 1976). I am not suggesting that the only reason that men are not as involved with their children is that their jobs keep them from getting involved. The fact that many women also contend with inflexible and highly demanding job schedules and still are relatively involved with their children would counter such an assertion. Rather, the point is that the level of achievement in market work expected of men in America generally is higher than the level of achievement in market work expected of women and that this socio-historical reality must be entered into any equation which attempts to explain why fathers are not more involved.

When we will begin to see significant changes in the conduct of fatherhood is hard to say. The past generally provides the data to help predict the future. But, as the historian John Demos (1982) once noted, "Fatherhood has a very long history, but virtually no historians" (p. 425). Hence, our ability to make informed predictions about the future of fatherhood is severely limited. Hopefully, as more empirical research—historical and otherwise—on fatherhood is carried out, we will be in a better position to not only see what is coming but to deal with what is at hand.

REFERENCES

Barnett, R. C., & Baruch, G. K. (1987). Determinants of fathers' participation in family work. *Journal of Marriage and the Family*, **49**, 29–40.

Belsky, M. R. (1986). Scott's and Julie's Daddy. In C. Kort & R. Friedland (Eds.), *The father's book: Shared experiences* (pp. 63–65). Boston: G. K. Hall.

Benokraitis, N. (1985). Fathers in the dual-earner family. In S. M. H. Hanson & F. W. Bozett (Eds.), *Dimensions of fatherhood* (pp. 243–268). Beverly Hills, CA: Sage Publications.

Berger, M. (1979). Men's new family roles—Some implications for therapists. *Family Coordinator*, **28**, 638–646.

Blumer, H. (1969). *Symbolic interactionism: Perspective and method.* Englewood Cliffs, NJ: Prentice Hall.

Caplow, T. with Bahr, H. M., Chadwick, B. A., Hill, R., & Williamson, M. H. (1982). *Middletown families: Fifty years of change and continuity.* Minneapolis: University of Minnesota Press.

Day, R. D., & Mackey, W. C. (1986). The role image of the American father: An examination of a media myth. *Journal of Comparative Family Studies*, **17**, 371–388.

Demos, J. (1982). The changing faces of fatherhood: A new exploration in American family history. In S. H. Cath, A. R. Gurwitt, & J. M. Ross (Eds.), *Father and child: Developmental and clinical perspectives* (pp. 425–445). Boston: Little, Brown.

Gustatis, R. (1982, August 15). Children sit idle while parents pursue leisure. *Atlanta Journal and Constitution*, pp. 1D,4D.

Hanson, S. M. H., & Bozett, F. W. (1985). *Dimensions of fatherhood.* Beverly Hills, CA: Sage Publications.

Hanson, S. M. H., & Bozett, F. W. (1987). Fatherhood: A review and resources. *Family Relations*, **36**, 333–340.

Harte, S. (1987, June 21). Fathers and sons. Narrowing the generation gap: Atlanta dads reflect a more personal style of parenting. *Atlanta Journal and Constitution*, pp. 4G,6G.

Juster, F. T. (1985). A note on recent changes in time use. In F. T. Juster & F. P. Stafford (Eds.), *Time, goods, and well-being* (pp. 313–332). Ann Arbor, MI: Institute for Social Research.

Kaplan, D. (1987, Early Summer). The great $39.00 2" TV catch. *DAK Industries Inc.*, p. 32A.

Kort, C., & Friendland, R. (Eds.). (1986). *The fathers' book: Shared experiences.* Boston: G. K. Hall.

Lamb, M. E. (1987). Introduction: The emergent American father. In M. E. Lamb (Ed.), *The father's role: Cross-cultural perspectives* (pp. 3–25). Hillsdale, NJ: Lawrence Erlbaum.

Lamb, M. E., Pleck, J. H., & Levine, J. A. (1987). Effects of increased paternal involvement on fathers and mothers. In C. Lewis & M. O'Brien (Eds.), *Reassessing fatherhood: New observations on fathers and the modern family* (pp. 109–125). Beverly Hills, CA: Sage Publications.

LaRossa, R. (1983). The transition to parenthood and the social reality of time. *Journal of Marriage and the Family*, **45**, 579–589.

LaRossa, R. (1988, November). *Toward a social history of fatherhood in America.* Paper presented at the Theory Construction and Research Methodology Workshop, Annual Meeting of National Council of Family Relations, Philadelphia, PA.

LaRossa, R., & LaRossa, M. M. (1981). *Transition to parenthood: How infants change families.* Beverly Hills, CA: Sage Publications.

LeMasters, E. E. (1957). Parenthood as crisis. *Marriage and Family Living*, **19**, 352–355.

LeMasters, E. E., & DeFrain, J. (1983). *Parents in contemporary America: A sympathetic view* (4th ed.). Homewood, IL: Dorsey.

Levine, J. A. (1976). *Who will raise the children?* New York: Bantam.
Lewis, C. (1986). *Becoming a father.* Milton Keynes, England: Open University Press.
Lewis, C., & O'Brien, M. (1987). *Reassessing fatherhood: New observations on fathers and the modern family.* Beverly Hills, CA: Sage Publications.
Lutwin, D. R., & Siperstein, G. N. (1985). Househusband fathers. In S. M. H. Hanson & F. W. Bozett (Eds.), *Dimensions of Fatherhood* (pp. 269–287). Beverly Hills, CA: Sage Publications.
Lynd, R. S., & Lynd, H. M. (1929). *Middletown: A study in American culture.* New York: Harcourt & Brace.
Lynd, R. S., & Lynd, H. M. (1937). *Middletown in transition: A study in cultural conflicts.* New York: Harcourt & Brace.
Mackey, W. C., & Day, R. D. (1979). Some indicators of fathering behaviors in the United States: A crosscultural examination of adult male-child interaction. *Journal of Marriage and the Family,* **41,** 287–297.
Margolis, M. L. (1984). *Mothers and such: Views of American women and why they changed.* Berkeley: University of California Press.
McKee, L., & O'Brien, M. (Eds.). (1982). *The father figure.* London: Tavistock.
Mead, M. (1967). Margaret Mead answers: How do middle-class American men compare with men in other cultures you have studied? *Redbook,* **129,** 36.
Mills, C. W. (1959). *The sociological imagination.* London: Oxford University Press.
Parke, R. D. (1981). *Fathers.* Cambridge, MA: Harvard University Press.
Pleck, J. H. (1979). Men's family work: Three perspectives and some data. *Family Coordinator,* **28,** 481–488.
Pleck, J. H. (1983). Husbands' paid work and family roles: Current research issues. In H. Z. Lopata & J. H. Pleck (Eds.), *Research in the interweave of social roles,* Vol. 3, *Families and jobs* (pp. 251–333). Greenwich, CT: JAI Press.
Pleck, J. H. (1985). *Working wives/Working husbands.* Beverly Hills, CA: Sage Publications.
Pleck, J. H. (1987). American fathering in historical perspective. In M. S. Kimmel (Ed.), *Changing men: New directions in research on men and masculinity* (pp. 83–97). Beverly Hills, CA: Sage Publications.
Rotundo, E. A. (1985). American fatherhood: A historical perspective. *American Behavioral Scientist,* **29,** 7–25.
Scanzoni, J. (1979). Strategies for changing male family roles: research and practice implications. *Family Coordinator,* **28,** 435–442.
Scott, M. B., & Lyman, S. M. (1968). Accounts. *American Sociological Review,* **33,** 46–62.
Stokes, R., & Hewitt, J. P. (1976). Aligning actions. *American Sociological Review,* **41,** 838–849.
Straus, M., Gelles, R. J., & Steinmetz, S. K. (1980). *Behind closed doors: Violence in the American family.* New York: Anchor/Doubleday.
Trudeau, G. B. (1985, March 24 & March 25). *Doonesbury.* United Press Syndicate.
Zerubavel, E. (1979). *Patterns of time in hospital life: A sociological perspective.* Chicago: University of Chicago Press.

ARTICLE 24
Parent Care as a Normative Family Stress

ELAINE M. BRODY

As life expectancy and longevity have increased, three- and even four-generation families are becoming more commonplace. What happens to the dependent elderly under these circumstances? The author contends that, contrary to popular belief, the elderly are largely cared for by their adult children, although it can be a very stressful experience for the "sandwich generation."

A CENTRAL THEME in Donald Kent's work was the importance of linking research about aging to practice and policy. He wrote:

> "Research, policy and practice are . . . not the same, but . . . they are not unrelated . . . policy that is not informed by knowledge may well be worse than worthless; it may be dangerous" (1972).

The subject of filial behavior in caring for disabled elderly parents is a case in point. The question "What should adult children do for their dependent elderly parents?" illustrates how values determine whether knowledge is used or ignored in shaping policy decisions. Values also influence the filial behavior of millions of people for whom the question is a salient personal issue. Though the topic of parent care excludes important aspects of family help to the old, it ultimately concerns almost all of us who have had, how have, or may in the future have a parent who is elderly, and all of us who have children and hope to grow old ourselves.

Elaine M. Brody, "Parent Care as Normative Family Stress." *The Gerontologist*, 25 (1985):19–29. Copyright © 1985 The Gerontological Society of America.

[I] will argue that parent care has become a normative but stressful experience for individuals and families and that its nature, scope, and consequences are not yet fully understood. Some of the extraordinarily complex factors that interact to determine filial behavior will be explored. A hypothesis will be advanced that may account in part for the myth that adult children nowadays do not take care of their elderly parents as they did in the good old days. I [also] will comment on some of the ways in which social policy responds to knowledge about filial responsibility.

HISTORICAL PERSPECTIVES

Answers to the question "What should adult children do . . .?" are profoundly influenced by the pervasive myth that adult children nowadays do not take care of their elderly parents as they did in the good old days.

In 1963, [there was] a symposium to examine the facts in the case. The conveners felt that the three-generation family required consideration. They agreed that many programs for older people were based on social myths that had persisted because the assumptions on which they were founded had not been scrutinized by scholars. In the same year in which the conference papers were published (Shanas & Streib, 1965), Kent characterized a related myth (that of the idyllic three generation household of earlier times) as the "illusion of the Golden Past" (Kent, 1965).

Fifteen years later, the assumptions had been further scrutinized and rejected by much additional research. To the bewilderment of many scholars, the myth had survived nonetheless, prompting Shanas (1979a) to call it a Hydra-headed monster (the monster of Greek mythology that could not be killed).

The 1963 Symposium was a significant watershed in the study of intergenerational relations. There was consensus on facts that are now familiar. Rosow called the conference a "bench mark of the final respects paid to the isolated nuclear family before its interment" (Rosow, 1965, p. 341). Studies had produced compelling evidence to the effect that older people are not alienated from their families. On the contrary, it was clear that strong and viable ties exist among the generations. A consistent theme was the responsible behavior of adult children in helping their parents when need be. Important for our present concern, however, was the conferees' acknowledgement that the effects on those caregivers were hardly touched upon (Streib & Shanas, 1965).

At that time, the number of adults 65 years of age or older had increased by 80% in the previous 20 years. But we were not yet fully aware of the second demographic revolution that was occurring—the change in the age structure of the elderly population with increasing proportions of *very* old people.

Less than 400,000 older people were in nursing homes and homes for the aged, a number that would more than double in the next decade. Services and service-supported living arrangements for the noninstitutionalized elderly were virtually nonexistent.

Social Security was beginning to take hold in improving the income position of those who were covered, but the income floor was low and incomplete and there was no social insurance against the costs of catastrophic illness in old age. Schorr's classic monograph on the destructive effects of compulsory family economic support of the aged had been published (1960). Yet in most states, the expectation that adult children should provide such support for their parents was still operationalized by harsh LRR (Legally Responsible Relatives) provisions of public assistance programs, imposing severe strains on families (Brody, 1967a).

At the very time that the Symposium was concerned with the *three-generation family*, a cross-national study by Shanas and her colleagues was underway. The data being collected would show that 40% of older people with children had great-grandchildren (Shanas et al., 1968, pp. 140–145). The *four-generation family* already had become a common phenomenon.

In those early 1960s, most intergenerational research focused on noninstitutionalized older people. Our view at the Philadelphia Geriatric Center (PGC) was looking outward from the doors of a facility whose limited mandate was to provide long-stay residential care for the "well" aged. We were experiencing increasing pressure to admit a special subgroup of the elderly—those who were mentally and/or physically disabled. Older people with dementia were prominent among them. The PGC set a precedent by making a deliberate decision to admit people with that diagnosis, and signaled its determination to provide them with treatment rather than custodial care by convening the first national conference on Alzheimer's disease and related disorders (Lawton & Lawton, 1965).

A series of studies of the changing characteristics of our applicants and of the experiences that brought them to the institution led at once to their families. We found evidence of the impact on all family members of having a dependent elderly relative (Brody, 1966a, 1966b, 1967b, 1969; Brody & Gummer, 1967) and began to explore the social cost of care to families (Lawton & Brody, 1968).

It became clear that institutionalization of the aged did not reflect "dumping" or abandonment, a conclusion reached by others (e.g., Lowenthal, 1964; Townsend, 1965). Rather, it resulted from the chronic disabilities and dependencies of very old people combined with the absence, loss, or incapacities of caregiving families, and a glaring lack of supportive community services. After prolonged and strenuous efforts to care for their parents, adult children reached their limits of endurance.

Our dependent applicants, whom we described as the "older old," had aging children many of whom were grandparents; three-fourths of those children were in their 50s and 60s (Brody, 1966b). The crushing reality strains they had experienced often were accompanied by emotional family crisis which peaked during the admission process (Brody & Spark, 1966; Spark & Brody, 1970). The older people felt abandoned, their children were conflicted and suffered intensely from guilt, and multiple relationship problems erupted to create a searing experience for members of all generations in the family.

PARENT CARE AS A NORMATIVE EXPERIENCE

What had been happening was that *having a dependent elderly parent was becoming a normative experience for individuals and families* and was exceeding the capacities of some of them.

To illustrate—Between 1900 and 1976, the number of people who experienced the death of a parent before the age of 15 dropped from 1 to 4 to 1 in 20, while the number of middle aged couples with two or more living parents increased from 10% to 47% (Uhlenberg, 1980). At the time of the 1963 Symposium, about 25% of people over the age of 45 had a surviving parent, but by the early 1970s, 25% of people in their late 50s had a surviving parent (Murray, 1973). By 1980, 40% of people in their late 50s had a surviving parents as did 20% of those in their early 60s, 10% of those in their late 60s and 4% of those in their 70s (NRTA-AARP, 1981). Ten percent of all people 65 years or older had a child over the age of 65!

Moreover, while the population of older people was increasing, the birthrate was falling, resulting in a marked alteration in the ratio of potential filial caregivers to those in need of care. The odds of being called upon for parent care were increasing radically, and for increasingly older parents and children.

There are no definitive data on the number of people involved in parent care. One of the difficulties in making an estimate is that surveys identify the proportions of older people in need of services but large studies do not gather detailed data from the perspective of all of the various people in the family who are service providers. A problem in collecting data is that more than one child may be helping the same elderly parent, while some may be helping more than one parent or parent-in-law.

Some notion of the dimensions of the situation can be gleaned from various studies, however. For example, estimates of the overall proportion of noninstitutionalized elderly in need of help range from 17% to 40% (see Brody, 1977a for review). For every disabled person who resides in a nursing home, two or more equally impaired elderly live with and are cared for by their families (Comptroller General of the United States, 1977a). Soldo calculates that two and one quarter million women between the ages of 40 and 59 share their households with elderly kin (1980) and over a million households contain an older person in need of assistance with activities of daily living or mobility—an extreme level of caregiving (Myllyuoma & Soldo, 1980). Soldo's figures, though they are not limited to filial care, reflect only intra-household caregiving. An even larger number of people provide help to old people who do not share their households.

Taken together, these and other findings suggest a very conservative estimate that well over 5 million people are involved in parent-care at any given time. But such cross-sectional data do not speak to the lifetime chances of needing to provide parent care—that is, they do not include people who have provided parent care in the past or who will do so in the future as they and their parents age.

Not only do more people now provide parent care than in the past, but there are differences in the nature and duration of the care provided. Gerontologists need no reminder that chronic illnesses have replaced the acute diseases accounting for most deaths early in this century. As a result, our health systems are struggling to make a major shift in emphasis from acute (i.e., temporary) to chronic (i.e., sustained) care (Brody, S., 1973). People are living longer today after the onset of chronic disease and disability (a phenomenon that has been called "The Failures of Success," Gruenberg, 1977); the number of years of active life expectancy decreases with advancing old age (Katz et al., 1983), and few people reach the end of life without experiencing some period of dependency. More years of dependency mean more years during which there must be someone on whom to depend.

It is *long-term parent care* that has become a normative experience—expectable, though usually unexpected.

The phrase *long-term care* emerged to describe the formal system of government and agencies needed to provide the continuum of sustained helping services dictated by chronicity, though attempts to define it were not made until the late 1970s (Brody, 1977; U.S. National Committee on Vital and Health Statistics, 1978). But the family, virtually unnoticed, had invented long term care well before that phrase was articulated. The family made the shift from episodic, short-term acute care sooner and more flexibly, willingly, and effectively than professionals and the bureaucracy.

The irony of the myth is that *nowadays adult children provide more care and more difficult care to more parents over much longer periods of time than they did in the good old days.* There is also evidence that adult children now provide more emotional support to the elderly than in the past (Bengtson & Treas, 1980; Hareven, 1982).

At a time when there is a call for new roles for aging adults, a major new role that has emerged for Neugarten's young old (Neugarten, 1974) is that of caregiver for the old old. Can our social values come to regard this role as being as satisfying as second careers of work, volunteer activities, or creative pursuits?

Research on Filial Behavior

During the 1960s and 1970s, several major research themes developed, producing a literature too immense to be reviewed here. Particularly relevant are the studies of the role of the family (the informal support system) vis-à-vis government and agencies (the formal support system) in helping the disabled aged. That stream of research found that families, not the formal system, provide 80 to 90% of medically related and personal care, household tasks, transportation, and shopping. The family links the old to the formal support system. The family responds in emergencies and provides intermittent acute care. The family shares its home with severely impaired old people who live in the community (Brody, S. et al., 1978), with rates of shared households rising with the advancing age and poor health of the parent(s) (Mindel, 1979; Troll, 1971). It is the dependable family that provides the expressive support—the socialization, concern, affection, and sense of having someone on whom to rely—that is the form of family help most wanted by the old, but that is not usually counted as a service in surveys.

The members of the family who are the principal caregivers were identified as adult daughters (and to some extent daughters-in-law). They are the main helpers to the old who care for their impaired spouses and the main providers of help from the spouse-less majority of very old people. They predominate among those who share their homes when the elderly cannot manage on their own. (See Brody, 1978; Horowitz, 1982; Myllyuoma & Soldo, 1980; Shanas, 1979b; Troll, 1971.)

The prominence of women in the parent care role should not obscure the efforts of men, however. Sons also sustain bonds of affection, perform certain gender-defined tasks, and become the "responsible relatives" for the old who have no daughters or none close by. And some sons-in-law are unsung heroes.

Parent Care as a Stress

Recently, research on the effects of caregiving has been accelerating. To put the matter in perspective—In the main, having an elderly parent is gratifying and helpful. Older people are a resource to their children, providing many forms of assistance. Most people help their parents willingly when need be and derive satisfaction from doing so. Some adult children negotiate this stage of life without undue strain and experience personal growth during the process. However, when there is an increase in reliance on children to meet a parent's dependency needs, the family homeostasis—whether it is precarious or well-balanced—must shift accordingly. Such shifts have potential for stress, particularly because they augur increasing dependency in the future.

Some people experience financial hardship and some experience declines in their physical health from the arduous tasks of caring for a disabled parent. Certainly, such problems require attention. However, study after study has identified the most pervasive and most severe consequences as being in the realm of emotional strains. A long litany of mental health symptoms such as depression, anxiety, frustration, helplessness, sleeplessness, lowered morale, and emotional exhaustion are related to restrictions on time and freedom, isolation, conflict from the competing demands of various responsibilities, difficulties in setting priorities, and interference with lifestyle and social and recreational activities (see Archbold, 1978; Cantor, 1983; Danis, 1978; Frankfather et al., 1981; Gurland et al., 1978; Hoenig & Hamilton, 1966; Horowitz, 1982; Sainsbury & Grad de Alercon, 1970).

Though most such research has focused on the "principal caregiver," there are many findings about the effects on the family. The family is affected by interference with its life-style, privacy, socialization, vacations, future plans, and income, and by the diversion of the caregiver's time from other family members and the negative effects on her health.

Emotional support from spouses (Sussman, 1979), siblings (Horowitz, 1982), and other relatives (Zarit et al., 1980), mitigates the caregivers' strains. But when changes in the family homeostasis stimulate interpersonal conflicts, relationships are affected negatively between husbands and wives, among adult siblings, and across the generations.

In short, filial care of the elderly has become normative but stressful, it affects the entire family, and adult children provide more care and affective support than in the good old days. But some aspects of parent care are not well understood as yet: its place in the individual and family life cycle, the inner processes of individuals and families when parent care becomes necessary, and the interaction of values with personal, situational, and environmental factors indetermining filial behavior.

Is Parent Care a "Developmental Stage"?

Parent care, though normative, does not appear in conceptualizations of what happens during the life course of individuals and families.

In a paper given at the 1963 Symposium, Margaret Blenkner made a seminal attempt to conceptualize the inner experience of adult children when parent care becomes necessary. She described the need for the adult child to have the capacity to be depended on by the aging parent and characterized parent care as a developmental stage of life called "filial maturity"—a transitional stage preceding old age. Therapeutic approaches, she urged, should help adult children to meet their parents' dependency needs (rather than to relieve their guilt) and thus to achieve filial maturity (Blenkner, 1965).

Though there are flaws in Blenkner's particular conceptual and therapeutic approach, at the least she issued an implicit challenge to develop appropriate models.

A basic problem with Blenkner's model is that *parent care is not a development stage*. Developmental stages are specific to age-linked periods of time while parent care is not.

The "normal" life crises of earlier life usually occur in a somewhat orderly progression as people move serially through more or less well-defined age categories. Those categories are linked to age-specific cognitive, emotional, and physiological developments and capacities. In sharp contrast, the demands of parent care often are incompatible with the adult child's psychological, emotional, and physiological capacities. In fact, the upward trajectory of the increasing demands on aging children often runs counter to the downward trajectory of their declining abilities to meet those demands.

Parent care is not a single "stage" that can be fitted neatly into an orderly sequence of stages in the life course. Among the elderly, age and stage are not the same (Peck, 1968). Young children are "programmed" developmentally for a gradual reduction of dependency, while the dependencies of old age appear with great variability and irregularity, over much wider time spans, and in different sequential patterns. In addition, the timing of the marriages and parenthood of both parent and child influence the ages and stages of adult children when their parents need help. Parent care, therefore, can overlay many different ages and stages in different people and different families, occurring as it does in young adulthood, in middle age, or even in old age. Moreover, since parent care often is a time-extended process (some of the women in our PGC studies had been helping a parent for more than 20 years), it may span several of the caregiver's age periods or stages.

While the largest proportion of parent caring daughters are in their 40s and 50s, as many as one-third are either under 40 or over 60. The caregiver may be a grandmother who is experiencing the decrements of aging or she may have young children at home.

Even when they are in the same age group, the situations of parent caring children are extraordinarily variable. One woman in middle age may be engaged in adapting to the onset of chronic ailments and disability; another may be running for Vice President. Health, marital and economic status, living arrangements, geographic distance from the parent, personality, adaptive capacities, and the quality of parent-child relationships vary. The caregiver may or may not be working. Her retirement or that of her spouse may be imminent or already have taken place. Meeting a parent's dependency needs may be concurrent with the "letting go" of one's young adult children. Or, the theoretically empty nest may contain young adult children who have not left it or have returned to it, a phenomenon that has been increasing.

Among the people who called the PGC for help in one typical day were: an exhausted, 70-year-old woman who could no longer go on caring for her disabled, 93-year-old mother; a recently widowed 50 year old who had just completed her education in preparation for a return to work, but found that her mother had Alzheimer's disease and could not be left alone; a couple in their late 60s with three frail parents between them; a divorcee of 57 who was caring for two disabled sons, a 6-year-old grandchild, and an 87-year-old wheelchair-bound mother; and a young couple in their early 30s, about to have a first child, who had taken two older people into their home—the wife's terminally ill mother and the confused, incontinent grandmother for whom the mother had been caring.

Such caregivers do not share a single developmental stage of life. A most important consequence of that fact is the absence of behavioral norms for this normative life crisis. Since behavior in different people and families cannot be measured by the same yardstick, there is no simple answer to the question "What should adult children do . . .?"

The Inner Meaning of Parent Care: A Dialectic of Dependence/Independence

At whatever age or stage the need for parent care arises, the dialectic tension of dependence/independence is a central issue. People vary in the extent to which they have the capacity to meet the dependency needs of others, though growth and change are possible.

As an explanation of the processes that occur, role reversal is a superficial concept at best. (See Goldfarb, 1965 for a discussion of the reasons "role reversal" is inaccurate as a description of dependency on one's child from the perspective of the older person.) Being depended on by one's elderly parent and being depended on by one's young child have different inner meanings. When caring for an infant or child, the future holds promise of a gradual reduction in dependency; caring for an impaired older person presages continuing or increasing dependence. Caregivers have very different reactions to manifestations that are normal and will be dealt with developmentally in the child, but are symptomatic of pathology in the elderly adult—incontinence, for example.

The issue of the older person's dependency on adult children has its origin in the dependency of the helpless infant on the young parent. The inevitable shift in the delicate balance of dependence/independence of the elderly parent and adult child reactivates that child's unresolved conflicts about dependency.

Parent care also stimulates anticipation of the final separation from the parent and of one's potential dependence on one's own children as well. If successful adaptation is to be made, not only must the adult child have the capacity to permit the parent to be dependent, but the parent must have the capacity to be appropriately dependent so as to permit the adult child to be dependable.

There is general acceptance of the proposition that the inevitable vestiges of incompletely resolved crises of earlier stages are reprised and qualify the extent to which later crises are resolved. Since personality continues to develop until the end of life, the way in which the filial crisis is negotiated not only depends on the past, but has implications for the future of the caregiver when she becomes old—and indeed, for that of succeeding generations.

Reactions to the need to provide parent care, of course, range along the theoretical spectrum from health to pathology, as do responses to other life crises. Complex parent care situations occur in the context of the individual's and family's personality and history, qualitative relationships, and coping capacities—all of which qualify the ability to achieve and adapt to the new homeostasis that is required. But the best integrated individual and the best functioning family can be shaken to the core when confronted with reality demands that they cannot meet. It cannot be assumed, as the myth would have it, that the family *is* the problem; more often, the family *has* a problem. Interpretation of "filial maturity" to mean that all of the concrete services needed by the old should be provided by adult children (clearly, a distortion of Blenkner's concept), reinforces the myth by implying that they could do so if only they were "emotionally mature."

When interpersonal problems occur, they are not caused by parent care. Rather, the pressures are such that family relationship problems are reactivated or exacerbated (Brody, 1979). The caregiver's spouse or children may compete with the old person for time and attention. New battles may be fought in the old wars among the siblings. "I do everything for my mother, but my sister/brother is still her favorite." Old loyalties and alliances as well as old rivalries operate.

Given the reality pressures, given the interpersonal and intrapsychic tensions, it is not surprising that the emotional aspects of caregiving have been a consistent theme in research reports. Nor is it surprising that some adult children relinquish tasks of parent care before others think they should. What *is* remarkable is that so many transcend the strains and take so long to reach their limits of endurance.

But to romanticize the family is just as inappropriate as to be judgmental. The romantic view admires those who continue to care for an impaired older person under conditions of such severe strain that there is deprivation and suffering for the entire family. People in such families may be psychologically unable to place the older person in a nursing home, or, as every service worker knows, may be unable to use formal support services that are badly needed. Whatever dynamics are at work—symbiotic ties, the gratification of being the "burden bearer," a fruitless search for parental approval that has never been received, or expiation of guilt for having been the favored child—excessive caregiving may represent not emotional health or heroism or love, but pathology (Brody & Spark, 1966).

Successful resolution of the filial crisis, then, may involve acceptance by adult children of what they can *not* do as well as acceptance of what they can and should do. For their part, successful adaptation to dependency by the elderly involved *their* acceptance of what their adult children cannot do. It is a curious value that encourages others to continue caregiving no matter the personal cost, but ignores the need of some people to be helped to reduce the amount of care they provide.

Interaction of Inner Processes with Values and Socioeconomic Trends

Such inner processes interact with values, socioeconomic trends, and other factors in determining behavior.

As the demand for parent care increased dramatically, a broad socioeconomic trend occurred that is associated with changing values. The rapid entry of middle-aged women—the traditional providers of parent care—into the labor force held the potential for affecting their availability for parent care and for increasing the pressures on them and their families.

Betty Friedan's book, which set in motion the women's movement with its changes in values about women's roles, was published in the same year in which the Symposium was held (Friedan, 1963). It was one of a number of factors that were operating to account for women's march to the workplace, not the least of which was that the money was needed. Between 1940 and 1979 the proportion of working married women between the ages of 45 and 54 increased five-fold. At present, 69% of all women between the ages of 35 and 44 are in the work force as are 62% of those between the ages of 45 and 54, and 42% of those in the 55 to 64 age group (U.S. Bureau of Labor Statistics, 1984).

In order to explore the effects of the converging demographic and socioeconomic trends on filial caregiving, our PGC research group surveyed women who were members of families that included three generations of women. We examined possible changes in values about parent care—in attitudes about family care of the aged and filial responsibility, about gender-appropriate roles, and about filial care vis-à-vis help from the formal system. (For methodology and detailed findings see Brody et al., 1982a, 1982b; Brody et al., 1983; Brody et al., 1984a; Lang & Brody, 1983.)

In contradiction to the myth, we found value continuity in that all three generations expressed firm commitment toward filial help for the aged. Value change was apparent in that large majorities of all generations favored equal roles for men and women—in, for example, the sharing of traditionally female roles such as child care and parent care (though each successively younger generation expressed progressively more egalitarian attitudes).

However, there were many findings indicating tension and conflict between the "new" values about women's roles and the "old" values. For example—Despite the general endorsement of feminist views of the roles of men and women, and though two-thirds of the middle generation women were working, they were more likely to expect working daughters than working sons to adjust their work schedules for parent care. But at the same time, a majority of all generations agreed that it is better for a working woman to pay someone to care for her elderly parent than to leave her job to do it herself.

The potentially conflicting values and multiple roles of the middle generation women whom we called the "women in the middle" (Brody, 1981) often led them to have incompatible views. They wanted to be responsible as daughters but not to become dependent on their children in their own old age. Similarly, the granddaughters, at an average age of 23, were the generation most in favor of egalitarian gender roles, but also were the ones most in favor of family care of the aged and the most in favor of grandchildren helping the old—an expression of what we called "grandfilial responsibility." Moreover, those young women expected to work more years than their mothers had expected to work when they were young, but they also expected to marry and have as many children as their mothers had.

Clear statements of these women's values—their "normative expectations [that] serve as guidelines for behavior" (George, 1980)—related to emotional support. Overall, emotional support is what members of all three generations wanted most from their adult children in their own old age. As in other studies, they strongly preferred households separate from their children and did not wish to be financially dependent on them. Family bonds were not equated with economic help, shared households, personal care and instrumental services. But there was variability as well, with preferences differing with the women's lineage position in the family, different situations, social and health status, ethnic backgrounds (Johnsen & Fulcomer, 1984), and according to the specific kind of help needed.

However, the actual behavior of the middle generation women, all of whom had a living elderly mother, demonstrates once again that attitudes and opinions are not always reflected in behavior. Despite their attitudinal acceptance of formal services and their consensus about egalitarian roles, the middle-generation daughters behaved not only in accordance with their unchanged values about family care of the elderly, but in accordance with "traditional" values about women's roles. They were the major source of help to their mothers even though their responsibilities rose steeply as they grew older. In response to the new demography, the older of the daughters (those in their 50s and 60s) provided many more hours of help and did more difficult tasks for their older and more dependent mothers. They also were more likely than the younger daughters to share their households with their mothers—a phenomenon we called the "refilling of the empty nest" (Brody, 1978). In comparison with their elderly mothers when the latter were in their middle years in the good old days, they also provided more emotional support to their elderly parents, provided more emotional and financial support to their own children, and had worked more (Brody et al., 1982b). When faced with competing demands on their time, what these women gave up was their own free time and opportunities for socialization and recreation. Findings such as these led us to be concerned about the mental and physical health of "women in the middle."

CAREGIVING CAREERS

But being in the middle because of parent care is not a single time-limited episode in the life-course, as data from more recent PGC studies show.

In this research we compared working and nonworking women with respect to their parent care behavior and the effects they experience from caregiving. All of the women in the study were married and were acting as principal caregivers for widowed elderly mothers who required varying amounts of help.

Care of a particular parent at a particular time proved to be only one phase of these women's careers in caregiving, caregiving careers that extend well into late middle age and early old age. Almost half of them had helped an elderly father before his death and one-third of them had helped other elderly relatives. Twenty-two percent were currently providing help to another elderly relative as well as to their own mothers—to parents-in-law, grandparents, aunts, cousins, and more distant relations. And two-thirds of them had children living at home, most under 18 years of age and some (about 10%) younger than six. Given the discrepancy in life expectancy for men and women, it is inevitable that many of these women will care for dependent husbands in the future.

To emphasize—*for many women, parent care is not a single time-limited episode in the life course*. Not only can it begin at widely differing ages and be superimposed on more than one of the other individual and family life stages, but dependence/independence issues may be replayed many times. They can be multiple and multi-layered as one's parents and parents-in-law and even grandparents and other elderly relatives require help sequentially or simultaneously. And all of these complex factors operate for the other adult children and their spouses as well, combining to affect parent care in almost infinite variations.

Do Work and Parent Care Compete?

Another finding from the same study speaks directly to the potential competition between work and parent care. It illustrates the subtle interplay of values, reality pressures, personal characteristics, and other factors in determining filial behavior.

The working and non-working women were providing roughly equal amounts of care to their dependent mothers. Substantial proportions of both groups were experiencing many of the various strains and mental health symptoms referred to above. But simply comparing all other working women with all of the nonworking women obscured those who were under the most pressure.

We found that *28% of our sample of nonworking women had quit their jobs because of their elderly mothers' needs for care. They had been displaced from the work force. A similar proportion of the working women were conflicted: they were considering giving up their jobs for the same reason and some had already reduced the number of hours they worked.*

Women's capacities may indeed be elastic in accommodating many roles, as some researchers have observed. But ultimately, those data indicate, elastic snaps if stretched too thin. To illustrate—

Compared with the other working and non-working women in the study, the women who had left their jobs were in the most difficult parent care situations and the ones who were considering doing so were very close behind. Both of those groups had more functionally dependent mothers. They experienced more interferences with their life styles and time for their husbands. They had been helping their mothers for longer periods of time and they tended to be the only ones providing that help. And they more often felt that parent care made them feel tied down and as though they had missed out on something in life.

The women who had already quit their jobs were older than any of the other women in the study and they had older mothers. They also had an additional set of problems: they more often shared their households with their mothers (a living arrangement which is a strong predictor of strain), they reported that parent care had resulted in more deterioration in their health and more of certain mental health symptoms, and they had the lowest family incomes. (See Brody et al., 1984 and Kleban et al., 1984 for detailed reports on these findings.)

Values and socioeconomic considerations also proved to be influential. Compared with the women who had quit their jobs, the women who were thinking of doing so were better educated, held higher level jobs and to a much greater extent viewed their work as part of a career rather than as "just a job." Within 2 years after the study, one-quarter of all the women in the study had changed their work status; some of the nonworkers entered the labor force (most because the money was needed—to send children to college, for example) and some of the working women had increased or decreased their working hours or were no longer working.

Obviously, patterns of parent care, work, and other role performance must be viewed as long-term processes. As yet, we have no data about this extraordinarily diverse and complex mosaic depicting responses to parent care over the individual and family life-course. Study of women's shifting work and family roles has focused on the earlier stages of their lives; the full story is yet to be written about the shifting of their roles later in life.

Virtually nothing is known about the processes by which different options are selected—processes which have profound implications for clinical approaches and social policy. Caregivers who were not part of our sample may have exercised other options such as nursing home placement or the parent of the redistribution of care in other ways along the informal and formal support systems. Other paths might have been taken by daughters who were not married or by sons.

Given the increasing diversity in women's life courses (cf. Lopata & Norr, 1980), we do not know what choices will be made by future cohorts of women as they move into the parent care years. We do not know how the old behavioral borders that have been measured by research will respond to lifestyle changes, to possible changes in family structure and size, to economic changes, or to changes in mobility patterns, for example.

And what of the myth? How did it fare in the views of the women we studied? To recapitulate the experiences of these "women-in-the middle"—

- They were the principal caregivers to their dependent mothers.
- They were in the middle of competing demands on their time and energy.
- They were experiencing many strains as a result of parent care.
- Their "empty nests" had been refilled—for some quite literally, and for all in terms of increased responsibilities.
- Care of their mothers was but one episode in time-extended "caregiving careers" to older relatives.
- Some had quit their jobs to care for their mothers and others were considering doing so or had cut back on the number of hours they worked.

Yet three-fifths of those very same women said that "somehow" they felt guilty about not doing enough for their mothers, and three quarters of them agreed that nowadays children do not take care of their elderly parents as was the case in the good old days.

THE MYTH: A HYPOTHESIS

Why is that myth so tenacious in the face of the factual evidence that refutes it? It is important to understand the myth because of its power to inhibit constructive practice and policy approaches.

Many explanations have been advanced for the myth's apparent immortality and it is probable that each of them plays a role. For example—observation of increased mobility and the geographic distance of adult children from their parents; the proliferation of nursing homes and age segregated living arrangements; the visibility of concentrations of old people in places with favorable climates; the taxpayer's fear of the escalating costs of formal system care; the fact, as Shanas (1963) suggested, that those in the helping professions see only the problem situations; and the tendency to romanticize and idealize some vague time in the past.

A hypothesis suggested here is that one possible contributant to the myth's vitality lies at a deeper level and is related to the dependence/independence dialectic:

The myth does not die because at its heart is a fundamental truth.

At some level of awareness, members of all generations may harbor the expectation that the devotion and care given by the young parent to the infant and child—that total, primordial commitment which is the original paradigm for caregiving to those who are dependent—should be reciprocated and the indebtedness repaid in kind when the parent, having grown old, becomes dependent.

The "truth" to which the myth speaks is that adult children cannot and do not provide the same total care to their elderly parents that those parents gave to them in the good old days of their infancy and childhood. The roles of parent and child cannot be reversed in that sense. The good old days, then, may not be earlier periods in our social history (after all, the myth existed then too), but an earlier period in each individual's and family's history to which there can be no return.

The myth exists because of the disparity between standards and expectations on the one hand and the unavoidable realities on the other hand. The disparity leads to guilt. The myth persists because the guilt persists, reflecting a universal and deeply rooted human theme. That may be why we hear over and over again from adult children "I know I'm doing everything I can for my mother, but somehow I still feel guilty." The fantasy is that "somehow" one should do more. That may be one reason that so many adult children are overwhelmed with guilt when a parent enters a nursing home. It is experienced as the total surrender of the parent to the care of others—the ultimate failure to meet the parent's dependency needs as that parent met the child's needs in the good old days.

Guilt may be a reason that people assert that they and their own families behave responsibly in caring for their old, but that most people do not do so as was the case in the good old days. They need to defend against the guilt and to deny their own negative and unacceptable emotions (emotions such as resentment, anger, and the wish not to be burdened, which add another dimension to the guilt), by feeling that others do not behave as well. "*They* are *really* guilty; I am not."

In completing the feedback loop, by exacerbating the guilt the myth contributes to the strains of parent care. Not only does the myth persist because the guilt persists, but the guilt persists because the myth persists.

To quote Erma Bombeck, "Guilt is the gift that keeps on giving" (1984).

SOCIAL POLICY

Since the 1963 symposium, social policy (which expresses the values of the time), has made some progress in applying knowledge about filial behavior. Medicare and Medicaid came into being (1965) and an income floor was established by Supplemental Security Income (SSI, 1974). Medicaid and SSI together eliminated compulsory financial support of the old by their adult children. With Social Security (1935) as a base, the proportion of older people who were wholly dependent on family for economic support dropped from about 50% in 1937 to 1.5% in 1979 (Upp, 1982). (Note that these figures do not speak to adequacy of income.) Those programs (together with savings, private pensions, etc.) enabled more of the aged to live as they prefer (close to, but not in the same household with their children) and to realize their wish not to depend on their children for income or the costs of catastrophic illness. There has been considerable development of services and living facilities, though many more are needed.

At present, however, in expressing current values, social policy echoes, uses, and perpetuates the myth, exerting psychological pressure on adult children, increasing their guilt, and adding to their strains by failing to provide services and facilities that are urgently needed to back up their efforts.

The myth is being invoked as a rationale for a philosophy that would shrink the formal support system and encourage its non-use to save public funds. The call to restore the good old days of family values is being operationalized in a variety of ways. For example—

- The States have been encouraged to reinstitute the archaic requirement that people in the grandparent generation be compelled to pay the costs of nursing home care for the great-grandparent generation.
- A variety of cost-containment efforts are limiting nursing home beds, frustrating efforts at quality care, and effectively closing nursing home doors to those who need them most—the "heavy care" Medicaid patients (U.S. GAO, 1983) such as those with Alzheimer's disease. As a result, aging caregivers who have gone beyond the limits of endurance will have no relief. This, though scientists on both sides of the "compression of morbidity" controversy agree that the number of those in need of long-term chronic care will continue to increase, at least for the next few decades (e.g., see Fries, 1984; Schneider & Brody, J., 1983). And this, though it has been shown that community care is not cheaper than nursing home care for severely disabled older people (Comptroller General of the United States, 1977b; Fox & Clauser, 1980).
- Services that would relieve the unrelenting strains on families of non-institutionalized old people should be increasing but are being cut back. Family focused services—notably respite care and day care—are sparse, uneven regionally, and are not funded consistently.

The language used is revealing. The injunction issued is not to "supplant" family services, though research evidence indicates that services strengthen family caregiving (Horowitz, 1982; Zimmer & Sainer, 1978). There are suggestions for "incentives" for families to care, implying that they need to be induced, rather than helped, to do what they want to do and have been doing. Issues are framed artificially as competing propositions such as institutionalization *versus* community care, family (informal) care *versus* formal (government and agencies) care, even respite services to provide temporary relief for caregivers *versus* training programs to build their caregiving skills.

When a "family policy" means cheering the family on to increase its efforts, the effect is to undermine the very family the rhetoric purports to save. The call for filial responsibility masks social irresponsibility, disadvantaging the elderly and the young as well as the middle generation. Binstock (1983) has called attention to the scapegoating of the old. Many policies scapegoat their adult children.

In the future, there could be radical changes in demands for parent care and other long-term support services if bio-medical breakthroughs result in prevention or cure of conditions causing chronic dependency—Alzheimer's disease, for example. But social policy cannot await such major advances. The informal system, which protects the formal system from being overwhelmed, should be supported, not weakened. Overburdening family members can increase the costs to the community of the mental and physical health problems they experience as a result.

Since knowledge has not dispelled the myth, and if the hypothesis advanced here means that one of its aspects is relatively immutable, perhaps the realistic goal is not to slay the Hydra monster but to render it powerless to impede constructive clinical approaches and a sound social policy. As gerontologists, we provide facts which are correctives so that policy based on bias and myth does not go unchallenged.

In a paper presented by co-authors Steve Brody and Don Kent at the 1968 GSA meetings, they said "The union of social research and social action is a long way off, but there are at least signs that such a bridge can be built . . ." (Brody & Kent, 1968). We have made progress in building that bridge, and our efforts have been increasing. Since the 1963 Symposium, the membership of this organization has risen from 2,000 to 6,000, which an exponential increase in the amount of research.

We cannot do it all, of course. Adult children will continue to care for and about their elderly parents. They will continue to be concerned, to provide affection and emotional support, to do what they are able, and to arrange for the needed services that they cannot supply. (Perhaps those are the only appropriate norms for filial behavior.) The strains families experience are not completely preventable or remediable. But policy should rest on knowledge rather than a myth if it is to create a dependable formal system that forges an effective partnership with the dependable family. Knowledge, properly used, can do much to prevent families from reaching the limits of endurance and can help us as a society to meet our collective filial responsibility.

REFERENCES

Archbold, P. (1978). Impact of caring for an ill elderly parent of the middle-aged or elderly offspring caregiver. Paper presented at the 31st Annual Meeting of the Gerontological Society, Dallas, TX, November.

Bengtson, V. L., & Treas, J. (1980). The changing context of mental health and aging. In J. E. Birren & R. B. Sloane (Eds.), *Handbook of mental health and aging*. Englewood Cliffs, NJ: Prentice-Hall.

Binstock, R. H. (1983). The aged as scapegoat. *The Gerontologist, 23*, 136–143.

Blenkner, M. (1965). Social work and family relationships in later life with some thoughts on filial maturity. In E. Shanas & G. F. Streib (Eds.), *Social structure and the family: Generational Relations*. Englewood Cliffs, NJ: Prentice-Hall.

Bombeck, Erma, quoted by Skow, John (1984). "Erma in Bomburgia," *Time*, July 2, p. 56.

Brody, E. M. (1981). "Women in the middle" and family help to older people. *The Gerontologist, 21*, 471–480.

Brody, E. M. (1979). Aged parents and aging children. In P. K. Ragan (Ed.), *Aging Parents*. Los Angeles, CA: University of Southern California Press.

Brody, E. M. (1978). The aging of the family. *The Annals of the American Academy of Political and Social Science, 438*, 13–27.

Brody, E. M. (1977). *Long-term care of older people: A practical guide*. New York: Human Sciences Press.

Brody, E. M. (1977a). Environmental factors in dependency. In Exton-Smith, A. N. & Evans, J. G. (Eds.), *Care of the Elderly: Meeting the Challenge of Dependency* (pp. 81–95). London: Academic Press; New York: Grune & Stratton.

Brody, E. M. (1969). Follow-up study of applicants and non-applicants to a voluntary home. *The Gerontologist, 9*, 187–196.

Brody, E. M. (1967a). Aging is a family affair. *Public Welfare*, 129–140.

Brody, E. M. (1967b). The mentally-impaired aged patient: A socio-medical problem. *Geriatrics Digest, 4*, 25–32.

Brody, E. M. (1966a). The impaired aged: A follow-up study of applicants rejected by a voluntary home. *Journal of the American Geriatrics Society, 14*, 414–420.

Brody, E. M. (1966b). The aging family. *The Gerontologist, 6*, 201–206.

Brody, E. M., & Gummer, B. (1967). Aged applicants and non-applicants to a voluntary home: An exploratory comparison. *The Gerontologist, 7*, 234–243.

Brody, E. M., Johnson, P. T., & Fulcomer, M. C. (1984a). What should adult children do for elderly parents: Opinions and preferences of three generations of women. *Journal of Gerontology, 39*, 736–746.

Brody, E. M., Johnsen, P. T., Fulcomer, M. C., & Lang, A. (1982a). The Dependent Elderly and Women's Changing Roles. Final report on Administration on Aging Grant #90-A-1277.

Brody, E. M., Johnsen, P. T., & Fulcomer, M. C. (1982b). "Women in the middle" and care of the dependent elderly. Final Report on AoA Grant #90-AR-2174.

Brody, E. M., Johnsen, P. T., Fulcomer, M. C., & Lang, A. M. (1983). Women's changing roles and help to the elderly: Attitudes of three generations of women. *Journal of Gerontology, 38*, 597–607.

Brody, E. M., Kleban, M. H., & Johnsen, P. T. (1984). Women who provide parent care: Characteristics of those who work and those who do not. Paper presented at the 37th Annual Meeting of The Gerontological Society of America, San Antonio, TX, November.

Brody, E. M., Lawton, M. P., & Liebowitz, B. (1984). Senile dementia: Public policy and adequate institutional care. *American Journal of Public Health, 74*, 1381–1383.

Brody, E. M., & Spark, G. (1966). Institutionalization of the aged: A family crisis. *Family Process, 5*, 76–90.

Brody, S. J. (1973). Comprehensive health care of the elderly: An analysis. *The Gerontologist, 13*, 412–418.

Brody, S. J., & Kent, D. P. (1968). Social research and social policy in a public agency. Paper presented at the 21st Annual Meeting of the Gerontological Society, Denver, CO.

Brody, S. J., Poulshock, S. W., & Masciocchi, C. F. (1978). The family care unit: A major consideration in the long-term support system. *The Gerontologist, 18*, 556–561.

Cantor, M. H. (1983). Strain among caregivers: A study of experience in the United States. *The Gerontologist, 23*, 597–604.

Cantor, M. H. (1980). Caring for the frail elderly: Impact on family, friends and neighbors. Paper presented at 33rd Annual Meeting of The Gerontological Society of America, San Diego, CA.

Comptroller General of the United States (1977a). *The well-being of older people in Cleveland, Ohio*, U.S. General Accounting Office, #RD–77–70, Washington, DC, April 19.

Comptroller General of the United States (1977b). *Report to Congress on Home Health— The Need for a National Policy to Better Provide for the Elderly*, U.S. General Accounting Office, HRD–78–19, Washington, DC, December 30.

Danis, B. G. (1978). Stress in individuals caring for ill elderly relatives. Paper presented at 31st Annual Meeting of the Gerontological Society, Dallas, TX.

Fox, P. D., & Clauser, S. B. (1980). Trends in nursing home expenditures: Implications for aging policy. *Health Care Financing Review*, 65–70.

Frankfather, D., Smith, M. J., & Caro, F. G. (1981). *Family care of the elderly: Public initiatives and private obligations*. Lexington, MA: Lexington Books.

Friedan, B. (1963). *The feminine mystique*. New York: Dell.

Fries, J. F. (1984). The compression of morbidity: Miscellaneous comments about a theme. *The Gerontologist, 24*, 354–359.

George, L. K. (1980). *Role transitions in late life*. Monterey, CA: Brooks/Cole.

Goldfarb, A. I. (1965). Psychodynamics and the three-generation family. In E. Shanas & G. F. Streib (Eds.), *Social structure and the family: Generational relations* (pp. 10–45). Englewood Cliffs, NJ: Prentice-Hall.

Gruenberg, E. M. (1977). The failures of success. *Milbank Memorial Fund Quarterly*, Health and Society, 3–24.

Gurland, B., Dean, L., Gurland, R., & Cook, D. (1978). Personal time dependency in the elderly of New York City: Findings from the U.S.-U.K. cross-national geriatric community study. In *Dependency in the elderly of New York City*. New York: Community Council of Greater New York, 9–45.

Hareven, T. K. (1982). The life course and aging in historical perspective. In T. K. Hareven & K. J. Adams (Eds.), *Aging and life course transitions: An interdisciplinary perspective* (pp. 1–26). New York: Guilford Press.

Hoenig, J., & Hamilton, M. (1966). Elderly patients and the burden on the household. *Psychiatra et Neurologia*, Basel, *152*, 281–293.

Horowitz, A. (1982). The role of families in providing long-term care to the frail and chronically ill elderly living in the community. Final report submitted to the Health Care Financing Administration, DHHS, May.

Johnsen, P. T., & Fulcomer, M. C. (1984). "Culture's consequences" in attitudes, opinions, and preferences affecting family care of the elderly. Paper presented at the 37th Annual Meeting of The Gerontological Society of America, San Antonio, TX, November.

Katz, S., Branch, L. G., Branson, M. H., Papsidero, J. A., Beck, J. C., & Greer, D. S. (1983). Active life expectancy. *The New England Journal of Medicine, 309*, 1218–1224.

Kent, D. P. (1972). Social policy and program considerations in planning for the aging. In D. P. Kent, R. Kastenbaum, & S. Sherwood (Eds.), *Research planning and action for the elderly* (pp. 3–19). New York: Behavioral Publications.

Kent, D. P. (1965). Aging—fact or fancy. *The Gerontologist, 5*, 2.

Kleban, M. H., Brody, E. M., & Hoffman, C. (1984). Parent care and depression: Differences between working and nonworking adult daughters. Paper presented at the 37th Annual Meeting of The Gerontological Society of America, San Antonio, TX, November.

Lang, A., & Brody, E. M. (1983). Characteristics of middle-aged daughters and help to their elderly mothers. *Journal of Marriage and the Family, 45*, 193–202.

Lawton, M. P., & Brody, E. M. (1968). The social cost of care for the elderly. Final report, U.S.P.H.S. Grant #CD00137.

Lawton, M. P., & Lawton, F. (Eds.) (1965). *Mental impairment in the aged: Institute on the mentally impaired aged*. Philadelphia, PA: Philadelphia Geriatric Center.

Lopata, H. Z., & Norr, K. F. (1980). Changing commitments of American women to work and family roles. *Social Security Bulletin*, June, 43, 3–14.

Lowenthal, M. F. (1964). *Lives in distress*. New York: Basic Books.

Mindel, C. H. (1979). Multigenerational family households: Recent trends and implications for the future. *The Gerontologist, 19*, 456–463.

Murray, J. (1973). Family structure in the preretirement years. *Social Security Bulletin*, October, 36, 25–45.

Myllyuoma, J., & Soldo, B. J. (1980). Family caregivers to the elderly: Who are they? Paper presented at the 33rd Annual Meeting of the Gerontological Society, San Diego, CA.

Neugarten, B. L. (1974). Age groups in American society and the rise of the young-old. *The Annals of the American Academy of Political and Social Science, 415*, 187–198.

NRTA-AARP (National Retired Teachers Association-American Association of Retired Persons) (1981). National survey of older Americans.

Peck, R. C. (1968). Psychological developments in the second half of life. In B. L. Neugarten (Ed.), *Middle age and aging: A reader in social psychology* (pp. 88–92). Chicago, IL: University of Chicago Press.

Rosow, I. (1965). Intergenerational relationships: Problems and proposals. In E. Shanas, & G. F. Streib (Eds.), *Social structure and the family: Generational relations* (pp. 341–378). Englewood Cliffs, NJ: Prentice-Hall.

Sainsbury, P., & Grad de Alercon, J. (1970). The effects of community care in the family of the geriatric patient. *Journal of Geriatric Psychiatry, 4*, 23–41.

Schneider, E. L., & Brody, J. A. (1983). Aging, natural death, and the compression of morbidity: Another view. *The New England Journal of Medicine, 309*, 854–856.

Schorr, A. L. (1960). *Filial responsibility in the modern American family*. Washington, DC: U.S. DHEW, Social Security Administration, Government Printing Office, June.

Shanas, E. (1979a). Social myth as hypothesis: The case of the family relations of old people. *The Gerontologist, 19*, 3–9.

Shanas, E. (1979b). The family as a social support system in old age. *The Gerontologist, 19*, 169–174.

Shanas, E. (1963). The unmarried old person in the United States: Living arrangements and care in illness, myth and fact. Paper presented at the International Social Science Research Seminar in Gerontology, Makaryd, Sweden, 1963.

Shanas, E., & Streib, G. F. (Eds.) (1965). *Social structure and the family: Generational relations*. Englewood Cliffs, NJ: Prentice-Hall.

Shanas, E., Townsend, P., Wedderburn, D., Friis, H., Milhøj, P., & Stehouwer, J. (Eds.) (1968). *Old people in three industrial societies*. New York: Atherton Press.

Soldo, B. J. (1980). The dependency squeeze on middle-aged women. Presented at Meeting of the Secretary's Advisory Committee on Rights and Responsibilities of Women, Department of Health and Human Services.

Spark, G., & Brody, E. M. (1970). The aged are family members. *Family Process, 9*, 195–210.

Streib, G. F., & Shanas, E. (1965). An introduction. In E. Shanas, & G. F. Streib (Eds.), *Social structure and the family: Generational relations*. Englewood Cliffs, NJ: Prentice-Hall.

Sussman, M. (1979). Social and economic supports and family environment for the elderly. Final report to Administration on Aging, Grant #90-A-316, January.

Townsend, P. (1965). The effects of family structure on the likelihood of admission to an institution in old age: The application of a general theory. In E. Shanas, & G. F. Streib (Eds.), *Social structure and the family: Generational relations* (pp. 163–187). Englewood Cliffs, NJ: Prentice-Hall.

Troll, L. E. (1971). The family of later life: A decade review. *Journal of Marriage and the Family, 33*, 263–290.

Uhlenberg, P. (1980). Death and the family. *Journal of Family History, 5*, 313–320.

U.S. Bureau of Labor Statistics. (1984). *Employment and earnings*, Table 3, January.

U.S. General Accounting Office. (1983). *Medicaid and nursing home care: Cost increases and the need for services are creating problems for the States and the elderly*. Washington, DC: U.S. General Accounting Office, October 21.

U.S. National Committee on Vital and Health Statistics. (1978). *Long-term health care: Minimum data set*, preliminary report of the Technical Consultant Panel on the Long-Term Health Care Data Set, NCHS, September 8.

Upp, M. (1982). A look at the economic status of the aged then and now. *Social Security Bulletin*, March, *45*, 16–22.

Zarit, S. H., Reever, K. E., & Bach-Peterson, J. (1980). Relatives of the impaired aged: Correlates of feelings of burden. *The Gerontologist, 20*, 649–655.

Zimmer, A. H., & Sainer, J. S. (1978). Strengthening the family as an informal support for their aged: Implications for social policy and planning. Paper presented at the 31st Annual Meeting of the Gerontological Society, Dallas, TX.

ARTICLE 25
Styles and Strategies of Grandparenting

ANDREW J. CHERLIN AND
FRANK F. FURSTENBERG, JR.

Grandparents, Cherlin and Furstenberg note, are not all alike. Some are highly detached from their grandchildren, some are essentially passive, while others are actively involved in the lives of their grandchildren. However, grandparenting styles change over the life course, they differ somewhat by race, and they may be altered when the grandparents' adult offspring divorce.

THERE IS A GREAT AMOUNT of variation in the kinds of relationships that American grandparents have with their grandchildren. Some grandparents are actively involved in their grandchildren's lives, but many others are quite passive and distant. In addition, as we will show in this chapter, the relationship can vary from grandchild to grandchild. Some grandchildren may live far from the grandparent, other grandchildren may live with parents who don't get along with the grandparents; and still others may no longer be living with the grandparent's son or daughter as a result of divorce. Under circumstances such as these, grandparents sometimes devote most of their attention to a few grandchildren—or even to just one. This strategy—which we call selective investment—allows them to act like grandparents and feel satisfied with their role, even though they aren't as close to the rest of their grandchildren.

Andrew J. Cherlin and Frank F. Furstenberg, Jr., "Styles and Strategies of Grandparenting." In *Grandparenthood*, Vern L. Bengston and Joan F. Robertson (Newbury Park, Calif.: Sage Publications, 1985): pp. 97–98 and 113–116. Copyright 1985 by Sage Publications, Inc. Reprinted by permission of Sage Publications, Inc.

The variation in the styles and strategies of grandparenting is consistent with the general principles that determine the nature of kinship ties in American society. Individuals are allowed to exercise a great deal of discretion in their relations with kin. In his classic account of American kinship, Schneider (1980) characterizes our system as highly voluntaristic. Blood and marriage circumscribe the available pool of kin, but within this pool it is up to individuals to cultivate and maintain ties. Kinship, therefore, has an achieved as well as an ascribed dimension.

This discretionary feature of American kinship is especially salient when divorce and remarriage occur. Our study, which will be described below, was originally designed to investigate what happens to the ties between grandparents and grandchildren when the grandchildren's parents divorce. We found a wide range of responses. Many grandparents became heavily involved in their grandchildren's lives, sometimes to the point of becoming surrogate parents, whereas others drifted apart from their grandchildren. There were no fixed rules about how grandparents should react to a divorce, although a pattern did emerge: With some exceptions, the ties between maternal grandparents and their grandchildren were maintained or strengthened after a divorce; but the ties between paternal grandparents and their grandchildren were often weakened. This difference emerged because mothers usually retain custody of their children after a divorce and many divorced fathers have infrequent contact with their children (Furstenberg, Nord, Peterson, & Zill, 1983). It is therefore more difficult for paternal grandparents to retain close ties to their grandchildren after the disruption of the parents' marriage.

[Here] we will focus on the more general issue of variation in the grandparent-grandchild relationship in intact as well as disrupted families. There have been a number of attempts to classify the styles and meanings of being a grandparent (Neugarten & Weinstein, 1964; Wood & Robertson, 1976; Robertson, 1977; Kivnick, 1982a; 1982b). All find a diversity of responses that form a continuum from substantial involvement to remoteness. These and other studies (Troll & Bengtson, 1979) also suggest the widespread acceptance in the United States of what we might call the "norm of non-interference": the idea that grandparents should not interfere with the parents in the rearing of the grandchildren.

The previous studies have provided much useful information, but they also have been quite limited. They have tended to be exploratory; geographically, socially, and ethnically limited; and small in size. They cannot tell us whether styles of grandparenting vary systematically by age, ethnicity, or other social and economic characteristics. Moreover, these studies leave us with a rather static view of grandparenting, as if we could pin a label on a grandmother shortly after her first grandchild was born ("fun seeker" or "distant figure") and be sure that the label would remain accurate for all her grandchildren for the rest of her life. As that seems implausible, we need to think more about whether there is a life-course of grandparenting and about the ways in which grandparents may simultaneously maintain different kinds of relationships with different grandchildren. In this chapter we hope to provide some insight into these unresolved issues of styles and strategies of grandparenting.

SELECTIVE INVESTMENT

It appears to us that many grandparents invest more heavily in their relationships with some grandchildren than with others. There are many reasons why selective investment may be common: Some grandchildren may live closer, some may have parents who get along better with the grandparent, or some may be more in need of help because of a family crisis. Moreover, some may just be more appealing to the grandparent because they are the first born, the last born, or the most outgoing. Consequently, the payoff is likely to be greater for investment in some grandchildren than in others. Often, we suspect, a close tie to one or two grandchildren, coupled with a more distant, ritualistic relationship with the rest, may be sufficient to make grandparents satisfied with their role. They may generalize to all their grandchildren their satisfaction with their relationships with their favorites. Thus, it may not be necessary for grandparents to have equally intense ties to all grandchildren in order to feel good about being a grandparent. Furthermore, equally intense relationships might even be burdensome for an older person with lots of grandchildren. Consciously or not, then, some grandparents have evolved a strategy of selective investment in which a few close ties to grandchildren suffice—in which the part substitutes adequately for the whole.

Given the flexible nature of the American kinship system, grandparents often can chose the grandchildren to whom they pay more attention and can change loyalties as they and their grandchildren age or change places of residence. To be sure, there are constraints on their ability to choose: geographical distance, poor relationships with the middle generation, the limited number of grandchildren they may have, and so forth. Still, this strategy of selective investment fulfills the function of allowing older persons to act as grandparents and to feel as though being a grandparent is an important part of their lives. It may also give grandchildren, who may not have close relations with both sets of grandparents, a better opportunity to experience intense ties to at least one grandparent.

Within families, then, all grandparent-grandchild relations are not equally close, despite the oft-repeated (and usually true) statements of grandparents that they love all their grandchildren. Instead, one often finds wide differences in the strength of the grandparent-grandchild bond, differences that appear to serve the needs of both grandparents and grandchildren to have meaningful, intense relationships with at least some members of the opposite generation.

CONCLUSION

That there is no single, dominant style of grandparenting is clear from our sample of grandparents. At one extreme are the "detached" grandparents, as we have labeled them. Some of them seem to be remote from all their grandchildren—truly distant figures for whom intergenerational ties, by choice or circumstance, play a small role in life. Older, less imbued with familistic values, perhaps far removed geographically, or emotionally estranged from their children, these people are grandparents only in a symbolic sense. They are recognized by kin and friends as grandparents, but they do little more than fill slots in a genealogy. Other grandparents, however, are detached from some but not all of their grandchildren. They may have little to do with the teenager in our study, but they have regular, rewarding contact with other grandchildren. Having adopted a strategy we labeled "selective investment," they focus their efforts and emotions on one or more of the grandchildren who live nearby or are especially personable or in need of help. In this way, they are able to act as grandparents and to compensate for weak ties to other kin.

Thus, a grandparent can be simultaneously detached and involved. Mrs. James, for example, who lives in a northeastern city, has nine children and 40 grandchildren. With such a large family, she can compensate for relationships that are dormant. She sees little of the study child, Henry, who lives with one of her daughters about 20 miles away; but she resides with another daughter and her children, with whom she is deeply involved. Personality differences and geographical mobility constrain the choices of grandparents like Mrs. James concerning involvement with kin. But the flexibility of American kinship patterns allows grandparents like her to selectively take on the grandparent role when and where they can. Grandparents often cannot manage an active, involved role with all of their grandchildren, but in our society they need not do so in order to regard themselves—and to be regarded by others— as "good" or "normal" grandparents. They can achieve the status of grandparenthood by investing in a small proportion of the possible kin ties open to them.

The "passive" grandparents we identified differ from the detached grandparents by their regular contact with the study children. Despite their inactivity, they may serve useful functions merely by being around. They may, for instance, be the "family watchdogs," in Troll's (1983) phrase, who stand ready to offer assistance when needed but otherwise are loath to interfere in the raising of the grandchildren. Most passive grandparents, we believe, drive substantial satisfaction from their relationships with their grandchildren. They consider the regular but often superficial contact with their teenaged grandchildren to be acceptable, proper, and unavoidable given the nature of adolescence. Although they may be nostalgic for the days when the grandchildren were younger, they also can derive satisfaction from watching them mature. Some of the passive grandparents in our study selectively invested in other grandchildren to compensate for the increasing independence of the teenaged study child. The passive grandparents, we submit, best fit the popular image of American grandparents: the loving older person who sees the grandchildren fairly often, is ready to provide help in a crisis, but under normal circumstance leaves parenting strictly to the parent.

We found other grandparents who take on more active roles. They exchange services with the teenaged grandchildren or, in some cases, advise, discipline, and even help rear them. At the extreme are the "influential" grandparents, who see the grandchildren quite often and are major figures in the grandchildren's day-to-day lives. The influential grandparents are younger and perhaps therefore more energetic; and they tend to have a familistic value orientation. But the key prerequisite for this style of grandparenting is frequent, almost daily contact with the grandchildren.

Indeed, a sizable minority of the influential grandparents resided in the same home with the study children, where they often took on a pseudo-parental role. It is therefore a style that is not open to the large number of grandparents who cannot—because of distance, health, or poor relations with the middle generation—visit so regularly. It is a style that seems to be quite rewarding—90 percent of these grandparents reported that they were "extremely close or quite close" to the study children. But it also can exact costs: It demands a great commitment of time, energy, and sometimes money. It is a style that we often celebrate and mythologize (as if it were the common arrangement in some bygone era—an unproven assertion); but it can be both a joy and a burden for the grandparents involved—"heaven and a hassle," as one grandparent said. On balance, though, we received the impression that the heavenly aspects outweighed the hassle for most of the influential grandparents in our sample.

We found little evidence that social class made a difference in grandparenting styles. Black grandmothers were much more likely to retain some authority over the rearing of the grandchildren. We say grandmothers rather than grandparents because we were not able to talk to many Black grandfathers. (Of our 51 interviews with Black grandparents, 44 were with grandmothers. Our lack of success in gaining interview access to Black men may be an indicator of their lesser role.) As mentioned above, the authority of Black grandmothers holds up nearly as well when the grandchildren are in two-parent homes as compared to one-parent homes. From our follow-up interviews, as well as from some preliminary interviews at a predominantly Black senior citizen's center in Baltimore, we received the impression that a strong grandmother is an accepted part of Black family patterns. Perhaps this role dates back to family disruptions during slavery or perhaps it is a more recent reaction to high rates of marital disruption or to the difficult economic position of Black men. Regardless, the Black grandmothers with whom we spoke often evinced a degree of authority, intensity, and warmth that made manifest their central roles in their children's and grandchildren's lives.

Although our study focused on grandparents with teenaged grandchildren, we were able to present evidence suggesting that the grandparental role changes as grandparents and grandchildren age. There is, then, a life course of grandparenting, although this life course can follow several diverse patterns. Early on, some grandparents offer substantial assistance in the form of baby-sitting, gifts, or even co-residence, and they seek leisure-oriented fun from their young grandchildren. The pattern of assistance continues for some, although it is transformed from baby-sitting to direct exchanges of services with the grandchildren. As grandchildren enter adolescence, the "fun seeking" style seems to fade. It can be superseded by mutual assistance, advice-giving, and discussions of problems; or it can be superseded by a passive style in which the grandparent still sees the teenaged grandchildren regularly but is increasingly removed from their world. And as the grandchildren enter adulthood, the grandparents prepare to let go of the relationship, just as parents do. Perhaps the relationship is strengthened again when the grandchildren marry and renew the cycle by producing great-grandchildren.

The styles and strategies we have described . . . show the kinds of relationships that emerge when the grandchildren are adolescents. There has been speculation that this lifecycle stage is a low-point in grandparent-grandchild relations. Perhaps so. But we found some grandparents who were deeply involved with their adolescent grandchildren and many others who, though passive in style, derived substantial satisfaction from being around to watch their grandchildren grow up.

REFERENCES

Furstenberg, F. F., Jr., Nord, C. W., Peterson, J. L., & Zill, N. (1983). The life course of children of divorce: Marital disruption and parental conflict. *American Sociological Review, 48*, 656–668.

Kivnick, H. Q. (1982a). *The meaning of grandparenthood*. Ann Arbor, MI: University of Michigan Research Press.

Kivnick, H. Q. (1982b). Grandparenthood: An overview of meaning and mental health. *Gerontologist, 22*, 59–66.

Neugarten, B. L., & Weinstein, K. K. (1964). The changing American grandparent. *Journal of Marriage and the Family, 26*, 199–204.

Robertson, J. F. (1977). Grandmotherhood: A study of role conceptions. *Journal of Marriage and the Family, 39*, 165–174.

Schneider, D. (1980). *American kinship: A cultural account*. (2nd ed.) Chicago: University of Chicago Press.

Troll, L. E. (1983). Grandparents: The family watchdogs. In T. Brubaker (Ed.), *Family relationships in later life* (pp. 63–74). Beverly Hills, CA: Sage.

Troll, L. E., & Bengtson, V. L. (1979). Generations in the family. In W. R. Burr, R. Hill, F. I. Nye, & I. L. Reiss (Eds.), *Contemporary theories about the family* (Vol. 1) (pp. 127–161). New York: Free Press.

Wood, V., & Robertson, J. F. (1976). The significance of grandparenthood. In J. F. Gubrium (Ed.), *Time, roles, and self in old age* (pp. 278–304). New York: Human Sciences Press.

PART THREE
Dissolution and Its Aftermath

NO SOCIETY EVER has been organized to ensure perfect marriages. However, most societies have provided a means for marital partners to exit from unsatisfactory relationships. Most commonly, this has involved legal divorce, although various societies have recognized only separation and annulment as legitimate means for terminating marriages. In the absence of these mechanisms, informal methods, such as desertion or informal separation, have always existed.

Worldwide, almost all societies are experiencing a significant upturn in their divorce rates. In some countries, the United States most prominently, this virtually amounts to a divorce revolution, with the experience of divorce becoming a commonplace event for a large segment of the population. Many of the past impediments to divorce are giving way as societies become increasingly industrialized and modernized. Arranged marriages are on the decline, because more and more societies recognize the individual's right to select a marriage partner. Corporate kin groups, which in tribal societies have a large stake in the marriages of their members, are gradually disintegrating. Dowry and bride price payments are becoming less frequent, lowering the financial investment families make in the marriages of their offspring. There is a movement toward a conjugal family system, freeing family units from broader kin obligations but, simultaneously, restricting an important source of social support.

Particularly in western societies, women are gaining increased independence. Because industrialization fosters an ideology of individualism and asserts each individual's right to choose, women are gradually escaping the yoke of a patriarchal past. Greater sexual freedom and greater equality with men in many spheres of life, most notably in terms of paid employment, are the result. Women are attaining higher levels of education and thereby enhancing their status. With all of these changes, marriage has come more and more to be defined as a companionate, expressive relationship, devoid of many of its more utilitarian purposes of the past. In becoming so, the continuance of the marital bond increasingly depends on the emotional—and easily changeable—relations between husband and wife.

Divorce is not unique, however, to the twentieth century or contemporary times. In American society, almost from the inception of the colonies, divorce has been a factor. Shortly after their founding, the New England and Middle Atlantic colonies adopted procedures and grounds for legally dissolving marriages, despite their faith in the injunction that "those whom God hath joined together, let no man put asunder." The colonists, whatever else might be said about them, were generally a very practical people. While divorce may have been a measure of last resort, most colonies recognized that some marital circumstances were intolerable and could be rectified only by freeing the spouses from each other. Most importantly, these situations involved cruelty toward the spouse, adultery, and desertion. Bigamy also was a common ground for seeking to end a marriage; at the time, it was relatively easy to migrate from one colony to another, forming a new marriage, which was later discovered.

Although the records are almost certainly incomplete, the recognition of divorce, carrying with it the right to remarry, did not translate into actual divorce with any great frequency. An analysis of Massachusetts divorce proceedings from 1692 to 1786, a little short of 100 years, reveals only 229 petitions being brought before the governor and his council. (Divorce was then awarded by legislative act rather than by a court.)

The first reasonably reliable statistics on divorce were not collected until 1860, at which point there was slightly more than one divorce for every 1,000 marriages, a rate that was probably characteristic of the early nineteenth century. During the entire nineteenth century, marriages were far more likely to be broken by the death of one spouse than by divorce. In the period 1860 to 1864, for example, marital dissolution by the death of a spouse occurred in 32 of every 1,000 existing marriages. Ever since, though, the divorce rate has climbed steadily, constituting a larger and larger proportion of the overall dissolution rate.

There always have been significant variations in who divorces and how the termination of marriages affects men and women. Although many societal and economic conditions influence divorce-proneness, two of the major social factors are social class and race.

An inverse relationship between social class and the rate of divorce is well documented, with those on the lower rungs of the socioeconomic ladder having the highest rate. Whether measured by occupational prestige or income, the rate consistently declines as one moves up in socioeconomic status. The rate also varies by specific occupations. Farm owners, for example, divorce half as frequently as business owners. The relationship between social class and divorce often has been interpreted as the result of the relative stress on the marriages of people in different social strata. Those in the lower strata are more likely to encounter personal and financial problems, and they are more vulnerable to economic downturns and the attendant unemployment. However, recent evidence suggests this may be changing and that the traditional differences between the lower, middle, and upper strata may be declining. Much of the dramatic upsurge in the divorce rate in the period 1965 to 1980 involved an increase in the divorce of middle and upper socioeconomic couples.

Substantial racial and ethnic differences in divorce also have been traditionally observed. Among the three largest racial and ethnic groupings in American society—whites, blacks, and Hispanics—blacks have had the highest rates, whites the lowest, with Hispanics in between but more similar to the rate of whites than blacks. While historically the trend in the divorce rate has been upward, the extent of that change has been greater for blacks than any other group. Current projections suggest that if the present rates continue, about two-thirds of all black marriages will end in divorce, compared to one-half of the marriages among whites. Most of the discrepancy in black-white rates of dissolution has come about in the last 50 years, so it seems unlikely this has anything to do with the experience of slavery, which ended 125 years ago. Much more significant is the relative economic well-being of the two racial groups. Blacks are the most disadvantaged segment of American society. They are the least educated, most vulnerable to unemployment, have the most unstable work histories, and have the lowest incomes. Three times the percentage of blacks compared to whites live below the poverty line. All of these economic hardships make black marriages more stressful and subject to disruption.

But economics alone does not totally account for racial and ethnic differences in divorce. Hispanics have many of the same characteristics as blacks. They, too, are undereducated, unemployed, have erratic work histories, and are disproportionately poor. Their rates of divorce, though, are similar to whites. Part of this may be explained by another cultural difference: Most Hispanics are Catholic, and the Catholic church is absolute in its condemnation of divorce.

Not only do we find class and racial differences in divorce, but its impact on men and women varies as well. Because men are typically the major breadwinners in the family, they often are financially better off following divorce. Particularly with the advent of no-fault divorce, courts assume men and women are equal at the time of divorce. Seldom is this the case, at least in a financial sense. Furthermore, the awarding of alimony has become more infrequent as the courts have assumed equality of the spouses. Only in more affluent situations is alimony likely to be mandated. The result is that economically needy women become more so, creating what has been called the "feminization of poverty." A second major gender difference concerns the living arrangements of ex-husbands and ex-wives. If the couple has children, which is the case in about two-thirds of all divorces, the children are most likely to reside with the mother, allowing the father greater freedom. Mothers are thrust into a situation of solo parenting that may compound the stress they experience in trying to survive economically.

The articles in Part Three document the complexities of terminating a marital relationship, pointing to the various problems and needed adjustments inherent in the process. The impact of divorce on children is also assessed. Because divorce most often signals dissatisfaction with a particular relationship and not disillusionment with marriage itself, for most divorced individuals there will be new beginnings. Remarriage means confronting new developmental tasks. The articles dealing with remarriage note the difficulties of these new beginnings, particularly when children are part of the new relationships.

ARTICLE 26
Major Variations in the Family Life Cycle: Divorce and Remarriage

BETTY CARTER AND MONICA McGOLDRICK

Divorce has become so commonplace that it is close to the point of occurring in the majority of families. It represents a major departure from the traditional family life cycle discussed in Article 11. Here, the dislocations associated with divorce are discussed. Divorce necessitates crucial shifts in one's social relationships and raises numerous developmental issues that need to be resolved in order to effectively cope with future relationships. Stepfamily integration may be especially problematic because of unresolved emotional issues stemming from a prior divorce.

WHILE THE STATISTICAL MAJORITY of the American middle and upper classes still go through the traditional family life cycle stages as outlined [in Article 11], the largest variation from that norm consists of families in which divorce has occurred. With the divorce rate currently at 50% and the rate of redivorce at 61% (Glick, 1984), divorce in the American family is close to the point at which it will occur in the majority of families and will thus be thought of more and more as a normative event. In our experience as clinicians and teachers, we have found it useful to conceptualize divorce as an interruption or dislocation of the traditional family life cycle, which produces the kind of profound disequilibrium that is associated

"Major Variations in the Family Life Cycle: Divorce and Remarriage." From *The Changing Family Life Cycle: A Framework for Family Therapy,* Betty Carter and Monica McGoldrick (eds.), 2nd ed. Allyn and Bacon, Inc., Boston, 1989, pp. 20–24. Copyright © 1989 by Allyn and Bacon.

throughout the entire family life cycle with shifts, gains, and losses in family membership (Ahrons & Rodgers, 1987). As in other life cycle phases, there are crucial shifts in relationship status and important emotional tasks that must be completed by the members of divorcing families in order for them to proceed developmentally. As in other phases, emotional issues not resolved at this phase will be carried along as hindrances in future relationships.

Therefore, we conceptualize the need for families in which divorce occurs to go through one or two additional phases of the family life cycle in order to restabilize and go forward developmentally again at a more complex level. Of women who divorce, at least 35% do not remarry. These families go through one additional phase and can restabilize permanently as post-divorce families. The other 65% of women who divorce remarry, and these families can be said to require negotiation of two additional phases of the family life cycle before permanent restabilization.

Our concept of the divorce and postdivorce family emotional process can be visualized as a roller-coaster graph, with peaks of emotional tension at all transition points:

1. At the time of the decision to separate or divorce
2. When this decision is announced to family and friends
3. When money and custody/visitation arrangements are discussed
4. When the physical separation takes place
5. When the actual legal divorce takes place
6. When separated spouses or ex-spouses have contact about money or children
7. As each child graduates, marries, has children or becomes ill
8. As each spouse is remarried, moves, becomes ill, or dies.

These emotional pressure peaks are found in all divorcing families—not necessarily in the above order—and many of them take place over and over again, for months or years. A more detailed depiction of the process appears in Table 1.

The emotions released during the process of divorce relate primarily to the work of emotional divorce—that is, the retrieval of self from the marriage. Each partner must retrieve the hopes, dreams, plans, and expectations that were invested in this spouse and in this marriage. This requires mourning what is lost and dealing with hurt, anger, blame, guilt, shame, and loss in oneself, in the spouse, in the children, and in the extended family.

In our clinical work with divorcing families, we subscribe to the basic systems view that cutoffs are emotionally harmful, and we work to help divorcing spouses continue to relate as cooperative parents and to permit maximum feasible contact between children and natural parents and grandparents. Our experience supports that of others (Hetherington et al., 1977; Ahrons, 1980), who have found that it takes a minimum of two years and a great deal of effort after divorce for a family to readjust to its new structure and proceed to the next life cycle stage, which may or may not include remarriage.

Families in which the emotional issues of divorce are not adequately resolved

TABLE 1 Dislocations of the Family Life Cycle Requiring Additional Steps to Restabilize and Proceed Developmentally

Phase	Emotional Process of Transition Prerequisite Attitude	Developmental Issues
Divorce		
1. The decision to divorce	Acceptance of inability to resolve marital tensions sufficiently to continue relationship	Acceptance of one's own part in the failure of the marriage
2. Planning the breakup of the system	Supporting viable arrangements for all parts of the system	a. Working cooperatively on problems of custody, visitation, and finances b. Dealing with extended family about the divorce
3. Separation	a. Willingness to continue cooperative coparental relationship and joint financial support of children b. Work on resolution of attachment to spouse	a. Mourning loss of intact family b. Restructuring marital and parent-child relationships and finances; adaptation to living apart c. Realignment of relationships with extended family; staying connected with spouse's extended family
4. The divorce	More work on emotional divorce: Overcoming hurt, anger, guilt, etc.	a. Mourning loss of intact family: giving up fantasies of reunion b. Retrieval of hopes, dreams, expectations from the marriage c. Staying connected with extended families
Post divorce family		
1. Single-parent (custodial household or primary residence)	Willingness to maintain financial responsibilities, continue parental contact with ex-spouse, and support contact of children with ex-spouse and his or her family	a. Making flexible visitation arrangements with ex-spouse and his family b. Rebuilding own financial resources c. Rebuilding own social network
2. Single-parent (noncustodial)	Willingness to maintain parental contact with ex-spouse and support custodial parent's relationship with children	a. Finding ways to continue effective parenting relationship with children b. Maintaining financial responsibilities to ex-spouse and children c. Rebuilding own social network

TABLE 2 Remarried Family Formation: A Developmental Outline*

Steps	Prerequisite Attitude	Developmental Issues
1. Entering the new Relationship	Recovery from loss of first marriage (adequate "emotional divorce")	Recommitment to marriage and to forming a family with readiness to deal with the complexity and ambiguity
2. Conceptualizing and planning new marriage and family	Accepting one's own fears and those of new spouse and children about remarriage and forming a stepfamily Accepting need for time and patience for adjustment to complexity and ambiguity of: 1. Multiple new roles 2. Boundaries: space, time, membership and authority 3. Affective Issues: guilt, loyalty conflicts, desire for mutuality, unresolvable past hurts	a. Work on openness in the new relationships to avoid pseudomutuality b. Plan for maintenance of cooperative financial and coparental relationships with ex-spouses c. Plan to help children deal with fears, loyalty conflicts, and membership in two systems d. Realignment of relationships with extended family to include new spouse and children e. Plan maintenance of connections for children with extended family of ex-spouse(s)
3. Remarriage and reconstitution of family	Final resolution of attachment to previous spouse and ideal of "intact" family: Acceptance of a different model of family with permeable boundaries	a. Restructuring family boundaries to allow for inclusion of new spouse-stepparent b. Realignment of relationships and financial arrangements throughout subsystems to permit interweaving of several systems c. Making room for relationships of all children with biological (noncustodial) parents, grandparents, and other extended family d. Sharing memories and histories to enhance stepfamily integration

*Variation on a developmental scheme presented by Ransom et al. (1979).

can remain stuck emotionally for years, if not for generations. The predictable peaks of emotional tension in the transition to remarriage occur at the time of serious commitment to a new relationship; at the time a plan to remarry is announced to families and friends; at the time of the actual remarriage and formation of a stepfamily, which takes place simultaneously and as the logistics of stepfamily life are put into practice.

The family emotional process at the transition to remarriage consists of struggling with fears about investment in a new marriage and a new family: one's own fears, the new spouse's fears, and the children's fears (of either or both spouses); dealing with hostile or upset reactions of the children, the extended families, and the ex-spouse; struggling with the ambiguity of the new family structure, roles, and relationships; rearousal of intense parental guilt and concerns about the welfare of children; and rearousal of the old attachment to ex-spouse (negative or positive). Table 2 depicts the process in somewhat greater detail.

Our society offers stepfamilies a choice of two conceptual models, neither of which work: families that act like the intact family next door; glorified in the situation comedies of TV; and the wicked stepparents of the fairy tales. . . . Stepfamilies . . . lack . . . social support and clarity in the paradigm of family they are offered.

In our experience the residue of an angry and vengeful divorce can block stepfamily integration for years or forever. The rearousal of the old emotional attachment to an ex-spouse, which characteristically surfaces at the time of remarriage and at subsequent life cycle transitions of children, is usually not understood as a predictable process and therefore leads to denial, misinterpretation, cutoff, and assorted difficulties. As in the case of adjustment to a new family structure after divorce, stepfamily integration seems also to require a minimum of two or three years before a workable new structure permits family members to move on emotionally.

REFERENCES

Ahrons, C. R. (1980). Redefining the divorced family: A conceptual framework. *Social Work,* Nov: 437–441.

Ahrons, C. R. H. & Rodgers, R. (1987). *The divorced family.* New York: Norton.

Glick, P. C. (1984). Marriage, divorce, and living arrangements. *Journal of Family Issues* 5: 7–26.

Hetherington, M. E., Cox, M., & Cox, R. (1977). The aftermath of divorce. In E. M. Hetherington & R. D. Parke, *Contemporary readings in child psychology*, 3rd ed. New York: McGraw-Hill.

ARTICLE 27
Uncoupling

DIANE VAUGHAN

How do relationships come to an end? This article discusses the complex process of coming apart, noting the transitions each of the partners makes. In order to uncouple, both husband and wife go through the same stages. The author emphasizes, however, that the transitions begin and end at different times for each of the partners, depending on whether the partner is an initiator or the one being left behind. Because the phasing of the transitions are different for each party, reconciliation, even at the desire of the initiator, becomes almost impossible.

> *Uncoupling is a railroader's term. When a relationship ends, it's like when a locomotive uncouples from a car or a car uncouples from another car. They're hooked together with knuckle couplers. They interlock, like your knuckles do when you clasp your hands together. When a locomotive uncouples, you pull a coupling pin on one side and one lets go, or you pull a coupling pin on the other side and the other lets go, or you pull both pins and they both let go. I know. I was a brakeman. I used to do that. Get the mechanical aspect of it? It's like a relationship. One can let go, the other can let go, or they can let go at the same time. But it's also a mechanical letting go because they no longer live together. They live separately. They do different things. They're no longer hooked up in mechanical ways.* [Mechanic, age 39, divorced after 12 years]

ALTHOUGH NOW APART, each partner witnesses the other person's transition. Formerly participants in each other's life, they are now observers. They see the

From UNCOUPLING: HOW RELATIONSHIPS COME APART by Diane Vaughan. Copyright © 1986 by Oxford University Press, Inc. Reprinted by permission.

home transformed, or with new occupants. They see physical changes. They see the other person master new skills and demonstrate unexpected ones. They see the other person with someone else. For both initiator and partner, what they see brings with it some sense of exclusion and loss. Equally as important is what they don't see. Being physically excluded from the routine of life with the partner does not diminish one's awareness of it.[1] Knowing it's the other person's birthday and not being present, hearing they are having a personal crisis and not giving a hand, realizing it's Sunday and they are at the ballgame—all contribute to each partner's redefining self and other as separate.

Both people also witness changes in themselves, which feed into this redefinition process. As they negotiate life on their own, they begin learning who they are without the other person. They gain insight about the relationship as they remove themselves from the patterns developed with the former partner. People describe this experience as one of discovery:

> *I lived all my life with 18th century antiques. I went out to buy furniture and discovered that I liked Swedish modern.* [Lawyer, age 50, separated after 26 years of marriage]

> *Alex left, he said, because I didn't give him good enough sex. He said there wouldn't be anyone who would want me, as soon as they found out. Well, what I discovered was that Alex was a lousy lover.* [Office manager, age 27, separated after living together 5 years]

> *I doubted that anyone would really come to visit just me. I discovered that they would.* [Housewife, age 60, separated after 39 years of marriage]

> *She used to always want me to come watch TV with her after supper. I always had work to do. After we separated, I discovered myself watching TV in the evenings. I seldom worked. It must have just been my way of avoiding being with her.* [Potter, age 32, separated after living together 9 years]

Some of the discoveries are pleasant; some are not. In the other person's absence, we have no ready scapegoat for the ills that befall us. When the same things keep happening over and over, but under different circumstances, we eventually have to confront the painful fact that we must be contributing to them.

> *I always thought Jamie was holding me back in my career. I discovered after she was gone that it wasn't her.* [Lawyer, age 32, divorced after 9 years]

> *I always complained about the house. When I left, I moved in with a friend and discovered piles of newspapers, books, pencils, scraps of paper everywhere. I went home to visit and it was neat and clean. I was shocked*

to discover it was me all that time. [Teacher, technical school/writer, age 39, divorced after 18 years]

I never had fun when we went out with other people. I thought it was because of who I was with. Since I've been seeing other people, I discovered I'm just not very good in groups. I get feeling inadequate, and that depresses me. [Leather craftsman, age 42, separated after living together 12 years]

For those married, the decision to seek a lawyer and initiate legal proceedings adds formal confirmation to the relationship's demise. Institutional legitimacy may grant stability to an ongoing relationship, yet legal ties hinder the dissolution of a relationship in trouble. In order to uncouple, the married not only must redefine themselves as separate entities for relatives, friends, and acquaintances, but must also do so in official records. While those living together may feel the absence of legal ritual is to their advantage, formal proceedings facilitate the redefinition process that is essential to the transition. By taking legal action, the two people announce the change in the relationship to a broad audience. Partners display their discontent in a formal setting. The adversary proceedings sharpen and reinforce the separation of the joint biography, as each partner, seeking separate ends, attempts to manipulate public definitions.[2] The formal division of property, custody decisions, final removal of the rings, and the legal termination all convey the message that the relationship is over, not only to outsiders, but to the two main participants.

I had really wanted out of the relationship for ten years. It was all I had thought about. When he left, I did not once regret it or miss him. Yet when I read the separation agreement and saw his name and my name, the date and place of our marriage, the names and birthdates of our children, I was overwhelmed. Twenty years of a life were ending and reduced to a few pieces of paper. We were really doing this to ourselves. [Housewife, age 41, divorced after 20 years]

I felt like an anvil had been lifted off me that day, so that it was over at last, because it was over two times before and two times back and I just wanted peace. The rest was a formality and the courthouse was that final scene, the curtain had dropped, you know, these are legalities that made it all real. It was scary. It was like it was this staged thing. It was a necessity that you had to go through. So much had happened. It was a final scene that I needed. I felt a great sense of loss, a great sense of failure. And this doom had set in. [Secretary, age 38, divorced after 10 years]

As the change in the relationship has become increasingly public, the result is a continuing decline in the precariousness of the new arrangement. Yet this is not synonymous with uncoupling, which is complete when the participants define themselves and are defined by others as separate and independent of each other—when being partners is no longer a major source of their identity. Instead, that identity comes from other sources. Arriving at this point depends on a complex intermingling of redefinition of self, other, and relationship. And this takes an unpredictable amount of time—separation or divorce are seldom the final stage.[3] People can live apart or be divorced and still not be uncoupled.[4]

> *The divorce didn't end it. When it took place, that day, you know, we weren't sure what had happened. Really, I mean we went to dinner and so on. She gives a kiss, I give a kiss. We went away on a vacation together. And when we visited her sister's house, we share the same bed, and her sister says, "Are you people divorced for real?" We went out. For six months we were very close. But she didn't want the marriage. I wanted it, but she didn't.* [Social services worker, age 44, divorced after 19 years]

> *I knew that I was in better shape than she was because I was the one who pushed for the split. Still, even a year later I was still very vulnerable to her actions. If I saw her at the supermarket, or someone brought her name up, or if she called about something, which she seemed to do pretty often—like she was trying to find stuff to talk to me about, did I see the exhibit, so-and-so called, the dog got sick, you know—I was always upset by it, by talking to her, being reminded of her. I just wanted it to be over and it just took a long time for that to happen, for that connection to be broken.* [Dental assistant, age 27, separated after living together 3 years]

Uncoupling does not occur at the same moment for each participant. Both, to uncouple, make the same transition, but begin and end at different times. Initiators, as we have seen, have a head start. But ultimately, aided by the initiator's behavior, by comparison with alternatives, and with a little help from their friends, partners begin to put the relationship behind them. They acknowledge that the relationship is unsaveable. Through the social process of mourning they, too, eventually arrive at an account that explains this unexpected denouement.[5] "Getting over" a relationship does not mean relinquishing the part of our life that we shared with another, but rather coming to some conclusion that allows us to accept and understand its altered significance.[6] Once we develop such an account, we can incorporate it into our lives and go on.

Over time, partners' accounts change from the self-blame that characterizes first attempts to understand this experience. When partners believe they are at fault, they assume the relationship can be saved—for what they have ruined, they also can fix. As they come to the conclusion that it is unsaveable, their accounts will correspondingly justify the relationship's demise on the basis of something beyond their ability to correct.[7] Like initiators before them, partners conclude that the failure was the result of an unavoidable external circumstance, or some fatal flaw in the relationship—or perhaps the seeds of destruction were in their beginnings.

I really didn't feel like she left me. I felt like she was the victim of people who pulled her away from me. I think that if she had left me for another man because she didn't love me or whatever, that I could have handled that. But it was almost like those old Shirley Temple movies. Someone kidnaps her. I felt like it just wasn't fair, that she had been taken away— that somebody took her away from me and that was terrible and I was just overwhelmed with this feeling of there's no chance to get her back. [Student, age 24, separated after living together 4 years]

She was the most emotionally demanding person that I've ever met because of the fact that she was emotionally starved her whole life. I blame everything that happened to us on her parents because they were just awful, miserable. They hated each other and they took it out on her. [Psychologist, age 36, separated after living together 6 years]

I think basically I blame the fact that I became divorced on the early age that I was married. I was married at 19 and he was 21 and I think our value systems weren't formed at that time and later we just grew apart. [Executive secretary/supervisor, age 34, divorced after 9 years]

Why he started this behavior is all tied up with the fact that all of a sudden he found himself a father of teenage girls and he wasn't a father of little kids anymore. He was feeling old and going through a crisis of middle life. In his case he had an illness already, so it hit him worse than normal people. He just started acting crazier than usual. It just brought me to my senses. I thought he's never going to get better, in fact he's getting more nutty as he gets older. I think once I saw that, which was about six months or whatever after we separated, I was definitely sure that I didn't want him anymore. [Housewife/handcraft goods supplier, age 35, separated after 15 years of marriage]

The partner will define the relationship as unsaveable in ways that reduce both the personal sense of failure and the possibility of social stigma. When the partner develops an account that seems to be complete and makes sense, the time spent in reflective thought and conversation about the relationship diminishes. Partners, too, arrive at a point when the other person seems to be someone they no longer know.[8]

He's changed. He's gotten a permanent, and it's kind of frosted on top. The curls seem strange for him. He's changed his appearance so much that he doesn't seem like the same man I lived with. At this point he has changed drastically personally. I'm quite sure he is on drugs. He was the three-piece business suit, responsible man who went to gold chains, tight dungarees, open necked shirts overnight and his eyes were all glassy and pupils dilated. [Teacher, age 35, divorced after 11 years]

I see his face and I remember him as a person. But I've totally erased even what I thought at that point was an exorbitant amount of pain that I went through for all those years. I have no animosity toward him. I don't have any bad feelings at all. It's like looking at a stranger. Basically I must have dealt with him in a sound way because I came out on top. I can talk with him in a rational way. I can laugh with him, I can joke with him, and it's like talking to somebody that I knew a long time ago and just had not seen for a long time. [Accountant, age 38, separated after living together 13 years]

I didn't feel divorced when we separated. I guess you could say that something clicked inside of me in terms of feeling divorced when I realized that this woman who I supposedly loved so much responded to what I perceived at that particular time to be putting my life on the line to save her—when she responded to this with trying to send me to jail, something clicked inside of me and the rest was just over a period of time I felt more and more divorced and I began to live my life independently, not tied by emotional responses to her. [Machinist, age 29, divorced after 6 years]

We came from the same kind of family background, and shared a lot of similar values. Manners and politeness were important to both of us, you know, respect for the other person. And then he abandoned that toward the end, and became wild and reckless and crazy. Rude and loud and disrespectful of others. He almost became a different person. [Student/service coordinator, age 28, separated after living together 1 year]

Many partners do not totally accept the idea that the relationship is over until the initiator becomes coupled with someone new. With that step, the tentativeness is gone. When the initiator recouples soon after parting from the partner, the news often shocks the partner and others close to the relationship. How could the initiator have found someone else so quickly? What others perceive to be a sudden incomprehensible change is, of course, not sudden at all, but a consequence of a transition that has prepared the initiator for this step. The shock is accompanied by a sense of loss, even when the partners have ceased being in touch in any regular way. When the other person forms a new partnership, it changes and limits interaction. For those who hope for reconciliation, it seals off the possibility. Children, friends, and family who have held on to a similar hope must also finally lay it aside.[9] For the initiator, the partner's recoupling is also a significant event, which often generates an unexpected emotional response.

When people have truly uncoupled—established a life confirming their independent identity—they will again be free to see both the positive and negative qualities of the former partner and the relationship. Negative definitions are essential to transition, but they are often temporary. When people achieve a valid self-identity, they no longer have to work at dissociating by focusing on negative attributes and displaying discontent. They are then able to reconstruct the history of the relationship to again include the good memories of the times shared.[10] Instead of discontent, they may display apathy. ("I don't hate him. I don't love him. I don't want anything awful to happen to him. I don't care if anything good happens to him either. I just feel neutral.") They may speak kindly and sincerely of the partner to others. ("He's a good father." "She's a hard worker.") They may even demonstrate good will and affection to the partner.

The initiator may be able to acknowledge the good in partner and relationship before the separation. When the partner is still dependent on the relationship, however, the initiator feels less free to reveal positive sentiments for fear of reinforcing the partner's hope that the relationship will continue. If, on the other hand, *both* partners are well along in their transitions prior to the physical break, vivid differences appear at separation. Each is free to take care of the other, appreciate the other, mourn the loss with the other, and, as in the case of the couple who held each other tenderly on the floor of their empty house, they may literally and figuratively help each other out of the door.[11]

Not only do the former partners tend to concede that the other has positive characteristics, but their generous reassessment can extend to other relationships left behind in the wake of uncoupling. Once they have achieved an independent identity, partners no longer need to dissociate from their former lifestyle. They are free to acknowledge the good qualities of former friends and family and perhaps incorporate them in their life once again. Sometimes these ties are renewed many years later, as when a lawyer at age 29 saw his father for the first time since his parents separated; the last time they were together, the son was 3. Ties with family and friends are often renewed when one or the other recouples. Having made a public commitment to a new relationship, initiator or partner may return to the previous social circle, picking up the threads of the former lifestyle with the new person—naturally with some alterations and embellishments to account for the changed cast of characters.

Each partner's account of the relationship's demise makes still another shift, as each arrives at a stable explanation that either removes them both from blame or joins them in the responsibility.[12] As independence frees the partners to see both positive and negative aspects of the other, so eventually they are able to look back and assess their own contribution to the fall. They're aided by their discovery of who they are without the other person, for chances are they've learned some things about themselves that alter their view of the past.

> *I wasn't even looking at things and evaluating things like I should have been. You know, looking at me and saying, "What were you doing? How did you get hooked up with this other person?" I had to do all that in retrospect, after it was really over, after all the pain was gone, after all the problems were gone, after I could look him in the face and after my heart didn't skip a beat to see people walking down the street that looked like him. But that took time.* [Student, age 21, separated after living together 2 years]

And when that dependence was broken on both our parts, that is when I said OK now, let me evaluate the whole situation in realistic ways. I'm not going to make excuses, I don't need to make excuses anymore. Then I began to think back—what did I say, what did I do—what did she put up with, what did I put up with—how did we stifle each other—and we paid a terrible price. Nineteen years of living a substandard existence. We have a lot to make up for. What she lost, what I lost. [Social services worker, age 44, divorced after 19 years]

For some, uncoupling can never be complete. One or both of the partners may not be able to develop a new life that becomes self-validating. When this is the case, the display of discontent signals their continued connection.[13]

I've spent a great deal of time talking about this, and thinking the whole thing through. And frankly, I've thought about it just as much as I think I want to. The thing is continuously a part of my life. No matter what I do, and no matter who I am with, those experiences and those memories are still going to be a part of my being. And a lot of them I don't want to get rid of. I know that I still have a lot of anger and hostility in relation to him that I have not expressed completely. I continuously think about those things but they're never any different. And I find myself on certain occasions allowing all of the anger and all of the hurt that I've suppressed to resurface at certain times. And then, I guess I say to myself that . . . I'm sorry, apparently I'm feeling some need to cry here, I'm feeling insecure here or something or other . . . that I need to do this thing, to re-evaluate the situation, or I get real angry, and hit this pillow, and say "God damn you, I really resent what you've done to me." [Graduate student, age 30, separated after 12 years of marriage]

CONTINUITIES

Even though people separate, move away, or divorce, visible indications of the bond between partners often remain.[14] Much as a vanished glacier is traced by a terminal moraine, relationships leave behind social reflections of the intimate connection. After formal termination, the bonds between partners are visible both in continued interaction patterns and in similarities of habit and lifestyle.

Former partners often continue to interact because they have in common something else that survives the demise of the relationship, drawing the two together. Most important and obvious of these are shared loved ones—children, in-laws.[15] Though in-laws may, of necessity, be excluded from the new life,[16] children rarely can be, and their very existence is not only a reminder of the relationship, but often causes the parents to keep in touch.[17] Former partners may also be thrown together because of shared ownership of some property,[18] or because of some event that grows out of their shared history. The partnership momentarily may be resurrected when, for example, a teenage child is arrested for drunken driving; a former landlord demands reimbursement for a damaged apartment; the IRS decides to conduct a tax audit of a joint return. The former partners are sometimes rejoined at moments of great sorrow or great joy. The relationship is temporarily renewed because the time spent together has made each an expert on the other. When a major life event occurs, sometimes only the former partner can thoroughly understand its significance. For both partners, the other is the one they want by their side at such moments.

I didn't sleep with him when his father died, but I kind of acted like his wife for the weekend. To make things easier, I did. You know, he was very sad about this thing and I helped him. It's OK to still care about somebody that you lived with all that time, you know. When his father died, I had a history with him, a history that his present wife doesn't know. She only met his father once, so I think it's appropriate to comfort him when he called to tell me his father is dead, to comfort him and to say remember the times, remember this, that, and that he never really was happy since your mother died. [Secretary, age 38, divorced after 10 years]

The promotion was something I had worked for for years, and I had to admit she had worked for it, too, in her own way. She had helped me in a lot of ways and I had recognized that it had cost both of us. When it was time to celebrate, there was no one who understood better than her what it meant to me, and she was the one I wanted to celebrate with. (Lawyer, age 36, separated after living together 6 years]

My lover of several years died unexpectedly at age 40. My ex-husband had been divorced a second time, and he suggested a trip together, so we went to Europe on a tour. The other couples on the trip commented that they were going to get divorced when they got home because, of all the couples on the trip, we seemed to get along best. [Antique jewelry dealer, age 54, divorced after 18 years]

Ironically, while divorce is usually taken as a sign of the end of a relationship, the divorce process itself can bind partners to each other, inhibiting them from going on. Two people are forced to continue to focus on the relationship and each other. The legal struggle consumes energies that would otherwise be spent in other directions. Suits and countersuits may take several years. The working and re-working of custody, visitation, and financial support can have people back in court long after what was thought to be the final judgment.[19]

In many cases, partners continue to interact not because of their previous role connections, but for reasons that seem to be actively created by one or both of the participants after or during the formal termination of the relationship. These "manufactured interactions" also reflect the bond between former partners. They illustrate the difficulty of severing the bond with the other person because, even when the continued contact is full of anger and conflict, the effect is to keep the relationship going.[20] Some examples from my interviews:

The initiator moves out. The partner spends the weekend helping with the relocation—hanging pictures, moving furniture.

The initiator moves out, leaving a set of tools behind. Several years later, even after the initiator's remarriage, the tools are still there. The initiator comes to borrow them one at a time. The partner is planning to move within the same city. The tools are boxed up, ready to be taken along.

The initiator moves out, but is slow to change the mailing address. Rather than marking a forwarding address on the envelopes and returning them by mail, the partner either delivers them once a week or the initiator picks them up.

The initiator moves out. The partner resists surrendering the initiator's grandmother's sewing machine. The conflict necessitates many phone calls and visits.

Sexual abuse was a constant part of the relationship. After separating, they each formed new partnerships. Nonetheless, the two kept a monthly rendezvous at a local motel, where they continued their abusive pattern.

The terms of the property settlement stated that a payment was to be made to the initiator every six months. Instead of mailing the check, the partner handed it over during an elegant semi-annual lunch.

The child support check was always late or missing, resulting in the partner making phone calls and writing letters, but getting no response. The partner got the check only by making a personal appearance.

Interaction between former partners tends to diminish, however.[21] As time passes, the partners become more engaged in their separate lives, thereby decreasing both their need and ability to interact with each other. For example, the creation of a new family often reduces the time and attention available for the old: visitation (and support checks) decrease; the elegant lunches no longer occur.[22] Some of the reasons to interact disappear. The children grow up, relatives move away, pets die, joint property is sold.[23]

As post-separation interaction decreases, the reality of their separate existences is sometimes again confirmed years later, surprising the former partners with a recurring sense of loss and a reminder of the finality of what they've done. Divorced for three years, two former partners decided to sell the family home that neither had lived in for some time. Instead, one of their grown daughters lived there, perpetuating the sense of family by reigning over the easy comings and goings of both parents, two younger children who lived with their mother, four other children, who, now single adults, lived nearby, plus miscellaneous friends of the family and assorted roomers. The week the new owners were to take possession of the house, the family organized a combined yard sale and party, billed in invitations as "A Celebration of New Beginnings." But, as one of the parents said, the effect of the divorce was nothing compared to the effect on everybody of the dismantling and sale of the family home. With the loss of the past and future locus of activity came the realization that for the nine of them, family life would never be the same.

Even though contact between former partners lessens, the bonds between them are reflected in similarities of habit and lifestyle that seem to persist after separation or divorce. Some people tend to take on certain traits characteristic of their partners after parting. Some examples: During a ten-year relationship, one person reported that his partner could not fall asleep at night with the bedroom closet doors open. He frequently left them open, which resulted in her getting up and closing them. (The impact of this near-nightly scenario on their bedroom intimacy is easily imagined.) After they separated, he found that *he* could not sleep with the closet doors open, and three years later was still compulsively getting up and closing them if a sleeping partner left them open. A woman, whose former husband complained during their marriage that she never was dressed appropriately when they went out, found that she spent her first vacation alone shopping for clothes. In the six years since the divorce, she has taken great pride in maintaining a fashionable wardrobe. Another person constantly fought with the partner during the relationship over the condition of their apartment.

> *I hated being chased by the vacuum cleaner and the washing machine was going all the time and she would empty ashtrays before the ashes got in the ashtray. I mean, I went out of my mind! We had fights like you wouldn't believe, and here I find myself today, obsessive-compulsive behavior about my apartment. It has to be neat and clean! I never figured out why I ended up being the same way she is. The very one thing I dislike a lot.* [Advertising salesman, age 38, divorced after 8 years]

These examples involve small habits or values that could be explained simply by our unerring ability to locate the other's vulnerable points and "thrust home," as Cyrano said.[24] Equally possible as an explanation, however, is that in dissociating from the other person, we dissociate from that part of ourselves that is like them. When we uncouple, behaviors previously undemonstrated are expressed because they then become a reflection of our own identity, not our former partner's.

Sometimes, however, the similarities between the former partners are more encompassing. Instead of a similarity of habit, one takes on the lifestyle of the other. A married minister fell in love with someone else. The minister divorced his wife and moved away with his new partner. The former wife began working in the counseling center of the church he used to head, went back to school, earned a Ph.D. in counseling, and became a full-time staff member. A man who was an English professor found that soon after he and his partner separated, the partner enrolled as a graduate student in his department. He remarked with dismay that he had moved out of her bedroom and she had moved into his work space. Lifestyle similarities like these may occur, in part, because of shifting interdependence. No longer can either rely on the other person to carry out former tasks connected to the relationship. While ways exist to get around this problem (find someone else to do it; forget it), often each partner has to take on the duties of the other, in addition to his or her own. The classic example is a marriage with children, where divorce requires that the husband become more domestic and the wife be a wage-earner.[25] In the process, their lifestyles become more similar.

But lifestyle similarities also result because our merging is more than physical when we couple. Relationships develop an intangible complement consisting of tastes, opinions, attitudes, values, and ideas that we exchange and learn from each other. We create a common culture. While the physical aspects of our life are readily separable, the intangible ones are not. And so when we separate, we may take our bodies and our material belongings, but leave behind other signs that we were there.[26] In retrospect, we may think of our former partners as transitional people, for they play a major role in preparing us for whatever comes next. Both by what they teach us that we incorporate and what we reject, they change our course.

We may formally terminate our relationships and reconstruct a life without the other person. But our relationships continue to affect us, for past history affects the future and memory lies waiting to take us on unexpected journeys into the past. A friend wrote, "One never checks memory at the door. It is there to be evoked, even when unrecognized. It is perhaps because we come to accept it or can recognize and deal with it that we mature. But one is never free! Only free-er—or more/less chained."

Coupling changes us and so does uncoupling. But in most cases relationships don't end. They change, but they don't end. When both individuals develop an identity of their own, they're free to acknowledge the ties.[27] Some don't choose this option. But others transform their relationship with the former partner. Many evolve a new character, significantly different from the past and suited to present needs.[28] Former partners may become friends or confidants, turning to each other for occasional advice or support. They may become occasional lovers. They may develop a professional relationship that allows them to be included in each other's life in a regular way. It's almost as if we need to know that the period of our life we shared with another was not in vain.

> *I don't know that people ever lose that, that want, that wish, to be important to someone who's been, you know, such an important part of your life. And I think it has been good for me to have the feeling that he still feels the urge to come around and let off steam, or discuss something that was on his mind.* [Bank teller, age 23, separated after living together 3 years]

> *I accept the fact that I'm angry with him but I'm also . . . there'll never be another man that I'll have children with. Just for the fact that we married and had children, he will always be special and because I understand his parents and his problems. I just can look at him and say,*

you know, the man is miserable, you know, but he is the children's father, so even though there is anger there's a certain amount of compassion I feel for him. [Housewife/handcraft goods supplier, age 35, separated after 15 years of marriage]

That's the mother of my kids, and I may not feel romantic about her, but I still have a sense of responsibility and she always will be somebody in my life. But there's still a sense of loss and of grieving. You know how, if someone you loved dies, you visit the grave because you want to remember. And maybe that's where you can feel the closest to them. I think that's it, there's a grief from that kind of profound loss, somebody you loved enough that you lived with for awhile, that they're gone, and it's almost, I think the emotional grief is almost as if someone died. But they're not really dead, so you want to hear them, see them and touch them once in a while. It's like going to the grave. It's like having a chance to have them come back from the dead and maybe something kind can pass between you. I don't want to possess her, I don't want to be her husband, I don't even want to have a necessarily on-going relationship, but there is that something—I want to know that she's OK and just every once in a while I want to touch base. [Administrator, age 44, separated after 23 years of marriage]

And so we keep in touch, or we take something the other person gave us, incorporate it in our lives, and go on.

RECONCILIATION

Uncoupling is not a compelling journey that, once embarked on, allows no turning back. Granted, as the problems in the relationship become more and more public, resurrecting the relationship becomes more and more difficult.[29] Each phase closes yet another door. Yet the process may be interrupted at any point. Even after separation or divorce, a couple may reconcile.

Reconciliation can and does occur, but it is both a delicate and difficult enterprise. To achieve a true reconciliation (as opposed to just moving back in together), both partners must redefine the other person and relationship positively. In addition, they must change the definitions others hold. By deciding to reunite, both partners risk social embarrassment, for they have chosen to again create a life with the person whose flaws they have been announcing publicly for some time. They must, in other words, display their content, legitimating the reconciliation.

A further difficulty is that, for both partners, reconciliation will entail the same sifting and sorting of relatives, friends, and associates that accompany every coupling and uncoupling. Other relationships must be gained and lost, if the partners are to reconstruct a world they can share. Confidants and transitional people are often left behind—either because they're links to a lifestyle now to be forsaken, or because the secrets they know about the partners preclude their being included. By definition, reconciliation entails a comparison of possible alternatives—both partners must redefine being in the relationship as superior to other possibilities.

Reconciliation is not simply a return to what used to be. It is yet another transition, with its own costs. Both partners must be willing to endure the social, emotional, and financial disruption that accompanies the rearrangement of their physical and social worlds. Under what circumstances do people consider it? Initiators may find that, once separated, the cost of terminating the relationship turns out to be higher than they thought.[30] They are overwhelmed by the ill will of family and friends, the loss of other relationships, missing the other person or the home environment, or the guilt associated with causing others pain. The lifestyle they have opted for may be disappointing: single life is harder than they thought; the lover proves difficult or unfaithful; work without someone to share life with is more drudgery than challenge; their income does not adequately meet their needs.

But if the initiator seeks reconciliation simply because going it alone is tough, but doesn't redefine self, other, and relationship, the contradiction between the self-concept and the social niche will remain. The two may stay together, nonetheless, because the initiator hasn't sufficient alternatives to manage the transition, or because the initiator finds some alternative to make staying in the relationship possible. Sometimes the reunion turns out to be temporary.

We were married for 18 years and fought like cats and dogs. Finally we divorced. We were apart for three years and we both were so goddamned lonely that we decided to remarry. After three years, all the old problems finally got to us again, and we got divorced. My father said, "Alan, if you do that one more time, I'm going to have you committed." [Interior decorator, age 52]

Alternatively, the initiator may seek reconciliation after the requisite redefinitions. Separation changes the initiator, causing a reordering of priorities and commitments. The irony—rather, one of the many ironies—of uncoupling is that while separation imposes social barriers to reconciliation, living apart can itself bring about changes that leave both partners better prepared to interact: changes that, had they happened during the relationship, might have prevented all of this. Once the initiator is physically separate and has achieved some measure of autonomy, negative definitions are no longer required. Now free to compare the new life with the old on a more equitable basis, the initiator may conclude that more has been lost than won.

The initiator's ability to again redefine partner and relationship positively may occur not simply because the separation experience changes the initiator, but because it changes the partner.[31] An initiator who complained the partner was boring reconsidered on seeing the effects of a new job and regular aerobics classes six months after separation. One initiator who wanted to feel needed and care for the partner became resentful when the partner got an interesting and exciting job. As a result of the separation, the partner had a mental breakdown, and was unable to keep his job, becoming again needy and dependent. Another initiator complained about the partner's involvement with work. After divorce, the partner decided to cut back on the 60-hour-a-week job and attend to the more personal aspects of life. Another initiator felt that the partner never communicated feelings well, never spoke of love or demonstrated affection. Faced with the responsibility for the children after divorce, the partner sought therapy and began taking courses in communication. He learned to deal with his children in ways that might have made him a better partner if the problem had been rectified during the relationship.[32]

Post-separation changes in either or both people can precipitate a reconciliation, even though the partners have experienced many phases of the transition, as in the following case.

> *Ellen met Jack in college. They fell in love and married. Jack had been blind since birth. He had pursued a college career in education and was also a musician. Both admired the independence of the other. In the marriage, she subordinated her career to his and helped him pursue a master's degree, as well as his musical interests. Her time was consumed by his needs for transportation and the taping and transcribing of music for the musicians in his group. He was teaching at a school for the blind by day and performing as a musician at night. They had a son. Ellen's life, instead of turning outward, as the husband's, revolved around family responsibilities. She gained weight. Jack, after 12 years of marriage, left Ellen for his high school sweetheart. Ellen grieved for a while, then began patching up her life. She got a job, established her own credit, went back to college, and lost weight. She saw a lawyer, filed for divorce, joined Parents Without Partners, and began searching out singles groups. She dated. Throughout, Jack and Ellen saw each other occasionally and maintained a sexual relationship. The night before the divorce was final, they reconciled.*

More often, however, post-separation changes reflect still another ironic twist in uncoupling. They happen too late.[33] Initiators may be unaware of changes in their partners. Or, if aware, initiators may have found their new social niche comfortable and confirming. So while they may note (and, in some cases, take pride in) the partner's accomplishments, they do not seek reconciliation. On the other hand, if the initiator does wish to get back together, it may be too late. The partner may have uncoupled. Often what makes the partner once again attractive to the initiator is that the partner has gone on. In creating a new life, the partner acquires the basic means of salvation. If reconciliation is what the partner desires, achieving it lies not in seeking it, but, perversely, in turning away. By giving up the past and building a future, the partner begins to create a different identity. In the process, the partner regains the sense of self that has been lost. Being once again "self-possessed," the partner interacts out of strength, not weakness.

To arrive at this point, the partner must have settled on an account of the breakup that has legitimated it. The partner has reordered the history of the relationship, concluding that it did not and could not meet his or her needs. Consequently, the partner may be unwilling to return to life as it was or to create a new one with the other person. The initiator wants to get back together. The partner says no. Now the initiator experiences rejection, and, focusing on the positive aspects of what has been lost, sinks into the morass from which the partner has so arduously climbed. Reconciliation, it turns out, is not only a matter of redefining self, other, and relationship, but of timing.

NOTES

1. Murray S. Davis, *Intimate Relations* (New York: Free Press, 1973), p. 179. Simmel describes isolation as interaction between two parties, one of whom leaves, after exerting certain influences. The isolated individual is isolated only in reality, however; for in the mind of the other party, the absent person continues to live and act. Kurt H. Wolff, ed. and tr., *The Sociology of Georg Simmel* (New York: The Free Press, 1950), p. 119.

2. See also Judith S. Wallerstein and Joan B. Kelly, *Surviving the Breakup: How Children and Parents Cope with Divorce* (New York: Basic Books, 1980), pp. 26–29.

3. Paul Bohannan, ed., *Divorce and After* (New York: Doubleday, 1971), pp. 33–34. Hart, examining the length of time between separation and divorce, found that some people took months or years to rule out the possibility of reconciliation. She reports, "In some cases, it was not until the individual had finalized some other plans for the future, either in the shape of another partner, or perhaps a new occupational career, that the old life could be abandoned. Arranging for the legal dissolution of the bond was often deferred until this state of affairs had been reached." Nicky Hart, *When Marriage Ends: A Study in Status Passage* (London: Tavistock, 1976), pp. 116–117.

4. Gram (pp. 12–13). Wallerstein and Kelly (p. 149), and Hagestad and Smyer (p. 183) also note that divorce date and separation date are seldom accurate measures of the actual end of a marital relationship. In fact, in William J. Goode's classic study *After Divorce* (Glencoe, Ill.: Free Press, 1956), 22% of the couples hadn't separated when the divorce suit was filed. Seven percent hadn't separated when the decree was granted. See also William H. Gram, "Breaking Up: A Study of Fifty-Nine Case Histories of Marital Collapse" (Ph.D. dissertation, Northwestern University, 1982); Wallerstein and Kelly, *Surviving the Breakup*; and Gunhild O. Hagestad and Michael A. Smyer, "Dissolving Long-Term Relationships: Patterns of Divorcing in Middle Age" in Steve Duck, ed., *Personal Relationships. 4: Dissolving Personal Relationships* (London: Academic Press, 1982), pp. 155–188.

5. Marvin B. Scott and Stanford M. Lyman. "Accounts," *American Sociological Review* 33 (1968): 46–62.

6. John H. Harvey et al., "An Attributional Approach to Relationship Breakdown and Dissolution," in Duck, p. 125.

7. Hart, pp. 196–197; Willard Waller, *The Old Love and the New* (New York: Liveright, 1930), pp. 172–185.

8. See also Abigail Trafford, *Crazy Times: Predictable Stages of Divorce* (New York: Harper & Row, 1982), p. 141.

9. Wallerstein and Kelly, pp. 38–39.

10. As Berger so elegantly puts it, "Old markers may be retrieved from the debris of

discarded chronologies." Peter L. Berger, *Invitation to Sociology: A Humanistic Perspective* (New York: Anchor, 1963), p. 59; Waller, p. 140.

11. Barney G. Glaser and Anselm L. Strauss, *Status Passage* (London: Routledge and Kegan Paul, 1971), pp. 90–97.

12. Scott and Lyman, pp. 46–62; George McCall, "Becoming Unrelated: The Management of Bond Dissolution," in Duck, p. 225; Wallerstein and Kelly, p. 158.

13. Waller, p. 185; Wallerstein and Kelly, pp. 154–157, 187, 193.

14. McCall describes five types of bonds: attachment, social structural bonds, commitment, benefit-dependability, and investment. George McCall, "The Management of Bond Dissolution," in Duck, pp. 212–217. See also Robert S. Weiss, "The Emotional Impact of Marital Separation," *Journal of Social Issues* 32 (1976): 138; John Bowlby, *Attachment and Loss, I: Attachment* (New York: Basic Books, 1969); John Bowlby, *Attachment and Loss, II: Separation* (New York: Basic Books, 1973); Hagestad and Smyer, pp. 161–166.

15. Jean Goldsmith, "Relationships between Former Spouses: Descriptive Findings," *Journal of Divorce* 4 (1980): 1–20. In a sample of one hundred fifty separated and divorced men and women, Baker found that 23% said that they never saw their former spouses at all. Those who never saw their former spouses tended to be childless. Maureen Baker, *Support Networks and Marriage Dissolution*, Final Report (Toronto: Connaught Foundation Project, University of Toronto, 1980), p. 23.

16. Weiss notes that men seem generally to drop relationships with in-laws, even if they have custody of the children, while women tend to maintain them. Robert S. Weiss, *Marital Separation* (New York: Basic Books, 1975), p. 144.

17. Kristine M. Rosenthal and Harry F. Keshet, *Fathers Without Partners: A Study of Fathers and the Family After Marital Separation* (Totowa, N. J.: Rowman and Littlefield, 1981), pp. xiii, 157. Wallerstein and Kelly report the tendency for couples with children to maintain geographic proximity in order to continue their parenting. They also note that "the visit is an event continually available for the replay of anger, jealousy, love, mutual rejection and longing between divorced adults," p. 125. In addition one-third of both parents in their study were in active competition for the affection and loyalty of the children, p. 125. Not only for these reasons do former partners initiate interaction, but the children sometimes actively work to get their parents together. Hoping to achieve a reconciliation, some children arrange for their parents to bump into each other or create scenes and problems that will bring them together. Wallerstein and Kelly, pp 73–74.

18. Patricia Leigh Brown, "Sharing the Pet After a Breakup," *New York Times*, November 1983.

19. Lenore J. Weitzman, *The Divorce Revolution: The Unexpected Social and Economic Consequences for Women and Children* (New York: Free Press, 1985). See also Weiss, *Marital Separation*, pp. 102–112; Wallerstein and Kelly, p. 30; Carol Smart, *The Ties That Bind: Law, Marriage, and the Reproduction of Patriarchal Relations* (Boston: Routledge and Kegan Paul, 1984). Unruh notes that documents can have a similar effect when one of the partners dies. Those who are dying use their wills to solidify their identity, affecting others' lives even after they are gone by creating or maintaining interdependencies. David R. Unruh, "Death and Personal History: Strategies of Identity Preservation," *Social Problems* 30, No. 5 (February 1983): 343. For a marvelous example, see Book 5: The Dead Hand, in George Eliot, *Middlemarch: A Study of Provincial Life* (Edinburgh and London: William Blackwood and Sons, 1871).

20. Weiss also found that expressions of hostility are attempts to maintain contact. Robert S. Weiss, "The Emotional Impact of Marital Separation," in Peter J. Stein, ed., *Single*

Life: Unmarried Adults in Social Context (New York: St. Martin's, 1981), p. 76; Weiss, *Marital Separation*, p. 114. See also Wallerstein and Kelly, p. 193.

21. Davis, p. 258.

22. Rosenthal and Keshet, p. x.

23. "Dog is Ruled Couple's 'Child' in Custody Case in California," *New York Times*, 8 September 1983.

24. Edmond Rostand, *Cyrano de Bergerac: An Heroic Comedy in Five Acts*, trans. Brian Hooker (New York: Henry Holt and Company, 1924), pp. 44–46.

25. For description of some gender differences in post-separation change, see Wallerstein and Kelly, pp. 157–159. See also Rosenthal and Keshet, pp. 121–123.

26. Davis, pp. 176–177.

27. Weiss notes that "Often the spouse who took the lead in the separation will also attempt to establish a friendly post-marital relationship. This spouse, perhaps, has less to be angry at and stronger feelings of continued obligation," *Marital Separation*, p. 115. According to my interviews, initiators are more likely to try to pick up the ties because they are ahead of the partner in the transition and thus have worked through their negative feelings. Consequently, initiators are first to be able to again see the positive characteristics of the partner.

28. See also Lindsy Van Gelder, "Is Divorce Ever Final? Ten Woman Talk about Their Ex-Husbands," *MS* (February 1979): 61–70; Kathy E. Kram, "Phases of the Mentor Relationship," *Academy of Management Journal* 26, No. 4 (December 1983): 608–625; Rosenthal and Keshet, pp. 89–111, 157.

29. Weiss notes this also, stating "the farther along a couple is in their course toward divorce, the less likely reconciliation seems to be." Weiss, *Marital Separation* p. 121.

30. George J. McCall and J. L. Simmons, *Identities and Interactions* (New York: Free Press, 1966), pp. 235–244; Barney G. Glaser and Anselm L. Strauss, *Status Passage* (London: Routledge and Kegan Paul, 1971), p. 106.

31. Waller, pp. 142, 167–168.

32. See also Wallerstein and Kelly, pp. 261–263.

33. For extensive examples, see William H. Gram, "Breaking Up: A Study of Fifty-Nine Case Histories of Marital Collapse" (Ph.D. dissertation, Northwestern University, 1982), pp. 43–50.

ARTICLE 28
The Divorce Process

PAUL K. RASMUSSEN AND KATHLEEN J. FERRARO

It is often thought that divorce is the culmination of a series of disruptive events or the inability to deal with problems, such as extramarital affairs, excessive drinking, or finances. This study shows that while these problems are often cited by divorced couples, they are not the cause of divorce. Perceived problems, instead, serve as a tool or crisis to break the marital bond. Couples use these crises to form allegiances with relatives and friends to support their actions.

IN THE PAST, divorce has been regarded as a regrettable deviation from the normal pattern of marriage. But today the projected rates of divorce are [50%] for first marriages and [60%] for second marriages. These divorce rates have climbed to a level at which divorce can no longer be classified as deviance or pathology. The prevalence of divorce suggests that it be examined as a natural, routine aspect of social order.

Traditional marriage and family research has been based on the premise that the nuclear family is the cornerstone of American society. Structural functionalism has dominated the field. Standard texts treat the family in its functional matrix in terms of its contributions to and dependence on political, economic, and religious spheres (Burgess, 1953; Blood and Wolfe, 1960). The most functional families are most rewarding to their members and least likely to dissolve. Marital disintegration is examined in connection with numerous social situations producing various levels of functionality. Social class, geographic location, race, religion, and age at marriage have been studied to determine which variables are most closely associated with high divorce rates (Burgess and Wallin, 1953; Cavan, 1963; Renne, 1970; Laner,

Paul K. Rasmussen and Kathleen J. Ferraro, "The Divorce Process." *Alternative Lifestyles* 2:443–460. Copyright 1979 by Human Sciences Press. Reprinted by permission.

1978). Marital adjustment scales have been devised to predict which characteristics have the greatest probability of association with a happy marriage.

Clearly, there is a bias in favor of marriage as a positive social force and against divorce as a social evil. Most scholarly work has treated divorce only in conjunction with marriage as the aberrant case. Research devoted to divorce as an independent phenomenon has been rare until the last 15 years. Waller wrote the first sociological study of divorce in 1930. Nine years later, Schroeder completed his dissertation on the social determinants of divorce in Peoria, Illinois. The major research effort on divorce was conducted by Goode (1956). He interviewed 425 divorced women to discover the causes and consequences of their divorces. Although there are severe limitations to Goode's research, the most notable being that it is outdated, it remains one of the few large-scale investigations of divorce. More recently, several studies focus specifically on postmarriage life and the feelings involved in divorce (Scanzoni, 1972; Fisher, 1974; Weiss, 1975; Levinger, 1976).

The attitude conveyed by previous research on divorce is that getting divorced is the consequence of a series of disruptive events within the marriage. The assumption is that something went wrong in the marriage which then caused a divorce. The focus for research, then, is the causes of divorce and the circumstances which disposed the couple to involvement in the causes. The logical conclusion of this line of thought is that elimination of the causes would result in a successful marriage. Our findings suggest that the causal approach to divorce—and the assumptions it applies—are inappropriate and contrary to fact. The basic error lies in confusing the reasons for divorce with how a divorce occurs.

Rejection of causal theories of divorce does not mean that the conditions cited as causes were not features of the marriage. Extramarital sex, excessive drinking, and/or financial problems were present in nearly all of the marriages we studied. Yet their mere presence does not establish their causal significance. The canons of logic make three requirements of a relationship before establishing causality. The causal variable must occur prior to the effect, the result must be observed to occur when the causal event has occurred, and there can be no third event explaining the occurrence of both cause and effect. This study indicates that the apparent causes of divorce do not meet the criteria of causality.

Divorce is not a simple, unidimensional phenomenon. It is an intricate interactive process occurring between married individuals. As such, it is subject to all the front work, power struggles, and negotiations of any social interaction. Divorce requires personal and social sensemaking techniques to understand and relay to others the changes in circumstance it entails. This article will attempt to describe the divorce process.

METHODS

Both authors have been divorced, and hence have an interest and understanding stemming from personal experience (see Reimer, 1977). The lack of correspondence between the sociological literature and one's own personal feelings and perceptions motivated us to systematically investigate the experiences of others who had been through divorce. Unstructured taped interviews were conducted with a convenient sample of friends and acquaintances. A total of 32 people, in most cases both husband and wife, were interviewed. With five couples, only one spouse was accessible to us. The ages of subjects ranged from 28 to 50, with males being slightly older. All subjects came from middle-class backgrounds and live at that level now.

The cross-gender of the researchers was important in being able to elicit responses unaffected by inhibitions relating to gender (see Warren and Rasmussen, 1977). Rasmussen could obtain information from males which would have been withheld from female researchers. Wives, on the other hand, spoke freely to Ferraro, presenting their side of the story. Interviews were also facilitated by knowledge that the researchers themselves were divorced, thus diminishing fears of disapproval.

FINDINGS

Our interviews indicated that situations typically presented as causes for divorce were present in most cases. Extramarital sex was the most common feature of marriages that ended in divorce. Most couples also reported excessive drinking and financial problems. Yet, it is difficult to accept these situations as the causes for divorce. In some cases these activities were the aftereffects of crises or problems which derived from other sources. In others, the behaviors had occurred prior to dating, through dating, during the marriage, and afterward. As Pete explains:

> *I was really blown away when Mary came down on me for being a drunken slob. I mean, I've always had a weakness for the taste of the grape and I do get loaded a lot, but I've always done that. While we were dating I got so loaded that I passed out with a cigarette in my hand. It burnt a straight line on my chest and I've still got a scar from it. Like most of our dating was about alcohol. We'd sit around drinking, watching TV, and talk. She didn't seem to mind then, but all of a sudden drinking becomes the biggest thing of the day.*

Conversely, many people remain committed to marriages in which the offending behaviors are both present and openly acknowledged. Pat, for example, accepted her husband's extramarital affairs as an unavoidable consequence of his occupation:

> *I'm married to a man in the Navy and every three years he goes on tour for nine months. It just isn't right to expect someone to go that long without some sex. When they come back from their tour they talk and joke a lot about how the sheets turn a darker shade of yellow as the days pass, but I know he and all his buddies go to prostitutes while they're overseas. I don't ask him about it and he doesn't ask me.*

Some divorces occurred in which the respondents were unable to locate the cause in a specific problem. Jim's divorce falls into this category. He came home to an empty house and a note from his wife asking for a divorce. As far as Jim knew, both had remained faithful, neither drank in excess, and they had plenty of money.

The causes of divorce, then, may have existed for years without creating any serious problems, may exist without leading to divorce, or may be totally absent when there is a divorce. The conclusion that divorce is caused by problem behaviors is contradicted by these situations described by respondents. If drinking, adultery and financial problems do not qualify as causes of divorce, what role do they play in the process of becoming divorced?

One important feature about divorce which is often slighted is the tremendous emotional investment married people have in each other. All of the marriages in our sample involved long-term friendships between the spouses. In one case, a total of two-thirds of their lives were involved in the relationship. The emotional bonds that develop over these years are deep and strong. They do not dissolve simply by deciding to get divorced (Ferraro, 1979). Long-standing feelings of love and affection cannot be easily dismissed, as Beth described:

> *I just had to sell the house and all the furniture just to forget about him. The neighbors, the place, all reminded me of him. The worst time I had was when I saw a fixture I'd been after him to fix. You wouldn't believe how the sight of that made me feel. There are times when I get really depressed and I'd go back to him in a minute. Over the years I guess I've built up a lot of feeling for him.*

In order to end this long-term feeling of friendship and trust, the marriage bonds must be cut with the knife of a crisis. Couples who have lived together for any length of time soon learn all the shortcomings and faults of their mate. Documenting them is usually the first stage of creating a crisis. One partner begins counting the amount of liquor consumed, searching for evidence of adultery, or monitoring the checking account. This is what happened to Roger and his wife:

> *I really couldn't believe it. All of a sudden Judy got really uptight about my playing around. She was checking mileage on my car, looking for strange cigarette butts in the ashtrays, sheets on the bed which had been used, you name it, she thought of it. It was like being married to Sherlock Holmes. It wasn't any big secret, my playing around. I even told her if she wanted to know all she needed to do was ask, but she kept on looking for things she could throw up in my face.*

People will sometimes devise elaborate schemes to collect incriminating evidence. Tom explained the extreme efforts he went through to catch his wife with another man:

> At first, I simply would check her underwear to see if I could find traces of "cum" in them. Then I got into attacking her the moment she got home to see if she was wet or horny. Finally, I borrowed a pair of binoculars from my dad and went down to where she worked and checked that out. I just knew she was playing around and I had to catch her at it.

In this instance, the custody of a child was in question and, while Tom had little moral objection to his wife playing around, he needed evidence.

All couples have periods of crisis. But those who choose divorce tend to escalate the crises. By the escalation of crisis, we mean that whatever behavior has come to be defined as a problem becomes a focus for concern and comment. The alleged offender in the relationship may increase or flaunt involvement in the problem activity. Jeff explains how his adulterous behavior became increasingly common:

> I'd done a few numbers on the side. I was always very careful how I did it and who would know. I never appeared in public with any woman and I was always certain they couldn't get back to me. I'd change my name, tell them I was from out of town, or pick up women who were married or living with someone. Before the divorce this all changed. I was picking up ladies anywhere, not guarding my ass. If it moved, I moved. The whole thing came to a head and we finally split. Thank God.

Terry related how she stopped trying to conceal her affairs and intentionally arranged to be caught in the act by her husband:

> I guess you could say that I had several affairs during the time that I was married. The type of work I did required a good deal of traveling and I just assumed that both of us would have outside friends. I always kept my friends separate from the town we lived in, and in most cases they were even from out of state. When my husband started following me in his car, I really got mad. Then one day I asked to go over to dinner at my parents'. I had to talk my husband into going along, but after dinner I had set up a meeting with a friend who I had been seeing. I told him I was going out with some of the girls from work and he followed me. I knew it but just didn't care. He caught me and that was the end of the marriage.

Some spouses choose to focus on the misbehavior of their partner, rather than create a problem with their own actions. The escalation of crisis then becomes a matter of increasing the significance of situations previously accepted as an aspect of the relationship. Dawn explained how she began to nag her husband about his contribution to their income, to the point where violence erupted:

> Tom had never made much money, or even had a decent job. He was just not ambitious, and I knew that when we got married. As I became dissatisfied with our marriage, though, his laziness really started to bother

me, and I got on him about it. He just hated it when I threw it up to him how little money he made and that I was really supporting us. But I kept it up, until one night he got so mad he hit me. Once that happened, I knew I really had good reason to leave him.

In this way, a divorce becomes a mutual "working out." Both parties contribute to the escalation of crises which will justify their decision to split up. The causes of divorce, then, are important only in the sense that they become tools used by those involved in the process of divorce. The causes create situations which are impossible to live with. The situation becomes impossible to live with because the situation is defined as impossible by those who want a divorce. The impact of realizing this impossibility involves a release of emotion, as Janet described:

John had been playing around with other women for some time and I knew it. But one night we had some friends over and John walked a single lady out to her car, for protection and all that. I kinda thought they had something going and went out on the back patio to see. He was out there with her, hugging and kissing her good night. I caught myself thinking what a lovely couple they made, and then realized that it was too much.

These confrontations symbolize the general dissatisfaction with the relationship and become "good reasons" to leave it. In much the same way a couple decides to marry, they decide to divorce. The reasons for either are intangible and nonrational, yet relate to the experience of immediate life situations.

ESTABLISHING FAULT

Crisis isolation may well serve the needs of those who want a divorce and need some way to break the close bonds that exist in the marriage. However, the fabricated crisis also has an important impact on relations with friends and relatives. What were once the grounds for divorce now become the battlegrounds for friends and family. The behavior which was used by both partners to create a crisis becomes evidence to prove that one partner was at fault. The guilty party can then be legitimately ignored. The decision of who becomes ignored depends largely on the relationship which existed prior to the divorce.

The reactions of close single friends or relatives are relatively unproblematic. Their sympathy will lie with the partner they have ties to, regardless of fault or blame. Pete found this to be true in his case:

The fact that I was getting a divorce didn't have much effect on my relations with my family. I had no idea what they would think of it and had not told them until after they had called me, which was a good two months after I had left my wife. They said they had always thought she was not my type and were pleased that we had gotten a divorce. Even some of my closest friends didn't seem to mind too much. Jim, my roommate from college, even called and congratulated me for "joining the club."

Mutual friends of the divorced couple are much more difficult to deal with. These friends feel ties to both partners of the divorce and try to remain friends equally. The problem of continued friendship with both partners of a divorce rests on the felt betrayal should any social interaction occur. Steve explained how his divorce affected his friendships:

I'd been separated for about six months and hadn't been asked out to any of my old friends' houses for dinner yet. At that point, I was pretty much happy with just being left alone and being by myself. I started to feel better about the divorce and myself though and was really pleased to receive an invitation by an old friend for dinner. I thought nothing more about it until later, when my friend expressed some feeling of doubt about his wife's feelings about getting together. He was very embarrassed about it all and suggested that we wait until things had cooled off some. After some discussion we agreed that his wife had been good friends with my wife and she was feeling strange about having me over for dinner.

Steve later won the battle and was invited to dinner. He found out that his wife had been having an affair and had told all their mutual friends.

CONCERNS OF FRIENDS

We have seen how married couples use crises to create situations that produce a divorce. We have also seen how these crises become the weapons used in the battle to win mutual friends. The private lives of friends are also important because they influence the relationship to divorced partners. This interrelationship between the private lives of friends and the social interaction with divorced persons is demonstrated by Steve's discovery:

When I found out what had happened I was really surprised. I had always thought they had the perfect marriage. I learned about their problems quite by chance. My girlfriend and I had gone out to this bar to listen to some friends of hers perform and ran into the husband with another woman. Actually, neither of us saw him with her, but he thought we did and called the next day to make certain that my girlfriend would not call his wife. I assured him that she wouldn't and then he went into all the problems he had had over the years with his marriage. I asked him if that was why his wife had felt so uptight around me and he said yes.

In this case, the wife was conscious of the problems in her own marriage and feared any confrontation with a divorced person.

A related issue with married couples is what might be called the domino theory. Much of the fear married couples have of divorced friends stems from their worry that the divorced friend will try to talk one partner into a divorce. The end of one marriage is believed to trigger a string of divorces. This theory is not totally without warrant. Married couples who socialize with a divorced friend sometimes do get a divorce, too, as was the case with Rick and Beth. Pete explained how his wife influenced their divorce:

> *Rick and Beth were neighbors at the time of my divorce. They were definitely having problems of their own and we knew it. This was probably the reason they became friends of ours. Before our divorce, Mary and Beth would get together and have woman-to-woman talks. Mary was 100% behind Beth's doing it [getting divorced]. After we got divorced, these conversations continued to increase. Rick began to wonder what was going on. I knew. They separated about three months later and Beth moved in with Mary.*

In this case, it is not likely one divorce caused the other. However, there is reason for concern when a married person associates with a divorced one. The divorce may represent acceptance of the behavior the troubled spouse is contemplating.

Another major problem which divorced persons have with married friends stems from subtle flirtations which occurred in the past. A wife or husband often flirts with the wife or husband of another couple and when there is not another mate present to balance the situation, it becomes very awkward. Larry explained how his weekly game of bridge ended with his divorce:

> *When I was married, we all got together at least once a week for bridge. The women would play [against] the men and we kept a running tab on who was winning. We really had a lot of fun and would sometimes even get tight. When that happened we had the most fun, although we paid for it the next day. There was always a lot of kidding around with the guys chasing each other's wife around or the other wife playing "footsie" with the husband. It never got serious and it was all in fun but I could not even consider any attempt to continue with the weekly game after the divorce. All concerned dropped it like it was the plague.*

While the fun that couples have while flirting with each other often makes that friendship enjoyable, it also sets the stage for feelings of jealousy and competition if one of the players in the game is absent.

NEW FRIENDSHIPS

The problems of friendship ties, the split of allegiance between husbands and wives, the interpersonal problems that married friends have, the fear of others being drawn into the same thing, and subtle flirting all contribute to a difficult social setting. Because of all these problems, most divorced people develop new friends (Weiss, 1975).

> *I had some good friends when I was married that you could trust and respect. I would have done anything for them and I know they would for me. It's hard to find friends like that and I figure in my whole life they number less than 10. But what can you do when you become a threat to their lives? You can't mess up someone else's life. So I went underground and am waiting for a better time to surface. Since good friends usually stay together in spite of distance and time, I figure it's a good bet.*

The problems involved with divorce extend into all social relationships. The impact of marital dissolution on long-standing friendships is often devastating. As a result, the divorced person is bereft of the sources of emotional support that had previously provided solace in times of stress. For most of the individuals interviewed, this void was soon filled by new, unmarried or divorced friends. The divorced person gradually moves from a social network revolving around married life to one consisting of singles. The lifestyle and interests of singles are more compatible with the needs of divorced people and help contribute to their reentry into the "marriage market."

COMMUNITY RELATIONS

More casual relationships are also upset by news of a divorce. One's reputation in the community is based on general impressions and sketchy knowledge about the kind of life one leads. When a divorce takes place, the character of both spouses is up for review. Opinions of acquaintances develop on the basis of rumors and speculation about the reasons for and the initiator of the divorce. Whether one maintains an image of respectability through this period of review is important in relation to one's social and economic standing. Pete's social life, for example, went through some lasting changes after his divorce:

> *I've always been the blond, blue-eyed star of the community. I worked hard at it, doing favors for people, going out of my way to be friends with everyone. It's important, too. People can do you in just as easily as they can help you out. You need that support to get anywhere in life. Did that change when people found out I was divorced. People that would talk your ear off pass me off now with a simple "hello." That really bothers me. I'll have to do some fast repair work with my public image or get out.*

Jim found relations at work so difficult that he decided to change jobs:

> *I had worked for this guy for five years. I started at the very bottom and had worked my way up. It was pretty much assumed by all that I was being groomed to take over the whole operation when my boss went into retirement. Besides the training and all of the job, my boss went even further. He always made certain that I had enough money, a nice car to drive, and an apartment close to work. Not many people would go to the extremes that he did. When word of the divorce came out he called me aside and told me that I really ought to grow up and take the responsibility of my marriage seriously. Being the man of the house, I was supposed to make sure that the marriage worked. When the divorce became certain, it was clear that I had fallen from his good graces. I finally quit and moved on to a different job.*

Public opinion is important to most people, and since that opinion is based on second-hand knowledge, control of information about the divorce becomes an important tool for manipulating public sentiment. Strategies develop for creating the impression most advantageous to oneself. One strategy is selective disclosure of facts related to the breakup. By keeping certain particulars of the divorce secret and making other aspects known, one increases the chance of maintaining a favorable image. This was clearly Beth's approach when she went to visit her mother:

> *I'd gone back home to live with my mother. She owns a small bar in town and just about everyone knows her and her kids. Before I left, Rick and I had this big fight and he hit me around and even tried to strangle me. I really had a good set of bruises so I wore a low-cut dress with short sleeves to show them off. The friends in town were very sympathetic and offered to defend me if Rick should come back and try to hurt me again.*

Only half the story was told by Beth, according to her ex-husband:

> *Beth had gone off on a visit to her mother for a week but I became suspicious when I could never find her at home when I called. When she returned from her visit she confessed that she had stayed with an old boyfriend and had been sleeping with him. It took place during her fertile cycle and she thought she was pregnant by him. She told me she wanted to keep the child should she be pregnant. At first I was mad about her affair, then I was totally devastated by her wanting to keep the child. But after long discussions and talking to friends, I decided that we both could deal with it, so I agreed to let things be. Things went well for a couple of weeks until one night after we had made love. I asked her if she still had any feelings for her boyfriend and she told me she still loved him. I'm ashamed to say I lost control and beat her up. She went back to her mother and boyfriend after that.*

The public life of the divorced person must be conducted in a manner which will elicit sympathy rather than recrimination. Being seen out on the town or failing to appear appropriately saddened opens the way to suspicions of lack of concern over the marriage. A divorced person who appears too happy too soon provides documentation for outsiders that he is unperturbed by the divorce.

Receiving more than a fair portion of the property settlement is also out of line with trying to sway public favor. It is hard to portray oneself as the underdog when receiving most of the property shared in marriage. For this reason, people are often anxious to arrive at equitable property settlements, or actually try to give away large sums of money. Bernie told me how he tried to give away his house:

> I'd talked Laura into taking just about everything we had, except an old junk car. We had collected a lot of expensive things over the years. I even tried to get her to take the house which had about 12 thou in equity. She wouldn't go for that so we split the profit. I really don't know why Laura wouldn't take it, that's a lot of money. I knew why I wanted to give it up. It would have been nice to be able to say that Laura ripped me off.

Selectively planting information is another image management technique used by the divorced. Key members of a community are in positions which place them at the center of the information network. By planting information with these key people which discredits one's past mate, it soon becomes common knowledge. Jim used this technique when he disclosed suspicions about his wife's sexual preference:

> There were a group of some 10 people who had often worked together that were all friends. They had known my wife and were very interested about why we were getting divorced. I couldn't come right out and say bad things about her to them because they probably wouldn't believe it or simply think I was acting emotionally. What I did do was tell one of my friends that I suspected my ex-wife had homosexual leanings which explained her lack of interest in sex with me. I knew this would get around to the others he knew and it would be much better coming from him.

By using this method of planting information, Jim was able to pass alleged disreputable information about his wife without being its direct source. Laura, in turn, got back at Pete by not changing her name after the divorce:

> I kept my married name after the divorce which really pissed Pete off. I didn't tell anyone about our divorce either and let them find out on their own. Pete even offered to pay the legal fees to have me change it and he always uses my maiden name when he writes or calls. His biggest complaint is that he runs into people when he is out with other dates and they think he is cheating on me. There are good reasons to keep my old name. I would have to change all my credit cards and my accounts. I am known by all the people at work by my married name. And, I receive mail

under that name. But I must admit I do get a kick out of knowing that it really upsets Pete.

By acting out the role of bereavement and spreading information to discredit their ex-mate, the divorced are able to both maintain a respectable public image and draw sympathy for their plight. However, since both partners are involved in disclosing information beneficial to their own image, friends and acquaintances may receive conflicting stories. The validity of both accounts is then called into question. Jerry's parents, for example, found his version of his divorce to be at variance with what they heard from his ex-wife's parents:

I'd been having an affair with my secretary for about a year and got emotionally involved with her. I'd get drunk at home and sit around with my wife crying about the whole thing. This got to be too much for her and she threw me out. Her father found out about it all and called mine. He told them everything and recommended I start therapy. Boy, did I get my ass chewed about that. My folks are pretty religious and found the whole thing hard to accept. I was able to smooth things out some by telling them I hadn't had sex with my wife for over a year. I needed that part of life and couldn't help myself. But there were two children involved and they were very concerned about their welfare.

Jerry's wife attested to the fact that they had not had sex in over a year. However, the affair had begun prior to that. On the other hand, his wife kept her sex life a secret, and may have been having an affair herself.

CONCLUSION

Divorce is a difficult, complex issue for everyone involved either directly or through association. Husbands and wives who share strong emotional ties require an equally significant crisis to break the bond. While the typically listed causes of divorce played an important role in all the divorces studied, it was in their use as tools to facilitate the divorce rather than as direct causes. The "knife of crisis" used as a means of ending a marriage was often adultery, heavy drinking, or financial ineptitude. Spouses either indulged in or complained of problem behaviors in building a case for divorce.

The impact of divorce on friendships was found to create awkward and sometimes painful problems for the divorced and their friends. Competition between spouses for the allegiance of old friends, fear of the domino effect, and remembrance of past flirtations combine to end friendships that have been the source of pleasure and emotional support.

Similarly, one's reputation within the broader community of casual acquaintances is called into question with widespread knowledge of the divorce. A political struggle for the sympathy of friends and acquaintances develops between ex-spouses. Elaborate strategies are devised to discredit one's ex-spouse and maintain a favorable self-image. Yet, regardless of the couple's skills in image management, both are certain to lose relationships which had been important both emotionally and socially.

Casual explanations of divorce have served the needs of couples in providing some cognitive closure on the reasons their marriage ended. Nevertheless, they are oversimplified and misleading. It is our hope that this research will contribute to the understanding of the *process* of divorce. Perhaps awareness of the process will help those encountering divorce to avoid those attitudes and actions which have made divorce so difficult. If not, Ted's story will be repeated:

You want the story of my divorce? It's a story of how my wife got me to substitute alcohol for sex, how drinking kept me from having sex, how the lack of sex became the reason for me becoming an alcoholic and caused the divorce, and how I used the divorce to become an alcoholic.

REFERENCES

Blood, R. O. and D. M. Wolfe (1960) *Husbands and Wives: The Dynamics of Married Living*. New York: Free Press.
Burgess, E. W. and H. J. Locke (1953) *The Family*. New York: American Book Co.
Burgess, E. W and P. Wallin (1953) *Engagement and Marriage*. Philadelphia, PA: J. B Lippincott.
Cavan, R. S. (1963) *The American Family*. New York: Thomas Y. Crowell.
Ferraro, K. J. (1979) "Hard love: letting go of an abusive husband." *Frontiers* 4(2): 35–45.
Fisher, E. O. (1974) *Divorce: The New Freedom*. New York: Harper & Row.
Goode, W. J. (1956) *Women in Divorce*. New York: Free Press.
Laner, M. R. (1978) "Love's labors lost: a theory of marital dissolution." *J. of Divorce* 1: 213–232.
Levinger, G. (1976) "A social psychological perspective on marital dissolution." *J. of Social Issues* 32: 54–66.
Reimer, J. (1977) "Opportunistic research." *Urban Life* 5: 467–480.
Renne, K. S. (1970) "Correlates of dissatisfaction in marriage." *J. of Marriage and the Family* 32: 54–66.
Scanzoni, J. (1972) *Sexual Bargaining: Power Politics in the American Marriage*. Englewood Cliffs, NJ: Prentice-Hall.
Warren, C. A. B. and P. K. Rasmussen (1977) "Sex and gender in field research." *Urban Life* 6: 349–369.
Weiss, R. V. (1975) *Marital Separation*. New York: Basic Books.

ARTICLE 29
Divorce and Marital Instability over the Life Course

ALAN BOOTH, DAVID R. JOHNSON, LYNN K. WHITE, AND JOHN N. EDWARDS

This study explores a variety of factors that affect divorce proneness over the life course. It finds several substantial differences between recent marriages and those of longer duration. Low income, early and late age at marriage, the lack of community involvement, and ill health all have a strong adverse effect on short marriages and younger individuals. The accumulation of financial assets serves as a crucial barrier to divorce among people who have been married for longer than five years.

THE HIGHEST LEVELS OF DIVORCE are among young people and those in short marriages. Recently, the divorce rate was 33 per 1000 married women at ages 20 to 24, 18/1000 at ages 30 to 34, and 6/1000 at ages 50 to 54. The same pattern is evident by duration of marriage: The divorce rate was 39/1000 women married 3 years, 17/1000 women married 10–14 years, and substantially lower in longer durations (U.S. National Center for Health Statistics, 1978).

A variety of explanations have been offered for these trends. On the one hand, older people and people in longer marriages are thought to be tied together by bonds of finance, children, and community integration that increase the barriers to divorce. In addition, older people are thought to value stability more than their younger counterparts. However, there have been no systematic empirical or theoretical attempts to examine the process of divorce by age.

This study uses a national sample of married persons, interviewed in 1980 and again in 1983, to study systematically differences in divorce and marital instability by age and duration of marriage. These dependent variables identify, respectively, those marriages that ended in divorce or permanent separation between 1980 and 1983 and those that became unstable or shaky in this period but did not end. Marital instability is indicated by thoughts and actions that may lead to divorce, such as thinking about divorce and consulting an attorney. Because instability is conceptually distinct from divorce and because the linkage between instability and divorce may vary by age, we treat them as substantively different marital outcomes.

BACKGROUND LITERATURE

Theoretical Perspective

In studying the relationship of divorce and marital instability by age and duration, we have been guided by expectations drawn from the life course perspective. *Life course* refers to the combination of roles and relationships associated with a cohort's moving through the age scale (Clausen, 1972). Hence, we expect that marriages become more stable as individuals and marriages age, because of developmental changes. Among those changes, we look at some that are expected or normative, such as increases in economic well-being and community integration, decreases in health, and, perhaps, growing religiosity.

In the study reported in this article, we examine changes (divorces and changes in marital stability) that occurred during a three-year period in an age-heterogenous sample. In such data, the effects of age and duration of marriage are confounded with any effects of membership in different birth and marriage cohorts, and there is no way to unconfound the effects. Furthermore, we know on the basis of evidence from outside of the data set that there are both age and duration of marriage effects and birth and marriage cohort effects reflected in the data. For instance, a particular nonlinear pattern of divorce by duration of marriage (concentration of divorces in the earlier years of marriage) has existed in this country for a long time, and such a pattern cannot be accounted for by differences in divorceproneness among the cohorts. Furthermore, persons who have recently married have been so much more divorceprone during the early years of marriage than persons who married three or four decades ago that intercohort differences in lifetime divorce rates is inevitable. Thus, we know that one reason the older people in our sample were less likely to divorce during the three-year period was that they are members of less divorce-prone birth and marriage cohorts.

Our theoretical interest, however, is only in those differences that reflect developmental changes. By selecting intervening variables known to be affected more by age or duration of marriage than by cohort, we are able to isolate a portion of the overall relationship that is of theoretical interest to us. The goal of this study is not greatly hampered by the fact that the remainder of the relationship reflects, in unknown proportions, both of the major kinds of effects.

In examining age/cohort effects on marital stability, we also consider the possibility of interactions by gender. Norms regarding roles and status differ for men and women and, important for this issue, the salient transition points over the life course are different (Neugarten and Hagestad, 1976). Because aging is qualitatively and normatively different for men and women, we anticipate that the interplay between history and aging represented by the life course perspective will be different by gender. Specific hypotheses are developed in more detail below.

Prior Research

Marital Satisfaction
The difference in divorce and marital instability by age and marital duration might suggest that older marriages are happier. However, cross-sectional studies of marital satisfaction over the life cycle have shown distinctly lower satisfaction after the first few years of duration (Rollins and Cannon, 1974). Although cross-sectional data cannot prove change, it appears that marital satisfaction declines while the divorce rate also declines. Thus we do not anticipate that marital satisfaction will explain the negative correlation between age/duration and divorce. Rather, we expect an interaction: a weaker link between satisfaction and stability during later stages of the life course.

The relationship between marital satisfaction and marital instability over the life course may vary by gender. Divorce is less advantageous for women than men (Weitzman, 1985) and women's disadvantage increases with age. For this reason, we expect that as individuals age, the link between marital satisfaction and dissolution will be stronger for men than women.

Age at Marriage
Research shows that individuals who marry early experience higher risks of divorce (Thornton and Freedman, 1983). To a lesser extent, people who marry late may also experience higher risks (Booth and Edwards, 1985). How long these effects last is the subject of some controversy. Glick and Norton (1977) show that the effects of early marriage are limited to the first five years of marriage, although more recent research shows a lasting effect (Heaton et al., 1985; Morgan and Rindfuss, 1985). We expect to find that age at marriage becomes a weak predictor of divorce and instability in longer marriages. No sex differential is expected.

Economic Status
Substantial evidence suggests that those with less income and fewer financial assets are more likely to divorce (Glick and Norton, 1977). Other evidence shows an

increase in divorce with unemployment and economic insecurity (Glenn and Supancic, 1984). Economic problems may aggravate marital problems and increase the desire to divorce; they may also decrease the costs of divorce. This effect may be stronger for women than men. Although women in poor families may feel that they can support themselves as well on their own earnings, few women in affluent families could support themselves at the level that a professional or executive husband could. Thus we anticipate an interaction by gender in the effect of economic status.

Generally, wealth and income increase with age. This wealth accumulation has been stressed as a reason that older people and those in longer marriages are reluctant to divorce (Becker et al., 1977). We test the hypothesis that intervening variables of wealth or income explain the correlation between age/duration and marital stability.

There are also reasons to believe that the effects of income on marital instability increase with age (Aldous, 1977). Economic insecurity and low income are frequent among people just starting their careers, but when economic problems persist into middle age, they clearly violate normative expectations. Thus, we anticipate that low income, economic insecurity, and low assets will be more damaging to older marriages than to younger ones. Similarly, because assets and income at middle age may be seen as the products of a life's work, we expect assets to have a stronger stabilizing effect in older than in younger marriages.

Wife's Labor Force Participation

Several studies have established a positive link between wife's labor force participation and marital instability (see Booth et al., 1984). Although the association is more pronounced when the wife has been employed only a short time, it is also evident when the wife has worked for many years. This apparent effect has been attributed to marital strains caused by the wife's working and to the greater freedom to divorce provided by the wife's independent income.

The effect of wife's labor force participation may vary over the life course in complex ways. Because traditional sex-role values are more common among older people, they might experience greater strains from the wife's working. On the other hand, men and women with young families are more apt to experience role overload and, perhaps, marital instability. Because role overload falls more heavily on the wife, this effect may be stronger for women. For these reasons, we examine the interaction of age and gender in the apparent impact of female labor force on marital stability.

Social Integration

Glenn and Supancic (1984) argued that divorce is associated with low social integration, in part because those with few ties will face fewer barriers to the dissolution of an unsatisfactory marriage. At least one form of social integration, voluntary association membership, has been shown to be associated with age and to peak at ages 40 to 59 (Babchuk and Booth, 1969). We hypothesize that organizational affiliation may help explain the differences in marital instability and divorce by age/duration.

Traditional values

The greater religiosity and traditionalism of older people (Riley and Foner, 1968, pp. 494–496) are plausible intervening variables between age and marital instability. We do not, however, anticipate any interactions; at all ages and marital durations, we expect that traditional and religious individuals will be less likely to consider divorce or get divorced in actuality.

The Problem

In this article, we use panel data on 1741 married men and women under age 55 to explore differences in the correlates of divorce and marital instability by age and marital duration. First, we examine whether intervening variables such as economic situation and social integration help explain the association between age/duration and marital instability. Second, we test whether there are two-way interactions between marital instability/divorce and the proposed determinants of divorce over the life course. We also test for three-way interactions with gender.

STUDY DESIGN

The Sample

This research is based on a national sample interviewed first in 1980 and again in 1983. In 1980, telephone interviews were conducted with 2033 married individuals. Sample households were chosen through a random-digit-dialing procedure and the husband or wife was selected for interview by a second random procedure. Only married individuals under age 55 were included in the sample.

Response rate to the 1980 survey was estimated to be 65%. This compares favorably to an average response rate of 70% reported by Groves and Kahn (1979) for random-digit telephone surveys conducted by the Survey Research Center at the University of Michigan. Refusal by respondents was slightly higher (12% versus 9%) than they reported, as was "other" reasons for nonresponse (13% versus 9%). These rates may not be directly comparable because of the extensive screening used in this study to locate intact marriages of persons under 55 years of age. The 1980 sample did not differ from the national distribution of married people under 55 on age, race, household size, tenure, and region.

In 1983, completed interviews were obtained with 1569 people from the original sample. Reliable information on current marital status was obtained for an additional 179, bringing the percentage for which we had reliable information to 86%. Our panel response rate is similar to other national personal interview panels.[1]

Using the first stage of a procedure developed by Heckman (1979), we tested for the presence of selection bias in panel attrition. A probit model, using presence of reliable information on 1983 marital status as the dependent variable, was estimated using all the independent variables. None of the variables was significantly related to attrition at the .01 level and only 2 were significant at the .05 level: lower family income and higher husband unemployment were associated with greater attrition. Selection bias from panel attrition, therefore, is minimal.

Measures of the Dependent Variable

Divorce is measured by whether respondents divorced or permanently separated between 1980 and 1983. Approximately 6% of the respondents divorced or permanently separated, paralleling the national rate of just over 2% of marriages ending in divorce each year.

Marital instability is a scale of divorceproneness that includes thoughts and actions that chart progress toward divorce. Development of the scale and information on its validity and reliability are reported elsewhere (Booth, Johnson, and Edwards, 1983; Booth et al., 1985). The measure used here is a dichotomy identifying individuals who increased in marital instability between 1980 and 1983. To avoid overinterpretation of minor fluctuations, the distribution of positive difference scores was cut at the median. . . .[2]

Life Course Measures

We rely on two related measures of the life course: respondent's age and marital duration. Although long marriages are still the exclusive province of middle age, there are enough cases of short marriages among older people to treat the two variables as separate in their impact.

Independent Variables

Age at marriage is age at first marriage. . . .

Economic status was measured in three ways: income, assets, and husband's unemployment. Total family income was measured in 1980. Family assets were measured by questions about the value of their home and their other assets. . . .

Husband's unemployment problems were measured by a question asking whether there had been a time in the last three years in which the husband did not have a job and was not bringing money into the family for one month or longer.

Marital satisfaction was measured by an 11-item summated scale with an alpha reliability of .87. The scale includes seven items asking about happiness with specific aspects of marriage (understanding, love, agreement, sexual relationship, taking care of things around the house, companionship, and faithfulness) and four global satisfaction items (overall happiness of marriage, rating of own marriage compared to others, strength of love for spouse, and whether the marriage is getting better or worse). Scores were collapsed into a three-category variable.

Wife's labor force participation was measured by a dichotomous variable indicating whether she worked outside the home for pay or not.

Social integration was measured by the question, "Some people are members of different organizations such as church groups, unions, or job-related groups, fraternal or civic groups, or recreation groups like bowling or card clubs. Do you belong to any groups or clubs?" More than half indicated such affiliation, consistent with affiliation rates found in other studies.

Religiosity was measured by the question, "In general, how much would you say your religious beliefs influence your daily life—very much, quite a bit, some, a little, or none?" Traditional values were tapped by an agree/disagree question, "Marriage is for life even if the couple is unhappy."

FINDINGS

The analysis section is divided into two parts. In the first part, we examine variables that might intervene between age/duration and marital instability/divorce. In the second, we test for interactions testing the hypothesis that determinants of divorce operate differently across stages in the life course.

Before beginning this more complex analysis, we [looked at] the simple associations of life course variables with divorce and marital instability. The results show significant differences in divorce and marital instability by age and duration. The divorce rate varies more by age and marital duration than does marital instability, supporting the contention that lasting marriages are not equivalent to happy marriages.

Because more and more middle-aged individuals may be found in new marriages, it would be desirable to estimate the joint effects of age and duration. The two variables are so highly correlated (r = .73), however, that it is not possible to estimate joint effects with the size of sample we have—some cells are empty and others have too few cases for meaningful analysis. Therefore, age and marital duration are analyzed separately.

Analysis of Intervening Variables

The following were hypothesized as possible intervening variables between age/duration and marital instability/divorce: economic status, organizational affiliation, and religiosity and traditional values. Measures of all of these variables are in fact statistically related to age and duration in the expected direction. To test whether they explain the relationship between life course and marital instability, we regressed the instability and divorce measures on each of the life course measures, and then introduced the hypothesized intervening variables separately to see whether the initial coefficients were reduced. . . . The coefficients are strong and negative. . . . Only one variable, joint assets, appears to explain any of the association between age or duration and divorce: The estimated effect of age and duration on divorce (although not on marital instability) is roughly halved after assets are controlled. This suggests that one of the reasons older people and those in older marriages are less likely to divorce is because the value of their homes and assets is more substantial. Assets do not seem to explain why older people think less about divorce, but they do help explain the lower divorce rates. None of the other factors thought possibly to explain reduced divorce over the life course (other economic measures, religiosity, traditional values, or organizational affiliation) have any effect on the coefficients between life course and the dependent variables. A final equation including all seven intervening variables reveals no greater decline than that produced by the assets variable alone.

We also tested to see whether the older respondents' failure to consider divorce (low marital instability) explained the link between life course and divorce. It does not. Control for marital instability does not reduce the correlation between age or duration and divorce.

Thus, we conclude that one reason older people are less apt to divorce is because they have greater assets. This does not appear to make their marriages any happier (since it does not reduce their likelihood of thinking of divorce), but it does reduce the chance that they will actually divorce. This suggests that the satisfactoriness of joint economic situation and perhaps the complexity of financial ties deter financially damaging divorces.

These results fail to support some of the most frequent hypotheses of why older people are less apt to divorce. Any reductions in divorce and marital instability over the life course cannot be attributed to greater conservatism, more traditionalism, more income, or even failure to consider divorce. This absence of direct intervening variables suggests that the determinants of divorce may differ across the life course. That is, factors that produce divorce and instability in young people and young marriages may have less impact as individuals age. To test this hypothesis, we turn to tests of interaction.

Differences Over the Life Course: Interaction Effects

In the following sections, we evaluate the significance of two- and three-way interactions over the life course. . . .

The Effect of Economic Status

Twelve models were investigated to test the three-way interactions of marital outcome (two measures) × life course (two measures) × gender × economic status (three measures). Only one of these was statistically significant at the .05 level: family income × gender × marital duration × marital instability. We also tested for two-way interactions involving gender or the life course variables. Again, only one was statistically significant: family income × marital duration × divorce.[3]

This analysis suggests that two measures of economic status (assets and husband's unemployment) do not operate differently at different stages of the life course, nor do they seem to operate differently for men and women. Family income, however, interacts with marital duration in its estimated effect on divorce and with duration and gender in its estimated effect on marital instability. . . . Contrary to our expectations, low income seems to increase divorce rates more among short marriages than among long. Among long marriages, those with high incomes are more rather than less apt to divorce.

When we switch dependent variables to marital instability—thinking about divorce. . . . the data illustrate a three-way interaction in which the joint estimated effects of income and duration depend on gender. For men, we find the same general pattern noted above: a negative relationship between income and instability for short marriages and a positive relationship between income and instability for long marriages. For women, the pattern is the opposite: high income is associated with very high instability in short marriages and has little apparent effect in long marriages.

It appears that family assets and husband's employment have similar effects at all ages and marital durations. The estimated effect of family income is also about the same at all ages, but it does differ significantly by marital duration. Contrary to our expectations, when we focus on divorce, we find that the deleterious estimated effects of low income are stronger in short marriages than long. When we focus on marital instability, we find the same pattern, but for males only. The most general conclusion that these data suggest is that income is more important in short marriages than in long. The exception to this finding is important to note, however, and it is that low income seems more likely to lead young husbands than young wives to consider divorce.

Age at Marriage
Because age at marriage may mean different things for people in second marriages than in first, the analysis of effect of age at marriage was limited to respondents in first marriages. Tests of interaction for age at marriage, marital duration, and marital outcome revealed one statistically significant interaction: The estimated effect of age at marriage on marital instability differs significantly by years married. There was no three-way interaction with gender. . . .

As expected, the negative estimated effects of early marriage are limited to the first 5 years of marriage. In short marriages, 40% of the early married are considering divorce compared to only 22% of those who married at conventional ages. At all subsequent durations, there is no apparent negative effect of early marriage. An apparent negative effect of late marriage, however, shows up strongly in both short- and medium-duration marriages. These data indicate that a late age of marriage is associated with substantially higher marital instability through the first 15 years of marriage. Thus, it would appear that the negative effect of late marriage is as strong as that of early marriage and is, moreover, longer lasting.

Female Labor Force Participation
We anticipated a positive association of female labor force participation with instability and divorce that might differ by age and gender. We find that any apparent

damaging effect of wife's labor force participation is virtually absent at all ages in this sample. Instead, we find a surprising and significant interaction effect: The *absence* of wife's labor force participation is strongly related to marital instability among young people, but is virtually unrelated to it among older people. . . . There was no three-way interaction, so this pattern is similar for male and female respondents. We considered the possibility that the estimated effect for unemployed young wives might be due to a presence of preschoolers, but a test of the three-way interaction between participation, age, marital instability, and children was not significant. Thus, it would appear that the positive relationship between marital instability and a nonworking wife for young people exists whether or not children are present.

Marital Satisfaction

It was proposed that marital satisfaction was a less important determinant of divorce as people and marriages age. This hypothesis was tested using divorce as the only dependent variable and using both marital satisfaction and marital instability as independent variables. The tests for interaction were insignificant. The relationships between satisfaction and instability and divorce did not differ by age or marital duration nor did they differ for men and women.

Health

There was a significant interaction between respondent's health, both life course variables, and the probability of divorce. . . . Poor health seems to increase the likelihood of divorce among young people (16–34) and those married less than 15 years, but may actually decrease divorce among older people and older marriages. The same pattern is found for marital instability. These results suggest that, as hypothesized, ill health has a more deleterious effect when it is least normative and expected, that is, among young people and young marriages.

Traditional Values

None of eight tests of traditional values ("How important is religion in your life?" and "Marriage is for life even if you are unhappy") was significant at the .05 level. Three-way interactions with gender were also insignificant. Taken together with the null results of the intervening variable analysis, these results suggest that the greater religiosity and traditionalism of older people do not help explain why they are less likely to consider divorce or get divorced.

Social Integration

Tests for social integration showed one significant two-way and one significant three-way interaction. Social integration, as measured by organizational affiliation, seems to have reduced divorce only among those married for a short time. . . . Among individuals over 45, voluntary association membership apparently suppresses divorce for women but not men. . . . The data modestly support Glenn and Supancic's (1984) suggestion that social integration reduces divorce, but they suggest that the relationship may be conditional. More complete measures of social integration would be necessary to test this hypothesis fully.

Summary

. . . . Relatively few interactions were found, demonstrating that most predictors of divorce and instability work similarly among old and young, long and short marriages, and men and women. Nevertheless, there are some meaningful findings that help make sense of the link between life course and marital instability. To summarize as follows:

(1) Low family income seems more apt to lead to divorce in short marriages than long.
(2) Low family income seems more apt to cause thoughts of divorce in short marriages than long—but this apparent effect is restricted to husbands. New wives appear to be stimulated to consider divorce by high family income.
(3) An early age at marriage apparently ceases to destabilize marriages after the first 5 years; a late marriage age seems to have a destabilizing influence throughout the first 15 years of marriage.
(4) Wife's *absence* from the labor force seems to have a destabilizing effect on marriages when the respondent is under age 25. At other ages and durations, there is no difference in marital instability by wife's labor force activity.
(5) Ill health apparently increases the likelihood of divorce only among younger people (16–34) and those in short marriages. At the other end of the life course, the effects of ill health may even be positive.
(6) Social integration, as measured by our item on organizational affiliation, seems to provide protection from divorce only for those married fewer than 5 years.

CONCLUSIONS

In this analysis, we have explored the reasons older people and those in longer marriages are less apt to consider divorce or to divorce in actuality. First, we tested whether older people and those in older marriages are less prone to marital instability *because* they are more conservative, better off, better integrated, or less likely to consider divorce. The answer is, most generally, "no," but there is an important exception. The value of family assets—not income or unemployment, but the dollar value of assets—appears to explain roughly half of the association between age and duration and the likelihood of actually divorcing. We conclude that an important reason for the link between life course and divorce is material interest. Assets, especially homes, are not easily divisible and divorce may mean loss of the assets entirely for one or both partners. As marriages accumulate assets, a process generally linked to age and duration, the barriers to divorce appear to mount. It is important to note that assets apparently do not keep individuals from considering divorce, rather they seem to erect a barrier to actually getting divorced.

Second, we considered whether some of the predictors of divorce might operate differently across various stages of the life course. In general, the results summarized above suggest that many predictors of divorce—low income, early or late age at marriage, absence of social integration, ill health—operate more strongly among short marriages and younger individuals. These factors do not predict marital failure as well among individuals farther along in the life course.

In evaluating the results of our analysis, it is vital to remember that we are dealing with a truncated panel covering a three-year time span. The differences that we observe could be caused by timing differences rather than differences in the likelihood that older individuals or older marriages will ever divorce or consider divorce. In addition, we have not ruled out selection effects. The differences between older and younger marriages could reflect the selection of less stable marriages out of the married pool through divorce, thus producing the appearance of developmental or cohort effects. An examination of the selection hypothesis with the same data set used here, however, found that the pattern of reductions in instability with age and duration persisted when selection effects were controlled (Johnson, n.d.).

Despite these important caveats, the results reported here raise important issues. First, of course, they suggest a closer look at asset accumulation as a factor that keeps marriages—at all ages and durations—together. Second, they suggest that older individuals and longer marriages are less vulnerable than younger marriages. The results suggest qualitative differences in the older cohort of marriages—differences that may or may not be experienced by the current cohorts of young marriages as they age. We are inclined to believe that conditions and norms have changed sufficiently that today's young marriage cohorts cannot count on age giving them the immunity to breakup that characterizes their seniors.

NOTES

1. The Panel Study of Income Dynamics (Morgan et al., 1972), a national panel sample originally interviewed in 1968 and reinterviewed in 1971, reported an 84% reinterview rate. A more complete description of our panel and a comparison with others is found in Booth and Johnson (1985).

2. We only measure increases because the instability score in 1980 has a floor (49% reported no instability at all in 1980), but no effective ceiling as no respondent had the theoretical maximum score on the scale. Because downward change was not limited for any respondents, coding in terms of score increases is less affected by the distributional properties of the scale. Because all 1980 marriages were intact, those divorcing by 1983, by definition, increased their instability over 1980 levels. Since our concern is with how marriages move toward termination, these marriages becoming more stable between waves are not our concern here, but have been studied in more detail elsewhere (Booth et al., 1985).

3. Strictly speaking, of course, there should be no interactions between gender and

divorce because divorce, by definition, occurs equally to men and women. Nevertheless, because reliability problems could have resulted in such a relationship, we tested for it. Happily, no such interactions occurred.

REFERENCES

Aldous, Joan. 1977. "Family Interaction Patterns." *Annual Review of Sociology* 3:105–135.
Babchuk, Nicholas and Alan Booth. 1969. "Voluntary Association Membership: A Longitudinal Analysis." *American Sociological Review* 34:31–45.
Becker, Gary, Elizabeth Landes, and Robert Michael. 1977. "An Economic Analysis of Marital Instability." *Journal of Political Economy* 85:1141–1187.
Booth, Alan and John Edwards. 1985. "Age at Marriage and Marital Instability." *Journal of Marriage and the Family* 47:67–75.
Booth, Alan and David R. Johnson. 1985. "Tracking Respondents in a Telephone Interview Panel Selected by Random Digit Dialing." *Sociological Methods and Research* 14:53–64.
Booth, Alan, David R. Johnson, and John N. Edwards. 1983. "Measuring Marital Instability." *Journal of Marriage and the Family* 45:387–394.
Booth, Alan, David R. Johnson, Lynn K. White, and John N. Edwards. 1984. "Women, Outside Employment, and Marital Instability." *American Journal of Sociology* 90:567–583.
Booth, Alan, David R. Johnson, Lynn K. White, and John N. Edwards. 1985. "Predicting Divorce and Permanent Separation." *Journal of Family Issues* 6:331–346.
Clausen, John A. 1972. "The Life Course of Individuals." Pp. 457–514 in *Aging and Society*, Vol. 3: *Sociology of Age Stratification*, edited by Matilda W. Riley et al. New York: Russell Sage.
Glenn, Norval D. and Michael Supancic. 1984. "Social and Demographic Correlates of Divorce and Separation in the United States: An Update and Reconsideration." *Journal of Marriage and the Family* 46:563–576.
Glick, Paul and Arthur J. Norton. 1977. "Marrying, Divorcing, and Living Together in the U.S. Today." *Population Bulletin* 32:1–42.
Groves, Robert and Robert Kahn. 1979. *Surveys by Telephone: A National Comparison with Personal Interviews*. New York: Academic Press.
Heaton, Tim B., Stan L. Albrecht, and Thomas K. Martin. 1985. "The Timing of Divorce." *Journal of Marriage and the Family* 47:631–663.
Heckman, James J. 1979. "Sample Selection Bias as a Specification Error." *Econometrica* 47:153–161.
Johnson, David R. n.d. "Marital Instability over the Life Course: Separating the Effects of Cohort, Marital Duration, Age, and Selection." (unpublished)
Morgan, James et al. 1972. *A Panel Study of Income Dynamics: Study Design, Procedures, and Available Data for 1968–71 Interviewing Years*. Ann Arbor, MI: Survey Research Institute.
Morgan, S. Philip and Ronald R. Rindfuss. 1985. "Marital Disruption: Structural and Temporal Dimensions." *American Journal of Sociology* 90:1055–1077.
Neugarten, Bernice L. and Gunhild O. Hagestad. 1976. "Age and the Life Course." In *Handbook of Aging and the Social Sciences*, edited by Robert H. Binstock and Ethel Shanas. New York: Van Nostrand Reinhold.

Riley, Matilda and Anne Foner. 1968. *Aging and Society*, Vol. 1: *An Inventory of Research Findings*. New York: Russell Sage.

Rollins, Boyd C. and Kenneth L. Cannon. 1974. "Marital Satisfaction over the Family Life Cycle: A Reevaluation." *Journal of Marriage and the Family* 36:271–283.

Thornton, Arland and Deborah Freedman. 1983. "The Changing American Family." *Population Bulletin* 38:1–42.

U.S. National Center for Health Statistics. 1978. "Divorces and Divorce Rates, U.S." Series 21, No. 29, *Vital and Health Statistics*.

Weitzman, Lenore J. 1985. *The Divorce Revolution: The Unexpected Social and Economic Consequences for Women and Children in America*. New York: Free Press.

ARTICLE 30
The Impact of Divorce on Children

DAVID H. DEMO AND ALAN C. ACOCK

As the divorce rate has accelerated, more children are spending at least some of their lives in single-parent families. It has generally been thought that departures from the nuclear family adversely affect children's development and well-being. This article reviews the voluminous research dealing with how family structure relates to children's personal adjustment, self-concept, cognitive functioning, interpersonal relationships, and antisocial behavior. It concludes that divorce may not necessarily have the disastrous effect many have assumed.

HIGH DIVORCE RATES in the United States over the past 20 years have resulted in numerous changes in American family life, with perhaps the most important consequences bearing on children whose families were disrupted. In 1970, 12% of American families with children under age 18 were headed by single parents. By 1984, one-fourth of American families and nearly 60% of black families were headed by single parents. Millions of other children live in two-parent but reconstituted families, separated from at least one biological parent. In fact, Furstenberg, Nord, Peterson, and Zill's recent analysis (1983) indicates that less than two-thirds of American children live with both biological parents.

A number of studies use recent social and demographic trends to predict children's future living arrangements, and while these predictions vary, the consensus is that most youth will spend some time prior to age 18 in a single-parent

David H. Demo and Alan C. Acock, "The Impact of Divorce on Children." *Journal of Marriage and the Family,* 50:619–648. Copyrighted © 1988 by the National Council on Family Relations, 3989 Central Ave. N.E., Suite #550, Minneapolis, MN 55421. Excerpted and reprinted by permission.

household (Bumpass, 1984, 1985; Furstenberg et al., 1983; Hofferth, 1985, 1986; Norton and Glick 1986). Hofferth (1985) suggests that the percentage of black youth who will live with one parent for some period of time prior to age 18 may be as high as 94%, while for white children the corresponding figure is 70%. Norton and Glick's (1986) analysis yields a lower estimate but still projects that 60% of American children will live in a single-parent family before reaching age 18.

These trends in family composition have major implications for the life course of children and their well-being. The purpose of this article is to review and assess recent empirical evidence on the impact of divorce on children, concentrating on studies of nonclinical populations published in the last decade. We also direct attention to a number of important theoretical and methodological considerations in the study of family structure and youthful well-being. We begin by briefly describing some of the theoretical propositions and assumptions that guide research in this area.

THEORETICAL UNDERPINNINGS

Consistent with the Freudian assumption that a two-parent group constitutes the minimal unit for appropriate sex-typed identification (Freud, 1925/1961), anthropologists, sociologists, and social psychologists have long maintained the necessity of such a group for normal child development. Representative of structural-functional theorizing, Parsons and Bales (1955: 16–17) argued that one of the basic functions of the family is to serve as a stable, organically integrated "factory" in which human personalities are formed.

Similarly, social learning theory emphasizes the importance of role models, focusing on parents as the initial and primary reinforcers of child behavior (Bandura and Walters, 1963). Much of the research adopting this perspective centers on parent-child similarities, analyzing the transmission of response patterns and the inhibitory or disinhibitory effect of parental models. The presence of the same-sex parent is assumed to be crucial in order for the child to learn appropriate sex-typed behavior. This assumption is shared by developmental and symbolic interactionist theories, various cognitive approaches to socialization, and confluence theory, as well as anthropological theories (Edwards, 1987).

It logically follows that departures from the nuclear family norm are problematic for the child's development, especially for adolescents, inasmuch as this represents a crucial stage in the developmental process. Accordingly, a large body of research literature deals with father absence, the effects of institutionalization, and a host of "deficiencies" in maturation, such as those having to do with cognitive development, achievement, moral learning, and conformity. This focus has pointed to the crucial importance of both parents' presence but also has suggested that certain causes for parental absence may accentuate any negative effects. Lynn, for example, asserts (1974: 279):

> The research on the relationship between father absence and the general level of the child's adjustment reveals that the loss of a father for any reason is associated with

poor adjustment, but that absence because of separation, divorce, or desertion may have especially adverse effects.

Some researchers suggest even more dire outcomes whenever parental separation, divorce, or desertion occur. Among these are vulnerability to acute psychiatric disturbances, the child's aversion to marriage, and proneness to divorce once they do marry (Anthony, 1974). In sum, two general propositions are suggested:

1. Children reared in households where the two biological parents are not present will exhibit lower levels of well-being than their counterparts in intact nuclear families.
2. The adverse effects on youthful well-being will be especially acute when the cause of parental absence is marital separation, divorce, or desertion.

Divorce and Family Structure

In examining research that addresses these two propositions, it is important to distinguish between studies investigating the effects of family structure and those investigating the effects of divorce. Most studies compare intact units and single-parent families, guided by the assumption that the latter family structure is precipitated by divorce. Of course, this is not always the case. Single-parent families consist of those with parents who have never married, those formed by the permanent separation of parents, and those precipitated by the death of a parent. Simple comparisons between one- and two-parent families are also suspect in that *two-parent families are not monolithic*. First-time or nondivorced units differ from divorced, remarried units in which stepparents are involved. In addition, little recognition has been given to the fact that families of different types may exhibit varying levels of instability or conflict, a potentially confounding variable in establishing the effects of family structure. In short, most investigations of the linkage between family structure and youthful well-being have failed to recognize the complexity of present-day families.

While family composition is a critical consideration in assessing the impact of divorce on children, we must also examine the unique events, disruptions, and transitions characterizing the divorce process that are not experienced by children and other members of nondivorced families. In particular, there are significant *changes* in family composition, parent-child interaction, discipline, and socioeconomic circumstances, as well as the emotional reactions that parents and children have to divorce. These events are accompanied by changes in extrafamilial relations and social networks, often as a result of stigma attached to divorced parents and their children. Although stepfamilies are beyond the scope of this review, researchers must also distinguish the consequences of divorce from those of remarriage and subsequent changes in family composition (see Ganong and Coleman, 1984, for a review of the emerging literature on reconstituted families and their impact on children).

Bearing in mind these conceptual distinctions, we now move to a systematic review of recent evidence on the impact of divorce on children and adolescents.

EXISTING RESEARCH

A substantial amount of research has examined the effects of family structure on children's social and psychological well-being. Many studies document negative consequences for children whose parents divorce and for those living in single-parent families. But most studies have been concerned with limited dimensions of a quite complex problem. Specifically, the research to date has typically (*a*) examined the effects of divorce or father absence on children, ignoring the effects on adolescents; (*b*) examined only selected dimensions of children's well-being; (*c*) compared intact units and single-parent families but not recognized important variations (e.g., levels of marital instability and conflict) within these structures; and (*d*) relied on cross-sectional designs to assess developmental processes.

Social and psychological well-being includes aspects of personal adjustment, self-concept, interpersonal relationships, antisocial behavior, and cognitive functioning. It should be noted that some of these variables (e.g., personal adjustment) have been the subject of voluminous research, while others (e.g., interpersonal relations) have received relatively little attention. . . .

Personal Adjustment

Personal adjustment is operationalized in various ways by different investigators but includes such variables as self-control, leadership, responsibility, independence, achievement orientation, aggressiveness, and gender-role orientation. . . . The overall pattern of empirical findings suggests temporary deleterious effects of parental divorce on children's adjustment, with these effects most common among young children (DeSimone-Luis, O'Mahoney, and Hunt, 1979; Hetherington, Cox, and Cox, 1979; Kurdek, Blisk, and Siesky, 1981; Wallerstein and Kelly, 1975, 1980a). Kurdek and Siesky (1980b, c) suggest that older children adjust more readily because they are more likely to discuss the situation with friends (many of whom have had similar experiences), to understand that they are not personally responsible, to recognize the finality of the situation, to appreciate both parents for their positive qualities, and to recognize beneficial consequences such as the end of parental fighting and improved relations with parents.

On the basis of her review of research conducted between 1970 and 1980, Cashion (1984: 483) concludes: "The evidence is overwhelming that after the initial trauma of divorce, the children are as emotionally well-adjusted in these [female-headed] families as in two-parent families." Investigations of long-term effects (Acock and Kiecolt, 1988; Kulka and Weingarten, 1979) suggest that, when socioeconomic status is controlled, adolescents who have experienced a parental divorce or separation have only slightly lower levels of adult adjustment.

In two other studies Kinard and Reinherz (1984, 1986) observed elementary school children in three different family situations (never-disrupted; disrupted prior to starting school; and recently disrupted) and found that children in recently disrupted families suffered pronounced and multidimensional effects: problems in attentiveness at school, lowered academic achievement, withdrawal, dependency and hostility. While their findings are not definitive, Kinard and Reinherz speculate that either "the effects of parental divorce on children diminish over time; or that the impact of marital disruptions is less severe for preschool-age children than for school-age children" (1986: 291). Children's age at the time of disruption may also mediate the impact of these events on other dimensions of their well-being (e.g., self-esteem or gender-role orientation) and thus will be discussed in greater detail below (also, see Rohrlich, Ranier, Berg-Cross, and Berg-Cross, 1977, for a clinical perspective on the impact of divorce on children of different ages). But two variables that critically affect children's adjustment to divorce are marital discord and children's gender.

Marital Discord
A significant pattern in the empirical literature is that personal adjustment, like other dimensions of well-being, is not related to family structure but is adversely affected by parental discord (Ellison, 1983; Rosen 1979). Kurdek and Siesky's (1980b) extensive data on children who had experienced their parents' divorce indicated that, although learning of the divorce and adjusting to the loss of the non-custodial parent were painful, children indicated that these adjustments were preferable to living in conflict. Many studies report that children's adjustment to divorce is facilitated under conditions of low parental conflict—both prior to *and* subsequent to the divorce (Guidubaldi, Cleminshaw, Perry, Nastasi, and Lightel, 1986; Jacobson, 1978; Lowenstein and Koopman, 1978; Porter and O'Leary, 1980; Raschke and Raschke, 1979; Rosen, 1979).

Children's Gender
Children's gender may be especially important in mediating the effects of family disruption, as most of the evidence suggests that adjustment problems are more severe and last for longer periods of time among boys (Hess and Camara, 1979; Hetherington, 1979; Hetherington, Cox, and Cox, 1978, 1979, 1982; Wallerstein, 1984; Wallerstein and Kelly, 1980b). Guidubaldi and Perry (1985) found, controlling for social class, that boys in divorced families manifested significantly more maladaptive symptoms and behavior problems than boys in intact families. Girls differed only on the dimension of locus of control; girls in divorced households scored significantly higher than their counterparts in intact households.

One explanation for boys' greater difficulties in adjusting to parental divorce is that typical postdivorce living arrangements are quite different for them than for girls. While custodial mothers provide girls with same-sex role models, most boys have to adjust to living without same-sex parents. In examining boys and girls living in intact families and in different custodial arrangements, Santrock and Warshak

(1979) found that few effects could be attributed to family structure per se, but that children living with opposite-sex parents (mother-custody boys and father-custody girls) were not as well adjusted on measures of competent social behavior. While father custody is rare, this study illustrates the importance of examining variations in postdivorce family structures (and specifically the combination of parent's gender and child's gender) for estimating the effects of divorce on children.

Along related lines, a number of researchers have examined gender-role orientation and, specifically, the relation of father absence to boys' personality development. Most of the evidence indicates that boys without adult male role models demonstrate more feminine behavior (Biller, 1976; Herzog and Sudia, 1973; Lamb, 1977a), except in lower-class families (Biller, 1981b). A variety of studies have shown that fathers influence children's gender role development to be more traditional because, compared to mothers, they more routinely differentiate between masculine and feminine behaviors and encourage greater conformity to conventional gender roles (Biller, 1981a; Biller and Davids, 1973; Bronfenbrenner, 1961; Heilbrun, 1965; Lamb, 1977b; Noller, 1978). Lamb (1977a) argues that because gender identity is usually developed by age 3 and because family influences are central to this process, the effects of father absence on gender-appropriate behavior may be most pronounced among boys who are very young (ages 5 and under) at the time of family disruption. Beyond early childhood, gender roles are largely established and children experience increasingly diverse extrafamilial social contexts and relationships that bear on their development. But it should be reiterated that these effects have been attributed to father absence and thus would be expected to occur among boys in all female-headed families, not simply those that have experienced divorce.

The claim has also been made that boys' adjustment problems are often compounded by custodial mothers' denigrating the masculinity of absent fathers, an occurrence that is particularly likely in black matriarchal families (Biller and Davids, 1973). The assumption here is that boys are trying to be masculine without the benefit of the same-sex role model and that the absent role model is portrayed as undesirable. However, most of the research on boys' adjustment fails to consider the quality or quantity of father-child contact or the availability of alternative male role models (e.g., foster father, grandfather, big brother, other male relatives, coach, friend, etc.), which makes it difficult to assess the impact of changing family structure on boys' behavior. There are also limitations imposed by conceptualizing and measuring masculinity-femininity as a bipolar construct (Bem, 1974; Constantinople, 1973; Worell, 1978), and there is evidence that boys and girls in father-absent families are better described as androgynous (Kurdek and Siesky, 1980a).

Positive Outcomes of Divorce

While much of the literature on divorce and children seems ideologically driven and biased toward emphasizing negative effects on children (Edwards, 1987; Raschke and Raschke, 1979), the tendency of children in single-parent families to display more androgynous behavior may be interpreted as a beneficial effect. Because of father absence, children in female-headed families are not pressured as strongly as their counterparts in two-parent families to conform to traditional gender roles. These children frequently assume a variety of domestic responsibilities to compensate for the absent parent (Weiss, 1979), thereby broadening their skills and competencies and their definitions of gender-appropriate behavior. Divorced parents also must broaden their behavioral patterns to meet increasing parenting responsibilities, thereby providing more androgynous role models. Kurdek and Siesky (1980a: 250) give the illustration that custodial mothers often "find themselves needing to acquire and demonstrate a greater degree of dominance, assertiveness, and independence while custodial fathers may find themselves in situations eliciting high degrees of warmth, nurturance, and tenderness."

Aside from becoming more androgynous, adolescents living in single-parent families are characterized by greater maturity, feelings of efficacy, and an internal locus of control (Guidubaldi and Perry, 1985; Kalter, Alpern, Spence, and Plunkett, 1984; Wallerstein and Kelly, 1974; Weiss, 1979). For adolescent girls this maturity stems partly from the status and responsibilities they acquire in peer and confidant relationships with custodial mothers.[1]

Finally, the relationship between family structure and personal adjustment (and other dimensions of well-being) must be viewed as reciprocal. The child's psychological state prior to changes in family structure is an important element in the child's ability to adjust to new situations and relationships. There is evidence (Kurdek et al., 1981) that children and adolescents with an internal locus of control and a high level of interpersonal reasoning adjust more easily to their parents' divorce and that children's divorce adjustment is related to their more global personal adjustment.

Self-Concept

. . . . A series of studies by Parish and his collaborators indicates that children in divorced, non-remarried families have lower self-esteem than children in intact families (Parish and Dostal, 1980; Parish and Taylor, 1979; Young and Parish, 1977). Measuring children's self-evaluations in 1979 and again in 1982, Parish and Wigle (1985) demonstrated that children whose family structure was intact throughout the study had the highest self-evaluations, while those whose parents divorced in the intervening years experienced declining self-evaluations, and those whose parents were divorced throughout the 3-year period apparently adjusted to their new situations and reported higher self-evaluations than they had previously. As is the case for most research on children of divorce, however, the studies conducted by Parish and his associates did not investigate pre- or postdivorce levels of family conflict.

Marital Discord
The bulk of evidence is consistent with the findings on personal adjustment; that is, family structure is unrelated to children's self-esteem (Feldman and Feldman, 1975; Kinard and Reinherz, 1984; Parish, 1981; Parish, Dostal, and Parish, 1981), but parental discord is negatively related (Amato, 1986; Berg and Kelly, 1979; Cooper,

Holman, and Braithwaite, 1983; Long, 1986; Raschke and Raschke, 1979; Slater and Haber, 1984). Because this conclusion is based on diverse samples of boys and girls of different ages in different living arrangements, the failure to obtain effects of family structure suggests either that family composition really does not matter for children's self-concept or that family structure alone is an insufficient index of familial relations. Further, these studies suggest that divorce per se does not adversely affect children's self-concept. Cashion's (1984) review of the literature indicates that children living in single-parent families suffer no losses to self-esteem, except in situations where the child's family situation is stigmatized (Rosenberg, 1979). Cautioning that considerably more research is needed before firm conclusions can be drawn, Long (1986: 26) suggests that future work investigate "Hetherington's (1979) idea that a stable home in which parents are divorced is better for a child than is a 'conflict-ridden' home where both parents are present." . . . Two important reviews of research on children in fatherless families produce different conclusions: Herzog and Sudia (1973) conclude that children's school achievement is not affected by father absence, but Shinn (1978) concludes that father absence has a number of detrimental effects on children's intellectual performance. Basing her conclusions on 30 studies that met reasonable methodological criteria, Shinn reports that "financial hardship, high levels of anxiety, and in particular, low levels of parent-child interaction are important causes of poor performance among children in single-parent families" (1978: 316). In the next section we summarize the differential effects of family disruption on academic performance by gender and social class and offer some insights as to the mechanisms by which these effects occur.

Cognitive Functioning

Most of the research relating cognitive functioning to family structure has assessed cognitive performance by using standardized intelligence and academic achievement tests or scholastic grade-point averages. Many of these studies find that family conflict and disruption are associated with inhibited cognitive functioning (Blanchard and Biller, 1971; Feldman and Feldman, 1975; Hess and Camara, 1979; Kinard and Reinherz, 1986; Kurdek, 1981; Radin, 1981).

Children's Gender
Some studies suggest that negative effects of family disruption on academic performance are stronger for boys than for girls (Chapman, 1977; Werner and Smith, 1982), but most of the evidence suggests similar effects by gender (Hess and Camara, 1979; Kinard and Reinherz, 1986; Shinn, 1978). While females traditionally outscore males on standardized tests of verbal skills and males outperform females on mathematical skills, males who have experienced family disruption generally score higher on verbal aptitude (Radin, 1981). Thus, the absence of a father may result in a "feminine" orientation toward education (Fowler and Richards, 1978; Herzog and Sudia, 1973). But an important and unresolved question is whether this pattern results from boys acquiring greater verbal skills in mother-headed families or from

deficiencies in mathematical skills attributable to father absence. The latter explanation is supported by evidence showing that father-absent girls are disadvantaged in mathematics (Radin, 1981).

Children's Race
There is a limited amount of evidence that father absence is more harmful to the intelligence and academic achievement of black children (Sciara, 1975), especially black males (Biller and Davids, 1973), but most studies show academic achievement among black children to be unaffected by family structure (Hunt and Hunt, 1975, 1977; Shinn, 1978; Solomon, Hirsch, Scheinfeld, and Jackson, 1972). Svanum, Bringle, and McLaughlin (1982) found, controlling for social class, that there are no significant effects of father absence on cognitive performance for white or black children. Again, these investigations focus on family composition and demonstrate that the effects of family structure on academic performance do not vary as much by race as by social class, but race differences in the impact of divorce remain largely unexplored. . . .

Family Socioeconomic Status
A review by Hetherington, Camara, and Featherman (1983) underscores the importance of social class as a mediating variable. They note small differences favoring children in two-parent families on standardized tests of intelligence and academic achievement that decrease when socioeconomic circumstances are controlled. Differences remain, however, on measures of school performance (e.g., grade-point average), with children in one-parent families at a disadvantage. In a study of predominantly white working-class children, Kinard and Reinherz (1986) investigated the impact of marital disruption on specific dimensions of school performance. Fourth-graders whose families were recently disrupted (i.e., children whose parents divorced since the children entered school) had lower scores on language aptitude and a composite measure of academic achievement than children in never-disrupted families or families in which disruption had occurred several years earlier. But no group differences were detected in mathematics achievement. When maternal education was controlled, there were no differences in reading achievement. In fact, maternal education had a stronger effect on school performance than did marital disruption. Differences in teacher assessments of productivity disappeared when gender and maternal education were controlled (Kinard and Reinherz, 1984).

These findings direct attention to a major methodological problem indicated in earlier reviews (Herzog and Sudia, 1973; Shinn, 1978), namely, inadequate attention to the role of social class in moderating the effects of family disruption on children's academic performance. When social class is controlled, children in female-headed families fare no worse than children from two-parent families on measures of intelligence (Bachman, 1970; Kopf, 1970), academic achievement (Shinn, 1978; Svanum et al., 1982), and educational attainment (Bachman, O'Malley, and Johnston, 1978). . . .

Family Processes
In recent years important insights have been gained into the specific processes by which marital disruption may affect children's school performance. First, family disruption alters daily routines and work schedules and imposes additional demands on adults and children living in single-parent families (Amato, 1987; Furstenberg and Nord, 1985; Hetherington et al., 1983; Weiss, 1979). Most adolescents must assume extra domestic and child care responsibilities, and financial conditions require some to work part-time. These burdens result in greater absenteeism, tardiness, and truancy among children in single-parent households (Hetherington et al., 1983). Second, children in recently disrupted families are prone to experience emotional and behavioral problems such as aggression, distractibility, dependency, anxiety, and withdrawal (Hess and Camara, 1979; Kinard and Reinherz, 1984), factors that may help to explain problems in school conduct and the propensity for teachers to label and stereotype children from broken families (Hess and Camara, 1979; Hetherington et al., 1979, 1983). Third, emotional problems may interfere with study patterns, while demanding schedules reduce the time available for single parents to help with homework. In support of the latter point, Furstenberg and Nord (1985) examined parent-child interaction patterns in different family types and found few differences in time spent together in social and recreational activities, but found that resident parents in reconstituted and single-parent families were much less likely than parents in intact families to help with homework. In sum, a variety of personal, family, and school processes operate to the detriment of academic performance among children of divorce.

Interpersonal Relationships

Compared to the large bodies of research on personal adjustment, self-concept, and cognitive functioning, relatively few studies have examined interpersonal relations among children and adolescents in different family structures. Generally, investigations have focused on peer relations among children and dating patterns among adolescents.

Peer Relations
Studies of preschool children (Hetherington et al., 1979) and preadolescents (Santrock, 1975; Wyman, Cowen, Hightower, and Pedro-Carroll, 1985) suggest that children in disrupted families are less sociable: they have fewer close friends, spend less time with friends, and participate in fewer shared activities. Stolberg and Anker (1983) observe that children in families disrupted by divorce exhibit psychopathology in interpersonal relations, often behaving in unusual and inappropriate ways. Other studies suggest that the effects are temporary. Kinard and Reinherz (1984) found no differences in peer relations among children in intact and disrupted families, but those in recently disrupted families displayed greater hostility. Kurdek et al. (1981) conducted a two-year follow-up of children whose parents had divorced and showed that relationships with peers improved after the divorce and that personal adjustment

was facilitated by opportunities to discuss experiences with peers, some of whom had similar experiences. However, Guidubaldi and Perry (1985) observed a much different pattern: among boys, those from divorced families had greater contact with friends, and among girls there were no differences by family structure.

Dating Patterns
Hetherington (1972) reported that adolescent girls whose fathers were absent prior to age 5 had difficulties in heterosexual relations, but Hainline and Feig's (1978) analyses of female college students indicated that early and later father-absent women could not be distinguished on measures of romanticism and heterosexual attitudes.

An examination of dating and sexual behavior among female college students found that women with divorced parents began dating slightly later than those in intact families, but women in both groups were socially active (Kalter, Riemer, Brickman, and Chen, 1985). Booth, Brinkerhoff, and White (1984) reported that, compared to college students with intact families, those whose parents were divorced or permanently separated exhibited higher levels of dating activity, and this activity increased further if parental or parent-child conflict persisted during and after the divorce. Gender did not mediate the effects of divorce on courtship, nor did the age at which parental divorce occurred. Regarding adolescent sexual behavior, the findings consistently demonstrate that males and females not living with both biological parents initiate coitus earlier than their counterparts in intact families (Hogan and Kitagawa, 1985; Newcomer and Udry, 1987). But Newcomer and Udry propose that, because parental marital status is also associated with a broad range of deviant behaviors, these effects may stem from general loss of parental control rather than simply loss of control over sexual behavior. Studies of antisocial behavior support this interpretation.

Antisocial Behavior

Many studies over the years have linked juvenile delinquency, deviancy, and antisocial behavior to children living in broken homes (Bandura and Walters, 1959; Glueck and Glueck, 1962; Hoffman, 1971; McCord, McCord and Thurber, 1962; Santrock, 1975; Stolberg and Anker, 1983; Tooley, 1976; Tuckman and Regan, 1966). Unfortunately, these studies either relied on clinical samples or failed to control for social class and other factors related to delinquency. However, a number of studies involving large representative samples and controlling for social class provide similar findings (Dornbusch, Carlsmith, Bushwall, Ritter, Leiderman, Hastorf, and Gross, 1985; Kalter et al., 1985; Peterson and Zill, 1986; Rickel and Langner, 1985). Kalter et al. (1985) studied 522 teenage girls and found that girls in divorced families committed more delinquent acts (e.g., drug use, larceny, skipping school) than their counterparts in intact families. Dornbusch et al. (1985) examined a representative national sample of male and female youth aged 12–17 and found that adolescents in mother-only households were more likely than their counterparts in intact families to engage in deviant acts, partly because of their tendency to make decisions independent of parental input. The presence of an additional adult (a grandparent, an uncle, a lover, a friend) in mother-only households increased control over adolescent behavior and lowered rates of deviant behavior, which suggests that "there are functional equivalents of two-parent families—nontraditional groupings that can do the job of parenting" (1985: 340). Peterson and Zill (1986) examined children of virtually the same ages (12–16) and found a higher incidence of behavior problems among children who had experienced marital disruption.

A tentative conclusion based on the evidence reviewed here is that antisocial behavior is less likely to occur in families where two adults are present, whether as biological parents, stepparents, or some combination of biological parents and other adults. Short-term increases in antisocial behavior may occur during periods of disruption, however, as children adjust to restructured relationships and parents struggle to maintain consistency in disciplining (Rickel and Langner, 1985). It is reasonable to expect that an important variable in predicting antisocial behavior is the level of family conflict, but most research has failed to examine the nature and quality of familial relationships in intact and other family structures. Peterson and Zill (1986) demonstrated that, when social class was controlled, behavior problems were as likely to occur among adolescents living in intact families characterized by persistent conflict as among those living in disrupted families. A related and often overlooked concern in tracing the effects of family structure on children's well-being is the quality of parent-child relationships experienced by children in different living arrangements. Peterson and Zill found that "poor parent-child relationships lead to more negative child behavior, yet maintaining good relationships with parents can go some way in reducing the effects of conflict and disruption" (1986: 306). Hess and Camara's (1979) analyses of a much smaller sample yielded a similar conclusion: aggressive behavior in children was unrelated to family type but was more common in situations characterized by infrequent or low-quality parent-child interaction and parental discord.

Summary of Empirical Evidence

The empirical evidence on children of divorce, although inconsistent in places, is punctuated by a number of consistent findings. Research on personal adjustment suggests that young children, particularly boys, suffer temporary deleterious effects when their parents divorce, while adolescents are not as much affected by family structure as by parental discord. Adolescents living in single-parent families also acquire certain strengths, notably a sense of responsibility, as a consequence of altered family routines. Likewise, the evidence on self-concept indicates that family structure is unrelated but parental discord is negatively related to children's self-esteem. We cannot be certain of the degree to which family structure influences children's academic performance (or other aspects of cognitive functioning) because the effects of race and social class have not been controlled. But the available body of research demonstrates that children in single-parent families are slightly disadvantaged in school performance. The evidence on interpersonal relationships is sparse but suggests that children in disrupted families experience problems in peer relations, while adolescents in such families tend to be more active in dating and sexual relations. Research on antisocial behavior consistently illustrates that adolescents in mother-only households and in conflict-ridden families are more prone to commit delinquent acts.

LIMITATIONS OF PRIOR RESEARCH

In this section we discuss some of the principal limitations of research assessing the impact of divorce on children. In most cases we do not cite individual studies because many of the problems pertain to virtually all of the extant research. However, the reader should consider these problems in evaluating the findings of particular studies.

Nonrepresentative Samples

Sampling is a virtually universal dilemma for researchers. There are excellent national surveys that analyze demographic variables but largely ignore social psychological issues such as personal adjustment or self-concept. Alternatively, there are excellent studies that incorporate these social psychological factors but are based on convenience samples.

Among the most problematic nonrepresentative samples are those that rely on clinical populations. While these studies are crucial to our understanding of children and adolescents who are most severely influenced by divorce, they tell us little or nothing about the typical experience following divorce. Since most children whose parents divorce do not receive professional help, such studies can be very misleading about the consequences of divorce for the majority of youth.

While nonrepresentative samples have shortcomings, national surveys typically involve reanalysis of data collected for other purposes and for which the effects of divorce are not a central concern. Because these surveys are not designed to investigate the consequences of divorce, many theoretically important variables are either excluded or poorly operationalized and important control variables are often absent.

What Family Structures Are Being Compared?

Generally, investigations of family structure rely on classification schemes, such as father absence, in which the types derive from different events. For example, many military families are classified as father-absent, but the absence is temporary, the father's income is available to the family, and no social stigma is attached. Alternatively, a single-parent household may consist of a 25-year-old never-married woman and her five children. Other families are father-absent as the result of death, permanent separation, or divorce. A central problem in identifying the effects of family structure is that all of these families are frequently classified as one monolithic family form called "father-absent." One investigation involved five types of black family structures (male-headed, parent-incarcerated, separated, divorced, and widowed) and found that these arrangements varied in role structure, family cohesiveness, and parent-child relationships (Savage, Adair, and Friedman, 1978). For example, separated parents spent considerably less time with their children than parents in other family structures, and women with incarcerated husbands were most inclined to use corporal punishment on their children. Until family researchers distinguish father-absent families in terms of the cause and length of father absence, the quality of mother-child interaction, and the availability of other male role models, the conclusions drawn must be viewed with skepticism.

Failure to Control for Income or Social Class

Perhaps the most significant limitation of research linking family structure and children's well-being is a failure to examine the moderating or mediating effects of income or social class. With very few exceptions, the studies rely on samples of children in one socioeconomic category, usually the middle class, for whom the economic consequences of divorce are dissimilar to those of children in lower socioeconomic categories. As a result, it is impossible to distinguish the effects of divorce and family structure from those of socioeconomic conditions. In explaining academic achievement, for example, the classic study by Coleman et al. (1966) demonstrated that income is more important than family structure (see also Herzog and Sudia, 1973; Rainwater and Yancey, 1967). Thus, effects that appear to be caused by divorce may actually be the result of inadequate income—the loss of the father being relatively less critical than the loss of his financial contribution.

Economic factors are important considerations in explicating causal processes for several reasons (see Greenberg and Wolf, 1982; Hill and Duncan, 1987; Kinard and Reinherz, 1984; McLanahan, 1985). First, low-income, single-parent mothers are more likely to work and, as a result, may provide inadequate supervision (Colletta, 1979). Children's behavioral problems associated with "mother-absence" (Hill, Augustyniak, and Ponza, 1986) may therefore be attributable to low income and the need for maternal employment rather than being the result of single-parent family structure per se. Second, the effects of marital disruption on children may be indirect, operating through the economic and emotional impact of divorce on custodial mothers (Longfellow, 1979; Shinn, 1978). As mothers adjust to divorce, single-parenthood, and lower economic status, their anxiety and emotional distress may induce anxiety and stress in children, which in turn may hinder children's academic performance (Kinard and Reinherz, 1986). Failure to examine socioeconomic variation in single-parent families thus obscures the specific processes through which marital disruption affects children. Third, children in single-parent households are more likely to assume adult roles at an early age—for example, working full-time and being responsible for younger siblings, responsibilities that require many adolescents to leave school (Kelly and Wallerstein, 1979; Weiss, 1979). The effects (both positive and negative) of these accelerated life course transitions are consequences of economic deprivation.

Other issues related to income and social class need to be considered. First, it is not clear whether the effect is due to inadequate family income or loss of family income. Single-parent families precipitated by divorce may be poor as a result of a sudden loss of income. Dramatic changes in lifestyle, financial instability, and loss of status may affect children indirectly through custodial parents' loss of control and altered childrearing practices. Increased labor force participation or increased transfer payments may help, but the net effect is still a dramatic loss of income (Cherlin, 1981; Hoffman, 1977; Weitzman, 1985).

While many families lose a stable middle-class environment and encounter stigmatization and financial instability, other families experience relatively minor changes. Santrock and Warshak (1979) report that postdivorce income losses were severe for mother-custody families but not for father-custody families. Further, the source of income is an important consideration, in that welfare dollars may stigmatize the poor and child support payments are unreliable (Bould, 1977).

The generally negative effects of divorce on family income must also be distinguished from the effects of divorce on female labor force participation and single mothers' personal income. Using the National Longitudinal Survey to trace the marital and work careers of women over a 10-year period, Porter (1984) found that divorced, never-remarried women earned more than the continuously married or the currently married (also see Corcoran, 1979). The long-term positive effect of divorce on the earning power of women needs to be recognized and may explain why most of the adverse effects of divorce diminish over time. Employed single mothers may provide stronger role models than dependent mothers in intact families, fostering egalitarian sex role attitudes among both women and men whose parents divorced (Kiecolt and Acock, 1988).

Ecological Fallacy

A common error in social research is termed the "ecological fallacy," occurring when relationships examined at the aggregate level are assumed to apply at the individual level. Herzog and Sudia (1973), for example, report several studies that correlate the proportion of single-parent households with the incidence of delinquency and other behavior problems in census tracts. But even substantial correlations tell us *nothing* about whether the delinquents come from two-parent or single-parent families. Rather than providing information on family structure, such correlations may indicate the aggregate effects of poverty, discrimination, inadequate education, and lack of opportunity.

Failure to Examine Contextual Factors

A number of contextual factors that distinguish the living conditions of children in intact and disrupted families may be linked to behavioral differences between the two groups. Glenn and Supancic (1984) note that divorced persons participate less in church activities than married persons. While parents' religious orientations are individual-level factors, involvement in church activities provides a contextual variable. If children living in single-parent households are systematically less likely to be exposed to other children who are active in a church, this may have a substantial impact on their adjustment. Evidence supporting this kind of contextual effect is provided by Coleman, Hoffer, and Kilgore (1982). They found that, although children from single-parent households were much more likely than those from two-parent families to drop out of public schools, there was no difference in Catholic schools—a result that illustrates a contextual effect involving norms and social networks operating in the Catholic community.

Another contextual variable is urban residence. Single-parent households are far more common in urban areas. Urban areas provide a different environment for children than do suburbs, rural areas, or small towns. The quality of the educational system and the exposure to deviant subcultures are two correlates of residential patterns that may affect children who live in a female-headed household. Contextual factors have an important influence on all children, regardless of family structure, adequacy of parenting, or income. Other contextual factors that influence children include the number of fatherless children in their school, neighborhood SES, presence of a gang subculture, presence of peer groups using drugs (Blechman, Berberian, and Thompson, 1977), and the geographic mobility of peers. Research has yet to disentangle such contextual factors from the direct effect of family structure. Contextual factors may prove as important as the immediate family history of the child.

Lack of Longitudinal Designs

Among the hundreds of studies on children of divorce, there are only a pair of widely cited longitudinal studies (Hetherington et al., 1978, 1979; Wallerstein and Kelly, 1980b), and even these studies have serious methodological limitations (Blechman, 1982; Cherlin, 1981). Yet adjustment to changes in family structure is a developmental process. Retrospective data are rarely used, so typical cross-sectional comparisons of children living in disrupted families with children in intact families provide very little, if any, information on the socioeconomic history of these families, level of family conflict, parent-child relations, and so on. If, for example, children from single-parent households were formerly in two-parent households that were poor and conflict-ridden, any problems the children now have may be scars from long ago rather than a direct consequence of the divorce. A partial solution is to collect retrospective information on numerous theoretically relevant dimensions of family life prior to the divorce (and to collect the same retrospective information on intact families). Unfortunately, most of the extant studies rely on cross-sectional information, and family researchers must therefore be cautious in interpreting results.

CONCLUSIONS

There is reason to question the validity of the family composition hypothesis. Theoretically, it has been assumed that the nuclear family is the norm and, by implication, that any departure from it is deviant and therefore deleterious to those involved. Even if this were the case, no theoretical perspective recognizes that these effects may be short-lived or otherwise mitigated by compensatory mechanisms and alternative role models. In the absence of a parent, it is possible that developmental needs are met by other actors.

It is simplistic and inaccurate to think of divorce as having uniform consequences for children. The consequences of divorce vary along different dimensions of well-being, characteristics of children (e.g., predivorce adjustment, age at the time of disruption) and characteristics of families (e.g., socioeconomic history, pre- and postdivorce level of conflict, parent-child relationships, and maternal employment). Most of the evidence reviewed here suggests that some sociodemographic characteristics of children, such as race and gender, are not as important as characteristics of families in mediating the effects of divorce. Many studies report boys to be at a greater disadvantage, but these differences usually disappear when other relevant variables are controlled. At present, there are too few methodologically adequate studies comparing white and black children to conclude that one group is more damaged by family disruption than the other.

Characteristics of families, on the other hand, are critical to youthful well-being. Family conflict contributes to many problems in social development, emotional stability, and cognitive skills (Edwards, 1987; Kurdek, 1981), and these effects continue long after the divorce is finalized. Slater and Haber (1984) report that ongoing high levels of conflict, whether in intact or divorced homes, produce lower self-esteem, increased anxiety, and a loss of self-control. Conflict also reduces the child's attraction to the parents (White, Brinkerhoff, and Booth, 1985). Rosen (1979) concludes that parental separation is more beneficial for children than continued conflict, and Blechman (1982) proposes that parent absence is not the key to adjustment problems but simply a surrogate for more fundamental causes, including family conflict and a hostile family environment. Such conflict and hostility may account for adolescent adjustment problems whether the family in question goes through divorce or remains intact (Hoffman, 1971). The level of conflict is thus an important dimension of family interaction that can precipitate changes in family structure and affect children's well-being.

Maternal employment is another variable mediating the consequences of divorce for children. Divorced women often find the dual responsibilities of provider and parent to be stressful (Brofenbrenner, 1976). But studies indicate that women who work prior to the divorce do not find continued employment problematic (Kinard and Reinherz, 1984); the problem occurs for women who enter the labor force after the divorce and who view the loss of time with their children as another detriment to the children that is caused by the divorce (Kinard and Reinherz, 1984). As a practical matter, the alternative to employment for single-parent mothers is likely to be poverty or, at best, economic dependency. The effects of maternal employment on children's well-being need to be compared to the effects of nonemployment and consequent poverty.

Other bases of social support for single-parent mothers and their children must also be examined. The presence of strong social networks may ease the parents' and, presumably, the child's adjustment after a divorce (Milardo, 1987; Savage et al., 1978). However, women who are poor, have many children, and must work long hours are likely to have limited social networks and few friends. Typically, the single mother and her children are also isolated from her ex-husband's family (Anspach, 1976). By reuniting with her family of origin, the mother may be isolated from her community and new social experiences for herself and her children (McLanahan, Wedemeyer, and Adelberg, 1981). Kinship ties are usually strained, as both biological parents and parents-in-law are more critical of the divorce than friends are (Spanier and Thompson, 1984). Little has been done to relate these considerations about kinship relations and social networks of divorced women to the well-being of children and adolescents. We believe that these social relations are important, but empirical verification is needed.

Methodologically, research in support of the family composition hypothesis has been flawed in a number of respects (Blechman, 1982). As described above, most studies (*a*) rely on simplistic classifications of family structure; (*b*) overlook potentially confounding factors such as income and social class; (*c*) use nonrepresentative samples; (*d*) examine limited dimensions of social and psychological well-being; (*e*) fail to assess possible beneficial effects deriving from different family structures; and (*f*) rely on nonlongitudinal designs to detect developmental processes.

In order to address the deficiencies of previous research, future studies must compare the four most prevalent family structures: (*a*) intact nuclear families with parents in their first marriage; (*b*) reconstituted families where one biological and one stepparent are present; (*c*) single-parent families consisting of a divorced or separated mother and child; and (*d*) mother-child units where the parent has never been married. Important variations *within* these structures must also be examined—for example, mother-custody and father-custody families. Our review suggests that researchers need to explore the effects of factors that may intervene between family structure and youthful well-being—factors mediating the impact of changing family forms. Social class, marital quality, parent-child relations, and contextual factors are important considerations in tracing the effects of family structure on children's social and psychological well-being. Not least, longitudinal designs should be employed, allowing estimation of the duration of any detected adverse effects. To the extent that we lack systematic evidence of this kind, the processes through which divorce and family structure affect children's well-being remain largely unknown.

NOTE

1. This is not to say that such responsibilities and status have uniformly positive effects. Weiss (1979) contends that these arrangements may have benefits for older children

but may lead to excessive self-reliance among younger children. Even for adolescents, however, the nature of confidant relations is important in that discussions of adult issues (e.g., mother's sex life, work stress) may be deleterious. There is also the risk of losing this status when the mother remarries, thus creating further problems.

REFERENCES

Acock, Alan C., and K. Jill Kiecolt. 1988. "Is it family structure or socioeconomic status: Effects of family structure during adolescence on adult adjustment." Paper presented at the annual meetings of the American Sociological Association, Atlanta.

Amato, Paul R. 1986. "Marital conflict, the parent-child relationship, and child self-esteem." *Family Relations* 35: 403–410.

Amato, Paul R. 1987. "Family processes in one-parent, stepparent, and intact families: The child's point of view." *Journal of Marriage and the Family* 49: 327–337.

Anspach, Donald F. 1976. "Kinship and divorce." *Journal of Marriage and the Family* 38: 323–330.

Anthony, E. James. 1974. "Children at risk from divorce: A review." In E. James Anthony (ed.), *The Child in His Family: Children at Psychiatric Risk* (Vol. 3). New York: John Wiley and Sons.

Bachman, Jerald G. 1970. *Youth in Transition, Vol. 2: The Impact of Family Background and Intelligence on Tenth Grade Boys*. Ann Arbor, MI: Survey Research Center, Institute for Social Research.

Bachman, Jerald G., Patrick M. O'Malley, and Jerome J. Johnston. 1978. *Youth in Transition, Vol. 6: Adolescence to Adulthood: A Study of Change and Stability in the Lives of Young Men*. Ann Arbor, MI: Survey Research Center, Institute for Social Research.

Bandura, Albert, and Richard H. Walters. 1959. *Adolescent Aggression*. New York: Ronald Press.

Bandura, Albert, and Richard H. Walters. 1963. *Social Learning and Personality Development*. New York: Holt, Rinehart and Winston.

Bem, Sandra L. 1974. "The measurement of psychological androgyny." *Journal of Consulting and Clinical Psychology* 42: 155–162.

Berg, Berthold, and Robert Kelly. 1979. "The measured self-esteem of children from broken, rejected, and accepted families." *Journal of Divorce* 2: 363–369.

Biller, Henry B. 1976. "The father and personality development: Paternal deprivation and sex-role development." Pp. 89–156 in Michael E. Lamb (ed.), *The Role of the Father in Child Development*. New York: Wiley.

Biller, Henry B. 1981a. "The father and sex role development." Pp. 319–358 in Michael E. Lamb (ed.), *The Role of the Father in Child Development* (2nd ed.). New York: Wiley.

Biller, Henry B. 1981b. "Father absence, divorce, and personality development." Pp. 489–552 in Michael E. Lamb (ed.), *The Role of the Father in Child Development* (2nd ed.). New York: Wiley.

Biller, Henry B., and Anthony Davids. 1973. "Parent-child relations, personality development, and psychopathology." Pp. 48–77 in Anthony Davids (ed.), *Issues in Abnormal Child Psychology*. Monterey, CA: Wadsworth.

Blanchard, Robert W., and Henry B. Biller. 1971. "Father availability and academic performance among third-grade boys." *Developmental Psychology* 4: 301–305.

Blechman, Elaine A. 1982. "Are children with one parent at psychological risk? A methodological review." *Journal of Marriage and the Family* 44: 179–195.

Blechman, Elaine A., Rosalie M. Berberian, and W. Douglas Thompson. 1977. "How well does number of parents explain unique variance in self-reported drug use?" *Journal of Consulting and Clinical Psychology* 45: 1182–1183.

Booth, Alan, David B. Brinkerhoff, and Lynn K. White. 1984. "The impact of parental divorce on courtship." *Journal of Marriage and the Family* 46: 85–94.

Bould, Sally. 1977. "Female-headed families: Personal fate control and provider role." *Journal of Marriage and the Family* 39: 339–349.

Bronfenbrenner, Urie. 1961. "The changing American child: A speculative analysis." *Journal of Social Issues* 17: 6–18.

Bronfenbrenner, Urie. 1976. "Who cares for America's children?" Pp. 3–32 in Victor C. Vaugh and T. Berry Brazelton (eds.), *The Family—Can It Be Saved?* Chicago: Yearbook Medical Publishers.

Bumpass, Larry L. 1984. "Children and marital disruption: A replication and update." *Demography* 21: 71–82.

Bumpass, Larry L. 1985. "Bigger isn't necessarily better: A comment on Hofferth's 'Updating children's life course.'" *Journal of Marriage and the Family* 47: 797–798.

Cashion, Barbara G. 1984. "Female-headed families: Effects on children and clinical implications." Pp. 481–489 in David H. Olson and Brent C. Miller (eds.), *Family Studies Review Yearbook*. Beverly Hills, CA: Sage.

Chapman, Michael. 1977. "Father absence, stepfathers, and the cognitive performance of college students." *Child Development* 48: 1155–1158.

Cherlin, Andrew J. 1981. *Marriage, Divorce, Remarriage*. Cambridge, MA: Harvard University Press.

Coleman, James S., et al. 1966. *Equality of Educational Opportunity*. Washington, DC: U.S. Government Printing Office.

Coleman, James S., Thomas Hoffer, and Sally Kilgore. 1982. *High School Achievement*. New York: Basic Books.

Colletta, Nancy D. 1979. "The impact of divorce: Father absence or poverty?" *Journal of Divorce* 3: 27–35.

Constantinople, Anne. 1973. "Masculinity-femininity: An exception to a famous dictum?" *Psychological Bulletin* 80: 389–407.

Cooper, Judith E., Jacqueline Holman, and Valerie A. Braithwaite. 1983. "Self-esteem and family cohesion: The child's perspective and adjustment." *Journal of Marriage and the Family* 45: 153–159.

Corcoran, Martha. 1979. "The economic consequences of marital dissolution for women in the middle years." *Sex Roles* 5: 343–353.

DeSimone-Luis, Judith, Katherine O'Mahoney, and Dennis Hunt. 1979. "Children of separation and divorce: Factors influencing adjustment." *Journal of Divorce* 3: 37–42.

Dornbusch, Sanford M., J. Merrill Carlsmith, Steven J. Bushwall, Philip L. Ritter, Herbert Leiderman, Albert H. Hastorf, and Ruth T. Gross. 1985. "Single parents, extended households, and the control of adolescents." *Child Development* 56: 326–341.

Edwards, John N. 1987. "Changing family structure and youthful well-being: Assessing the future." *Journal of Family Issues* 8: 355–372.

Ellison, Edythe S. 1983. "Issues concerning parental harmony and children's psychosocial adjustment." *American Journal of Orthopsychiatry* 53: 73–80.

Feldman, Harold, and Margaret Feldman. 1975. "The effects of father absence on adolescents." *Family Perspective* 10: 3–16.

Fowler, Patrick D., and Herbert C. Richards. 1978. "Father absence, educational preparedness, and academic achievement: A test of the confluence model." *Journal of Educational Psychology* 70: 595–601.

Freud, Sigmund. 1961. "Some psychical consequences of the anatomical distinction between the sexes." In J. Strachey (ed. and trans.), *The Standard Edition of the Complete Psychological Works of Sigmund Freud* (Vol. 19, 1923–1925). London: Hogarth Press. (Original work published 1925)

Furstenberg, Frank F., Jr., and Christine Winquist Nord. 1985. "Parenting apart: Patterns of childrearing after marital disruption." *Journal of Marriage and the Family* 47: 893–904.

Furstenberg, Frank F., Jr., Christine Winquist Nord, James L. Peterson, and Nicholas Zill. 1983. "The life course of children of divorce: Marital disruption and parental contact." *American Sociological Review* 48: 656–668.

Ganong, Lawrence H., and Marilyn Coleman. 1984. "The effects of remarriage on children: A review of the empirical literature." *Family Relations* 33: 389–406.

Glenn, Norval, and Michael Supancic. 1984. "The social and demographic correlates of divorce and separation in the United States: An update and reconsideration." *Journal of Marriage and the Family* 46: 563–576.

Glueck, Sheldon, and Eleanor Glueck. 1962. *Family Environment and Delinquency*. Boston: Houghton Mifflin.

Greenberg, David, and Douglas Wolf. 1982. "The economic consequences of experiencing parental marital disruption." *Child and Youth Services Review* 4: 141–162.

Guidubaldi, John, Helen K. Cleminshaw, Joseph D. Perry, Bonnie K. Nastasi, and Jeanine Lightel. 1986. "The role of selected family environment factors in children's post-divorce adjustment." *Family Relations* 35: 141–151.

Guidubaldi, John, and Joseph D. Perry. 1985. "Divorce and mental health sequelae for children: A two-year follow-up of a nationwide sample." *Journal of the American Academy of Child Psychiatry* 24: 531–537.

Hainline, Louise, and Ellen Feig. 1978. "The correlates of childhood father absence in college-aged women." *Child Development* 49: 37–42.

Heilbrun, A. B. 1965. "An empirical test of the modeling theory of sex-role learning." *Child Development* 36: 789–799.

Herzog, Elizabeth, and Cecilia E. Sudia. 1973. "Children in fatherless families." Pp. 141–232 in B. M. Caldwell and N. H. Riccuiti (eds.), *Review of Child Development Research* (Vol. 3). Chicago: University of Chicago Press.

Hess, Robert D., and Kathleen A. Camara. 1979. "Post-divorce family relationships as mediating factors in the consequences of divorce for children." *Journal of Social Issues* 35: 79–96.

Hetherington, E. Mavis. 1972. "Effects of father absence on personality development in adolescent daughters." *Developmental Psychology* 7: 313–326.

Hetherington, E. Mavis. 1979. "Divorce: A child's perspective." *American Psychologist* 34: 851–858.

Hetherington, E. Mavis, Kathleen A. Camara, and David L. Featherman. 1983. "Achievement and intellectual functioning of children in one-parent households." Pp. 205–284 in Janet T. Spence (ed.), *Achievement and Achievement Motives: Psychological and Sociological Approaches*. San Francisco: Freeman.

Hetherington, E. Mavis, Martha Cox, and Roger Cox. 1978. "The aftermath of divorce." In J. H. Stevens, Jr., and M. Mathews (eds.), *Mother-Child, Father-Child Relations*. Washington, DC: National Association for the Education of Young Children.

Hetherington, E. Mavis, Martha Cox, and Roger Cox. 1979. "Play and social interaction in children following divorce." *Journal of Social Issues* 35: 26–49.

Hetherington, E. Mavis, Martha Cox, and Roger Cox. 1982. "Effects of divorce on parents and young children." In M. Lamb (ed.), *Nontraditional Families: Parenting and Child Development*. Hillsdale, NJ: Erlbaum.

Hill, Martha S., Sue Augustyniak, and Michael Ponza. 1986. "Adolescent years with parents divorced or separated: Effects on the social and economic attainments of children as adults." Paper presented at the meetings of the Population Association of America, Detroit.

Hill, Martha S., and Greg J. Duncan. 1987. "Parental family income and the socioeconomic attainment of children." *Social Science Research* 16: 39–73.

Hofferth, Sandra L. 1985. "Updating children's life course." *Journal of Marriage and the Family* 47: 93–115.

Hofferth, Sandra L. 1986. "Response to a comment by Bumpass on 'Updating children's life course.'" *Journal of Marriage and the Family* 48: 680–682.

Hoffman, Martin L. 1971. "Father absence and conscience development." *Developmental Psychology* 4: 400–406.

Hoffman, Saul. 1977. "Marital instability and the economic status of women." *Demography* 14: 67–76.

Hogan, Dennis P., and Evelyn M. Kitagawa. 1985. "The impact of social status, family structure, and neighborhood on the fertility of black adolescents." *American Journal of Sociology* 90: 825–855.

Hunt, Janet G., and Larry L. Hunt. 1977. "Race, daughters, and father-loss: Does absence make the girl grow stronger?" *Social Problems* 25: 90–102.

Hunt, Larry L., and Janet G. Hunt. 1975. "Race and the father-son connection: The conditional relevance of father absence for the orientations and identities of adolescent boys." *Social Problems* 23: 35–52.

Jacobson, Doris S. 1978. "The impact of marital separation/divorce on children: II. Interparent hostility and child adjustment." *Journal of Divorce* 2: 3–19.

Kalter, Neil, Dana Alpern, Rebecca Spence, and James W. Plunkett. 1984. "Locus of control in children of divorce." *Journal of Personality Assessment* 48: 410–414.

Kalter, Neil, Barbara Riemer, Arthur Brickman, and Jade Woo Chen. 1985. "Implications of parental divorce for female development." *Journal of the American Academy of Child Psychiatry* 24: 538–544.

Kelly, Joan B., and Judith Wallerstein. 1979. "Children of divorce." *National Elementary Principal* 59: 51–58.

Kiecolt, K. Jill, and Alan C. Acock. 1988. "The long-term effects of family structure on gender-role attitudes." *Journal of Marriage and the Family* 50: 709–717.

Kinard, E. Milling, and Helen Reinherz. 1984. "Marital disruption: Effects of behavioral and emotional functioning in children." *Journal of Family Issues* 5: 90–115.

Kinard, E. Milling, and Helen Reinherz. 1986. "Effects of marital disruption on children's school aptitude and achievement." *Journal of Marriage and the Family* 48: 285–293.

Kopf, Kathryn E. 1970. "Family variables and school adjustment of eighth grade father-absent boys." *Family Coordinator* 19: 145–151.

Kulka, Richard A., and Helen Weingarten. 1979. "The long-term effects of parental divorce in childhood on adult adjustment." *Journal of Social Issues* 35: 50–78.

Kurdek, Lawrence A. 1981. "An integrative perspective on children's divorce adjustment." *American Psychologist* 36: 856–866.

Kurdek, Lawrence A., Darlene Blisk, and Albert E. Siesky, Jr. 1981. "Correlates of children's

long-term adjustment to their parents' divorce." *Developmental Psychology* 17: 565–579.
Kurdek, Lawrence A., and Albert E. Siesky, Jr. 1980a. "Sex role self-concepts of single divorced parents and their children." *Journal of Divorce* 3: 249–261.
Kurdek, Lawrence A., and Albert E. Siesky, Jr. 1980b. "Children's perceptions of their parents' divorce." *Journal of Divorce* 3: 339–378.
Kurdek, Lawrence A., and Albert E. Siesky, Jr. 1980c. "Effects of divorce on children: The relationship between parent and child perspectives." *Journal of Divorce* 4: 85–99.
Lamb, Michael E. 1977a. "The effects of divorce on children's personality development." *Journal of Divorce* 1: 163–174.
Lamb, Michael E. 1977b. "The development of mother- and father-infant attachments in the second year of life." *Developmental Psychology* 13: 637–648.
Long, Barbara H. 1986. "Parental discord vs. family structure: Effects of divorce on the self-esteem of daughters." *Journal of Youth and Adolescence* 15: 19–27.
Longfellow, Cynthia. 1979. "Divorce in context: Its impact on children." Pp. 287–306 in George K. Levinger and Oliver C. Moles (eds.), *Divorce and Separation: Context, Causes, and Consequences*. New York: Basic Books.
Lowenstein, Joyce S., and Elizabeth J. Koopman. 1978. "A comparison of the self-esteem between boys living with single-parent mothers and single-parent fathers." *Journal of Divorce* 2: 195–208.
Lynn, David B. 1974. *The Father: His Role in Child Development*. Monterey, CA: Brooks/Cole.
McCord, Joan, William McCord, and Emily Thurber. 1962. "Some effects of parental absence on male children." *Journal of Abnormal and Social Psychology* 64: 361–369.
McLanahan, Sara S. 1985. "Family structure and the reproduction of poverty." *American Journal of Sociology* 90: 873–901.
McLanahan, Sara S., Nancy V. Wedemeyer, and Tina Adelberg. 1981. "Network structure, social support, and psychological well-being in the single-parent family." *Journal of Marriage and the Family* 43: 601–612.
Milardo, Robert M. 1987. "Changes in social networks of women and men following divorce: A review." *Journal of Family Issues* 8: 78–96.
Newcomer, Susan, and J. Richard Udry. 1987. "Parental marital status effects on adolescent sexual behavior." *Journal of Marriage and the Family* 49: 235–240.
Noller, Patricia. 1978. "Sex differences in the socialization of affectionate expression." *Developmental Psychology* 14: 317–319.
Norton, Arthur J., and Paul C. Glick. 1986. "One parent families: A social and economic profile." *Family Relations* 35: 9–17.
Parish, Thomas S. 1981. "The impact of divorce on the family." *Adolescence* 16 (63): 577–580.
Parish, Thomas S., and Judy W. Dostal. 1980. "Evaluations of self and parent figures by children from intact, divorced, and reconstituted families." *Journal of Youth and Adolescence* 9: 347–351.
Parish, Thomas S., Judy W. Dostal, and Joycelyn G. Parish. 1981. "Evaluations of self and parents as a function of intactness of family and family happiness." *Adolescence* 16 (61): 203–210.
Parish, Thomas S., and James C. Taylor. 1979. "The impact of divorce and subsequent father absence on children's and adolescents' self-concepts." *Journal of Youth and Adolescence* 8: 427–432.
Parish, Thomas S., and Stanley E. Wigle. 1985. "A longitudinal study of the impact of

parental divorce on adolescents' evaluations of self and parents." *Adolescence* 20: 239–244.

Parsons, Talcott, and Robert F. Bales. 1955. *Family Socialization and Interaction Process*. Glencoe: Free Press.

Peterson, James L., and Nicholas Zill. 1986. "Marital disruption, parent-child relationships, and behavior problems in children." *Journal of Marriage and the Family* 48: 295–307.

Porter, Beatrice, and K. Daniel O'Leary. 1980. "Marital discord and childhood behavior problems." *Journal of Abnormal Child Psychology* 8: 287–295.

Porter, Karen. 1984. The Scheduling of Life Course Events, Economic Adaptations, and Marital History: An Analysis of Economic Survival after Separation and Divorce among a Cohort of Midlife Women. Unpublished PhD dissertation, Syracuse University.

Radin, Norma. 1981. "The role of the father in cognitive, academic, and intellectual development." Pp. 379–427 in Michael E. Lamb (ed.), *The Role of the Father in Child Development* (2nd ed.). New York: Wiley.

Rainwater, Lee, and William L. Yancey. 1967. *The Moynihan Report and the Politics of Controversy*. Cambridge, MA: MIT Press.

Raschke, Helen J., and Vernon J. Raschke. 1979. "Family conflict and the children's self concepts." *Journal of Marriage and the Family* 41: 367–374.

Rickel, Annette U., and Thomas S. Langner. 1985. "Short-term and long-term effects of marital disruption on children." *American Journal of Community Psychology* 13: 599–611.

Rohrlich, John A., Ruth Ranier, Linda Berg-Cross, and Gary Berg-Cross. 1977. "The effects of divorce: A research review with a developmental perspective." *Journal of Clinical Child Psychology* 6: 15–20.

Rosen, Rhona. 1979. "Some crucial issues concerning children of divorce." *Journal of Divorce* 3: 19–25.

Rosenberg, Morris. 1979. *Conceiving the Self*. New York: Basic Books.

Santrock, John W. 1975. "Father absence, perceived maternal behavior, and moral development in boys." *Child Development* 46: 753–757.

Santrock, John W., and Richard A. Warshak. 1979. "Father custody and social development in boys and girls." *Journal of Social Issues* 35: 112–125.

Savage, James E., Jr., Alvis V. Adair, and Philip Friedman. 1978. "Community-social variables related to black parent-absent families." *Journal of Marriage and the Family* 40: 779–785.

Sciara, Frank J. 1975. "Effects of father absence on the educational achievement of urban black children." *Child Study Journal* 5: 45–55.

Shinn, Marybeth. 1978. "Father absence and children's cognitive development." *Psychological Bulletin* 85: 295–324.

Slater, Elisa J., and Joel D. Haber. 1984. "Adolescent adjustment following divorce as a function of familial conflict." *Journal of Consulting and Clinical Psychology* 52: 920–921.

Solomon, Daniel, Jay G. Hirsch, Daniel R. Scheinfeld, and John C. Jackson. 1972. "Family characteristics and elementary school achievement in an urban ghetto." *Journal of Consulting and Clinical Psychology* 39: 462–466.

Spanier, Graham B., and Linda Thompson. 1984. *Parting: The Aftermath of Separation and Divorce*. Beverly Hills, CA: Sage.

Stolberg, Arnold L., and James M. Anker. 1983. "Cognitive and behavioral changes in children resulting from parental divorce and consequent environmental changes." *Journal of Divorce* 7: 23–41.

Svanum, Soren, Robert G. Bringle, and Joan E. McLaughlin. 1982. "Father absence and cognitive performance in a large sample of six- to eleven-year-old children." *Child Development* 53: 136–143.

Tooley, Kay. 1976. "Antisocial behavior and social alienation post divorce: The 'man of the house' and his mother." *American Journal of Orthopsychiatry* 46: 33–42.

Tuckman, J., and R. A. Regan. 1966. "Intactness of the home and behavioral problems in children." *Journal of Child Psychology and Psychiatry* 7: 225–233.

Wallerstein, Judith S. 1984. "Children of divorce: Preliminary report of a ten-year follow-up of young children." *American Journal of Orthopsychiatry* 54: 444–458.

Wallerstein, Judith S., and Joan B. Kelly. 1974. "The effects of parental divorce: The adolescent experience." In E. James Anthony and Cyrille Koupernik (eds.), *The Child in His Family*, (Vol. 3). New York: Wiley.

Wallerstein, Judith S., and Joan B. Kelly. 1975. "The effects of parental divorce. The experiences of the preschool child." *Journal of the American Academy of Child Psychiatry* 14: 600–616.

Wallerstein, Judith S., and Joan B. Kelly. 1980a. "Children and divorce: A review." *Social Work* 24: 468–475.

Wallerstein, Judith S., and Joan B. Kelly. 1980b. *Surviving the Breakup: How Children and Parents Cope with Divorce*. Basic Books: New York.

Weiss, Robert S. 1979. "Growing up a little faster: The experience of growing up in a single-parent household." *Journal of Social Issues* 35: 97–111.

Weitzman, Lenore. 1985. *The Divorce Revolution: The Unexpected Social and Economic Consequences for Women and Children in America*. New York: Free Press.

Werner, Emmy E., and Ruth S. Smith. 1982. *Vulnerable but Not Invincible: A Study of Resilient Children*. New York: McGraw-Hill.

White, Lynn K., David B. Brinkerhoff, and Alan Booth. 1985. "The effect of marital disruption on child's attachment to parents." *Journal of Family Issues* 6: 5–22.

Worell, J. 1978. "Sex roles and psychological well-being: Perspectives on methodology." *Journal of Consulting and Clinical Psychology* 46: 777–791.

Wyman, Peter A., Emory L. Cowen, A. Dirk Hightower, and JoAnne L. Pedro-Carroll. 1985. "Perceived competence, self-esteem, and anxiety in latency-aged children of divorce." *Journal of Clinical Child Psychology* 14: 20–26.

Young, Earl R., and Thomas S. Parish. 1977. "Impact of father absence during childhood on the psychological adjustment of college females." *Sec Roles* 3: 217–227.

ARTICLE 31
The Six Stations of Remarriage: Developmental Tasks of Remarriage after Divorce

ANN GOETTING

Just as the divorce process involves coping with various developmental tasks, remarriage is a complex process requiring many personal changes and adjustments. Goetting suggests that there are six stations of remarriage, each presenting a challenge to forming a new couple identity.

WHILE THERE ARE CLEAR FACTORS favoring remarriage after divorce such as experience and maturity, it remains a trying experience for most who pursue it. . . . [A] great portion of the problems associated with remarriage are related to the complexities introduced by children from former marriages. The complexity of an institution in itself need not present problems, but if society fails to provide guidelines for the relationships involved, the outcome may be one of chaos and conflict. For lack of such guidelines in Western culture, the remarried pair is often expected to function in the same way as does a first married pair, despite the fact that in addition to the

Ann Goetting, "The Six Stations of Remarriage: Developmental Tasks of Remarriage after Divorce." *Family Relations*, 31:213–222. Copyrighted © 1982 by the National Council on Family Relations, 3989 Central Ave. N.E., Suite #550, Minneapolis, MN 55421. Reprinted by permission.

new husband and wife there may be two former spouses, two sets of children, four sets of grandparents, and numerous other relatives and friends associated with a former marriage. In addition, there may be many unresolved feelings carried over into the new marriage.

Undoubtedly, remarriage after divorce is a complex process with several interrelated components. That process is described here through [the] use of Bohannan's (1970) model outlining developmental tasks of divorce. His six "stations" of divorce consist of those tasks which must be mastered in order to exit successfully from an existing marriage. They include the emotional, legal, economic, coparental, community and psychic divorces. Those stations are revisited here in the course of moving from divorce to remarriage. As Furstenberg (1979) pointed out, a successful remarriage must involve undoing or refashioning many of the adaptions made to a successful divorce. As is true of the divorce stations, all six stations of remarriage need not necessarily occur to all remarrying people with the same intensity and in the same order. In fact, some individuals may avoid some stations altogether. The six stations of remarriage are ordered here in such a way that the first three can occur independent of the existence of children from a former marriage, while the last three assume the involvement of such children.

EMOTIONAL REMARRIAGE

Typically the remarriage process begins with the emotional remarriage. This is the often slow process by which a divorced person reestablishes a bond of attraction, commitment and trust with a member of the opposite sex. After having experienced severe disappointment in a previous relationship, the divorcee learns to release emotions in an effort to once again secure comfort and love. Often this process is wrought with the fear that this emotional investment will lead to loss and rejection. Such fears may justifiably be intense because an additional failure [of] relationships threatens not only to leave the individual once again disappointed and alone, but also to damage identity and self-concept. Another divorce could strongly suggest to others as well as self a deficiency in those skills, whatever they may be, which are necessary to sustain a marriage. While there is always ambiguity in terms of cause and fault with one divorce—possibly it was at least partially the fault of the other spouse, or maybe the divorce could be blamed on a situation which surrounded that particular marriage—additional failures begin to single out an individual as a "loser." Due to the loss, rejection and failure that are typically associated with divorce, the emotional remarriage is a unique and often arduous and volatile process which is not satisfactorily completed by all who attempt it.

PSYCHIC REMARRIAGE

Psychic remarriage is the process of changing one's conjugal identity from individual to couple. It involves relinquishing the personal freedom and autonomy established by their psychic divorce, and resuming a lifestyle in which a person is expected to be viewed as one component of a partnership. . . .

Since the role of adult males in our society dictates a primary identity with occupational status, thereby deemphasizing conjugal identity, men are likely to experience a relatively mild identity shift as they pass from the status of single person to that of mate. In other words, since the social status and therefore personal identity of a man is relatively independent of his marital status, a shift in his marital status would not represent an extreme alteration in personal identity. But the situation may be very different for women, who in accordance with traditional gender roles, identify strongly with their marital status. While the occupational sphere tends to be the domain of the man, the conjugal sphere is seen as the domain of the woman. It is the woman, then, who is faced with the more extreme identity shift when there is an alteration in marital status.

But the shift is not of equal intensity among all women. The traditional women would suffer a great loss with psychic divorce, a true identity crisis. But upon remarriage these women would adjust easily in the psychic realm. For them psychic remarriage represents the recovery of their valued identity as wife. Non-traditional women, on the other hand, are likely to view the psychic divorce in positive terms as a period of growth into autonomous identity, an opportunity to do away with the restraints of couple identity. It is these women who are likely to have adjustment problems associated with psychic remarriage. To them the wife role is less important, and psychic remarriage represents [a] loss of a more highly valued independence and freedom. . . .

COMMUNITY REMARRIAGE

The community remarriage like the community divorce represents an alteration which a person often must make in relationships with a community of friends. Where the community divorce involves breaking away from the world of couples, entering what Hunt (1966) called "the world of the formerly married," the community remarriage involves reentrance into the couple's world. Like the community divorce, the community remarriage may be a turbulent process. Unmarried friends are typically lost for lack of a common lifestyle, especially friends of the opposite sex. These friends are replaced by married couples, often remarried couples with whom remarrieds share important aspects of biography.

In some ways the process of community remarriage has potential for being more strenuous than does the process of community divorce because it can result in the loss of closer friends. With the community divorce one must give up couples, that is *pairs* of friends who were shared with a spouse. Often the friendships had not been intimate. Instead, they were secondary to, convenient to, and dependent upon, the marital relationship. They were not one's own friends, selected as a reflection of one's interests and needs. They were relationships based on the combined interests and needs of the spouses. But with the community remarriage, one may be put in a position of severing the close personally tailored ties established while divorced, and replacing them with less intimate, couple-oriented relationships. Furthermore, those bonds of friendship established during that period of time when one was divorced may be particularly valuable because they lent support at a time of personal crisis. These were the friends who were there to help the individual through the typically devastating experiences associated with the divorce process.

So the community remarriage, while representing reentrance into the "normality" of the couples' world, also may mean the eventual loss of valuable friendship bonds. Married life is often intolerant of relationships with unmarried friends. Its structure discourages those connections with the past, those ties with the world of the formerly married.

PARENTAL REMARRIAGE

The parental remarriage is necessary if there are children. It is the union of an individual with the children of this new spouse. Parental marriage . . . has received the most attention in the literature as is indicated by the fact that a series of bibliographies on steprelationships, the product of parental remarriage, is periodically compiled and distributed for the use of social scientists (Sell, 1977). Unprecedented numbers of people find themselves living with other people's children, and many view the process of combining with them to form a family unit as challenging at best.

Fast and Cain (1966) suggested that the problems of stepparenthood are based on the fact that the role definition of stepparent in this society is poorly articulated, and implies contradictory expectations as "parent," "stepparent" and "nonparent." The stepparent cannot fully assume any of these roles, and therefore must individually work out behavior patterns for interacting with [his or her] spouse's children. Folk tradition describes the stepmother as wicked and cruel—in a word, unparentlike—so to enact that role would be socially unacceptable. Instead, the stepparent is encouraged to assume the role of parent, for which there is legal support in the explication of the rights and duties entailed by the "in loco parentis" relationship. But the stepparent cannot totally assume the role of father or mother. The natural parent is typically still active in the parental role, which requires that the stepparent gracefully accede to the parental rights of another and behave as [a] nonparent. The stepparent and the natural parent are placed in a position of sharing the residential, education, financial, health, and moral decisions incumbent on the parental role. Society provides no guidelines for this sharing of rights and responsibilities which can easily lead to confusion, frustration and resentment.

Another explanation for the difficulties associated with parental remarriage and the associated steprelationships is that marital role expectations between husband and wife are not worked out prior to the assumption of parental roles. Spouses are not allowed the opportunity to develop workable and comfortable marital relationships and to establish a primary husband-wife bond prior to the birth of children.

Marital and parental adjustment must be confronted simultaneously which could encourage the inappropriate involvement of children in marital dissension. Marital and parental problems could easily confound one another. The natural parent's prior relationship to his child can serve as a threat to the establishment of a primary husband-wife bond. In that way it may detract from the integration of the new family unit.

One problem relating to stepparenthood that appears often in the literature is discipline. The stepparent is often reluctant to provide discipline because the clear authority vested in a natural parent is lacking. If the stepparent does actually attempt to discipline, such action may not be well-received by the child or may not be interpreted as acceptable by the spouse. This problem of discipline would seemingly be more common for stepfathers than stepmothers, since children typically stay with their mothers after divorce. It is the stepfather who most often enters a formerly single-parent family unit and who, therefore, actually experiences daily interactions with his stepchildren. The stepmother, on the other hand, usually spends limited time with her visiting stepchildren.

Another specific problem associated with parental remarriage concerns children as a link to the former marriage, and was expressed by Messinger's (1976) subjects. Some felt that continued ties through the children with previous family members made it more difficult for the new spouse to integrate into the new family unit. In this way they saw the children as a source of marital disruption. New mates frequently felt that such continued ties made them feel as though they were outsiders.

ECONOMIC REMARRIAGE

The economic remarriage is the re-establishment after divorce of a marital household as a unit of economic productivity and consumption. Like the parental remarriage, it is a particularly difficult developmental task of remarriage, as evidenced by the Messinger study, which suggested that the problem of finances in remarriage was surpassed in severity only by problems associated with children. The economic remarriage as a developmental task can be considered as being an extension of the parental remarriage in that its main difficulties stem from the existence of children from a former marriage. When there are such children involved, the economic remarriage becomes complex in that it emerges as an open system, dependent on or at least interrelated with the economic behavior of individuals other than the two spouses.

Typically the standard of living increases at remarriage due to the simple fact that financial resources which had formerly maintained two residences are combined to support only one. So the problem is not so much one of insufficient funds as it is one of financial instability and resource distribution. One source of instability stems from the sporadic nature of incoming child support payments, especially after the mother has remarried. Many reconstituted families are simply unable to predict how much money will be available from month to month because of the uncertainty associated with the arrival of child support payments. . . .

A second source of economic instability lies in the unpredictable nature of the needs of the husband's children, who typically reside with their mother. While outgoing child support payments may be constant, the possibility of unexpected needs requiring extra financial cost (medical, educational, etc.) can loom as a dark cloud over the remarriage. It can bring the same kind of uncertainty and consequent inconvenience into the remarriage household as [the] lack of continuity associated with incoming child support payments.

The problems of *resource distribution* refers to the issue of how the money should be spent: who should get how much of what is available? For example, if *his* daughter is given ballet lessons, should not *her* son be allowed tennis lessons, even though the sources of support for the two children are quite different? If the resources available to her son from her ex-spouse preclude such tennis lessons should the stepfather finance such lessons for the sake of equity? Messinger (1976) reported frequent statements of discomfort and embarrassment on the part of the mothers over the financial cost incurred for her new husband on behalf of her children. Society fails to provide guidelines for these kinds of situations, which can lead to stress in the remarital relationship.

The economic remarriage unites individuals from two different family systems and two different generations who have learned different and possibly opposing earning and spending habits. The problems involved in integrating such persons into a smooth functioning economic unit may provide a true challenge for all involved.

LEGAL REMARRIAGE

Remarriage as a form of marriage is a creature of the law. Since it is such a relatively newly recognized way of life, its legal ramifications are only beginning to be explored. By the time a remarriage takes place, alimony, child support, and the division of property have already been set regarding the former marriage. The new marriage may cause additional legal considerations concerning responsibility toward relationships from the former marriage. The complexity of what Bohannan (1970) referred to as the pseudokinship system created by remarriage after divorce requires decisions regarding his and her financial resources, his and her former spouses, and his, her, and their children. . . .

Remarriage after divorce does not mean that a person exchanges one family for another; instead it means that the individual takes on an additional family. Since legal responsibilities associated with this action have not been clearly charted, individuals are left to base legal decisions on their own moral guidelines. For some this can be a difficult process because it involves assigning weights of importance to members of their complicated pseudokinship networks. Such questions arise as to which wife deserves the life and accident insurance, medical coverage, retirement benefits, pension rights and property rights. Is it the former wife who played a major role in building the estate or is it the current wife who has contributed less but is currently in his "good graces"? Also, to which children should he lend support for college education—his children, her children or their children? Since state inheritance laws typically favor a person's current spouse and natural children, inheritance rights need to be clearly defined at the point of legal remarriage if the person wishes to will benefits to a former spouse or to stepchildren.

Until the time that state legal codes respond to the needs of the remarried, individuals will continue to be left to work out the legal problems and decisions of remarriage after divorce. The imposition of structure by the state in this area not only would make the legal remarriage logistically simpler, but might contribute to increased affability for the relationships involved. The implementation of a standard procedure for the distribution of resources, for example, would eliminate the sense of competition and jealousy which is now encouraged by the lack of guidelines. If, for example, it was predetermined by the state that the resources of remarried persons would be divided among all of their surviving spouses in proportions corresponding to the length of each marriage, bitterness on the part of any of those spouses toward one another before or after death regarding equity in inheritance rights might be reduced. The burden of responsibility for distribution of resources would have been lifted from the individual by the state. Such legal structure could relieve tension among spouses, former spouses, parent-child relationships and steprelationships, and therefore contribute to the maintenance of the complex pseudokinship structure created by remarriage after divorce.

CONCLUDING STATEMENT

As divorce and subsequent remarriage become increasingly common, adjustment to their developmental tasks becomes a greater concern for family practitioners. While individuals face different tasks in varying orders, it has been suggested here that the six developmental tasks of divorce outlined by Bohannan are also important developmental tasks of remarriage. Remarriage can be a complex process, and its adjustment accordingly difficult. The problems associated with remarital adjustment are often heightened by the fact that partners in remarriage may still be adjusting to their divorces. At remarriage, a person may be compelled to commence the stations of remarriage while having not yet completed the stations of divorce. For example, as an individual struggles with establishing bonds of affection, commitment and trust with a new partner, he or she may still be contending with the severance of emotional ties with the former spouse. . . .

REFERENCES

Bohannan, P. The Six Stations of Divorce. I. P. Bohannan (Ed.), *Divorce and After*. New York: Doubleday and Co., 1970.

Fast, I., and A. C. Cain. The Stepparent Role: Potential for Disturbances in Family Functioning. *American Journal of Orthopsychiatry,* 1966, *36,* 485–491.

Furstenberg, F. F. Recycling the Family. *Marriage and Family Review,* 1979, *2*(3), 1, 12–22.

Hunt, M. M. *The World of the Formerly Married.* New York: McGraw-Hill Book Co., 1966.

Messinger, L. Remarriage between Divorced People with Children from Previous Marriages: A Proposal for Preparation for Remarriage. *Journal of Marriage and Family Counseling,* 1976, *38,* 193–200.

Sell, K. D. *Divorce in the 1970s.* Salisbury, N.C.: Department of Sociology, Catawba College, 1977.

ARTICLE 32
From Nuclear to Stepfamily Ideology: A Stressful Change

BARBARA FISHMAN AND BERNICE HAMEL

Most people who divorce eventually remarry. However, there are few rules or prescriptions as to how stepfamilies are to behave. This article discusses how stepfamilies function, noting the ways in which they differ from first-time married families in the use of space, time, and money. In the absence of institutionalized norms, most stepfamilies experience considerable stress, which only begins to decline when they begin to develop new rules consistent with their expanded family structure.

STEPFAMILIES ARE A PRODUCT of the changing social construction of family life resulting from today's high incidence of divorce and remarriage (Bohannon, 1971; Cherlin, 1978; Furstenberg, 1979). This article proposes that people experience stress as they try to function within a stepfamily structure using an ideology which is more applicable to a nuclear family. The relationship between social change and ideology is observed as stepfamilies long for familiarity—a nuclear family style of life—and experience frustration trying to recreate it in a contemporary American remarriage. Stress diminishes if and when participants come to recognize that stepfamily structure has its own behavioral imperatives.

Barbara Fishman and Bernice Hamel, "From Nuclear to Stepfamily Ideology: A Stressful Change. "*Alternative Lifestyles* 4:181–204. Copyright 1981 by Human Sciences Press. Reprinted by permission. Barbara Fishman, Ph.D., is in the private practice of family therapy and the author of a book on coupling entitled *Resonance: For People Who Want Autonomy as Well as Intimacy in Their Relationships* to be published by Jeremy Tarcher, Inc., during 1990. Bernice Hamel is a writer situated in the Philadelphia area.

Across the centuries, changes in the organization of family life have been documented: the structure of the family, the numbers of people considered family members, the use of time and space to meet the normative expectations of members—indeed, the very nature of those expectations—have changed. The emergence of the idea of childhood and the rising status of children is but one example of how family life has altered over time (Aries, 1962).

We are now in a period of accelerated change, which occurs within one's lifetime rather than across generations. Current modifications in marital patterns often now include initial marriage, separation, divorce, and then remarriage: For three couples recently married, one will probably divorce. Out of every four people who divorce, three remarry within a three to five year period. Between 32% and 46% of the children who have grown up in this country during the 1970s have experienced either separation or divorce of their natural parents, and, in 1978, fully 10% of American children under 18 lived in stepfamilies (Norton and Glick, 1976; Glick, 1977, 1979).

People in a culture share an ideology or a set of beliefs about what family life should be. The nuclear family ideology in this culture prescribes rules about when to marry, male and female role behavior, and even how to have a family meal. These well-learned rules are "basic truths" by which family life is understood and daily behavior is constructed, although sometimes pragmatic needs may demand a different set of rules. For instance, families hold to the idea that the evening meal should be taken together and that it should be a pleasant event, reflecting family unity at the conclusion of the day. But with men and women working at long distances from their homes, with children participating in after-school activities, with no one at home to assume responsibility for preparing a meal, the experience of the dinner hour can be quite different from the expectation. This poor fit between expectation and reality is an example of how people, using the nuclear family ideology as a measure by which to construct and evaluate their lives, may feel that they have failed.

Often, people expect that habituated behavior will work in novel contexts. When the structure of the family changes, as in the case of stepfamilies, the gap between expectation and reality widens. For example, many stepparents expect that the role of parent is similar to the role of stepparent. They may be frustrated by the outcome of their stepparenting efforts because they are behaving according to nuclear family rules which do not apply. There are those who keep using inappropriate rules in the face of failure, unable to find or invent alternatives. On the other hand, some people over time and accumulated experience perceive that the stepparent role is qualitatively different from biological parenting. With this perception, more suitable role expectations emerge, behavior is modified, and a "stepfamily ideology" develops which is realistically matched to the family's new structure.

Stepfamilies, of course, have existed throughout history as an anomalous family form—a consequence of high maternal death rates resulting in frequent remarriage. However, the modern American stepfamily is created most often following divorce rather than widowhood. The contemporary union of two previously married people may incorporate children from prior marriages, and ex-spouses are often active in the lives of their children. Bohannon describes the linkages of family and former family members in what he refers to as a "divorce chain"—a new version of the extended family (Bohannon, 1971). Students of the family and cultural change are beginning to research this increasingly common family form. The intention of this study is twofold:

(1) To understand how the stepfamily functions, given its extended structure;
(2) To ask whether ideology accommodates to the new structure and if so, in what ways?

DESIGN OF THE STUDY

As defined in this study, the stepfamily is a merger of two households resulting from remarriage. At least one partner has lost a previous spouse through divorce and each has children from a former union who now live, or have lived, in the new household for some portion of the time. Children who live with their fathers and stepmothers compose only 5% to 10% of stepfamilies—as opposed to those living with their mothers and stepfathers (Glick, 1980). Recent evidence, however, indicates that men are increasing their commitment to parenting (Lewis and Pleck, 1979). All the fathers chosen for this study have had at least some custodial care of their children so that their biological and stepparenting behaviors could be compared, and because the study hypothesizes that parents who retain some level of connection with former spouses in the interest of their children may best illustrate in ideology and behavior the shift from nuclear to stepfamily living.

The sample consisted of 16 white, middle-class stepfamilies, all from the greater Philadelphia metropolitan area. Class status was defined by level of education, place of residence, and income. The sample reflected an equal representation of Protestant, Catholic, and Jewish faiths. Families were recruited through contacts with self-help groups, the clergy, and referrals from the larger community. By and large, those stepfamily members contacted were willing to cooperate and even eager to tell their stories. Longitudinal in design, the first measures were taken in 1980. Each researcher interviewed 8 stepfamilies in depth. Members of each stepfamily household were interviewed separately (husbands, wives, and their respective children). When available, grandparents (parents of the remarried couple) were interviewed or contacted by telephone. Former spouses and their current mates were not included in the study. All interviews were taped in natural surroundings, either in the homes or offices of family members. The researchers used semistructured interview schedules constructed around a core of specific questions. For each family, a total of approximately 6 hours of interviewing time was spent over a span of several weeks. The design of the study allowed observation of individual family members in natural contexts so that in-depth interviews could take place.

SUMMARY OF FINDINGS

In certain respects, the 16 families sampled are typical of others in their age cohort (Glick, 1977). The women of the sample have a median age of 40.4, having been born about 1940. On average, they married at 20.8 years, had 3.2 children, and separated at 32. The men had a median age of 43.4 years, having been born in the mid-1930s. On average, they married at 22 years, had 2.9 children, and separated when they were 34.8 years of age.

In other respects, this group is different from their age cohort. They remained in their first marriages longer than most who divorce: The women separated after 11.5 years and the men after 12.5 years. These men met their new spouses within an average of 7 months after their earlier marriages dissolved. The women, at considerable disadvantage in the marriage market, required 4 years to accomplish this same goal.

All but 3 of the women in this sample have full custodial care of their children. These 3 share parental responsibilities with former spouses. By definition of the study, the men are committed to childrearing: Of the 16, 8 have full custodial care of their biological children, 4 share equal parental responsibilities with ex-spouses, and the remaining 4 fathers have periodic custodial obligations, such as weekends or summer and winter vacations.

The sample represents an anomalous family life course pattern, if the family life course is described with references to ages of children (Feldman and Feldman, 1975). Since it takes people considerable time to marry, separate, divorce, and remarry, the stepfamilies in this sample contain no preschool age children, with the exception of one child born to a remarried couple. While the stepfamilies sampled have been living together for an average of 3.6 years, 14 families are rearing adolescent children. Traditional families reach this point after at least 13 years of marriage. These stepfamilies are in the anomalous position of being at a later point in their family life course and at an earlier point in their marital career.

Of the families studied, 6 merged with children of markedly different ages, so that two "age groups" of children, each from different primary families, are contained within one household. For example, in one stepfamily, although the husband and wife are the same age, the husband's children are from 6 to 9 years old and the wife's children are adolescents from 14 to 18 years. In another family, the spread of ages includes school-age children, teenagers, and young adults living away from home. These findings indicate that the modern stepfamily often spans more than one point in the family life course and the commitment to childrearing becomes longer and more intensified.

Regarding sex-linked work preferences, the men indicate economic functions similar to those of their previous marriages (none changed careers to accommodate their new families), although most reported an increased involvement in their present homes and greater parenting responsibilities than in prior marriages. All but one is employed full time, and some moonlight for additional income or career enhancement. At the time of the interviews, five women were employed full time, six were unemployed and at home full time, and five had sought ways to accommodate family and professional needs by working part time. Indeed, three women designed for themselves entrepreneurial careers which operate out of their homes, in order to maintain family and mothering functions without sacrificing economic and professional functions.

NUCLEAR FAMILY IDEAL AND STEPFAMILY REALITY

The modern nuclear family, idealized as a "haven in a heartless world" (Lasch, 1977), has its hallmarks in romantic love, privacy, and autonomy. Born in sexual excitement and nurtured in the privacy of their courtship, a couple's love is supposed to set the stage for the new marriage. Once married, the maintenance of privacy and autonomy are essential operating rules. These rules take the form of a separate household and clear boundaries that limit the access of kin and other community members. Shielded from the outside by these boundaries, the family is supposed to develop self-sufficiency in such matters as finance and child rearing. Considerable research, however, disputes this picture of the family as separate and autonomous from kin (Bott, 1975; Sussman and Burchinal, 1962; Lee, 1980). Nevertheless, it is often this picture that is operative as the ideal.

For the contemporary stepfamily, the nuclear ideal of privacy and autonomy is rarely experienced. From the outset, people in stepfamilies report a disparity between what they had expected and what they actually experience. The consequence of this disparity between expectation and reality is personal and family stress.

Even the courtships are different. But, not unlike those who marry for the first time, many people seeking remarriage ardently wish for that idyllic state of romantic love. Yet many describe their actual courtships and subsequent marriages in businesslike metaphors, such as "mergers," rather than in romantic terms. A typical woman complained that her courtship was over almost as soon as it began. Her husband-to-be was short of both time and funds, and she felt uneasy leaving her young children in order to date him. They decided it was simply more practical for economic reasons, as well as living arrangements, to get married:

> *The romance never had a chance. Once we were married, we had to spread ourselves across the crowd. We do well now. We share household and family tasks very nicely. But I sometimes wonder how we will do when the kids are grown and we're alone, just the two of us.*

The new couple wants time to create their conjugal world. Berger and Kellner (1964) propose a necessary marital function of time spent together when "shared understandings" emerge which are basic to the "nomic" processes of marriage. The couples who courted in this study have had trouble finding this kind of private time.

One man reported that by his second date with the woman he was to marry, they included all their children on an outing to the movies—his three and her three.

He said, "If it doesn't work with the children, it's not going to work at all." In reporting on the "absurdity" of two adults attempting to get to know one another while surrounded by six demanding children, he said:

The only privacy we could find was in my automobile. We felt like kids again, but until we were sure of each other, we did not want our children exposed to any evidence of sexuality.

The newly married couple finds it hard to create a circle of privacy which excludes children or past mates. The implications of this rebound throughout stepfamily life.

Designing the New Family

Separation and divorce have taken their toll in each of the families interviewed. Respondents say that they remarried after experiencing failure, but they did so because they value family life and wish to succeed within its context. This motivation provided them with the stamina and goodwill necessary for a new and challenging project.

The formal stepparent role comes with a new marriage contract, but beyond that, it is a status achieved (Walker and Messinger, 1979). By and large, adults in this study say that they did not expect to have to work so hard to attain a parenting status with stepchildren. One woman reports on the discrepancy between her expectations and the reality:

The hardest part for me is that I wanted an "instant" family. I felt these kids would be mine. My position was you didn't vote for me and I didn't vote for you. But, by God, we are stuck with each other. With that simple philosophy, we should all love each other and be one big happy family. But, it doesn't work that way.

The ideological shift to an active, planning role in stepfamily formation is difficult for the two adults, since children often resist the new stepfamily relationships as an expression of loyalty to their biological parents (Visher and Visher, 1979). For example, one adolescent girl contrasts two relationships:

We never see eye-to-eye. She's so different from my mother. Just the constant comparison—that she doesn't cook as well as my mother, that she lays down more rules. Different kinds of things are expected, and we never really developed much of a relationship. I feel she tries to become more involved in my affairs than she's welcome to. That particularly causes me to draw away from her.

Other children often feel that a stepparent interferes with the closeness they shared with a parent who, perhaps during a "single" period, had more time to give. A child's resentment was described by his stepmother, as follows:

> *My stepson is angry at me because he feels I replaced him (when I married his father). I took his father away from him. I'm aware of that, but I don't think that there is much I can do about it. It happened, and he will have to get some living under his belt to appreciate me. But for now, he gets nice meals and he has a lovely house, which he never had before—and he's got clean underwear!*

This stepmother is defining the relationship with her stepson so that its limits are acknowledged and its possibilities remain attainable. Given the absence of institutional norms, the stepfamily must design its own relationships, a task made more difficult by loyalty to biological relationships and nuclear family ideals.

Space, Time, and the Family Economy

The comparison between nuclear family and stepfamily lifestyles is often made by people in the early and most stressful days of the new marriage. This is a period when old expectations are put to the test and many new rules must be developed. For example, middle-class nuclear families desire livingspace that comfortably accommodates their numbers, often preferring that children have separate bedrooms when possible. But the enlarged numbers of the new stepfamily may mean that they must give up the idea of a separate bedroom for each child. Even if the new stepfamily could afford to move to a home with enough bedrooms, they would have to find one, and finding or deciding on a place to live is always a stressful issue. Repeatedly, people say that they would prefer to begin their new marriages in a neutral place, like those who marry for the first time (neither his nor hers). But other factors, such as economics or location, may prevent this solution. For example, in one family a woman and her two daughters moved into her new husband's small home because it was located in a "better neighborhood." In order to accommodate themselves into his house, she moved much of his furniture into the garage and displaced her stepson to a basement room. Her eight-year-old daughter reported:

> *We feel like guests in Jim's house. We are careful of what we do. It is like we are the intruders. And I feel very bad that we took Tommy's room. They fixed up a room for him in the basement, with posters and all, but he's still mad at us for taking his room.*

Metaphorically, space can be used to define relationships. That Jim's furniture was moved to the garage and his son was moved to the basement may describe the beginning distribution of power and affect in this new stepfamily. Stepfamily living demands a change in expectations regarding use of space. People still desire privacy, but the reality of living with more people in often crowded space requires a new set of behavioral rules. The middle-class act of walking into one's room and closing the door for privacy is a behavior that works in a nuclear family but perhaps not in stepfamilies.

The pressures associated with *time* constitute another central issue for new stepfamilies. The lack of sufficient time to meet a stepfamily's needs is related to its increased numbers, and complexity of structure, as well as its point in the family life course. Adults in their early forties with school-age children are usually heavily committed in many ways to parenting, as well as to their careers. Also, their recent marriage requires additional time commitments if they are to build a satisfying conjugal relationship.

The demands of the new marriage require time; interacting with new family members requires time. Many adult stepfamily members sacrifice their personal time, while others set up rigid schedules to guard it. Time must be distributed such that people do not feel cheated, as one woman does:

> *Stevie was home from school last week with a high fever. I resented it greatly. I was supposed to be completing a report for my job—and there I was, nursing a child that is not even my own. I felt that he should have gotten sick on his mother's time, but it happened when he was here with us.*

Money is of such importance in this culture that it too may be used as a metaphor of commitment to the new stepfamily. Often, the most stressful issue for a stepfamily is how to support it financially. A nuclear family economic model does not easily fit, as income may come from multiple sources rather than from a primary source. Where monies come from, for whom and how funds should be spent are issues that must be dealt with. For example, should child support be included in the general family budget, or should it be spent only for the children? The stepfamily's economic structure may reflect an "incomplete state of the merger." People who shared financial responsibilities with former spouses may now face a different reality. Consider one couple: married for seven months, the wife does not know how much her husband earns, how much and where he invests additional capital, which family members are named as his insurance beneficiaries, or how his will reads.

While all the families interviewed are middle class, seven have less financial flexibility. They do not have significant savings to draw from or families to rely upon. These stepfamilies pool available resources for the well-being of the entire household. Issues such as children's future inheritances are not of immediate concern. One man's statement illustrates the complexity of having to cope with old and new financial obligations.

> *I have a lot of expenses—lawyer's fees, custody payments, my car is falling apart. I can't seem to pull my own weight in this new household. Joan [his new wife] resents that, and it causes a lot of strain between us.*

> *If I could hold up a bank tomorrow, I'd consider it. Don't think that I haven't thought about it.*

Issues of income distribution, property, and inheritance rights are of major concern to the nine families with greater financial resources—those with significant savings or inherited money. These families often reported their use of prenuptial agreements and wills with clearly spelled out ownership of assets. Of these nine more affluent families, five use money to starkly differentiate biological relationships. One stepchild reports on the stress that can develop when one partner and one set of children are more affluent than the other:

> *My stepmother and her kids are well off, and that creates a lot of conflict—within me, mostly. Because, for example, my stepsister has been to Europe three times and gets everything she wants. I resent having had to work from the time I was fifteen, just to survive! My stepmother doesn't understand why I have so many clothes, when I'm so hard-pressed for money. Well, clothes are important to me, so I'll work hard for a nice wardrobe. But I get a lot of digs in there about how I ought to be saving instead of spending.*

The other four of these nine more affluent families distribute their assets so that current income is pooled but wills provide for the children differentially, acknowledging financial ties to biological heirs.

Stepfamily members tend to look closely at who gives gifts and who receives them. Among grandparents, recognition of the stepfamily (or lack of it) may be reflected in their distribution of resources or gifts. Most grandparents interviewed report that they give gifts to all their grandchildren, stepgrandchildren included, but that their wills recognize only their biological heirs. Most stepfamilies in this sample retain loyalty to biological inheritance patterns but with a sharing of resources for everyday living.

Nuclear or Extended Family: Nonpermeable or Permeable Boundaries

To be included in this study, a household must consist of a parent, a stepparent, children, and stepchildren. This stepfamily may also be part of a chain of households, which can include other parents and other children. The existence of multiple parents and extended kin demands the development of rules to regulate their access to one another. Starting with custodial arrangements for children, the flow of traffic across several households is designed. In some cases, ex-spouses deny themselves or are denied access to their children by their previous mates. Some families experience a loss of kin as a consequence of divorce. Many divorced couples are, however, keeping themselves available to one another for the child-rearing process (Ahrons, 1980). A new extended stepfamily structure is developing to serve the needs of these people, and with it, a new family ideology is evolving. The form that child care sharing takes differs from family to family. One household includes "her" children all the time and "his" half the time. Another has "his" children spending weekends. Still another household divides their time so that they have custodial care for each parent's children during the same portion of the week: All children are "home" half the week and the house is empty of all children for the other half. The members of this family express satisfaction with the arrangement. The adults are pleased to have time which allows for their conjugal relationship, as well as personal time for career interests. The children feel that the arrangement is fair to all their parents, and they enjoy spending time with their stepsiblings.

Some stepfamilies report an air of excitement, particularly when members acquire steprelationships that they like. One thirteen-year-old girl was pleased to gain a new sister of the same age. They go to school together, have the same friends, and share secrets. After years of living with a single parent who was preoccupied with working and dating, this girl has gained a sister-friend with whom she could be close. A boy of seventeen talked of the positive experience of acquiring new siblings:

Until my dad remarried, all I had was my younger brother—then all of a sudden here comes four new people! It was great! I really looked up to my oldest stepbrother. I idolized him. It was good that we became so close because when my dad became involved with Greta (his new wife), he had little time for me. So, at least, I had somebody I could turn to.

Many of the children in this sample were ready to give up the isolation of nuclear family or single-parent households for the benefit of acquiring stepsiblings. A child might have great difficulty adjusting to his/her new stepparent, but may thoroughly enjoy his/her stepsiblings. The stepfamily is best understood, therefore, as a series of subsystems: at the conjugal level, the children's level, and between the two levels (Minuchin, 1974; Keshet, 1980). When analyzed in this way, certain relationships can be understood to function successfully, while others may be less successful.

The stepfamily is less autonomous and more interlinked with other households than is the nuclear family. Stepfamilies that range across several households may have permeable boundaries such that information can flow between units (Walker and Messinger, 1979). The shift to permeable boundaries, and the stress it may cause, is described by one woman:

There just has to be more awareness because there are so many different components inside and outside the house. Many a night we did not get to bed until two o'clock in the morning because there were so many crises. My first husband would pull something on one of the kids that I didn't agree with—or one of the kids would play him against us. Those were the bad days.

Figure 1 is an example of an extended stepfamily. Each household is outlined such that the children's overlapping memberships are illustrated.

In the adult subsystem, the Cooper/Stone household has boundaries that clearly separate it from the Miller/Stone or Cooper/Ross households. Becky and Charlie, former spouses, have few claims on each other. Becky barely knows Charlie's wife, and has no desire to share confidences with adults in either of these other households. Yet her life is intimately connected to them through their children, in a shared parental subsystem.

In the children's subsystem, the overlapping memberships are evident. Resources from several households are available to the children in the Miller/Stone-Cooper/Stone intersection, as Becky, mother of the Stone children, illustrates:

> *Charlie (Stone) was always an absentee father. He sees the kids when he's in town. The children have added resources now that he's married again. I may not like it, but I must admit that the kids enjoy Charlie's new family. From what I can gather, they get along well with his new wife.*

Peter Stone says his life is better because of his extended family. He talks of a forthcoming trip with enthusiasm:

> *My dad is married to a woman named Dorothy. I see her at holidays when I visit down in Florida. Anyway, Dorothy's parents also come to Florida on holidays. They're really good people, and they've invited me to visit them when they live in California. They said I could stay as long as I like. I'm going to take advantage of this opportunity—planning to go next summer.*

The Miller/Stone-Cooper/Stone overlapping memberships permit traffic across family boundaries. Each household is linked with the other, clearly operating less autonomously than nuclear units. Eric Stone's relationship to his biological father, Charlie, is very close, though they see each other only sporadically. He is, in fact, the son slated to go into Charlie's business. Feelings of competitiveness or animosity between Charlie and Paul Cooper are kept to a minimum. There is a sense of collaboration between them, and Charlie is grateful that Paul has been such a conscientious "parent" to his sons. Paul described a meeting between them that occurred at Peter's high school graduation:

> *One of the nicest things that ever happened to me was that Charlie thanked me for what I have done for his kids. And, coming from a guy who doesn't usually give compliments, I felt terrific! Well, we've all worked hard, in our own ways—and we agree that the kids turned out well.*

The Miller/Stone-Cooper/Stone extended family structure has boundaries which allow for the sharing of resources. Paul Cooper said:

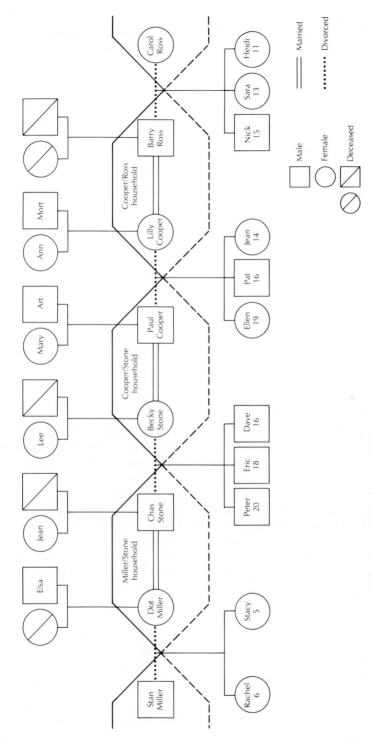

FIGURE 1 The Miller-Stone-Cooper-Ross Extended Structure

> When Charlie's in town, he comes to the house and visits. He's welcome here, and why not? His kids live here!

In contrast, the Cooper/Stone-Cooper/Ross intersecting boundaries are less permeable; at times, nonpermeable. Parents never exchange information about children. Lilly Cooper-Ross is not welcome in the Cooper/Stone home. When she comes to pick up her children, she honks her horn from the street. The animosity between Paul Cooper and his former wife, Lilly, had its culmination in a bitter court fight for full-time custody of the Cooper children during which Paul and his current wife, Becky, negated Lilly's parental role. At the time of the suit, the Cooper children were in collusion with their father and stepmother. Pat remembers the period with feelings of remorse:

> I suppose we needed more of a mother than mom was able to be. It wasn't that she didn't want to spend more time with us. I know that now. We just didn't realize that she worked full time during the week and we saw her only at night when she was exhausted and irritable. On weekends, we stayed with dad and Becky. And because dad had free time on the weekends, we had a better deal with dad. So we wanted to live with him.

The schism between the Coopers and Lilly Ross has intensified their children's conflict over divided loyalties and has denied them access to her and the resources of her new stepfamily. Indeed, though the Stone children have close and loving ties to their Cooper stepsiblings with whom they live, they scarcely know Lilly's stepchildren.

The Miller/Stone-Cooper/Ross extended constellation demonstrates how stepfamilies can organize in two different ways. The family intersection on one side has permeable boundaries, with information and resources flowing. The children easily move between households, although the adults maintain distance. On the other hand, the second family intersection has boundaries that are less permeable. The resources of the Cooper/Ross household and their associated kin are less available.

For children, dual-family membership means that they must learn to live in two systems. In one family, watching TV late at night may be acceptable, while in another, TV viewing may be strictly limited. A child described this difference, saying, "I have to figure out what I can do and cannot do in each house." Dual-family living gives the child a comparison in lifestyles, and, at least for some, an opportunity to think critically. One ten-year-old boy assessed his two homes in this way:

> My dad always gets so angry. I don't know why, he's supposed to be a grown-up. My mom, in my other house, will be nicer if I do something wrong. She won't just yell—she'll ask me to explain why it happened. Now my stepmother, she doesn't know how to deal with me. If I ask her for something, she'll say, "Ask your father." Really, if they're married now, I think I should get an answer from her.

Stepfamily members reported that parenting children from dual households calls for cooperation of both adults in the stepfamily—or, even more desirable, the collaboration of all adults between households.

Role Changes

Roles between men and women or between children and adults are prescribed in the nuclear family ideology, whereas stepfamily members say they must be more flexible and design roles appropriate to their lives. From this study, it appears that men have more freedom to carve out a variety of flexible roles with their stepchildren than do women. Perhaps because the role of the nurturing father has been more marginal in traditional families, men can experiment with the stepfather role. One man said: "I'm just a boarder in the house." Still another says: "I want to be a father to my stepson. He can have two fathers. There's no law against that."

Women show less flexibility in their expectations of relationships with their stepchildren. Repeatedly, many women in the sample value their parental function as paramount, investing heavily in its success. This leads to a sense of frustration and fear of failure when there is difficulty in the relationship, as one woman's statement shows:

I want to be her mother. I am fighting, bleeding to be her mother. But what I can't be is her mother. Little things hurt me. On her college application form, she filled in my name but added "step" to the word "mother." I cried for the rest of the day.

Men and women in this sample report role changes in their new marriages. Men share in household and parenting tasks, and women expect more participation from them than from previous husbands. Child rearing is less strictly the woman's role. Generally, men and women feel obliged to manage their "own" children. When asked how his new family differed from his first, one man said:

It's different, but it's hard to say how. There's a little bit of distance between me and Julie (his current wife) that wasn't there in my relationship to my former wife. When Lynn and I were together, if I was busy, it was automatic that she would take care of the kids, allowing me to do my thing. With Julie we have to negotiate it more.

STEPFAMILIES IN THE LARGER COMMUNITY

Evidence from this and other studies indicates that the absence of institutional norms impeded stepfamily development (Cherlin, 1978). Generally, the shift from nuclear to stepfamily behavior and ideology occurs without benefit of education, little contact with other stepfamilies, and almost no help from established institutions. For example, many adults in the sample could identify several single-parent households, but only three couples could identify other stepfamilies known to them, with whom, presumably, they could share experiences and provide mutual support, but did not. Several of the stepfamilies are linked together through remarriage and some interaction among parents does occur, although limited. Children report contact with other stepfamilies through their stepfamily linkages and through school and social affiliations.

Because family privacy is a powerful guide for behavior, schools are often hesitant to inquire about specifics, such as which parent school reports should be sent to or who should be invited to school conferences. Of the 16 families, 10 send one or more of their children to private schools, and 3 to parochial schools, often at a considerable financial sacrifice. Because private and parochial schools are less tied to neighborhoods, ex-spouses who share child care but who live at a distance from one another find these schools to be an advantage. They do not wish their children to be connected only to one neighborhood. Private schools are also chosen because parents believe that their children, disrupted by the changes in their lives, require more shelter and support than can be offered in public schools. One man, for example, connected his son's difficulty in learning to read to the dissolution of his first marriage. The boy experienced learning and social problems for several years, and now in the fifth grade, he is just beginning to read with fluency. The father reports, however, that private school tuition is causing financial stress for the entire family.

Several families complained about the absence of literature to guide them in the development of new rules for living. Many were surprised to learn that their family form is of interest to the academic community, that "the blended family" or the "reconstituted family" are terms being used to describe them. At the tail end of the data-gathering period of this study, several magazine articles (for example, see Norman, 1980) were published about stepfamily life, and people who read them commented on their usefulness. Several families referred to a popular TV program called *The Brady Bunch,* which was a favorite among many of the children in the study. As one woman said, "My kids were constantly trying to live up to the *Brady Bunch* mystique of fun and games. It didn't work that way, but it was the only thing they could identify with."

Only 5 of the 16 families report active involvement in their religious communities, and these report having received little religious counsel in formulating guidelines for stepfamily living. However, the individuals who actively participated in their religious communities during their marital transitions reported that the support they received through their churches and synagogues provided a stabilizing influence during those periods.

Counseling has been the one institutionalized means of support that many families have received—either during their marital transitions or in their stepfamilies. Of the families in this sample, 12 have had counseling at some point. On the whole, therapists were regarded positively. When old behaviors did not work and troublesome symptoms appeared, families sought help from the therapeutic community from whom they feel they found support in their search for alternative behavior.

CONCLUSION

Each of the families sampled in this study made the shift to stepfamily living without institutionalized norms and little education, resulting in stress. Previous nuclear family living taught them to expect romantic love, a private and autonomous life style, and an easily acquired sense of family identity. Some families resisted the change, trying—and to some extent, succeeding—to maintain a nuclear family lifestyle, with its sharply defined household boundaries. Others, however, designed their behavior to fit the new extended structure—stretching, as it does, across several households, with its more public and interdependent functioning. Those parents who kept themselves available to each other for the child-rearing process after divorce and remarriage to new partners permitted information to flow across boundaries—so that resources of available kin remained accessible to their children. All families included in the study invented, at least to some degree, new rules for behavior in keeping with their new family structure. Stepfamily members have the opportunity to design their lives such that they use rules from the nuclear family ideology that work and combine them with rules specific to an emerging stepfamily ideology. Stress diminishes if and when stepfamilies make this ideological adaptation.

REFERENCES

Ahrons, C. R. (1980) "Redefining the divorced family: a conceptual framework." *Social Work* 25, 6: 437–441.

Aries, P. (1962) *Centuries of Childhood*. New York: Knopf.

Berger, P. and H. Kellner (1964) "Marriage and the construction of reality," pp. 49–72 in H. P. Dreitzel (ed.) *Recent Sociology*. Volume 2. New York: Macmillan.

Bohannon, P. (1971) "Divorce chains, households of remarriage, and multiple divorcers," in P. Bohannon (ed.) *Divorce and After*. Garden City, NY: Doubleday.

Bott, E. (1975) Family and Social Network. New York: Macmillan.

Cherlin, A. (1978) "Remarriage as an incomplete institution." *Amer. J. of Sociology* 84, 3: 634–649.

Feldman, H. and M. Feldman (1975) "The family life cycle: some suggestions for recycling." *J. of Marriage and the Family*. 37, 2: 277–283.

Furstenberg, F. (1979) "Recycling the family: perspectives for a neglected family form." *Marriage and Family Rev.* 2 (Fall): 12–22.

Glick, P. (1980) "Remarriage: some recent changes and variation." *J. of Family Issues* 1, 4: 455–478.

——— (1979) "Future American families." *Washington COFO Memo* 2 (Summer/Fall): 2–5.

——— (1977) "Updating the life cycle of the family." *J. of Marriage and the Family* 39, 1: 5–13.

Keshet, J. K. (1980) "From separation to stepfamily: a subsystem analysis." *J. of Family Issues* 1, 4: 517–532.

Lasch, C. (1977) *Haven in a Heartless World: The Family Besieged*. New York: Basic Books.

Lee, G. R. (1980) "Kinship in the seventies: a decade review of research and theory." *J. of Marriage and the Family* 42, 4: 923–934.

Lewis, R. A., and J. H. Pleck (1979) "Special issue on men's roles in the family." *Family Coordinator* 28, 4.

Minuchin, S. (1974) *Families and Family Therapy*. Cambridge, MA: Harvard Univ. Press.

Norman, M. (1980) "The new extended family." *N.Y. Times,* November 23.

Norton, A. J., and P. C. Glick (1976) "Marital instability: past, present, and future." *J. of Social Issues* 32, 1: 5–20.

Sussman, M., and L. Burchinal (1962) "Kin family network: unheralded structure in current conceptualizations for family functioning." *J. of Marriage and Family Living* 24: 231–240.

Visher, E., and J. Visher (1979) *Stepfamilies: A Guide to Working with Stepparents and Stepchildren*. New York: Brunner/Mazel.

Walker, K., and L. Messinger (1979) "Remarriage after divorce: dissolution and reconstruction of family boundaries." *Family Process* 18, 2: 185–192.

ARTICLE 33
Children in Stepfamilies

MARILYN IHINGER-TALLMAN
AND KAY PASLEY

When divorce occurs, who gets custody of the children? Does joint custody work? What are the consequences of remarriage for children? How is their well-being affected by living in stepfamilies? What effect do children have on remarriages? Why is the divorce rate higher in remarriages when stepchildren are present? This article provides an overview of the research regarding these questions, pointing out the diverse consequences of custody arrangements and living in reconstituted families.

> *Once there was a gentleman who married, for his second wife, the proudest and haughtiest woman ever seen. By her former husband she had two daughters who were exactly like her. Her new husband had a daughter, too, by an earlier marriage, but this child was the sweetest and best creature one could imagine.*
>
> *As soon as the wedding ceremony was over, the wife began to show her true nature. She could not bear it that her husband's pretty daughter with all her goodness made her own daughters appear the more hateful. She began to use her for the meanest housework. She ordered her to scour the pots and to scrub the tables and the floors. She gave her a wretched straw pallet for a bed in the garret while her own daughters lay below upon soft new beds and had full length mirrors in which to admire themselves.*

Marilyn Ihinger-Tallman and Kay Pasley, "Children in Stepfamilies." In *Remarriage* (Newbury Park, Calif.: Sage, 1987) pp. 78–96. Copyright 1987 by Sage Publications Inc. Reprinted by permission of Sage Publications, Inc.

The poor girl bore all this with patience and dared not tell her father, for she saw that he was ruled completely by his new wife . . .
—Cinderella

WHEN FOLK TALES about mistreated stepchildren such as Cinderella were first told, being a stepchild was not an uncommon event. . . . Even though the current remarriage rate is similar to the earlier one, a primary difference is that most remarriages today follow first marriages that were ended by divorce instead of death. Thus one of the major differences that distinguishes stepchildren of the past from those of the present is the way the majority of children "lose" their biological parent. This is reflected in the term *step*, which originally meant orphan. The stories of Cinderella, Snow White, and Hansel and Gretel are more likely the first source of knowledge about being a stepchild for children today, rather than actual experience. Nevertheless, a large minority of today's children have a reasonable probability of experiencing stepfamily life firsthand. In 1980 it was estimated that there were 2.3 million households with stepparents who were raising stepchildren (Cherlin and McCarthy, 1985). Estimates of the probability of experiencing a parental divorce are about 33% (Glick, 1984). Sandra Hofferth (1985) estimates that 64% of white children and 89% of black children will live at some point in their lives in a single-parent household by the time they reach the age of 17. Of these, more than half will gain a stepparent when the mother or father with whom they reside remarries. This [article] explores the effects on children of living in a stepfamily, beginning with a discussion of child custody practices.

CUSTODY DECISIONS AND PRACTICES

Child custody practices have changed over the past 150 years, from a "parental rights" premise to a "tender years" doctrine to a "best interests of the child" policy. The parental rights premise regarded children as the property of their father, whereas the tender years doctrine entrusted the care of (young) children to their mother. The doctrine of best interests of the child has translated into an equal rights doctrine, wherein both parents have equal rights and responsibilities for minor children and neither parent's share is superior. This latter ruling is better known as joint custody.

Father Rights

From Roman law into nineteenth-century England and America, the father's right to the custody of his children was almost absolute. Under common law children were considered to be a father's property. Under his guardianship children were entitled to support, education, and religious training, and he was entitled to their labor and service (Derdeyn, 1976). The link between provision of support and custody is illustrated with this excerpt from an 1891 law text: "As the first duty to support the child rests on the father, he is prima facie and before all others . . . entitled to the custody" (Bishop, 1891: 453). This point is illustrated again by an 1840 custody decision that "a positive unfitness in the father must be shown before children can be withheld or withdrawn from his charge" (Ahrenfeldt v. Ahrenfeldt, 1840: 501). Mothers were not viewed as fit guardians since they were seen as needing protection themselves.

Only gradually, with the advent of the industrial revolution and the social changes that accompanied it, did mothers begin to gain custody rights. Andre Derdeyn (1976: 1371) describes the changes this way:

> Women began to vote, to own property in their own right, and to be gainfully employed in great numbers. At the same time, the country's new interest in children began to be manifested by the development of public education, children's aid societies . . . and child labor laws. . . . Not only did women start to develop more rights and more economic competence, but society, influenced by early interest in child development, stressed the importance of maternal care.

Mothers first won custody of very young children. Such custody was seen as a temporary exemption to the rule. Custody was awarded to the mothers of infants or toddlers (presumably those who were still nursing), and custody reverted to fathers when children reached the age of four, or sometimes age seven. Both girls and boys, but especially the latter, were given back to the care and custody of their fathers, who were viewed as the proper persons to administer discipline and moral guidance to children.

Mother Custody

In the early twentieth century, mothers were increasingly awarded custody under the principle of the "tender years" doctrine. This doctrine held that the well-being of children was enhanced if they were kept in their mother's care. Several factors influenced this change. Derdeyn (1976: 1372) summarizes these as follows:

> In addition to women's generally increasing rights and economic capability, child support from former spouses became more consistently available . . . mother's right to custody was a moral one based on a developing cultural assumption that the woman was better suited to caring for children.

Over time the policy of mother custody was eventually given preference. By 1960 mothers were given custody in over 90% of contested cases (Derdeyn, 1976), an estimate that prevails today.

The phrase "best interests of the child" was introduced into state statute in 1925. Here the intention was the child's best interest as the first criterion for placement. This policy was intended to shift the focus away from the conflicting parents in order to protect the child. It resulted in an inclination or "presumption for" maternal custody. Thus until about 1970 mother custody was the preferred placement (Luepnitz, 1982). As the struggle for social equality pervaded American society, the legal climate also was changing. "Between 1969 and 1975 nine states passed legislation explicitly stipulating that the sex of the parent should not be a factor in determining custody" (Weitzman, 1985: 466).

Joint Custody

In 1980 California became the first state to adopt a joint custody preference. Law was established to maintain the child's ties to both parents. Joint custody is variously called shared custody, cocustody, and coparenting. California's policy also encourages parents to work out their own custody arrangements; if they need assistance because of irreconcilable differences there are court affiliated mediators and counselors to help. The doctrine has proved to be popular. According to Lenore Weitzman (1985), by 1985 at least some form of joint custody legislation had been adopted in 30 states. She summarizes four alternative forms of joint custody legislation:

(1) *Joint custody as an option*. This is the least specific of joint custody forms, and it permits the court to order joint custody for parents who have not requested it.
(2) *Joint custody when parents agree*. This statute permits joint custody only when both parents request it. According to Weitzman, these laws follow the growing consensus that the agreement to the parties is a prerequisite for making joint custody work.
(3) *Joint custody at one party's request*. This policy permits the judge to award joint custody when only one parent requests it. Weitzman feels this can be detrimental to children because it places children at the center of their parent's conflict.
(4) *Joint custody preference or presumption*. These are the most coercive forms of joint custody because they require judges to give preference to joint custody. Joint custody presumption is the strongest of the two, since it assumes that joint custody is in the child's best interests. In order to overcome this presumption, a parent is required to prove that joint custody would be detrimental to the child. In these cases sole custody is the exception and requires special justification.

In actuality, the way in which joint custody is translated into daily living arrangements varies considerably. One study of 50 divorced couples reported that no two joint arrangements were alike, but four general patterns emerged: (a) children split the day between two homes; (b) children spent varying amounts of time during the week between two homes; (c) children split the year living in two homes (usually the summer and one or two major holidays in one home and the rest of the time with the other parent); and (d) children lived alternate years in two homes (Luepnitz, 1982). These alternatives all center on joint *physical* custody. *Legal* custody means the "child's legal custodian is responsible for the education and welfare of a child under 18; he or she may control the religious training the child is or is not taught, and has the power to authorize medical care for the child" (Weitzman, 1985: 227). Legal custody does not specify who the child lives with. Joint legal custody means that both parents have the right to be involved in making important decisions about the child's upbringing, schooling, religious training, health care, and so on.

Accurate reporting on a child's custodial/living arrangements involves an awkward terminology. That is, the customary term to describe a child's living situation would be to say he or she is in a mother-custody or father-custody home. However, that term is not accurate if the child's biological parents have joint legal custody but the physical custody of the child is with the mother. To eliminate inaccurate implications, we use the term *residential* to mean living arrangements, and *custody* to mean the child's legal custodial situation. Unfortunately, the consequence of this precision is a sometimes cumbersome phrasing.

An excellent study by Weitzman (1985) shows that the California no-fault divorce legislation did not result in any significant increases in father requests for child custody. In fact, even the new joint custody law has effected little change in custody awards. Weitzman (1985: 250) suggests that what has occurred in California is a change in labeling:

> Arrangements that would have been called "liberal visitation" before 1980, under the old law, are now called "joint custody." The shift may have important psychological consequences for fathers who can now define themselves as joint parents after divorce, but it has not changed the day-to-day arrangements for the care of most children.

The Ideal versus the Real: Joint Custody versus Visiting

One of the concerns of family scholars as well as those in the helping professions is the large number of children who are growing up without the continued involvement of their biological father. Information on the amount of child-father contact after divorce overwhelmingly confirms that, over time, father involvement diminishes in the majority of cases. One of the earliest studies of divorce documented this tendency (Goode, 1965), and researchers have continued to affirm it. E. Mavis Hetherington and Martha and Roger Cox (1976) conducted a two-year longitudinal study of children of divorce and found that father-child contact decreased steadily over time. A recent national study found that nearly 50% of the children in the study had not seen their nonresidential parent in the past five years. Of those children who had visited this parent in the past five years, 20% had not seen him or her in the past year. Only 16% of these children saw their absent parent an average of once a week (Furstenberg et al., 1983). Furstenberg and Spanier's (1984) study of Pennsylvania remarried couples supports the findings of other studies, again suggesting that father-child contact decreases over time. Their data also suggested that contact was reduced if a remarriage took place. When neither parent was married, two-thirds of the nonresidential parents visited with their children at least a few times a month. When one of the partners was married, the proportion dropped to 40%. When both parents had remarried the proportion who visited their children a few times a month dropped further to 34%.

Similar findings are reported by Walter Tropf (1984) in a study of 101 divorced fathers. Here again visitation decreased after divorce, decreased more after the father's remarriage, and still more after the remarriage of the ex-wife. Tropf noted, however, that although frequency dropped after remarriage, duration of visits increased: Children visited less frequently but stayed for longer visits. Tropf acknowledged that a decrease in visiting frequency did not necessarily denote a decline in father's interest or involvement. "The findings on phone calls, plus the increase in visiting length accompanying the decline in frequency, indicate a reordering of roles" (1984: 70). However, in this study an increasing number of fathers ceased contact with their children altogether: 12% never visited their children after the divorce. After their own remarriage, 23% ceased visitation, and 31% did so after the remarriage of their ex-wife.

Weitzman's (1985) California study showed the same gradual decrease in contact between nonresidential fathers and their children. What's more, California court records show that 23% of fathers did not see their children at all after the divorce.

In contrast to the general trends, one study that examined the behavior of parents who held joint legal custody found a higher rate of involvement with children. In her study of 41 joint custody families, Ahrons (1981) found that about two-thirds of the nonresidential parents saw their children at least once a week or more.

Most studies of nonresidential mothers report that visitation is both more regular and more frequent than nonresidential father visitation. In the Furstenberg and Spanier study reported earlier, 86% of the children who did not live with their biological mothers had contact with them in the past year. Only 48% of children with nonresidential fathers had such contact. Of nonresidential mothers, 31% saw their children at least once a week compared to 16% of nonresidential fathers.

We must interpret the figures relating to mother-visiting with some caution, however, since in most studies the number of nonresidential mothers is quite small (there were only 35 visiting mothers in the Furstenberg and Spanier study). However, the trends are consistent. Mothers visit their nonresidential children more frequently than fathers.

We should note that in some studies the high rate of father involvement may be affected by the way the samples were selected. The Ahrons study selected samples in order to examine family interaction in a binuclear family. Thus families included in the study held joint legal custody. An incentive to cooperate with a study of mother custody families was built into a study conducted by clinicians Judith Wallerstein and Joan Kelly (1980). These researchers found a high degree of father contact after divorce. This may have been because the researchers offered the study families a six-week prevention program designed to help children and adolescents cope with divorce in exchange for their participation (Kelly, 1981).

Age of children and geographic distance are said to influence visitation. The national study designed by Furstenberg, Peterson, and Zill that was reported on earlier, however, found that sex and age of child did not seem to affect contact with father. Residential closeness was a salient factor. Weekly contact was reduced by half when the father lived over an hour's drive from the child. However, visitation rates of "once a month or more" were not affected by geographic distance (Furstenberg et al., 1983). It seems that geographic closeness facilitates visitation, but does not determine it. Tropf (1984) examined the differences in frequency of visitation of fathers living within 150 miles of the child and those living farther away. As reported earlier, he found that frequency of visitation decreased still further upon an ex-wife's remarriage when fathers lived within 150 miles. A similar, but more dramatic, pattern of decreased visitation occurred when the father lived more than 150 miles away.

The evidence is clear that the marital status of one or both former spouses influences the frequency of contact between children and their nonresidential parent in a negative way. There also is a connection between visitation, remarriage, and financial support of children. Furstenberg et al. (1983) found that fathers who paid some child support were more likely to see their children on a regular basis than fathers who did not. Tropf (1984) found that requests for additional support were more likely met if the father had remarried, but were reduced if his ex-wife remarried.

These findings may be explained in several ways. Remarriage means that energy, attention, and resources must be divided among prior and current families. Redirecting resources to a new family means there is less for members of the prior family, children included. Should the remarriage also include children, the demands on resources multiply. Also, a new spouse may not encourage the continued contact with a former spouse and children, seeing such contact as a constant reminder of the past. There is a strong desire to "put the past behind us" among remarried couples (Visher and Visher, 1979). Some ex-spouses engage in conflict over support payments, visitation, child-rearing practice, and so forth. Poor relations between former-spouses can readily discourage and dishearten fathers' attempts to maintain a relationship with their children (Fox, 1985). Further, the visits between fathers and their children can be painful due in part to their intensity, brevity, and insufficiency. Guilt feelings on the part of the father may result. When negative feelings accompany or follow visitation, it is likely that contact will decrease.

The other half of the binuclear family, residential mothers, also report problems. They say that children are unruly and emotionally drained after visiting their nonresidential fathers (Weiss, 1979). They complain that the father commonly fails to enforce rules and offers only "good times" instead of enforcing the rules necessary for ordinary child rearing. Visitation sometimes means seeing a former spouse when one would prefer not to have that contact. Consciously or unconsciously, mothers may act in ways to disrupt or discourage continued contact.

Custody and Residence Shifting

There is no precise information on the number of children whose legal custody changes or who shift their residence from one parent's home to another's, or on why these changes are made. Some studies offer limited information regarding the prevalence of such shifts. One noteworthy characteristic associated with children's shift of residence is that such changes do not necessarily involve all children in the family. One or more children may continue to live with one parent while another child moves in with the other parent. In a study of 517 mothers without custody Geoffrey Greif (1986) reported 61% of the mothers had physical custody when the marriage ended, but subsequently lost it or gave it up. Of these mothers 26% had split physical custody, with at least one child under age 18 living with them. In another study Greif (1985) found that 19.6% of his father-custody sample (N = 1136) had children living with them because their former wife could no longer handle them. Similar estimates are suggested by Furstenberg and Spanier (1984) who reported that almost 20% of the Centre County, Pennsylvania, respondents experienced a change in custody arrangements. Julie Fulton (1979) reported a 33% shift rate in her study of Minnesota divorces. In a study of single-parent fathers, Barbara Risman (1986) reported that among 141 fathers, 62% said they had little choice in assuming responsibility for the care of their children because their wives had deserted, died, or refused the responsibility. A total of 18% had negotiated for custody while they were still married, and 20% had obtained custody by legal action against the wishes of their wives.

Overall, fathers are unlikely to obtain sole custody, regardless of the life conditions of the mother. Fathers are somewhat more likely to have custody of all children if their former partners have remarried. They are also more likely to gain custody if all children in the family are boys, and least likely to have custody if all children are girls. Finally, it is estimated that about half of the fathers with custody of any children have custody of only part of the sibling group, and about half have custody of all the children in the family (Spanier and Glick, 1981).

Many times, a change in residence occurs several years after an initial custody award. The reasons for these changes are not straightforward and may not always be for the good of the child. Behavior may be motivated by the wish to disrupt the new marriage of an ex-spouse, or a new stepmother may have a "rescue fantasy" and wish to provide better mothering for her stepchildren than she perceives their biological mother provides. Other reasons for child shifting include illness in a custodial parent, a desire on the part of children to move, a mother's desire to further her education or career that involves a large time commitment, or a mother's feeling that she cannot handle a particular child.

The following statements serve to illustrate the reactions of three parents about child shifting. First, a mother's perspective on her child's move to his father's home, followed by the comments of two fathers about their children's moves.

(Mother, age 27, homemaker, married 6 years): One of the biggest problems seems to be the children. Accepting the stepparent. Once you have convinced the child that the stepparent does not wish to take the place of the real parent, tension eases and the child begins to love the stepparent for himself. Often children of this age don't understand that they can feel love for a stepparent without losing the love of his real parent. This was a serious problem with our oldest boy until recently. He has been living with his real father for 2 months and is ready to return home. Now he is secure about his feelings for his real father and stepfather. We think this separation will ultimately bring us closer together and now we can stay together where we now *all* want to be. This was the hardest thing we had to do, but we felt we had to "let him go before we could bring him back."

(Father, age 41, salesman, married 5½ years): I am very pleased with my marriage. My two younger children lived with us by choice for a period of time, the girl returned to her mother by choice after 9 months, the boy by consensus after 16 months. My wife and I are both in career situations and lacked the time to supervise properly. The children brought problems into our marriage and did not respond to *our* expectations. We both made our best effort to have a family that worked well, but did not have available adequate supervision. I was raised by a stepfather who was without a doubt the best, but I never realized it until I was an adult, and stepchildren like stepparents can be very cruel and very cold with very little effort.

(Father, age 37, carpet cleaner, married 4 years): We have a total of 7 children in our marriage. Four from my wife and three from myself. Not all these children get along super but for the most part are doing OK together. There are two children who don't live with us anymore. One needed to be with her mother. Seems to be OK. The other ran away. Couldn't handle her own problems. Nine people together from a marriage and most of them benefiting from the union.

CONSEQUENCES OF REMARRIAGE FOR CHILDREN

The Adjustment of Children to Parental Remarriage

Empirical findings suggest that the age of the child at the time of parental divorce and remarriage, sex of the child, and sex of the stepparent are important factors for understanding and predicting the influence of family change on children.

A few studies have investigated the relationship between age of child and children's adjustment to parental remarriage. Wallerstein and Kelly's (1980) study mentioned earlier suggests that school-aged children are particularly vulnerable to the stress associated with the remarriage of a residential parent. Their findings are supported by others (Rosenberg, 1965; Kaplan and Pokorny, 1971). Parental remarriage that occurs early in the child's life (before age five) has been found to have positive effects on the child's I.Q. and school performance.

Early studies generally neglected to study sex differences, but more recent research has consistently found that boys in stepfamilies have fewer adjustment problems and less negative outcomes than do girls. Several studies have reported that girls have more difficulty in their relationship with their stepparents than do boys, particularly with stepmothers (Clingempeel and Segal, 1986; Peterson and Zill, 1986). Lucile Duberman (1975) reported that stepmothers and stepdaughters have more problematic relationships than stepfathers and stepsons.

In a study asking adolescent members of stepfamilies about stressful aspects of stepfamily life, Lutz (1983) found boys with stepfathers reported less stress associated with living in a stepfamily than did girls. Clingempeel and Segal's (1986) recent study emphasizes the association between good relations in stepfamilies and psychological adjustment. They found that the more positive this relationship was (between stepmother and stepchild) the better the psychological adjustment. This finding was particularly pronounced for girls.

It has been suggested that the stepparent-stepchild relation may be influenced by the quality of the marital relationship. In Brand and Clingempeel's (1985) study, remarried mothers with good marital adjustment had daughters who reported less positive relationships with their stepfathers. In stepmother families, the more positive the stepmother's marital adjustment, the less positive their relationship with their stepdaughter. This finding was not true for stepmothers with stepsons.

Although the current empirical evidence suggests that girls in stepfamilies may be at greater "risk" than boys, this conclusion should be considered with caution. The majority of these studies have used small, middle-class, Caucasian samples. However, one study with a large, random sample of respondents did affirm these findings (Peterson and Zill, 1986). Still, more studies are needed before we can trust this finding about sex differences.

Academic Achievement and Cognitive Functioning

Several studies have examined the influence of remarriage on the academic performance and/or cognitive functioning of children. Four studies concur that being reared in a stepparent family does not negatively influence either the academic achievement or the cognitive functioning of children. For example, no differences were found in school grades for children reared in stepfamilies compared to those reared in first families (Bohannan and Yahraes, 1979). John Santrock's (1972) study reported similar findings in a sample of grade school children. I.Q. and achievement scores were the same for boys living with stepfathers and those living with biological fathers. Boys living with stepfathers also were found to have higher I.Q. and achievement scores than boys living in single-parent households. Living with a stepfather, however, did not have the same effects for girls in Santrock's study. Girls in stepfather families performed significantly lower on achievement tests than girls in intact first families. There were no differences in girls' performance when comparing girls in stepfather families and girls in single-parent families.

Self-Esteem, Self-Confidence, and Personality Variables

A child's sense of "self" has been a popular topic of investigation in stepfamily research. The majority of studies found no differences in self-concept and self-image between children reared in first families, single-parent households, and stepparent families. Two studies found that children reared in stepfamilies had lower self-images than children reared in first families. Of these two, only one strongly demonstrated that children in stepfamilies had lower self-images. The other found self-esteem was negative only if parental remarriage had occurred when the child was older than age eight. Overall, these studies have failed to consider the variety of factors beyond family structure that likely influence self-esteem; factors such as family size, length of time in remarriage, and so on.

Psychological Functioning

Many researchers have been interested in studying the psychological functioning of children in stepfamilies. However, comparing the findings from one study with those of another is difficult because researchers have measured psychological functioning in a variety of ways. We believe the use of diverse measures and methods contributes to the conflicting findings.

Harvey Oshman and Martin Manosevitz (1976) found that males in father-present families (both first and step-) had a higher psychological functioning than males in father-absent families. One characteristic of this study was that the males had lived in their stepfather families for several years, suggesting that length of time in a stepfamily might be an important mediator of any possible negative effects of remarriage on boys.

Most studies assessing psychological functioning by measuring frequency of psychosomatic complaints found no difference between children reared in stepfamilies and those reared in other types of families. However, there is little recent data on general psychological functioning. More study is needed on this particular topic before general conclusions can be drawn.

Family Relationships

Overall, it becomes clear after reviewing the literature that the relationships within stepfamilies are not terribly different from those in other families. Similar issues face children and parents in all types of families. The nature of these issues, however, may be different due to the complexity of remarriage and kinship relationships, and the "newness" of family rituals, routines, and habits.

Ganong and Coleman (1984: 400) reviewed the studies that compared family relationships in stepfamilies and other types of families. They summarize the findings from several studies this way:

> No differences were found in relationships with stepfathers . . . perceptions of parental happiness . . . perception of amount of family conflict . . . socioemotional relationships between mothers and daughters . . . sharing of household tasks . . . reciprocal confiding, supportiveness, and trust between mothers and daughters . . . positive family relationships . . . and observed stepparent-child and parent-child interactions. . . . Wilson et al. (1975) found no differences in adult family relationships between adults raised in stepfather families and adults raised in nuclear families. Most stepchildren

reported liking stepparents (stepfathers as well as stepmothers) and getting along well with them.

On the other hand, there are some studies that do report poorer adjustment in stepfamilies. As suggested earlier, the relationship between stepparent and stepchild is more negative than the one with a residential biological parent. Less affection is reported between stepparents and stepchildren, and stepchildren see the stepparent in a negative light (Bowerman and Irish, 1962; Halperin and Smith, 1983). One recent study on the effects of stepfamily interaction on child well-being suggests that children of divorce and remarriage exhibited more stress and more disruptive behavior than children in the general population (Jacobson, forthcoming; Peterson and Zill, 1986). We are cautious, however, not to interpret this as meaning stepchildren need psychological treatment.

It has been suggested that the stepparent-stepchild relationships is central to expressions of satisfaction with one's remarried family (Crosbie-Burnett, 1984). Further, the quality of the stepparent-stepchild relationship appears to be a better predictor of child adjustment than the quality of the relationship with the nonresidential biological parent (Furstenberg and Selzer, 1983; Furstenberg et al., 1983). This is a consistent finding across the majority of studies regardless of sample size. For example, a recent study by Pink and Wampler (1985) compared the responses from 28 stepfamilies with the responses from 28 first-marriage families on measures of family functioning and the quality of the stepfather-adolescent relationship. Their findings indicate that the ratings from the mother, stepfather, and adolescent were lower in family cohesion and adaptability and lower in quality in the stepfather-adolescent relationship than that reported by members of first families. The findings did not hold true for the mother-adolescent relationship.

Studies have examined other aspects of the stepparent-stepchild relationship. For example, research by Clingempeel et al. (1984) reported lower scores for stepchildren, stepparents, and biological parents when they rated the stepfather-stepdaughter relationship. In this study girls were found to emit less positive verbal communication and more negative problem-solving behaviors toward their stepparents than boys. Stepparents did not differ in their response toward either their stepdaughters or stepsons. Similar findings were reported in another study by these psychologists (Clingempeel et al., 1985). Here, however, the researchers were interested in determining the possible effects of structural complexity on stepparent-stepchild interaction. Findings revealed that simple (wife had custody of a child from a previous marriage and husband had no children) and complex (wife had custody of a child from a previous marriage and husband was the father of a noncustodial child) stepfather families did not differ on any of the measures of love detachment, positive-negative verbal communication, and problem-solving behaviors.

Other Social Relationships

Most studies of the influence of remarriage and stepparenting on children's social interaction with friends, peers, and in other institutional settings suggest that stepchildren do not have any more trouble than other children do. Again, Ganong and Coleman (1984: 108) have best summarized these findings:

> Stepchildren did not differ from nuclear family children in peer relationships . . . delinquent behaviors . . . delinquent companions . . . drug use . . . school behaviors . . . and church attendance.

The findings from Furstenberg, Nord, Peterson, and Zill's 1983 National Survey of Children suggest less positive outcomes for stepchildren. These researchers conclude that children reared in stepfamilies are more vulnerable to all kinds of behavior problems than children reared in families that have not experienced divorce. Some earlier studies support the results from the National Children's Survey. For example, Barbara Dahl, Hamilton McCubbin, and Gary Lester (1976) found poorer social adjustment in stepchildren, and Shepard Kellam, Margaret Ensminger, and Jay Turner (1977) concluded that children being reared in stepfamilies are almost as "at risk" in social adaptation as children being reared in mother-custody single-parent households. These two studies were conducted with newly established stepfamilies. The National Survey of Children data demonstrate that the "at risk" concern can be applied even to children in stepfamilies that have survived the early stages of stepfamily formation.

In summary, it is still too soon to draw firm conclusions about the impact of remarriage on children's development. What we can say is that there may be some potential for risk and careful attention must be paid to children who are subjected to parental divorce and remarriage. Most marital status transitions occur within a relatively short period of time, forcing children to adjust and adapt to a multitude of changes rather quickly. It may be that the rapidity of change rather than the change itself is a primary influence on the outcomes of such change for the children involved. This question has not been thoroughly explored. In terms of the overall effects of remarriage on children, we quote Furstenberg et al.'s (1983: 667) summary of the situation: "The increasingly common pattern of divorce and remarriage is profoundly altering the practice of parenthood. The experience of growing up has probably changed as much in the past several decades as in any comparable period in American history."

CHILDREN'S POWER TO BREAK UP THE MARRIAGE

Several researchers have reported that the divorce rate is higher in remarriages with stepchildren (Becker et al., 1977; Cherlin, 1978; White and Booth, 1985). There are at least three reasons that this may be true. First, the presence of children makes adjustment harder for a remarried couple. To illustrate, read the words of a 29-year-old woman married 5½ years:

My husband's kids are from two different marriages. Two live with one [ex-wife] and one with the other. I have no kids and we don't want anymore. The two oldest lived with us for 1½ years and I about went crazy, but things worked out and they are gone and life is great! My marriage is wonderful and we are really happy. I think we'll keep each other.

We do not know why the children were problematic in this particular marriage. . . . We do know that children limit a couple's privacy and the opportunity for intimacy. We know that stepmothers have a particularly difficult time parenting other women's children. We also know that remarried couples with children must accommodate to their marriage at the same time they are dealing with family matters.

It is important to differentiate between *marriage* and *family*. Although a couple may see eye-to-eye on matters that concern their behavior and personal relationship, they may differ in marked ways in their perceptions of what constitutes "good" child behavior, or rules that children "ought to" follow. They may also differ markedly in what they believe to be a proper means of disciplining when the rules are broken. First-married partners may also have disagreements about these aspects of child rearing, but a major difference is that the child in a stepfamily is not the biological offspring of both spouses. Unless the child was living with a never-married mother he or she has a history of being parented by another "father" or "mother."

Second, the discipline of children is a source of conflict between remarried spouses. There is little dispute that discipline of children is among the most frequently cited areas of difficulty reported by remarried adults, and adolescents share this perception. Discipline refers to the establishment and enforcement of family rules. It is not uncommon for a stepparent to feel that changes need to be made in the way things were done in the "old" family, and to set new rules with different expectations for children's behavior. In one study 80% of the adolescents reported they had experienced firsthand this type of discipline. They had to "adjust to living with a new set of rules from a stepparent," "accept discipline from a stepparent," and "deal with the expectations of a stepparent." These situations were judged to be stressful by the adolescents (Lutz, 1983).

Disciplining children is also stressful for adults. Because of the emotional attachment parents have to children it is very difficult to arbitrate between one's child and new spouse over matters of discipline and types or severity of punishment. This is confounded by the interpretation of behavior. Often it is not so much a matter of the actual behavior of the child but the motive behind the behavior that is important. For example, the behavior of a 16-year-old adolescent boy who takes the family car without permission may be viewed quite differently by the boy's parent and stepparent. Both may agree that the behavior was against the rules but they may disagree about the motive, his moral character, or the importance of following through with punishment under all circumstances. Different interpretations can result in conflict and disunity between parent and stepparent. Further, the parent and child can team together against the stepparent.

Third, although children typically have no say in their parent's decision to remarry and form a new family in the first place, they do have incredible power to break it up. Children can create divisiveness between spouses and siblings by acting in ways that accentuate differences between them. Children have the power to set parent against stepparent, siblings against parents, and stepsiblings against siblings. Finally, because a child is the link that unites the binuclear family, he or she has the capabilities to make uncomfortable comparisons between the two households, or to bring quasi kin and members of the extended family into the family's business. That interference is a potential source of conflict.

In summary, we began by discussing the history of custody arrangements and defining different types of custody. The most common custodial arrangement in our time is for the children to reside with their mother and for fathers to "visit." We learned that father involvement decreases over time, especially as former spouses find new partners and remarry. Studies suggest that about 10%–25% of fathers do not contact their children at all after divorce. Nonresidential mothers tend to stay involved with their children more than nonresidential [fathers]. A child's residential status after divorce may change and he or she may move to the second parent's home. The most frequent move seems to be for adolescent boys to move from their mother's residence to their father's. It is estimated that about 11%–20% of children change residence (Ihinger-Tallman, 1985). Data on the adjustment of children to stepfamily life indicates that boys have an easier time than girls, and children in stepfather families have an easier time than children in stepmother families. The findings are somewhat mixed with regard to self-esteem, psychological functioning, family relationships, and children's other social relations. We depicted the vulnerability of children regarding their powerless position when the remarriage is contracted, but the strength of their position if they decide to pull against the parent's efforts to create cohesion and unity.

REFERENCES

Ahrenfeltd v. Ahrenfeldt (1840) 1 Hoff Ch. 497. New York.

Ahrons, C. R. (1981) "The binuclear family: two stepfamilies, two houses." *Stepfamily Bulletin* 1: 5–6.

Becker, G. S., E. M. Landis and R. T. Michael (1977) "An economic analysis of marital instability." *Journal of Political Economics* 85: 1141–1187.

Bishop, J. P. (1891) New Commentaries on the Law of Marriage, Divorce, and Separation. Vol. 2, Mass 187, Mass.

Bohannan, P. and H. Yahraes (1979) "Stepfathers as parents," pp. 347–362 in E. Corfman (ed.) *Families Today: A Research Sampler on Families and Children*. National Institute of Mental Health Science Monograph. Washington, DC: Government Printing Office.

Bowerman, C. E. and D. P. Irish (1962) "Some relationships of stepchildren to their parents." *Marriage and Family Living* 24: 113–121.

Brand, E. and G. W. Clingempeel (1985) "The interdependencies of husband-wife and stepparent-stepchild relationships in stepmother and stepfather families: a multimethod study." Unpublished manuscript, Pennsylvania State University, Harrisburg.

Cherlin, A. (1978) "Remarriage as an incomplete institution." *American Journal of Sociology* 84: 634–650.

Cherlin, A. and J. McCarthy (1985) "Remarried couple households: data from the June 1980 Current Population Survey." *Journal of Marriage and the Family* 47: 23–30.

Clingempeel, W. S., E. Brand and R. Ievoli (1984) "Stepparent-stepchild relationships in stepmother and stepfather families: a multimethod study." *Family Relations* 33: 465–473.

Clingempeel, W. S., R. Ievoli, and E. Brand (1985) "Structural complexity and the quality of stepfather-stepchild relationships." *Family Process* 23: 547–560.

Clingempeel, W. S. and S. Segal (1986) "Stepparent-stepchild relationships and the psychological adjustment of children in stepmother and stepfather families." *Child Development* 57: 474–484.

Crosbie-Burnett, M. (1984) "The centrality of the step relationship: a challenge to family theory and practice." *Family Relations* 33: 459–463.

Dahl, B. B., H. I. McCubbin and G. R. Lester (1976) "War-induced father absence: comparing the adjustment of children in reunited, non-reunited and reconstituted families." *International Journal of Sociology of the Family* 6: 99–108.

Derdeyn, A. P. (1976) "Child custody contests in historical perspective." *American Journal of Psychiatry* 133: 1369–1376.

Duberman, L. (1975) *The Reconstituted Family: A Study of Remarried Couples and Their Children*. Chicago: Nelson-Hall.

Fox, G. L. (1985) "Noncustodial fathers," pp. 393–415 in S.M.H. Hanson and F. W. Bozette (eds.) *Dimensions of Fatherhood*, Beverly Hills, CA: Sage.

Fulton, J. A. (1979) "Parental reports of children's post-divorce adjustment." *Journal of Social Issues* 35: 126–139.

Furstenberg, F. F., Jr., C. W. Nord, J. L. Peterson and N. Zill (1983) "The life course of children of divorce: marital disruption and parental contact." *American Sociological Review* 48: 656–668.

Furstenberg, F. F., Jr., and J. A. Seltzer (1983) "Divorce and child development." Presented at the annual meeting of the American Orthopsychiatric Association, Boston.

Furstenberg, F. F., Jr., and G. B. Spanier (1984) *Recycling the Family: Remarriage After Divorce*. Beverly Hills, CA: Sage.

Ganong, L. H. and M. Coleman (1984) "The effects of remarriage on children: a review of the empirical literature." *Family Relations* 33: 389–405.

Glick, P. C. (1984) "Marriage, divorce, and living arrangements." *Journal of Family Issues* 5: 7–26.

Goode, W. J. (1965) *Women in Divorce*. New York: Free Press.

Greif, G. L. (1985) "Single fathers rearing children." *Journal of Marriage and the Family* 47: 185–191.

Greif, G. L. (1986) "Mothers without custody and child support." *Family Relations* 35: 87–93.

Halperin, S. M. and T. A. Smith (1983) "Differences in stepchildren's perceptions of their stepfathers and natural fathers: implications for family therapy." *Journal of Divorce* 7: 19–30.

Hetherington, E. M., M. Cox and R. Cox (1976) "Divorced fathers." *Family Coordinator* 25: 417–428.

Hofferth, S. L. (1985) "Updating children's life course." *Journal of Marriage and the Family* 47: 93–115.

Ihinger-Tallman, M. (1985) "Perspectives on change among stepsiblings." Presented at the annual meeting of the National Council on Family Relations, Dallas, TX.

Jacobson, D. S. (forthcoming) "Family type, visiting patterns, and children's behavior in the stepfamily: a linked family system," in K. Pasley and M. Ihinger-Tallman (eds.) *Remarriage and Stepparenting Today: Theory and Research*. New York: Guilford.

Kaplan, H. B. and A. D. Pokorny (1971) "Self-derogation and childhood broken home." *Journal of Marriage and the Family* 33: 328–337.

Kellam, S. G., M. E. Ensminger and R. J. Turner (1977) "Family structure and the mental health of children: concurrent and longitudinal community-wide studies." *Archives of General Psychiatry* 34: 1012–1022.

Kelly, J. B. (1981) "The visiting relationship after divorce: research findings and clinical implications," in I. R. Stuart and L. W. Abt (eds.) *Children of Separation and Divorce*. New York: Van Nostrand Reinhold.

Luepnitz, D. A. (1982) *Child Custody: A Study of Families after Divorce*. Lexington, MA: D. C. Health.

Lutz, P. (1983) "The stepfamily: an adolescent perspective." *Family Relations* 32: 367–375.

Oshman, H. P. and M. Manosevitz (1976) "Father absence: effects of stepfathers upon psychosocial development in males." *Developmental Psychology* 12: 479–480.

Peterson, J. L. and N. Zill (1986) "Marital disruption, parent-child relationships, and behavior problems in children." *Journal of Marriage and the Family* 48: 295–307.

Pink, J. E. and K. S. Wampler (1985) "Problem areas in stepfamilies: cohesion, adaptability, and the stepfather-adolescent relationship." *Family Relations* 34: 327–335.

Risman, B. L. (1986) "Can men 'mother?' Life as a single father." *Family Relations* 35: 95–102.

Rosenberg, M. (1965) *Society and the Adolescent Self-Image*. Princeton, NJ: Princeton University Press.

Santrock, J. W. (1972) "Relation of type and onset of father absence to cognitive development." *Child Development* 43: 455–469.

Spanier, G. S. and P. C. Glick (1981) "Marital instability in the United States: some correlates and recent changes." *Family Relations* 30: 329–338.

Tropf, W. D. (1984) "An exploratory examination of the effects of remarriage on child support and personal contact." *Journal of Divorce* 7: 57–73.

Visher, E. B. and J. S. Visher (1979) *Stepfamilies: A Guide to Working With Stepparent and Stepchildren*. New York: Brunner/Mazel.

Wallerstein, J. S. and J. B. Kelly (1980) *Surviving the Break-Up: How Children and Parents Cope with Divorce*. New York: Basic Books.

Weiss, R. S. (1979) *Going It Alone*. New York: Basic Books.

Weitzman, L. (1985) *The Divorce Revolution: The Unexpected Social and Economic Consequences for Women and Children in America*. New York: Free Press.

White, L. K. and A. Booth (1985) "The quality and stability of remarriages: the role of stepchildren." *American Sociological Review* 50: 689–698.

Wilson, K. L., L. A. Zurcher, D. C. MacAdams and R. L. Curtis (1975) "Stepfathers and stepchildren: an exploratory analysis from two national surveys." *Journal of Marriage and the Family* 37: 526–536.

PART FOUR
Intimate Alternatives and Issues for the Future

THROUGHOUT THE BOOK we have documented the tremendous changes that have occurred over the past three decades in family-related values, attitudes, norms, and behaviors. Family diversity and a broader range of intimate relationships are acceptable in the 1990s. Many people are pursuing open marriage, extramarital sexual experiences, or homosexual relationships to fulfill emotional and developmental needs for intimacy, affection, and self-realization. But what might the future hold for us?

For the majority who choose traditional, conjugal, monogamous marriage, there will be numerous variations, with many forms signaling that marriage will be less socially and emotionally exclusive. Greater sexual diversity within and outside of marriage, commuter marriages, weekend couples, and childless families are all likely to be part of our future. The family life cycle, as a consequence, is in the process of being redefined. Postponed marriage and parenthood, when coupled with low fertility rates, high divorce rates, and longer life expectancy, mean that singlehood and the postparental or "empty nest" years are becoming relatively long stages in the life course. On the other hand, marriage and parenthood will be central, organizing themes of family life for a relatively short period of the total adult life cycle. Further, we can expect to see continued movement toward more egalitarian gender roles, accompanied by increasing levels of educational and occupational attainment among women and increased pressures to redefine family roles for men.

Family diversity will be manifest in other ways as a wide variety of emerging family forms become more prevalent. With regard to children, it is estimated that 90 percent of black children and 70 percent of white children will live with one parent before reaching age eighteen. Among the arrangements that will be replacing the traditional family, in which two once-married parents rear their natural children, are: single-parent families headed by never-married women; single-parent families formed by divorce or by death of a spouse; reconstituted families with stepchildren from previous marriages combined with mutual children from current relationships; and couples raising biological or nonbiological children born through the assistance of new reproductive technologies.

An important theme underlying many of these developments is the separation of what were traditionally interconnected activities of marriage: sexual intercourse, reproduction, and parenthood. The separation of sex from marriage gained considerable momentum in the 1960s and 1970s with the increased acceptance of premarital and extramarital sexual experiences. The widespread incidence of single-parent families reflects a separation of parenthood from marriage, and many reconstituted families involve nonbiological relationships between stepparents and stepchildren. With the advent of different reproductive technologies discussed in this section, we are embarking on the next phase of this process in which reproduction and parenthood are separated from sexual intercourse. The new reproductive techniques raise numerous legal and ethical issues which are similar to the heated national debate surrounding abortion.

Rapidly changing demographic patterns also have serious implications for the future. The proportion of the population that is sixty-five or over is steadily increasing, a trend that is fueled by low fertility rates and longer life expectancy. As the baby boomers leave the work force, the financial costs for supporting them will mount, and there will be a relatively small segment of the population to support them—financially or emotionally. At the same time, the proportion of families living below the poverty level—most of them female-headed families with young children—continues to increase. The family of the 1990s bears little resemblance to the family of twenty years ago, and the implications for public policy are substantial.

ARTICLE 34
Multiple Marriage, Swinging, Adultery, and Open Marriage

ROBERT N. WHITEHURST

Diversity in living arrangements and life styles is part of our social landscape. Whitehurst describes some of the more visible alternative relationships to monogamous marriage: serial marriage, adultery, cohabitation, homosexual relationships, open marriage, multiple marriages, and swinging. Although people can freely choose their life styles, the author observes that there are varying degrees of social support for the alternatives, which has implications for their legitimacy and longevity.

RELATIONSHIP OPTIONS

Lifetime Monogamy

Although few people go into marriage believing they will get a divorce, increasing numbers have that experience, and in the near future it may become a norm to have experienced two marriages (one that might be chalked up to inexperience, or perhaps we will come to allow one marriage period to be for personal growth and the next for stability). Whether monogamous marriage in fact continues to dominate the

Robert N. Whitehurst, "Multiple Marriage, Swinging, Adultery, and Open Marriage." In *Current Controversies in Marriage and Family,* Harold Feldman and Margaret Feldman, eds. (Beverly Hills, Calif.: Sage, 1982): pp. 263–273. Reprinted by permission of Margaret Feldman.

relationship scene (or if it even does today) is a matter of some debate. The ideal is one to which most persons still adhere when they marry. What they do in later years is another problem, but the increased tenuousness of long-term marriages makes it problematic as a future dominant form. Traditional monogamous marriage has the most strength of custom, law, religion, and community supports to prop it up; thus we might speculate that it remains in part as a perseverance of an older form that in some respects simply does not provide people with clear options and will only decline when more options are open and available.

Adultery

This form of marital violation is obviously as old as man/woman, since it is generously mentioned in the Bible. In terms of modern practices, we ought to recognize variations in the dimension of openness and permission related to nonmonogamy. All couples have rules, whether written or not, spoken or not, and clearly understood or not. Some partners maintain nonverbal rules that, in essence, admonish the person sexually active outside the marriage to act as though it does not happen or to otherwise protect the other from this knowledge. Therapists relate many tales of spouses who in fact "know" that their spouses have affairs. There are thus many complications in comprehending the nature of "monogamy," unless both partners in fact declare and adhere to its ideals and in fact practice monogamy. If we had clear statistics showing how many did this, it is quite likely that monogamy would not be the most usual form of marriage, even though it is still held as the ideal one.

If we persist in selectively seeing only that which upholds our own preferred view of reality, we will continue to have a situation of uneasy pluralism. If we are able to comprehend the complexity, ambivalence, and mixed nature of life about us, we stand more chance of accepting and adapting more peacefully to pluralism. For example, the media give us not only messages of free-choice and open sexuality, but messages of hoped-for permanence in relationships too. It is possible to support virtually any belief or lifestyle by being highly selective in use of materials. There are without doubt a number of sources to support adultery as a lifestyle choice if one were so inclined to find these. In second place as most popular lifestyle adaptation, we must recognize that the rules of affairs have been well codified, even in writing; thus, conducting these becomes simpler as more people gain personal freedoms and the know-how to create and sustain them without severe consequences (Hunt, 1969; Ellis, 1972).

Perhaps the best way to characterize adultery as a lifestyle is to suggest that its supports are informal, rather than inhering within accepted institutions, and that its constituency lies somewhat outside the pale of the conventional, but not really very far, since most practitioners are also legitimate members of the establishment. Since such extramarital behavior shows no signs of abating, it may be safe to conclude that adultery will continue to be a very popular (at least part-time) added feature to otherwise normal marriages. Since recent experience with sexually open marriages has suggested generally that such arrangements are fluid and explosive (if not ephemeral), then what many find positive and useful in their marriages (stability) will not normally be endangered by extramarital sexual affairs. Thus, my conclusion is that such affairs will not only continue, but will proliferate. The vagaries of love, however, will continue to take their toll in divorce and create a larger remarriage pool, which in all likelihood will not be materially happier (nor more sexually satisfied) than other persons (Cargan et al., 1984).

Nonmarital Cohabitation

In the United States most cohabiting relationships are still at the courtship phase of their relationship (Macklin, 1983: 60). It is likely that in the early 1980s most persons who cohabit do so with the intent of getting married at some time (to someone), if not in the immediate future. It is not difficult at the same time to find couples who have lived together for long periods of time (either after being divorced or before their first marriage) and still not contemplate marriage. Also, people sometimes get married for various reasons after highly varied periods of cohabitation.

Macklin distinguishes five types of cohabitation, each varying in seriousness of intent and meaning to the participants (Macklin, 1983: 56). If we lump together all of these five types, it is easy to conclude that cohabitation is popular. It is not so often seen as an alternative to legal conventional marriage; it thus has rather limited validity in this respect in terms of our definition. It has somewhat more validity as a kind of semilegitimized relationship of convenience, trial, or comradeship. It may be proper to view cohabiting as a variable-term stop-gap, not as a permanent alternative. At the least, many persons will have had some experience with cohabiting in their life-cycle relationships. Whether some cohabiting experience implies liberalization for and further potential for other sexual experimentation is not well known. It may, at least for some persons, mean that the wild-oats period is past and people are ready to settle down into conventional roles and lifestyles.

What we have been discussing so far by way of lifestyles might be considered as relatively normal behaviors, given that the three adaptations above tend to approximate statistical (or social) normality in our society (Whitehurst and Booth, 1980). The remaining adaptations are less frequently found, even though densities in certain places (such as gay subcultures) may make this less frequent occurrence seem doubtful.

Except for the gay alternative to be described in the following, the reader might suppose that all of the adaptations are statistically insignificant and socially acceptable to only a very small minority of persons. This is true today, but it is unwise to be so certain about futures that we cannot envision circumstances that would change our view and potentials for other relationship futures. Anyone presently over five or six decades of age will attest to the dramatic and seemingly radical changes that have occurred in their lifetimes. Projecting technological and social changes forward is risky, but the point is worth nothing that change continues, and may well do so at an even faster rate.

The Homosexual Adaptation

Even though there is still a large area of common concern and consensus among gay people with respect to human rights and political actions, there is no longer much of a monolithic gay community anywhere. It has become diversified, split, and pluralistic within its ranks. Gays have become more accepted into other parts of the community, and job discrimination is beginning to be seriously questioned where gays are involved. Many who formerly lived active and variety-filled sex lives now are monogamous and conventional in most respects other than their sexual choice of partner. The larger community has yielded to political pressures in some ways and has become liberalized and educated and more frequently finds gays among their friends and acquaintances. All of this makes for easier assimilation of gays into the larger culture and may well make for more gays refusing to stay in the closet.

Popular thought is now divided as to whether homosexuality is an acquired choice deeply ingrained, perhaps at birth in some ways we poorly understand now. Depending on which view prevails in the future, we may see more rapid hastening of homosexuals' acceptance in the large community and therefore the potential legitimacy of gay marriages and couple relationships not unlike the variety that heterosexuals experience. Barring unforeseen political repression on a wide scale, the clear trend is for validity of gay lifestyles' enhancement and legitimization; when or how soon this might come to include legal gay marriages is speculative.

Open Marriages

There is overlap between open marriages and adultery, since SOM (sexually open marriages) may involve consensual adultery. In another respect, ROM (role open marriages) are becoming in some circles the ideal. The latter imply the flexibility that accompanies gender-free activities, both inside and outside of the home. Although very few marriages persist for long with open sexual arrangements, they do sometimes persist and thrive in some contexts. Those that do persist without a great deal of support from networks of persons of similar persuasion are likely a very small number. For most, if interests in open sexuality persist beyond some experimentation phase, they will most likely turn to one of several adaptations: Nonsexual (or sexually clandestine) friendship in an intimate network, swinging, or a kind of adaptation fostered by the Kerista communities, in which several persons form a kind of group-marriage household. Marriages characterized by the SOM adaptation are likely to remain small in number, since it appears to take a pair of highly individualistic persons to make for the easing of strains of such complexity and potential feelings of being left out of many activities (Whitehurst, 1977: 323). Marriages that have elements of ROM, however, are likely to expand; whether or not this ultimately leads to the more open choice of more SOM potential is speculative.

Multiple Marriage

If we mean by multiple marriage the simultaneous bonding of two or more partners with one or more others, then the concept is not at all valid in our context of the socialization system today. The relatively low level of familism (putting the group first, not the self) makes for a low probability of success in group or communal ventures in marriage. This may be why religious communities more often succeed where more secular organizations fail, since they are sometimes able to call forth loyalty to a higher power or more noble motives that supersede one's personal desires. Groups that stress doing your own thing and personal satisfaction are usually of short duration in terms of stability of membership. Depending on the exact definition of multiple marriage, we cannot expect this form to be visible on the scene in the foreseeable future.

Swinging

This form of recreational (and generally uncommitted) sex involves consensus and a relatively high degree of solidarity between the partners as to goals and values. With high-volume turnover in marriages and divorces, it is possible that people with more similar values, such as swinging, may more likely find each other the second time around and be able to make swinging a slightly more long-term adaptation in their lives.

Swinging by its nature tends to have a short half-life. By this I mean that the male's fantasy of a candy-store freedom to grab all the sex one can from anyone nearby is rapidly replaced by a more discriminatory approach to such casual sex. Male appetites are notorious for being large in prospect but small in retrospect (wanting lots before the fact but becoming sated more easily than one had imagined). Thus, where women are more reluctant to begin swinging, men are more reluctant to continue such behavior. Fear of diseases also gives pause to many who otherwise might feel more free to participate.

The commercialization of swinging in the past decade has made for a mixed scene: some people like it because of the convenience, selectivity, and ease of access to parties and conventions. There are elements of festivals, Halloween, and other ritual escapes that make them popular. To others, it is too depersonalized, commercialized and—in short—Americanized. Those desiring discretion, friendship, and longevity of relations may try such swinging conventions but then revert to more informal networks of low-key activity.

In short, hothouse sex is seen as basically undesirable by many. The fact that these organizations have prospered in the recent past attests to something of the demand for them. One Midwest organization regularly turns out 400 to 600 persons for weekends on occasion. Whatever its growth or decline, swinging likely attests to the advance of a pluralistic acceptance of variety in lifestyle.

SUMMARY, IMPLICATIONS, AND CONCLUSION

The concept of "valid" as used to describe various relationship forms has been relativized and used in terms of social acceptance and longevity of form. Since no statistical base is available that would empirically verify the numbers of persons practicing each form, we are left with estimates and are free to interpret what each might mean for life today and tomorrow. Depending on definition and context, we might well come to the conclusion that monogamous marriage is no longer the only way to practice an adult relationship style. Although monogamy is not the only form, it is still the most accepted, most visible, and simplest lifestyle. But many persons opt for complexity and novelty, not simplicity or tradition. These are likely to be found practicing a variety of other ways of being sexual and of carrying on relationships.

Some rationales were provided to suggest that our budding pluralism will support many lifestyles now and in the future; barring radical political and economic changes, current trends will likely be continued, ensuring some variety, but not the phasing out of the most popular forms of today. Some of the trends noted involve the increased use of clear contracts, networks, and commercialism (Whitehurst, 1984). The tendency to prepackage and commercialize many aspects of life may be accompanied by further development of more highly specialized networks, which will serve to make for easier access to and sustenance of variety lifestyles.

The dominant nature of the idea of monogamous lifetime commitment in traditional marriage is not likely to fade, even though it may increasingly become at least partly invalidated by more frequent violations. This may not keep people in such a position from holding it forth as an ideal simply on sentimental and symbolic grounds. The need for nostalgic ties remains strong and "monogamy" may coexist with more modern needs for self-expression, legitimized by a more immediately hedonistic society.

REFERENCES

Cargan, L., R. N. Whitehurst, and G. R. Frisch (1984) "Social life and happiness: the differences among singles." Presented at the Popular Culture Association Annual Meeting, Toronto, Ontario, March 29.

Ellis, A. (1972) *The Civilized Couple's Guide to Extramarital Adventure*. New York: Peter Wyden.

Hunt, M. (1969) *The Affair*. New York: World.

Macklin, E. D. (1983) "Non-marital heterosexual cohabitation: an overview," pp. 49–76 in E. D. Macklin and R. H. Rubin (eds.) *Contemporary Families and Alternative Lifestyles*. Beverly Hills, CA: Sage.

Whitehurst, R. N. (1984) "Alternatives to legal marriage and the nuclear family," in M. Baker (ed.) *The Family: Changing Trends in Canada*. Scarborough, Ontario: McGraw-Hill Ryerson.

——— (1977) "Changing ground rules and emergent lifestyles," pp. 319–334 in R. W. Libby and R. N. Whitehurst (eds.) *Marriage and Alternatives: Exploring Intimate Relationships*. Glenview, IL: Scott, Foresman.

——— and G. V. Booth (1980) *The Sexes: Changing Relationships in a Pluralistic Society*. Agincourt, Ontario: Gage.

ARTICLE 35
The Intimate Relationships of Lesbians and Gay Men

LETITIA ANNE PEPLAU AND STEVEN L. GORDON

This article looks at several issues important to both gay and heterosexual couples: What do people want from their relationships, how do gender roles affect them, how satisfying and committed are the relationships, are they sexually exclusive or open? The authors conclude that there are many commonalities in the relationships of homosexuals and heterosexuals. Most people, regardless of sexual orientation, seek intimate and enduring relationships. However, compared to heterosexuals, gays are less likely to adhere to traditional gender roles and are more apt to have egalitarian relationships.

CONFUSION ABOUT GENDER ROLES and sexuality is perhaps greatest in response to homosexuality. Stereotypes often depict gay men and lesbians as individuals who are uncomfortable with their gender identity and who want to change their gender. Cultural images of the effeminate gay man and the masculine, "butch" lesbian are common. In relationships, homosexuals are thought to mimic heterosexual patterns, with one partner acting as the "wife" and the other partner playing the "husband." But current research shows that these stereotypes are inaccurate and misleading. Although these stereotypes may characterize a small minority of homosexuals, they fail to fit the lifestyles of most gay men and lesbians.

Where do these stereotypes come from? In part, they stem from the faulty assumption that three components of human sexuality are inseparable. These compo-

"The Intimate Relationships of Lesbians and Gay Men." From *Changing Boundaries: Gender Roles and Sexual Behavior*, edited by Elizabeth Rice Allgeier and Naomi B. McCormick by permission of Mayfield Publishing Company. Copyright © 1983 by Mayfield Publishing Company.

nents are *sexual orientation* (attraction to same-gender versus other-gender partners), *gender identity* (our belief that we are male or female) and *gender-role behavior* (acting in traditionally "masculine" or "feminine" ways). Many people wrongly believe that, if an individual differs from the norm on one of these components, he or she must differ on the others as well. In North American culture, a typical heterosexual woman is attracted romantically and sexually to men (sexual orientation), she knows without doubt that she is female (gender identity), and she frequently enacts the roles or behaviors that society defines as appropriate for women. A lesbian differs from this pattern in that her sexual and romantic attraction is to women. The stereotype assumes that the lesbian must also differ in her gender identity and gender-role behavior. This assumption is wrong.

Homosexuals are not confused about their gender identity: lesbians are not different from heterosexual women in their sureness of being female, nor do gay men differ from heterosexual men on this dimension. In terms of behavior, research indicates that most gay men are not effeminate in dress or manner, nor are lesbians usually "masculine" in their behavior (see DeLora & Warren, 1977; Gagnon, 1977; Gagnon & Simon, 1973; Warren, 1974).

This [article] reviews research findings about the love relationships of lesbians and gay men. We begin by asking what people want in love relationships and by examining how relationship values are affected by sexual orientation. We next look at the question of whether homosexuals adopt heterosexual scripts for relationships. . . . Are homosexual relationships more similar to heterosexual "marriages" or to same-gender "best friendships"? We then consider love and commitment in the relationships of lesbians and gay men. Finally, we investigate sexual behavior and the issue of sexual exclusivity in gay relationships.

METHODOLOGICAL ISSUES AND LIMITATIONS

Before beginning our investigation of homosexual relationships, however, a few methodological issues deserve mention. First, terms need to be defined. The term *homosexual* is appropriately used to refer to both men and women whose primary sexual and affectional orientation is toward same-gender partners. But many gay men and lesbians dislike the term, believing that it overemphasizes the sexual aspect of their lifestyle. Instead, most prefer "gay" (for both men and women) or "lesbian" (for women).

Second, research on gay relationships, like studies of heterosexual relationships (see Hill et al., 1979), is limited in several ways. Most research uses questionnaires or interviews. Self-report responses can be biased because people lack insight into their relationships or because they want to present a favorable image to researchers. Whatever their sexual orientation, people are not always truthful in describing their relationships to themselves or to researchers. People who volunteer for studies may differ from nonvolunteers in being more interested in social science research, more liberal or permissive in their views, or more trusting of psychologists. In addition, studies of gays or of any partially hidden population encounter special problems. There is no such thing as a representative sample of lesbians and gay men (Morin, 1977). Some gay people are secretive about their sexual orientation and would not volunteer for psychological research. Those gays who have participated in research tend to be younger, educated, middle-class, white adults. Because of these limitations, we can place greatest confidence in findings that have been replicated in several different studies. And we need to be cautious in assuming that research findings adequately describe the entire gay population in America. Our primacy focus is on voluntary relationships. Generalizing our conclusions to forced sex in institutions (for example, prisons or the military) would be inappropriate. With these warnings in mind, we turn to the questions of what gay men and lesbians are looking for in an intimate relationship.

VALUES ABOUT INTIMATE RELATIONSHIPS

What do lesbians and gay men want from their close relationships? Do gays want a long-term relationship with a single partner, or do they prefer to live pretty much in the present? Is their view of love romantic or cynical? Do homosexuals have a distinctive set of values about relationships unique to lesbians and gay men, or do gays and heterosexuals seek similar goals in relationships? Research is beginning to answer these questions.

Most gays want to have steady love relationships. Few would be satisfied to have only casual liaisons. One study (Bell & Weinberg, 1978) asked homosexuals how important it was to them to have "a permanent living arrangement with a homosexual partner." Of the lesbians, 25 percent said this was "the most important thing in life," and another 35 percent said it was "very important." Less than one woman in four said that a permanent relationship was not important. Gay men showed a similar pattern: 15 percent said a relationship was the most important thing in life; 22 percent said it was very important; and only a third said it was not important at all. Thus a somewhat higher proportion of women than men said that having a permanent relationship was extremely important.

Most gays, like most heterosexuals, value steady love relationships (for example, see Hill, Rubin & Peplau, 1976). What are the characteristics that gays seek in such partnerships? Lesbians, gay men, and heterosexuals were asked to rank nine possible relationship goals (Ramsey, Latham, & Lindquist, 1978). All groups ranked affection, personal development, and companionship as most important; least importance was given to having "a place in the community" and to religion. Other goals such as economic security and having an attractive home were ranked in the middle. Lesbians, gay men, and heterosexuals have also been asked to rank the qualities that they seek in partners (Laner, 1977). All groups gave greatest importance to honesty, affection, and intelligence; these traits ranked above having "good looks," a sense of humor, and money.

Matched samples of lesbians, gay men, and heterosexual women and men rated the importance of various features of love relationships (Peplau & Cochran, 1980). These included such issues as revealing intimate feelings, spending time together, holding similar attitudes, having an equal-power relationship, and having sexual exclusivity. Participants gave varied answers. For example, although some considered it essential to share many activities with a partner, others viewed joint activities as relatively unimportant. Despite such individual differences, remarkably few overall group differences were found between heterosexuals and homosexuals. For example, on average, both groups gave greatest importance to "being able to talk about my most intimate feelings" with a partner.

One major difference between homosexuals and heterosexuals did emerge, however. Sexual exclusivity in relationships was much more important to heterosexuals than to homosexuals. Lesbians and gay men gave sexual fidelity an average rating of somewhat more than 5, compared with a rating of just over 7 for the heterosexuals (the highest possible importance rating was 9). Homosexuals were less likely than heterosexuals to endorse monogamy as an ideal for relationships. Two interesting gender differences also emerged. Whatever their sexual orientation, women gave greater importance than men did to emotional expressiveness and the sharing of feelings. This finding is consistent with the emphasis in North American gender-role socialization that men should conceal their feelings and present a tough exterior (David & Brannon, 1976). Second, lesbian and heterosexual women cared more than did men about having egalitarian relationships. Perhaps because of the women's movement, women showed greater sensitivity to equal power in love relationships.

Finally, Peplau and Cochran (1980) examined how "romantic" gays were in their attitudes about love. Participants were asked how much they agreed or disagreed with statements about love such as "Lovers ought to expect a certain amount of disillusionment after they have been together for a while" and "To be truly in love is to be in love forever." No differences were found in the answers of lesbians, gay men, and heterosexuals; most people took a middle-of-the-road position. Homosexuals and heterosexuals were equally likely to be starry-eyed romantics or cold-hearted cynics. In sum, the picture that emerges from these studies is that most people, whatever their sexual orientation, want much the same things from love relationships; namely, affection and companionship.

RELATIONSHIP SCRIPTS: MARRIAGE OR BEST FRIENDSHIP?

Of the myths about homosexual relationships, none is more persistent—or wrong—than the belief that in gay partnerships one person adopts the role of "husband" and the other the role of "wife." According to this stereotype, gay partners "make believe," in some sense, that one of them is male and the other female. One partner is the breadwinner, takes the initiative in sex, and generally assumes the conventional role of dominant male. The other partner keeps house and acts the part of the submissive female.

Scientific research refutes this stereotype. More typical of actual gay relationships are the following personal descriptions:

> *[Gay man:]* My involvement with other men is always like we are buddies, or at least that's what I strive for. . . . I very much want to have a man-to-man relationship with my friend and I value this element of masculinity. . . . I believe masculinity can be realized as readily through another man as it can through a woman. [Quoted by Spada, 1979, p. 168]

> *[Lesbian:]* In a heterosexual relationship, you are playing a role . . . in a gay relationship, you don't have that. You have two people on an equal level living together, sharing responsibilities. In a heterosexual relationship you are not going to get it 50:50 (division of labor). You'd be lucky if you get it 60:40, so there is a certain amount of role playing that you are going to have in a heterosexual relationship that you don't have in a gay relationship. [Quoted by Tanner, 1978, pp. 90–91]

Most lesbians and gay men actively reject traditional husband-wife roles as a model or script for love relationships. One study (Jay & Young, 1977) asked lesbians and gay men their feelings about "role playing." Most of the lesbians and half of the men said they felt negatively about role playing. One lesbian explained, "I don't like role playing because it copies the traditional male-female relationship. I'm proud I'm a woman. And I love women, not pseudo-men" (cited in Jay & Young, 1977, p. 320). Many gays value their relationships precisely because they feel freed from the restrictions imposed by gender roles in traditional heterosexual relationships. A gay man commented, "Role playing seems to me by nature to involve dominance and control, both of which make me feel uncomfortable" (cited in Jay & Young, 1977, p. 369). Three possible areas of masculine-feminine role playing in gay relationships have been investigated: the division of household tasks, sexual behavior and decision making (Bell & Weinberg, 1978; Caldwell & Peplau, 1980; Cardell, Finn, & Marecek, 1981; Harry & DeVall, 1978; Jay & Young, 1977; Saghir & Robins, 1973).

In most heterosexual marriages, clear distinctions are made between the husband's work (for example, being the breadwinner, doing household repairs) and the wife's work (for example, doing the cooking and other domestic chores). Is there a similar division of household tasks among gay couples who live together? Research finds little evidence for this idea. For example, Bell and Weinberg (1978) asked gay men and lesbians which partner in the relationship does "the housework"; 61 percent of gay men and 58 percent of lesbians said that housework was shared equally. When asked if one partner consistently does all the "feminine tasks" or all the "masculine tasks," about 90 percent of the gay men and lesbians said no. As one gay man commented, "When I am asked who is the husband and who is the wife, I would say we're just a couple of happily married husbands" (quoted by Saghir & Robins, 1973, p. 74). The predominant pattern is one of role flexibility, with partners sharing in housekeeping and financial expenditures. Because it is common in gay relationships for both partners to have jobs, both are usually able to contribute financially to the relationship and neither can devote all their time to homemaking. . . .

In the area of sexual behavior, role playing might be reflected in which partner initiates sexual interactions or in personal preferences for particular sexual activities. . . . Some studies have asked gays which partner is more "active" or "passive" in sex. A majority of lesbians and gay men say that both partners are equally active or that partners alternate from situation to situation (Califia, 1979; Harry, 1976; Marmor, 1980; Saghir & Robins, 1973). Jay and Young (1977) asked gays if they role played sexually when they were sexually intimate. Only 12 percent of gay men and 8 percent of lesbians said they did this frequently; some said they took an active or passive role occasionally, and the largest group responded "never." Studies of gay men have investigated men's preferences for particular sexual activities, such as receiving versus giving anal intercourse. Again, many men indicate enjoying both roles. When a man does have a preference for one kind of sexuality, this preference is not linked to more general dominance in decision making in the relationship (Harry & DeVall, 1978). Few homosexuals consistently engage in sexual role playing. When role playing does occur, it may be more common among gay men than lesbians.

A third component of traditional marriage is the idea that the masculine partner should be the "boss" and leader in decision making. Gay men and lesbians largely reject this model, preferring a relationship in which partners share equally in power (for example, see Harry, 1979; Spada, 1979). One study (Peplau & Cochran, 1980) asked matched samples of heterosexual and homosexual college students about power in their current love relationship. Virtually everyone (over 95 percent in each group) said that ideally both partners should have "exactly equal say" in their relationship. Unfortunately, only about half the lesbians, gay men, and heterosexuals thought that their current relationships lived up to this ideal.

What are some of the factors that tip the balance of power away from equality in gay relationships? In gay relationships, power is more likely to be wielded by the partner who has greater personal resources, in terms of greater education, income, age, or other characteristics (Caldwell & Peplau, 1980; Harry & DeVall, 1978). In addition, when there is an imbalance of involvement or commitment in a relationship, the partner who is less interested often has greater power. Gay relationships, like heterosexual ones (Peplau, 1979), seem to have the greatest chance for equality when partners have similar resources and commitments to the relationship.

Although most lesbians and gay men do not engage in gender-role playing, a small minority does. One lesbian described her experience: "When I am with a younger girl, I like to act 'male'—that is, protect her—and I like it very much if she lets me buy drinks, etc. . . . What I like best about the 'male' or 'butch' role is the protective angle, even though I realize intellectually that this is a lot of sexist shit" (quoted by Jay & Young, 1977, p. 322). A gay man expressed these views:

> I put strong emphasis on roles, more sexually than nonsexually. But, and this is the distinctive part, I can feel perfectly comfortable in either set of roles . . . but I like to

keep these roles clearly defined with any given person. . . . I like the stability and clarity of it, the ease of prediction and minimal conflict it provides; the communications are so much easier, more familiar. [Quoted by Jay & Young, 1977, p. 367]

For a minority of homosexuals, some elements of gender-role playing are an important and comfortable part of relationships, just as they are for many heterosexuals (see Peplau, Rubin, & Hill, 1977).

Because a few gays do engage in some gender-role playing, it is informative to examine factors that may affect the adoption of these patterns. It appears that such role playing was more common in the "old gay life" prior to the recent evolution of homophile organizations, gay liberation, and the women's movement. One older lesbian commented, "I was 'butch' in experience prior to 1960, but never heavy butch. Just a wee bit more the aggressor, paying the way of my partner, for example. . . . Since 1964 I haven't engaged in role playing. [Now] we are equal women together" (cited in Jay & Young, 1977, p. 321). There has been a historical decline in gender-role playing in the United States. One possible consequence is that such role playing may be more common among older gay men and lesbians than among younger ones.

Gender-role playing may be more common among gays and lesbians from lower socioeconomic and educational levels (Gagnon & Simon, 1963; Harry & DeVall, 1978; Wolf, 1979). It has also been suggested that role playing is part of the "coming-out" experience of some gays (Gagnon & Simon, 1973; Saghir & Robins, 1973). For example, a young woman new to the lesbian community may initially dress in a "butch" manner in order to be more easily identified as lesbian (Wolf, 1979).

In some cases, gender-role playing may result from temporary situational factors. Saghir and Robins (1973) found that only 12 percent of lesbians and 17 percent of gay men had engaged in domestic role playing for a period of three months or longer. Role playing usually occurred because one partner was temporarily unemployed or attending school. Finally, role playing occurs in prison settings; prison culture sometimes defines masculine-feminine roles as the acceptable form for sexual or love relations between same-gender prisoners (for example, see Gagnon & Simon, 1973).

The idea that most lesbians and gay men engage in masculine-feminine role playing is a myth. Although a small minority of homosexuals does show these patterns, the vast majority does not. Why, then, does the role playing stereotype persist? One reason is that this, like other common stereotypes, is seldom subjected to careful scientific scrutiny. In addition, those gays who do engage in role playing may be much more visible to the general public than the majority of gays who do not. Movies and television often perpetuate the stereotype. Finally, in North America, heterosexual marriage is so powerful a script for love relationships that many people find it difficult to imagine an intimate relationship that does not involve husband-wife roles. In North American society, the imagery of romance, love, and "living happily ever after" is heavily colored by the symbolism of marriage.

Although most gays reject husband-wife roles as a model for intimacy, they do want a loving, committed relationship. Therefore, lesbians and gay men must find or create alternate scripts for relationships. Harry and DeVall (1978) suggest that gay relationships are often modeled after friendship, with the added component of erotic and romantic attraction. As such, gay relationships may most closely resemble best friendships.

A friendship script fosters equality in relationships. The norms or rules for friendship assume that partners will be relatively equal in status and power; this contrasts sharply with the institution of marriage, in which the husband is traditionally expected to be the "boss" or leader. Friends also tend to be similar in interests, resources, and skills. In contrast, spouses have traditionally brought different gender-linked qualities to a marriage. For heterosexuals, these differences often foster male dominance rather than equality. As one sociologist has observed,

> Take a young woman who has been trained for feminine dependencies, who wants to "look up" to the man she marries. Put her at a disadvantage in the labor market. Then marry her to a man who has a slight advantage over her in age, income, and education, shored up by an ideology with a male bias. . . . Then expect an egalitarian relationship? [Bernard, 1972, p. 146]

Because of the divergent socialization of males and females in our society, partners in heterosexual relationships often find it difficult to break out of traditional patterns. Research on same-gender relationships suggests that when partners are more similar in their interests and abilities, equality between partners is more easily (although not inevitably) achieved. Feminists have long argued that heterosexual couples *should* abandon gender-based differences in behavior and power. Studies of homosexual relationships demonstrate that successful love relationships *can* be built on models other than traditional marriage. We now turn to studies describing what gay relationships are actually like.

LOVE AND COMMITMENT IN GAY RELATIONSHIPS

A starting point for our discussion is the question of how many lesbians and gay men are actually involved in steady relationships. Although stereotypes often portray gays as unable to develop enduring relationships, empirical evidence argues to the contrary. In studies of lesbians, between 45 percent and 80 percent of the women surveyed were currently in a steady relationship (for example, see Bell & Weinberg, 1978; Jay & Young, 1977; Peplau et al., 1978; Raphael & Robinson, 1980; Schäfer, 1977). In most studies, the proportion of lesbians in an ongoing relationship was close to 75 percent. Studies of gay men show that between 45 percent and 60 percent of the men surveyed were currently involved in a steady relationship (for example, see Bell & Weinberg, 1978; Jay & Young, 1977; Peplau & Cochran, 1981; Spada, 1979). The best estimate about the proportion of gay men in such relationships is about 50 percent. Many lesbians and gay men in steady relationships live with their partners. Although these figures should not be taken as representative of all lesbians and gay men, they do suggest that at any particular point in time a large proportion of homosexuals have stable love relationships. It appears that relatively more lesbians than gay men are involved in steady relationships.

We should emphasize that those lesbians and gay men who do not currently have steady relationships are a diverse group. They include people who have recently ended relationships through breakups or the death of partners, people who are eager to begin new relationships, and others who do not want committed relationships.

Love and Satisfaction

We saw earlier that most homosexuals want close love relationships. How successful are lesbians and gay men in achieving this goal? Unfortunately, information about love, satisfaction, and commitment in gay relationships comes from a few studies based on fairly small samples. So the following results are presented cautiously. They suggest that gays do find their relationships highly rewarding.

One study (Cardell, Finn, & Marecek, 1981) compared lesbian, gay male, and heterosexual couples on a standardized measure of couple adjustment. Most couples were very satisfied with their relationships, and gay men and lesbians did not differ significantly from each other or from the heterosexuals. Another study (Ramsey, Latham, & Lindquist, 1978) compared lesbian, gay male, and heterosexual couples on the Locke-Wallace Scale, a widely used measure of marital adjustment. All couples scored in the "well-adjusted" range, and the homosexuals were indistinguishable from the heterosexuals.

Only recently have social psychologists attempted to measure love systematically, spurred by Rubin's (1973) development of scales to measure "love" and "liking" for a romantic partner. Peplau and Cochran (1980) compared matched samples of lesbians, gay men, and heterosexuals on these measures. Lesbians and gay men reported high love for their partners, indicating strong feelings of attachment, caring, and intimacy. They also scored high on the liking scale, reflecting feelings of respect and affection toward their partners. On other measures, lesbians and gay men rated their current relationships as highly satisfying and very close. When comparisons were made among lesbians, gay men, and heterosexuals on these measures, no significant differences were found.

Peplau and Cochran also asked lesbians, gay men, and heterosexuals to describe in their own words the "best things" and "worst things" about their relationships. Consider these observations by people listing the best aspects of their relationships: "The best thing is having someone to *be* with when you wake up" and "We like each other. We both seem to be getting what we want and need. We have wonderful sex together." Or these descriptions of the worst aspects of relationships: "My partner is too dependent emotionally" and "Her aunt lives with us!" All these remarks could have been made by heterosexuals, but they are actually all responses made by lesbians. Systematic analyses (Cochran, 1978) found no significant differences in the responses of lesbians, gay men, and heterosexuals—all of whom reported similar joys and problems. To examine the possibility that more subtle differences among groups existed that were not captured by the coding scheme, the "best things" and "worst things" statements were typed on cards in a standard format, with information about gender and sexual orientation removed. Panels of judges were asked to sort the cards, separating men and women and separating heterosexuals and homosexuals. The judges were not able to identify correctly the responses of lesbians, gay men, or heterosexual women and men.

Taken together, these findings suggest that many gay relationships are highly satisfying. Lesbian and gay male couples appear, on standardized measures, to be as "well adjusted" as are heterosexual couples. This does not mean, of course, that gays have no difficulties in their relationships. They undoubtedly have many of the same problems as heterosexuals in coordinating joint goals, resolving interpersonal conflicts, and so on. In addition, lesbian and gay male couples may have special problems arising from the hostile and rejecting attitudes of many people toward homosexuals (see Mendola, 1980; Silverstein, 1981). Overall, however, existing research shows that homosexual relationships can be as personally satisfying as heterosexual ones.

Commitment

It is a sad truth that love is no certain guarantee that any relationship will endure. In homosexual relationships, as in heterosexual ones, relationships begun hopefully and lovingly can and do fall apart. Do homosexual relationships last as long as heterosexual ones?

There is no easy answer to this complex question. The U.S. Bureau of the Census records with considerable accuracy the proportion of the population who are heterosexually married and divorced, but no comparable statistical information exists describing any aspect of homosexual relationships. We simply do not know how long the "average" lesbian or gay male relationship lasts. It is useful to remember that for an adolescent, whether lesbian or heterosexual, a relationship of three months may seem "long"; for a 25-year-old, a relationship of 2 years may be relatively "long"; for a 50-year-old, a relationship of 20 years may be long. In other words, a person's age determines to some extent the length of time that it is possible or likely for a relationship to endure.

A recent study of homosexuals in San Francisco (Bell & Weinberg, 1978) inquired about the length of people's *first* homosexual relationships. On the average, lesbians in this sample were 22 years old when they had their first "relatively steady relationships." Nearly 90 percent said they had been "in love" with these first woman partners, and the typical relationship lasted for a median of one to three years. For a third of the lesbians, these relationships lasted four years or longer. Gay men in this sample were, on the average, 23 years old when they had their first steady relationships. About 78 percent said they had been in love with these first male partners, and the typical relationship lasted for a median of one to three years. For 22 percent of the men in this sample, the first steady relationship lasted four years or longer.

Several studies have asked homosexuals to describe the length of their current love relationships (for example, see Bell & Weinberg, 1978; Jay & Young, 1977; Peplau & Amaro, in press; Saghir & Robins, 1973). In these studies, most participants have been young people in their 20s. The typical length of relationships is about two to three years for both men and women. Studies of older gays would be especially useful in understanding the length of homosexual relationships, but such research is strikingly absent from the available literature. A few studies that have included older lesbians and gay men document that relationships of 20 years or more are not uncommon (for example, see Mendola, 1980; Raphael & Robinson, 1980; Silverstein, 1981). Finally, although it is sometimes thought that lesbians have more long-lasting relationships than gay men, evidence about gender differences in the duration of gay relationships is inconsistent (for example, see Bell & Weinberg, 1978; Jay & Young, 1977; Schäfer, 1977).

What factors influence the permanence of gay relationships? Probably many of the same forces that operate in heterosexual relationships. Permanence is affected by two separate factors (Levinger, 1979). The first concerns the strength of the positive attraction that make a particular partner and relationship appealing. We have seen that homosexuals do not differ from heterosexuals in the love and satisfaction they feel in steady relationships. But the possibility always exists that attractions may wane and that people may "fall out of love." Thus, a decrease in attraction can lead to the ending of a relationship.

The second set of factors affecting the permanence of relationships consists of barriers that make the ending of a relationship costly, in either psychological or material terms. For heterosexuals, marriage usually creates many barriers to the dissolution of a relationship, including the cost of a divorce, a wife's financial dependence on her husband, joint investments in property, children, and so on. Such factors may encourage married couples to "work" on improving a declining relationship, rather than ending it. In some cases, these barriers can also keep partners trapped in an "empty-shell" relationship.

Gay men and lesbians probably encounter fewer barriers to the termination of relationships, as these quotations illustrate:

> *[Gay Man:]* I see differences and I see similarities between gay and straight couples. A big difference is that gays are less frequently obliged "to stay together." Ed and I don't have the kids, the high cost of divorce, the in-laws, and the financial entanglements to keep us together. We also don't have all the support systems that straights enjoy. [Quoted by Mendola, 1980, pp. 122–123]
>
> *[Lesbian:]* Marje and I are no different from any straight couple. We've got a lot of problems to work out. And the problems aren't any different from the problems straights have: financial, sexual, in-laws. . . . However, what's different is we don't have a lot of the structures straights have to help them solve their problems. We have to do it on our own, and so it's harder for a gay couple to stay together and make their relationship work. [Quoted by Mendola, 1980, p. 123]

Because of weaker barriers to relationship dissolution (Lewis et al., 1980), lesbians and gay men are less likely to become trapped in hopelessly unhappy relationships. They may also be less motivated to rescue deteriorating relationships.

SEXUAL BEHAVIOR IN GAY RELATIONSHIPS

Most people view gays largely in terms of their sexuality. Stereotypes sometimes depict lesbians and gay men as "highly sexed" people whose lives are organized around the pursuit of sexual pleasure to a much greater extent than is true for heterosexuals. Such a characterization is both far-fetched and wrong. Few of us, whether gay or heterosexual, have sexuality as the organizing principle in our lives (Gagnon & Simon, 1973). For most of us, sex is only one aspect of our lives, along with work, friendship, and other activities. Research suggests that, when it comes to sexuality, differences between men and women are much greater than differences between heterosexuals and homosexuals.

The Physiology of Sexual Arousal

Studies of the physiological aspects of sexuality (Kinsey et al., 1948, 1953; Masters & Johnson, 1979) have found no major differences in the pattern of sexual response of lesbians and heterosexual women, nor in the response of gay and heterosexual men. This should not be surprising. The physiological mechanics of sexual arousal and orgasm are human characteristics, unaffected by sexual orientation.

Heterosexual Experiences

Before considering sexuality in steady relationships, it is useful to provide some background about the more general sexual experiences of gay men and lesbians. Only a minority of lesbians and gay men have had exclusively homosexual experiences throughout their lives. Most homosexuals have had sex with other-gender partners, often before they adopted a homosexual lifestyle (Gundlach & Reiss, 1968; Jay & Young, 1977; Kinsey et al., 1948, 1953; Saghir & Robins, 1973). For example, a recent study (Bell & Weinberg, 1978) found that 83 percent of lesbians and 64 percent of gay men had had heterosexual intercourse. For many people, these heterosexual experiences occurred in the context of dating relationships (Peplau et al., 1978; Peplau & Cochran, 1981). A significant minority of lesbians and gay men have been married. Bell and Weinberg (1978) found that 35 percent of the lesbians and 20 percent of the gay men surveyed had been in heterosexual marriages. Research findings lead to two conclusions. First, most homosexuals have had sexual experience with other-gender partners. Second, a greater proportion of lesbians than of gay men have had heterosexual experiences, including marriage.

Sex in a Steady Relationship

For most lesbians, sex is an enjoyable part of a steady relationship. In one study (Peplau et al., 1978), 75 percent of lesbians reported that sex with their steady partners was extremely satisfying, and only 4 percent said that it was not at all satisfying. One factor contributing to satisfaction was the reported lack of guilt among lesbians; 80 percent said they never felt guilty about their sexual activity with their partners, and only 4 percent said they usually or always felt guilty. Another major factor was the frequency with which lesbians experienced orgasms with their current partners. Over 70 percent of women said they almost always experienced orgasms; only 4 percent said they never had orgasms. Other studies (Jay & Young, 1977; Kinsey et al., 1953) confirm that most lesbians do not usually have difficulty in having orgasms during sex.

Comparative studies suggest that lesbians may have orgasms more regularly during sex than do heterosexual women (for example, see Hunt, 1974; Jay & Young, 1977; Pietropinto & Simenauer, 1979; Tavris & Sadd, 1977). Kinsey researchers (1953) compared heterosexual women who had been married for five years with lesbians who had been sexually active for an equal number of years. Among these women, 17 percent of the heterosexuals compared to only 7 percent of the lesbians had never had an orgasm. And only 40 percent of heterosexual women had orgasms consistently (that is, 90 to 100 percent of the times they had sex), compared to 68 percent of lesbians. These differences may, as Kinsey suggested, reflect differences in the knowledge and sexual techniques of women's partners. But differences in the emotional and interpersonal aspects of lovemaking may be equally important. Schäfer (1976) asked 57 lesbians who had had sexual relations during the past year both with women and with men to compare these experiences. Most lesbians said that compared to sex with men, sex with women was more tender (94 percent), intimate (91 percent), considerate (88 percent), partner related (73 percent), exciting (66 percent), and diversified (52 percent).

Lesbian couples have sex about as often as do heterosexual couples of the same age. Among the younger lesbians typically studied by researchers, the average frequency of sex is about two to three times per week. This figure varies widely from couple to couple, however. Among the lesbians surveyed by Jay and Young (1977), only 5 percent reported having sex with their partners daily. Most women (57 percent) had sex two to five times per week; 25 percent had sex once a week, and 8 percent had sex less often. Little is known about factors that influence the actual or desired frequency of sex in lesbian relationships. The picture that emerges from these statistics is that most lesbian couples find sex an enjoyable and rewarding part of their relationships.

Research on sexuality in gay men's relationships presents a fairly similar picture. In general, gay men report high satisfaction with sex in their relationships (Peplau & Cochran, 1981). Gay men have sex with their steady partners as often or more often than do heterosexual couples (Lewis et al., 1980; Schäfer, 1977). Among gay men studied by Jay and Young (1977), 11 percent reported having sex with their partners daily, 38 percent had sex three to four times per week, 40 percent once or twice a week, and 11 percent less than once a week. Researchers assume that sex usually leads to orgasm for men, and so questions specifically about orgasms have not been included in most studies of gay men's relationships.

It has been suggested (for example, by Saghir & Robins, 1973) that long-term gay men's relationships often decline in sexual activity and interest. Adequate empirical evidence on this point is, however, lacking. We do not know how often such sexual "devitalization" occurs in gay men's relationships, whether it is any more common among gay male couples than among lesbian and heterosexual couples, or what factors might create such a situation.

Sexual Exclusivity

Today many couples, both heterosexual and homosexual, are questioning whether it is better for relationships to be sexually monogamous or sexually "open." As we discussed earlier, Peplau and Cochran (1980) found that more heterosexuals than homosexuals strongly valued sexual exclusivity in a steady relationship. It is important to emphasize, however, that gays are a diverse group with varied views about sexual behavior. Some gays are strong advocates of sexual exclusivity, as this quotation from a gay man illustrates: "I want my lover to be mine and only mine, and I want to be his and only his. He is my life, and I am his life, and that's the way I want it to be" (cited in Silverstein, 1981, p. 141). Other gay men and lesbians reject the idea of sexual exclusivity. One gay man explained,

> I still feel that a commitment to a relationship . . . has very little to do with what I choose to do with my body. My commitment is more intellectual and in the heart. I differentiate between sex and making love. . . . When I feel strongly toward a person, I make love. When I don't, I have sex. And I can enjoy both of them very much. [Quoted by Silverstein, 1981, p. 143]

Although these two quotations are from gay men, it is easy to imagine lesbians and heterosexuals who would agree with these views.

In actual practice, the relationships of gay men are less likely to be sexually exclusive than are those of lesbians or heterosexuals. Studies suggest that most gay men who are in a steady relationship also have sex with men other than their primary partner (for example, see Bell & Weinberg, 1978; Blasband & Peplau, 1980; Harry & Lovely, 1979; Plummer, 1978; Warren, 1974). In some studies, all the men whose relationships had continued for several years reported having had outside affairs. Why is sexual openness so common in the relationships of gay men? Several factors are relevant.

First, gender-role socialization in America teaches men to be more interested in sex and sexual variety than are women. One gay man suggested that "Promiscuity is inbred in all boy children, and since most boy children don't find out they're gay until later in life, their promiscuity has nothing to do with their gayness. It has to do with their *male*ness" (quoted by Mendola, 1980, p. 55). In contrast, for many women, whatever their sexual orientation, sex and love are closely linked; thus casual sex may be less appealing.

In Jay and Young's survey (1977), 97 percent of lesbians said that emotional involvement was important to sex, and 92 percent said that emotional involvement always or very frequently accompanied their own sexual relations. In comparison, 83 percent of the gay men said that emotional involvement is important in sex, and

45 percent said that involvement always or usually accompanied sex. Gay men more often than lesbians separate sex and love and can enjoy casual sex for its own sake, without emotional involvement. In Schäfer's (1977) survey, gay men were more likely than lesbians to say that many of their sexual partners were people they had never met before (70 percent of gay men, 26 percent of lesbians) and were partners with whom they had sex only once (64 percent of gay men; 18 percent of lesbians). Gay men were less likely than lesbians to say they were in love with most of their sex partners (19 percent of gay men, 64 percent of lesbians).

Basic differences in men's and women's orientations toward love and sex may be more important here than sexual orientation. Equal proportions of lesbians and heterosexual women (64 percent) told Gundlach and Reiss (1968) that they could have sex only if they were in love with their partners. Similarly, just as gay men are more likely than lesbians to have sexually open relationships, so too are heterosexual husbands more likely than wives to have extramarital affairs (Hunt, 1974; Kinsey et al., 1948, 1953; Pietropinto & Simenauer, 1979). Gender has a major influence on the kind of relationship people want. Whereas most men and women want a steady relationship with one special partner, men are more likely to want—and to have—sexual relations with other partners as well.

For gay men, the norms of the gay community may also encourage sexual openness rather than exclusivity. Especially in urban centers, the gay men's community provides many opportunities for casual sex. Gay men can find new partners at gay bars, public baths, and other places. The important point to remember is that for many gay men, as for many heterosexual men, casual sexual affairs are a complement to a steady relationship, not a substitute for it.

In growing up, men and women learn different lessons about sexuality. As adults, the genders are exposed to different opportunities for sexual exploration, and men continue to receive greater social support for sexual experimentation. Thus, we believe, differences in the sexual attitudes and behaviors of men and women are largely a result of socialization. But others attribute these gender differences to biology. For example, sociobiologist Donald Symons (1979) proposes that evolutionary pressures have encouraged a desire for sexual exclusivity in females and a desire for sexual diversity in males. In Symons' view, "the sex lives of homosexual men and women—who need not compromise sexually with members of the opposite sex—should provide dramatic insights into male sexuality and female sexuality in their undiluted states" (1979, p. 292). Symons is referring to the fact that heterosexual relationships are, in some measure, a compromise between the goals and desires of the male and female partners—a compromise that can obscure underlying gender differences. In relationships with same-gender partners, individuals may be able to express their personal dispositions more fully.

For gays as for heterosexuals, decisions about sexual exclusivity can have varied consequences for a love relationship. For some people, sexual exclusivity is a sign of love and commitment to their partners. For such individuals, sexual exploration with other partners might only occur if there were problems in the primary relationships. For others, however, secure and rewarding primary relationships are enhanced by the excitement and novelty of outside liaisons. Indeed, some people view sexual fidelity as excessively restrictive and unnecessary (see Harry, 1977; Jay & Young, 1977; Silverstein, 1981; Warren, 1974). In other words, the meaning of sexual openness and its implications for the continuation of a relationship can be quite diverse.

Research on the relationships of lesbians and gay men leads to several broad conclusions. There are many similarities between the relationship values of homosexuals and heterosexuals. Few significant differences have been found between gay and heterosexual couples on measures of relationship adjustment, love and satisfaction, or sex with one's partner. There appear to be many commonalities among intimate relationships, regardless of sexual orientation. However, a major difference between gay and heterosexual relationships did emerge. Heterosexual relationships usually emphasize gender-based differences between partners and adopt husband-wife roles as a relationship script. In contrast, lesbians and gay men usually reject traditional marital roles. Instead of treating one another as husband and wife, homosexuals treat their partners like best friends. The patterns of interaction that develop in gay couples are more likely to be based on the unique individual characteristics of the partners than on predetermined cultural scripts.

Our review has also highlighted several gender differences between the relationships of lesbians and gay men. Homosexuals are not a unitary group; it is unwise to assume that all homosexuals, regardless of gender, are necessarily similar. Lesbians are more likely than gay men to be in stable relationships. Lesbians give greater emphasis to emotional intimacy and to equality in relationships than do gay men. Lesbians are more likely to view sexuality and love as closely linked, and to prefer having sex only with partners they care about. Gay men, in contrast, are more likely to separate sex and love. Gay men enjoy sex with loved partners, but they are also more likely than gay women to enjoy recreational sex with casual partners. Gay men are more likely than lesbians to be in a sexually open relationship and to have had sex with a considerably larger number of partners. Cultural gender-role socialization undoubtedly touches all of us, regardless of sexual orientation. Gay men and lesbians bring to love relationships many of the same expectations, values, and interests as heterosexuals of the same gender.

REFERENCES

Bell, A. P., & Weinberg, M. S. *Homosexualities: A Study of diversity among men and women.* New York: Simon & Schuster, 1978.

Bernard, J. *The future of marriage.* New York: Bantam Books, 1972.

Blasband, D., & Peplau, L. A. *Open and closed long-term relationships of gay men: A comparative study.* Unpublished manuscript, Department of Psychology, University of California, Los Angeles, 1980.

Caldwell, M., & Peplau, L. A. *Power in lesbian relationships.* Unpublished manuscript, Department of Psychology, University of California, Los Angeles, 1980.

Califia, P. Lesbian sexuality. *Journal of Homosexuality.* 1979, *4*, 255–266.

Cardell, M., Finn, S., & Marecek, J. Sex-role identity, sex-role behavior, and satisfaction in heterosexual, lesbian, and gay male couples. *Psychology of Women Quarterly,* 1981, *5,* 488–494.

Cochran, S. D. *Romantic relationships: For better or for worse.* Paper presented at the annual meeting of the Western Psychological Association, San Francisco, April 1978.

David, D. S., & Brannon (Eds.) *The forty-nine percent majority: The male sex role.* Menlo Park: Addison-Wesley, 1976.

DeLora, J. S., & Warren, C. A. B. *Understanding sexual interaction.* Boston: Houghton Mifflin, 1977.

Gagnon, J. H. *Human sexualities.* Glenview, Ill.: Scott, Foresman, 1977.

Gagnon, J. H., & Simon, W. *Sexual conduct: The social sources of human sexuality.* Chicago: Aldine, 1973.

Gundlach, R. H., & Reiss, B. F. Self and sexual identity in the female: A study of female homosexuals. In B. F. Reiss (Ed.), *New directions in mental health* (Vol. 1). New York: Grune & Stratton, 1968.

Harry, J. On the validity of typologies of gay males. *Journal of Homosexuality,* 1976, *2,* 143–152.

Harry, J. Marriage among gay males: The separation of intimacy and sex. In S. G. McNall (Ed.), *The sociological perspectives: Introductory readings* (4th ed.). Boston: Little, Brown, 1977.

Harry, J. The "marital" liaisons of gay men. *Family Coordinator,* 1979, *28,* 616–621.

Harry, J., & DeVall, W. *The social organization of gay males.* New York: Praeger, 1978.

Harry, J., & Lovely, R. Gay marriages and communities of sexual orientation. *Alternative Life Styles,* 1979, *2,* 177–200.

Hill, C. T., Rubin, Z., & Peplau, L. A. Breakups before marriage: The end of 103 affairs. *Journal of Social Issues,* 1976, *32,* 147–168.

Hill C. T., Rubin, Z., Peplau, L. A., & Willard, S. G. The volunteer couple: Sex differences, couple commitment and participation in research on interpersonal relationships. *Social Psychology Quarterly,* 1979, *42,* 415–420.

Hunt, M. *Sexual behavior in the 1970s.* Chicago: Playboy Press, 1974.

Jay, K., & Young, A. *The gay report.* New York: Summit, 1977.

Kinsey, A. C., Pomeroy, W. B., & Martin, C. E. *Sexual behavior in the human male.* Philadelphia: Saunders, 1948.

Kinsey, A. C., Pomeroy, W. B., Martin, C. E., & Gebhard, P. H. *Sexual behavior in the human female.* Philadelphia: Saunders, 1953.

Laner, M. R. Permanent partner priorities: Gay and straight. *Journal of Homosexuality,* 1977, *3,* 21–39.

Levinger, G. A social psychological perspective on marital dissolution. In G. Levinger & O. C. Moles (Eds.), *Divorce and separation: Context, causes, and consequences.* New York: Basic Books, 1979.

Lewis, R. A., Lozac, E. B., Milardo, R. M., & Grosnick, W. A. *Commitment in lesbian and gay male living-together relationships.* Paper presented at the annual meeting of the American Sociological Association, New York, August 1980.

Marmor, J. (Ed.). *Homosexual behavior.* New York: Basic Books, 1980.

Masters, W., & Johnson, V. *Homosexuality in perspective.* Boston: Little, Brown, 1979.

Mendola, M. *The Mendola report: A new look at gay couples.* New York: Crown, 1980.

Morin, S. F. Heterosexual bias in psychological research on lesbianism and male homosexuality. *American Psychologist,* 1977, *32,* 629–637.

Peplau, L. A. Power in dating relationships. In J. Freeman (Ed.), *Women: A feminist perspective* (2nd ed.). Palo Alto, Calif.: Mayfield, 1979.

Peplau, L. A., & Amaro, H. Lesbian relationships. In W. Paul & J. D. Weinrich (Eds.), *Homosexuality as a social issue*. Beverly Hills, Calif.: Sage, in press.

Peplau, L. A., & Cochran, S. D. *Sex differences in values concerning love relationships*. Paper presented at the annual meeting of the American Psychological Association, Montreal, September 1980.

Peplau, L. A., & Cochran, S. D. Value orientations in the intimate relationships of gay men. *Journal of Homosexuality*, 1981, *6*, 1–19.

Peplau, L. A., Cochran, S., Rook, K., & Padesky, C. Loving women: Attachment and autonomy in lesbian relationships. *Journal of Social Issues*, 1978, *34*, 7–27.

Peplau, L. A., Rubin, Z., & Hill, C. T. Sexual intimacy in dating couples. *Journal of Social Issues*, 1977, *33*, 86–109.

Pietropinto, A., & Simenauer, J. *Husbands and wives*. New York: Berkeley, 1979.

Plummer, K. Men in love: Observations on male homosexual couples. In M. Corbin (Ed.), *The couple*. New York: Penguin, 1978.

Ramsey, J., Latham, J. D., & Lindquist, C. U. *Long term same-sex relationships: Correlates of adjustment*. Paper presented at the annual meeting of the American Psychological Association, Toronto, August 1978.

Raphael, S. M., & Robinson, M. K. The older lesbian: Love relationships and friendship patterns. *Alternative Lifestyles*, 1980, *3*, 207–230.

Rubin, Z. *Liking and loving: An invitation to social psychology*. New York: Holt, Rinehart & Winston, 1973.

Saghir, M. T., & Robins, E. *Male and female homosexuality*. Baltimore: Williams & Wilkins, 1973.

Schäfer, S. Sexual and social problems of lesbians. *Journal of Sex Research*, 1976, *12*, 50–69.

Schäfer, S. Sociosexual behavior in male and female homosexuals: A study in sex differences. *Archives of Sexual Behavior*, 1977, *6*, 355–364.

Silverstein, C. *Man to man: Gay couples in America*. New York: Morrow, 1981.

Spada, J. *The Spada report: The newest survey of gay male sexuality*. New York: New American Library, 1979.

Symons, D. *The evolution of human sexuality*. New York: Oxford University Press, 1979.

Tanner, D. M. *The lesbian couple*. Lexington, Mass.: Heath, 1978.

Tavris, C., & Sadd, S. *The Redbook report on female sexuality*. New York: Delacorte, 1977.

Warren, C. A. B. *Identity and community in the gay world*. New York: Wiley, 1974.

Wolf, D. G. *The lesbian community*. Berkeley: University of California Press, 1979.

ARTICLE 36
Asexual Reproduction and the Family

JOHN N. EDWARDS

This article describes dramatic new biosocial innovations that separate sex from reproduction. These include in vitro fertilization, cryopreservation, artificial insemination, genetic engineering, ovum transfer, cloning, ectogenesis, sperm banks, and surrogacy. Combined, these technologies render marriage unnecessary, and they radically alter the nature of parenthood and what we mean by "family."

TO ARTIFICIALLY CREATE LIFE is not a new dream. In 1818, Mary Shelley, the wife of the poet, published *Frankenstein, or The Modern Prometheus*. It is well known as a fable of failure—the result being a man-monster. But the tale clearly reflects an abiding desire to learn the secrets of life in order to artificially create it. Today, that desire is rapidly becoming a reality. Most instrumental among the biological innovations in bringing this about are the technologies associated with in vitro fertilization (IVF), cryopreservation, artificial insemination (AI), genetic engineering, ovum transfer (OT), and the promise of cloning and ectogenesis, the creation of an embryo without a host. Augmenting these on the social side are sperm banks and the practice of surrogacy.

John N. Edwards, "New Conceptions: Biosocial Innovations and the Family." *Journal of Marriage and the Family* (in press, May 1991). Copyrighted © 1991 by the National Council on Family Relations, 3989 Central Ave. N.E., Suite #550, Minneapolis, MN 55421. Adapted and reprinted by permission.

NEW CONCEPTIONS

In Vitro Fertilization

In vitro fertilization, prompted largely by infertility problems, basically involves the insemination of oocytes in a sterile Petri or organ-transplant dish. The procedures are highly complex (Fredericks, Paulson, and DeCherney, 1987; Wood and Trounson, 1984). They include the harvesting of the oocyte through laparoscopy or by using ultrasonic techniques. The oocytes must be at a proper stage of maturity. Once aspirated, they are placed in a proper medium and incubated in a carbon dioxide atmosphere with a high level of humidity (98 percent). Meanwhile, fresh semen must be collected, inspected for motility, washed, and placed in a culture medium that induces sperm capacitation. After a proper interval, 100,000 to 800,000 spermatozoa are added to the medium of the oocyte. Once fertilization has taken place, the embryos are carefully monitored and assessed with respect to their size, shape, density, and the presence of fragments. Those with the proper cleavages are then transferred to the uterus. Up to four embryos are returned to the womb, as the chance of pregnancy begins to approximate natural fecundity with more than one embryo (Fredericks, Paulson, and DeCherney, 1987; Wood and Trounson, 1984; Jones, Jones, Hodgen, and Rosenwaks, 1986). The rate of successful pregnancies can be enhanced by the use of fertility drugs, making it more likely that the embryo will implant in the womb (Singer and Wells, 1985). The insertion of multiple embryos, combined with the use of fertility drugs, also increases the probability of bearing twins, triplets, or quadruplets.

Cryopreservation

Cryopreservation, or the freezing of embryos, is fast becoming commonplace (Lieber, 1989). Ordinarily, only one oocyte at a time will develop. With the use of fertility drugs, upwards of forty eggs may be produced, although the typical range is five to ten. Cryopreservation makes it possible to store the excess embryos for later use in the event earlier attempts at implantation are unsuccessful. It further reduces the costs of IVF procedures, running about one-seventh of the cost of a full IVF cycle using a fresh embryo. Moreover, many clinicians prefer cryopreservation in the belief that the embryos surviving freezing and thawing are thought to be the hardiest and most capable of producing a live birth. Cryopreservation further allows for the possibility of embryo adoption. Employing cryoprotectants, which act like antifreeze to prevent crystallization, it is estimated that frozen embryos may be kept potentially viable for 600 years and perhaps up to 10,000 years (Lieber, 1989; Singer and Wells, 1985).

Artificial Insemination and Sperm Banks

Compared to IVF, artificial insemination (AI) has a long and rather successful history, having served as a basic technique in animal husbandry. As with IVF, AI is medically indicated in certain cases of infertility, especially those instances of male infertility (Amirikia and Booker, 1980).

Four major methods of insemination are now employed: intrauterine, intracervical, vaginal, and cervical cap. The general assumption is that the vagina presents the most hostile environment to spermatozoa, so a combination of methods is frequently used. Cervical-cap insemination is considered the method that best mimics the nature process (Belaisch, Kremer, Stenno, and Paulson, 1980).

Where, with respect to the family, artificial insemination begins to raise fundamental issues stems from the fact that there are three different types: artificial insemination homologous (AIH), insemination by donor (AID), and a combination of the two (AIC). AIH is homologous insemination using the husband's semen. It poses no significant ethical or legal problems because any resulting child is the biological offspring of the husband and wife. However, if the husband's sperm are subgrade in number or motility, other procedures may be needed to achieve a pregnancy, assuming the wife is potentially fertile. AID and AIC are the available alternatives.

There are now over seventy commercial and university-based sperm banks worldwide, the greatest number of them located in the United States (Alsoform, 1985). In the United States alone, it is estimated that artificial insemination contributes to 65,000 births each year (Office of Technology Assessment, 1988).

Proponents of AI emphasize its clinical applications. Those who are oligospermic (having a low sperm count) may be aided by pooling and concentrating sperm samples. Men undergoing chemical or radiological therapy may preserve and store their semen. Males who have had a vasectomy, which is usually irreversible, can save their sperm and still father children at a later date.

Genetic Engineering

Having separated human reproduction from the act of sexual intercourse, IVF procedures plainly create the opportunity for further manipulation of the final product. Putting embryos into an external laboratory environment makes them directly accessible for genetic manipulation. Paralleling developments in fertilization technology, significant advances have been taking place over the last fifteen years in recombinant DNA research and genetic engineering. The latter advances are being used to produce various transgenic animals (pigs and mice), which have foreign DNA integrated into their germ line cells. All of the body cells carry the new gene, making it possible to pass it on to future generations. Thus far, techniques have not been perfected for gene insertion in humans, but many scientists consider it only a matter of time and further experimentation before it becomes feasible (Kucherlapti and Skoultchi, 1984).

A worldwide project to map the entire human genome is now underway. Ostensibly, the aim is to identify and manipulate "bad" genes linked to inheritable conditions and diseases, including psychological disorders such as manic depression. But there are no barriers preventing the technology to be used for eugenic purposes, even the predetermination of the sex of the child (Ewing, 1988). Nothing prevents even embryos conceived in the "old-fashioned way" from being flushed from the womb, genetically screened, having the "necessary corrections" made, and then being reimplanted for gestation.

Ovum Transfer

Ovum transfer (OT) is a relatively new procedure for humans. As an infertility treatment, OT consists of a donor female and a recipient, who will carry the embryo to term. The procedure, in comparison to IVF, is relatively simple, less invasive, and more successful. It has the added advantage of being nonsurgical; the transfer from donor to recipient is accomplished by a specially designed catheter. But the use of the procedure need not be confined to infertile women. It can allow fertile women who are concerned about adverse genetic transmissions to bear a child. Ovum transfer could further serve as an intermediate process to diagnose genetic makeup and to detect potential health problems early in embryonic development (Chapman, 1984; Lancaster, 1984).

Cloning and Ectogenesis

Advances in IVF and OT are leading the way for other new and even more dramatic reproductive techniques, such as cloning and ectogenesis. In principle, cloning is straightforward. The procedure involves the removal of the nucleus of a mature unfertilized egg and replacing it with the nucleus of a body cell (other than a germ cell) from an adult organism. The donor body cell, in effect, fertilizes the egg, with the result that the new organism is genetically identical to the donor, including its sex. The procedure has been used with varying degrees of success in reproducing frogs, salamanders, and fruit flies. A second, and simpler, type of cloning consists of taking an egg fertilized in vitro. When the egg goes through its first division, it consists of two cells. Because the cells of an early embryo are not specialized, they share a common genetic constitution. By splitting the embryo at the two-cell stage, identical twins will develop (Singer and Wells, 1985). Technically, the procedure is difficult and remains in a primitive stage (Walters, 1982). Yet, the theoretical possibility fosters many startling scenarios about cloning being the ultimate in asexual reproduction.

Only slightly less dramatic are the prospects of ectogenesis. This is the term applied to the insemination of an ovum and development of an embryo without a host, or outside of the uterus. Ectogenesis is now a first-stage procedure in IVF. True ectogenesis, though, would entail developing the embryo throughout the gestational period. To date, no artificial placenta has been successfully designed to support the fetus during the first half of gestation. The prospects for such may not be too distant, however. Currently, premature infants, some less than 1,000 grams in weight, are being kept alive in incubators (Walters, 1982).

Proponents of ectogenesis hail it as a procedure that not only may aid infertile couples, who might eschew the services of a surrogate, but view it as a process that could supply spare parts needed to replace diseased organs. If ectogenesis were possible and if there were a demand for such fetuses (for organ transplants or adoption), abortions could become obsolete (Singer and Wells, 1985). Abortion, in effect, would become early births.

Surrogacy

Surrogacy has received considerable attention as a part of the new reproductive technologies. The practice typically does not involve sexual intercourse, relying instead on artificial insemination with the husband as donor. Strictly speaking, such arrangements do not involve true surrogacy since the birth mother is also the genetic mother. Only when the birth or carrying mother does not contribute her ova do we have a true case of surrogacy, a distinct possibility with current IVF techniques. However, the term "surrogate motherhood" is used widely in referring to all arrangements where the social or nurturing mother does not give birth to the child.

As with IVF procedures, surrogate motherhood has been seen as a boon to those with infertility problems, in this case those of the wife. The most obvious cases have been women with diseased wombs that have been removed or who have dysfunctional fallopian tubes. Surrogacy also has been sought by women suffering from medical conditions that would make pregnancy dangerous, such as kidney disease, drug-resistant high blood pressure, or multiple sclerosis as in the case of Elizabeth Stern, the sociological mother in the celebrated "Baby M" dispute. Increasingly, though, surrogates are being sought by women avoiding pregnancy for career or cosmetic purposes (Singer and Wells, 1985).

THE PREVALENCE OF THE NEW REPRODUCTIVE TECHNOLOGIES

Although statistics on some techniques and practices are difficult to ascertain, reliable figures and estimates on the adoption of others are available. The first successful in vitro conception and embryo transfer, for example, took place in England in 1978 with the birth of Louise Brown. This was followed by a second birth later that year in India. Scotland saw its first "test-tube" child in 1979, Australia in 1980. The United States and France followed in 1981, West Germany in 1982 (Arditti, Klein, and Minden, 1984). By the mid-1980s, there were more than 270 IVF clinics spread throughout First World countries, and the number of clinics continues to proliferate. There are over a hundred in the United States alone. Worldwide, by 1986, more than five thousand babies have been born as a result of this technique, and annually the number climbs rapidly (Laborie, 1988).

Since 1960, artificial insemination has been extensively practiced worldwide. It is estimated, perhaps conservatively, that there are as many as 350,000 individuals in the United States who have been conceived in this fashion (Isaacs and Holt, 1987). The practice is widespread in other industrialized countries, but precise figures are difficult to obtain.

Moreover, it seems reasonable to assume that the practice of AI will increase. There are several reasons for this. Some members of the male population desire children but are themselves infertile. Because of environmental causes, such as radiation and chemical pollution, this portion of the population is thought to be growing. Basically, AI is a simple, inexpensive, and highly effective procedure, with a reputed success rate of 80 percent (Shaman, 1980). In the case of infertile couples, AI satisfies the desire to have a normal pregnancy and have some input into the genetic makeup of the child, an impossibility with adoption, which is also a more costly process. With the advent of cryopreservation, AI permits flexibility. A male can store his sperm, have a vasectomy, and later father children. A female could, with cryopreservation, produce "legitimate" children in the event of her husband's death. There is the further demand for AI on the part of single women, both heterosexuals and lesbians (McGuire and Alexander, 1985). As work in genetic engineering proceeds, AI probably will become a standard adjunct procedure in the sex determination of offspring, the demand for which may be enormous, involving a very large segment of the population.

The universal desire for the "perfect" child virtually assures continued research in genetic engineering. As simple as gene splicing is in principle, normal hemoglobin-gene DNA cannot as yet be placed correctly in the total genetic code of the embryo. The more realistic means to minimize human defects for the foreseeable future is through the use of IVF. Carriers of genetic defects and diseases could use it with artificial stimulation to produce several embryos that could be genetically screened, transferring only those without defect to the birth mother.

For the time being, the cloning of humans does not appear feasible. There has been only one report of a successful experiment with mammals, this involving the cloning of mice, but other experimenters have not been able to replicate it (Singer and Wells, 1985). If the process is ever perfected, the most likely use of the technique will be to allow gene typing and to provide spare biological material. These uses would avoid the psychological problems that might face sets of identical people and also avoid the specter of an army of clones. Most of the medical objections to cloning, in fact, have centered on the prospect of multiple cloning (Singer and Wells, 1985).

Although true ectogenesis is not now possible, medical science may well back into its development. By finding methods to routinely save infants earlier and earlier in the gestational period, ectogenesis may eventually be achieved. The demand for partial ectogenesis to supply spare body organs would certainly increase the technique's adoption and diffusion.

More than 500 known babies had been born to surrogate mothers by the mid-1980s. The contractual nature of surrogacy, involving a third party as it does, has opened the practice to legal interpretation, with varying results. To critics, surrogate motherhood represents "baby-selling" and the commercialization of childbearing, and some state courts have agreed. Several courts, though, have upheld the legality of the practice, maintaining it is protected by the constitutional right of privacy (Isaacs and Holt, 1989). A large number of international, as well as U.S., commissions and professional associations remain divided over whether it should be permitted, indicating that even the experts do not represent a united front. In the absence of any reliable statistics, the legal challenges to surrogate arrangements have probably slowed the practice, but they are unlikely to stop it. As long as all parties to an agreement are satisfied, the practice can continue in an extralegal manner. Furthermore, combined with IVF and ovum transfer (OT), the status of the child and who its parents are become moot legal issues. The surrogate is plainly the gestational or carrying mother, and the contracting husband and wife are the genetic parents. To make regulation even more problematic, many women in Third World countries are participating in a flourishing surrogate industry that could become available to potential parents in industrialized nations, even if the practice were outlawed there (*India Today,* 1986).

Ultimately, the high value society places on parenthood drives the demand for the new reproductive technologies. The desire for a child is so intense for many that, in the face of difficulties, they will go to any lengths to achieve their goal.

Given the growing prevalence of these biosocial innovations, they clearly have profound implications for the future. Not the least of these concerns parenthood as an institution and what may constitute a family.

FUTURE PARENTS AND FAMILIES

In theory, if not yet in practice, the new reproductive technologies signal the obsolescence of marriage and the family as we presently know these institutions. While the separation of sexual intercourse from reproduction has had major consequences for these institutions, most of these biosocial innovations make intercourse itself superfluous. They enable the ultimate separation. In the short term, the new technologies at the very least present the need for redefining "family" relations, for the innovations pointedly illustrate the impoverishment of our kin vocabulary. The combination of surrogacy and AID alone create the possibility of a child having five parents, perhaps even six parents if one considers the partner of the genitrix. In consequence, we have had to fall back on strictly biological-legal terms, rather than a more organic sense of the concept, to describe what we mean by "family." Some of the combinations are illustrated in Table 1.

As complex as the parental roles listed in Table 1 are, they do not fully reflect the entire range of the impact of asexual reproduction on parenting. What is designated as "holistic motherhood" may appear to be traditional parenting until we consider that it may not involve marriage, having been initiated through artificial insemination, and could involve either a heterosexual or homosexual mother. Likewise, the status of "holistic fatherhood" might be achieved by cloning or ectogenesis, a radically different form of fatherhood. If nothing else, the new means of conception fragment parental roles, paving the way for new parent-child relationships.

To be sure, the biosocial innovations in reproduction represent responses to

TABLE 1 Reproductive Means and Parental Roles

Contributing Mother	Holistic Mother
Genetic Mother (Donor)	
Carrying Mother (True Surrogate)	Genetic/Carrying/Nurturing Mother
Nurturing Mother (Recipient, Adopter, or Surrogate Employer)	
Genetic/Carrying Mother (Surrogate)	
Carrying/Nurturing Mother (Donor Recipient)	
Genetic/Nurturing Mother (Surrogate Employer)	
Contributing Father	Holistic Father
Genetic Father (Donor)	Genetic/Nurturing Father
Nurturing Father (Recipient, Adopter, or Surrogate Employer)	

an age-old quest—the desire for parenthood. The new reproductive technologies unquestionably solve some problems, but they create many others. The technologies clearly suggest that marriage is unnecessary. More fundamentally, they present a direct challenge to what we know as "family." Although current legal responses generally reflect prevailing norms and existing social arrangements, it remains to be seen how long this will be the case as wider segments of the population, particularly the unmarried, avail themselves of asexual means of reproduction. Implicitly, the innovations suggest that the family of the future may merely consist of one socialized adult and an offspring. Even this group need not be based on any consanguineal tie between the adult and child. Given the variety of permutations brought about by asexual reproduction, the psychology of parenting will undoubtedly be different than it is today. It will be possible for each child in the "family" to be conceived in a different way, making the parent (her, him, or them) a different type of parent to each child.

REFERENCES

Alsoform, Judy. 1985. "Sperm banking issues debated." *American Medical News* (October): 3.

Amirikia, H., and J. H. Booker. 1980. "Legal and ethical aspects of artificial insemination."

Pp. 221–228 in J. C. Emperaire, A. Audebert, and E. S. E. Hafez (eds.), *Homologous Artificial Insemination*. The Hague: Martinus Nijhoff Publishers.

Arditti, Rita, Renate Klein, and Shelley Minden. 1984. "Test-tube babies and clinics, where are they?" Pp. 52–53 in R. Arditti, R. Klein, and S. Minden (eds.), *Test-Tube Women*. London: Pandora Press.

Belaisch, J., J. Kremer, O. Stenno, and J. Paulson. 1980. "Insemination techniques." Pp. 186–197 in J. C. Emperaire, A. Audebert, and E. S. E. Hafez (eds.), *Homologous Artificial Insemination*. The Hague: Martinus Nijhoff Publishers.

Chapman, Fern. 1984. "Going for gold in the baby business." *Fortune* (September 17): 41–77.

Ewing, Christine M. 1988. "Tailored genes: IVF, genetic engineering, and eugenics." *Reproductive and Genetic Engineering* 1: 31–40.

Fredericks, Christopher M., John D. Paulson, and Alan H. DeCherney (eds.). 1987. *Foundations of In Vitro Fertilization*. Washington, D.C.: Hemisphere.

India Today. 1986. "Renting wombs." (July 15): 80–84.

Isaacs, Stephen, L., and Renee J. Holt. 1987. "Redefining procreation: Facing the issues." *Population Bulletin* 42: 3–37.

Jones, Howard H., G. S. Jones, G. D. Hodgen, and Z. Rosenwaks (eds.). 1986. *In Vitro Fertilization, Norfolk*. Baltimore: Williams & Wilkins.

Kucherlapti, R., and A. Skoultchi. 1984. "Introduction of purified genes into mammalian cells. *Critical Reviews in Biochemistry* 16: 349–379.

Laborie, Francoise. 1988. "New reproductive technologies: News from France and elsewhere." *Reproductive and Genetic Engineering* 1: 77–85.

Lancaster, Hall. 1984. "Firm offering human-embryo transfers for profit stirs legal and ethical debates." *Wall Street Journal* (March 7): 33.

Lieber, James. 1989. "A piece of yourself in the world." *The Atlantic Monthly* (June):76–80.

McGuire, Maureen, and Nancy Alexander. 1985. "Artificial insemination of single women." *Fertility and Sterility* 43: 182–184.

Office of Technology Assessment. 1988. *Artificial Insemination Practice in the United States: Summary of a 1987 Survey*. Washington, D.C.: U. S. Government Printing Office.

Shaman, Jeffrey M. 1980. "Legal aspects of artificial insemination." *Journal of Family Law* 18: 331.

Singer, Peter, and Deanne Wells. 1985. *Making Babies: The New Science and Ethics of Conception*. New York: Scribner's.

Walters, William A. W. 1982. "Cloning, ectogenesis, and hybrids: Things to come?" Pp. 110–118 in W. A. W. Walters and P. Singer (eds.), *Test-Tube Babies*. Melbourne: Oxford University Press.

Wood, Carl, and Alan Trounson (eds.). 1984. *Clinical In Vitro Fertilization*. Berlin: Springer-Verlag.

ARTICLE 37
Age Wars: The Coming Battle between Young and Old

PHILLIP LONGMAN

The elderly constitute a steadily increasing proportion of the population, commanding an ever greater portion of governmental expenditures in terms of financial support and health care. This article forcefully argues that the well-being of today's senior citizens is being financed at the expense of future generations. Unless dramatic policy changes are undertaken, by the time the baby-boom generation reaches retirement we may have a war between young and old.

AMERICANS HAVE ALWAYS been an exceptionally optimistic people—and never more so than now. In the late 1970s, it was fashionable to question whether the country had at last entered an "era of limits," but the rallying cry these days is "America is back!" Inflation is down, employment is up, the military is strong, and energy is plentiful. This is not the season to peddle unhappy thoughts about the future of America, much less to call for sacrifice.

Yet today's prosperity is being purchased at the eventual expense of today's younger citizens and those yet unborn. As a result, the early decades of the next

Phillip Longman, "Age Wars: The Coming Battle between Young and Old." Reprinted, with permission, from THE FUTURIST, published by the World Future Society, 4916 St. Elmo Ave., Bethesda, MD 20814.

century may well bring a war between the generations, as tomorrow's elderly attempt to compel the young to honor the compounding debts of the present era.

The United States is now using an almost endless variety of means to distribute wealth and opportunity away from future taxpayers. After more than two decades of declining expenditures for public works, the cost of repairing the nation's dilapidated bridges, roads, waterways, and other infrastructure is conservatively estimated at more than $1 trillion.

By failing to pay for the safe disposal of toxic wastes, today's generations shove this cost on to those who follow. Similarly, by running down supplies of clean water, topsoil, energy, and other natural resources required to maintain future production, all Americans gain a higher standard of living today but at the eventual expense of the young and future generations.

The most brazen example of how we rob future taxpayers is today's massive federal deficits. With each month that goes by, these deficits are dramatically reducing the future standard of living of today's younger Americans. Just to finance the interest charges on *this year's* deficit will cost the average citizen now entering the work force an extra $10,000 in taxes over his or her lifetime, according to a conservative estimate by the Congressional Research Service.

At prevailing interest rates, every additional dollar the government borrows will cost future taxpayers $22 in service charges over the next 30 years. With the burden of paying compounding interest charges on the ever-mounting national debt, today's young families will find it increasingly difficult to save for a new home or for their children's education—much less for their own retirement.

As long as the deficits continue, capital that could otherwise be used for rebuilding the nation's dilapidated infrastructure, for robotics, space manufacturing, education, and other productive investments is instead committed to servicing the national debt. Already, 15% of the federal budget is consumed by interest charges on previous deficits. To meet this expense, the government is borrowing still more.

THE GRAYING OF AMERICA

The true measure of how far Americans are living beyond their means is revealed not just by the magnitude of federal borrowing, nor by the other examples given above. Also to be counted in the balance is the nation's failure to save up for one of the greatest and most predictable challenges to the American standard of living in the next century: the enormous social cost of the baby-boom generation's retirement.

Comprising 75 million Americans born between 1946 and 1964, the baby boomers are now and will remain for several more decades a source of bulging cash flow for the government. The youngest baby boomers have now become adults, and most—men and women alike—are working and paying taxes. Fully 91% of all baby boomers hold down jobs—the highest percentage of any generation of Americans thus far.

Moreover, while few baby boomers are experiencing the same upward mobility

CHART 1 Social Security Tax

Maximum combined employer/employee Social Security tax paid annually:

1949	1972	1986	1990
$60	$936	$5,710	$8,690

enjoyed by their parents in the 1950s and 1960s, their incomes will tend to rise, along with their taxes, as they gain experience and seniority in the workplace. Finally, the baby boomers are, for the moment, both too old and too young to be entitled to many government benefits.

With all these trends running together, the Social Security system is, not surprisingly, in strong shape for the near term. But as the baby boomers begin to take their own turn at retirement, all these trends will be thrown into reverse. Today, there are 3.4 workers available to support each retiree. Accordingly, the per capita cost of providing old age benefits, while very high, is still bearable. Because of the baby boomers' exceptionally low fertility rates and increased life expectancy, however, there could well be fewer than two workers for each retiree by 2035.

THE PREDICAMENT OF THE BABY BOOMERS

How can the baby boomers avoid an impoverished old age without presenting an impossible encumbrance to their children? The essential predicament faced by most members of the generation is that they have inordinately great need to save for retirement but little ability to do so. The baby boomers will probably live longer in retirement than any previous generation in American history, yet they cannot prudently rely on receiving anywhere near the same level of benefits enjoyed by today's senior citizens.

In the meantime, most baby boomers are struggling to get by with lower real wages than their parents enjoyed at a similar time of life, while also paying much higher taxes and housing expenses. This leaves little left over for retirement savings, however paramount the need—for both individuals and for the generations as a whole—to build up capital and to invest in the future.

The prevailing "upwardly mobile" stereotype notwithstanding, most baby

CHART 2 Tax Rate for Young Families

Average tax rate for households headed by persons aged 25–34:

1960	1982
10%	23%

Higher taxes account for much of the downward mobility of the so-called "upwardly mobile" baby boomers, says author Longman.

boomers are now in the grip of real downward mobility. According to Census Bureau data, 42% of all baby boomers earn less than $10,000 a year. Between 1973 and 1983, the real, after-tax income of households headed by a person 25–34 declined by nearly 19%. After adjusting for inflation, today's young families have slightly less disposable income than did their counterparts in the early 1960s, even though the labor force participation rate of young wives has more than doubled since then, from 29% to 62%.

One important cause of this downward mobility, which further underscores the need for baby boomers to increase their savings for retirement, is the dramatic increase in the cost of housing during the post-war era.

The already alarming rise in the incidence of poverty among today's children further increases the baby boomers' objective need to save for retirement. Since 1973, the poverty rate among Americans under 18 has increased by more than 50%. More than one out of five children are now living in poverty. Experts predict that a third of all American children will experience poverty sometime before reaching adulthood.

Poor children tend to grow up to be poor adults. Even if other members of the "baby-bust" generation do comparatively well, they will still be responsible for supporting an expanding under-class within their own age group. This will leave fewer resources available to cover the enormous cost of providing even minimum retirement benefits for the baby-boom generation, as well as all other social needs.

For these and other reasons, the baby boomers' prospects for retirement lie not only with increased *financial* saving, but with "human capital" formation as well.

As the baby boomers, in their large numbers, move into retirement, the nation's per capita output of goods and services will decline, along with its standard of living, unless the next, very small generation of workers becomes correspondingly more efficient. To achieve this end requires, first, that we cease to borrow so much against the future earnings of today's children for the purpose of subsidizing current consumption, and, second, that we increase the savings rate.

Yet, no matter how large the pool of financial savings available for productive investment during the period of the baby boomers' retirement, if the next generation lacks the skills and knowledge to put it to good use, no one's interest will be served. Individual baby boomers may scrimp and save to build a nest egg for retirement, but their dollars won't go very far if their children, for lack of education, are unable to develop or use new technologies required to compete in the world economy of the next century.

WHAT MUST BE DONE

Younger Americans must encourage government to institute reforms in their own and the nation's long-term interest. Policies that have worked well for today's elderly

> ## The High Cost of Housing
>
> Two-thirds of today's elderly own their own homes with the mortgage fully paid off. Many seniors have paid much less in mortgage payments over the years than their houses are now worth. Since 1950, the median price of existing homes has increased sevenfold (see Chart), while the general cost of living has increased only fourfold.
>
> This happy circumstance allows many of today's senior citizens to convert the inflated equity in their homes into a substantial nest egg for retirement. But few of the baby boomers are likely to enjoy such an advantage in their later years. Between 1977 and 1983, the rate of home-ownership among persons 25 to 34 declined from 41% to 34%. Yet even those young people who do manage to afford a house are unlikely to reap the windfalls of the previous generation of homeowners.
>
> In the early 1950s, a young family with an income of $4,000 (the median income at the time) could purchase a house in Levittown for $7,990, paying $60 a month with no money down.
>
> ### Price of Housing
>
> | Median price of existing homes: | |
> |---|---|
> | 1950 | 1985 |
> | $10,050 | $73,800 |
>
> Today, for the privilege of living in the same house, a young couple must surrender as much as $90,000, or put $18,000 down and assume monthly mortgage payments of about $880—which will most likely rise with inflation. At prevailing interest rates, their total expenditure for the home will be $316,800 over the next 30 years. Yet when the house is finally paid off and the owners are ready to retire, it will only be worth what some member of the very small—and so far, very poor—baby-bust generation will be able or willing to pay.
>
> —Phillip Longman

will fail the baby boomers and their children, who must plan against an entirely different set of economic and demographic circumstances.

The baby-boom generation is the first in American history to be larger than the one that follows. This by itself creates a need for the baby boomers to save more toward the cost of their retirement than did the present older generation. Moreover, unless we soon reduce the deficits, the few workers who will be available to support the baby boomers in old age will already be encumbered with enormous public debts and a declining standard of living.

In the meantime, baby boomers must pay an unprecedented share of their income to provide benefits to today's elderly—rich and poor alike. Unless we move toward equitable reform of Social Security and Medicare, this burden will make it all the more difficult for the baby boomers to save up against the near inevitability that these benefits will not be available to them when they retire.

Finally, the generation as a whole can't afford *not* to spend more of its income for the rigorous education of the young and for the repair and retooling of the nation's obsolete factories and sagging infrastructure. Like their Victorian forebears who built up America into a great industrial power, the baby boomers will have to rediscover an ethos of thrift and sacrifice for the future.

The oldest baby boomers are now but 23 years away from reaching current average age of retirement. The longer today's generations fail to reduce the deficits, increase savings, and invest in the future of the next generation, the more likely it is that the American future will consist of depression and a war between the young and old.

ARTICLE 38
The Politics of the Family

STEVEN MINTZ AND SUSAN KELLOGG

The family has become the subject of heated public debate. With the loosening of family bonds and the growth of family-related problems, politicians of both parties claim to be "pro-family." However, liberals and conservatives, as well as the electorate itself, remain deeply divided over specific policies as to how to deal with family issues. Among the most pressing issues of the near future, Mintz and Kellogg suggest, are those concerning the growing number of children living in poverty, child care for working mothers, and the complex ethical and legal issues surrounding the new reproductive technologies.

EACH RECENT DECADE has witnessed explosive public controversy over questions of sex and the family. It was during the 1960s that the family became the focus of an angry and ongoing public debate. Environmentalists warned of the dangers posed by a worldwide "population explosion"; feminists called for abortion law reform, day-care centers, and shelters for battered wives; mounting campus unrest generated fears about a "generation gap"; and government policymakers debated whether poverty and street crime were related to "family disorganization." In the 1970s public controversy swirled around a new set of issues raised by the sexual revolution, the increasing divorce rate, and the growing number of working mothers, such as day care, abortion, single parenthood, and gay rights.[1]

During the 1980s, as anxiety mounted over the consequences of the sexual and social revolution that reshaped family life in recent years, public debate has focused on new issues. Milk cartons, subway billboards, and utility bills began to carry pictures of missing children, abducted by strangers or a noncustodial parent

"The Politics of the Family." Reprinted with permission of The Free Press, a division of Macmillan, Inc. from DOMESTIC REVOLUTIONS: A Social History of American Family Life by Steven A. Mintz and Susan M. Kellogg. Copyright © 1988 by The Free Press.

after a divorce. Big-city high schools opened clinics to dispense contraceptives in an attempt to reduce teenage pregnancy and out-of-wedlock births.

Television stations started to broadcast advertisements for condoms in order to slow the spread of AIDS (Acquired Immune Deficiency Syndrome) and other sexually transmitted diseases. New terms—such as "test-tube baby," "genetic engineering," "surrogate motherhood," and "safe sex"—became a part of public discourse, and abused children, pregnant teenagers, and battered wives became subjects of television documentaries and miniseries.

State legislators, shocked by reports of abducted and abused children, strengthened child pornography laws, increased penalties for sexual abuse, set up registries of missing children, and required applicants for jobs in day care centers to undergo checks for criminal records. Other legislation allowed wages and income tax refunds to be withheld from parents who fell too far behind on child support. A host of family problems, until recently considered private matters, became public political issues.[2]

During the 1980s the "family" became a buzzword, invoked by politicians of both parties to advance their agendas. Conservatives used the term as a synonym for "traditional social values" and as a way of expressing opposition to the growth of government and liberal welfare policies. Liberals, in turn, used the word as a synonym for "compassion" and as a way of defending government programs designed to help individuals suffering from poverty, abuse, and other problems. For both Democrats and Republicans, the concept of "family" became a symbol of two divergent views of the role and responsibilities of government.[3]

In the 1980 presidential campaign, Ronald Reagan tried to stake out the family issue for conservatives. "Family, work, and neighborhood" were at the top of his rhetorical agenda. In his campaign speeches he argued that federal programs that were supposed to provide family services had, in actuality, promoted "acceptance of indolence, promiscuity, easy abortion, casual attitudes toward marriage and divorce, and maternal indifference to child-rearing responsibilities." In many former Democrats and religious activists—concerned over abortion, school prayer, and pornography as well as by sharp increases in illegitimacy and single-parent families—the call for a return to traditional family values struck a responsive chord.[4]

In office President Reagan launched a counterrevolution against the New Deal, the Fair Deal, the New Frontier, and the Great Society. He halted the growth of social welfare programs and limited benefits to those he called the "truly needy." Although the president repeatedly said that he reduced only the rate of growth in social spending, not the actual level, spending was in fact curtailed in a variety of social welfare programs. Between 1981 and 1984, spending on AFDC was reduced 13 percent; food stamps, 13 percent; child nutrition, 28 percent; job training for young people, 53 percent; programs to prevent child abuse, 12 percent; and mental health services, 26 percent. The Reagan administration also eliminated cash welfare assistance for the working poor, reduced federal subsidies for child care services for low income families, and cut grants used to pay for the regulation of child care programs. At the same time that the Reagan administration tried to cut the role of government, it also attempted to use the power of government to encourage citizens to live by "traditional" family values. To this end, the administration supported legislation that would deny federal funding to any program that allowed unmarried teenagers to obtain contraceptives and abortions without their parents' knowledge.[5]

Following Reagan's election, Democrats began to emphasize family questions. In part the Democrats embraced family issues as a way of demonstrating that they were still in touch with the concerns of mainstream middle-class Americans, but the new emphasis on families also reflected the increasing number of baby-boomers who were marrying and having children. The Democrats declared that the president's concern about the family was hypocritical and that the Reagan administration's cuts in social spending seriously harmed children and families. They called for concrete programs—such as flexible work hours, maternity and paternity leaves, federal financial support and uniform standards for child care, increased spending on nutrition and health care for poor children, and federal enforcement of court-ordered child support payments—to strengthen families and to assist parents in caring for their children.[6]

In the 1984 presidential election, the Democrats unsuccessfully attempted to wrest the family issue away from the Republicans. Democrats used the family issue to dramatize such issues as poverty, federal budget deficits, and child care. Conservative Democrats focused on the family issue as a way to emphasize the sharp increase in federal budget deficits under the Reagan administration. The nation's $2 trillion debt was, they declared, a threat to the well-being of future generations of families. Jesse Jackson used the metaphor of family to describe the need to build a sense of community to replace the inward-looking individualism associated with the years of the Reagan presidency. New York Senator Pat Moynihan focused attention on a new generation of poor children and adolescents—accounting for nearly one-quarter of all Americans under eighteen—growing up in single-parent households and mired in a cycle of poverty.[7]

A common theme uniting the Democratic arguments was that government had a responsibility to help meet the needs of the nation's families. The Democratic view of society as a family that should share benefits and burdens was expressed most eloquently at the 1984 Democratic National Convention by New York Governor Mario Cuomo. "We believe in a government strong enough to use the words 'love' and 'compassion,'" Cuomo declared. "We must be the family of America, recognizing that at the heart of the matter we are bound to one another."[8]

Today the angry controversy that surrounded child care and family issues in the late 1970s and early 1980s has quieted as both political parties have pledged support for the American family. Yet, beneath the surface calm, serious differences of opinion remain. While abstract support for pro-family policies is widespread, the electorate remains deeply divided over such specific issues as abortion, provision of family planning materials to adolescents, tax treatment of working mothers, and federal funding of day care. These policy disagreements, in turn, reflect divergent moral judgments of such issues as women's rights, the prerogatives of parents, the authority of husbands, adolescent sexuality, the rights of children, and mother-centered versus public approaches to child care. The result has been a national deadlock on family issues.[9]

As the stalemate drags on, family-related problems continue to grow. In particular, liberal and conservative politicians will have to address three major family-related issues in the years ahead. One unsolved problem involves the growing number of children who live in poverty as a result of family breakups. Today nearly half of all marriages end in divorce, and many others end in legal separation or desertion. At the same time, an increasing number of mothers are not married. As a result, an enormous number of children are living with a single parent, and all too frequently their economic plight is grave. There are now 12 million children who live in poverty. Since 1968 the number of poor American children has increased by 3 million while the real value of assistance through AFDC has declined by one-third.[10]

Another set of problems grows out of the continuing influx of mothers of young children into the work force. Families today face hard choices as they try to reconcile their children's need for quality care and young mothers' needs to work outside the home to help support their families. Since 1977 the number of children five years old or younger whose mothers are employed has increased by more than 50 percent to nearly 10 million. Today more than 50 percent of all mothers of children six or younger have jobs outside the home. Despite the explosive growth in women's employment, more than 60 percent of women have no right to get their jobs back if they take time off during pregnancy or following childbirth. And, decent, reliable, and affordable child care remains in short supply.[11]

Other changes such as new reproductive technologies—like artificial insemination, in vitro fertilization, embryo transfer, and surrogate mothering—that enable people who could not otherwise have babies to have them raise perplexing ethical and legal issues. With infertility increasing—as a result of venereal disease, exposure to dangerous chemicals, use of intrauterine birth control devices, and the growing number of couples waiting until their thirties or later to start a family—and adoption growing more difficult as the number of the most desired babies has dropped—many prospective parents have turned to artificial techniques of reproduction. These techniques present a wide range of dilemmas, from the rights of children to know their biological parents and the rights of egg or sperm donors to know their children to the question of responsibility if a child is born with a handicap. Surrogate mothering, in which a woman is artificially inseminated with the semen of another women's husband or has the couple's embryo implanted in her uterus, has aroused particularly bitter controversy. Among the issues it has raised are the right of a surrogate mother to change her mind about relinquishing a child and the question of whether women should be encouraged to carry a child for financial gain.[12]

History offers no simple solutions to the problems facing today's families, but it does offer a bit of reassurance as we look toward the future. Ours is not the first generation of Americans to worry about a loosening of family bonds or to complain that parents are growing more selfish and irresponsible or that children are becoming more defiant of adult authority. History reminds us that American families have been through periods of crisis before and that despite recurrent fears for the impending demise of the family, the institution as such has not disappeared.

The history of American family life suggests that we need not be disturbed by change in and of itself, because change—and not stability—has been the norm. American families have repeatedly had to change in order to adapt to novel circumstances—from the challenges of New World colonization to the commercial and industrial revolutions, enslavement, immigration, depression, and war—and the changes that have taken place in family structure, roles, and conceptions have been so far reaching that they might be considered revolutions. Nor do we need to worry obsessively about the increasing diversity of family arrangements, since ethnic, religious, and economic diversity has always been a defining characteristic of American family life. Instead of focusing our attention on the futile question of whether the family will survive, we would do better as a society to confront the concrete problems that face families today, such as problems of employment, income, and child care and issues raised by changing legal norms and technologies.

The difference between our predicament and past concerns is that unlike earlier Americans, who relied upon the family as a valuable resource in adapting to difficult circumstances, many Americans today tend to regard familial responsibilities as an impediment to individual self-fulfillment. We have failed to take the steps necessary to resolve the tensions between our domestic arrangements and changing social and economic circumstances, and the results are apparent in the growing number of poor families and the declining well-being of children.

For nearly four centuries, the family has been our primary unit of nurture and emotional sustenance in the United States. Whether it can continue to perform these functions effectively will ultimately depend on whether we take the steps necessary to help the institution adapt to the unique conditions of our time.

NOTES

1. *NYT,* December 25, 1969, I, 37.
2. *NYT,* March 24, 1985, IV, 5; *NYT,* July 8, 1985, I, 1; *NYT,* March 15, 1987, V, 1.
3. *NYT,* August 20, 1984, C15.
4. *Ibid.; NYT,* September 28, 1986, I, 1. On the conservative critique of federal family initiatives, see Steiner, *Futility of Family Policy,* 17.
5. *NYT,* October 20, 1984, I, 18; *NYT,* October 24, 1984, I, 13; *NYT,* August 20, 1984, C15; *NYT,* September 28, 1986, I, 1.
6. *NYT,* September 1, 1985, I, 37.
7. *Newsweek* (February 17, 1986), 31; Laura Gellott, "Staking Claim to the Family," *Commonweal* (September 20, 1985), 488ff.
8. Refer to note 7.
9. Andrew Hacker, "Farewell to the Family," *New York Review of Books* (March 18, 1982), 37ff.; Steiner, *Futility of Family Policy,* 20, 50.
10. On the new generation of poor Americans, see *NYT,* October 20, 1985, I, 1; *NYT,* February 6, 1987, I, 30; *NYT,* February 19, 1987, 1, 12; Barbara Bergmann, *The Economic Emergence of Women* (New York, 1986).

In three states, California, Maine, and Wisconsin, maximum AFDC benefits for a family of four remained stable between 1970 and 1985. In all other states, the value of benefits declined. In Texas the decline was 59 percent; in Massachusetts, 46 percent; in New York City, 38 percent. See Moynihan, *Family and Nation*, 15.

One proposed solution to the exploding rate of child poverty is strict enforcement of court-ordered child support payments. Unfortunately, the average court-ordered payment is so low—$2,460 a year, or roughly $47 a week—that it is unlikely to make a major difference in the actual lives of poor children. See *NYT* (Carol E. Curtis letter), February 17, 1987, I, 28.

Although the most rapid growth in the number of poor children has occurred in single-parent families, it needs to be stressed that half of all poor families contain both a husband and a wife. While there is no generally accepted explanation for the increase in single-parent families, there can be little doubt that a major contributor is the increasing number of men unable to support a family. Over the past decade, 80 percent of the new jobs created were in the service sector of the economy, and most of these jobs have gone to women. Today half the young black males between the ages of sixteen and twenty-four have never held a job. See *NYT* (Jane J. Young letter), February 27, 1987, I, 34; Richard B. Freeman and Harry J. Holzer, *The Black Youth Employment Crisis* (Chicago, 1986), 3–18.

11. On child-rearing dilemmas of working mothers, see *NYT*, March 11, 1985, C11; *NYT*, September 2, 1984, I, 1; *NYT*, September 4, 1984, B11.

On January 13, 1987, the U.S. Supreme Court upheld a California law that gave women up to four months unpaid disability leave for pregnancy. In a related decision, issued January 21, 1987, the Court ruled that states can deny unemployment benefits to anyone who leaves a job for reasons unrelated to work, including pregnancy.

Many women today are forced to choose between their job and their child. No more than 40 percent of the nation's 49 million working women have job-protected, paid maternity leaves of at least six weeks duration. Ten states have adopted laws that guarantee workers jobs after they return from maternity leave. Five states provide temporary disability insurance to replace income lost during a maternity leave. In contrast, at least 75 other countries guarantee women the right to leave work for a specified period to care for a baby and provide job guarantees and cash payments to compensate for time lost from work because of pregnancy or childbirth. See *NYT*, March 11, 1985, C11 and refer to note 71, chapter 10.

12. On new reproductive techniques, see *NYT*, February 15, 1987, E22; *NYT*, October 1, 1986, C1; *NYT*, February 11, 1986, C1; *NYT*, March 20, 1985, III, 8; *NYT*, November 16, 1984, A20, A21.

APPENDIX Correlation Chart

This chart correlates the thirty-eight articles in this anthology with thirteen of the more widely used marriage and the family texts. To the right of the selected articles in Marriage and Family in Transition *appear the corresponding chapter number(s) in which a given topic is discussed. Depending on the text used, the instructor may wish to rearrange the order in which the articles are assigned.*

Part	Article	Broderick	Coleman	Cox	Dickinson & Leming	Eshleman
One	1	7	2,7	4	8	9
	2	8	—	3	—	—
	3	4	3	4	8	10
	4	—	7	4	—	—
	5	2	4	4	9	10
	6	8	6	4	8	9
Two	7	9	14	2	4	4
	8	3	8	—	7,9	—
	9	9	9	9	5	4
	10	9	9	9	5	4
	11	16	8,11	14	4	12–15
	12	11	8	10	10	11
	13	16	8	10	10,12,13	12–15
	14	16	7	5	9	12
	15	14	11	5	16	11
	16	15	11	6	13	16
	17	18	—	14	—	15
	18	18	11	14	13	15
	19	13	10	13	11	13
	20	9	9	7	5	4
	21	—	—	13	12	10
	22	17	12	13	14	7
	23	13	10	13	11	13
	24	18	—	—	—	15
	25	16	11	14	12	15
Three	26	17	12,13	15,16	14	17
	27	17	12	15	14	17
	28	17	12	15	14	17
	29	17	12	15	14	17
	30	17	12	15	14	17
	31	17	13	16	14	17
	32	17	13	16	14	17
	33	17	13	16	14	17
Four	34	14	8	—	8,9	11
	35	3	8	—	9	—
	36	12	—	11	—	—
	37	18	—	—	13	15
	38	—	14	11	5,7	4,7

Kammeyer	Lamanna & Reidmann	Lasswell	Melville	Rice	Saxon	Scanzoni	Strong & Devault
4	6	4,6	3	6,7	7	4	6
3	—	2	3	7	3	—	5
5	6	6	3	7	5	4	6
—	—	—	—	6	—	—	15
2	13	3	4	1	5	5	4
6	6	5	3	10	5	6	6
7	7,8	1	1	10	10	7	1
9	7,8	2,3	7	6	2	6,8	6
12	12	—	8	12	6	8	11
12	12	12	8	13	6	9	11
—	—	—	11	11	10	14,16	10
9	13	—	10	9	5	10	8,10
9	13	—	10	11	10	10	8,10
8	19	7,8	11	4	9	10	10
9	19	3	—	22	5	10	8
13	11	12	—	17	10	12	15
14	—	15	13	11	—	16	10
14	18	15	—	22	10	16	10
10	14	11	12	20	10	14	12
11	14	12	—	13	10	9	12
11	14	—	—	—	—	—	—
—	—	13	14	20	10	16	17
11	14	11	12	20	13	14	12
14	—	—	11	21	—	16	10
14	—	15	13	21	10	16	10
15,16	16,17	13,14	14,15	23,24	11,12	17	16,17
15	16	13	14	23	11	17	16
15	16	13	14	23	11	17	16
15	16	13	14	23	11	17	16
15	16	13	14	23	11	17	16
16	17	14	15	24	12	17	17
16	17	14	15	24	12	17	17
16	17	14	15	24	12	17	17
9	19	5	7	22	5	6	8
—	7	3,5	7	—	4	6	6
10	9	9	1	19	—	13	9
14	—	15	—	—	—	16	—
2,11	—	—	—	—	10,11	8	11,12